Resources,
Values and Development

Resources,

Values and Development

AMARTYA SEN

Harvard University Press
Cambridge, Massachusetts
London, England

First Harvard University Press paperback edition, 1997

Library of Congress Cataloging-in-Publication Data

Sen, Amartya Kumar.
  Resources, values and development.

  Includes index.
  1. Economic development—Addresses, essays, lectures.
  2. Resource allocation—Addresses, essays, lectures.
  3. Welfare economics—Addresses, essays, lectures.
  4. Social values—Addresses, essays, lectures. I. Title.
  HD82.S439 1984   338.9   84-9091
  ISBN 0-674-76525-7 (cloth)
  ISBN 0-674-76526-5 (pbk.)

Contents

Preface

I was once asked (in Geneva, by a patrician sizing up a doubtful visitor) whether I liked culture. Yes, I heard myself saying, and felt immeasurably stupid. That sense of fatuity is slightly revived in calling this selection of essays *Resources, Values and Development*. Good enough subjects, but can any economics get away from them? Informative titles are hard to devise, but it may be explained that these essays are mainly concerned with development economics as it is normally understood, and that many of them deal with various aspects of resource allocation in that context and in particular with the role of motives and values in resource use and its assessment.

The essays are not directly concerned with welfare economics, unlike many of the papers included in a previous selection, *Choice, Welfare and Measurement* (Basil Blackwell and MIT Press, 1982). But the welfare economic perspective has been widely used. That perspective influences the assessment of allocational rules and motivational features (Part I), investment strategies and discounting procedures (Part II), shadow pricing and project evaluation (Part III), global inequalities and international transfers (Part IV), social poverty and intra-family disparities (Part IV), real income and economic inequality (Part V), food availability and entitlement failures (Part V), and even the nature of economic development (Part V). The welfare-economic approach often departs from traditional formats, and there is also some reassessment of the moral foundations of policy making and resource allocation (Essays 12 and 13).

Apart from traditional problems of resource allocation, the investigations focus particularly on some uncomfortable subjects, including inequality, deprivation, sex bias, undernourishment, morbidity, hunger and famines. The descriptive and predictive analyses go specifically into institutional features at different levels, involving the state, the legal system, the wage system, the market mechanism, the family, and even the media and pressure groups.

There is a fairly long introductory essay. This deals with inter-connections between the various themes of these papers as well as the related literature. Some of the essays included here have provoked a fair amount of discussion (in the form of extensions, applications and disputations), and many of the issues raised have been taken up in the Introduction.

The idea of publishing this selection of essays (like the last one, *Choice, Welfare and Measurement*) came from René Olivieri of Basil Blackwell, and he has once again been enormously helpful in advising on which essays to select and how to arrange them. I am also most grateful to Patricia Williams for encouragement and helpful suggestions.

I would also like to thank Nicola Harris for looking after the production and presentation of the book with superb efficiency, and Jocelyn Kynch for greatly helping me with proof correction and indexing.

A.K.S.

Introduction

Much of economics is neat and elegant; but some of it is not. The essays included in this volume belong distinctly to the latter category. They deal with institutional complexities of economic development, the untidy parts of the theory of resource allocation, the peculiar role of values in social behaviour, the conflicts and contradictions of normative assessment, and the challenges to economic theory and policy presented by informational lacunae and conceptual ambiguity.

Some of the issues also call for going beyond what are often taken to be the boundaries of economics — into political, social and philosophical matters. These boundaries are often defined very narrowly, involving partitions that classical economists, such as Smith or Marx, would not easily have recognized. Some of modern economics seems indeed to be based on the corset-maker's old advice: 'If madam is entirely comfortable in it, then madam most certainly needs a smaller size.'

1 *Institutions and Motivation*

1.1 *Non-wage systems and the peasants*

The wage system was born yesterday. For ages, people have toiled in hunting, fishing, gathering, husbanding animals and cultivating land with other systems of reward. Even today a majority of the labour force of the world work in institutional arrangements that involve little or no use of wages. In contrast, the bulk of modern economic theory sees employment strictly in terms of the wage system and investigates resource allocation within that specific format. There is, of course, no mystery in this contrariness, since much of modern economic theory confines itself — explicitly or by implication — to the advanced capitalist economies. The first two papers in this selection are devoted to exploring the logic of various non-wage

1

systems – peasant agriculture, dual economies and cooperative allocation.

In my *Choice of Techniques*, written in the fifties,[1] there was an attempt, among other things, to contrast the allocational rules of peasant agriculture with those of wage-based industry. Essay 1 ('Peasants and Dualism with or without Surplus Labour') extends that analysis within an explicit framework of maximizing behaviour. The subject is not, of course, new, and various authors, such as Chayanov, have produced models of non-wage agricultural allocation.[2] Even Alfred Marshall had argued that 'the cultivator working with his own hands often puts into his land as much work as he feels able to do, without estimating carefully its money value in relation to its product'.[3] The analytical structure of peasant allocation developed and used in Essay 1 accepts this departure from profit-maximization and money-value calculation, but does not attribute the departure to behaviour that is not 'careful'. Rather, the goal is seen to be maximizing some notion of the well-being of the family, and institutional constraints are seen as limiting transactions. In this context, 'careful' calculations can and do lead to different results from profit-maximization at market prices.

This exercise in pure theory also relates to some apparently puzzling empirical findings about Indian agriculture. Official studies of 'farm management' done in the fifties produced a wealth of information about Indian agriculture.[4] But they made rather a mess of interpreting these data by trying to fit them into a framework of a wage economy, e.g., by valuing family labour at imputed market wages. For example, the reports expressed 'alarm' at finding that '50 per cent or more of the farmers are carrying on the business at a loss'. Indian agriculture does, of course, offer genuine scope for much alarm; but this one is really due to illegitimate application of imported concepts, to wit, valuing all family labour at market wages even when there is no option of such employment. While there is no great difficulty in making *ad hoc* corrections to interpret the results of Indian 'farm management' studies (and to explain away the

1. *Choice of Techniques* (Oxford: Blackwell, 1960), Chapter 1 and Appendix A. (This was presented as a Prize Fellowship dissertation at Trinity College, Cambridge, in 1957). See also 'The Choice of Agricultural Techniques in Underdeveloped Countries', *Economic Development and Cultural Change*, 7 (1959).

2. A. V. Chayanov, *The Theory of the Peasant Economy*, English translation, edited by D. Thorner, B. Kerblay and R. E. F. Smith (Homewood, Ill.: Irwin, 1966).

3. A. Marshall, *Principles of Economics*, 8th edition (London: Macmillan, 1949), p. 540.

4. See the series of *Studies in the Economics of Farm Management*, done by the Ministry of Food and Agriculture, beginning in 1954–55, for Bombay, Madhya Pradesh, Madras, Punjab, Uttar Pradesh and West Bengal, published by Government of India, New Delhi.

apparent puzzles),[5] what is needed is a more complete theory of resource use in peasant and mixed agriculture. Essay 1 is an attempt to take up that challenge. It presents a structure of fully peasant allocation (respectively, with *and* without markets for products and for non-labour inputs) and also of dual economies with peasant agriculture coexisting with wage-based capitalist enterprises.

Among the various 'responses' that can be calculated in terms of such a structure is the response of total output to the withdrawal of a part of the labour force (equation (37), Essay 1, p. 50 below). The special case of zero response represents the existence of 'surplus labour' — a subject of some interest and much controversy. The analysis showed that contrary to some well-known statements,[6] marginal product of labour being zero is neither a necessary, nor a sufficient, condition for the existence of surplus labour (or 'disguised unemployment'). That depends more on the extent to which the effort per person left behind can be expected to increase as a part of the labour force moves away, and it is this relation that equation (37) expresses.

These issues have been discussed a good deal in the literature.[7] I shall not try to review those extensive discussions here,[8] but it may

5. See my 'An Aspect of Indian Agriculture', *Economic Weekly*, 14, Annual Number, February 1962, and 'Size of Holdings and Productivity', *Economic Weekly*, 16, Annual Number, February 1964. There has been an extensive controversy on the reading of the empirical relationships and the explanations offered. That literature up to the early seventies is reviewed in my *Employment, Technology and Development* (Oxford: Clarendon Press, 1975), Appendix C ('Labour Cost, Scale and Technology in Indian Agriculture'). Later contributions on this subject include, among others, Krishna Bharadwaj, *Production Conditions in Indian Agriculture* (Cambridge: Cambridge University Press, 1974); G. R. Saini, *Farm Size, Resource-Use Efficiency and Income Distribution* (New Delhi: Allied Publishers, 1979); and Ashok Rudra and Amartya Sen, 'Farm Size and Labour Use: Analysis and Policy', *Economic and Political Weekly*, 5, Annual Number, February 1980.

6. See, for example, R. Nurkse, *Problems of Capital Formation in Underdeveloped Countries* (Oxford: Blackwell, 1953), p. 33; J. Viner, 'Some Reflections on the Concept of "Disguised Unemployment"', *Contribuções a Analise do Desenvolvimento Economico*, 1957, p. 18; G. Myrdal, *Asian Drama* (New York: Pantheon, 1968), p. 2053.

7. See particularly S. Wellisz, 'Dual Economies, Disguised Unemployment and the Unlimited Supply of Labour', *Economica*, 35 (1968); S. Hymer and S. Resnick, 'A Model of an Agrarian Economy with Non-agricultural Activities', *Review of Economic Studies*, 36 (1969); D. W. Jorgenson and L. Lau, 'An Economic Theory of Agricultural Household Behaviour', presented at the Far Eastern meeting of the Econometric Society, Tokyo, 1969; C. Nakajima, 'Subsistence and Commercial Family Farms: Some Theoretical Models of Subjective Equilibrium', in *Subsistence Agriculture and Economic Development*, edited by C. R. Wharton (Chicago: Aldine, 1969); J. Stiglitz, 'Rural–Urban Migration, Surplus Labour, and the Relationship between Urban and Rural Wages', *East African Economic Review*, 1 (1969); J. S. Uppal, 'Work Habits and Disguised Unemployment in Underdeveloped Countries: A Theoretical Analysis', *Oxford Economic Papers*, 21 (1969); W. C. Robinson, 'The Economics of Work Sharing in Peasant Agriculture', *Economic Development and Cultural Change*, 19 (1971); H. N. Barnum and L. Squire, *A Model of an Agricultural Household: Theory and Evidence* (Baltimore, Md.: Johns Hopkins Press, 1979); M. R.

be appropriate to make a few remarks on this subject, supplementing what is said in Essay 1. First, the necessary and sufficient conditions for the existence of surplus labour can become much less exacting than those derived from equation (37) if the objective function of the family is not taken to be separable into consumption and leisure. This point is, in fact, made in Essay 1 (p. 45), but has tended to be ignored in the subsequent literature, in taking the flatness of both marginal utility of consumption and of marginal disutility of work as being necessary for the existence of surplus labour. What is necessary is the constancy − as some labourers move away − of 'the real cost of labour', i.e. of the marginal rate of substitution between income and leisure (Essay 1, pp. 44–5), and this can be the case even when the marginal utility and disutility schedules are not respectively flat, provided they interrelate (i.e. have non-zero 'cross partials'). For example, if more income and consumption (e.g. greater intake of food) reduces the drudgery of work, then the marginal rate of substitution can be constant as both work and income per head increase, due to a reduction in peasant labour force, even when the marginal utility of income has the conventional downward slope and the marginal disutility of work the conventional upward incline.[9]

Second, surplus labour is only one special case and the importance of the 'response analysis' does not lie only in dealing with that case − interesting and controversial though that case may be. Labour emigration leads to a number of adjustments in a peasant economy, of which a change in the hours of work of those remaining behind is one. Often there may be no disguised unemployment at all, and yet the net reduction of total labour effort, and consequently of output, may be small in comparison with the size of migration. It is possible to estimate these expected responses, and the relevance of these calculations goes well beyond merely checking whether the output response happens to be exactly zero or not.[10]

Rosenzweig, 'Neoclassical Theory and the Optimizing Peasant: An Econometric Analysis of Market Family Labour Supply in a Developing Country', *Quarterly Journal of Economics*, 94 (1980); C. J. Bliss and N. H. Stern, *Palanpur: The Economy of an Indian Village* (Oxford: Clarendon Press, 1982); P. Bardhan, *Land, Labour and Rural Productivity: Essays in Development Economics* (Cambridge: Cambridge University Press, forthcoming).

8. See, however, my *Employment, Technology and Development* (1975).

9. Barnum and Squire (*A Model of Agricultural Household*, 1979) have argued for extending this analysis by taking note of the adjustment of labour hiring in peasant agriculture following migration from it, and this can make the conditions for unchanged agricultural output less exacting still.

10. For example, Barnum and Squire (1979) estimate in their case study that 'in the study area of northwest Malaysia ... 38 percent of the reduction of household labour supply following the departure of one working family member is replaced by the extra effort on the part of the remaining family members, ceteris paribus' (p. 93).

Third, as is argued in Essay 1, because of the seasonal nature of agricultural production, it is 'misleading to speak in terms of a homogeneous unit of labour'. The problem can be dealt with by either assuming strict proportionality between labour use in different seasons (e.g. harvesting labour and planting labour going up or down in proportion with each other), or limited complementarity (with positive cross-partials of marginal productivity of one type of labour vis-à-vis another) (Essay 1, pp. 58–9). There is no great difficulty in extending the response analysis, including the conditions for the existence of surplus labour, to the seasonal case.[11] A simple case – sufficient for this purpose – involves flat 'real cost of labour' (marginal rate of substitution between income and leisure) in *each* season.[12]

How common and how extensive surplus labour may, in fact, empirically be is, of course, a different question. There is some considerable evidence that lean-season idleness may often go with much tightness in other seasons,[13] and the indifference curves between income and leisure may well be far from straight in the peak seasons. Essay 1 makes no claim about the actual existence, or size, of surplus labour,[14] but presents some necessary and sufficient conditions for surplus labour to exist in peasant economies. More generally, the

11. There has been some misunderstanding of this particular point. In an otherwise illuminating paper, Stiglitz has argued: 'we have proved that, provided leisure is a superior good and labour supplied at harvest and planting times and at other times of the year are complementary, output must fall as labour migrates to the urban sector: labourers cannot be in surplus' (J. Stiglitz, 'Rural–Urban Migration, Surplus Labour, and the Relationship between Urban and Rural Wages', *East Africa Economic Review*, 1 (1969), p. 11). This claim is not correct, and Stiglitz gets this odd result only because he assumes 'for simplicity' that in one of the two seasons labourers 'work the maximum that is possible at those times' (p. 3). See Essay 11 below, pp. 262–3.

12. This would permit surplus labour with any degree of substitutability between labour in different seasons – even with perfect complementarity (see Essay 1).

13. See, for example, B. Hansen, 'Employment and Wages in Rural Egypt', *American Economic Review*, 59 (1969); P. Bardhan, *Land, Labour and Rural Poverty*, forthcoming.

14. Empirical tests of the existence of surplus labour have been few and rather limited. T. W. Schultz is one of the few to offer a serious statistical test, based on output reductions after the influenza epidemic of 1918–19 in India (*Transforming Traditional Agriculture*, New Haven: Yale University Press, 1964). I have argued elsewhere that Schultz's test is, however, rather seriously flawed; see my 'Surplus Labour in India: A Critique of Schultz's Statistical Test', *Economic Journal*, 77 (1967), and the exchange with Schultz in the same number. See also S. Mehra, 'Surplus Labour in Indian Agriculture', *Indian Economic Review*, 1 (1966); D. W. Jorgenson, 'Testing Alternative Theories of the Development of a Dual Economy', in I. Adelman and E. Thorbecke (eds), *The Theory and Design of Economic Development* (London: Johns Hopkins Press, 1967); A. R. Khan, *The Economy of Bangladesh* (London: Macmillan, 1972); Raj Krishna, 'Unemployment in India', *Economic and Political Weekly*, 8, 3 March 1973; M. Alamgir, *Bangladesh: A Case of Below Poverty Level Equilibrium Trap* (Dacca: BIDS, 1978); A. Rudra, *Indian Agricultural Economics: Myths and Realities* (Delhi: Allied Publishers, 1982).

essay presents the response relations and the parameters on which the size of those responses would depend. Surplus labour merely corresponds to a special case of one of the responses analysed.[15]

1.2   *Cooperation and motives*

The motivational assumption underlying the model of peasant alloca-tion in Essay 1 is simple — perhaps even naïve. The entire allocation is guided by the objective of maximizing 'family welfare', which is given a utilitarian form. While there may be conflicts of interest within the family (e.g. between the members involved primarily in agricultural work and those primarily homebound), the model does not permit these conflicts to play any serious part in determining the economic activities of the peasant family.

This type of motivational format is often thought to be appropriate for characterizing the role of families in other types of economies as well. For example, in standard general equilibrium theory dealing with capitalist market economies, intra-family relations are kept completely out of the picture, presumably on the basis of some simpli-fying assumption like this one. One of the later essays in the volume (Essay 15) critically evaluates this tradition, and others (Essays 16, 19 and 20) pursue these matters more. I shall come back to this question later on in this Introduction.

While conflicts within the family have come into formal economics only relatively recently, those within other non-wage organizations,

---

15. There is also a brief discussion in Essay 1 of resource allocation under share-cropping. Much depends on what types of institutional assumptions we make, e.g. whether the shares of the landowners and the cultivators are taken to be fixed, given by established conven-tion and norms, or whether they are assumed to be flexible, determined by market forces. The model of fixed shares presented in Essay 1 yields inefficiency (Section 4.2), whereas a model of competitive determination of shares need not (see S. N. Cheung, *The Theory of Share Tenancy*, Chicago, Ill.: University of Chicago Press, 1969). The results depend on the institutional assumptions about related markets, (e.g. those of labour, land and credit), the nature of technology, input cost sharing, and also on features of uncertainty. There is by now quite a rich literature on the subject. See, among others, P. K. Bardhan and T. N. Srinivasan, 'Crop Sharing Tenancy in Agriculture: A Theoretical and Empirical Analysis', *American Economic Review*, 61 (1971); J. Stiglitz, 'Incentives and Risk Sharing in Share-cropping', *Review of Economic Studies*, 61 (1974); C. Bell and P. Zusman, 'A Bargaining Theoretic Approach to Cropsharing Contracts', *American Economic Review*, 66 (1976); D. M. G. Newbery, 'Risk Sharing, Sharecropping and Uncertain Labour Markets', *Review of Economic Studies*, 44 (1977); A Braverman and T. N. Srinivasan, 'Credit and Sharecropping in Agrarian Societies', *Journal of Development Economics*, 9 (1981); A. Braverman and J. E. Stiglitz, 'Sharecropping and the Interlinking of Agrarian Markets', *American Economic Review*, 72 (1982); Bliss and Stern, *Palanpur: The Economy of an Indian Village* (1982); T. J. Byres (ed.), 'Sharecropping and Sharecroppers', Special Issue, *Journal of Peasant Studies*, 10 (1983), including contributions by T. J. Byres, R. Pearce, Utsa Patnaik, Amit Bhaduri, Juan Martinez-Alier, José Maria-Caballero and Jay R. Mandle.

such as cooperatives, have been discussed extensively for a long time. Essay 2 ('Labour Allocation in a Cooperative Enterprise', 1966) is concerned with this question. It takes explicit note of the combination of congruent and conflicting interests that characterize the problem of cooperative allocation. Essay 2 starts off with the distinction between payment according to work and that according to need — a contrast that has been discussed a great deal since Marx's classic analysis of it in his *Critique of the Gotha Programme* (1875).[16]

Assuming that each individual constituting the cooperative is concerned only with his own well-being, it is easily checked that a system of distribution entirely according to needs would tend to lead to inoptimal use of labour in the sense that too little effort would be put in. There is nothing odd or unusual about this conclusion. Already in 1875, Marx had criticized 'the Gotha Programme' of the German Workers' Party for overlooking this basic incentive problem. What might be a little more surprising was the result that labour use would be inoptimal also with distribution entirely according to work. That system would make people perform *too much* labour, since work points give them 'entitlement' to parts of the *total* production (not just to the marginal output). Both the directional results (i.e. too little effort with distribution according to need, and too much with distribution according to work) remain true even when people are not selfish and have concern for others (Essay 2, Section 5), so long as they do not have perfect 'social consciousness' (in the form of valuing the gains to others just as much as those to themselves).

The optimal rule of part-work–part-need distribution is easy to derive.[17] The rule, interestingly enough, is independent of the actual extent of 'sympathy' that people have for each other,[18] though the

16. K. Marx, *Critique of Gotha Program*; English translation (New York: International Publishers, 1933), and K. Marx and F. Engels, *Selected Works*, Vol. II (Moscow: Foreign Language Publishing House, 1967).

17. Equations (14) and (14b) in Essay 2, p. 82. In an ingenious contribution, Louis Putterman has shown how this optimal rule for division of income can get chosen through democratic voting by self-interested individuals ('On Optimality in Collective Institutional Choice', *Journal of Comparative Economics*, 5 (1981)). See also L. Putterman and M. DiGiorgio, 'Simulation Results for a Model of Democratic Semi-Collective Agriculture', *Oxford Economic Papers*, forthcoming.

18. There is an obvious analogy here — indeed analytical equivalence (under a different interpretation) — with the fact that some competitive efficiency results are unaffected by particular types of externality. Some of these issues were later explored illuminatingly by S. G. Winter, Jr. ('A Simple Remark on the Second Optimality Theorem of Welfare Economics', *Journal of Economic Theory*, 1 (1969)), and G. C. Archibald and D. Donaldson ('Non-paternalism and Basic Theorems of Welfare Economics', *Canadian Journal of Economics*, 9 (1976)), among others.

size of the loss from inoptimal rules would vary with it. However, in the special case of perfect 'social consciousness', any rule of division between payment according to work and that according to need will do. To put it another way, within the structure of this type of cooperative allocation, the conditions that make distribution purely according to need fail (as in the 'early stages of communism' in Marx's schema) would also make distribution according to work inefficient. It is only with perfect social consciousness that work-wise distribution − like needwise distribution − will be itself adequate.

At the time Essay 2 was written (during 1964–65), Benjamin Ward's pioneering study of 'market syndicalism'[19] had begun to revive interest in the pure theory of cooperative allocation.[20] In Ward's model the work per person was fixed (the number of members in the cooperative being the variable that was studied). The main thrust of Essay 2 was to take up the question of variable effort and the incentive problems associated with this. The literature on cooperative allocation has expanded enormously in recent years, and the incentive problems have been extensively studied, both in terms of pure theory, and also drawing on the lessons learned from experiences in such countries as China, the USSR, Yugoslavia and Israel.[21]

The Chinese experience, in particular, has been the subject of a great deal of international interest, and there can be no doubt that China has experimented with bolder schemes of cooperative alloca-

19. 'The Firm in Illyria: Market Syndicalism', *American Economic Reivew*, 48 (1958). See also his later article, 'Organization and Comparative Economics: Some Approaches', in A. Eckstein (ed.), *Comparison of Economic Systems* (Berkeley, Calif.: University of California Press, 1971), and his book *The Socialist Economy* (New York: Random House, 1967).

20. See also E. D. Domar, 'The Soviet Collective Farm as a Producer Cooperative', *American Economic Review*, 56 (1966).

21. Among other contributions, see J. Vanek, *The General Theory of Labour-Managed Market Economies* (Ithaca, New York: Cornell University Press, 1970); N. E. Cameron, 'Incentives and Labor Supply in Cooperative Enterprises', *Canadian Journal of Economics*, 6 (1973); A. K. Sen, *On Economic Inequality* (Oxford: Clarendon Press, 1973), Chapter 4; C. Riskin, 'Incentive Systems and Work Motivations: The Experience of China', *Working Papers for a New Society*, 1 (1974); E. S. Phelps (ed.), *Altruism, Morality and Economic Theory* (New York: Russel Sage, 1975); C. Riskin, 'Maoism and Motivation: A Discussion of Work Incentives in China', in V. Nee and J. Peck (eds), *China's Uninterrupted Revolution* (New York: Pantheon, 1975); J. M. Montias, *The Structure of Economic Systems* (New Haven, Conn.: Yale University Press, 1976); M. D. Berman, 'Short-run Efficiency in the Labor-Managed Firm', *Journal of Comparative Economics*, 1 (1977); J. P. Bonin, 'Work Incentives and Uncertainty on a Collective Farm', *Journal of Comparative Economics*, 1 (1977); D. L. Chinn, 'Team Cohesion and Collective Labour Supply in Chinese Agriculture', *Journal of Comparative Economics*, 3 (1979); L. D. Israelsen, 'Collectives, Communes and Incentives', *Journal of Comparative Economics*, 4 (1980); L. Putterman, 'Voluntary Collectivization: A Model of Producers' Institutional Choice', *Journal of Comparative Economics*, 4 (1980); Putterman, 'On Optimality in Collective Institutional Choice' (1981); L. Putterman, 'Incentives and the Kibbutz: Toward an Economics of Communal Work Motivation', *Zeitschrift für Nationalökonomie*, 43 (1983).

tion than any other country in the world. At the time Essay 2 was written, the Great Leap Forward (1958–60), with its attempt at communal distribution emphasizing needs, had come to an end, and the starvation and famine (1959–61) that followed (on this see Essay 19, pp. 501–3 below) had also passed. The Chinese economy was being consolidated with the use of more traditional incentives; and the radical experiment of the Cultural Revolution would soon be launched.

The 'Sixteen Points' programme, adopted in 1966, ushering in the Cultural Revolution, pleaded for 'an education to develop morally, intellectually and physically and to become labourers with socialist consciousness and culture'.[22] It declared that 'the aim of the Great Proletarian Cultural Revolution is to revolutionize people's ideology and as a consequence to achieve greater, faster, better and more economical results in all fields of work'.[23] I remember wondering whether the case of 'perfect social consciousness' discussed in Essay 2, which happened to be published just as the 'Sixteen Points' were being adopted, would prove to be actually realizable, making that particular 'optimal solution' (among the two, (14a) and (14b), outlined in Essay 2) to be something more than a purely theoretical possibility.

It is tempting to think that this question has been answered firmly in the negative, since the Cultural Revolution is now regarded by the Chinese government as a total failure. This may well be the correct answer, but it is difficult to be sure. It is undoubtedly true that the official Chinese assessment of the Cultural Revolution is now as firmly negative as it had been firmly positive earlier, and that 'eating from the same big pot' and 'stirring up a communist wind' (two colourful phrases used these days to describe the philosophy of the Cultural Revolution) have been condemned in no uncertain terms. But it is difficult to separate out the problems created by the reliance on moral incentives from the chaos of the political movement that went with it.[24] With screaming Red Guards taking over factories,

22. 'The Decision of the Central Committee of the Chinese Communist Party Concerning the Great Proletarian Cultural Revolution', adopted on 8 August 1966, reproduced in Joan Robinson, *The Cultural Revolution in China* (Harmondsworth: Penguin, 1969), p. 93. The language partly mirrored Marx's concern in *Critique of the Gotha Programme* of an early socialist economy being 'economically, morally and intellectually, still stamped with the birthmarks of the old society' (p. 21).

23. Quoted in Robinson, *The Cultural Revolution*, p. 95.

24. It is also worth noting that judged in terms of over-all growth rate the Chinese economy did rather well in the period of the Cultural Revolution. While Professor Ma Hong, the President of the Chinese Academy of Social Sciences, may well be right in saying that 'needless to say, none of these successes can be attributed in any way to the "Cultural

intellectuals being banished to rural areas, etc., more was happening in China during the Cultural Revolution than just the use of a different incentive system — with emphasis on social consciousness.[25]

The goal of 'perfect social consciousness' is undoubtedly a hard one to achieve, and certainly the Cultural Revolution has not been able to establish the feasibility of 'moral incentives' in the way Mao had anticipated. But nor has it demonstrated its unfeasibility in a definitive way, since the theory and practice of the Cultural Revolution have been so far apart.[26] The possibility of transforming the parameters that affect cooperative allocation, including social consciousness, will no doubt continue to attract serious attention.

The importance of motives other than individual profits is inescapable in cooperative allocation, and in other forms of non-capitalist systems (including peasant economies). But even for capitalist economies the adequacy of the profit motive is far from clear. This is so not only because of the 'welfare state' features of modern capitalism (e.g. unemployment benefits, poverty relief), which may

---

Revolution", without which we would have made far greater achievements' (*New Strategy for China's Economy*, Beijing: New World Press, 1983, p. 13), the period of the Cultural Revolution was certainly not one of economic disaster in the way in which the Great Leap Forward was.

25. Also the inappropriateness of the relative prices (e.g. low agricultural prices vis-à-vis those of industrial goods) played a role in generating inefficiency that must be distinguished from the part played by the distributional rule *within* an enterprise. It is plausible to argue that the problem of loyalty to others (in particular, the values of a_{ij} in the model of Essay 2) depends on the distance — physical and social — between the persons involved (that is, between i and j respectively). For example, loyalties to each other are easier to cultivate within a production 'brigade', which is a relatively small unit, than in larger units, like a commune. Identification is especially difficult when the beneficiaries are far away (e.g. for the agricultural workers to identify with the urban population enjoying the benefits of lower agricultural prices).

26. Andrew Walder describes the nature of the contrast thus (in the specific context of industrial wages policy):

Despite all the elaborations by Western observers of Maoist incentive principles, most workers experienced the much-vaunted experiment as little more than (1) discontinuation of regular wage raises, (2) cancellation of bonuses tied to work performance, and (3) intensification of political study, campaigns, and criticism sessions. In actual practice, there was never any attempt to blend moral with material incentives, to balance collective and individual material incentives. The mixed collective and individual incentive structure already in use in the early 1960s was dismantled during the Cultural Revolution, and nothing at all put in its place. The consequence was not only a complete severing of the link between work performance and either collective or individual pay, but also, over time, a growth of new kinds of inequality, perceived inequities, and real economic difficulties for certain age cohorts within the labor force. The ultimate effect was a quite predictable erosion of employee motivation and work discipline. Increased ideological appeals as a remedy appear only to have bred growing political cynicism or indifference. ('Some Ironies of the Maoist Legacy in Industry', in M. Selden and V. Lippitt (eds), *The Transition to Socialism in China*, Armonk, New York: Sharpe, 1982, p. 222.)

involve incentive problems similar to need-based distribution. Even the basic productive operations of a capitalist economy draw heavily on motives other than profits. Essay 3 ('The Profit Motive', 1983) is concerned with this question.

The picture of an all-embracing price system, well served by uncomprising profit-seekers, may have the pride of place in standard textbooks of economics, but the working of a capitalist economy relies substantially on other motives as well. For example, a society in which people renege on contracts whenever it is in their personal interest to do so will have difficulty with efficient capitalist transactions. Legal redress is expensive and slow, and of course, reneging may still be a 'fair bet' despite the penalty that might possibly be incurred. Similarly, in production processes requiring teamwork, the pursuit of pure self-interest is often an inefficient motivation, and there may even be a tendency for it to be weeded out by 'fitter' motivational patterns.

These issues, taken up in Essay 3 relate closely to some general behavioural questions that were discussed in 'Rational fools' and other essays included in my *Choice, Welfare and Measurement* (1982). I shall not go further into this topic here, but it is worth emphasizing that the problem of 'moral incentives' is not a peculiar feature of cooperative allocation only. Indeed, the relative success of capitalism in societies with strong codes of 'obligation' (most notably Japan) also underlines this need for taking a more sophisticated view of the motivational requirements of capitalist economies (Essay 3).

The issue, incidentally, is of a certain amount of immediate interest in this country. As I write this Introduction, I read one of Mrs Thatcher's senior Cabinet Ministers announcing: 'We are seeking to build an entrepreneurial society in which the pursuit of profit is the fuel of the system and individual reward is the prime incentive.'[27] Given the pervasive interdependences in modern production and the importance of teamwork, it might well turn out that this piece of no-nonsense wisdom is a lot less cunning than it appears. A romantic belief need not be taken as realistic just because it is crude.

2 Isolation and Social Investment

2.1 Group rationality and social choice

The combination of congruent and conflicting interests gives the incentive problem in group behaviour much complexity and richness.

27. *The Sunday Times*, 12 February 1984. The remark was made, in fact, by Michael Heseltine, one of the less 'dry' members of Mrs Thatcher's cabinet.

Some of these issues can be fruitfully studied in terms of certain distinguished games. The one that has been most used – for good reason – is the so-called 'Prisoners' Dilemma'.[28] While it is not invoked in the analysis of sub-optimality of savings in Essay 4 ('On Optimizing the Rate of Saving', 1961), the 'isolation paradox' discussed in that paper (and later in Essay 5) is, in fact, a case of the Prisoners' Dilemma extended to an n-person world. Each person is willing, in the circumstances specified, to save more for the future generation if this is a condition for inducing others to save more also, but will not save on their own, given whatever others do. The solution explored is the contractual one – through public investment.[29] The social contract is seen as the obvious solution, and the problem of its adoption is simplified by the fact that everyone is ready to vote for a compulsory contribution programme (even though none will contribute on their own). Rousseau's 'general will' takes over from Smith's 'invisible hand'.

This way of analysing the problem, it can be argued, is deeply flawed, for two distinct reasons. First, there will not typically be just one contractual outcome superior to the atomistic one, but *many* such outcomes – each preferred to none by all, but themselves ranked quite differently by the different participants. This is a game of the type that J. F. Nash called 'the bargaining problem'.[30] Cooperation can improve the lot of each, but differently in different cooperative solutions. Superimposed on the desirability of cooperation there can thus be a problem of conflict – possibly intense. This introduces a substantial difficulty in arriving at an agreed cooperative solution even when communication and collusion are possible and enforcement can be guaranteed.[31] Theories of collectivism based on

---

28. R. D. Luce and H. Raiffa, *Games and Decisions* (New York: Wiley, 1957).

29. See Essays 6 and 7, and also S. A. Marglin, 'The Social Rate of Discount and the Optimal Rate of Investment', *Quarterly Journal of Economics*, 77 (1963). Also E. S. Phelps, *Fiscal Neutrality Toward Economic Growth* (New York: McGraw-Hill, 1965). See also the earlier contributions of W. J. Baumol, *Welfare Economics and the Theory of the State* (Cambridge, Mass.: Harvard University Press, 1953; reprinted 1966), and O. Eckstein, 'Investment Criteria for Economic Development and Intertemporal Welfare Economics', *Quarterly Journal of Economics*, 71 (1957).

30. J. F. Nash, 'The Bargaining Problem', *Econometrica*, 18 (1950). See also my *Collective Choice and Social Welfare* (San Francisco: Holden-Day, 1970; reprinted Amsterdam: North-Holland, 1979), Chapter 8.

31. The necessity of enforcement is one of the respects in which the 'isolation paradox' differs from the 'assurance game' (see Essay 6), which is a game of some considerable interest of its own; see A. Deaton and J. Muellbauer, *Economics and Consumer Behaviour* (Cambridge: Cambridge University Press, 1980), Chapter 1. On the difficulties of arriving at a solution of the Prisoners' Dilemma because of problems of collusion and of enforcement, see Mancur Olson's important and influential work, *The Logic of Collective Action* (Cambridge, Mass: Harvard University Press, 1965).

the Prisoners' Dilemma and the isolation paradox are, I have tried to argue elsewhere, 'a great deal more successful in showing the inefficiency of individualistic allocation than in developing a precise collective alternative'.[32]

The issue of isolation and social contract links up here with general problems of 'social choice', and in particular, that of dealing with conflicts of interests and of judgements. The thrust of the 'isolation' discussion has been on the criterion of Pareto improvement.[33] That leaves us with a problem of choosing between various Pareto-improving contracts. There is no serious possibility of discussing these issues of failure of atomism (and the superiority of a contractual outcome) without taking on the complex problems that form the subject-matter of social choice theory. Rousseau has to face Arrow in addition to Smith.[34]

This does not, of course, imply that the problem must be insoluble, as is often suggested in simple-minded interpretations of Arrow's classic 'impossibility theorem'. Arrow's theorem shows the impossibility of getting a system of social choice based on a particular informational structure and a particular set of regularity and reasonability requirements. The former restriction — that of informational constraints — is especially limiting. While it corresponds exactly to the informational basis of traditional welfare economics (used since the thirties), it can be argued that one of the main messages of Arrow's far-reaching result is to reject that restriction. I have tried to

32. 'A Game-Theoretic Analysis of Theories of Collectivism in Allocation', in T. Majumdar (ed.), *Growth and Choice* (London: Oxford University Press, 1969), p. 15. In addition to problems arising from conflicts of interests and plurality of values, a further difficulty in the choice of a generally acceptable collective solution relates to the possible opaqueness of the *contents* of the alternative solutions. The simple game-theoretic models, with transparent solutions, are seriously misleading in this respect. The 'interpretation' of alternative outcomes may itself require quite a deep probe, especially in economic matters, e.g. in dealing with income distributions (on this see A. B. Atkinson, *Social Justice and Public Policy* (Brighton: Wheatsheaf, 1983), and Assar Lindbeck, 'Interpreting Income Distributions in a Welfare State', *European Economic Review*, 21 (1983)).

33. Indeed, the only welfare criterion used in this entire approach is the Paretian one. This raises the interesting question as to how individual valuations (e.g. of the rate of discount) could possibly differ from social valuations (the social rate based on Paretian — unanimous — aggregation of individual valuations). The peculiar problems of specification involved in this relationship is discussed in Essay 8 ('Approaches to the Choice of Discount Rates in Social Benefit–Cost Analysis'), below.

34. The literature on 'social choice' has grown enormously since its beginning with Kenneth Arrow's pioneering contribution, *Social Choice and Individual Values* (New York: Wiley, 1951). For a recent attempt at sorting out the main ideas developed in this large and technical literature, see my 'Social Choice Theory', in *The Handbook of Mathematical Economics*, ed. by K. J. Arrow and M. Intriligator, vol. 3 (Amsterdam: North-Holland, forthcoming).

discuss these issues elsewhere,[35] and will not further pursue them here. But the need to take on the difficulties of social choice in dealing with problems of 'isolation' (and the related questions of investment planning and public economics) does require emphasis.

The second problem concerns motivation and conduct. In the formulation of the isolation paradox and the Prisoners' Dilemma, the nature of individual behaviour is simplified by seeing it in terms of maximizing according to an individual preference ordering. This is, of course, entirely in line with traditional economic theory, in which too the assumption of invariable pursuit of a given individual ordering rules out important issues of motivation and behaviour. It can be seen that even if the participants in a Prisoners' Dilemma were maximizers of *moral* (rather than selfish) orderings – different for different persons – the same 'dilemma' could result.[36] The real issue concerns the tying-up of individual behaviour with individual goals (no matter whether self-interested or moral). The requirements of 'collective rationality' may call for a more sophisticated approach. 'Rational fools'[37] can be foolish moralists as easily as foolish egoists.

Social demands on *conduct* in situations of interdependence can go well beyond modifying the preference ordering of a person (e.g. in a more 'social' direction) and may involve systematic departures from the pursuit of one's preference orderings.[38] The obligations towards others may not just take the form of giving weights to their interests (or goals) in one's own goals, but may also require that one's choice of actions not be naïvely tied to one's goals (even moral goals). This does not necessarily involve the rejection of what moral philosophers call 'consequentialism',[39] but it does at least require a more sophisticated approach to the instrumental and strategic aspects of consequential pursuits.[40]

35. 'On Weights and Measures: Informational Constraints in Social Welfare Analysis', *Econometrica*, 45 (1977), reprinted in my *Choice, Welfare and Measurement* (1982), which also includes other papers on related subjects.

36. See particularly Derek Parfit, 'Prudence, Morality and the Prisoners' Dilemma', in *Proceedings of the British Academy for 1979* (London: Oxford University Press, 1981), and *Reasons and Persons* (Oxford: Clarendon Press, 1984).

37. 'Rational Fools: A Critique of the Behavioural Foundations of Economic Theory', *Philosophy and Public Affairs*, 6 (1977), reprinted in my *Choice, Welfare and Measurement* (1982).

38. See my 'Choice, Orderings and Morality', in S. Körner (ed.), *Practical Reason* (Oxford: Blackwell, 1974), reprinted in my *Choice, Welfare and Measurement* (1982).

39. See Bernard Williams, 'A Critique of Utilitarianism', in J. J. C. Smart and B. Williams, *Utilitarianism: For and Against* (Cambridge: Cambridge University Press, 1973). See also Essay 12 below.

40. Some discussion of the issues involved in this problem can be found in my *Choice, Welfare and Measurement* (1982: 'Introduction', and Essays 2–4); and in 'Liberty and Social Choice', *Journal of Philosophy*, 80 (1983), and 'Rationality, Interest and Identity', to be

The question of *rules of conduct* as opposed to the *contents of preference* is not, of course, a new one in social analysis. Even the father of modern economics, the much-misinterpreted Adam Smith, had argued: 'Those general rules of conduct, when they have been fixed in our mind by habitual reflection, are of great use in correcting misrepresentations of self-love concerning what is fit and proper to be done in our particular situation.'[41] Marx's analysis of 'ideology' and its role in social behaviour relates closely to these questions.[42] It has both moral and prudential bearings on the behaviour of groups, such as classes, occupation groups and communities.

While the discussions of 'isolation' problems (including those in Essays 4 and 5, republished in this volume) may have had a useful role in raising some important questions; nevertheless as explorations they have been limited and incomplete. This is especially so in (1) the failure to deal with the problem of non-uniqueness of possible social contracts, and (2) taking an oversimple view (in line with standard economic theory) of motivation and conduct.

2.2 *Savings and discount rates*

There has been quite a lively debate on the 'isolation paradox' applied to the problem of optimal savings and discounting – identifying the possible inoptimality of private savings and the inappropriateness of market discount rates.[43] The more general issues discussed in the last section (concerning the non-uniqueness of possible social contracts and the rationale of counterpreferential behaviour) did not figure much in this debate. The focus was more on what could be reason-

published in a volume of essays in honour of Albert Hirschman. See also T. Schelling, 'Self-Command in Policy, and in a Theory of Rational Choice', *American Economic Review*, 74 (1984), D. H. Regan, *Utilitarianism and Co-operation* (Oxford: Clarendon Press, 1980), Parfit, *Reasons and Persons* (1984) and K. Basu, *The Less Developed Economy* (Oxford: Basil Blackwell, 1984).

41. Adam Smith, *The Theory of Moral Sentiments*, III.4.12; republished edited by D. D. Raphael and A. L. Macfie (Oxford: Clarendon Press, 1974, p. 160.

42. See particularly *Grundrisse* and *The German Ideology*.

43. See the contributions referred to in footnote 29 above; the articles and books referred to in Essays 5 and 8 below (including those by Feldstein, Harberger, Lind, Tullock, Usher, Arrow); and also R. Layard (ed.), *Cost-Benefit Analysis* (Harmondsworth: Penguin. 1972); E. J. Mishan, *Cost-Benefit Analysis* (London: Allen & Unwin, 1972); R. Lecomber, 'The Isolation Paradox', *Quarterly Journal of Economics*, 41 (1977); S. Wellisz, 'Savings in Isolation and under a Collective Decision Rule', *Quarterly Journal of Economics*, 41 (1977); D. Collard, *Altruism and Economy* (Oxford: Martin Robertson, 1978); R. W. Boadway, *Public Sector Economics* (Cambridge, Mass.: Winthrop, 1979); P. Dasgupta and G. Heal, *Economic Theory and Exhaustible Resources* (Cambridge: Cambridge University Press and London: Nisbet, 1979); R. Sugden, *The Political Economy of Public Choice* (Oxford: Martin Robertson, 1981); P. G. Warr and B. D. Wright, 'The Isolation Paradox and the Discount Rate for Benefit–Cost Analysis', *Quarterly Journal of Economics*, 45 (1981).

ably assumed about the marginal values of the relevant parameters given an atomistic equilibrium with rational (preference-based) choice. Some of the criticisms of the 'Sen–Marglin results' (from Tullock, Lind, Usher, Harberger and others), I have had the occasion to discuss already in Essay 5 ('Isolation, Assurance and the Social Rate of Discount'), and will not discuss here any further.

In a later paper, Stanislaw Wellisz has argued that while 'Sen and Marglin have demonstrated that the atomistic and collective equilibrium savings rates do not necessarily coincide, ... it is impossible to tell on any *a priori* grounds which regime will lead to a higher rate of savings'.[44] Similarly, Peter Warr and Brian Wright (who have – as they generously say – 'cast no doubt on the analytical validity, intellectual interest, or potential social importance of the isolation paradox argument *itself*, or of other similar forms of the "prisoner's dilemma" framework') have disputed 'the claim that, in an economy where private savings for benevolent purposes and public (or private) investment coexist, projects should be discounted at a rate below the market rate of discount'.[45]

These points are quite correct, and the questioning well deserved. However, there is some difficulty in relying on arguments that require the existence of an 'interior' equilibrium in which *all* the activities concerned actually do take place. For example, one of Wellisz's arguments involves assuming that the person 'has a $20,000 income, saves $500 for his heirs, $400 for his nonheirs, but gives only $1 in charity', and on the assumption that this is an optimum, 'he derives equal utility from the marginal dollar devoted to any of the four activities' (p. 664).[46] But some of these activities can quite plausibly not figure *at all* in an optimal private equilibrium. Warr and Wright also make use of interior-equilibrium properties, involving (among other things) significant 'private savings *for beneficial purposes*' (p. 144, italics added). Indeed, that is how they derive the result that 'the appropriate rate of discount is the market rate'.[47]

44. Wellisz, 'Savings in Isolation and under a Collective Decision Rule' (1977), p. 65.

45. Warr and Wright, 'The Isolation Paradox and the Discount Rate for Benefit–Cost Analysis' (1981), p. 144.

46. Wellisz uses two arguments, of which this figures in the first, dealing with preferences being 'revealed through the market mechanism'. In his second argument he can see no *a priori* reason for taking values of parameters that would yield a below-optimal private savings. See also Lecomber, 'The Isolation Paradox' (1977).

47. 'What underlies these results is a "smoothing" of the impact of public projects both within and between generations via the private donations of individuals. If one generation or individual is initially affected adversely by a project, ... this is compensated for by a contraction in the voluntary donations of those individuals to the next generation, so as to restore the donor's private savings equilibrium' (Warr and Wright, p. 140). The economy moves from one 'interior' equilibrium to another, with private voluntary donations to future generations fully adjusted (without vanishing).

The 'marginalist' methodology imposes many restrictions anyway, but to assume further that all the activities – including donations – actually figure (with non-zero values) in *each* equilibrium is by no means just a slight addition to that load.

As far as the social discount rate is concerned, it is shown in Essay 8 ('Approaches to the Choice of Discount Rates in Social Benefit-Cost Analysis', 1982) that the contrast between the private and the social discount rates – as presented in Essay 5 – is in fact quite misleading, since they do not deal with the same interpersonal *composition* of consumption. Also it is easily seen that this contrast is not the same as that between the *market* rate and the social rate of discount. Indeed even if all the conditions of Essay 5 (and 'the Sen-Marglin model') were to hold, it is still possible for the social rate to be *either* above *or* below the market rate (Essay 8, pp. 178–84 below).

Essay 8 also goes into the nature of social choice decisions underlying the selection of social rates of discount. Attempts at avoiding this question by relying only on the Pareto criterion do not work, for reasons discussed already in the last section. And when social choice problems are explicitly faced, they are seen as involving not merely questions of utility gains and losses, but also those of equity and rights. Environmental issues, among others, figure prominently in this discussion (Essay 8, pp. 190–7).[48]

Two of the other papers in this section deal with rather different types of issues. Essay 6 ('Terminal Capital and Optimal Savings', 1967) is concerned with the formulation of finite-horizon optimal accumulation exercises, and argues for specifying a terminal margin of savings rather than a terminal stock of capital (cf. formulations of Graaff, Dobb, Chakravarty and others cited in Essay 6). The argument rests partly on showing that the results can vary quite sub-

---

48. See also the illuminating comments of Robert Dorfman, Mark Sherefkin and Talbot Page, on my essay in R. C. Lind *et al.*, *Discounting for Time and Risk in Energy Policy* (Washington, DC: Resources for the Future, 1982). On one point raised by Robert Dorfman, a brief response may be useful. In arguing against my rejection of 'welfarism' (social welfare being a function of individual utilities only), Dorfman notes – rightly – that individual utilities 'may also take note of animosity, envy, concern for their country's honor and prestige, dedication to civil liberties, devotion to justice and entitlements, esteem for democratic procedures, and all other such values'. He goes on to argue that 'on this interpretation, the [welfarist] SWFL is immune to criticisms that Sen levels at it in his section on "the inadequacy of welfarism"' (p. 354). The point has some plausibility, but there is a difference between valuing, say, *civil liberties* and valuing the *utility derived from civil liberties*. Welfarism requires not merely that nothing can be valued that does not give utility to someone, but also that the exact value of anything (e.g. liberty) must be based *entirely* on the utilities generated by it. On the inadequacies of this view, see my 'Utilitarianism and Welfarism', *Journal of Philosophy*, 76 (1979), and 'Rights and Agency', *Philosophy and Public Affairs*, 11 (1982). Also Essay 13 below.

stantially with the choice of terminal capital stock, and also that we shall not know *a priori* whether the terminal stock specified would be adequate to avoid the necessity of a fall in consumption immediately beyond the horizon specified. Fixing the terminal margin at a non-negative level guarantees that — other things given — there will be no such necessity, and further, it turns out that for certain ranges of values of factual and valuational parameters, commonly considered in the literature,[49] the determined terminal capital stock would vary within quite narrow limits for substantial variations of the terminal margin. These choices are, of course, ultimately political and involve all the 'social choice' difficulties referred to earlier. But 'if people would subscribe to the value judgment that the *necessity* of a future fall in consumption immediately beyond the horizon should be avoided', then 'the choice of terminal capital stock becomes considerably simpler' (Essay 6, p. 161).

Essay 7 ('On Some Debates in Capital Theory', 1974) is a somewhat impertinent attempt at discussing a great debate — on the measurement and use of aggregate capital — without the dedicated seriousness that the involved practitioners demand. A sceptical view is presented in Essay 7, though the *format* clearly suffers from the vice of ethnicity.

3   Shadow Pricing and Employment

3.1   Savings and the cost of labour

One of the elementary questions of development planning is why the unemployed labour force — open *and* 'disguised' — cannot be easily given jobs, creating full employment. Since many types of jobs require very little complementary capital goods (e.g. the making of rough rural roads, or the digging of ponds or irrigation channels), the constraint cannot be the absence of complementary capital goods. It was argued in my *Choice of Techniques* (1960)[50] that the primary constraint may come from the shortage of savings (see also Essays 9–11). Extra employment in the wage system involves expansion of purchasing power and greater consumption, leading to less savings,

49. See Sukhomoy Chakravarty, 'Optimal Savings with Finite Planning Horizon', *International Economic Review*, 3 (1962). See also his *Capital and Development Planning* (Cambridge, Mass.: MIT Press, 1969).

50. See especially Chapter V ('Labour Cost and Technological Choice'). Also my 'Labour Cost and Economic Growth', *Economic Weekly*, 8, 29 September 1956, and 'Some Notes on the Choice of Capital-Intensity in Development Planning', *Quarterly Journal of Economics*, 71 (1957). See also M. H. Dobb, *An Essay on Economic Growth and Planning* (London: Routledge, 1960).

unless the output can be correspondingly increased. The cost of labour use can thus be seen in terms of diverting resources from savings to consumption – leading to a social loss if savings are valued correspondingly more than consumption.

The argument was not really new (it goes back to Ricardo and Marx), nor entirely convincing. It is certainly based on a variety of institutional assumptions, which were spelt out (*Choice of Techniques*, Chapters II and V). The result is contingent on these assumptions holding. First, it depends on savings being suboptimal – an issue discussed in Essays 4, 5 and 8, and touched on in Section 2 of this Introduction. This requires not merely the suboptimality of market savings, but also that this suboptimality not be easily curable through public investment (Essay 9, pp. 208–12).

Second, it has plausibility only when the extra consumption resulting from extra employment cannot be avoided by extra taxation and other fiscal means. The assumption of the limitation of the fiscal machinery in raising taxes and savings was partly based on the reading of the Indian economy.[51] Interestingly enough, both the taxation ratio and the savings rate have gone up a great deal even in the poorer developing countries, including India, in the course of the last two decades,[52] and the assumption may be less appropriate now.

Third, the nature of the argument rests on the use of the wage system as the form of employment. The possibility of non-wage mobilization of labour – as in China – provides an alternative.[53] One of the arguments for breaking away from the wage system is this possibility of dissociating the expansion of employment from the necessity of an immediate addition to consumption, permitting the postponement of consumption benefits until the output expands. This type of strategy is not unrelated to the perceived rationale of the Cultural Revolution, which was briefly discussed in Section 1.2.[54]

Fourth, it is very misleading to think in terms of total consumption only, since the case for expanding the consumption of the poorest stratum may be very strong on its own rights. Employment expan-

51. See my 'Labour Cost and Economic Growth' (1956), and *Choice and Techniques* (1960). See also A. K. Das-Gupta, 'Disguised Unemployment and Economic Development', *Economic Weekly*, 8, 25 August 1956, and I. M. D. Little, 'The Real Cost of Labour and the Choice between Consumption and Investment', *Quarterly Journal of Economics*, 75 (1961).

52. See Essay 19 ('Development: Which Way Now?') below. Also I. M. D. Little, *Economic Development: Theory, Policy and International Relations* (New York: Basic Books, 1982).

53. See my 'Working Capital in the Indian Economy: A Conceptual Framework and Some Estimates', in P. N. Rosenstein-Rodan (ed.), *Pricing and Fiscal Policies* (London: Allen & Unwin, 1964), and *Employment, Technology and Development* (1975).

54. See my *On Economic Inequality* (1973), Chapter 4.

sion for the most deprived groups may not involve anything that can be regarded as a *net* 'cost' in terms of social welfare.[55] Indeed, employment can be a very useful means of getting consumption to the people for whom it is most important, and this policy may have a crucial strategic role in programmes to combat hunger and starvation (see Essay 18).

Essays 9–11 deal *inter alia* with these questions. They also tackle some rather more technical issues, in particular the meaning (or, more accurately, the meaning*s*) of the shadow price of labour and the parameters on which the shadow price (or prices) would depend. A variety of other questions are also addressed, e.g. integrating the determination of shadow wage with optimal investment planning (Essay 9), labour cost in the presence of extra migration (Essays 10 and 11), alternative concepts of unemployment (Essay 11), dual economy equilibria (Essay 11), trade in second-hand machinery (Essay 11).[56] There is clearly no point in trying to rediscuss these issues in this Introduction.[57]

3.2   *Constraints, control and project appraisal*

It is easy to see that investment planning involves many things that are 'essentially political in nature' (Essay 4, p. 125),[58] and the planning exercises have to obey 'constraints imposed by political factors' (Essay 9, p. 211). In Essay 10 ('Control Areas and Accounting

---

55. See Essays 10 and 11, and also my *Choice of Techniques* (1960), pp. 78–9.

56. On the last, see also my 'On the Usefulness of Used Machines', *Review of Economics and Statistics*, 44 (1962); M. A. M. Smith, 'Wage Differentials and Trade in Second-Hand Machines', *Journal of International Economics*, 6 (1976); and A. K. Dixit, *The Theory of Equilibrium Growth* (London: Oxford University Press, 1976), Chapter 4.

57. One class of problems of investment planning not taken up in any of the papers included in this selection is that of *intersectoral* allocation of investment, which relates closely to issues of optimal savings and project evaluation (discussed in several of the papers in this volume); see my 'Interrelations between Project, Sectoral and Aggregate Planning', *Economic Bulletin for Asia and the Far East*, 21 (1970). One particular type of sectoral problem, involving investment respectively in the intermediate goods sector and sectors producing machinery, was discussed in my joint paper with K. N. Raj, 'Alternative Patterns of Growth under Conditions of Stagnant Export Earnings', *Oxford Economic Papers*, 13 (1961). There was an exchange on this, involving J. Bhagwati, J. P. Lewis, G. Rosen, M. Scott and the two authors, in *Oxford Economic Papers*, 14 (1962). Important extensions of the analysis have been presented by A. B. Atkinson, 'Import Strategy and Growth under Conditions of Stagnant Export Earnings', *Oxford Economic Papers*, 21 (1969), and C. Cooper, 'Extensions of the Raj–Sen Model of Economic Growth', *Oxford Economic Papers*, 35 (1983).

58. This was one of the starting points of *Choice of Techniques* (1960), and it was argued that even some apparently technical exercises were 'not entirely a matter of positive economics', e.g. 'the calculation of the time series of national income' (p. 78); on that particular question, see Essay 17 ('The Welfare Basis of Real Income Comparisons') below.

Prices: An Approach to Economic Evaluation', 1972), importance is attached to the distinction between the political elements in the choice of planning *objectives*, on the one hand, and the political elements that *constrain* public policy, making the choice of 'control variables' (e.g. tax rates) significantly 'constrained within certain ranges' by administrative or political considerations, such as fear of military coup or political agitation.[59]

In contrasting the methods of project evaluation presented respectively by Dasgupta, Marglin and myself in the so-called UNIDO *Guidelines*,[60] and by Little and Mirrlees in their *Manual*,[61] the differences in the respective readings of the political elements (especially of the constraints imposed on the control variables) turn out to be important. In addition to discussing the general issue of control and planning, Essay 10 goes into this contrast between the two approaches to project appraisal and investment planning.[62] When the readings of the political constraints are similar, the framework of shadow prices is similar too, e.g. in the discussion of accounting wages,[63] for which the Little–Mirrlees formula does not differ essentially from the formulation used by Marglin and myself (see Essay 9).[64] The differences (including the important one of the reliance on

59. The constraints can, of course, be formally linked up with the objectives through 'Lagrangean multipliers' in a *reformulated* maximization exercise. That formal point can well be worth making (as it has sometimes been made), but there is no reason to confound *real* objectives, on the one hand, and the *derived* values of removing constraints, on the other.

60. P. Dasgupta, S. Marglin and A. Sen, *Guidelines for Project Evaluation*, UNIDO (New York: United Nations, 1972).

61. I. M. D. Little and J. A. Mirrlees, *Manual of Industrial Project Analysis in Developing Countries* (Paris: OECD, 1969), and *Project Appraisal and Planning for Developing Countries* (London: Heinemann, 1974). A third approach to project evaluation can be found in L. Squire and H. G. Van der Tak, *Economic Analysis of Projects* (Baltimore, Md.: Johns Hopkins Press, 1975). See also R. Layard, ed., *Cost-Benefit Analysis* (Harmondsworth: Penguin, 1972).

62. See also P. Dasgupta, 'A Comparative Analysis of the UNIDO *Guidelines* and the OECD *Manual*', *Bulletin of the Oxford Institute of Economics and Statistics*, 34 (1972).

63. For illuminating discussions, see L. Taylor, *Macro Models for Developing Countries* (New York: McGraw-Hill, Chapter 13, 1979), and A. P. Thirlwall, *Growth and Development with Special Reference to Developing Countries* (London: Macmillan, 3rd edn, 1983), Chapters 8 and 9.

64. The formulation was first derived by Stephen Marglin in his unpublished 'Industrial Development in the Labour-Surplus Economy' (1966); later published in a revised version, as *Value and Price in the Labour-Surplus Economy* (Oxford: Clarendon Press, 1976). A part of Essay 9 (1968) drew, as is acknowledged, on Marglin's analysis. The rationale for this way of seeing labour cost was discussed in my 'Some Notes on the Choice of Capital-Intensity in Development Planning' (1957) and *Choice of Techniques*, Chapter V ('Labour Cost and Technological Choice'); by Maurice Dobb in *Essays on Economc Growth and Planning* (1960); and by Ian Little, 'The Real Cost of Labour and the Choice between Consumption and Investment' (1961).

'world prices' in the Little–Mirrlees *Manual* in contrast with the UNIDO *Guidelines*[65]) relate to divergent readings of who can control what, and the contrasts are discussed in Essay 10.[66]

I have nothing much to add on this subject here, but I shall take the liberty of making one brief remark on a question that seems to have attracted some attention; to wit, whether the Little–Mirrlees *Manual* and the UNIDO *Guidelines* are essentially 'equivalent'.[67] Whatever the importance of this question (there is room for much scepticism here), it certainly cannot be resolved (as has been often attempted) by checking whether we shall get the same shadow prices and same evaluation if we make exactly the same assumptions about objectives and constraints (economic *and* political). The result of that checking exercise must be an affirmative one, which merely reflects that despite the use of different accounting procedures (and different numeraires), there are no obvious *analytical* errors – relevant to this comparison – in either work. The real contrast between the two approaches lies precisely in the choice of assumptions regarding objectives and constraints – especially political constraints. For example, the different relevance of world prices in the two approaches relates ultimately, as is argued in Essay 10, to differences in the respective views of what is 'a good theory of government action' – in particular who can control what.[68]

---

65. The issue, I believe, is not whether world prices are invariably correct or invariably incorrect, but the contingent nature of their appropriateness depending on substantive assumptions about who controls what.

66. See also E. Bacha and L. Taylor, 'Foreign Exchange Shadow Price: A Critical Review of Current Theories', *Quarterly Journal of Economics*, 85 (1971); P. Dasgupta and J. Stiglitz, 'Benefit–Cost Analysis and Trade Policies', *Journal of Political Economy*, 81 (1973); C. Blitzer, B. Clark and L. Taylor, *Economy-Wide Models and Development Planning* (London: Oxford University Press, 1975); J. Mirrlees, 'Social Benefit–Cost Analysis and the Distribution of Income', mimeographed, Nuffield College, Oxford, 1977; Akira Takayama, 'Alternative Policies under Fixed Exchange Rates', *Quarterly Journal of Economics*, 92 (1978); P. G. Warr, 'Shadow Pricing, Information and Stability in a Simple Open Economy', *Quarterly Journal of Economics*, 92 (1978); Taylor, *Macro Models for Developing Countries* (1979); C. Blitzer, P. Dasgupta and J. Stiglitz, 'Project Appraisal and Foreign Exchange Constraints', *Economic Journal*, 91 (1981).

67. See, for example, Deepak Lal, *Methods of Project Analysis – A Review* (Baltimore, Md.: Johns Hopkins Press, 1974); Frances Stewart, 'Social Cost–Benefit Analysis in Practice: Some Reflections in the Light of Case Studies Using Little–Mirrlees Techniques', *World Development*, 6 (1978); Janos Kornai, 'Appraisal of Project Appraisal', in M. Boskin (ed.), *Economics and Human Welfare* (New York: Academic Press, 1979).

68. For an illuminating analysis of the different political and economic assumptions underlying the UNIDO *Guidelines* and the Little–Mirrlees *Manual* (and respective criticisms of each), see Bimal Jalan, *Essays in Development Policy* (New Delhi: Macmillan, 1975), Essays 6 and 7. See also Taylor, *Macro Models for Developing Countries* (1979).

3.3 Ignorance and partial orders

The difficulties of correct specification do not, of course, apply only to political aspects of investment planning. Many of the economic variables are also hard to estimate and there is scope for different modelling of such features as wage determination, migration, and so on,[69] which would affect the calculations underlying investment planning. One of the most elementary aspects of investment planning is the way of handling informational lacunae and valuational ambiguity.

The literature on the rational treatment of uncertainty and ignorance is relevant to choosing sensible ways of proceeding in these cases.[70] It is also important to note that the extent of our ignorance is partly a matter of the time and effort we put into the empirical investigations providing the background to project appraisal. Given the limitations of resources and constraints on time, it is often necessary to choose between alternative investigations that would respectively reduce different areas of ignorance. In choosing between alternative inquiries, sensitivity analysis has much to offer, as was emphasized in the UNIDO Guidelines (Chapter 18).[71] Since the facilities and speed of computation are, in general, immensely superior to those of data gathering, the case for directing empirical attention on the basis of relative sensitivities of results to empirical knowledge is strong. The object is not really to get as much information as possible, but rather to be content with as little as would be adequate for a definite judgement.

The approach of making do with partial ignorance is discussed in Essay 11 ('Employment, Institutions and Technology: Some Policy Issues', 1975), Section 7. The values of variables on which there is some ignorance are specified partially, each value lying within a certain 'range'. The greater the ignorance, the wider the range. Informational lacunae can apply to shadow prices (e.g. the rates of discount) as well as particular factual parameters (e.g. rates of saving).

69. See, for example, J. Stiglitz, 'Alternative Theories of Wage Determination and Unemployment in LDCs: The Labour Turnover Model', Quarterly Journal of Economics, 88 (1974); M. Todaro, Internal Migration in Developing Countries (Geneva: ILO, 1976); O. Stark, 'On the Optimal Choice of Capital Intensity in LDCs with Migration', Journal of Development Economics, 9 (1981).

70. See K. J. Arrow, Essays in the Theory of Risk-Bearing (Amsterdam: North-Holland, 1971). Also UNIDO Guidelines, Chapter 10.

71. See also M. Datta-Chaudhuri and A. K. Sen, 'Durgapur Fertilizer Project: An Economic Evaluation', Indian Economic Review, 5 (1970), for an empirical exercise in sensitivity analysis applied to an Indian project.

Given all the range-specifications, the net present value (NPV) can be shown to lie within a certain range itself. If the *maximum* NPV is negative, the project would seem to be rejectable without having to narrow down the ranges. Similarly, if the *minimum* NPV is positive, then the project would seem to pass, despite the partial ignorance about several – possibly many – determining variables. The case for further investigation arises only when the maximum value is positive and the minimum negative. If this were to occur, sensitivity analysis can be used to decide which particular ignorance-range should have priority in terms of investigation aimed at narrowing that range. The object is to get the set of all NPV values on one side or the other of the zero line.[72]

The ignorance-ranges can reflect not merely gaps in factual knowledge, but also normative ambiguities. It is often hard to decide what weights to attach to different objectives and values, e.g. expanding longevity vis-à-vis raising real income.[73] Also, as Kornai notes, every 'real' society 'consists of interest groups': he argues that cost–benefit analysis may, within limits, 'successfully promote the tasks of planning: cognition and reconciliation of interests'.[74] When dealing with interest conflicts – reconcilable or not – weighting of the respective advantages of different groups is a crucial exercise, and these judgements tend inevitably to be both political and imprecise.

Some exercises in social choice theory have been concerned with ambiguities of values and information, and with obtaining, nevertheless, partial orders of alternatives.[75] The use of ranges of variable-values in project evaluation and cost–benefit analysis is one example of addressing informational lacunae or intrinsic ambiguity. To try to follow a procedure of investment planning that insists on complete information and precise valuational parameters is like seeing a Greek tragedy – the doom is never in doubt.

The issue of conflicts of interests raises another question, to wit, whose interests are the planner or the project evaluator supposed to serve. Frances Stewart has argued that 'use of government values as widely advocated is illegitimate because governments represent particular classes'.[76] This is, of course, a very general problem – not just

72. See Datta-Chaudhuri and Sen (1970). Also my *Employment, Technology and Development* (1975), Chapter 13.

73. See Essays 19 ('Development: Which Way Now?' 1983) and 20 ('Goods and People').

74. Kornai, 'Appraisal of Project Appraisal' (1979), p. 96.

75. See my *Collective Choice and Social Welfare* (1970) and *Choice, Welfare and Measurement*, pp. 21-5, 203-79. See also my joint paper with Mukul Majumdar, 'A Note on Representing Partial Orderings', *Review of Economic Studies*, 43 (1976), and Partha Dasgupta, *The Control of Resources* (Oxford: Blackwell, 1982), Chapter 3.

76. Frances Stewart, 'A Note on Social Cost–Benefit Analysis and Class Conflict in LDCs', *World Development*, 3 (1975), p. 31.

of cost–benefit analysis – and applies to advising any government in any sphere of action. There are really two distinct issues here. The first concerns the decision whether or not to help a government, and the second how best to help a government that one has chosen to help. Much of the project appraisal literature is really addressed to the second question, though there is no great difficulty in doing project evaluation for purposes of non-government evaluation, including social criticism (even arguing for a rebellion), using values different from those adhered to by the government in power.[77] But the former question (i.e. whether to help a particular government) is an important personal one for the practising economist, and is at once moral and political. In dealing with this particular question, the usual techniques of cost–benefit analysis certainly offer little help.

4 *Morals and Mores*

4.1 *Information, ethics and policy*

Essays 12 ('Ethical Issues in Income Distribution: National and International', 1981) and 13 ('Rights and Capabilities', 1983) deal with normative economics. The dominant moral approach in economics has undoubtedly been the utilitarian one, and that tradition still exercises a good deal of influence on the way normative problems are posed and dealt with in economics.[78] In Essay 12 utilitarianism is contrasted with other moral approaches. Their respective bearings on judgements of income distribution are examined and also used to assess some controversies on international inequalities and their policy implications.

There is not much point in going over the ground again in this Introduction, but the relevance of 'informational' issues to ethical judgements may be worth spelling out a little more, especially since it is of particular relevance to normative economic analysis. Any moral principle uses certain types of information and ignores others. The decision to use that principle implies willingness to be guided by that class of information, and – perhaps more importantly – to *exclude* the use of other types of information.

---

77. See *Collective Choice and Social Welfare* (1970), pp. 191-2; *UNIDO Guidelines*, p. 259; Essay 8, pp. 173-203; Marglin, *Value and Price in the Labour-Surplus Economy* (1976); Dasgupta, *Control of Resources* (1982).

78. See my 'Personal Utilities and Public Judgments: Or What's Wrong with Welfare Economics?' *Economic Journal*, 89 (1979), reprinted in my *Choice, Welfare and Measurement* (1982), and a volume of essays jointly edited with Bernard Williams, *Utilitarianism and Beyond* (Cambridge: Cambridge University Press, 1982), including our 'Introduction'.

The exclusion aspect of moral principles can be illustrated with the case of, say, utilitarianism. In judging between two alternative actions the utilitarian approach would exclude the use of all information other than that about the consequent states of affairs (this is the feature of 'consequentialism' discussed in Essay 12), and in judging the consequent states of affairs the approach would exclude all information other than utility information related to those states (this feature is called 'welfarism').[79]

If these excluded types of information were to be non-available, then the exercise of justifying the utilitarian approach is to that extent made easier. And the same, of course, applies to other approaches as well. In Essay 12 it is shown how the case for a specific moral approach may rest on 'the dual characteristic of the *presence* of some information *and* the *absence* of others' (p. 291). Informational limitations have been used – often implicitly – in disputes about international policy to tilt the moral balance in one direction or another (pp. 299–300).

While there is no real attempt in Essay 12 to argue in favour of one moral theory over another, it is shown that many *derived* moral beliefs and attitudes are not easy to sustain, even when the theory allegedly supporting them is accepted. For example, Robert Nozick's 'entitlement theory',[80] which is often invoked to justify global conservatism and the refusal to offer international assistance, does in fact impose quite demanding conditions for its use, making its application in the chosen contexts deeply problematic (p. 293). Essay 12 is mainly devoted to clarifying different moral approaches and their implications on distributional questions in general and international inequalities in particular.

In contrast, Essay 13 is more assertive, and argues against certain positions (e.g. utilitarianism, the Nozickian entitlement theory, the Rawlsian focus on 'primary goods',[81] Dworkin's approach of 'equality

---

79. Of the three components into which utilitarianism is factorized in Essay 12 (pp. 277–8, 'sum-ranking' has not been invoked here. This is because sum-ranking is *not* an 'informational' restriction. It only requires that the utility information (to which attention is restricted by the other two requirements, viz. consequentialism and welfarism) should be used in an *additive* way. Examples of consequentialist-cum-welfarist moral approaches that violate sum-ranking include the 'maximin' (and 'lexicographic maximin') approach – sometimes called 'Rawlsian' – used in welfare economics. See E. S. Phelps (ed.), *Economic Justice* (Harmondsworth: Penguin, 1973); J. E. Meade, *The Just Economy* (London: Allen & Unwin, 1976); A. B. Atkinson, *Social Justice and Public Policy* (Brighton: Wheatsheaf, 1983).

80. R. Nozick, *Anarchy, State and Utopia* (Oxford: Blackwell, 1974).

81. J. Rawls, *A Theory of Justice* (Oxford: Clarendon Press, 1981). My debt to Rawls in developing an alternative perspective (the 'capability' approach) is, however, enormous.

of resources'[82]). It also argues in favour of an informational format that focuses on positive freedom and capabilities. I am well aware of the difficulties and uncertainties of substantive moral arguments of this kind (especially ones that are ambitious, as indeed these are). I am also aware that the arguments used here cannot, in any way, be seen to be definitive, and furthermore that the vital question of 'founding' moral judgements[83] has been left unanswered here. Some of these issues have been further pursued elsewhere.[84] Whether or not these other arguments carry any conviction, Essay 13 is best seen in the present context as spelling out the implications of using a particular informational format for normative analysis and outlining some advantages of approaching questions of judgement and policy in that way.

One further point to make concerns the fact that the capability perspective can be used in many different ways, since an informational format for ethical analysis does not provide a specific moral formula.[85] In particular, the question of the 'trade-offs' between 'equality' of capabilities and the overall 'size' has not been at all addressed here. In fact, much of the focus of Essay 13 is on the more primitive normative question as to how to judge a person's 'advantage', and on what type of information to base judgements of states, actions, institutions and societies.

In Essay 14 ('Poor, Relatively Speaking', 1983) the capability approach is used to throw light on certain aspects of our perception of poverty and deprivation. In particular the coexistence of 'absolute' and 'relative' considerations in the judgement of poverty can be understood and analysed in terms of this approach. Certain capabilities (e.g. the capability to be well-nourished) may largely depend on the person's *absolute* intake of food, whereas other capabilities (e.g. that of appearing in public without shame) depends crucially on what clothing, etc., the person possesses *relative* to others and in relation

82. R. Dworkin, 'What is Equality? Part 1: Equality of Welfare', and 'What is Equality? Part 2: Equality of Resources', *Philosphy and Public Affairs*, 10 (1981).

83. Cf. T. Scanlon, 'Contractualism and Utilitarianism', in Sen and Williams, *Utilitarianism and Beyond* (1982).

84. See my 'Equality of What?' in S. McMurrin (ed.), *Tanner Lectures on Human Values*, vol. I (Cambridge: Cambridge University Press, 1980), reprinted in my *Choice, Welfare and Measurement* (1982); 'Rights and Agency', *Philosophy and Public Affairs*, 11 (1982); *Commodities and Capabilities* (Amsterdam: North-Holland, forthcoming); John Dewey Lectures (1984), to be published.

85. The distinction is similar to the one discussed in footnote 79, in the context of 'sum-ranking', which induces a particular formula on an informational (in this case, utility-based) format. With a capability-based format the need for specific formulations would have to be faced as an additional exercise – not, of course, unrelated to the informational exercise, but nevertheless distinct from it.

to established standards in that community.[86] Thus the demand for a minimum capability for all relates to some *absolute commodity requirements* (more accurately, to some absolute 'characteristic' commands, in the sense of Gorman and Lancaster) and other *relative commodity requirements* (or relative characteristic commands).[87] What is entirely absolute in one space (capabilities) is partly relative in another (commodities), translating into minimum income requirements with some 'relative' features. Essay 14 analyses the problem of identification and measurement of poverty in that perspective.

4.2 *Family relations*

The conception of poverty in terms of deprivation of capabilities links up issues of morals with those of mores. Mores and norms are especially important when intrafamily allocations and distributions are considered. Essay 15 ('Family and Food: Sex Bias in Poverty', 1981) is an empirical paper with rather little analytical content. It presents some evidence in favour of the diagnosis of sex bias in intrafamily divisions in a part of South Asia, in India and Bangladesh.

The capability approach is also used here, examining certain achievements in terms of avoidance of undernourishment, morbidity and premature mortality. The often-used procedure of checking sex bias by comparing commodity consumptions (e.g. food intakes) of particular family members is found to be empirically inconvenient as well as conceptually unsound. Using the informational framework of certain elementary achievements is more promising, and is utilized here to identify certain *prima facie* evidence of sex bias in intra-family divisions. Essay 14 has been followed up by other empirical studies,[88] which extend these findings. They indicate considerable heterogeneity of observed sex bias even between very closely located communities, raising interesting questions of causal influence.[89]

86. This point goes back, in fact, to Adam Smith, as is explained in Essay 14 (p. 335).

87. This is not, strictly speaking, correct, since the relation between commodity vectors and capability bundles may be a 'many–one' correspondence. On this see Essay 20, pp. 510–11. Rather, we should refer to *sets* of absolute and relative commodity requirements respectively. But the *minimum income requirement*, at given commodity prices, to achieve a certain capability bundle, is of course a well-defined problem.

88. Including two papers with co-authors, viz. J. Kynch and A. K. Sen, 'Indian Women: Well-being and Survival', *Cambridge Journal of Economics*, 7 (1983), and A. K. Sen and S. Sengupta, 'Malnutrition of Rural Children and the Sex Bias', *Economic and Political Weekly*, 18, Annual Number (May 1983).

89. For example, in West Bengal the sex bias in malnutrition of children aged 5 or less in a village called Sahajapur was found to be rather little, whereas that in another called Kuchli within 10 kilometres of Sahajapur turned out to be quite severe (Sen and Sengupta, 'Malnutrition of Rural Children and the Sex Bias' (1983)). Some of the questions raised are briefly discussed in Essay 16, pp. 380–1.

The last section of Essay 15 goes into the economic analysis of families, and in particular into the ways of characterizing conflict and congruence of interests within families. The question of *perception* of interest is an important one in this context, and the contrast between observed inequalities and perceived harmony makes this a particularly hard area of economic analysis.

Approaches to family economics are also discussed in Essay 16 ('Economics and the Family', 1983). Part of the paper is negative, disputing various approaches involving assumptions of 'the glued-together family', 'the super-trader family', or 'the despotic family'. On the more positive side, it is argued that a serious attempt to deal with family economics must come to grips with the problem of 'cooperative conflicts', of which a Nash-type 'bargaining problem' is an illustration. The parties can gain from cooperation, but there are many cooperative solutions, and the choice between them involves conflicts of interest. The problem of cooperative conflict can be trivially resolved through some special formula, e.g. an 'implicit-market-based' outcome (family relations determined by *as if* price-taking market behaviour), or some implicit mechanism for an 'optimal' distribution within the family.[90] But these stories hide more than they reveal. It seems plausible to argue that the nature of co-operative conflicts has to be clearly characterized in the analysis of family economics.

The format of the Nash-type 'bargaining problem' is helpful in bringing out the inescapable combination of 'cooperative' and 'conflicting' features of family economics.[91] But the format is also rather limited because of the assumptions of *unambiguous* perception of individual interest and preference, representable for each by an 'ordering' (indeed, one with 'cardinal' properties, as assumed by Nash and those following him). It is arguable that a more plausible approach

90. A good example of the 'optimal' allocation view of the family can be found in P. A. Samuelson, 'Social Indifference Curves', *Quarterly Journal of Economics*, 70 (1956). The 'implicit market' approach is well developed by G. S. Becker, *A Treatise on the Family* (Cambridge, Mass.: Harvard University Press, 1981). But Becker combines this 'implicit market' approach with some very special assumptions of preferences of family members, the result of which is that 'all beneficiaries voluntarily maximize family income and the utility of the altruist [head]' and 'the "group preference function" is identical to that of the altruistic head' (pp. 191-2). While this assumed pattern of 'altruism and voluntary contributions' eliminates some of the oddities of the 'implicit market' view of family behaviour, the crucial features of 'cooperative conflicts' continue to remain well-hidden (here, in the unanimous pursuit of the preference function of the 'altruistic head'), thanks to the special assumptions made by Becker.

91. I have argued in that direction in Essay 16, and also in 'Cooperative Conflicts: Technology and the Position of Women', mimeographed, All Souls College, Oxford, 1983. See also the contributions of Clemhout and Wan, Manser and Brown, McElroy and Horney, Rochford and Pollak, cited in footnote 10 of Essay 16.

would formalize cooperative conflicts in a way that admits ambiguities of interest perception and also gives explicit roles to notions of 'normality' and 'legitimacy' of accepted patterns of intra-family distributions. Our normative rejection of such notions of 'legitimacy' (e.g. of the family head getting more, or those earning incomes from outside having larger claims) need not make us overlook the important descriptive and predictive roles that such perceptions of legitimacy, obligations and interest have. Many of the inequities of the world survive by making allies out of the deprived and the abused (an issue discussed in Essay 13). The rigid format of the 'bargaining problem' with each party clearly perceiving and pursuing its own interests (whether or not cardinally representable) tends to mis-specify the nature of the problem, even though it has the merit of pointing towards the combination of cooperative and conflicting features of family economics.

The nature of family economics would seem to require a substantial departure from many models that have proved useful in analysing other types of economic problems. Seeking 'qualitative' relationships (characterizing 'directional' responses, rather than firmly identifying a particular outcome) may well be a more realistic – though less ambitious – way of modelling family relations.[92] It is easier to see family relations as involving 'cooperative conflicts', and to reject approaches that hide that view, than to determine what precise approach will do justice to that perspective.

5   Goods and Well-being

5.1   Entitlements and development

Essay 18 ('Ingredients of Famine Analysis: Availability and Entitlements', 1981) presents an analysis of hunger and famines in terms of 'entitlement analysis'.[93] Entitlements refer to the bundles of commodities over any of which a person can establish command, by using the rules of acquirement that govern his circumstances. Essay 19 ('Development: Which Way Now?', 1983) views the process of development as an expansion of people's entitlements and the capabilities enjoyed by the use of these entitlements.

---

92. This 'qualitative' approach is defended and used (mainly in the context of sex bias in developing countries) in 'Women, Technology and Sexual Divisions', a paper prepared for the Technology Division of UNCTAD and INSTRAW (United Nations), 1984.

93. This has close links with my book *Poverty and Famines: An Essay on Entitlement and Deprivation* (Oxford: Clarendon Press, 1981).

Empirical analyses of actual hunger and famines are used to illustrate the point that starvation – even large-scale famines – can take place in situations of good food availability if the entitlements enjoyed by particular occupation groups collapse for some reason. The reasons for such collapse can be various, e.g. reduction of endowment (e.g. land alienation), or changes in terms of trade (e.g. fall in the food-equivalent of money wages), or failure of trade (e.g. unemployment), or failure of production – 'exchange with nature' (e.g. peasant output failure).[94] They may or may not be associated with a decline in food availability per head.

The term 'entitlement' might not have been well chosen. It is liable to be confused with a moral right, though it *was* warned that this would be a mistake (Essay 18, p. 453).[95] The focus was more on legality, and the fact that in many cases, 'the law stands between food availability and food entitlement, and famine deaths can reflect legality with a vengeance' (Essay 18, p. 480). The term also suggested that not only the analysis and the applications, but also the concept itself, might be novel, which certainly it is not. But whether 'entitlement' is a badly chosen term or not, the need for studying entitlement in order to understand the causation of hunger and famines is strong.[96] In the past, economic policies regarding food have often been ineffective, or worse, precisely because of concentrating on misleading variables, e.g. total food output, physical transport capacity. Unhappily, these mistakes are still made, and some of the case studies in Essay 18 deal, in fact, with the very recent past.[97]

Essay 20 ('Goods and People') goes, *inter alia*, into different aspects of food policy, dealing with entitlements of families, the division of food within the family, and ultimately the capabilities of different sections of the society to be well nourished. Entitlement analysis is important for food policy, but food policy calls for more than that. Entitlements are only part of the story; but it is an important part – and one that has been often neglected with tragic results.[98]

---

94. See Essay 18, and also *Poverty and Famines* (1981).

95. Also in *Poverty and Famines* (1981), p. 2.

96. See also K. J. Arrow, 'Why People Go Hungry', *New York Review of Books*, 29, 15 July 1982; M. J. Desai, 'A General Theory of Poverty?', mimeographed; forthcoming in *Indian Economic Review*.

97. See also my 'The Food Problem: Theory and Policy', *Third World Quarterly*, June 1982.

98. See also my 'Famines as Failures of Exchange Entitlement', *Economic and Political Weekly*, 11 (1976); K. Griffin, *International Inequality and National Poverty* (London: Macmillan, 1978); A. Ghose, 'Short Term Changes in Income Distribution in Poor Agrarian Families', ILO Working Paper WEP 10-6/WP28 (Geneva); M. Alamgir, *Famine in South Asia – Political Economy of Mass Starvation in Bangladesh* (Cambridge, Mass.: Oelgeschlager,

5.2   Well-being, utility and opulence

What is well-being? There are many views, but two in particular are commonly used in economics, viz. utility and opulence. The former view — that of well-being as utility — comes straight out of the strong utilitarian tradition in economics, though it is less exacting than the full utilitarian discipline would demand. No matter how the goodness of states of affairs or the rightness of actions is judged, the utility view of well-being identifies the *well-being of a person* with one of the various interpretations of utility, viz. happiness, desire-fulfilment, or the binary relation of choice. The last — an offshoot of the theory of revealed preference — is a bit of a non-starter since it is bizarre to suppose that whatever one chooses — no matter out of what motive — must be conducive to one's own well-being.[99] But happiness and desire-fulfilment are serious enough candidates for capturing the idea of personal well-being. The classical utilitarians (e.g. Jeremy Bentham) favoured the former view, whereas modern utilitarians (e.g. Richard Hare) seem more inclined towards the latter.[100] Pigou took the happiness view but rather hoped that the two concepts would empirically coincide.[101]

The opulence view goes back at least to Adam Smith, springing straight out of the motivating concern of *The Wealth of Nations*,[102] to wit, to determine what makes a nation 'better or worse supplied with all the necessaries and conveniences for which it has occasion' (p. 1) and to explain 'the different progress of opulence in different ages and nations' (p. 375). In a framework in which commodity bundles are evaluated through a utility function, opulence can be sensibly thought of as the *commodity basis of utility*. It is not, of

Gunn and Hain, 1980); E. Oughton, 'The Maharashtra Drought of 1970–73: An Analysis of Scarcity', *Oxford Bulletin of Economics and Statistics*, 44 (1982); M. Ravallion, 'The Performance of Rice Markets in Bangladesh During the 1974 Famine', *Economic Journal*, forthcoming; Q. M. Khan, 'A Model of Endowment Constrained Demand for Food in an Agricultural Economy with Empirical Applications to Bangladesh', *World Development*, forthcoming.

99. It also gets one to a rotten start on interpersonal comparison of well-being — surely one important part of understanding well-being. No one really faces the *choice* of becoming someone else, though it is sometimes nice to think about that mind-boggling possibility (especially in sticky situations, when absence of body would be even better than presence of mind).

100. For comparisons of the various approaches and two assessments of the respective advantages, see J. C. B. Gosling, *Pleasure and Desire* (Oxford: Clarendon Press, 1969); A. K. Sen, 'Plural Utility', *Proceedings of the Aristotelian Society*, 81 (1981).

101. A. C. Pigou, *The Economics of Welfare* (London: Macmillan, 4th edn, 1952), p. 24.

102. Adam Smith, *An Inquiry into the Nature and Causes of Nations*, 1776; reprinted, Everyman's Library (London: Dent, 1954), vol. I.

course, utility as such, though the temptation to confuse the two is evidently strong. The difference remains even with 'given tastes' (in the sense of a given indifference map). The distinction is easily seen by considering two utility functions $U_1(\cdot)$ and $U_2(\cdot)$ holding in two periods 1 and 2 when the commodity bundles enjoyed are x_1 and x_2, respectively. Take the following ordering of utilities: $U_1(x_2) > U_1(x_1) > U_2(x_2) > U_2(x_1)$. The person is clearly more opulent in period 2 since x_2 is valued higher than x_1 in both periods (with unchanged tastes), and nevertheless the person has more utility in period 1 than in period 2, since $U_1(x_1) > U_2(x_2)$.[103]

In Essay 17 ('The Welfare Basis of Real Income Comparisons', 1979) both opulence comparisons and utility comparisons are discussed. They are called respectively 'situational' and 'comprehensive' comparisons (Section 2.3). The two coincide when the utility function is unchanged – an assumption that is more justifiable for rational choice theory and for planning (comparing *alternatives* counterfactually) than in actual intertemporal or interpersonal comparisons of well-being. Various conceptual, strategic and interpretative issues of personal and interpersonal comparisons are discussed, and the essay then moves on to comparisons of *social* income, involving aggregation over persons. Here too various approaches are compared, contrasted and assessed (including the 'named good' approach presented elsewhere).[104]

While comparisons of utility and those of opulence have interest of their own, the claim of either concept to reflect well-being is disputed in Essay 20 ('Goods and People'). The ethical disputes raised in Essay 13 ('Rights and Capabilities') reappear here, in a somewhat different garb, and the informational format of the capability approach is defended in the context of development analysis and policymaking. Other approaches, e.g. that of 'basic needs', are compared and contrasted.

103. See Essay 17, pp. 406–8. See also H. Gintis, 'Alienation and Power: Toward a Radical Welfare Economics', Ph.D. dissertation, Harvard University, 1969; F. M. Fisher and K. Shell, *The Economic Theory of Price Indices* (New York: Academic Press, 1972); A. K. Sen, 'The Living Standard', *Oxford Economic Papers*, forthcoming in the special number in honour of John Hicks.

104. See my 'Real National Income', *Review of Economic Studies*, 43 (1976); reprinted in *Choice, Welfare and Measurement* (1982). See also P. Hammond, 'Economic Welfare with Rank Order Price Weighting', *Review of Economic Studies*, 45 (1978); J. Muellbauer, 'Distributional Aspects of Price Comparisons', in R. Stone and W. Peterson (eds), *Economic Contributions to Price Policy* (London: Macmillan, 1978); K. Roberts, 'Price Independent Welfare Propositions', *Journal of Public Economics*, 13 (1980); A. B. Atkinson and F. Bourguignon, 'The Comparison of Multidimensional Distributions of Economic Status', *Review of Economic Studies*, 49 (1982); S. R. Osmani, *Economic Inequality and Group Welfare* (Oxford: Clarendon Press, 1982).

The essays dealing with the capability approach are all fairly new, and I do not have much to add to what is said there. However, it may perhaps be worth emphasizing that the case for the utility approach is much less convincing in *inter*personal comparisons than in *intra*personal ones (especially in comparing *alternative* positions of the same person). A person's relative desires for various objects may *prima facie* provide a sensible basis for valuing these objects from his or her point of view. But in interpersonal comparisons the same procedure can produce arbitrarinesses of various sorts. The social underdog who has been taught — perhaps by bitter experience — to expect little from life may have learned to have easily fulfillable desires and may take pleasure in small mercies. But it is hard to think that the person, for that reason, has a lot of well-being; or that he or she is having an excellent deal if those disciplined desires get fulfilled.

The question can be of some importance in comparing well-beings across social classes, or of the illiterate vis-à-vis the educated, or of women vis-à-vis men in a sexist environment. 'He that desires but little has no need of much' may well be good advice for contentment and for coming to terms with a harsh reality. But it is not a formula for judging well-being. Nor is it a recipe for social justice.

Part I

Institutions and Motivation

1

Peasants and Dualism with or without Surplus Labour

This paper has four objects. In the first section the economic equilibrium of a peasant family is studied. In the second section we discuss the theory of surplus labour and disguised unemployment and, more generally, the response of peasant output to a withdrawal of the working population. The third section goes into an analysis of a dual equilibrium of a partly peasant, partly capitalist agriculture. In the last section some observations are made on the efficiency of resource allocation in peasant agriculture and in share-cropping. Illustrations on the working of peasant agriculture come mostly from India, though the general framework might be of somewhat wider interest.

1   *Economic Equilibrium of a Peasant Family*

1.1   *The simplest model*

Imagine a community of identical peasant families, with α working members, β total members ($\beta \geqslant \alpha$), and with a given stock of land and capital. The family output Q, at a given point of time, is a function of labour L alone, and the function is smooth (twice-differentiable throughout) and normal (with diminishing marginal productivity of labour).

$$Q = Q(L), \text{ with } Q''(L) < 0. \tag{1}$$

Furthermore, the marginal productivity of labour is assumed either (i) to become zero for a finite value of labour ($\bar{L}$), with a maximum

I have greatly benefited from the comments of Harry Johnson and Theodore Schultz, and from discussions with Amiya Bagchi, Dipak Banerji, Dale Jorgenson, John Mellor, Carl Riskin, and Daniel Thorner.

From *Journal of Political Economy*, 74 (October 1966), 425–50.

output ($\bar{Q}$); or (ii) to approach zero asymptotically.[1] The two alternative possibilities define (1) further.

$$\bar{Q} = \max_L Q(L) = Q(\bar{L}), \text{ and } Q'(\bar{L}) = 0, \tag{2}$$

or

$$\lim_{L \to \infty} Q'(L) = 0. \tag{3}$$

The peasants are guided in their allocational efforts by the aim of maximizing the happiness of the family.[2] The peasants have not heard of difficulties of interpersonal comparisons of utility, and make such comparisons blatantly. Furthermore, they know that every member of the family has a personal utility function U which is a function of individual income q, and every working member has a personal disutility function V related to his individual labour l, and the functions U and V are of the same shape for everyone.[3] The marginal utility from income is positive and non-increasing, and the marginal disutility from labour is non-negative and non-decreasing.[4]

$$U = U(q), \text{ with } U'(q) > 0, \text{ and } U''(q) \leqslant 0. \tag{4}$$

$$V = V(l), \text{ with } V'(l) \geqslant 0, \text{ and } V''(l) \geqslant 0. \tag{5}$$

Each person's notion of family welfare W is given by the net utility from income and effort of all members taken together, attaching the same weight to everyone's happiness. Attaching subscript i to the utility or disutility of the ith individual, we get the following expression for family welfare, W.

$$W = \sum_1^\beta U_i - \sum_1^\alpha V_i. \tag{6}$$

It is assumed further that work is equally divided between working members, and income equally between all members. This can either be taken as a rule of thumb or derived from welfare maximization. When the marginal utility of income is strictly diminishing and the marginal disutility of labour is strictly increasing, egalitarian distri-

1. For the substitutability assumptions underlying such a production function, see A. Guha (1963). We assume this for the existence of an equilibrium.
2. See Robinson (1960, Chapter I); see also Mellor (1963).
3. Alternatively one can modify the formulation of the problem by making the utility function variable with age; for example, children having greater (or less) needs than adults. No essential difference is made in our analysis by such a change.
4. We are ruling out satiety, that is, marginal utility being zero at very high income levels. No sleep need be lost on this assumption for a peasant economy.

bution will be the only one consistent with welfare maximization; and even under the less restrictive conditions given by (4) and (5), egalitarian distribution will be one of the rules consistent with welfare maximization, without being unique in this respect.

$$L = \alpha \cdot l, \tag{7}$$

$$Q = \beta \cdot q, \tag{8}$$

$$W = \beta \cdot U - \alpha \cdot V. \tag{9}$$

Leaving out the odd case of welfare maximization at zero labour, by assuming that $Q'(0) \cdot U'(0) > V'(0)$, it is easy to verify that family welfare is maximized when the following condition is met.

$$Q'(L) = \frac{V'(l)}{U'(q)} \equiv x. \tag{10}$$

We define x as the 'real cost of labour'; it is given by the individual rate of indifferent substitution between income and labour. The rule given by (10) is easy to interpret: labour is applied up to the point where its marginal product equals the 'real cost of labour'. Given the form of equations (1), (4), and (5), it can be verified that the second-order conditions are also fulfilled.

Two methods of implementation of the decision given by rule (10) are possible. One is that the head of the family takes the decision on behalf of the entire family and tells the individual members what to do. A second interpretation is that each working member is free to decide how much to work, but since he equates the interests of the other members of the family with his own, he is guided to the point given by (10). He equates his personal marginal disutility from work, that is, $V'(l)$, not with his personal marginal utility from his own share of the marginal product, which is

$$\left[\frac{Q'(L)}{\beta} \right] \cdot U'(q),$$

but β times that, which is the family's total gain from the extra unit of his effort.[5]

Finally, since $Q''(L) < 0$ throughout, not only is $Q'(L)$ a function of L, but L itself is a function of $Q'(L)$, that is, the inverse function exists. But $Q'(L)$ equals the real cost of labour at each point of equilibrium. The value of total family labour employed can, there-fore, be expressed as a function of the real labour cost given equili-

5. Cf. Harsanyi (1955).

brium. Similarly, the value of total family output and income can also be expressed as a function of the real labour cost. This relationship we shall find convenient later (Section 2.1).

$$L = \phi[Q'(L)] = \phi(x). \tag{11}$$

$$Q = \psi[Q'(L)] = \psi(x). \tag{12}$$

It is easy to check that ϕ and ψ are decreasing functions of x, that is, a higher equilibrium real labour cost goes with lower volumes of total family labour and output; if $x_2 > x_1$, we have $\phi(x_2) < \phi(x_1)$, and $\psi(x_2) < \psi(x_1)$.

1.2 Production for a market

In the last section we considered production for direct consumption only; but peasant economies often rely significantly on the sale of their product to markets. In fact, if the product in question is of the type of, say, jute, or rubber, or cocoa, the whole of the product might be sold. The amount of the product Q may be exchanged for an amount C of products directly enjoyable by the peasants. We relate individual utility to the individual share of this (c) and correspondingly modify equation (4) keeping it, however, of the same analytical type, with positive non-increasing marginal utility.

$$U = U(c), \text{ with } U'(c) > 0, \text{ and } U''(c) \leqslant 0. \tag{13}$$

The peasants are assumed to face a competitive market for the product, and the price of their output in terms of the commodity C is taken to be p per unit.

$$C = Q \cdot p = \beta \cdot c. \tag{14}$$

The allocational rule for maximization of family welfare, which is still given by (9), is:

$$Q'(L) = \frac{V'(l)}{U'(c)} \cdot \frac{1}{p}. \tag{15}$$

The right-hand side represents the appropriate definition of the 'real labour cost' being the marginal rate of indifferent substitution between labour and product, bearing in mind the rate at which the product can be substituted for the commodity C. The intuitive meaning of the allocational rule remains, therefore, very similar to that of (10).

A somewhat more complicated case occurs when a part of the product Q is sold in the market, and a part is consumed directly. Let y

stand for the proportion of the output that is marketed, c for the amount of the purchased commodity enjoyed per member of the peasant family, q for the amount of the self-produced output enjoyed per member of that family. We have a more complicated individual utility function involving both c and q. We assume that there is non-increasing marginal utility for each good when the amount of it is increased in isolation, or when both goods are raised in the same proportion. However, there is no satiety level for either good.

$$U = U(c, q), \text{ such that } U_q > 0, U_c > 0, U_{qq} \leqslant 0,$$
$$U_{cc} \leqslant 0, U_q(c, q) \geqslant U_q(\lambda \cdot c, \lambda \cdot q), \quad (16)$$

and $U_c(c, q) \geqslant U_c(\lambda \cdot c, \lambda \cdot q)$, when $\lambda > 1$.

$$Q(1 - y) = \beta \cdot q. \quad (17)$$

$$C = Q \cdot y \cdot p = \beta \cdot c. \quad (18)$$

By maximizing family welfare, given by (9), with respect to variations in family labour (L), and therefore of individual labour (l) and of output (Q), and with respect to variations in the share of the product marketed (y), we get the two following allocational rules:

$$U_q = U_c \cdot p. \quad (19)$$

$$Q'(L) = \frac{V'(l)}{U_q} \quad (20)$$

The intuitive explanations are, once again, quite simple. The first equation simply states that the product should be divided in such a manner between direct consumption and exchange in the market that the relevant marginal rate of indifferent substitution between the two commodities equals their price ratio. The second equation still equates the marginal product of labour with the real cost of labour at the margin, the latter being defined still as the individual indifferent rate of substitution between labour and the product.

1.3 Factor supply

If the peasants buy factors other than labour at fixed prices, it is easy to show that the equilibrium conditions will be very similar to those in the competitive model, with the exception of the labour allocational equation.[6] The marginal product of each factor will equal its price in terms of the product, and only labour will have a separate rule, given by the equality of its marginal product with the real labour cost. Assuming the prices (in terms of the good Q) of the n factors f_j (other than labour) to be p_j, we have in profit maximizing equilibrium:

$$\frac{\partial Q}{\partial f_j} = p_j, \quad \text{for } j = 1, 2, \ldots, n; \tag{21}$$

$$\frac{\partial Q}{\partial L} = \frac{V'(l)}{U_q}. \tag{22}$$

This is combined with the marketing rule (19).

2   Surplus Labour and the Relation of Peasant Output to the Working Population

We now discuss the circumstances under which surplus labour can exist.[7] We define surplus labour as that part of the labour force in this peasant economy that can be removed without reducing the total amount of output produced, even when the amount of other factors is not changed. It is easily seen that if the reduction in the working population reduces the amount of labour put into cultivation, then clearly there would be a reduction in the amount of output produced. Thanks to continually diminishing marginal productivity of labour given by equation (1), a reduction in total family labour (L) will make the marginal product of labour positive, even if it was zero to start with, so that a smaller volume of L must mean a smaller volume of output. Thus what is necessary for the existence of surplus labour under these circumstances is that a fall in the number of working members (α) should be compensated by a rise in the amount of work done per person. And this will be the case only if the real labour cost is insensitive to the withdrawal of a part of the population.

We discuss in detail the case of a peasant economy in isolation, namely the model outlined in Section 1.1, because the debate has usually been in the context of such a case. However, we discuss later

6. For an illuminating discussion of the competitive model as applied to agriculture, see Nerlove (1958).

7. The literature is enormous. A good survey of the discussions and a fairly complete bibliography on the topic can be found in Kao *et al.* (1964). The bibliography can be supplemented by including Dobb (1951), Dumont (1957), K. N. Raj (1957), Datta (1960), Robinson (1960), Mathur (1964), Myint (1964), and Das-Gupta (1965).

the case in which a part or the whole of the output is marketed, that is, the models of Section 1.2. Considerations raised in Section 1.3 will not, however, be relevant, because by the formulation of the question we are interested in the impact on output of a reduction of the labour force keeping other factors of production constant.

2.1 The possibility of surplus labour

Relation (12) shows that a reduction in output can occur only when the real labour cost rises; and in consequence of a reduction in the population such a rise in the real labour cost can take place for two different reasons. First, an emigration of labour from the family reduces the number of working members (α), and to maintain the same level of total family labour, each remaining member has to work longer, raising the marginal disutility of effort. Second, with such withdrawal of labour there will be a rise in income of the remaining members, because there will be a smaller number of people to share the family fortune, and this will reduce the marginal utility from income. Both these effects will tend to push up the real labour cost and will shift the equilibrium to a smaller volume of family labour and total output.

The existence of surplus labour depends, in this model, therefore, on the marginal utility schedule and the marginal disutility schedule being *flat* in the relevant region. Only under that circumstance will a rise in income leave the marginal utility unchanged and a rise in individual effort leave the marginal disutility unaffected.

The constancy of the marginal utility of income within a certain range implies an insensitivity of the usefulness of income to its quantity within this region. Given this assumption, with a suitable choice of units, we can make the constant value of marginal utility equal to unity, so that (10) reduces to the following:

$$Q'(L) = V'(l) = x. \tag{23}$$

If, furthermore, the marginal disutility of effort remains constant, say at value z, until a certain critical amount of effort l^* is reached, then we have:[8]

$$x = V'(l) = z > 0, \text{ for } l \leqslant l^*; \quad V''(l) > 0, \text{ for } l > l^*. \tag{24}$$

Assume that the withdrawal of labour in question starts in a situation when the amount of labour put in by each working member in a family is l, so that the total family labour is ($\alpha \cdot l$). If $l \geqslant l^*$, there

8. This violates the twice differentiability condition of the V function at $l = l^*$.

cannot be any surplus labour in this model. If, however, $l < l^*$, and withdrawal of labour can take place in divisible units, then some labour can be removed without affecting the output.

If, on the other hand, it is assumed that labour can be withdrawn only in units of one person (ruling out part-time outside work), and if reorganization of the land–labour allocation cannot take place after withdrawal of labour from some families, then the necessary and sufficient condition for the existence of surplus labour in this model is given by condition (25):

$$\frac{\alpha}{\alpha - 1} \, l \leqslant l^*. \tag{25}$$

If, however, land can be reallocated, after the transfer of labour, and if there are a very large number of families, then the necessary condition for the existence of surplus labour approximates that quoted in the divisible case, namely $l < l^*$.

2.2   Analysis of the assumptions underlying surplus labour

In the last section the existence of surplus labour was shown to depend on the flatness of the schedules of marginal disutility of effort and marginal utility of income, in the relevant regions. Of the two, perhaps the assumption of a flat marginal disutility schedule up to a critical value is less objectionable. The flatness of the schedule of marginal utility of income until a certain standard of living is reached may be thought to be more dubious. However, near the so-called level of subsistence, when the end of having a 'decent' standard of living has not yet been achieved, such non-diminution of the desire to earn more income may not be implausible.[9] This is a verifiable question, and more empirical work is called for to settle it.

Regarding the *necessity* of the two assumptions for the existence of surplus labour, a couple of reservations must be made. First, if the taxation system is such that the rise in income per head as a result of the departure of some members of the family is wiped away by extra taxes, then there will be no rise in *net* income per head, and the question of the invariance of the marginal utility with respect to the variations in income will not arise. This will happen if Nurkse's scheme of utilizing the so-called saving potential is carried out through

9. Cf. Alfred Marshall, 'It may be noticed here, though the fact is of but little practical importance, that a small quantity of a commodity may be insufficient to meet a certain special want; and then there will be a more than proportionate increase in pleasure when the consumer gets enough of it to enable him to attain the desired end' (1949, p. 79).

an appropriate system of taxation (see Nurkse, 1953). Nurkse had concluded that 'some form of collective saving enforced by the state may prove to be indispensable for the *mobilization* of the saving potential implicit in disguised unemployment'.[10] We find further that even the *existence* of 'disguised unemployment' and of the so-called saving potential may depend on taxation or other methods of state interference, unless the marginal utility schedule is flat in the relevant region.

The second point to make is that the flatness of the two schedules is necessary in this model only because the utility from income and disutility from work are taken to be independent of each other. If instead, more generally, we take net utility as a function jointly of income and work, we have to look not only at the 'double partial' derivatives, which we have been doing so far, but also at the 'cross-partials' between income and work. For example, if it is argued that the marginal disutility from work is less at higher income (since work may be less tiring when a person is well fed),[11] then it is no longer necessary to assume that the marginal utility of income and the marginal disutility of work are constant with respect to variations in income and work, respectively. We do not need then the flatness of the two schedules. All that is needed is the invariance of the 'real labour cost' (x) with respect to joint variations of income and work per person when the size of the family is reduced, and, given a joint utility function, this can come about in a variety of different ways.

2.3 Surplus labour and zero marginal productivity

The existence of surplus labour is sometimes identified with the marginal product of labour being zero. It is in this form that the doctrine has been most widely discussed (see Nurkse, 1953; Lewis, 1954; Georgescu-Roegen, 1960; Ranis and Fei, 1964; among others). And it is in this form that the thesis has been most strongly attacked (see Haberler, 1957; Viner, 1957; Schultz, 1964; and others). In terms of the model put forward here, this situation corresponds to the special case of $z = 0$, when the marginal disutility of labour is nil

10. Nurkse (1953, p. 43); italics added. For an earlier discussion of this problem of utilization of surplus labour, see Dobb (1951, Chapter II).

11. Contrast this argument with the surplus labour thesis discussed by Leibenstein (1957), Mazumdar (1959), Ezekiel (1960), and Wonnacott (1962), in which the productivity of people rises with their income. While they consider variations in the *marginal product* of labour with income, we consider variations in the *marginal disutility* of effort with income.

in the relevant region.[12] It is arguable whether such an assumption is realistic, but we need not go into the question here, for this is covered as a special case, though it is not a necessary assumption for the existence of surplus labour.[13]

Viner (1957) has claimed that

> as far as agriculture is concerned, I find it impossible to conceive of a farm of any kind on which, other factors of production being held constant in quantity and even in form as well, it would not be possible by known methods, to obtain some addition to the crop by using additional labour in more careful selection and planting the seed, more intensive weeding, cultivation, thinning, and mulching, more painstaking harvesting, gleaning, and cleaning of the crop.[14]

We need not enter here into a controversy with Viner on the empirical validity of his assertion, but we should point out that even if it were shown that the marginal productivity of labour in agriculture was not zero but positive, it will not follow that there is no surplus labour, as was shown above. Indeed, the assumption of zero marginal productivity is neither a necessary nor a sufficient condition for the existence of surplus labour. We can see from the analysis of the last two sections that it is not necessary. That it is not sufficient follows from considering the case when $z = 0$, but $l = l^*$, where marginal product of labour is zero, but any finite withdrawal of the peasant labour force will reduce the level of output.

A closely related point needs to be clarified here. It is sometimes asserted that the existence of surplus labour requires certain specific types of production functions, with limited possibilities of factor substitutability. This, it should be clear from the preceding analysis, is not the case. While it is true that with some production functions, for example, the Cobb–Douglas, or more generally, a CES production function with positive elasticity of substitution (Arrow *et al.*, 1961),

12. If we assume a significant discontinuity in the marginal productivity schedule so that it falls abruptly to zero from a positive value, then we do not have to assume that marginal disutility of effort is zero in order to assume a zero marginal productivity of labour. For possible reasons behind such a discontinuity, see Eckaus (1955). For a disagreement on the realism of such a discontinuity, see Viner (1957), Oshima (1958), and Schultz (1964).

13. There is, however, one advantage for the theory of surplus labour in the special case where $z = 0$, because then the existence of surplus labour will be independent of the constancy of marginal utility of income. On the other hand, this is a very strong assumption. Furthermore, with this situation surplus labour can arise only with certain types of production functions, namely, where the marginal product of labour falls to zero for a large L.

14. Viner (1957), from the extract in Meier (1964, pp. 79–80). Cf. Mellor and Stevens (1956); Rosenstein-Rodan (1957); Pepelasis and Yotopoulos (1962).

the marginal product of labour never falls to zero, this does not, in any way, rule out the existence of surplus labour. At equilibrium we require of course that the marginal product of labour should equal the 'real labour cost' (x), and also that the schedule of the 'real labour cost' should be *flat*, but it is not necessary that the 'real labour cost' be *zero*. Thus we do not have to restrict the class of production functions arbitrarily to admit the possibility of surplus labour.[15]

2.4 Quantitative response of peasant output to population withdrawal

It is easy to overestimate the importance of the problem of the existence of surplus labour. We shall show in Section 3 that some conclusions that are drawn with the assumption of surplus labour can be drawn just as easily without this assumption. Even for those problems where the existence of a surplus makes a genuine difference, much will depend on the *size* of the surplus and the *extent* of the response once the surplus is exhausted. If the latter response is very weak, the consequences may in general be similar to those of surplus labour. If, on the other hand, there is some, but little, surplus labour, and once this is exhausted output responds very sharply, the surplus labour models of the Lewis type may be of little relevance.

In studying the response of output to labour, we have to make a sharp contrast between units of labour hours and units of population. Sometimes these two concepts are merged together in the literature. When the hours of work are variable there is little justification for this, irrespective of whether labour is assumed surplus or not. This is a generalization of our point about surplus labour and the marginal productivity of labour, where we showed surplus labour can coexist with positive marginal productivity of labour, that is, the 'coefficient of labour hours' may be positive, while the 'coefficient of population' is zero. We are now making the more general proposition that the two coefficients can differ widely also in other circumstances. The identification of the two, which is appropriate in the advanced wage economies with more or less fixed hours of work per week, does not at all carry over to peasant economies.[16]

---

15. Note that conditions (2) and (3) are both unnecessary for the existence of surplus labour.

16. On the general question of the limited applicability of the concepts and assumptions of advanced wage economies to the situation in peasant economies, see Thorner and Thorner (1962, Chapters X, XI, and XIII). See also Daniel Thorner's discussion (1965) of the views of Chayanov on this question.

The distinction is worked out below in terms of a rather simplified model.[17] We take the peasant economy model of Section 1, and in addition make the following assumptions: (i) non-labour resources can be reallocated after withdrawal of labour from some families; (ii) there are constant returns to scale; (iii) non-labour resources are fully divisible; and (iv) there are a large number of peasant families in this economy. With these additional assumptions, the entire peasant economy can be treated as one production unit, applying a uniform production function, given by equation (1), with Q standing for total output for the economy and L for total labour hours for the economy. The allocational rule (10) will be uniformly followed, and there will be a uniform real cost and marginal productivity of labour. This uniformity will be achieved for each peasant family in spite of indivisibility of the number of persons in each family, through redistribution of non-labour resources. We shall be exploring the conditions for the equilibrium of the economy as a whole, and it will not matter whether the economy is divided into families of equal or unequal size, as long as uniformity of the ratio of non-labour resources to labour resources is maintained for each family. We shall also take α to be the total number of working members and β to be the total number of all members in all families taken together. Since we shall take the number of such families to be very large, we shall treat the newly defined α and β as continuously divisible. We also assume that marginal utility from income and disutility from work are both positive.

We assume further that the ratio of the number of working members to the total number of members is k, and this is a constant, that is, when one working member leaves for work elsewhere, he supports his share of the family, which is k members, so that the peasant economy is left with one less working member and k less consuming members.

$$\beta = k \cdot \alpha. \tag{26}$$

We know from (10):

$$\frac{dx}{d\alpha} = \left[\frac{dV'(l)}{d\alpha} U'(q) - \frac{dU'(q)}{d\alpha} V'(l) \right] \bigg/ [U'(q)]^2. \tag{27}$$

---

17. We have not discussed here the question of intensity of work per hour; that is, working hard or less hard for any given length of time. If such variations are considered in terms of the model outlined here, we can treat the value of individual labour (l) as the *effective* time equivalent of total hours of work.

From equations (4), (5), (7), (8), and (26), we know that:

$$\frac{dV'(l)}{d\alpha} = V''(l)\left[\left(\frac{dL}{d\alpha}\cdot\alpha - L\right)\Big/\alpha^2\right]. \tag{28}$$

$$\frac{dU'(q)}{d\alpha} = U''(q)\left[\frac{Q'(L)\,(dL/d\alpha)\,\beta - Q\cdot k}{\beta^2}\right]. \tag{29}$$

We know from equation (10), bearing in mind that $Q''(L)$ is uniformly strictly negative, that:

$$\frac{dx}{d\alpha} = \frac{dL}{d\alpha}\cdot\frac{1}{\phi'(x)} = \frac{dL}{d\alpha}\cdot Q''(L). \tag{30}$$

Using (27), (28), (29), and (30), and solving for $dL/d\alpha$, ignoring the possibility of $V'(l) = 0$, we get:

$$\frac{dL}{d\alpha} = \left[\frac{V''(l)}{V'(l)}\cdot L\cdot k - \frac{U''(q)}{U'(q)}\cdot Q\right]\Big/\left[\beta\cdot\frac{V''(l)}{V'(l)} - \alpha\cdot\beta\cdot\frac{Q''(L)}{Q'(L)}\right.$$
$$\left. - \alpha\cdot Q'(L)\frac{U''(q)}{U'(Q)}\right]. \tag{31}$$

We can now define a number of elasticities and can express our result as relationships between them. In particular, we define E as the elasticity of output with respect to the number of working members, m the (absolute value of) elasticity of the marginal utility of income with respect to individual income, n the elasticity of marginal disutility from work with respect to individual hours of work, G the elasticity of output with respect to hours of labour, and g the (absolute value of) elasticity of the marginal product of labour with respect to hours of labour. In the definition of these elasticities, there is of course no implication that they will be constant,

$$E = \frac{dQ}{d\alpha}\cdot\frac{\alpha}{Q}; \tag{32}$$

$$n = \frac{V''(l)\cdot l}{V'(l)}; \tag{33}$$

$$m = -\frac{U''(q)\cdot q}{U'(q)}; \tag{34}$$

$$G = \frac{Q'(L)\cdot L}{Q}; \tag{35}$$

$$g = -\frac{Q''(L) \cdot L}{Q'(L)}. \qquad (36)$$

We obtain from (1), (26), (31)–(36), the *response equation*:

$$E = G\left(\frac{n + m}{n + m \cdot G + g}\right). \qquad (37)$$

The extreme case of surplus labour corresponds in this model to $n = m = 0$, which is exactly the same as the case of having flat regions in the marginal utility and the marginal disutility schedules, as discussed in Section 2 earlier. It might look from equation (37) as if another such case is $G = 0$, but this does not strictly follow, since G being zero requires that the marginal productivity of labour be zero, which requires, thanks to (10), that the relevant marginal disutility of labour be zero too, and that was ruled out in deriving equations (31) and (37), involving division by $V'(l)$. However, with a slightly different formulation we can get substantially the same result of surplus labour by assuming $Q'(L) = V'(l) = 0$. To assume, however, that it does not only hold trivially for infinitesimally small changes around the point of equilibrium, we need the further assumption that $V'(l)$ stays at zero even when l is increased. Therefore, $V''(l)$ has to be zero over a certain range, which comes to the same thing as n being zero over this range. A slight bit of formalism might be helpful. Putting $n = 0$, that is, having a flat marginal disutility curve in the relevant region, we get from equation (37):

$$E = \frac{m \cdot G}{m \cdot G + g} \qquad (38)$$

The case of surplus labour discussed in Section 2, is that of $m = 0$, which makes $E = 0$. The other case, corresponding to zero marginal productivity ($G = 0$), can be seen heuristically by making G smaller and smaller, with an unchanged g, and this makes E indefinitely small. The limiting case of $G = 0$ is ruled out by the derivation, but that it will be approached can be verified from equation (38).

Another special case is $G = E$, that is, a case when the elasticity of output with respect to labour hours coincides with that with respect to working people. If we assume n to be very large, we shall approach this result. Heuristically this corresponds to the case of the marginal disutility schedule approaching the vertical position, which of course will tend toward constancy of the number of hours worked, making the change in labour hours proportional to the change in number of working people. This is probably the underlying assumption of taking fixed hours of work in traditional analysis. An alternative assumption yielding the same result is that the hours of work are institutionally fixed, which does not apply well to peasant agriculture but is reasonably realistic for capitalist industry.

There is also another very special case when the result of $E = G$ can be expected. This happens when $m = g/(1 - G)$, as can be checked from the *response equation* (37). This critical case can be understood in the following heuristic terms. When some people are withdrawn from the peasant economy, with an unchanged number of hours of work per person, the marginal physical return from work will increase. On the other hand, since the people left behind will now enjoy a higher income, the utility value of a unit of physical output will now be lower. The condition quoted corresponds to the special case when the two forces just cancel out each other.[18]

Leaving out these special cases, we would not in general expect the elasticity of peasant output with respect to the number of working men to coincide with the elasticity with respect to labour hours. The qualitative relationship between G and E can be checked from (37) to be the following:

$$E \begin{Bmatrix} \leq \\ = \\ > \end{Bmatrix} G \text{ according as } m \begin{Bmatrix} \leq \\ = \\ > \end{Bmatrix} \frac{g}{1 - G}. \tag{39}$$

With a constant elasticity production function (Cobb–Douglas type), we have, further, $g = (1 - G)$, so that the condition then reduces to:

$$E \begin{Bmatrix} \leq \\ = \\ > \end{Bmatrix} G \text{ according as } m \begin{Bmatrix} \leq \\ = \\ > \end{Bmatrix} 1. \tag{40}$$

Except under very special assumptions it will be illegitimate to equate the proportionate response of output to labour hours with that to the number of working members. This general point holds even when we relax the possibility of having continuous variations in α through the assumptions (i)–(iv) outlined at the beginning of this section. Alternatively, we might consider the consequences of a reduction of α by 1 for one family after another, and considerations similar to m, n, G, and g will also apply in this discrete case. Once again, unless we assume that either (a) the marginal disutility schedule is vertical, or (b) the number of hours worked is institutionally fixed even in the peasant economy, or (c) the effect of population withdrawal on marginal productivity is *exactly* counterbalanced by its effect on the marginal utility of income, there will be no reason to

---

18. It is easy to check that $m = g/(1 - G)$ corresponds to having simultaneously $dl/d\alpha = 0$, and $(d/d\alpha)[Q'(L) \cdot U'(q)] = 0$.

identify G and E. Assumption (b) is highly unrealistic, and assumption (c) will be the result of a pure coincidence, and even if it happens to be true at some positions of equilibrium, it is extremely unlikely that such a special coincidence will hold throughout. (It must be remembered that the values of m, n, G, and g are not necessarily constant.) Assumption (a) of a *vertical* schedule is, in some respects, the extreme case exactly opposite to the one associated with the theory of surplus labour, namely, that the marginal disutility schedule will be horizontal in the relevant region.

2.5   The product market and price response

When a part of the working force moves out of a peasant economy that markets its product (part or whole), the situation is more complex, because the result will depend on the impact of this labour movement on the relative price of the output, and the peasants' reaction to price changes. So we must first determine how the peasants will react to a price change, assuming that they cannot change the amount of other factors to be employed (ruled out by the definition of the problem of surplus labour).

First take the case in which the family markets its entire produce Q for the purchase of the outside commodity C (at an exchange rate p); the allocational rule is given, as we have seen, by equation (15).

$$Q'(L) = \frac{V'(l)}{U'(c)} \cdot \frac{1}{p}. \tag{15}$$

By differentiating this with respect to p, and solving for dL/dp, we get after simplifying:

$$\frac{dL}{dp} = \frac{Q'(L)[U'(c) + U''(c) \cdot c]}{[V''(l)/\alpha] - [U''(c)/\beta][Q'(L) \cdot p]^2 - U'(c) \cdot Q''(L) \cdot p}. \tag{41}$$

Now, since $V''(l) \geqslant 0$, $U''(c) \leqslant 0$, and $Q''(L) < 0$, the denominator is positive, and therefore the direction of the response of labour supply to the price of the product will depend entirely on the sign of the numerator, of which all items are non-negative except $U''(c)$. For the response of labour supply to product price to be negative, the following condition has to be fulfilled:

$$-\frac{U''(c) \cdot c}{U'(c)} > 1. \tag{42}$$

Now, the left-hand side of relation (42) is simply the absolute value of the elasticity of the marginal utility of income, identical with m

as defined by (34), except for the substitution of c for q; let us call this elasticity $\bar{m}$. The response of labour, and therefore of output (given positive marginal product, that is, non-zero marginal disutility of work) to the product price, will be positive or negative depending on whether the elasticity of the marginal utility is less than or greater than unity. To summarize:[19]

$$\frac{dQ}{dp} \begin{Bmatrix} > \\ = \\ < \end{Bmatrix} 0, \text{ according as} \frac{dL}{dp} \begin{Bmatrix} > \\ = \\ < \end{Bmatrix} 0, \text{ according as } \bar{m} \begin{Bmatrix} < \\ = \\ > \end{Bmatrix} 1. \quad (43)$$

In the case when a part of the produce is marketed and a part consumed, the position is more complicated, and we cannot analyse the situation without specifying the shape of the utility function more precisely than we have done so far. As an illustration, we can take the case of a utility function with unit elasticity of substitution, with given coefficients of the two types of goods.

$$U = A (c^{\mu} \cdot q^{1-\mu})^{k}, \text{ where } 0 < \mu < 1, \text{ and } 0 < k \leqslant 1. \quad (44)$$

Given (44), the allocational equation (19) implies that the two goods will be consumed in a ratio (r) that is simply proportional to the price p.

$$r = \frac{c}{q} = \frac{p \cdot \mu}{1 - \mu}. \quad (45)$$

From this relation (45) and the equations (17) and (18), giving the value of c and q in terms of the output level Q, price level p, and the marketing ratio y, it follows:

$$y = \mu. \quad (46)$$

That is, in this case the marketing ratio is fixed irrespective of the price level, because the income and the substitution effects of a price increase just cancel out.

The labour allocational rule was found earlier to be given by (20):

$$Q'(L) = \frac{V'(l)}{U_q}. \quad (20)$$

When the price p varies, $Q'(L)$ is affected through the resulting variation in L; $V'(l)$ is affected through variation in l related to the variation in L; and U_q responds to both changes in the consumption

---

19. Cf. result (40). If m and $\bar{m}$ could be identified, a positive response of total output to price will imply the coefficient of the number of labourers is less than that of labour hours, with a Cobb–Douglas production function.

ratio r and the size of consumption of q, both of which are themselves functions of the price, the latter through the intermediary of the volume of labour and the quantity of output produced (since the marketing ratio is fixed). Solving for dL/dp, we get:

$$\frac{dL}{dp} = x \cdot T_1 \bigg/ \left[\frac{V''(l)}{U_q} \frac{1}{\alpha} + x \cdot T_2 - Q''(L) \right], \qquad (47)$$

where

$$T_1 = \frac{\mu \cdot k}{p} > 0,$$

and

$$T_2 = \frac{(1-k)(1-\mu)}{q \cdot \beta} Q'(L) \geq 0.$$

Since, furthermore, $V''(l)$ must be non-negative, and $Q''(L)$ must be negative, and of course U_q must be positive, and x non-negative, we have the result that the application of labour cannot fall when the price of the product increases. Moreover, ruling out the case in which the disutility of labour (therefore, x) is nil, we shall always have a positive response of labour to price. And this together with positive marginal product (guaranteed also by the positivity of x) must imply a positive response of output to price. We find, therefore, the interesting result that with a utility function with fixed coefficients and unit elasticity of substitution (homogeneous of degree $k \leq 1$), the response of output to price must be positive.[20]

When such a positive response of output to the price level is assumed, the conditions for the existence of surplus labour become less exacting, assuming that the transfer of peasant labour will be accompanied by a rise in the price of their output. Indeed the literature on the problem of the creation of marketed surplus concerns itself precisely with the possibility that a transfer of peasant labour to work elsewhere may produce a shortage of food even when the peasant output is maintained.[21] This is because of the fact that out of

20. Without further empirical research, we cannot say how realistic are the cases covered here. However, it is interesting to note that empirical studies on the response of production to price in Indian agriculture have usually found the response to be positive (see Raj Krishna, 1963, and Dharm Narain, 1965). While these studies have been done mainly for individual crops, and one would expect more positive response there than in the case of peasant output in general (because of the substitution for the more lucrative crop against the others), so far there is relatively little indication of a negative response even for the total output of peasant economies vis-à-vis a general rise in the price level of the peasant output.

21. For one of the earliest and clearest discussions of this problem in the context of economic development, see Dobb (1951, pp. 45–8, 71–3).

the given output produced, the fraction sold in the market outside may not rise *pari passu* with the movement of the labour force out of the peasant economy. If this shortage of agricultural produce raised its price level, then, with our assumptions, the peasant output may respond positively to it. Thus, even if there is a tendency for the output level to fall when a part of the labour force moves out, *given* the price of the produce, this may be compensated, or more than compensated, by a positive response to the price level resulting from the movement of the labour force itself. In the case of a peasant economy that relies exclusively or inclusively on a product market, the conditions for the existence of surplus labour must take into account this price response.[22]

However, there is a stricter form in which the question of surplus labour can be posed. It may be asked whether the peasant output will remain constant if a part of the labour force moves out, given the amount of non-labour resources used, *and* assuming that the relative price of output does not change. Given this formulation of the question, the condition necessary for the existence of surplus labour is extremely similar in the case of a peasant economy with a product market, as in the case of a peasant economy without one, discussed in the earlier sections. In the case of the peasants who sell all of their product, with labour allocational rule (15), we now require, as before, that the marginal disutility to work and marginal utility from income (now in terms of c rather than q) both be flat schedules. In the case when a part of the output is directly consumed and a part sold in the market, the condition reduces to a flat marginal disutility schedule and constant marginal utility when the amount of the two commodities obtained goes up in the proportion indicated by the appropriate utility function. In the case of the fixed-coefficient homogeneous utility functions studied earlier, the requirement on utility simply boils down to the degree of homogeneity being 1, that is, $k = 1$ in equation (44), in the relevant region.

3   Dual Equilibrium of a Peasant Economy and Capitalist Farming

Typically peasant and capitalist agriculture coexist in varying proportions in many parts of the world. The nature and consequences of this dualistic equilibrium are studied in this section.

22. One exception to this rule is the extreme case of marginal disutility of labour being nil, for there the peasants will always apply enough labour to make the marginal product of labour zero, no matter what the price level is. In such a case, however, when the marginal disutility is nil and stays nil in the relevant range, the possible existence of surplus labour has already been shown, independently of the utility function.

3.1 *Positive wages with surplus labour and the wage gap*

As a preliminary, we discuss briefly a more familiar problem that has engaged a number of economists, namely, the explanation of a positive wage outside the peasant economy when there is surplus labour inside it. One explanation that has been put forward is the efficiency-enhancing effects of nutrition and, therefore, of higher wages.[23] Another approach is to postulate an institutional minimum wage rate.[24] A third approach suggests that a peasant leaving his family loses his income from the farm (roughly, the *average* product per person), and the wage rate outside must compensate for this.[25]

This question is, in some respects, ill-conceived. Surplus labour only implies that some people can move out without reducing output, that is, $E = 0$, but this does not require that the marginal product of labour be zero, that is, $G = 0$. If $G > 0$, this implies that there is some marginal disutility of effort, that is, $z > 0$. Why should we expect the wage rate to be zero, when there is some marginal disutility of effort?

While the question of the coexistence of positive wages with surplus labour can be dismissed as misconceived, there is a question closely related to it for which these theories have relevance. There is usually a substantial gap between the wage rates outside the peasant economy and the real cost of labour (and, therefore, of marginal productivity) inside it. To a great extent this can be explained in terms of the theories discussed above, supplemented in the case of the rural–urban differential by considerations of different costs of living and possible variations in earner-dependent ratios.

Insofar as wage employment takes the form of full-time work per day, though not necessarily per year, one further reason for the wage gap can be seen in the shape of the marginal disutility schedule, which will rise after a point at least, even if it is flat at the beginning. If the point l^*, where the marginal disutility schedule starts rising, is to the left of such full-time work, then the relevant marginal disutility will be higher in wage employment than that for the lower level of work per person in the peasant equilibrium. In this context it is interesting to note that an institutionally determined minimum number of hours of work per person in wage employment can serve

23. This was worked out by Leibenstein (1957) and has been further studied by Mazumdar (1959), Ezekiel (1960), and Wonnacott (1962).

24. See Nurkse (1953), Ranis and Fei (1964), and others. This is a modern extension of a Ricardian concept.

25. See Lewis (1954).

the same function as an institutionally determined minimum level of wages, namely, have the effect of causing a wage gap.

3.2 *Productivity of labour and of land*

The existence of a wage gap binds together such dissimilar models of growth as those of Lewis (1954) and Ranis and Fei (1964), on the one hand, and that of Jorgenson (1961), on the other. This wage contrast is sometimes taken to be one that applies between industry and agriculture only, and sometimes as one that relates to wage employment and family employment in general. We shall take it in the latter form, and assume the existence of such a gap even within the agricultural sector between wage-based farms and family-based farms.

We start by reinterpreting equation (1). Let us assume that there are constant returns to scale, and only two factors of production, namely, land and labour. Let Q stand for product per acre and L for labour per acre. We assume, temporarily, that the peasants and the capitalists use the same production function, but the former run their farms on family lines while the latter use hired labour, and there is a 'wage gap', that is, the wage rate (w) is higher than the equilibrium real cost of labour (x).[26]

The crucial relation to be used is equation (12), relating output per acre to equilibrium labour cost, and since $w > x$, we have immediately the result that the capitalist farms will have a lower output per acre than the peasant farms.

$$\psi(x) > \psi(w). \tag{48}$$

Thus while the capitalist farms will have a higher productivity of labour, the peasant farmers will have a higher productivity of land.

A special case of this result has attracted a lot of attention in the context of the debate over the relative efficiency of peasant farming and capitalist agriculture. If the real cost of labour in 'over-populated' peasant economies is zero ($x = 0$), and the wage rate in the capitalist sector is positive ($w > 0$), we have:

$$\psi(0) > \psi(w). \tag{49}$$

In his study of the rubber industry in Malaya and Indonesia, Bauer (1948) makes an observation that is substantially the same as

---

26. We can take any case of peasant farming, with or without a product market, and provided we are careful enough to take the right 'real labour cost', given respectively by the right-hand side of equations (10), (15) and (20), the analysis will apply equally well in each case.

inequality (49).[27] Georgescu-Roegen (1960) has traced the origin of this line of thought to the historical 'agrarian doctrine' and has related it to the logic of feudal agriculture.[28] It played an important part in the development of political thinking in Russia (see, for example, Lenin, 1893).

It should, however, be noted that while in these arguments inequality (49) is used (often implicitly), inequality (48) is more general. It is not necessary that the real labour cost in peasant farms be zero ($w > x = 0$), as assumed by Bauer (1948), Georgescu-Roegen (1960), and others; it is sufficient that there be a wage gap ($w > x$).[29]

3.3   Seasonal wage gap and productivity

Agriculture being a seasonal operation, it is somewhat misleading to speak in terms of a homogeneous unit of labour. A unit of labour at the time of harvesting is not replaceable by a unit of labour at a slack period. Indeed it has been found in many peasant economies that at the harvesting time many peasant families themselves hire outside labour. Around this busy season the labour market becomes much more perfect, and we could even assume that the wage gap disappears at this time of the year. How is the result of the last section affected by the existence of only a seasonal wage gap?

Let there be two seasons, one in which there is no wage gap ($x_1 = w_1$) and another in which there is one ($x_2 < w_2$). If it is assumed that the labour in the two seasons must be used in fixed proportions (say, with r units of season 1 labour with one unit of season 2 labour), then it is easy to see that the real labour cost of the composite unit of labour will be higher for the capitalist farm than for the peasant farm, and the old result of a higher output per acre of the peasant farms will still hold.[30]

$$\psi(r \cdot x_1 + x_2) > \psi(r \cdot w_1 + w_2). \tag{50}$$

27. 'In the choice of planting density the rational course is not the same for estates and small holders. The majority of small holders incur no cash wage costs and attempt to maximize the gross yield per surface unit. On their densely planted holdings the trees are of smaller girth and yield per tree – lower than on estates, but the yields per surface area are higher' (Bauer, 1948, p. 363).

28. Cf. Nicholls (1960), Dandekar (1962), Sen, *Economic Weekly* (1962), and Myint (1964).

29. This gap has to exist in comparable efficiency units so that a gap reflecting higher productivity of labour in capitalist enterprises (for example, in Leibenstein's model (1957)) will not serve this purpose.

30. This suggestion came up in the context of discussion on Indian data on agriculture; see Mazumdar, *Economic Weekly* (1963), and Sen, *Economic Weekly* (1964).

We can, however, dispense with the assumption of strict proportionality and simply assume that labour in different seasons is essentially complementary each to the other, with positive cross-partials. The marginal productivity of both kinds of labour is diminishing, and an increase in the application of slack-season labour (for example, transplanting) increases the marginal productivity of busy-season labour (for example, harvesting).

It can be shown that the fulfilment of the second-order condition of maximization of profits (the so-called stability conditions) guarantees that the use of a factor will increase when its equilibrium price falls.[31] Since the cross-partials are positive, this greater use of slack-season labour will increase the marginal productivity of the busy-season labour, and increase its use. Thus, a lower value of the real cost of slack-season labour will mean that more busy-season labour will also be used per acre in the peasant farms. Together this will guarantee that the output per acre will be higher for peasant farms with more labour being used in both seasons than in the capitalist farms. Thus there need not be a wage gap in each season; its presence in some seasons is sufficient, provided labour of each kind raises the others' productivity.[32]

3.4   The land market

So far we have assumed that the amounts of land held by peasant farmers and by capitalist farmers are given. Only in terms of this assumption has it been possible to work out the conditions of equilibrium with differential labour costs in different modes of production. We can now inquire what will be the effect of having a perfect market in renting land. If we consider a two-factor case (with land and labour) and continue with the assumption of constant returns to scale, the answer is immediately seen. Such an equilibrium cannot exist. As long as the marginal productivity of land is higher for peasant farmers than for the capitalist farmers, it will be in the interest of the capitalist farmer to rent his land out to the peasants. The process of transfer will continue until either the labour-cost gap vanishes or, alternatively, all land owned by the capitalists is rented out.

31. See Hicks (1946), Mathematical Appendix to Chapter VII; also Nerlove (1958, Chapter I).
32. In fact it can be checked that, for this result to hold, it is sufficient that the particular relationship that Hicks calls 'regression' does not take place between slack-season labour and output (Hicks, 1946, pp. 93–6, 320–3).

As a matter of fact, the imperfection of the land market is quite a fair assumption for most underdeveloped countries. For one thing, a variety of regulations, traditional and modern, makes renting out land a more hazardous occupation than lending capital; there are regulations about tenancy and customary rights of the cultivators. Also in most societies there are restrictions put on the maximum rent chargeable when there generally is no corresponding limitation on the profits to be enjoyed by using wage labour.[33] Imperfections arise from the other sources also.

3.5   An illustration from Indian agriculture

It has been noted by the *Studies in the Economics of Farm Management* (1954–57), produced by the government of India, that in most areas studied the value of output per acre, both gross and net, becomes smaller as the size of the holding increases.[34] It has also been observed that the amount of labour applied per acre decreases with an increase in the size of the farms and that the proportion of capitalist farms as opposed to peasant farms rises with size. These facts fit well with the explanation expressed in relation (48) or (49).[35] The data are not entirely conclusive (for example, there are some exceptions to this negative relation between output per acre and size); there are also some complications introduced by the existence of factors other than land and labour. There is some evidence that the amount of capital used per acre is also higher for the smaller farms than for the larger ones.[36] The measurement problems here are enormous, but taking the data at their face value, we face the question of which caused what. The higher cost of borrowing that the smaller farms face makes it unlikely that they have any price advantage in the use of purchased capital goods, so that the natural explanation would seem to be that the cheaper cost of labour may act indirectly to increase the amount of capital used per acre for smaller farms.

This can happen in at least two different ways. First, as exemplified by the case of labour of two seasons, in the previous section,

33. The imperfection of the land market is not a modern phenomenon produced by land reforms. The assumption of a perfect land market for a traditional peasant agriculture is a very weak one. For the situation in India in the pre-British period, see Gupta (1958) and Habib (1963). The importance of the problem in the thinking of the eighteenth-century British lawmakers has been studied by R. Guha (1963).

34. But the 'profits' per acre as defined by the *Studies* (1954–57) is higher for the larger farms. We discuss the concept of 'profits' later.

35. Discussed by Sen *et al.*, *Economic Weekly* (1962–64).

36. See the *Studies* (1954–57) and Randhawa (1960).

a lower price of one factor will tend to increase the use of its complementary factor; the lower labour cost of the smaller farms will have such an effect on the use of capital also.[37] Second, much of the capital used in smaller farms is not brought from outside but produced (or reared, in the case of the livestock) with direct labour in the family economy itself. Here the cheaper cost of labour will reflect itself directly in the cheapening of the capital goods, and the differential price advantage that the peasant farmers have in the use of labour will imply such an advantage also in the use of capital.[38]

Also there are some indications that the smaller farms may be inherently more fertile. There is relatively little data on this,[39] and what estimates there are tend to be partly circular in this context, being based on output per acre indirectly. However, such a correlation between the sizes of the farms and fertility can be expected for the following economic reasons. If there is a tendency for higher income to lead to a larger size of family (say, due to greater ability of the members of the family to survive famines and other crises), then there will be a tendency for the more fertile farms of a certain size to sustain bigger families than less fertile farms of the same size. Subdivision through inheritance will, therefore, be faster on the former, and a correlation will thus be established between natural fertility and smallness of the holdings.[40]

The evidence regarding Indian agriculture, therefore, cannot be viewed as conclusive at this stage. It is possible that part of the reason for the higher productivity per acre of the smaller farms is its cheaper labour, acting also on capital through complementarity and direct embodiment of cheap labour; but it is also possible that the explanation lies partly in natural fertility differences. Without more empirical work on this, these different elements cannot be separated out; however, it can be asserted that the expectation based on

37. Variation of the intensity of capital utilization may, however, make it difficult to take account of relationships of this kind in terms of simple neoclassical analysis, as has been discussed by Bagchi (1962). In an unpublished paper, 'Productivity and Disguised Unemployment in Indian Agriculture: A Theoretical Analysis', Bagchi has analysed the Indian farming situation in terms of a more complex model, emphasizing particularly the problem of seasonality.

38. There will be some saving of working capital also, because peasant agriculture is not based on wage advances so far as the marginal units of labour are concerned, and this reduces the need for work-in-progress (discussed in my note, 'Working capital in the Indian economy: a conceptual framework and some estimates', in Rosenstein-Rodan (ed.), 1964).

39. See Khusro (1964).

40. See Sen, *Economic Weekly* (1963, 1964).

relation (48) is not contradicted, and is, if anything, supported by Indian data, insofar as these data have been analysed.[41]

Certain methodological problems of cost accounting in Indian agriculture are also raised by this problem of the wage gap.[42] *The Studies in the Economics of Farm Management* (1955–57) computed 'profits' of different kinds of enterprises by imputing to family labour the market wage rate as shadow labour cost, and it came to the frightening conclusion that much of Indian agriculture is being run on 'losses'.[43] This illustrates the problems that arise if the wage gap is ignored. If the family-based farmers did have to pay the market wage rate for their labour, they would not have applied that much labour, and would have certainly avoided the 'loss'. But since they in fact faced a lower real labour cost, they applied labour beyond the point where the marginal product equals the market wage rate, and for these marginal units incurred fictitious 'loss'. And it appears that in many cases the 'loss' over these units overcompensated the profits on units prior to the critical point, leading to an over-all mythical 'loss'.[44] This illustrates the danger of analysing peasant equilibrium in terms of ideas borrowed from a capitalist economy.

4   *Labour Allocation and Different Economic Systems*

In this section we start by analysing the problems of allocational efficiency in a wage system as opposed to peasant agriculture. Then the question of share-cropping is discussed.

---

41. This relation has been observed in other economies as well, some even in Europe, for example, in prewar Poland. 'Labour productivity is unquestionably higher on the landed estates than on the peasant farms. The yield per acre, however, is higher in the latter owing to the use of more labour, especially in stock-breeding' (Pohorille, 'Development and rural overpopulation: lessons from Polish experience', in ILO, 1964).

42. For a general discussion on the confusion of categories in Indian farming, see Thorner and Thorner (1962, Chapters X–XIII).

43. Cf. 'This is an alarming situation, for if 50 per cent or more of the farmers are carrying on the business at a loss, the farming community cannot be considered to be comfortably placed in any sense of the term' (*The Studies in the Economics of Farm Management*, Report on Madras, 1955–56, p. 146).

44. In terms of the model outlined in Section 1.1, when the market wage rate is given by w, and the equilibrium real labour cost by x, the necessary and sufficient conditions for an over-all 'loss' are given by:

$$\psi(x) - \phi(x) \cdot w < 0. \tag{51}$$

No story of low and negative returns from family farms emerges from this.

4.1 *The wage system and allocational distortions*

Three different interpretations of the wage gap need to be carefully distinguished. Insofar as the wage gap reflects a pure distortion of the market, which is the form we have been studying, the efficiency implication is clear. The peasant family is guided properly by its calculation of the real labour cost, reflecting the rate at which the members are ready to substitute labour for output, but the capitalist farmer is misguided by an inefficient market mechanism. His allocation is, therefore, correspondingly distorted.

Two qualifications must, however, be made. First, insofar as the peasant faces a distorted capital market, with an unduly high price of borrowing capital from usurious moneylenders, he too may get a wrong signal from the market mechanism. Second, when the assumption of uniformity of all peasant families is dropped, different peasant families may equilibrate at different levels of real labour cost, and then the allocation of labour *between* different peasant enterprises may also suffer from the imperfection of the labour market.

A second interpretation of the wage gap is that it is not a market *distortion*, but a *genuine* reflection of the higher social cost of hired labour as opposed to own labour. If people prefer to work for themselves rather than be 'wage slaves', the capitalist farms are at a disadvantage, but there is no misallocation on this account.

A third interpretation of the wage gap is that it reflects the higher efficiency of wage labour. This can happen in at least two different ways: (i) higher wages attracting the cream of the labour force, peasant farming being left to the less efficient ones; and (ii) higher wages leading to greater efficiency through better nutrition.[45] Insofar as this is the case, labour in efficiency units may not be any more expensive for the wage farms than for the peasant farms. Consequently, there will not necessarily be any special advantage to peasant farming. But if this were the whole story, it would indeed be difficult to explain the observed difference between productivity per acre of peasant and capitalist farms (Section 3.5). Since capitalist farmers have cheaper access to capital, if the peasant farmer does not have the advantage of cheaper labour (in efficiency units) and cheaper capital goods made by directly embodying labour, then the explanation of the observed productivity difference has to rely exclusively on natural differences in the fertility of different kinds of land.

---

45. See Leibenstein (1957), Mazumdar (1959), and Galenson and Pyatt (1964).

Therefore, according to some interpretations of the wage gap, the wage system distorts, and the peasant farms have distinct allocational advantages. This is worth remembering because of the prevalence of facile generalizations about the superior efficiency of 'extensive, relatively mechanized, commercial agriculture' over 'small-scale, labour-intensive peasant agriculture'.[46]

On the other hand, it is not possible to conclude from the preceding discussion that peasant agriculture is necessarily more efficient than wage-based farming. The allocational efficiency discussed so far is a purely static one related to the utilization of *given* resources. It is indeed possible for peasant farming to yield more output but less savings, and make less contribution to future growth. This whole problem is analogous to the conflicts faced in the problem of the choice of techniques of production, which has been discussed a great deal, and which is unnecessary to repeat here.[47] Apart from savings, there is also the question of 'marketed surplus', which is generally assumed to be proportionately smaller for the smaller farms.[48]

Furthermore, it is illegitimate to eulogize peasant farming on the basis of an analysis in which every type of farm has access to the same production function and to the same factors of production. A peasant farmer in an underdeveloped area might be constricted to a less efficient set of production conditions for at least three different reasons: (i) he might not have access to economies of large scale; (ii) he might not have the necessary technical know-how or access to the same factors of production; and (iii) he might be forced to shun experimentation with new techniques, because the precarious nature of his existence makes him more averse to taking risks. The classical arguments for large-scale farming (both capitalist and cooperative) were based mainly on consideration (i), but it is possible that consideration (ii) is of greater importance, particularly 'where technically superior factors of production are a principal source of agricultural

---

46. See United Nations (1962). See also the frequent references to the 'losses' of the smaller farms in *The Studies in the Economics of Farm Management* (1954–57). The position is rather more complicated with co-operative farms; see Sen (1966).

47. Sen (1960), Chapters II and V. The question depends crucially on the fiscal possibilities. See also Ranis (1959), Ohkawa and Rosovsky (1960), and Johnston and Mellor (1961).

48. The importance of the marketed surplus was emphasized by several classical writers. In fact it was Adam Smith's preoccupation with this and his identification of this with 'supply' as such that Marx found to be 'a naïve misunderstanding' (Marx, 1957, p. 140). On the relevance of marketed surplus for economic development, see Dobb (1951). Regarding the empirical question as to whether the proportion of the output marketed does or does not increase with the size of the farms, see Dharm Narain (1961) and Raj Krishna (1963).

growth'.[49] Consideration (iii) might also be important in certain situations, for example, in the use of fertilizers in areas of uncertain rainfall. Thus while the 'wage gap' may distort the allocation of wage-based farms, and the peasant farms seem to have a distinct advantage in the utilization of labour, it is not possible for us to argue from this that peasant farming must be of superior economic efficiency.

4.2 Share-cropping and labour allocation

There is a widely prevalent system in many underdeveloped areas of the world, namely, share-cropping or tithe cultivation, by which the cultivator gets a certain proportionate share (h) of the produce (with $0 < h < 1$), while the landowner gets the rest. This fits in neither with peasant farming nor with capitalist farming. We examine now the allocation of labour under this system. In this case there is no proper 'wage gap', but the allocation is not according to the 'real cost' of labour either.

The sharing can take place either on the basis of the net product or on that of the gross product. And in the latter case, the landowner might be expected to pay for the value of the non-labour inputs, or alternatively, the cultivator may be expected to do this. We take first the case of the sharing of the net product, with the payments for the hired factors being made out separately.

It is easy to verify that the rule for the allocation of non-labour inputs will be the same as under peasant farming. When p_j are the prices (in units of output Q) of the factors f_j (other than labour), we have:

$$\frac{\partial Q}{\partial f_j} = p_j, \quad \text{for } j = 1, 2, \ldots, n. \tag{21}$$

The rule for labour allocation will, however, be different, even if each member of the cultivating family identifies his interests with those of his family (as assumed in the case of peasant farming).

$$Q'(L) = \frac{V'(l)}{U'(q)} \cdot \frac{1}{h}. \tag{52}$$

Since $h < 1$, the share-cropper's relevant labour cost is higher than the 'real labour cost'. Output will thus be restricted, and the marginal

49. Schultz (1964, p. 189, see also Chapters VIII–XII). See also Griliches (1960).

product of labour will exceed the 'real cost of labour'. There is, thus, misallocation under share-cropping.[50]

This result differs from the analysis of share-cropping by Georgescu-Roegen (1960), quoted earlier, who does not identify any misallocation of this type. This difference is due to Georgescu-Roegen's exclusive concern with the case when the marginal disutility of effort is nil, that is, $V'(l) = 0$. Then we have, irrespective of the value of h, the result:

$$Q'(L) = 0. \tag{53}$$

This is the same result as under peasant farming (with the assumption of no 'real cost' of labour), and explains Georgescu-Roegen's argument that in an overpopulated feudal economy, people will work up to the point where the marginal product of labour is zero, irrespective of the share of the produce they receive (Georgescu-Roegen, 1960, p. 26). The same assumption also explains Georgescu-Roegen's conclusion that in an over-populated economy, 'the feudal formula warrants maximum welfare' (p. 31).

We have seen before that the existence of surplus labour does not imply either that the marginal product of labour is zero or that the marginal disutility of effort is nil. Hence there is nothing contradictory in assuming the presence of surplus labour along with asserting that there is misallocation of resources under share-cropping.

We can now consider cases of sharing of the gross output. Here the misallocation is more pervasive. If the landowner pays for the non-labour inputs, the marginal product of these factors will exceed the price of them by the proportion $(1 - h)$.

$$(1-h) \cdot \frac{\partial Q}{\partial f_j} = p_j, \quad \text{for } j = 1, 2, \ldots, n. \tag{54}$$

This represents a marginal distortion of a restrictive nature.

A similar distortion will take place when the cultivator meets the non-labour costs and the sharing is on the basis of the gross output.

$$h \cdot \frac{\partial Q}{\partial f_j} = p_j, \quad \text{for } j = 1, 2, \ldots, n. \tag{55}$$

50. Furthermore, labour use under share-cropping would be less intensive than by a comparable peasant family. However, insofar as the share-cropper is poorer, his marginal utility of income will be higher, and that will probably compensate partially the influence of h being less than one.

To take a mixed case, when either side can provide the non-labour inputs in any amount they like, the following result can be seen to hold in equilibrium.

$$\max \left\{ \left(h \cdot \frac{\partial Q}{\partial f_j} \right), \; \left[(1-h) \cdot \frac{\partial Q}{\partial f_j} \right] \right\} = p_j, \quad \text{for } j = 1, 2, \dots, n. \quad (56)$$

As long as *either* side finds it worth its while (in view of its own share) to supply a given input, it does so. But even here, there will be some distortion of a restrictive nature, compared with peasant farming (equation (21)), since $0 < h < 1$.

When the gross output is shared, the non-labour factors will not be allocated according to the proper marginal costs and products, and this will create allocational distortions even if the labour application formula is the same as under peasant farming. That is, even if we make the assumption made by Georgescu-Roegen (1960) of no disutility of effort, and assume that labour is applied according to rule (53), there will still be resource misallocation if there is sharing of gross (as opposed to net) output.[51]

We can conclude that quite apart from problems of 'equity' and 'exploitation' involved in share-cropping, there is also a problem of inefficient allocation. This is present whenever the marginal disutility of effort in the relevant region is positive, even if the sharing is of the net product. Furthermore, when the sharing is of the gross product, there is misallocation even if the disutility of effort is assumed to be uniformly zero.

5 Concluding Remarks

In this paper we started with an analysis of a peasant family in economic equilibrium, by making explicit assumptions about its objectives and the economic circumstances. Equilibrium with direct consumption of own produce was contrasted with that involving the sale of a part or the whole of the product to the market. With this framework as the background, the paper ranged over a variety of issues involving resource allocation in backward agriculture. The main conclusions are the following.

(1) The existence of surplus labour does not necessarily require the assumption of zero marginal disutility of work (or that of a dis-

---

51. Sharing of gross, as opposed to net, output is quite common. See, for example, *Studies in the Economics of Farm Management* (1954-57).

continuity in the production function, or that of the effects of better nutrition on productivity). It is sufficient to assume flat sections in the marginal rate of indifferent substitution between income and work in the relevant region.

(2) Closely related to this point is the observation that the assumption of surplus labour does not conflict with an equilibrium at a positive marginal product of labour, labour being measured in terms of hours of work, rather than in terms of number of persons. It is also shown that the existence of surplus labour is consistent with a production function with any degree of substitutability between labour time and other factors.

(3) In a peasant economy that markets a part or the whole of its product, even complete flatness of the marginal rate of indifferent substitution is not necessary for the existence of surplus labour because under certain conditions the rise in the price of the peasant output resulting from the transfer of a part of the labour force will stimulate production by the remaining members of the peasant economy. The exact conditions for the existence of such a positive stimulus from a price rise were specified.

(4) The importance of the question of the *existence* of surplus labour may have been unduly exaggerated by both sides in the dispute. Some of the standard results derived from a model of surplus labour, for example, allocational advantages of peasant farming as opposed to capitalist farming, were shown not to require the assumption of surplus labour, only that of an imperfect labour market with a gap between the 'real cost of labour' in peasant farming and the market wage rate.

(5) Even for problems where the existence of surplus labour makes a crucial difference, much depends on the size of this surplus and the extent of the response of output to the withdrawal of the labour force once this surplus is exhausted. This response cannot be calculated without bringing in variations in hours of labour as a part of the population is withdrawn. In terms of the utility functions used for the peasant families, this variation can be quantified. The practice of relating the peasant output to the size of the peasant population, treating hours of labour as constant, seems to be legitimate only under some very special assumptions.

(6) The simultaneous existence of surplus labour and positive wages is not a genuine problem at all, except in the special model of surplus labour where zero marginal disutility of effort is assumed. However, the problem of a gap between the wage rate and the corresponding real cost of labour in the peasant economy is a genuine question, and the existing theories on why the wages are positive

throw considerable light on the rather different question of the existence of the 'wage gap'. Further explanations were suggested as possible additions to this list.

(7) Given the use of only two factors of production, namely, labour and land, higher output per acre of peasant farms over capitalist farms is usually explained in terms of disguised unemployment or seasonal unemployment. It was shown that it is sufficient to assume that there is a seasonal wage gap if labour applied in one season raises the productivity of labour in the other. The result is, of course, not contradicted by assuming seasonal unemployment, or year-round surplus labour, or zero marginal disutility of work, but the result does not depend on these assumptions being made.

(8) The simultaneous existence of capitalist farms and peasant farms, with different equilibrium labour cost, is possible only with the further assumption of an imperfect land market, if the two-factor production function has constant returns to scale. However, the assumption of such imperfection does not seem to be particularly unrealistic.

(9) The higher productivity per acre of the smaller farms compared with the larger ones in India may be related to these considerations. However, some alternative explanations are also possible. But the practice of imputing the market wage rate to family labour in peasant farming used in Indian official publications, which show a considerable part of Indian peasant agriculture having 'losses', seems to be based on a confusion of concepts.

(10) According to some interpretations of the wage gap, the wage system suffers from market distortions, and peasant farming has some distinct advantages in the allocation of labour. From this, however, a general conclusion in favour of the superior efficiency of peasant farming cannot be drawn.

(11) Even though share-cropping as a method is free from the wage system, it leads to inefficient allocation of resources when the relevant marginal disutility of effort is positive. Even when this disutility is nil, there are distortions when the sharing is on the basis of the gross product, as opposed to the net output.

Finally, a general remark. This paper is basically an attempt to apply the postulates of rational behaviour to the details of allocational decisions in peasant and dual economies. The differences between the allocational results of the peasant economies and those of the others are traced here to differences in objective circumstances. It is seen that the special features of peasant and dual agriculture made familiar by two decades of development economics can be fitted well into a framework of rational behaviour. Nevertheless, it is worth emphasizing that, for the purpose of this paper, rationality is an assumption that is explored and not a hypothesis that is tested.

References

Arrow, K. J., Chenery, H. B., Minhas, B. S. and Solow, R. M. (1961): 'Capital-Labour Substitution and Economic Efficiency', *Review of Economics and Statistics*, **63**.

Bagchi, A. K. (1962): 'The Choice of the Optimum Technique', *Economic Journal*, **72** (September).

Bauer, P. T. (1948): *The Rubber Industry* (London: Longmans, Green & Co.).

Dandekar, V. M. (1962): 'Economic Theory and Agrarian Reform', *Oxford Economic Papers*, **14** (February).

Das-Gupta, A. K. (1965): *Planning and Economic Growth* (Mystic, Conn.: Lawrence Verry, Inc.).

Datta, Bhabatosh (1960): *The Economics of Industrialization* (Calcutta: World Press).

Dobb, M. H. (1951): *Some Aspects of Economic Development* (Delhi: Ranjit Publishers).

Dumont, R. (1957): *Types of Rural Economy* (New York: Methuen & Co.).

Eckaus, R. S. (1955): 'Factor Proportions in Underdeveloped Countries', *American Economic Review*, **43** (September).

Economic Weekly (1962-64): Debate on Size and Productivity of Indian Farms. (1) A. K. Sen, 'An Aspect of Indian Agriculture' (Annual No., 1962); (2) D. Mazumdar, 'On the Economics of Relative Efficiency of Small Farmers' (Special No., 1963); (3) A. K. Sen, 'Size of Holdings and Productivity' (Annual No., 1964); (4) R. Agarwala, 'Size of Holdings and Productivity: A Comment' (11 April 1964); (5) A. K. Sen, 'A Reply' (2 May 1964); (6) K. Bardhan, 'Further Comment' (22 August 1964); and (7) R. Agarwala, 'Further Comments' (21 November 1964).

Ezekiel, H. (1960): 'An Application of Leibenstein's Theory of Underemployment', *Journal of Political Economy*, **68** (October).

Galenson, W. and Pyatt, G. (1964): *The Quality of Labour and Economic Development in Certain Countries* (Geneva: ILO).

Georgescu-Roegen, N. (1960): 'Economic Theory and Agrarian Reforms', *Oxford Economic Papers*, **12** (February).

Griliches, Z. (1960): 'Measuring Inputs in Agriculture: A Critical Survey', *Journal of Farm Economics*, **42** (December).

Guha, Ashok (1963): 'Scarcity of Specific Resources as a Limit to Output', *Review of Economic Studies*, **30** (February).

Guha, Ranajit (1963): *A Rule of Property for Bengal* (Paris: Mouton).

Gupta, S. C. (1958): 'Land Market in the North Western Provinces (Uttar Pradesh) in the First Half of the Nineteenth Century', *Indian Economic Review*, **4** (August).

Haberler, G. (1957): 'Critical Observations on Some Current Notions in the Theory of Economic Development', *L'Industria*, **2**.

Habib, Ifran (1963): *The Agrarian System of Moghul India* (Bombay: Asia Publishing House).

Harsanyi, John (1955): 'Cardinal Welfare, Individualistic Ethics, and Interpersonal Comparisons of Utility', *Journal of Political Economy*, 63 (August).

Hicks, J. R. (1946): *Value and Capital*, 2nd edn (Oxford: Oxford University Press).

ILO (1964): *Problems of Employment in Economic Development* (Geneva).

Johnston, B. F. and Mellor, J. W. (1961): 'The Role of Agriculture in Economic Development', *American Economic Review*, 51 (September).

Jorgenson, D. W. (1961): 'The Development of a Dual Economy', *Economic Journal*, 71 (June).

Kao, C. H. C., Anschel, K. R. and Eicher, C. K. (1964): 'Disguised Unemployment in Agriculture', in C. K. Eicher and L. Witt (eds), *Agriculture in Economic Development* (New York: McGraw-Hill Book Co.).

Khusro, A. M. (1964): 'Returns to Scale in Indian Agriculture', *Indian Journal of Agricultural Economics*, Silver Jubilee No. (July–December).

Krishna, Raj (1963): 'Farm Supply Response in India–Pakistan: A Case Study of the Punjab Region', *Economic Journal*, 73 (September).

—— (1964): 'The Marketable Surplus Function for a Subsistence Crop', *Economic Weekly* (Annual No.).

Leibenstein, H. (1957): 'The Theory of Underemployment in Backward Economies', *Journal of Political Economy*, 65 (April).

Lenin, V. I. 1893 (1963): 'New Economic Developments of Peasant Life', and 'On the So-called Market Question', in his *Collected Works*, Vol. I (Moscow).

Lewis, W. A. (1954): 'Economic Development with Unlimited Supplies of Labour', *Manchester School of Economic and Social Studies*, 22 (May).

Marshall, Alfred (1949): *Principles of Economics* (London: Macmillan Co.).

Marx, Karl (1957): In F. Engels (ed.), *Capital*, Vol. II (Moscow).

Mathur, Ashok (1964): 'The Anatomy of Disguised Unemployment', *Oxford Economic Papers*, 16 (July).

Mazumdar, D. (1959): 'The Marginal Productivity Theory of Wages and Disguised Unemployment', *Review of Economic Studies*, 26 (June).

Meier, G. (1964): *Leading Issues in Development Economics* (New York: Oxford University Press).

Mellor, J. W. (1963): 'The Use and Productivity of Farm Family Labour in Early Stages of Agricultural Development', *Journal of Farm Economics*, 65 (August).

—— and Stevens, R. D. (1956): 'The Average and Marginal Product of Farm Labor in Underdeveloped Economies', *Journal of Farm Economics*, 38 (August).

Myint, H. (1964): *The Economics of the Underdeveloped Countries* (London: Hutchison & Co.).

Narain, Dharm (1961): *Distribution of the Marketed Surplus of Agricultural Produce by Size Level of Holdings in India 1950-51* (New York: Asia Publishing House).

—— (1965): *The Impact of Price Movement on Areas Under Selected Crops in India 1900-1939* (Cambridge: Cambridge University Press).

Nerlove, M. (1958): *The Dynamics of Supply* (Baltimore, Md.: Johns Hopkins Press).

Nicholls, W. H. (1960): *Southern Tradition and Regional Progress* (Chapel Hill: University of North Carolina Press).

Nurkse, R. (1953): *Problems of Capital Formation in Underdeveloped Countries* (Oxford: Basil Blackwell).

Ohkawa, K. and Rosovsky, H. (1960): 'The Role of Agriculture in Modern Japanese Economic Development', *Economic Development and Cultural Change*, **9** (October).

Oshima, Harry T. (1958): 'Underemployment in Backward Economies: An Empirical Comment', *Journal of Political Economy*, **66** (June).

Pepelasis, A. and Yotopoulos, P. A. (1962): *Surplus Labour in Greek Agriculture 1953-1960* (Athens).

Raj, K. N. (1957): *Employment Aspects of Planning in Underdeveloped Economies* (Cairo).

Randhawa, N. S. (1960): 'Returns to Scale and Co-operative Farming', *Indian Journal of Agricultural Economies* (July-September).

Ranis, G. (1959): 'The Financing of Japanese Economic Development', *Economic History Review*, **11** (April).

—— and Fei, C. H. (1964): *Development of the Labour Surplus Economy: Theory and Policy* (Homewood, Ill.: Richard D. Irwin, Inc.).

Robinson, Joan (1960): *Exercises in Economic Analysis* (New York: St. Martin's Press).

Rosenstein-Rodan, P. N. (1957): 'Disguised Unemployment and Underemployment in Agriculture', *Monthly Bulletin of Agricultural Economies and Statistics*, **6** (July-August).

—— (ed.) (1964): *Pricing and Fiscal Policies* (Cambridge, Mass.: MIT Press).

Schultz, T. W. (1964): *Transforming Traditional Agriculture* (New Haven, Conn.: Yale University Press).

Sen, A. K. (1960): *Choice of Techniques* (Oxford: Basil Blackwell).

—— (1966): 'Labour Allocation in a Cooperative Enterprise', *Review of Economic Studies*, **33** [Essay 2 in this volume].

Studies in the Economics of Farm Management, 1954-55, 1955-56, 1956-57 (1954-57) (New Delhi: Directorate of Economics and Statistics, Ministry of Food and Agriculture).

Thorner, D. (1965): 'A Post-Marxian Theory of Peasant Economy: The School of A. V. Chayanov', *Economic Weekly* (Annual No.).

—— and Thorner, A. (1962): *Land and Labour in India* (Bombay: Asia Publishing House).

United Nations, Economic Commission for Asia and the Far East (1962): *Programming Techniques for Economic Development* (Bangkok).

Viner, Jacob (1957): 'Some Reflections on the Concept of "Disguised Unemployment",' *Contribucoes a Analise do Desenvolvimento Economico*; partial extract in Meier (1964), pp. 79-83.

Wonnacott, P. (1962): 'Disguised and Overt Unemployment in Underdeveloped Economies', *Quarterly Journal of Economics*, **76** (May).

2

Labour Allocation in a Cooperative Enterprise

1 *Introduction*

Two methods of income distribution have been particularly associated with socialist thinking: 'to each according to his needs' and 'to each according to his work'. In the literature on socialism it is the latter system that has been mostly studied. Marx felt the former system to be appropriate only at the 'higher phase of the communist society', and emphasized the principle of distribution 'proportional to the amount of labour they contribute', in the 'first phase' of the communist society.[1] While discussions in the Marxist literature have concentrated mainly on distribution according to work, in particular on the utilization of the wage system, actual methods of payments in socialist economies have often departed from this rule, the most notable example of this being in Chinese agriculture.

On the other plane of discussion, in the theoretical literature on resource allocation with decentralized planning, the emphasis has been on reaching Pareto-optimality, and that, with the usual assumptions, has been found to fit in well with a wage system.[2] There have of course been discussions on correcting the distribution according to work towards the goal of distribution according to needs through a set of taxes and subsidies, but the basic method of payment that has been considered has always been some variant or other of the wage system.

I am indebted to Peter Diamond for his helpful comments.

1. Marx [14], pp. 29–31; see also Sweezy [20], pp. 10–11.
2. See Lange and Taylor [10], Lerner [11] and Koopmans [8]. See also Robinson [16], Chapter II.

From *Review of Economic Studies*, 33 (July 1966), 361–71.

The actual organization of enterprises in communist countries tends to depart from a pure wage system in at least two different ways: (i) in the use of some variant of profit-sharing over and above a wage system,[3] and (ii) in having a part of the income distributed on some criteria other than that of work, e.g. some interpretation of 'needs'.[4] There is not yet a distinct body of literature on the *theory* of non-wage allocation of labour; nevertheless, in the context of policy debates, the following questions have repeatedly cropped up.

(1) What are the difficulties in having a system of distribution purely according to needs? While in the USSR and in Eastern Europe there has not been any large-scale attempt to have payments primarily according to needs, the Chinese leaders have tried to break through the problem of incentives involved in this, and it has even been claimed that 'ideally, the party leaders would like non-material incentives to become the main motive force impelling the masses on to greater output'.[5]

(2) What difficulties are there in having a system of distribution purely according to work, even profits being shared on that basis? Based on Yugoslav experience Ward [21] has discussed some problems of allocation that arise in this context when the cooperatives are allowed to vary the number of members, and they use it to maximize returns *per person*. The problem does not disappear even when the number of members cannot be varied by the cooperative for this purpose, for there is also the question of the amount of work done. Ward takes the amount of work done per person as given; we shall however treat this as a variable, and study the problem of incentives in that context.

(3) If a mixed system is attempted, what are the 'proper' shares of the two methods of distribution? In some respects, all systems actually used in these countries are mixed ones; even in the USSR the 'social insurance' is basically a method of payments according to needs, and it is 'usually considered to add something of the order of the magnitude of one-third to money earnings'.[6] In the Chinese attempt at communization of agriculture, heavy emphasis was put

---

3. See Ward [21]; the discussion is based on the experience of Yugoslavia. The 'enterprise funds' in the USSR also imply some profit-sharing (see Bergson [2], p. 109). See also Wiles [22], Chapters 1 and 2.

4. Attempted mainly in China, particularly in agriculture; see Li [13], Hoffman [6], Nove [15]. The rejection of the wage system in China may have a lot to do with the well-known problems of utilization of surplus (or near-surplus) labour arising from the rigidity of the wage rate. The efficiency problems arising from a positive wage rate in an economy with surplus labour are discussed in Sen [18].

5. Hoffman [6], p. 110.

6. Dobb [3], p. 448.

on the so-called 'supply portion' of income, distributed on some criteria of needs, and in some cases the proportion of this reached 'as high as 80–90 per cent with the slim remainder being distributed as money wages'. But by 1960 payments according to work gained predominance again, when the 'ideal' ratio of supplies to wages was put at 30 per cent.[7]

(4) To what extent are these problems dependent on the attitude of the members of the cooperative to each other? It is natural to expect that the results of cooperative efforts will depend crucially on how much concern people have for each other.

In this note we shall go into this collection of questions in terms of a highly simplified model. A cooperative is considered, consisting of N families, identical in every respect.[8] The cooperative uses its own homogeneous labour and its own land, and hires outside factors from a set of perfectly competitive markets. We shall confine our attention to the efficiency problems that arise *within* a cooperative enterprise, and not be concerned with allocational problems *among* them. Problems of taxation are not considered. Nor do we go into saving decisions in this paper, which we assume are left to individual families, and we relate utility to family income and not to family consumption. If the basic framework is found relevant, then the analysis can be easily extended in a variety of directions.

2 Individual and Social Welfare

There are N identical families that make up the cooperative. Member families of the cooperative like more and more income (y^i) and dislike more and more work (l^i), and each family has a given and identical utility function, U. Marginal utility from income is positive and diminishing, and marginal utility from work is negative and diminishing (i.e. marginal disutility from work is positive and increasing), and they are independent of each other.

$$U^i = U(y^i, l^i), \text{ with } U_y > 0, U_l < 0, U_{yy} < 0, U_{ll} < 0, U_{yl} = U_{ly} = 0. (1)$$

However, the families are not *necessarily* indifferent to the happiness of other families (though they might also be that), and their notion of 'social welfare" takes into account the utility of other families.[9]

---

7. Hoffman [6], pp. 104–5.

8. Since the families share the same needs and have the same productive abilities, we shall find that distribution according to needs as well as that according to work both tend to produce an equal distribution of income, but the *level* of income varies, and so does welfare.

9. For the underlying concepts, see Harsanyi [4].

Individual j attaches a weight a_{ij} to a unit of the utility of individual i in aggregating the social welfare,

$$W^j = \sum_{i=1}^{N} a_{ij} \cdot U^i. \tag{2}$$

The utility of his own family can serve as the unit of account ($a_{jj} = 1$), and it is assumed that he attaches a weight somewhere between 0 and 1 to a unit of the utility of other families ($0 \leqslant a_{ij} \leqslant 1$). This means that while he may like other people to be happy, he does not attach greater weight to the happiness of other families than he does to his own.[10] Equation (2) can now be rewritten as:

$$W^j = U^j + \sum_{\substack{i=1 \\ i \neq j}}^{N} a_{ij} \cdot U^i, \quad \text{with } 0 \leqslant a_{ij} \leqslant 1. \tag{2.1}$$

While (2) or (2.1) represents the welfare of the cooperative as viewed by individual j, we define the 'social welfare' (W) to be simply an aggregate of individual utilities. We assume that this is the Management's notion also, which is assumed to be non-discriminating.

$$W = \sum_{i=1}^{N} U^i. \tag{3}$$

The set of a_{ij} for any individual j defines, quite precisely, his attitude to the welfare of other families, and we shall find it convenient to extract from it an aggregate measure of his 'sympathy' for other families, which we shall call, in keeping with our subject matter, his 'social consciousness' (S^j).

$$S^j = \frac{1}{N} \sum_{i=1}^{N} a_{ij}. \tag{4}$$

In view of (2.1), S^j resides somewhere in the closed range $[(1/N), 1]$. The more he values other families' happiness vis-à-vis his own, the closer is the value of S^j to 1.

While S^j measures the sympathy that family j has for the other families, we can define a magnitude T^i that will measure the sympathy

10. Of course he can attach a greater weight to a unit of another family's *income* than to his own, if there is significant inequality.

that family *i receives* from the other families. This we call the 'social goodwill' of family *i*.

$$T^i = \frac{1}{N} \sum_{j=1}^{N} a_{ij}. \tag{5}$$

Once again, in view of (2.1), T^i resides somewhere in the closed range $[(1/N), 1]$, and the more 'goodwill' that this family has, the closer will be the value of T^i to 1.

We now introduce two crucial assumptions, one of which will be used immediately, and the other later. The assumption of *symmetric sympathy* is that all families have the same measure of 'social consciousness'.

$$S^j = S, \quad \text{for all } j. \tag{4.1}$$

The assumption of *symmetric goodwill* is that all families have the same measure of 'social goodwill'.

$$T^i = T, \quad \text{for all } i. \tag{5.1}$$

Note that neither assumption requires symmetry in the exact *distribution* of the values of a_{ij}. Both the notions of symmetry are *aggregate* ones.

3 Centralized Allocation

The cooperative owns a given amount of land (A) and hires m outside factors $(F^k$, with $k = 1, 2, \ldots, m)$ at constant prices $(P^k$, with $k = 1, 2, \ldots, m)$. Labour (L) is provided by members of the cooperative. The production function Q is given by (6).

$$Q = Q(L, A, F^1, F^2, \ldots, F^m). \tag{6}$$

Q is assumed to be a 'well-behaved' production function, with the usual nice properties, including differentiability throughout, and positive but diminishing marginal product of each factor.

Given (1), it is easy to check that welfare maximization requires equal division of total income (V) and of total work (L). Hence, *under centralized allocation*, we should have:

$$y^i = \frac{V}{N} \equiv y, \quad \text{for all } i \tag{7}$$

$$l^i = \frac{L}{N} \equiv l, \quad \text{for all } i. \tag{8}$$

Given (7) and (8), the social welfare function (3) simplifies into:

$$W = N \cdot U(y, l). \tag{3.1}$$

The income generated in the cooperative (V) is given by the difference between the value of the output (Q) and the purchase costs of the m inputs. We take the factor prices (P^k) to be expressed in units of the output.

$$V = Q - \sum_{k=1}^{m} F^k \cdot P^k. \tag{9}$$

Given (1), (3.1), (6), (7), (8) and (9), maximization of social welfare (W) under centralized allocation requires:[11]

$$Q_k = P^k, \quad \text{for } k = 1, 2, \ldots, m \tag{10}$$

$$Q_L = -\frac{U_l(y, l)}{U_y(y, l)} \equiv R. \tag{11}$$

Here R is defined as the individual marginal rate of indifferent substitution between income and non-labour (leisure). The rate is the same for all individuals. The interpretation of rules (10) and (11) is obvious.

Note that rules (7), (8), (10) and (11), which describe the allocation decisions, yield not only Paretian optimality (the usual competitive result), but also maximization of total social welfare. This completing of the incomplete Paretian ordering has been possible by assuming a social welfare function with additive cardinal utility.[12]

4   Voluntary Allocation of Labour

One feature of the allocational rules of the last section is that the individual members of the cooperative are not allowed to determine how much work they would like to put in; it is all decided for them by the Management. We now relax that assumption, and examine the voluntary allocational results given the system of rewards. It is assumed that a proportion α of income is distributed according to 'needs', and the rest $(1 - \alpha)$ according to 'work'. The value of α lies in the closed interval between 0 and 1. Needs are equal, and thus α

11. These are the first order conditions. The second order conditions are given by the usual restrictions on the 'bordered' determinants (see Hicks [5], p. 320). Q_k refers to the partial derivative of Q with respect to F^k, and Q_L that with respect to L.
12. We discuss this question further in Section 8.

proportion of the income is equally distributed; the rest is distributed in such a way that family i gets (l^i/L) proportion of it. We have then:

$$y^i = V\left(\frac{\alpha}{N} + (1-\alpha)\left(\frac{l^i}{L}\right)\right). \tag{7.1}$$

Individual j maximizes W^j for variations of his own labour l^j, given the amount of labour performed by others,[13] and given the use of other factors of production. He is thus guided by (1), (2.1), (6), (7.1) and (9), and his optimal allocation can be seen to require the following condition:

$$-U_l^j = \sum_{i=1}^N a_{ij} \cdot U_y^i\left[Q_L\left(\frac{\alpha}{N} + (1-\alpha)\left(\frac{l^i}{L}\right)\right) - \left(\frac{V}{L}\right)\left(\frac{l^i}{L}\right)(1-\alpha)\right]$$
$$+ U_y^j \cdot \left(\frac{V}{L}\right)(1-\alpha). \tag{12}$$

Given (1) and (4.1), we shall find at equilibrium, the same amount of labour offered by each family. As a result, the income of each family will also tend to be equal, as is seen from (7.1). Thus conditions (7) and (8) will also hold at equilibrium. There is no inconsistency between this and the assumption of labour allocation underlying (12). Each family decides on how much labour to apply given the amount of labour of other families; but since their calculations are identical they end up by offering the same amount.

Since (7) and (8) hold, and since everyone has the same utility function U, the marginal utilities of income and the marginal disutilities of work that enter in (12) are respectively identical for all families. It is easy to check that under these circumstances (12) simplifies into the following:

$$R = R^j = Q_L\left[S + (1-S)(1-\alpha)\left(\frac{\beta}{\eta}\right)\right], \tag{13}$$

where $\beta = V/Q$, the ratio of income to total output, $\eta = (Q_L \cdot L)/Q$, elasticity of output with respect to labour. S and R have been defined before as the measure of 'social consciousness' (see (4)) and the relevant individual marginal rate of indifferent substitution between income and leisure (see (11)). The voluntary allocational result (13) has to be compared and contrasted with the optimal rule (11).

---

13. We are abstracting from behaviour based on 'game' considerations. When the number of individuals (N) is small, this may be an important limitation.

5   Pure Systems and Optimality

If the system that is followed is one purely according to needs, then we have $\alpha = 1$. Under those circumstances, result (13) becomes:

$$R = Q_L \cdot S. \tag{13.1}$$

This corresponds to the optimum rule (11) only when $S = 1$, i.e. only when sympathy for other families is perfect, with each family attaching equal weight to the happiness of every family in the community.[14] Barring this special case, the allocation of labour will not be carried to the point required for optimality, but stopped before that, since $S < 1$, and therefore $R < Q_L$.

If, on the other hand, the system of distribution is one purely according to work, we have $\alpha = 0$. Then, result (13) becomes:

$$R = Q_L \left[S + (1 - S) \left(\frac{\beta}{\eta} \right) \right]. \tag{13.2}$$

This can coincide with the optimality requirement (11) if *either* there is complete sympathy for all, *i.e.* $S = 1$, *or* if $\beta = \eta$. The latter condition can be analysed a little further. It equates the relative share of the income of the cooperative in gross output to the elasticity of output with respect to labour. If we assume that the production function is homogeneous of the first degree,[15] and also that the co-operative does not own any factor (like land) other than labour, then this condition of β being equal to η will indeed be fulfilled. The proof is obvious from Euler's Theorem and the fulfilment of the allocational rules for other factors given by (10).

If, however, sympathy or 'social consciousness' is not perfect, i.e. $S < 1$, and the cooperative owns some factors other than labour (in our assumption, land), it is easy to show that with a production function homogeneous of the first degree, we have $\beta > \eta$. And it follows from (13.2) that $R > Q_L$, i.e. labour will be applied *beyond* the point required for optimization. Thus barring the special cases of complete sympathy for all, or of a cooperative devoid of non-

14. Cf. Marx's position that payments according to needs will not be the right system in the 'first phase' of socialism when the society is 'in every respect tainted economically morally, intellectually with the hereditary diseases of the old society from whose womb it is emerging' ([14], p. 29), and that it could work well only when 'all the springs of cooperative wealth are gushing more freely together with the all-round development of the individual' ([14], p. 31).

15. More generally, in an equilibrium with no 'abnormal' profits, as under perfect competition, this result will hold. Constant return to scale is not needed throughout; only at the point of equilibrium.

labour resources, a pure system of allocation according to work will tend to make the amount of labour offered to be greater than the optimum.

One comment on the distribution system according to work may be worth making here. We have assumed that the part that is distributed according to work is given out directly in terms of the proportion of labour contributed by each family. If instead a part is distributed as straightforward wages, and if the surplus after paying for wages and for the part of the income that is distributed according to needs (still α proportion of total income of the members) is again split up in proportion to the amount of labour contributed, the result will be the same as in our distributional equation (7.1), and all consequences will hold.

$$y^i = \frac{V \cdot \alpha}{N} + l^i \cdot w + [V(1-\alpha) - L \cdot w] \left(\frac{l^i}{L}\right)$$

$$= V\left[\frac{\alpha}{N} + (1-\alpha)\left(\frac{l^i}{L}\right)\right].$$

In particular, when nothing is distributed according to needs ($\alpha = 0$), the same tendency to over-contribute labour will follow, except in the special case of complete sympathy ($S = 1$), or no owned non-labour resource ($\beta = \eta$). This is a basic problem of syndicalism, in fact of any economic system with profit-sharing by workers according to work.

Of the two pure systems, the result that there is *too little* work done in a system of distribution according to *needs* is easier to see intuitively. The result of *too much* work done in a system of distribution according to *work* can be explained in the following heuristic terms. When an individual contributes an additional unit of labour, he gets two compensations for his troubles: first, the income of the cooperative goes up, and he gets a share of the marginal product, though not the whole of it; second, he gets an enlarged share of the *total* income because his share in the total labour contributed is larger. The former, on its own, is insufficient to make him offer the optimum amount of labour, since he gets only a part of his marginal product, but the latter over-compensates for it, as long as the average income per unit of labour is greater than the marginal product of labour. Hence the over-allocation of work. When, however, the cooperative possesses no factor other than labour, and the production function has constant returns to scale, the average income per unit of labour just equals the marginal product, and the two effects exactly balance out. Similarly, when he has complete sympathy for all other families, he does not mind other people getting a share of his marginal product, nor does he see any gain in getting a larger income at the cost of others; and once again the allocation is right. When, however, the cooperative possesses non-labour factors and the sympathy is not quite complete, there is a tendency towards over-contribution of work, arising from a desire to get a higher share of the existing income exploiting the system of distribution according to work.

6 The Optimal Rule

In order to achieve welfare maximization, result (13) has to coincide with the requirement (11). This coincidence holds if and only if:

$$S + (1 - S)(1 - \alpha)\left(\frac{\beta}{\eta}\right) = 1. \tag{14}$$

This is always satisfied when:

$$S = 1. \tag{14a}$$

If (14a) does not hold, and 'social consciousness' is not complete, we require then:

$$(1 - \alpha) = \frac{\eta}{\beta}. \tag{14b}$$

This means that the proportion of income to be distributed accord-ing to work should equal the ratio of the elasticity of output with respect to labour to the share of cooperative income in total output.

It should be noted that rule (14b) has a close affinity to the com-petitive rule. If the production function is homogeneous of the first degree, and if the allocational rule (9) for hired factors (F^k) is followed, then the share of the cooperative's income in total output, i.e. the value of β, will simply equal the sum of the elasticities of output with respect to all factors of production supplied by the cooperative. Also, under those circumstances, labour's share of output (Q) will be given by η and labour's share in the cooperative income (V) will be given by (η/β). And it is this portion that is to be distributed according to work if rule (14b) is followed. And the proportion of the cooperative income that is to be distributed according to needs should equal the rest, i.e. what would have been the competitive share of non-labour productive factors (land, in our example) owned by the cooperative.

However, the similarity with the competitive case, while striking, should not be over-stressed. First of all, the correspondence is not complete when we take a production function with diminishing returns to scale. Then it is not clear what the competitive distribution would have been. It is, however, clear from observing (14b) that the right proportion to be distributed according to work is what would have been the share of labour *if* it got its competitive share while the owned non-labour resources obtained the surplus that remained after paying all hired factors and labour their respective shares equal to their elasticities. The result quoted earlier that the right proportion to be distributed according to needs is what would have been the competitive share of non-labour factors of production (land) owned by the cooperative, does not any longer hold.

Second, while rule (14b) corresponds to the competitive solution, the method of distribution need not involve any wage system at all, and might therefore be free from sociological constraints that apply to boundary values of the wage rate as such. For example, the well-known allocational problems raised by the existence of a minimum level of the wage rate in preventing proper utilization of surplus or near-surplus labour in the underdeveloped countries,[16] might not necessarily apply to this case where no explicit use of a wage rate need be made. That is, if the constraint applies not to the minimum marginal return to labour (irrespective of the form of it) but to the minimum *wage rate* as such,[17] then rule (14b) need not be interfered with by such a constraint while the competitive solution might be.

Third, rule (14b) is not strictly necessary for optimality and condition (14a) is quite sufficient. That is if people do have complete social consciousness ($S = 1$), any choice of α will do just as well.[18] This introduction of external concern makes our model different from that of the usual competitive models. However, for any value of $S < 1$, rule (14b) is necessary for optimality in the voluntary system.

7   The Role of External Concern

It is interesting to note that the optimal rule (14b) is completely independent of the extent of external concern that people have for

16. See Sen [18], Chapters II, V, and Appendix A.

17. This will be the case when there is a conventional minimum level of the wage rate which does not come in when the method of rewards is altogether different from the wage system.

18. This might explain why the Chinese attempt at having a system of payment not closely related to work in agriculture in the 'Great Leap Forward' period was accompanied by attacks on the 'family-centred psychology' (Nove [15], p. 22; Hoffman [6], p. 100).

each other. The coincidence of (13) with the optimality requirement (11) when rule (14b) is followed, is independent of the value of S.

One reason why this appears surprising is the practice, in 'new welfare economics', of ruling out *all* types of external effects while deriving propositions about the optimality of competitive equilibrium.[19] But it can be checked that some types of external concern do not matter at all as far as the optimum allocation is concerned. At the competitive equilibrium an individual is paid at a rate just equal to the productivity of his last unit of labour, so that the real income enjoyed by the others is not affected by this allocational decision, and how much weight he wants to attach to other people's happiness does not make any difference to his choice. Similarly, since he stops at the point where his marginal net gain from the last unit of labour is nil, other people also do not care whether he applies this unit of labour or not, even though they may attach value to his utility.

It is to be noted that the external effects allowed here are of a kind different from the usual utilitarian presentation. In the utility functions of each family we have introduced only the labour and income of that family, but we have assumed that members try to maximize not this utility function of their family but a weighted sum of the utilities of all families, representing their notions of welfare. There is, however, a well-established tradition in economics of taking as people's 'utility' whatever it is that they try to maximize, so that family utility in this model might be taken to be equivalent not to our set of (U^i) but to the set of (W^j). The consequences of taking social welfare to be the sum of (W^j) rather than of (U^i) may be pursued.

$$\bar{W} = \sum_{j=1}^{N} W^j = \sum_{j=1}^{N} \sum_{i=1}^{N} a_{ij} \cdot U^i = N \cdot \sum_{i=1}^{N} T^i \cdot U^i. \qquad (3.2)$$

At this stage, the assumption of symmetric goodwill (5.1) is helpful. With that assumption, we have:

$$\bar{W} = N \cdot T \cdot W. \qquad (15)$$

Since N and T are given, maximization of W is equivalent to that of $\bar{W}$.[20] Aggregate social welfare is still maximized by following rule

19. 'The new welfare economists, despite their name, actually said little that was new. They accepted the usual simplifying assumptions of Pareto and Barone: to wit, the independence of different people's satisfactions and the absence of external economies and diseconomies.' (Scitovsky, in 'The state of welfare economics', in [17], p. 79.)

20. Even the condition of 'symmetric goodwill' can be relaxed when the object is to achieve only Pareto optimality through the competitive mechanism, as can be seen from the argument outlined in the previous paragraph in the text.

(14b), even though the identification of the set of individual utilities as the set (W^j) rather than the set (U^i), makes it a straightforward case of 'direct (i.e. non-market) interdependence', where 'the individual person's satisfaction ... depends not only on the quantities of product he consumes and services he renders but also on the satisfaction of other persons'.[21] The optimality of the rule seems to be completely independent of the exact size of such external concern.

One extreme case of *symmetric goodwill* is the case when people are completely egocentric (family-centric) and other people's (families') satisfactions simply do not enter into the individual utility functions, which is the favourite *neo-classical* assumption, which corresponds here to $T = 1/N$. The other extreme case is that of full 'social consciousness', which Marx expected in, and only in, the 'higher phase' of socialism,[22] and which corresponds here to the case of $T = 1$. The value of T can lie *anywhere* in the closed interval $[(1/N), 1]$, and irrespective of where it lies, rule (14b) yields the maximization of the aggregate welfare of the cooperative. However, in the extreme case of $T = 1$, we also have $S = 1$, i.e. condition (14a) holds, so that the policy implied by rule (14b), while still optimal, is redundant, and any proportion of total income (even all) can be distributed directly according to needs.

8   Concluding Remarks

We have examined the problem of labour allocation in a cooperative system both in terms of centralized decisions as well as in terms of voluntary allocation. The optimal rules of allocation in the former system are straight-forward (rules 7, 8, 10 and 11), and it is the latter system that raises interesting problems. The conflicting principles of distribution according to 'work' and according to 'needs' were specifically examined in terms of maximizing aggregate social welfare. The following are the main conclusions.

(1) Distribution purely according to 'needs' tends to result in an under-allocation of labour in the cooperative enterprise, and that purely according to 'work' tends to produce an over-allocation of it.

(2) Optimization requires a mixed system of distribution according to work and needs. More specifically, the proportion of income to be distributed according to work should equal the ratio of the elasticity of output with respect to labour *to* the relative share of

21. Scitovsky, 'Two concepts of external economies', in [17], pp. 70-1.
22. Marx [14], pp. 29-31.

cooperative income in the value of total output. The correspondence between this rule for a cooperative enterprise with the result of competitive equilibrium is striking, but some differences are also noted.

(3) An exception to conclusions (1) and (2) is provided by the case when there is complete 'social consciousness', i.e. in the case in which every individual attaches the same weight to his own happiness as he does to that of everyone else. In this case, a system of distribution according to work, or one according to needs, or *any* mixture of the two, produces the optimum allocation of labour.

(4) Barring the special case discussed in (3), the optimum proportion to be distributed according to needs, or according to work, is completely independent of the amount of sympathy that the members of the cooperative have for each other (i.e. is independent of their 'social consciousness').

(5) A corollary of conclusion (4) is that the optimal distribution rule, which closely corresponds to the competitive result, is not influenced by the existence or not of 'external effects' in the shape of concern for each other. An incidental observation is that to show the optimality of competitive equilibrium, all 'external effects' do not have to be ruled out, as is the practice in the now classic presentation of 'New Welfare Economics'.[23] Existence of concern for each other's happiness is seen to be harmless for the optimality of competitive allocation, provided there is symmetry (strictly defined as 'symmetric sympathy' and 'symmetric goodwill') in the pattern of such external effects. Zero external effects amount to no more than a *special case* of that symmetry.

So much about the conclusions. Now about the assumptions underlying the analysis. Some assumptions are easily removable, e.g. that the cooperative does not own any resource other than land. Even if the cooperative owns some other resource (e.g. capital goods) along with (or without) land, it makes no difference to the results. Some other assumptions are serious but not especially odd in this branch of economics. We have assumed well-behaved utility and production functions; automatic fulfilment of the second order conditions of welfare maximization and of equilibrium; no uncertainty; perfectly competitive markets; homogeneity of labour; and other assumptions commonly employed in this field.

We have also abstracted from some of the more perplexing problems in the practical running of a cooperative. In particular, we have avoided the complexities of resource allocation when different

23. Perhaps the best presentations are to be found in Lange [9], and Koopmans [8].

members have differently shaped utility functions, or have different degrees of 'social consciousness' (or of 'social goodwill'), if we take the social welfare function given by (3.2) as opposed to (3). These are relatively restrictive assumptions. However, both *symmetric sympathy* and *symmetric goodwill* are aggregate constraints and do not impose any detailed pattern of actual sympathies (a_{ij}). The values of (a_{ij}) can vary in many manners within the two sets of linear constraints.[24]

The nature of the social welfare function used, given by (3), (3.1) and (3.2), is also open to question. There are, first of all, the general difficulties of the impossibility of a social ordering based on individual orderings satisfying the set of conditions postulated by Arrow [1]. This problem we avoided by deliberately violating Arrow's condition of 'the independence of irrelevant alternatives'.[25]† The use of *cardinal* individual welfare to arrive at a social ordering always violates this condition.[26] The acceptability of the particular social ordering used depends on our assessment of the relevance of the condition of the 'independence of irrelevant alternatives'. Secondly, even within this general framework, the use of the Marshallian method of simply *aggregating* unweighted individual welfare indices may be found objectionable. However, its high intuitive appeal (from Bentham onwards) is an argument for the retention of this simple formula. Thirdly, non-utilitarian considerations are excluded from the social welfare function, which is a limiting assumption.

Similar problems arise with the individual welfare functions also. The general homogeneous, linear form (equation (2)) of individual

24. There are $2(N-1)$ linear constraints given by symmetric sympathy and symmetric goodwill.

$$\sum_{i=1}^{N} a_{i1} = \sum_{i=1}^{N} a_{i2} = \cdots = \sum_{i=1}^{N} a_{iN} \qquad (4.2)$$

$$\sum_{j=1}^{N} a_{1j} = \sum_{j=1}^{N} a_{2j} = \cdots = \sum_{j=1}^{N} a_{Nj}. \qquad (5.2)$$

The set of (a_{ij}), in number N^2, has to satisfy these $2(N-1)$ linear equations.

25. An alternative way out of the 'impossibility' problem is to assume that the individuals have a certain pattern of 'similarity', e.g. 'single peaked preferences', or more generally 'value restricted preferences' (see Arrow [1], Inada [7], and Sen [19]).

† [This is, I am afraid, wrong. It is possible to satisfy an appropriately defined condition of independence or irrelevant alternatives even with *cardinal* individual welfares, with or without interpersonal comparability; on this see my *Collective Choice and Social Welfare* (San Francisco: Holden-Day, 1970; reprinted, Amsterdam: North-Holland, 1979), Chapters 7*, 8* and 9*. The Arrow impossibility problem is avoided here by a richer informational base, in particular not ruling out interpersonal comparisons of utility.]

26. On this see Arrow [1], Chapter III.

welfare based on the set of individual utilities is open to challenge. While Harsanyi [4] has shown that this is the only acceptable form for an individual's judgements about social welfare, if a number of highly appealing postulates have to be fulfilled,[27] an individual may not act, even in a cooperative, to maximize what he recognizes to be the social welfare of that cooperative, as opposed to his own welfare.

However, even if we do not restrict ourselves to the linear form used in equation (2), our analysis need not require substantial change. Consider W^j in the more general form below:

$$W^j = W^j(U^1 \cdot U^2, \ldots, U^N), \text{ with } 0 \leqslant \frac{\partial W^j}{\partial U^i} \leqslant 1, \frac{\partial^2 W^j}{\partial U^{i2}} \leqslant 0,$$

and

$$\frac{\partial W^j}{\partial U^j} = 1. \tag{2.2}$$

Equation (12) will still give the first order conditions of individual equilibrium if we interpret a_{ij} as the partial derivative of W^j with respect of U^i, i.e. $a_{ij} = \partial W^j/\partial U^i$. The assumptions of symmetry will need to be redefined to take account of the variability of a_{ij}. *Symmetric sympathy* can be defined as equal 'social consciousness', i.e. equations (4.1), *whenever* the utilities of all individuals are equal. Similarly *symmetric goodwill* will now require the fulfilment of (5.1) in a situation of equal utility. It is easy to check that our main results stand even with this more general definition of the individual welfare function (2.2) instead of the homogeneous, linear form (2) used in the foregoing analysis.

References

[1] Arrow, K. J. *Social Choice and Individual Values* (New York, 1963).

[2] Bergson, A. *The Economics of Soviet Planning* (New Haven, 1964).

[3] Dobb, M. H. *Soviet Economic Development Since 1917* (London, 1951).

---

27. See Theorem V in Harsanyi [4]. Note that when Harsanyi speaks of 'social' preferences, he 'always mean[s] preferences based on a given individual's value judgement concerning "social welfare"' ([4], p. 310). Incidentally, to justify that equation (2) is of the right form for W^j using Harsanyi's proof, we may assume that (a) W^j for each j satisfies Marschak's Postulates I, II, III' and IV; (b) U^i for each i satisfies the same postulates, and (c) if each U^i is the same in two situations, W^j must have the same value in both the situations.

[4] Harsanyi, J. 'Cardinal Welfare, Individualistic Ethics and Interpersonal Comparisons of Utility', *Journal of Political Economy*, **43** (August 1955).

[5] Hicks, J. R. *Value and Capital* (Oxford, 1953).

[6] Hoffman, C. 'Work Incentive Policy in Communist China', *China Quarterly* (January-March 1964).

[7] Inada, K. I. 'A Note on the Simple Majority Decision Rule', *Econometrica*, **32** (October 1964).

[8] Koopmans, T. C. *Three Essays on the State of Economic Science* (New York, 1957), Essay I.

[9] Lange, O. 'The Foundations of Welfare Economics', *Econometrica*, **10** (1942).

[10] —— and Taylor, F. M. *On the Theory of Socialism* (Minneapolis, 1938).

[11] Lerner, A. P. *The Economics of Control* (New York, 1944).

[12] Lewis, W. A. *The Theory of Economic Growth* (London, 1959).

[13] Li, Choh-Ming. 'Economic Development', *China Quarterly* (January-March 1960).

[14] Marx, K. *Critique of the Gotha Programme* (New York, 1933).

[15] Nove, A. 'Collectivization of Agriculture in Russia and China', in E. F. Szcepanik (ed.), *Symposium on Economic and Social Problems of the Far East* (Hong Kong, 1962).

[16] Robinson, J. V. *Exercises in Economic Analysis* (London, 1960).

[17] Scitovsky, T. *Papers on Welfare and Growth* (Stanford, 1964).

[18] Sen, A. K. *Choice of Techniques* (Oxford, 1960).

[19] —— 'A Possibility Theorem on Majority Decisions', *Econometrica*, **34** (April 1966). [Reprinted in *Choice, Welfare and Measurement* (Oxford, 1982).]

[20] Sweezy, P. M. *Socialism* (New York, 1940).

[21] Ward, B. 'The Firm in Illyria: Market Syndicalism', *American Economic Review*, **48** (September 1958).

[22] Wiles, P. J. *The Political Economy of Communism* (Oxford, 1962).

3

The Profit Motive

In an important and influential paper called 'The Results of Human Action but not of Human Design', Friedrich von Hayek has noted the limitations of those theories – economic, political, legal or whatever – that have 'no room for anything which is "the result of human action but not of human design" '.[1] In this context Hayek pays particular attention to the achievements of self-seeking and profit maximization – producing public good through private motivation – and argues against the alleged virtues of 'deliberate design and planning'. He complains, with justice, about 'the uncomprehending ridicule' later poured on Adam Smith's 'expression of the "invisible hand" by which "man is led to promote an end which was no part of his intention" ', and the consequent undermining of what Hayek calls 'this profound insight into the object of all social theory'.

However, all's well that ends well, and Hayek notes that the basic idea – revived by Carl Menger – 'now... seems to have become widely accepted, at least within the field of social theory proper' (pp. 99–100). Certainly Adam Smith's version of it is now part of the standard tradition of economics. The professional economist is, by and large, much taken by the notion of private motivation achieving public good through the intermediary of the market mechanism. The results of two recent surveys of views of professional economists in

Text of the fourth Fred Hirsch Memorial Lecture given in Washington DC on 17 November 1982 at the Eugene R. Black Auditorium of the World Bank.

1. F. A. Hayek, *Studies in Philosophy, Politics and Economics* (Chicago: University of Chicago Press, 1967), pp. 96–105.

From *Lloyds Bank Review*, 147 (January 1983), 1–20.

the UK and the USA, analysed respectively by Samuel Brittan,[2] and Kearl, Pope, Whiting and Wimmer,[3] bring out the point forcefully.

In the British survey it is in fact also possible to compare the response of professional economists with those of members of Parliament. It is interesting to note that a very much higher percentage of professional economists than members of Parliament accepted the claim that 'in a free-enterprise economy, the presumed harmony between individual and public interest' is brought about by 'competitive markets and pursuit of self-interest by individuals' and/or 'a strong desire for profit maximization'. It is perhaps more interesting to observe that while 79 per cent of professional economists accepted this claim, the proportion of even *Conservative* MPs, not to mention the others, agreeing with that view was 20 per cent less than that figure, with a sizeable minority emphasizing the role of 'careful planning and coordination' and 'the exercise of social responsibility by private businessmen'.

Also rather interestingly, among the economists, the business economists were relatively the most sceptical of the claim. While 62 per cent of the business economists gave answers pinpointing markets, self-interest and profits, the proportions for academic economists and government economists were 82 per cent and 87 per cent respectively. The economists furthest from business had, it appears, the greatest respect for its ability to turn the pursuit of self-interest into a harmonious pursuance of public interest. Indeed, the academic economists who had devised the questionnaire had ticked the answer that the presumed harmony is brought about by 'competitive markets and pursuit of self-interest by individuals' as the 'correct' answer. One has to look only at standard textbooks to see the extent to which belief in that 'presumed harmony' and in that view of the correct answer is part of the basic training of the modern economist.

In this lecture I would like to re-examine the role of markets and self-seeking behaviour in achieving economic success. I would argue that the standard approach takes a remarkably limited view of the nature of the economic problem and of the tasks that an economy has to perform.

I am aware that there is a danger that the examination of private motivation and public interest may look like an annual event associated with the name of Fred Hirsch. Professor Frank Hahn gave the

2. Samuel Brittan, *Is There an Economic Consensus? An Attitude Survey* (London: Macmillan, 1973).

3. J. Kearl, C. Pope, G. Whiting and L. Wimmer, 'A Confusion of Economists?', *American Economic Review Proceedings*, 69 (1979).

third Fred Hirsch Memorial Lecture last year on the subject of 'Reflections on the Invisible Hand',[4] and he discussed with his characteristic clarity and elegance the economic theory of markets, and what self-seeking may or may not do in economic allocation. I am not daunted by the danger of asking much the same questions again, since the questions are important and also because I shall argue for a somewhat different reading of both the contents of the questions and, naturally, the answers that they call for. Also, I believe, it is not inappropriate to pay particular attention to the roles of self-interest and the invisible hand in a Fred Hirsch Memorial Lecture, since Fred Hirsch himself has done such outstanding work in this area. His *Social Limits to Growth*[5] presents some of the most interesting and far-reaching arguments on this issue.

1   Intentions and Results

The Hayekian claim regarding the profundity of the insight provided by the perspective of 'the results of human action but not of human design' seems to me to be difficult to sustain. That actions often have results different from and quite the opposite of their intended effects can, of course, be a matter of some significance. This possibility has been investigated in many different ways in social theory, one example being the Marxian study of dialectics, including the well-known argument that the actions of capitalists have the effect of ultimately destroying the system. Hayek himself has given several good examples of *contrariness* between design and outcome. It is, however, important to distinguish between those results of an action that are just not part of the design and those that are *opposite* to what was designed.

It is, I fear, a rather *un*profound thought to recognize that any action has many results that were not part of the design of the agent. This cannot but be the case. I cross the street at the pedestrian crossing, and this action has many results. First, I am now on the other side of the street, as indeed I intended to be. Second, you saw me crossing the street. Normally I would not give a damn whether you did or not, and almost certainly I did not have that vision of yours as part of my design. Third, I delayed a passing car slightly, which was not a part of my design. Fourth, the driver gets home slightly later; that was not my design. Fifth, the driver's delayed

4. F. Hahn, 'Reflections on the Invisible Hand', *Lloyds Bank Review*, **144** (April 1982).
5. F. Hirsch, *Social Limits to Growth* (London: Routledge and Kegan Paul, 1977).

arrival makes the actions at his home slightly different in timing and possibly even in content. These things did not figure in my choice. If this discourse is generating boredom, then I have succeeded in making my point. The recognition that many results of our actions are not reflections of our design can, in itself, scarcely be one of great profundity.

It would be, of course, quite a different matter if the interesting results happened to be the *opposite* of what we intended. But it is important to recognize that this is not the case with the invisible hand, by which – in Adam Smith's words – 'man is led to promote an end which was no part of his intention'. It is certainly the case, as Adam Smith made clear, that 'it is not from the benevolence of the butcher, the brewer, or the baker that we expect our dinner, but from their regard to their own interest'.[6] But the butcher, the brewer and the baker did not have a design that we should starve – a design that got frustrated by their pursuit of it. The butcher *et al.* wanted to make money and so indeed they did. We intended to have dinner, as indeed we did. There is nothing startling or deeply illuminating in the recognition that not *all* the results were part of the design of *every* agent.

2 Congruence and Conflicts

The reason why this point is important is that the Smithian argument partly rests precisely on the ability of the market to *achieve* the results intended by individuals, i.e., to fulfil the 'designs' of the participants – and *then* some more. I want bread and will happily give some money for it, and the baker wants money and will give me a loaf of bread in exchange. When we carry out the exchange, we do achieve what we set out to achieve, and in the process we have helped each other. In more complex cases too – with many agents and with production in addition to trade – the market works on the basis of congruence of interests of different participants. That is the essence of the Smithian perspective: different people have a common interest in exchange and the market gives them the opportunity to pursue their common interests – with success, *not* failure. Of course, they also have conflicting interests in many other matters, but the market is not concerned with resolving these conflicts.

6. Adam Smith, *An Inquiry into the Nature and Causes of the Wealth of Nations*, 1776, Book I, Chapter II; Everyman's Library (London: Dent, 1910), vol. 1, p. 13.

It is precisely because the market equilibrium is partly what the agents designed to achieve that it has the various efficiency properties that fill up the textbooks on market achievements. The market, on that analysis, turns out to be quite a good way of having results of human action that are *also* of human design. Given certain assumptions – especially the absence of interdependences working outside the market (the so-called 'externalities') – every competitive equilibrium is Pareto optimal, which means that no one can be made better off without making someone else worse off. Also, under certain – rather more stringent – assumptions (especially the absence of economies of large scale in addition to the absence of externalities), the converse is true. That is, every Pareto optimal state of affairs can be reached through some competitive market equilibrium corresponding to some initial distribution of 'endowments' or resources owned.

The latter result – the 'converse theorem' – has been thought to be a great result in favour of the market mechanism, and so in some ways it is. If Pareto optimality is taken to be a necessary even though not a sufficient condition for overall optimality, then the fact that every Pareto optimal outcome can be reached through the market mechanism does imply that – given the right initial conditions – the market mechanism can be used to reach even the very best social state.

However, three notes of caution should be introduced here. The first is the obvious one that the assumptions (such as no externality and no economy of large scale) are terribly demanding and will be often violated.

Second, while the 'converse theorem' is a tribute to the market mechanism, it is not a tribute to the invisible hand, i.e., to the market unassisted by political intervention. The initial distribution of resources has to be got right, and this of course does involve a political process, indeed – quite possibly – a totally revolutionary one requiring a thorough redistribution of the ownership of means of production, depending on the particular Pareto optimal outcome that is identified as socially best. The contrast between capitalism and socialism is not the same as that between market and non-market allocation. Indeed, many of the main results in the theory of resource allocation involving the market mechanism were first investigated and established by economists looking for socialist allocation procedures – Oscar Lange and Abba Lerner being two of the greatest of this class.

Third, while the result in question is a tribute to the market mechanism, it suggests the need to go beyond the market mechanism to get the information that would be needed to decide how best to distribute the resources initially. Under the market mechanism, given the right initial distribution and right prices, people may have the incentive to take the right decisions about production, consumption, etc. But they don't have a similar incentive to reveal information about themselves that makes decisions regarding the initial distribution of resources possible. Disclosures about productive abilities, tastes, etc, can go against one's own interests in the determination of the initial distribution of resources, e.g. confession of higher ability or lower needs may have the effect of one's getting a lower share of non-labour resources in the initial split up. There have been some suggestions about how to deal with this problem, but none really promises easy success.

Thus, the 'converse theorem' may, in fact, turn out to be of rather less practical interest than the first theorem, which simply asserts that under the specified conditions, no matter what initial distribution of resources we begin from, the outcome will be Pareto optimal. Of course, as already mentioned, even in getting this result there are formidable difficulties since the assumptions needed are by no means easily fulfilled.

In discussing this question – the relevance of the first theorem – it is also worth bearing in mind that while Pareto optimality is some achievement, it is not in itself a grand prize. All that Pareto optimality implies is that there is no other feasible alternative that is better for everyone without exception, or better for some and no worse for anyone. A state in which some people are starving and suffering from acute deprivation while others are tasting the good life can still be Pareto optimal if the poor cannot be made better off without cutting into the pleasures of the rich – no matter by how small an amount. Pareto optimality is faint praise indeed.

In most economic problems the interests of the different people involved are partly congruent, partly conflicting. The market mechanism on its own confines its attention only to issues of congruence, leaving the interest conflicts unaddressed. It could, of course, turn out that the process of meeting the congruent interests itself might have the effect of reducing disparities and inequalities. For example, it has been argued that market-based economic growth of the type seen in the newly industrializing economies such as South Korea, Hong Kong, Taiwan and Singapore tends to be particularly beneficial to the poor – the potentially unwaged and unemployed. I shall presently have more to say on possible pitfalls in reading the experiences of these newly industrializing countries, but I don't doubt that there must be many examples all over the world in which market-based pursuit of congruent interests has also reduced disparities. But there are also many examples in which precisely the opposite has happened. To take just one set of cases, there is strong evidence that the poor have shared relatively little in the fast economic growth in Latin America, and the congruent interests have been pursued in a way that has made the conflicts more sharp and violent.

Embedded in most problems of congruence is a problem of conflict, since the congruent interests can be pursued in many different ways with very different divisions of joint benefits. Both you and I may benefit from having some deal rather than none, and each may prefer having either of the deals, A and B, to no deal at all, but A may be better than B for you and B better than A for me. In the choice of *either* deal over *none*, our interests are congruent. In the choice *between* deals, they conflict. The situation in game-theoretic terms is one that J. F. Nash, the mathematician, has called a 'bargaining problem'.[7]

The market mechanism with each person pursuing his self-interest is geared to making sure that the congruent interests are exploited, but it does not offer a mechanism for harmonious or fair resolution of the problem of conflict that is inseparably embedded in the congruent exercise. The 'presumed harmony' referred to in the questionnaire discussed earlier, stands for, at best, a half-truth. The market division of benefits tends to reflect, roughly speaking, the economic 'power balance' of different individuals and groups – an idea that has been formalized in terms of the concept of the 'core'.[8]

3 Positional Goods and Public Interest

One of the remarkable achievements of Fred Hirsch's analysis of 'social limits to growth' is the weaving together of the different types of failures that the market mechanism produces and to get from it an understanding of the malaise and the preoccupations of modern Western society. I shall not try to summarize that analysis, but I will comment on two particular points of immediate relevance to my discussion. Hirsch's concept of 'positional goods' helps us to understand why the elements of conflict have tended to acquire a new importance in the modern world. Many sources of enjoyment depend on the relative position of a person vis-a-vis others, e.g., a person holding an eminent position in a job hierarchy, or – to take a different type of example – having access to an uncrowded beach. It is not

7. J. F. Nash, 'The Bargaining Problem', *Econometrica*, 18 (1950).
8. See K. J. Arrow and F. Hahn, *General Competitive Analysis* (San Francisco: Holden Day, 1971: reprinted by North-Holland).

possible to increase the supply of these positional goods, and one's ability to enjoy these goods depends on being ahead of others.

The increasing importance of positional goods has two important – and rather distinct – aspects. First, in case of any given positional good, there is no congruence of interest, since the total supply is fixed. In 'positional competition', as Hirsch explains, 'what winners win, losers lose' (*op. cit.*, p. 52). There is little scope for the market to enhance 'efficiency' through expanding the availability of positional goods.

However, this should not be taken to imply that the market cannot improve the well-being of all individuals in positional exchange, if exchange of different positional goods were possible. Indeed, the standard model of 'general equilibrium of exchange' also has the feature of having fixed total supply of goods. One positional good can be fruitfully exchanged for another *if* such exchanges were possible. This is where the second feature comes in. Most positional goods are not marketed and many of them are non-marketable. Thus the scope for mutually beneficial exchange of positional goods among the individuals happens to be severely limited. These two features together make the conflict elements dominate in the allocation of many of the positional goods, and make the congruent elements rather rare and difficult to exploit through the market mechanism.

Hirsch has pointed out that with material progress the pressure on positional goods has increased sharply. The fixity of total supply has made positional goods relatively scarce as the supplies of other goods have expanded. This has had the effect of making the market mechanism that much less adequate for the modern society.

Another force in the direction of making markets less adequate is the increasing importance of public goods – goods for which one person's consumption does not conflict with that of another. You and I both benefit from a clean city centre, or a better television programme, without interfering with each other's consumption. Public goods involve strong congruence of interests, and as such it might be thought that the market mechanism should be able to deal with it very well. But in fact it cannot, since the market operates by insisting on a price to be paid for *possessing* a good, whereas in the case of public goods like enjoying a clean city centre or a good TV programme, such a pricing arrangement is not easy to devise. The market is good at taking care of issues of congruence of a special type only. It cannot handle well issues of conflict (including that involved in positional goods); nor issues of congruence in which the good in question is not individually possessed (as in the case of public goods).

The failure of the market mechanism based on the profit motive to deal with public goods is a specific example of its failure to deal with interdependences that work outside the price system. These problems have received a great deal of attention in the literature and the underlying analytical issues have been illustrated by games such as the Prisoner's Dilemma. There are various different ways of responding to this type of difficulty. One way is to use state intervention and the public sector. Indeed, the enormous growth of the public sector in the recent years has not a little to do with this issue. Hirsch analyses this trend, but goes on to discuss another route, to wit, changing the behaviour norms, including the eschewal of the profit motive (*op. cit.*, p. 146).

4   *Motives and Outcomes*

The rationale of Hirsch's suggestion regarding behavioural reorientation lies in the argument that self-interested behaviour may be collectively self-defeating. The Prisoner's Dilemma illustrates the problem very clearly.[9] Given the actions of others, it is in the interest of everyone to pursue self-interest directly, and each has a dominant strategy. But, for everyone it would have been better if they all had pursued some other, not directly self-interest-oriented, strategy. I shall have more to say on this presently, but before that a more elementary type of failure is worth discussing.

It is possible for the active pursuit of self-interest to be not only collectively self-defeating but also individually self-defeating. Even without any interpersonal interdependence of the kind referred to earlier, aiming directly at self-interest may be bad for achieving it.

Henry Sidgwick − that great utilitarian philosopher and economist − has pointed out that trying actively to maximize personal happiness may have the effect of producing a disposition that makes happiness difficult to achieve. Hayek's 'results of human action but not of human design' take, incidentally, a rather serious form here. The question of choosing between dispositions has figured importantly in the writings of such philosophers as Richard Hare, Robert Adams, and Jon Elster. Having a roving eye for the quick 'utile' might well be disastrous for achieving happiness.

9. See my 'Behaviour and the Concept of Preference', *Economica*, **40** (1973), reprinted in my *Choice, Welfare and Measurement* (Oxford: Basil Blackwell, 1982), and Derek Parfit, 'Prudence, Morality, and the Prisoner's Dilemma', *Proceedings of the British Academy for 1979* (London: Oxford University Press, 1981).

The cultivation of achievement-oriented motivation in the modern society can indeed produce psychological and social barriers to personal happiness. Motivational uptightness can be a serious impediment to enjoying life. The activist who, to vary a famous Presidential description, can chew gum *only when* he is crossing the street, certainly has some problems. So has the person who relentlessly pursues positional success.

The agony of the maximizer may be less known to the economist than to the novelist, but it is no less important for that reason. Indeed, the neglect of serious psychological issues in traditional economics is truly remarkable, and it is only recently that this lacuna has begun to get some response in the writings of − in addition to Fred Hirsch − Albert Hirschman, Janos Kornai, Tibor Scitovsky, Harvey Leibenstein, Thomas Schelling, George Akerlof and William Dickens, and others.[10]

5   Procedural Assessment

I have so far been proceeding on the implicit understanding that the market mechanism has to be assessed in terms of its results. That implicit assumption has been shared by economists of very different schools of thought − from Milton Friedman to John Kenneth Galbraith. The differences between the schools on this issue have centred on the question as to what results the profit motive and the market mechanism, do *in fact*, have. There is, however, a well-developed philosophical approach in social theory arguing against end-state judgements. For example, Robert Nozick in his influential and important book, *Anarchy, State and Utopia*,[11] has argued in favour of downgrading consequence-based evaluation into a minor

10. A. O. Hirschman, *Exit, Voice, and Loyalty* (Cambridge, Mass.: Harvard University Press, 1970), and *Shifting Involvements: Private and Public Action* (Princeton: Princeton University Press, 1982); J. Kornai, *Anti-Equilibrium* (Amsterdam: North-Holland, 1971); T. Scitovsky, *The Joyless Economy* (Oxford: Oxford University Press, 1976); Harvey Leibenstein, *Beyond Economic Man: A New Foundation for Microeconomics* (Cambridge, Mass.: Harvard University Press, 1976); Thomas Schelling, *Micromotives and Macrobehaviour* (New York: Norton, 1978); George Akerlof and William T. Dickens, 'The Economic Consequences of Cognitive Dissonance', *American Economic Review*, 72 (1982); Howard Margolis, *Selfishness, Altruism and Rationality* (Cambridge: Cambridge University Press, 1982). See also the important critique of Robert Solow in his AEA Presidential Address, 'On Theories of Unemployment', *American Economic Review*, 70 (1980). For some sceptical notes by one of the founders, see John Hicks, 'The Measurement of Real Income', *Oxford Economic Papers*, 10 (1958), reprinted in his *Wealth and Welfare* (Oxford: Blackwell, 1981), pp. 148–50.

11. R. Nozick, *Anarchy, State and Utopia* (New York: Basic Books, 1974).

secondary position compared with the imperative of the right procedural rules. Nozick has seen a collection of rights, including that of ownership, and transfer, as central. Individuals have these rights and 'there are things no person or group may do to them'. Since the rights of ownership and transfer include exchange, markets are, in this view, justified by antecedent rights rather than by consequent outcomes. Nozick points to (what he calls) 'invisible-hand explanations' of the emergence of social institutions (such as markets), citing Adam Smith (*op. cit.*, p. 18), but there is no assessment of such institutions in terms of the goodness of interest-fulfilling outcomes. If this view is accepted, then the focus of traditional discussion of the merits and demerits of the market is quite misplaced, since the right to exchange exists no matter what the consequences of such market operations happen to be. The focus is on 'entitlements', not on results.

This approach involves a major philosophical departure and *inter alia* it rejects seeing markets in the way economists have typically done, i.e. in terms of what markets do to people's interests (rather than how people's rights require markets). I believe these procedural issues deserve a great deal more attention than economists have been inclined to give them, and Nozick's analysis represents just one example of non-consequentialist moral reasoning which is potentially of much relevance to welfare economics.[12] While I shall not pursue this complex philosophical question here, which I have tried to do elsewhere,[13] I should make two quick remarks on this approach specifically related to the main enquiry.

First, the justification of markets in terms of rights of ownership and transfer is independent of the exact nature of human motivation in a way that a consequence-based assessment of markets cannot be. What guides people in undertaking exchange in the market matters not at all in justifying the markets, since it is their privilege to be guided by whatever they like irrespective of consequences. Thus, while the Nozickian approach is pro-market, it need not be pro-profit-motive in any sense. People are free to pursue profits if they so choose, but they need not, and Nozick gives some good reasons as to why they may choose not to.[14]

Second, any consequence-independent justification suffers from the possibility that the consequences may be so disastrous that the

12. See A. Sen and B. Williams (eds), *Utilitarianism and Beyond* (Cambridge: Cambridge University Press, 1982).

13. Especially in 'Rights and Agency', *Philosophy and Public Affairs*, 11 (1982), and 'Liberty and Social Choice', *Journal of Philosophy*, 80 (1983).

14. Nozick, *Anarchy, State and Utopia*, Chapter 8.

entire approach may look altogether implausible. Nozick does not deal with this issue at all adequately, and states that 'the question of whether these side constraints reflecting rights are absolute, or whether they may be violated in order to avoid catastrophic moral horror, and if the latter, what the resulting structure might look like, is one I hope largely to avoid' (p. 30). But this is a serious issue to leave open, since permitting violation of allegedly consequence-independent rights is the thin end of the wedge. Once consequence-based arguments are accepted as relevant, then it is not clear what obvious stopping place there is for a theory that was set up on a purely procedural approach.

6   Consequences, Disasters and Achievements

Terrible consequences emerging from the exercise of rights in market situations are not only imaginable in theory, they are also observable in the real world. In my book *Poverty and Famines: An Essay on Entitlement and Deprivation*,[15] I have presented evidence to indicate that many famines – even very big ones – have taken place in the recent past with no over-all decline of food availability, and millions have died because of being deprived of food in terms of market command, reflecting sharp failures of entitlement. There is something deeply implausible about asserting that justification of rules of ownership, exchange and market operations can be really consequence-independent, and in this case unaffected by matters of life and death.

It is, of course, true that such terrible consequences have not occurred in the richer market-based economies of the West. People do not go begging for food in the countries that are now called, merciless to geography, the North. But this is not the result of any guarantee that the market or profit maximization has provided, but rather due to the social security that the state has offered. The magnitude of unemployment being what it is today in Western Europe or North America, the 'entitlements' of many millions of people in the moral system based on ownership have amounted to next to nothing. The reason why these countries have not been visited by disaster is precisely the existence of systematic transfers through the state of the kind that the moral entitlement theory does so much to reject.

I should not, however, concentrate my attention only on the failures of the market system; I must also look at the achievements.

15. Oxford: Clarendon Press, and New York: OUP, 1981.

Indeed, the last few decades have also been seen as years of great cheer for the market mechanism. Until fairly recently the richer market economies have grown very fast in economic terms. While over the last two decades the growth rate of gross national product per capita in the 'industrial market economies' (3.6 per cent over 1960–80), has been a little lower than that of 'non-market industrial economies', i.e. the richer communist countries (4.2 per cent),[16] the world record of fast growth among all the richer countries – market and non-market – is held by Japan (7.1 per cent). Also, the high growth of several 'non-market economies' has been combined with remarkable shortages in specific goods, including food.

As far as the poorer economies are concerned, if we concentrate attention on countries outside Europe and North America, the highest growth performers have been Singapore (7.5 per cent), South Korea (7.0 per cent), and Hong Kong (6.8 per cent), according to the *World Development Report* over 1960–80. These are, of course, all economies with private ownership and markets. The fact that these countries have combined fast economic growth with no noticeable worsening of the relative distribution of income has received, with justice, much admiration and many eulogies. The literature on the theory of economic development is beginning to reflect appreciation of these performances. One of the most distinguished examples of this type of analysis can be found in Ian Little's new book, *Economic Development*.[17] The 'old guards' at that side of the fence, such as Peter Bauer who wrote such a lonely – but excellent – book called *Dissent on Development*,[18] can rejoice at this trend, and Bauer can with justified pride write a new book reflecting the changing professional opinion, and call it, perhaps, *Assent at Long Last on Development*.

There is, however, some difficulty in reading the experiences of the East Asian newly industrializing countries – countries that Ian Little calls by the delightful name 'baby tigers' (*op. cit.*, p. 262). Hong Kong and Singapore are essentially city economies, and if we look at growth rates of cities, there are others that compare with the performance of these baby tigers, which benefit from being babies at least in size. There are no great rural masses to drag them down. But South Korea is a fairly large country, and is no city state. The difficulty, however, in reading great significance into the performance of South Korea as a success story for the 'invisible hand' is the fact

16. *World Development Report* (Washington, DC: World Bank, 1982), Table 1.
17. I. M. D. Little, *Economic Development: Theory, Policy, and International Relations* (New York: Basic Books, 1982).
18. P. T. Bauer, *Dissent on Development* (London: Weidenfeld, 1971).

that the hands that reared South Korean growth were very visible indeed. The government played a major part in fostering economic growth in South Korea, and as has been argued, 'no state outside the socialist bloc ever came anywhere near this measure of control over the economy's investible resources'.[19] Indeed, adding government savings to deposits in nationalized banks, the South Korean government had control over two-thirds of the investment resources in the country in the period of its rapid acceleration of growth. This governmental power was firmly used to guide investment in chosen directions through differential interest rates and credit availabilities. I have discussed this question in some detail elsewhere.[20] Even Korean export expansion was founded on building an industrial base through severe import controls before export promotion was promoted, and even now the import of many items is restricted or prohibited. The economic expansion was directly orchestrated by an activist central government.

In fact it is remarkable that if we look at the sizeable developing countries, the fast growing and otherwise high-performing countries have all had governments that have been directly and actively involved in the planning of economic and social performance. I don't mean that they have powerful governments – that is certainly the case but that is true of almost all developing countries anyway. I mean that the governments have been involved with economic planning and with deliberate and ambitious public action. The types of planning used have varied, say between China, Sri Lanka, South Korea and Yugoslavia, but their respective successes are directly linked to deliberation and design, rather than being just the results of unco-ordinated profit seeking or atomistic pursuit of self-interest. I have discussed these issues elsewhere,[21] and will not pursue them further here.

7   Motives and Behaviour

The issue of public action is, however, rather different from that of the best orientation of individual behaviour. In this respect, the ambitious Chinese attempt at replacing the profit motive and self-

19. M. K. Datta-Chaudhuri, 'Industrialization and Foreign Trade: An Analysis Based on the Development Experience of the Republic of Korea and the Philippines', ILO Working Paper WP II-4, Asian Employment Programme, ARTEP, ILO, Bangkok, 1979.

20. 'Public Action and the Quality of Life in Developing Countries', *Oxford Bulletin of Economics and Statistics*, 43 (1981).

21. 'Development: Which Way Now?' Presidential Address, Development Studies Association, given in Dublin, September 1982 [*Economic Journal*, 93 (December 1983); Essay 19 in this volume].

seeking by non-incentive systems seems to have been acknowledged as a failure. Certainly, the extent of cultural reorientation that was called for required such a drastic revision of human motivation that it would have been totally remarkable if it had been an easy success.

But it would be a mistake to think that the alternatives to the profit motive must, of necessity, take such a drastic form. In our day to day actions there is much scope for departing from self-seeking in a less grand way. There is, in fact, very little doubt that neither the family as a social unit nor the firm as an economic unit can really operate entirely on the basis of individual self-seeking. Norms of behaviour depart from that not only vis-à-vis other members of the family but in terms of loyalty to colleagues and to the firm.

To some extent this has been observed in all types of economies, but the scope for such non-profit behaviour also varies greatly between countries. It has been argued with much force and plausibility that the success of the Japanese economy owes not a little to what Michio Morishima has recently called 'the Japanese ethos',[22] which clearly has deep historical roots. The extent of loyalty, cooperations, sense of duty, and public spirit that is observed in Japanese factories is evidently in sharp contrast with what can be found in, say, Britain.

There is little doubt that the Japanese attitude to private gain and public duty differs greatly from that in other rich, industrial countries. Much has been written on that contrast. The differences in social psychology play a major part not only in economic performance but also in such other communal matters as the lower crime rate, much less frequent litigation (indeed, far fewer lawyers per unit of population), and so on. If the invisible hand does a great deal of visible good in Japan, the hand does not seem to work through the relentless pursuit of self-interest.

In fact, when one considers how production takes place in a modern industrial establishment, it is quite incredible to think that being actively self-interested can be such a virtue. Success in production depends greatly on team work, and while that interdependent picture provides incentive for a group, it is not an incentive that can be effectively translated into rewards and punishments related to individual work and performance.

Milton Friedman has argued in his *Essays in Positive Economics* that 'the process of "natural selection". . . helps to validate the hypothesis' of profit maximization.[23] The profit maximizing firms

22. Michio Morishima, *Why Has Japan 'Succeeded'? Western Technology and Japanese Ethos* (Cambridge: Cambridge University Press, 1982).
23. Milton Friedman, *Essays in Positive Economics* (Chicago: University of Chicago Press, 1983), p. 22.

survive and do better. This process may indeed work *if* deliberate attempts at profit maximization are likely to produce more actual profits and more expansion. However, when it comes to individual workers, the argument does not translate at all. Indeed, insofar as workers with better team spirit do better than self-interest maximizing workers, one might expect the argument to favour the development of team spirit rather than of maximization of individual interests or profits. Morishima's historical account of the emergence of the Japanese ethos may be supplemented by an argument for sustenance through better survival.

Fred Hirsch's analysis of the need to reorient behaviour norms is very relevant here. His argument is this:

> where individual preferences can be satisfied in sum only or most efficiently through collective action, privately directed behaviour may lose its inherent advantages over collectively oriented behaviour *even as a means to satisfying individual preferences themselves*, however self-interested. It follows that the best result may be attained by steering or guiding certain motives of individual behaviour into social rather than individual orientation, though still on the basis of privately directed preferences. This requires not a change in human nature, 'merely' a change in human convention or instinct or attitude of the same order as the shifts in social conventions or moral standards that have gone along with major changes in economic conditions in the past (p. 146).

In understanding this proposed solution, it is important to see that Hirsch is not arguing for a change of what people actually would like to achieve. It is not an argument for changing one's goals, which of course will be a defeatist solution to the problem at hand (no matter how desirable for other reasons). The argument is a strategic one for better achieving the given self-interested objectives. Self-interest-based objectives are achieved better for the group as a whole by the individuals *behaving* differently, *as if* they are maximizing some other objectives.[24] The so-called 'Japanese ethos' can be just the ethos of behaviour and not necessarily of having different ultimate objectives.

24. See my *On Economic Inequality* Oxford: Clarendon Press, 1973) and 'Choice, Orderings and Morality', in S. Körner (ed.), *Practical Reason* (Oxford: Basil Blackwell, 1974); reprinted in my *Choice, Welfare and Measurement*. See also George Akerlof, 'Loyalty Filters', *American Economic Review*, 73 (1983).

8 *Roles, Information and Self-interest*

At this stage of the discussion, a different type of difficulty altogether may be considered. Surely the Adam Smithian argument about the merits of self-interested behaviour in the context of exchange builds on the twin fact that (1) such behaviour gives everyone the *role* of protecting and pursuing his or her own interests, and (2) the interests of each person are best *known* by the person himself or herself. While such behaviour does not resolve conflicts, nor take care of pursuing congruent interests in the presence of interdependences of the kind specified, it does help in the fulfilment of many congruent interests. Are we not in danger of losing even the limited virtues of self-interest maximization (related to role division and informational efficiency) if the motivational parameters change?

More other-regarding behaviour, unless it is specially symmetrical, can certainly lead to very unequal coverage of different people's interests. An assumption of 'symmetric goodwill' will be quite exacting.[25] It can, however, be pointed out that the market mechanism, even with self-interested behaviour, does not deal with issues of equity at all satisfactorily, and indeed, as already discussed, does not properly address the question of interest conflicts at all. Nonsymmetric goodwill might introduce another element of asymmetry in the pursuit of different people's interests, but it would not necessarily make the over-all situation less just or more inequitable. Indeed, we can say very little in general about how the equity side of the picture will change with a motivational shift from self-interested behaviour, since so little can be said generally about equity under self-interest behaviour.

The change on the informational issue is, however, more easy to see and assess. Even if I pursue your interests with the same vigour that you would, and you pursue my interests in the same breathless way that I would, we may do worse jobs of these functions than if we were to look after our interests ourselves, respectively. This recognition does nothing to wash away the problems of interdependence identified by Fred Hirsch and others and the failure of self-interest-based behaviour to deal with those problems. But superimposed on those problems are also some problems of informed pursuit of different people's respective interests, and replacing

25. Cf my 'Labour Allocation in a Cooperative Enterprise', *Review of Economic Studies*, **33** (1966), Essay 2 in this volume; David Collard, *Altruism and Economy* (Oxford: Martin Robertson, 1978).

self-interested behaviour by other-regarding behaviour may punch a new hole as it plugs an old one.

It is interesting that there has been so little discussion of the impact of motivational change on the result of market equilibrium. There are, of course, some interesting and analytically important results about how special types of altruism might preserve some of the links between Pareto optimality and competitive equilibria.[26] But these results have been derived in quite a limited format, using strong assumptions, and they are in particular based on ignoring the force of the informational problem.

Some have seen relatively little difficulty in the market system being able to accommodate a great variety of motivational assumptions without losing its virtues. For example, in his lucid and illuminating report on the survey of the views of British economists (discussed earlier), Samuel Brittan refuses to be impressed by the assumption of the pursuit of self-interest in guaranteeing the achievements of the market. He remarks: 'the success of a competitive free enterprise economy, working under the right environmental policies, depends on people pursuing *self-chosen* interest, which can be altruistic, aesthetic or anything else'.[27] This is indeed so up to a point, in the sense that it may be possible to replace the achievement of, say, Pareto optimality by achieving a corresponding condition of non-improvability in terms of the different people's goals — whatever they are — rather than their self-interest or utilities.

On the other hand, other-regarding goals raise problems of consistency and coherence in a way that independent self-interests of different people do not. We can both try to do good to each other and end up failing to serve either person's interests. One has only to recollect O Henry's story 'The Gift of the Magi' to see how the pursuit of altruism can lead to frustration.

In his paper called 'Morality, Competition and Efficiency',[28] Robin Matthews has discussed lucidly how the information-revealing role of the pursuit of self-interest may be lost if people do behave according to some moral norms, e.g. those given by act utilitarianism. The person who knows an individual best is the individual himself or

26. See S. G. Winter, Jr, 'A Simple Remark on the Second Optimality Theorem of Welfare Economics', *Journal of Economic Theory*, 1 (1969); G. C. Archibald and D. Donaldson, 'Non-Paternalism and Basic Theorems of Welfare Economics', *Canadian Journal of Economics*, 9 (1976); Collard, *Altruism and Economy*.

27. Brittan, p. 53. See also R. Sugden, 'On the Economics of Philanthropy', *Economic Journal*, 92 (1982); A. J. Oswald, 'An Approach to the Economics of Unselfishness', mimeographed, St John's College, Oxford, 1982.

28. R. C. O. Matthews, 'Morality, Competition and Efficiency', *Manchester School* (1981).

herself, and this signalling function may well be quite lost if rather than acting on the basis of personal self-interest one pursues other goals. Doing good is not an easy matter with informational deficiency. (I remember the embarrassment of a friend who, staying as a guest of a family in Bombay, decided to be useful and expended the afternoon polishing up a small dirty-looking metal statue she found in the living room to discover later that she had made a thirteenth-century icon look sparklingly modern.)

There are, in fact, the horns of a dilemma here. If individuals pursue goals other than the pursuit of self-interest, they can mess up the market mechanism informationally and also produce problems of consistency and coherence. On the other hand, if they do act selfishly, then they prevent the market from achieving efficiency in the presence of interdependences, not to mention other goals such as addressing problems of conflict.

What has to be recognized clearly is the unreality – and over-ambitiousness – of the neat, harmonious picture of social good coming from coherent and independent choices of individuals – a picture that has so deeply influenced economics. That account misses the real world by many miles. It is not easy – perhaps impossible – to replace that old model of success based on self-interested individuals, by another one with the same degree of ambition, and to get with equal ease a similarly neat picture of social good coming from the individual pursuit of some other simple motivation.

9   *Some General Conclusions*

First, the central economic problem can be seen as that of fulfilling congruent interests of different people, along with dealing with conflicts of interest fairly. The 'invisible hand' in the form of the market mechanism is geared to the congruence exercise, leaving the conflict problem unaddressed and essentially left to the equilibrium of relative powers and muscles (formalized in the notion of the 'core'). Despite claims to the contrary, the market and the profit motive cannot guarantee bringing about a 'harmony' of interests.

Second, the profit motive is, of course, a very powerful force and it can certainly do wonders. Its success is partly due to the fact that quite often the interdependences underlying congruent interests can be captured within the market mechanism. The market mechanism succeeds, under these circumstances, because of the *fulfilment* of non-conflicting individual designs, and it is quite misleading to see this achievement as 'a result of human action but not of human design'.

Third, the conflict problem is, obviously, not amenable to solution in this way, and this failure can take a serious, even disastrous, form. Even the congruence problem may be insoluble through the market and the profit motive, if the congruence in the market mechanism cannot be split up with a price tag attached to each benefit and cost. The market is best at dealing with only one kind of congruence of interests.

Fourth, purely procedural justifications of the market independently of consequences – while interesting and challenging – ultimately lack plausibility. They do not, incidentally, do anything to support the profit motive.

Fifth, the profit motive and self-interest-based action can be self-defeating. Specialist maximizers can produce very general failures. There is the problem of being collectively self-defeating because of interdependences that elude the market, and these are of increasing importance, as Fred Hirsch has argued. There is, in addition, the problem of being individually self-defeating because of psychological conflicts between motivation and realization.

Sixth, while the problem of being individually self-defeating raises deep psychological issues, that of being collectively self-defeating raises questions of state action and cooperative efforts. It also points towards the case for behavioural modification. It is in that context important, as Hirsch has emphasized, to examine the possibility of behaviour norms that break away from the pursuit of self-interest by individuals to better achieve the fulfilment of those very interests. There is a clear link between this type of theory and the observed success of some economies, most importantly, Japan.

Seventh, departures from self-interest maximization help in some respects but also hinder in other ways. Self-interest maximization serves to channel information into the market procedures; each pursuing the interests of others can, in many contexts, be informationally defective. Indeed, it is not easy to see that some rule of behaviour of the same type of generality as the pursuit of self-interest can, in fact, avoid both the Scylla of interdependence failures and the Charybdis of informational deficiency.

What goes wrong with the traditional model of the invisible hand is not just the limitation of relying exclusively on self-interest, but the stunning ambitiousness of trying to guarantee social efficiency – not to mention social optimality – on the basis of *independent* pursuit by individuals of some general objective (such as profits).

This negative recognition, however, does nothing to undermine the importance of studying alternative behaviour norms and examining their consequences. Behaviour norms have to be assessed in the light of comparative achievements rather than just in terms of the attainment or not of efficiency or optimality. The effectiveness of non-profit behaviour is important in that less ambitious but more practical context.

Finally, I should point out that I have not had the opportunity to go into a fundamental question which Adam Smith had touched on and thought to be important. Should motivation be determined entirely by usefulness, or are there other important values to consider? Should the profit motive be recommended to all if it had proved impeccably useful? Should the 'Japanese ethos' be cultivated by all if it is really as useful as it seems to be? Adam Smith would have disputed that usefulness is all that is involved. Indeed, he did think that to praise a person for his useful qualities is to confuse him or her with something like a piece of furniture or a building:

> . . . it seems impossible that the approbation of virtue should be a sentiment of the same kind with that by which we approve of a convenient or well-contrived building, or that we should have no other reason for praising a man than that for which we commend a chest of drawers.[29]

While I have concentrated on assessing motivations in terms of their usefulness, I would not deny that Adam Smith is right and this cannot provide a full view of that important question. Even as economists we cannot altogether escape this deeper valuational issue. The subject is dismal enough as it is.

---

29. *The Theory of Moral Sentiments*, IV, 24, p. 188. The immediate provocation for Smith's remark is Hume's analysis of virtue in terms of 'utility' (in the sense of usefulness).

Part II

Isolation and Social Investment

4

On Optimizing the Rate of Saving

While the search for the 'optimum' rate of saving has not yet been vastly more successful than that for the holy grail, a number of possible methods of approaching the problem have emerged from the debate. The object of this paper is to examine some of these methods, and to discuss some other questions that seem to be relevant. The main conflict involved in the choice of the rate of saving is one between present consumption and future consumption, and naturally it cannot be solved without some intertemporal value judgements. In the first section we shall critically examine some methods of solving the problem that have been put forward in the economic literature. We shall also examine some attempts at avoiding the question altogether by some special assumptions. In the second section we shall try to make some general observations on the relationship between individual preferences and social judgements. In the final section we shall discuss some factors that limit the scope of the choice of the 'optimum' rate of saving.

1 Some Traditional Methods of Intertemporal Judgements

1.1 Utility maximization

Easily the most widely used method for solving the intertemporal allocation problem is to employ a utility function that is valid over time. In one of the earliest attempts at solving the problem, F. P.

I am indebted to Maurice Dobb, Richard Goodwin, Stephen Marglin and Robert Solow for their comments and criticisms.

From *Economic Journal*, 71 (September 1961), 479-96.

Ramsey used this tool of utility maximization.[1] His assumption of an identifiable state of maximum possible satisfaction, which he referred to as 'bliss', allowed him to obtain some very simple rules for determining the 'optimum' rate of saving. Being rather sceptical of the usefulness of the concept of an identifiable 'bliss', Professor Tinbergen has recently used a more general kind of utility maximization.[2] His apparatus includes a utility function, a rate of 'pure' time discount and a growth formula (of the 'Harrod–Domar' type) involving a (constant) capital coefficient and a variable saving rate. The saving rate is a policy variable, but the choice is assumed to be once for all, so that the saving rate once chosen is constant over time.[3] That saving rate is chosen which maximizes the sum of the discounted social utilities for all time to come.

The main strength of the utility maximization approach lies in the acceptability of the concept of diminishing marginal utility of increasing consumption. It is a widely observed phenomenon that we seem to care less for a unit of consumption when we are rich than when we are poor, and this provides a good common-sense ground against having too high a rate of saving, leading to an enormous inequality between the present and the future. The use of a specific utility function in the choice seems, however, to raise a number of other questions beyond this common-sense point.

There are two ways of defining 'utility'. We can use the term to represent a magnitude which we, according to our value judgements, wish to maximize. In this sense this is just a synonym for the equally vague expression 'welfare' defined by some 'welfare function'. Alternatively, and this is perhaps its more usual meaning, we can use the term as a synonym for the satisfaction of the people. In this sense an interpersonal comparison of utility is a non-normative comparison, possibly done on some sort of behaviouristic ground, like compari-

---

1. 'A Mathematical Theory of Saving', *Economic Journal*, 38 (December 1928). See also J. E. Meade, *Economic Analysis and Policy* (London, 1937), Part IV, Chapter III; and D. H. Robertson, *Lectures on Economic Principles* (London, 1958), Chapter VI.

2. 'The Optimum Rate of Saving', *Economic Journal*, 66 (December 1956).

3. In an unpublished paper, 'The Optimal Growth Path for an Underdeveloped Economy', Mr Richard Goodwin tries to find out the optimal *time path* of the rate of saving, rather than one optimal *rate* of saving for all time to come. Mr Goodwin uses the same type of utility function as Professor Tinbergen, but his results are very different, which seems to suggest that it is unfortunate to put the question in terms of the choice of a rate of saving once for all. One of the more exciting aspects of the problem of the rate of saving is the way it changes, or should change, with the process of development. [Goodwin's paper was later published in *Economic Journal*, 71 (December 1961).]

sons of anger or courage.[4] If this latter definition is used, then we run into two problems, in trying to use utility-maximization as our policy objective. First, it is difficult enough to find out the rate at which the marginal 'utility' of consumption declines in the case of any given individual; to discover it for the whole society, over time, is practically impossible. Secondly, if utility is defined in this non-normative sense there is, of course, no necessary reason for treating it as the thing to be maximized. Indeed, factors normally not included in the term satisfaction, e.g. national pride, altruism, preference for a 'just' distribution of satisfaction between different generations of the nation, have considerable relevance to the problem, and total utility maximization can no longer be axiomatically treated as the thing to be achieved.

We can, of course, use the term 'utility' in the other sense, viz. to mean the magnitude that is defined by the welfare function given by our value judgements, which becomes automatically the thing to be maximized. But then, with this definition we cannot *prove* that the 'marginal utility' of consumption will definitely decline with increasing consumption. We cannot even be sure that 'utility' will depend *only* on consumption. This problem is present in the other case as well, but it is much more obvious with the second definition. Capital-goods production can satisfy (and, in the case of many nations, has satisfied) the self-respect of nations, and may also affect the ability of a nation to help other countries. In spite of these questions, however, it seems reasonable to expect (a) that the main determinant of social 'welfare', according to the value judgements normally held, will be the level of consumption (or that of *per capita* consumption), and (b) that the common-sense belief in diminishing marginal 'utility' will have some validity in this sense as well. But how are we going to choose the precise utility function to be used? There are an endless number of functions with a negative second derivative (i.e. with diminishing marginal utility), and our results will depend considerably on the function actually employed. One method of choosing a utility function will be to place the problem before the public for a political debate. I must confess, however, that the possibility of a lively political debate on such questions as 'Should we maximize the logarithm of consumption?' appear to me to be limited. The trouble with the 'utility' approach, it seems to me, is that it introduces value judgements in such a way that the only people who can appreciate

4. See I. M. D. Little, *A Critique of Welfare Economics* (London, 1957), Chapter IV.

the meaning of these judgements are those who can be described as 'professionals' in the field. In a theoretical study a utility function can, of course, be used to make some general points about the nature of the choice,[5] but its use in actual saving decisions is very difficult. A popular ratification of a utility function seems to be out of the question, and it is not clear how, in the absence of political ratification, the planners should choose between different utility functions of the appropriate type. The temptation is to use a utility function that can be handled most comfortably, and we find ourselves in a slightly curious position where the implicit policy objective is making the planner's life comfortable, which is a worthy aim, but a limited one.

1.2   'Pure' time preference

The concept of a 'pure' psychological discount of the future is of respectable antiquity. A distant object 'looks' smaller, and we tend to value, it is claimed, a unit of consumption in the future less than we value the same now. There is a possible ambiguity in the use of this approach. If the difference is only due to the distance in time, then the position is symmetrical. A future object looks less important now, and similarly, a present object will look less important in the future. While it is true that the decision has to be taken now, there is no necessary reason why today's discount of tomorrow should be used, and not tomorrow's discount of today.

Ramsey was explicit in his rejection of 'pure' time discount as something that 'arises merely from the weakness of imagination',[6]

---

5. This was partly the object of Professor Tinbergen, and is also that of Mr Goodwin in the unpublished paper referred to above. Since this article was written, Professor Tinbergen has published another paper on the subject, viz. 'Optimum Savings and Utility Maximization over Time' (*Econometrica*, April 1960), where he himself makes an interesting criticism of approaching the problem from the utility angle. He shows that if the elasticity of marginal utility with respect to 'surplus consumption', i.e. consumption beyond the subsistence level, is low ($v \leqslant 1$), then 'it looks promising, at any time, to save "as much as possible" – i.e. everything beyond the subsistence level of consumption, because a higher contribution to "satisfaction" (utility) will be obtained "later". But this "later" is continually postponed and in fact never occurs' (p. 487). This particular result is apparently independent of the value of the capital–output ratio, and is not affected even if the capital–output ratio is dependent on the rate of savings. Since statistical investigations so far made indicate a low value of the relevant elasticity (v), Professor Tinbergen concludes that no 'clue for the establishment of an "optimum savings programme" can be derived from the simple maximization over time of instantaneous utility' (p. 488). It should be noted that here Professor Tinbergen uses the term 'utility' in the non-normative sense, so that its application to a welfare problem involves the difficulties that we have discussed above.

6. *Op. cit.*, p. 543. See also M. H. Dobb, *Essay on Economic Growth* (London, 1960), Chapter II.

and Sir Roy Harrod has described 'pure time preference' as 'a polite expression for rapacity and the conquest of reason by passion'.[7] Indeed, in so far as the 'pure' discount is just a result of 'irrationality', its use in a choice that aims at being 'rational' is unjustifiable. We should, however, examine two other possible lines of argument in defence of 'pure' time preference. From the point of view of the individual, the discount may not be purely 'irrational', for, the more distant the future, the less is his chance of being alive. Unless we assume that a person identifies his heirs' interests with his own, a 'pure' time discount is not an unreasonable assumption from the point of view of the individual. This does not, however, make its use in the determination of the social optimum rate of saving justifiable, unless we assume that the present generation's interests are all that matter. A second line of argument is put forward by Professor Otto Eckstein. He argues that 'a social-welfare function based on consumers' sovereignty must accept people's tastes including their intertemporal preferences'.[8] I am not sure that the principle of 'consumers' sovereignty' is very meaningful in this context. The consumers involved are not merely those of the present generation, but also those yet to be born and those who are now too young to express any preference. Of course, the views of the present generation may prove to be the decisive factor in this choice, for the simple reason that the views of the coming generations are not yet available; but this is a very different argument from that of 'consumers' sovereignty'. In Section 2 we shall discuss the method of using the values of the present generation for the choice, and shall find that even this does not justify the use of the individual's 'pure' time discount.

There is, however, an element in the 'pure' time discount that might be of significance for the social choice. One of the reasons for preferring a unit of present consumption to the same in the future is the uncertainty associated with the future. This might arise for reasons other than the possibility of death of the present consumers. Now, to a certain extent this uncertainty (say, about production) is present even for the society, and if an individual discounts the future yields because he does not know whether these yields will be obtained, the same argument may apply in the case of the society as well. It should, however, be added that (a) the uncertainty facing an individual is not the same as that facing the society as a whole, and (b) the individual's *assessment* of the uncertainty might be wrong because

7. *Towards a Dynamic Economics* (London, 1948), p. 40. See also *Economic Journal*, 70 (June 1960): 'Second Essay in Dynamic Theory'.
8. 'Investment Criteria for Economic Development and the Theory of Intertemporal Welfare Economics', *Quarterly Journal of Economics*, 71 (February 1957), p. 75.

he does not know how other individuals are acting. Thus, this partial justification of a time discount is not the same as justifying the use of the individual's 'pure' time discount in the social optimization problem.

1.3 *Some partisan solutions*

One possible way of avoiding the question of intertemporal judgements is to take a distinct stand, completely one way or the other. One can, for example, argue for the maximum possible saving allowed by political considerations, or the maximum possible consumption allowed by the maintenance of a 'decent' rate of growth. Another possible line is to avoid the question by leaving it entirely to the individual savers on some political grounds. For example, Professor Bauer argues:

> I regard the extension of the range of choice, that is, an increase in the range of effective alternatives open to the people, as the principal objective and criterion of economic development; and I judge a measure principally by its probable effects on the range of alternatives open to individuals. This implies that the process by which development is promoted affects the assessment, and indeed the meaning, of the result. The acceptance of this objective means that I attach significance, meaning, and value to individual acts of choice and valuation, including the individual time preference between the present and the future; and my position is much influenced by my *dislike of policies or measures which are likely to increase man's power over man, that is to increase the control of groups or individuals over their fellow men.*[9]

There are two distinct elements in the above argument. One involves a set of assumptions about the way the economic world behaves, e.g. whether the most effective way of extending the 'range of choice' is to leave the decisions to the market forces or whether the market mechanism properly reflects the 'individual time preference between the present and the future'. The other is a straightforward rejection of any policy that increases the power of the society, or the State, over the individual. Many empirical questions can be raised about the first line of the argument. It is not obvious that a higher rate of saving generated through interference with the market

9. *Economic Analysis and Policy in Underdeveloped Countries* (London, 1957), pp. 113–14; italics mine.

mechanism will not, in the long run, extend the 'range of choice' farther than would happen in the absence of interference.[10] It also seems doubtful that the 'individual acts of choice and valuation' reflect the time preference the individuals would like to apply in the choice between the present and the future, and Section 2 of this article will be devoted to this very question. On the other line of argument, however, there is not much that one can say, except that many of us find the role of the State (depending on the nature of the State) not as much of an evil as Professor Bauer seems to find. It is not possible to refute his argument by pointing out that 'man's power over man' is sometimes greater in a system of free enterprise than in a system where the State plays an important role, for Professor Bauer explains that what he really objects to is 'direct compulsion, as distinct from social compulsions affecting individual choices'.[11] If one has an enormous dislike of 'direct compulsion' as opposed to 'social compulsion', then Professor Bauer's stand is the natural one and cannot be criticised for internal inconsistency. And, of course, if this stand is taken, the whole problem of the 'optimum' rate of saving can be dismissed, for we are not allowed to have any alternative to the rate of saving that will emerge from individual decisions.

1.4   Horvat's solution

Another way of avoiding the problem of conflicting values can be observed in the criterion suggested by Mr Branko Horvat.[12] His approach is based on the dominating influence of the 'absorptive capacity' of an economy. Given the factors of organization, knowledge, requirements of personal consumption, etc., an economy can absorb only a limited amount of investment in any period of time. As investment is expanded, soon a point is reached where marginal investment leads to a negative return. Mr Horvat defines the 'optimum' investment as *the maximum investment which may be productively applied* in a given economy'.[13]

---

10. Cf. Mr P. J. D. Wiles, '. . . in the Soviet economy there are, as it were, always too few hairbrushes and too many nailbrushes in view of the resources available, while in a "capitalist" economy this proportion is always more nearly right. But the production of both these articles is growing at about 10 per cent per annum in USSR and at about 2 per cent per annum in "capitalist" countries. In the end the Soviet citizen will be supplied better even with hairbrushes' ('Scarcity, Marxism and Gosplan', *Oxford Economic Papers*, 5 (October 1953), pp. 315-16). One need hardly add that the rate of saving is one of the most important influences on the rate of growth, so that the question cannot be dismissed merely in terms of the widening of the 'range of choice'.

11. *Op. cit.*, pp. 121-2.

12. 'The Optimum Rate of Investment', *Economic Journal*, 68 (December 1958).

13. *Op. cit.*, p. 753.

While this criterion focuses attention on an important aspect of the problem,[14] it is undoubtedly a very partisan criterion. The level of maximum productive investment provides, it seems to me, an important *upper limit* of investment; while there are excellent reasons for not trying to invest *more* than this amount, it is not obvious why a rate of investment *below* this should be ruled out. Before investment becomes completely unproductive, it will have a very low rate of return, and a unit of consumption sacrificed at the margin may not be recovered in less than, say, several hundred years. Would we, then, be justified in undertaking this piece of investment with a *net* return rate less than, say, a fraction of 1 per cent per year? Mr Horvat's model is one of infinite social patience, which eliminates the problem of intertemporal preference altogether.

Mr Horvat does, at one stage, consider the method of 'period maximization', but concludes that maximization has to be carried out for an infinite period of time, as there is 'logically no possibility of confining it to a single period'.[15] This amounts to pushing the economy on to the path of maximum growth. This argument for maximizing the growth rate is rather weak. It may not be possible to ignore altogether the future beyond the maximizing period, but this is not a sufficient justification for treating all units of future consumption as *equally* important, no matter how distant it is. Mr Horvat uses a different argument in a later section, viz. that a sacrifice of present consumption will lead to a larger volume of additional consumption within a short period.[16] This is undoubtedly so in his arithmetical example[17] with a constant capital coefficient of 3, but cannot, of course, be treated as a ground for maximizing the growth rate in all cases.

Mr Horvat has an appendix on the proposition that 'any movement off the path of maximum growth is equivalent to the diminution of the welfare for some individuals without any increase in welfare for anybody else'.[18] His reasoning can be put in the following

14. One of the limitations of Professor Tinbergen's solution referred to above was his assumption of a constant capital coefficient independent of the saving rate. See in this connection 'A Note on Tinbergen on the Optimum Rate of Saving', by the present writer, *Economic Journal*, 67 (December 1957); also Branko Horvat, 'The Optimum Rate of Saving: A Note', *Economic Journal*, 68 (March 1958).

15. *Op. cit.*, p. 757.

16. *Op. cit.*, pp. 758-60. There seems to be a certain amount of ambiguity here. 'If it were for only 1 per cent of social product to be added annually to already existing investment funds, the whole thing might have practical value.... It is exactly those 1 or 2 per cent which are needed' (p. 758). For what? Maximizing the growth rate? Certainly not, unless it is being *implicitly* assumed that when an expansion of more than 1 or 2 per cent is attempted, the marginal capital–output ratio rises abruptly from the mentioned value of 3 to infinity.

17. *Op. cit.*, p. 759.

18. *Op. cit.*, Appendix II, Equivalence Theorem, pp. 766-7.

way. On the path of maximum growth, marginal productivity of investment is zero, so that 'the marginal utility of investment' is zero too. Since the latter must be equal to the marginal disutility of saving, this, too, must be zero. Once this becomes zero it will never again be positive, since with the rise in consumption over time there is a tendency for the marginal disutility of saving to fall rather than to rise. Hence, once an economy has chosen to be on the path of maximum growth, there will be no point in moving away from it. Thus, the proposition is correct, provided the economy happens to be on the path of maximum growth on grounds of utility calculus, i.e. if actually all the present wants *have been* met. It is, however, obviously no argument for moving *towards* the path if we happen to be away from it. This may not be obvious from the wording of the proposition, which is put in terms akin to those used for genuine Paretian conditions. In fact, using Horvat's line of argument itself, it can be shown that Horvat's 'optimum' cannot be the optimum for the world as we know it. The marginal usefulness of consumption is not in fact nil in any known community, so that the marginal disutility of saving is positive. And since the 'choice of maximum growth implies that the marginal disutility of saving is zero',[19] no existing economy should choose the path of maximum growth. This way of looking at the problem makes, therefore, the establishment of what Ramsey called 'bliss' to be a necessary condition for choosing Horvat's 'optimum'.

One can, of course, leave out all this utility calculation, and simply make the maximization of growth the policy objective, irrespective of the present level of consumption. Then the solution of the question becomes one example of the 'partisan' approach to the question. The rest of the paper is meant only for those who believe that there is a genuine conflict to be faced in the problem, that is, those who are not ready to make one of those overriding value judgements, in one direction or the other, that eliminate the problem altogether.

2 Individual Preferences and Assumed Values

If democracy means that all the people that are affected by a decision must themselves make the decision (directly or through representatives), then, clearly, there can be no democratic solution of the problem of the 'optimum' rate of saving. The rate of saving chosen today influences not merely the division of consumption between

19. Horvat, *op. cit.*, p. 767.

early and late dates for the same group of people, but also that between the consumption of different generations, some of which are yet to be born. This also disposes of, as we have mentioned earlier, any possibility of applying the principle of 'consumers' sovereignty' to this problem. From this it does not, of course, necessarily follow that decisions made by some authoritarian body will be more 'fair' to future generations than those made by the present generation voting collectively.[20] What would, however, be of very considerable interest to investigate is whether there is any reason to believe that individual decisions made by members of the present generation through the market mechanism would give us the same result as the one they would themselves choose if they were voting collectively on the question. This also involves the question whether the 'pure' discounts revealed by individuals in their personal choices indicate the present generation's views of the weights to be attached to the consumption of the present generation and that of future generations.

A number of difficulties can, of course, be easily pointed out. The distribution of votes in a political decision need not conform to the distribution of the capacity to save in the market mechanism. Thus, the over-all discount emerging from the market mechanism may not have much in common with the decision that will emerge from political voting. There is also a problem of knowledge. An individual's saving rate depends on the future prices, which are affected by the saving rate of others, and no one individual, acting separately, has any means of knowing what other individuals intend to do.[21] So the individual action must be based on imperfect knowledge, whereas a consistent political programme placed before the community need not have this particular imperfection.

A more fundamental question is involved in Rousseau's distinction between the 'general will' and the 'will of all', which we do not wish to go into here.[22] We should, however, point out that there is no reason to believe that a man acting as a responsible participator in a political debate will express exactly the same preferences as he does

20. Those who believe that 'political leaders' take a relatively less-biased view of the future, being concerned about their reputation to future generations, may question this proposition.

21. See J. de V. Graaff, *Theoretical Welfare Economics* (London, 1957), Chapter IV. There may also be some 'external economies'. A saver gets only a few per cent interest on his capital, the rest goes to others in the community. A person may, thus, gain from other people's saving, and this 'external economy' may provide a need for collusion. On the general question of this kind of external relationships see W. J. Baumol, *Welfare Economics and the Theory of the State* (London, 1952).

22. For a very lucid discusson of this question, see Kenneth J. Arrow, *Social Choice and Individual Values* (New York, 1951).

in his day-to-day life. This dichotomy in people's behaviour is very clearly noticeable in many fields, e.g. in the attitude of the people to regulations restricting the traffic. The assumption of a consistent set of values serving as the basis for action of individuals is most unlifelike.

Quite apart from these difficulties, however, there is, it seems, a fundamental problem involved in individual and social decisions arising from the different nature of the choice in the two cases. Let us assume that the individual has no imperfection of knowlege about how much others will save; he knows the exact amounts. Let us also assume that he is an individual with a constant and consistent set of preferences, so that the way he values alternative possibilities does not vary according to his position, i.e. according to whether he is acting in a political or a non-political capacity. He acts equally responsibly in all cases. The question is whether, even in these special circumstances, his saving decisions will properly reflect his views on how much should be saved by the members of the present generation for the future.

2.1   The isolation paradox

Now, this individual faces a choice, let us say, between one unit of consumption now and three units of consumption in twenty years time. He knows, for some reason, that in twenty years he will be dead. He cares for the future generations, but it is not enough, let us assume, to make him sacrifice a unit of his present consumption for three units for the generation living in twenty years' time. He decides, therefore, to consume the unit; but another man comes and tells him that if he saves one unit of consumption the other man will also save one unit. It would not be, by any means, irrational for the first man to change his mind now and to agree to save a unit. The gain to the future generation is much greater, and he can bring all this about by sacrificing himself only one unit of consumption. So he may, without any inconsistency, act differently in the two cases. This is a problem we may face in much larger scale in contrasting individual saving decisions with a political decision taken by the whole society. This paradox, which we shall refer to as the 'isolation paradox' for the rest of the paper, does not arise due to any inconsistency of values, but due to the differences in the nature of the choice involved in the two cases.[23]

23. This difference is often completely ignored. See, for example, Professor Bauer's rejection of 'compulsory saving' through taxation on the ground that (to quote Professor

Before we proceed farther, it may be useful to discuss a possible misunderstanding that may arise in interpreting the above case. Put in this form, it looks as if the conflict arises because the person concerned values the gains of the future generations but does not care at all about the sacrifices of the others in the present generation. This is not so. The possibility of the conflict is present whenever the person values the sacrifice (of one unit, in the above example) of present consumption of others less than the corresponding gain (three units) of the future generation, so that he would like them to save more.[24] In our example the person may value each of the three units of consumption of the future generation as equal to 0.3 unit of his own consumption now; and he may value the consumption of one unit by others in the present generation as equal to as much as 0.7 unit of his own consumption. If he saves one unit along with another person saving the same amount they produce (assuming the same rate of return) six units for the future generation, which he values at 1.8 units of his own consumption. And the sacrifice necessary for this is 1.7 units in his valuation. So while he is not ready to make the sacrifice alone, he is perfectly prepared to do it if others are ready to join in. *This possibility of the apparent paradox is present whenever his relative valuation of others' consumption is such that he would prefer them to sacrifice some consumption for the future generations; and sacrificing something himself might, because of the indivisibility of the political decision, be the means of achieving this to a sufficient extent to over-compensate the loss that he would incur from his own act of sacrifice.* This paradox could be put in terms of 'external economy', but this terminology is unhappy, because the basic framework of the concept of 'external economy' is that of the maximization of personal utility (with possibilities of *personal gain* from the action of others). This, however, is a case of a person's readiness to sacrifice his own pleasures for future generations provided others are ready to do the same. The 'isolation paradox' arises from not distinguishing between the assumption appropriate to a general

---

Bauer's slightly provocative understatement): 'I attach significance, meaning, and value to individual acts of choice and valuation, including individual time preference between the present and the future' (*loc. cit.*). See also Professor Eckstein's arguments for using the inividual's 'pure' time preference as revealed in economic operations (*loc. cit.*).

24. To put it in another way, each member of the present generation may want to raise the rate of saving of everybody, but may not wish to raise that of himself *in isolation*. A person is likely to be more 'biased' in favour of his *own* consumption vis-à-vis that of the future generations, than he would be in favour of the consumption of the present generation *as a whole*, which also contains people other than himself, vis-à-vis the consumption of future generations.

political decision as opposed to one of individual action in isolation. It seems to be an extremely simple distinction, yet it has been responsible for considerable confusion of thought about the nature of democratic decisions on economic matters.

2.2   Problems of political mechanism

It is one thing to recognize that the question that is being discussed is essentially political in nature and cannot be resolved by aggregating isolated decisions of individuals, it is another to decide on the type of political mechanism that will be most suited to the policy decision. The conflicts and paradoxes involved in voting are well known.[25] Without a certain degree of 'similarity' of the social values of the people, the voting procedure may not give us unambiguous results. But this is a problem that is present in all types of political decisions, and this does not prevent us from relying on some political mechanism or other for resolving all these questions. It is most important that the question should be debated in terms such that people know clearly what is the precise issue involved and the rest has to be left to the usual channels of political decision-taking, e.g. elections, public criticisms and, if necessary, referendum. The difficulty is no more (and, of course, no less) than that faced in other problems of political decision.

We must, however, pay some attention to the different ways of presenting the issues involved in the choice of an 'optimum' rate of saving. We have earlier expressed our doubts about the usefulness of putting the question in terms of utility functions, for it is not easy to appreciate what one is doing when one is voting for a certain specific utility function. On the other hand, the choice cannot be put as a once-for-all choice between a point-sacrifice of consumption and a consequent point-addition to consumption in the future. An investment creates productive capacity for a number of years, and the present sacrifice of consumption leads to a *flow* of additional consumption in the future. If production capacities are not specific and the current input requirements of corresponding units of consumer goods and investment goods are equal we can easily express both the investment and the consequent flow of output in terms of consumer goods. If the amortization necessary for the maintenance of the capacity is subtracted from the annual flow of output, we get something like a perpetual annuity that is one of the ways of looking at

25. See Kenneth J. Arrow, *Social Choice and Individual Values*.

the problem.[26] If we find that the annuity as a proportion of the amount of consumer goods sacrificed by a marginal unit of investment is, say, 10 per cent, we can then put the question before the people whether this is an acceptable rate of net return. This way of putting the problem has, however, two defects. First, in certain societies a question like this may not make much sense to the people who have to judge the acceptability of the rate of return. Familiarity with market rates of interest may not necessarily make the problem easier; in fact, in some cases it may make the appreciation of the true significance of the rate of return more difficult. The context in which interest rates enter the life of the people is often so different from the context in which this question is raised that the possibility of deception by a false sense of comparability might add to the difficulty. Secondly, the gestation lag between the investment and the beginning of the fruits of the project will add to the complication of the choice.

An alternative way of putting the same question is to calculate the number of years in which the lost consumption can be recovered from the output due to the investment. If we do not wish to commit ourselves about the rates of saving in the future we may try to calculate the shortest possible period of recovery (subject to the maintenance of the capacity). If, for example, the rate of *net* return is 10 per cent and the gestation lag is five years, we may put the question before the public whether they would be ready to give up a unit of present consumption that *can* be recovered fully (if so desired) in fifteen years, and from then onwards, once every ten years.[27] This way of presenting the question has two great advantages. In the first instance, it makes an aspect of the choice much clearer, and thus contributes to the understanding of those who will debate on the issue. Secondly, in so far as one of the most important reasons for social time preference is the degree of uncertainty associated with the future, the limitation of the time horizon is a useful way of introducing this factor, for the longer period of return, the more hazardous things may become.[28] We shall not, here, go farther into the question of the right way of presenting the problem. In certain political debates, though not in all, this may indeed be quite a useful method of putting the question.

26. The value of the annuity may change with the conditions of labour supply and of technological change.

27. Possibilities of technological advance and changes in labour supply will add to the complication of the question.

28. In Chapter VII of my *Choice of Techniques: An Aspect of the Theory of Planned Economic Development* (Oxford, 1960) I discuss the different types of uncertainty involved in the choice.

It may, however, be difficult to avoid committing ourselves about future rates of investment, because when we build new capacity with this year's investment we may have to know the specific composition of the future output. If this is so, the idea of *possible* (but not necessarily actual) periods of recovery of lost consumption will not be a very useful concept. On the other hand, the assumption of an unchanging saving rate is not fair to the future generations, for they may wish to alter the saving rate. While not denying the truth of this proposition, it must be pointed out that the economic world is such that (thanks to specificities and time lags) we *do* have to take decisions for future generations. We need not, of course, make the assumption (as Professor Tinbergen did) that we should choose the *same* rate of savings in the future as now, but the saving rates for a considerably long period may have to be decided now. The present-day counterpart of this proposition is that the rate of real saving that is possible now may similarly have been determined in the past, and given the specificity of the capacities, there is not much that we can do about it at the moment. This brings us to our final question: how much freedom do we, in fact, have in the choice of the 'optimum' rate of saving. This is discussed in the next section.

3 *Limits of Variation of the Saving Rate*

For a satisfactory solution of the problem of the 'optimum' rate of saving, we must have an idea of the width of the range from which the choice is to be made. We cannot assume that any rate of saving from 0 per cent to 100 per cent can be chosen, and a big part of our exercise in this problem will consist of finding the relevant range from which the 'optimum' is to be selected. The upper and the lower limits will depend on both social and technical factors, and we shall first discuss the former.

The level of consumption in any particular community cannot be suddenly pushed below a certain limit determined by the history of the community. One of the advantages that a post-revolutionary government has compared with the pre-revolutionary government in the same society is a certain relaxation of this barrier. By eliminating a certain high-consumption class from the top of the social hierarchy, which previously enjoyed a big part of the cake, a revolution might lead to a raising of the upper social limit of saving given by the difference between productive capacity and the socially accepted limit of minimum consumption. This, of course, involves the assumption that the disappearance of the previous upper class is not accompanied by: (a) an even greater reduction of productive capacity arising from dislocation, and/or (b) the creation of a new high-consumption upper class replacing the earlier set.

In a society where the proportion of luxury consumption is small the lower limit of consumption approximates to the real wages bill of the community, *plus* the necessary doles for those who are unemployed, or are otherwise dependent on the society. We shall not go into the question of what constitutes the 'minimum' wages, or doles; it is sufficient, for our purpose here, to recognize that there is a sociologically determined lower limit of consumption, and a corresponding upper limit of the saving rate.

Another possible upper limit may arise from the effect on the efficiency of production when the saving rate is raised too much. One of the merits of Mr Horvat's criterion discussed earlier was his emphasis on this limit. While we need not follow him in considering this upper limit to be the 'optimum', it is a limit that tends to reduce the width of the range of our choice. Beyond a point, an expansion of investment may actually lead to a negative return at the margin, and there is obviously no point in pushing the rate of investment beyond this point.[29] If this limit applies before we reach the limit given by the socially accepted level of minimum consumption this will naturally be the *effective* limit.

The lower limit of saving may arise from a number of different factors. One limit may be given by the investment necessary for the maintenance of the existing capacity of production. Another limit may be provided by the growth of population. Like the minimum consumption of the present period given by the social ideas and the size of the present population, there may be a minimum growth rate of consumption given by the growth of population. It is true, of course, that in certain societies this type of values (viz. objecting to a decline in the standard of living) may not yet be fully developed, and one can quote examples of this happening in some countries in the past. It is, however, extremely unlikely that a community that is at all interested in the question of the 'optimum' rate of saving will tolerate an actual decline in the standard of living. So for the type of society that is relevant for our analysis, this is likely to provide a lower limit to the rate of capital accumulation. It is of interest to note that in some countries, which are, on the one hand, very poor with a high rate of growth of population, and which are at the same

---

29. One can, however, think of a very special situation when the society might want to store some consumer goods for the future even at the cost of some loss over time. This is a case of investment in inventories with a negative rate of return.

time very keen on planned growth, i.e. interested in questions like that of the 'optimum' rate of saving, the upper and the lower limits may leave only a very small range in the short run from which the rate of saving can be chosen. Many countries in Asia provide examples of this. Maintenance of the standard of living might require the investment of nearly the whole of the possible surplus over minimum consumption. As the economy develops, the range of choice expands, and the problem of selecting the 'optimum' rate grows in significance.[30] The general point that, given other things, a higher rate of growth of population will tend to raise the 'optimum' rate of saving remains, however, true.[31]

3.1 Short-run limits

Even in societies where possibilities of variation are not restricted by poverty and population growth, the short-run scope of variation may be very little for two different reasons. First, at any point of time an actual curtailment of the standard of living is unlikely to be accepted, unless (a) there is some kind of emergency, e.g. a war, or unless (b) the political nature of the society changes radically, bringing about a shift of the balance of different social classes. But leaving out these political and social upheavals, it is reasonable to assume that an actual reduction of the standard of living enjoyed by the different groups of the community will not be easily acceptable. This limits the possibility of raising the saving rate from whatever it is in the short run without a social revolution. The proportion of saving of the *incremental* income, however, is a short-run variable.

A no less important short-run limit to the variation of the saving rate arises from the technical specificity of productive capacity. The possibility of real saving is restricted by the possibility of real investment, and it is not possible to switch immediately from the production of consumer goods to the production of investment goods.[32] In

30. Thanks to a desire to catch up with the richer countries, people in an underdeveloped economy may, however, be ready to make proportionately higher sacrifices than people in richer countries. The existence of surplus labour may also allow an expansion of saving without a curtailment of consumption. See Ragnar Nurkse, *Problems of Capital Formation in Underdeveloped Countries* (Oxford, 1953).

31. In so far as an expansion of consumption increases the rate of growth of population, the problem is more complex. The question can, then, be studied only in terms of a set of simultaneous equations.

32. Investment in 'working capital' may, however, be possible to a certain extent with a surplus of consumer goods. For example, in some poor economies a surplus of food and cloth (and a few primitive tools) may be sufficient for investment in building dams, or roads, with very labour-using techniques. The possibility of this type of investment is, however, limited.

the very short run, therefore, the real saving rate cannot be *raised* beyond a fairly close limit, and it is also pointless to *reduce* it beyond a limit in the very short run. The determination of the 'optimum' rate of saving must, therefore, be viewed as a long-term problem. The relevant question is not what should we make the rate of investment this year, but what should we make it after the lapse of several years. This raises some rather interesting problems of political evaluation. The values of the present-day society have to be used to allocate consumption between two different periods in the future. This is, of course, by no means a unique problem arising only with the determination of the 'optimum' rate of saving; in fact, most of the important political and economic decisions do involve such problems. This aspect of the question is, however, worth stressing, since it has not received much attention in the discussions on the 'optimum' rate of saving.[33]

Once the specificity of productive capacity is recognized to have an important bearing on the question, the problem of the *allocation* of investment between different sectors becomes the present-day equivalent of choosing future rates of saving. If, for example, we assume that investment goods are of two types, viz. those that make consumer goods and those that produce investment goods, the present-day allocation of productive *capital* between these two sectors comes to very much the same thing as the determination of the future division of national output between consumption and investment. The allocation of *investment* between the two becomes the means of influencing the rates of investment in the future.[34]

If one assumes further specificity, so that investment goods to make investment goods to make consumer goods are different from investment goods to make investment goods to make investment goods, the decision has to be taken one farther step backwards, and so on. The process need not, however, be continued indefinitely, for two distinct reasons. First of all, the various sectors of the economy are not related to each other in one long chain of 'earlier' to 'later' sectors, and there is a considerable element of circularity of technical relationships. Further, some types of investment goods can make other investment goods of their own kind. For example, machine tools (like cows) can reproduce themselves, and a point comes when one can find a sector which produces investment goods not merely for other sectors but also for itself. Secondly, the possibility of inter-

---

33. See, however, Maurice Dobb, *Essay on Economic Growth*, Chapter V.
34. This will require a corresponding change in the nature of the political question to be asked, which can no longer be put in the form used in Section 2.

national trade increases the degree of freedom that can be achieved in the allocation of investment. To some extent, this also increases the scope of varying the total rate of investment in the very short run. As an example, one may refer to the purchase of producer goods by the Soviet Union during her First Five Year Plan, by exporting grains, and 'a number of goods which were in short supply in the home market (tobacco and matches, sweetmeats, linen and dairy produce) at the expense of home consumption'.[35]

The scope of *short-run* variation of the investment rate through international trade is, however, restricted much by the possible adverse effects on terms of trade, so that it still remains true that the debate on the 'optimum' rate of savings must be a debate mainly of long-run policy variations. One can classify the questions involved in the determination of the 'optimum' saving into at least three groups. First of all, it is a problem of allocation of consumption for the present generation between near and distant future. Secondly, it is a question of allocating consumption between the present generation and the future generations. And finally, it is also a problem of allocating consumption *between* different generations in the future.[36] The longer the time period necessary for the execution of saving decisions given by the extent of specificities and gestation lags, the more important becomes the last question compared with the earlier two, and the second question compared with the first. The nature of the political questions asked will, thus, depend on these economic and technical factors. The formulation of the questions may, therefore, turn out to be no less difficult than the determination of the political methods of answering them.

4   *Summary and Conclusions*

In the first section we discussed some of the traditional methods of solving the problem of intertemporal allocation. We found the use of utility functions a totally unsatisfactory method of introducing the political element into the choice. We also discussed the case for using the 'pure' time discount of individuals and discovered that it could not be justified even on grounds of 'consumers' sovereignty'. We examined a number of other solutions published in this journal

35. Maurice Dobb, *Soviet Economic Development since 1917* (New York, 1948), p. 238.
36. As we have suggested earlier, the level of consumption might not be the only determinant of 'welfare', and the allocation of capital goods between different generations may also have to be considered.

and elsewhere, and found them to be various alternative methods of eliminating the problem altogether by taking very partisan views of the question.

In the second section we tried to compare the solution of the problem that will emerge from individual decisions in a free market with the one that will emerge from a political decision in which the whole population took part. In addition to differences arising from the necessarily incomplete knowledge of the individuals, the existence of 'external economies', and the considerations connected with Rousseau's distinction between the 'general will' and the 'will of all', we found a further, and in our opinion important, difference arising from the totally different nature of the two questions. The alternatives that are open to the people are completely different in the two cases, and the paths chosen may, therefore, be very different from one another. It is, for example, perfectly possible that in a society where no one saves anything, everyone might nevertheless be ready to vote for a political proposal requiring each member of the society to save, say, 20 per cent of his income for the sake of future generations. This apparent paradox, which arises due to a case of interdependence though not of 'external economy' in the usual sense, is readily understandable if it is recognized that while a person might apply a 'pure' discount to the consumption of the people of the future, he might apply a similar, if less severe, discount to the consumption of *others* in the *present* generation. We also discussed some alternative methods of posing the political question for popular debates.

In the final section the limits imposed on the problem by political and technological factors were discussed, explaining that the range of choice is quite narrow in the short run, and the real choice might concern the saving rates of the fairly distant future. The greater the strength of these factors, the more will the problem be one of allocation of consumption between *different* generations in the *future*, rather than one of allocation between the present generation, on the one hand, and the future generations, on the other. To the extent that this is true, the present generation will have to play a part in this problem that is totally different from the one usually attributed to it.

An Appendix on Harrod's Second Essay

In his 'Second Essay in Dynamic Theory',[37] Sir Roy Harrod discusses a number of things that are relevant to our problem. Sir Roy resolves

37. *Economic Journal*, 70 (June 1960).

the question of the optimum rate of saving in terms of the concept of the 'natural' rate of growth, which he first put forward in his well-known 'An Essay in Dynamic Theory'.[38] It is the rate given by the growth of population and that of technology, being, in the main, exogenously determined. This natural rate is taken by Harrod to be also the 'welfare optimum' rate.

At first glance this identification might appear to be a little puzzling. How can a growth rate given by a set of purely positive factors be automatically regarded as the 'welfare optimum' rate? In his article a utility function is employed, but its purpose is mainly to find out what interest rate, as an expression of intertemporal prefer-ence, is consistent with the natural rate of growth.[39] Even the con-flicting claims of an increase in the interest rate and the creation of a budget surplus as alternative counter-inflationary policies are dis-cussed in terms of establishing the 'natural rate of interest' derived from the natural rate of growth.[40]

In Harrod's system the natural rate of growth gives the only rate of growth consistent, in the long run, with maintaining full employ-ment. A lower rate of growth cannot be chosen if growing unemploy-ment is unacceptable. A higher rate of growth cannot be sustained, in the long run, because of the shortage of labour. This is certainly a very neat and ingenious method of solving this intertemporal problem using value judgements that are sufficiently widespread (at least, in some societies) to be taken for granted.

The reason why I find this solution unacceptable is my inability to accept technological progress as 'an almost entirely independent variable'.[41] It might be useful to contrast this with the empirical assumptions made by Professor Tinbergen in the article we discussed earlier.[42] There it was assumed that within the limit set by the given capital–output ratio, one can have any rate of growth by varying the rate of saving. A rise of x per cent in the saving rate is assumed to lead to a rise in x per cent in the growth rate also, without the capital–output ratio moving against one due to the limitation of labour supply or of technological improvement. This, as I tried to

38. *Economic Journal*, 49 (March 1939).

39. The natural rate of growth, in Harrod's system, is 'an almost entirely independent variable, but possibly depending to a slight degree upon the rate of interest' (paragraph 23).

40. *Op. cit.*, paragraphs 42–3.

41. Harrod adds that the 'natural' rate of growth depends 'to a slight degree upon the rate of interest'. It should be noted that it is not necessary for Harrod's equations to assume a dependence of only a slight degree, and this is, in fact, an additional empirical assumption. However, as far as other variables are concerned, they have no direct influence on the 'natural' rate of growth, in Harrod's system.

42. 'The Optimum Rate of Saving', *Economic Journal*, 66 (December 1956).

suggest elsewhere,[43] must assume that 'as soon as we try to speed up the full capacity of growth of output by choosing a higher rate of saving, progress of technological knowledge will also be speeded up to the required extent'. This assumes a very high dependence of technological progress on the experiences acquired in making new investments, and on the active pursuit of new techniques associated with a high rate of capital accumulation. Sir Roy Harrod makes the exactly opposite assumption, and the growth rates of technology and population, in his model, *cannot* be influenced by the rate of accumulation of capital. While I find the Tinbergen assumption too flexible, Harrod's assumption strikes me as being too rigid. This is, however, an empirical question, and can be resolved only by factual research, which has been, so far, sadly inadequate.

43. 'A Note on Tinbergen on the Optimum Rate of Saving', *Economic Journal*, 67 (December 1957), pp. 745-6.

5

Isolation, Assurance and the Social Rate of Discount

Some of the recent discussions on the relationship between private and social rates of discount have been concerned with a special instance of a very general problem, being an extension of the two-person non-zero-sum game known as the 'Prisoners' Dilemma'.[1] In the first section of this paper the general nature of this problem will be studied, and it will also be shown that there is another problem close to this one with which it is sometimes confused, but which has a very different logical structure and involves different policy implications. In the remaining three sections the application of this general framework to the question of optimum savings and the social rate of discount will be examined, particularly in the light of some recent controversies.[2]

---

1. Due to A. W. Tucker; see R. D. Luce and H. Raiffa, *Games and Decisions* (New York: Wiley, 1958), Sections 5.4 and 5.5. See also M. Shubik (ed.), *Game Theory and Related Approaches to Social Behavior* (New York: Wiley, 1964), Chapters 20 and 23.
2. W. J. Baumol, *Welfare Economics and the Theory of the State* (Cambridge: Harvard University Press, 1952); A. K. Sen, 'On Optimizing the Rate of Saving', *Economic Journal*, 71 (September 1961) [Essay 4 in this volume]; S. A. Marglin, 'The Social Rate of Discount and the Optimal Rate of Investment', *Quarterly Journal of Economics*, 77 (February 1963); G. Tullock, 'The Social Rate of Discount and the Optimal Rate of Investment: Comment', *Quarterly Journal of Economics*, 78 (May 1964); Robert C. Lind, 'Further Comment', *Quarterly Journal of Economics*, 78 (May 1964); D. Usher, 'Comment', *Quarterly Journal of Economics*, 78 (November 1964); M. S. Feldstein, 'The Social Time Preference Discount Rate in Cost-Benefit Analysis', *Economic Journal*, 74 (June 1964); A. C. Harberger, 'Techniques of Project Appraisal', Universities-National Bureau of Economic Research, Conference on Economic Planning, 27 and 28 November 1964 (mimeo); E. S. Phelps, *Fiscal Neutrality Toward Economic Growth* (New York: McGraw-Hill, 1965), Chapter 4.

From *Quarterly Journal of Economics*, 81 (February 1967), 112-24.

1 The Isolation Paradox and the Assurance Problem

Consider a community of N individuals, each of whom must do one and only one of two alternatives, A and B. The payoff to each individual is a function of the actions of all individuals. Let the preference ordering of each individual satisfy the two following conditions: (1) given the set of actions of the others (no matter what they are), the individual is better off doing A rather than B; and (2) given the choice between everyone doing A and everyone doing B, each individual prefers the latter to the former.[3]

Given the two features noted of the preference pattern, certain results follow immediately. In particular the following three.

(1) *Pareto-inferior outcome:* In the absence of collusion, each individual will prefer to do A rather than B, for no matter what the others do each is himself better off doing A. However, the outcome, viz., A by all, will be regarded as strictly worse by each than the alternative B by all. Thus the outcome is Pareto-inferior, and will be rejected by everyone in a referendum.[4]

(2) *Strict dominance of individual strategy:* The atomistic result is completely independent of the individuals' expectations of other people's actions. Irrespective of each person's expectations of the others' actions, each prefers to do A, i.e. the strategy of doing A strictly dominates over the alternative. Thus we do not have to make any assumption about the individual's behaviour when faced with uncertainty and conflict, with which much of game theory is concerned.

(3) *Need for enforcement:* Even if the policy of everyone doing B was adopted by resolution, this would not come about (assuming self-seeking) except through compulsory enforcement. Everyone would like the others to do B, while he himself does A, so that even if a contract is arrived at, it will be in the interest of each to break it.

3. If $i(x^i)$ stands for individual i pursuing strategy x^i, when x^i can be A or B, and if ϕ^i stands for the payoff to individual i in terms of his own welfare units, then:

$$\phi^i[1(x^1), 2(x^2), \ldots, i(A), \ldots, N(x^n)] > \phi^i[1(x^1), 2(x^2), \ldots, i(B), \ldots, N(x^n)] \qquad (1)$$

and

$$\phi^i[1(B), 2(B), \ldots, i(B), \ldots, N(B)] > \phi^i[1(A), 2(A), \ldots, i(A), \ldots, N(A)]. \qquad (2)$$

4. It is possible to argue that the difference between the non-cooperative equilibrium point and the collusive solution in this game corresponds precisely to Rousseau's distinction between 'will of all' and the 'general will'. See Marglin, *op. cit.*, p. 104, fn. 2. See also W. G. Runciman and A. K. Sen, 'Games, Justice and the General Will', *Mind*, 74 (October 1965); and R. R. Farquharson, 'An Approach to the Pure Theory of Voting Procedure', Ph.D. thesis, Oxford University, 1957-58 [later published, *Theory of Voting*, New Haven, Conn.: Yale University Press, 1959].

It is easy to check that in the special case when there are only two individuals, the above corresponds exactly to the game of Prisoners' Dilemma. In fact with $N = 2$, the conditions (1) and (2) on the preference pattern give a complete strict ordering of the individuals over the entire field of possible outcomes, which consists of four alternatives.[5] We shall, however, stick to the N-person version, and call it the 'isolation paradox'.[6]

The savings problem is only a special application of this. Suppose B stands for the policy of saving one more unit for the sake of the future of the community, and A for not doing it. Given the action of all others, each individual is better off not doing the additional unit of saving himself. Hence nobody will, but everyone would have preferred one more unit of saving by each than by none. This is the essence of the problem discussed by Marglin and myself.[7]

Consider now a somewhat different preference pattern. Let the individuals continue to hold (2), but let (1) be modified. In the special case when everyone else does B, the individual now prefers to do B himself. Excepting this special case, the individual continues to prefer doing A to B no matter what the others do, *given* their action.[8]

This is a near-cousin of the isolation paradox, but differs from it in some of the main results. Result (II), i.e. strict dominance no longer holds. Expectations about other people's behaviour must be brought in. If it is expected that the others will all do B, then this one would prefer to do B also; otherwise he may do A. Result (I) needs some modification also. If everyone has implicit faith in everyone else doing the 'right' thing, viz., B, then it will be in everyone's interest to do the right thing also. Then the outcome need not be Pareto-inferior.[9] However, if each individual feels that the others

---

5. A. K. Sen, *Choice of Techniques* (2nd edn; Oxford: Basil Blackwell, 1962), Appendix to Chapter VIII. We have in this case:

$$\phi^i[i(A), j(B)] > \phi^i[i(B), j(B)] > \phi^i[i(A), j(A)] > \phi^i[i(B), j(A)]. \qquad (3)$$

6. See Sen, 'On Optimizing the Rate of Saving' [Essay 4 above], Section 2.

7. See Phelps, *op cit.*, for an illuminating discussion of this problem in the context of others involving growth and public savings.

8. Formally, we impose the restriction on (1) that

$$Not\,[x^1 = x^2 = x^3 = \ldots = x^n = B]. \qquad (1^*)$$

And we supplement (1), thus restricted, by:

$$\phi^i[1(B), 2(B), \ldots, i(B), \ldots, N(B)] > \phi^i[1(B), 2(B), \ldots, i(A), \ldots, N(B)]. \qquad (1.1)$$

9. Note, however, that there is no guarantee that this will definitely not be Pareto-inferior. From (1), (1.1) and (2), we get an incomplete ordering for each individual, if $N > 2$.

are going to let him down, that is not do B, then he too may do A rather than B, and the outcome will be Pareto-inferior.

Result (III) does not hold any longer. Given that each individual has complete assurance that the other will do B, there is no problem of compulsory enforcement. Unlike in the case of the isolation paradox, it is not in the individual's interest to break the contract of everyone doing B. In this case assurance is sufficient and enforcement is unnecessary, and we shall refer to this case as that of the 'assurance problem'.

These two problems have often been confused with each other. Marglin's and my argument for the inoptimality of market savings is based on the assumption of a situation of the type of the isolation paradox. This problem however, has been identified with Vickrey's analysis[10] of 'the interdependence of the transfers of different donors', where 'an individual might be willing to make a gift to one of his fellows *if he knew* that others were doing so even if he would not make the gift on his own'.[11] This last is, however, a case of the assurance problem.[12] In our case an individual will not do the saving *even* if 'he knew that others were doing so', and this makes the inoptimality of the market result certain, which it is not in Vickrey's case.

The difference is a simple one when viewed in the context of game theory. In the assurance problem with which Vickrey is concerned,[13] everyone doing the 'right' thing, i.e. B, is an 'equilibrium point',[14] whereas in Marglin's case and in mine, this is definitely not so. Baumol's discussion of the optimum savings problem also fits in with the assurance problem, rather than with the isolation paradox, and it rests on an interdependence due to the indivisibility of public projects. The effect of trying to save alone for the sake of the future generation is 'negligible', so that the individual, though endowed with altruism, does not do this, 'except if he has grounds for assurance that others, too, will act in a manner designed to promote the future welfare of the community'.[15] In the case of the isolation paradox,

10. W. S. Vickrey, 'One Economist's View of Philanthropy', in F. G. Dickinson (ed.), *Philanthropy and Public Policy* (New York: National Bureau of Economic Research, 1962).

11. Tullock, *op. cit.*, p. 331; emphasis added.

12. The preference pattern corresponds to (1) subject to (1*) and (1.1).

13. Vickrey goes into more complex cases also. He introduces the possibility that an individual donating a sum might induce others to do the same. This restricts condition (1) even more than in the assurance problem, with the individual preference for A over B being not only not applicable when *all* others do B, but also when, say, a certain suitably large fraction of the total group does B.

14. See Luce and Raiffa, *op. cit.*, Section 7.8. For the classic analysis of the meaning and the existence of equilibrium points, see J. F. Nash, 'Equilibrium Points in N-person Games', *Proceedings of the National Academy of Sciences*, 36 (1950).

15. Baumol, *op. cit.*, p. 92.

however, the individual will not do the saving *even with* the assurance.[16]

2 Optimum Savings

Consider now the following ordering of individual i. He attaches a weight of unity to his consumption today (simply a normalization assumption), β per unit to the consumption of his contemporaries, γ per unit to the consumption of his own heirs in the future, and α per unit to the consumption of the others in the future generation.[17] For each person, only one marginal choice is considered, viz., whether to increase the saving by one unit (B), or not to do it (A). Also, the future consumption is taken to be a one-shot affair, though this assumption can be easily relaxed without losing anything essential. The marginal rate of return on one unit of saving (i.e. one unit less of consumption) today is an increase in the consumption in the future by k units, where $k > 1$. The individual expects that a proportion λ of the fruits of his saving will accrue to his heirs, and the rest $(1 - \lambda)$ to others in the future generation, when $0 \leqslant \lambda \leqslant 1$; we shall discuss presently the proper assumption about the value of λ. The individual figures that *given* the actions of other people today, the net gain $G(i)$ from one unit more of personal saving is the following:

$$G(i) = [\lambda \cdot \gamma + (1 - \lambda) \alpha] \cdot k - 1. \qquad (4)$$

If $G(i) > 0$, the individual i will clearly save the extra unit, i.e. do B. However, when we start with the amount of savings on which each has already made a decision (based on their atomistic calculation), and then consider the extra unit to be a tiny bit more, G clearly cannot be positive or they would not have been in atomistic equilibrium. Making the usual assumptions about well-behaved and continuously differentiable functions, we shall indeed find that in the atomistic equilibrium, $G = 0$ for every individual, which amounts to:

$$[\lambda \cdot \gamma + (1 - \lambda) \alpha] k = 1. \qquad (5)$$

16. 'This possibility of the apparent paradox is present whenever his relative evaluation of others' consumption is such that he would prefer them to sacrifice some consumption for the future generations; and sacrificing something himself might, because of the indivisibility of the political decision, be the means of achieving this to a sufficient extent to over-compensate the loss that he would incur from his own act of sacrifice' (Sen, *op. cit.*, pp. 488-9, Essay 5 above, p. 124). 'I am willing to abide by [the no-fix system], too, if this is the price I must pay for your adherence, although my first choice is that all of you abide by the no-fix system and I buy off the police force' (Marglin, *op. cit.*, p. 100).

17. These values can be interpreted as the relevant marginal utilities in the utility function of individual i, and can be taken as constant for small changes (see Marglin, p. 101).

Now, consider the possibility of a social contract of everyone (N in all) saving one more tiny unit, so that as evaluated by any individual the immediate loss is $[1 + (N-1)\beta]$, attaching the appropriate weights to the consumption of oneself and of one's contemporaries. This has to be set against the gain in the future. The total gain in physical terms is $(N \cdot k)$ for the future generation as a whole, and let the proportion of that enjoyed by one's own heirs be h; the appropriate assumptions for h will be discussed presently. However, the net gain $G(s)$ from the social contract, as viewed by any individual, will be of the general form:

$$G(s) = N \cdot k \cdot h \cdot \gamma + N \cdot k(1-h)\alpha - 1 - (N-1)\beta. \qquad (6)$$

We can now examine what conditions have to be satisfied for the isolation paradox to hold. Note that (5) indicates the weak form of the preference relation (1). Since we are starting from an atomistic market equilibrium, people, in isolation from the others, do not want to save more than they are doing already. Strictly speaking they should be indifferent between A and B, since the net gain from the change is exactly nil, but we can assume that they prefer not to save when there is no net gain. For condition (2) to hold, we need $G(s) > 0$, i.e. everyone prefers B (saving) by each rather than A (not saving) by each.

$$N \cdot k[h \cdot \gamma + (1-h)\alpha] > 1 + (N-1)\beta. \qquad (7)$$

When (7) is consistent with (5), we have the isolation paradox holding, and people are willing to join in the contract to save but not do so individually. To get this result, the assumption that was made by Marglin and myself has been found to be unacceptable by many, viz., that individuals do not discriminate between their own heirs and the rest of the future generation, i.e. $\gamma = \alpha$. As can be readily checked, exactly the same formula holds if $\lambda = h = 0$, i.e. if the fruits of my saving (both in individualistic saving and social contract) accrue to the future generation in general and not to my own heirs. Neither, I agree, is a good assumption, and it will be shown presently that neither is necessary. But before that, the consequence of this assumption, however bad, can be checked immediately. Then from (5), $k = (1/\alpha)$ and condition (7) reduces to:

$$1 > \beta. \qquad (7.1)$$

The result is independent of the value of N, provided, of course, $N > 1$. It is quite reasonable to assume that $\beta < 1$, i.e. I value my consumption more than that of my other contemporaries.

In a closely-reasoned note on this problem, commenting on Marglin's paper, Lind has suggested an alternative set of assumptions. In effect, he assumes that the individual can pass on (if he chooses) all the fruits of his own saving to his own heir without any part of it going to others in the future generation. Then: $\lambda = 1$, $h = 1/N$, and $k = 1/\gamma$, so that (7) reduces to:

$$\frac{1}{\gamma} > \frac{\beta}{\alpha}. \tag{7.2}$$

We cannot be so sure that (7.2) will hold as (7.1). If $(1/\gamma) > (\beta/\alpha)$, the individuals will be willing to join the contract; and if $(1/\gamma) < (\beta/\alpha)$, the individuals will not be willing to do so. Indeed, if the latter condition held, it would be easy to show that they will be prepared to join a contract to *reduce* savings; this too fits the isolation paradox, except it now runs the other way, with B standing for reducing the saving by one unit each, and A as before. In between these values lies the case where everything is fine with atomistic allocation, and the case of $(1/\gamma) = (\beta/\alpha)$ can be seen to be one where my relative evaluation of your heir's consumption (α) and your consumption (β), exactly corresponds to your relative evaluation of your heir's consumption (γ) vis-à-vis your own (1). Lind finds this a 'reasonable' assumption.[18]

The difficulty with Lind's assumption of the balance of emotions is that it makes insufficient allowance for the personal nature of egoism. My egoism might not extend as much to my heirs vis-à-vis yours, as it applies to me personally vis-à-vis you. The longer the distance in time that we consider the more is this likely to be the case. So that $(\alpha/\beta) > \gamma$, does not seem to be a particularly bad assumption. However, for the sake of argument, let us grant this balance of emotions, and assume that γ is exactly equal to (α/β), no more and no less. There is the further question of $\lambda = 1$, which is the only case Lind discusses. If it is assumed that there is a gap between the marginal productivity of capital and the rate of interest, λ must be below 1.[19] But even when there is no such gap, in a society with taxation this will happen again. Even if we assume, in a competitive

18. Lind, *op. cit.*, pp. 341–2, 345. In commenting on my *Economic Journal* paper on the subject, the same suggestion was made in a personal communication (dated 4 April 1962) by the late Sir Dennis Robertson.

19. In much of the literature on economic development, it is conventional to assume that the market wage rate is above the social opportunity cost of labour, which will also make $\lambda < 1$, since the marginal benefits to the owners of capital will fall short of the marginal benefits to the community. This is a sufficient assumption for $\lambda < 1$, but, of course, not necessary.

dream world, that no one is prevented from enjoying the full 'return' of his own investment through taxes, this does not rule out taxes, such as estate duties, that apply to unrequited transfers. And these too will make $\lambda < 1$. This is not to say that Marglin's and my assumption of $\alpha = \gamma$, or alternatively, of $\lambda = 0$, is a good assumption, but neither is the other special case of $\lambda = 1$, with exactly balanced emotions. The natural question to ask is what happens when λ takes a value in between these extremes, i.e. when it is selected from the open interval $]0, 1[$. The answer is that the condition for the isolation paradox remains *exactly* the same as with $\lambda = 0$. Lind's case of $\lambda = 1$ is the one exceptional value; the rest of the interval gives the same condition. This is shown below.

Let us assume first that in the case of the social contract to save more, my heir gets only λ part of my own savings, and nothing of other people's savings. In that case:

$$h = \frac{\lambda}{N}. \tag{8.1}$$

Then the required condition (7) reduces to:

$$[\lambda \cdot \gamma + (N - \lambda) \alpha] \cdot k > 1 + (N - 1) \beta. \tag{7.3}$$

In view of (5) and the Lindian balanced emotions $\gamma = (\alpha/\beta)$, this is equivalent to:

$$\beta < 1. \tag{7.1}$$

Precisely the same condition, as with $\alpha = \gamma$, or with $\lambda = 0$.

Now, this assumption of my heir getting only λ part of the fruits of my savings in the social contract with other people's heirs getting the whole of the fruit of their savings *plus* $(1 - \lambda)$ part of the result of my saving, seems a poor one. Surely my heirs will do better than this from the social contract; they can expect to get a part of the $(1 - \lambda)$ portion of other people's savings that goes to future generations in general. But, if this is the case, (7.1) will be *a fortiori* sufficient for the isolation paradox, as can be readily checked from the fact that $\gamma > \alpha$, since $\gamma = \alpha/\beta$, and $\beta < 1$. If (7.1) is sufficient to induce me to join the contract even with the minimum share of my heirs, it is naturally sufficient if they get a higher share.

3   The Rate of Discount

To derive the formula for the social rate of discount implicit in this, we have to specify the value of h more than working with its minimum magnitude. The symmetrical assumption is the following: each set of heirs get λ part of the results of their progenitor's savings, while $(1 - \lambda)$ goes to a general pool of the 'future generation', out of the total of which each set again gets $(1/N)$ portion. It is readily seen:

$$h = \frac{1}{N}. \tag{8.2}$$

And with this symmetrical sharing of the general pool, the social rate of discount (ρ) is given by exactly the same formula as that of Lind (except in the special case of $\lambda = 0$):[20]

$$\rho = \frac{1 + (N - 1)\,\beta}{\gamma + (N - 1)\,\alpha} - 1. \tag{9}$$

Marglin's formula coincides with this only when $\alpha = \gamma$, or when N is very large, which reduces this to $[(\beta/\alpha) - 1]$, and also reduces Marglin's to the same value. However, the difference between the private and the social rate of discount continues to hold, except when the knife-edge balance happens to occur. This is the dual to the problem of the optimum rate of saving, and (7.1) can be seen to be sufficient for the social rate to be below the private rate of discount.

Representing the private rate of discount by π, it is seen from (5) and (9) that:

$$\rho \underset{>}{\overset{<}{=}} \pi, \text{ according as: } \frac{1 + (N - 1)\,\beta}{1 + (N - 1)\,(\alpha/\gamma)} \underset{>}{\overset{<}{=}} \frac{1}{\lambda + (1 - \lambda)\,(\alpha/\gamma)}. \tag{10}$$

Lind gets $\rho = \pi$; by assuming the balance of emotions $(\alpha/\gamma) = \beta$, and that $\lambda = 1$. The more general set of conditions is given by taking (10) as an equality; there are pairs of values of (λ, γ) that satisfy this equality, of which Lind's is one. However, there is nothing at all in the market mechanism to guarantee that we shall indeed have one of these critical pairs holding. Of course, it *can* happen, but it will be an accidental outcome.

Marglin's case can be obtained from (10) by putting $\alpha = \gamma$, a different balance of emotions. This reduces (10) to:

$$\rho \underset{>}{\overset{<}{=}} \pi; \text{ according as } \beta \underset{>}{\overset{<}{=}} 1. \tag{10.1}$$

We would get the same condition if $\lambda = 0$, and $h = 0$, when the social rate of discount is as given in Marglin.[21] Suppose, however, we grant

---

20. Lind points out that the assumption of identical individuals is quite crucial for this formulation, and indeed the existence, of the social rate of discount, *op. cit.*, pp. 342-5.
21. Equation (13), Marglin, *op. cit.*, p. 106.

(as in our discussion of the dual problem to this) that Lind's emotional balance holds; i.e. $(\alpha/\beta) = \gamma$; then (10) becomes:

$$\rho \underset{>}{\overset{<}{=}} \pi, \text{ according as } \beta(1-\lambda) \underset{>}{\overset{<}{=}} (1-\lambda). \tag{10.2}$$

The quality holds only in Lind's special case of $\lambda = 1$. For any other value of λ, (10.2) reduces into (10.1). Thus, while $\lambda = 1$, and $\lambda = 0$, look like two extreme cases, they are not symmetrical in the generality of their respective results.

4 Rich They, Poor Us

Finally, the point has been raised[22] whether the isolation paradox in savings is at all likely to arise when it is borne in mind that the future generation is going to be a great deal more wealthy than the present generation. In the determination of the social rate of discount, this will undoubtedly be an important consideration. This can be checked readily by looking at (9), where the wealth of the future generation will tend to make the values of γ and α relatively lower. However, will this affect the condition for the isolation paradox to hold? Not at all! It is seen from (7.1) and (7.2) that a proportionate fall in γ and α (the values attached to the consumption of the future generation) vis-à-vis the values attached to the consumption of members of the present generation, will not make any difference to the fulfilment of the conditions.

The explanation is simple; the fact that the future generation will be wealthier has already been taken into account in the atomistic allocation of resources, and the average wealth of the future generation vis-à-vis that of the present generation does not affect the *relative* profitability of atomistic allocation and the social contract. Indeed substituting the value of k from (5) into (7), we find that (7) is equivalent to:

$$\frac{N[h \cdot \gamma + (1-h)\alpha]}{[\lambda \cdot \gamma + (1-\lambda)\alpha]} > 1 + (N-1)\beta. \tag{7*}$$

In this general condition a proportionate change in the values of γ and α would leave the fulfilment of the inequality entirely unchanged.

Exactly the same is true, naturally, in the dual to this problem, i.e. in the difference between the private and the social rate of discounts.

22. Tullock, *op cit.*, pp. 333–5; Harberger, *op. cit.*, Section 4.

A proportionate change in γ and α will leave condition (10) exactly the same, as is obvious from its form.

5 Conclusions

In Section 1 two specific problems concerning individual and social actions were studied. One, the isolation paradox, is an N-person extension of the two-person non-zero-sum game of the Prisoners' Dilemma. Here each individual has a strictly dominant strategy, and the pursuit of this by each produces an overall result that is Pareto-inferior. Individuals can do better than this by collusion, but the collusive solution requires enforcement.

The second, the assurance problem, which is sometimes confused with the first, has a different analytical structure and implies different policy questions. Here there is no strictly dominant strategy, and one of the equilibrium points in the non-cooperative game may be Pareto-optimal. Whether this will be the outcome of the non-cooperative game or whether the outcome will be Pareto-inferior depends on what each individual expects about the others' actions. To get out of the problem all that is necessary is that each individual is assured that the others are doing the 'right' thing, and then it is in one's own interest also to do the 'right' thing. No enforcement is necessary.

Marglin's and my discussion of the inoptimality of market savings corresponds to the isolation paradox, whereas that of Baumol, and of Vickrey (in the context of philanthropy), corresponds to the assurance problem. The distinction is important analytically as well as for policy decisions.

In the last three sections, Marglin's and my formulation of the problem of the inoptimality of market savings was examined as an application of the paradox of isolation. It should be conceded immediately that if one is ready to make some rather special assumptions, the problem can in fact be assumed away. Lind's conditions of balance ($\gamma = \alpha/\beta$, and $\lambda = 1$) achieve this,[23] and, as we have seen, so does a family of pairs of values of (γ, λ). However, there is nothing in the market mechanism that will ensure this achievement. This inoptimality of the market mechanism, and the possibility of a social contract by which everyone will agree to do something he would not

23. Lind's condition is not, of course, in conflict with the claim that 'this possibility of the apparent paradox is present whenever his relative valuation of others' consumption is such that he would prefer them to sacrifice some consumption for the future generations' (Sen, *op. cit.*, p. 488). With $\gamma = (\alpha/\beta)$, and $\lambda = 1$, the condition is not met, and the consequence does not, naturally, follow. See also Marglin, *op. cit.*, pp. 100-2.

be ready to do individually, is not a surprising result when viewed in the context of games such as the Prisoners' Dilemma. It is a paradox only as an apparent one, as most paradoxes are. Even from the point of view of usual theories of optimum allocation through decentralized decisions, the result need not be viewed as particularly contrary, for the basis of it lies in an *external* concern for members of the future generation vis-à-vis those of the present.

If the emotional balance of the type proposed by Lind is taken $(\gamma = \alpha/\beta)$, then the optimality of the market rate of saving and that of the market rate of discount are unlikely to hold in any economy that we know of. With this type of balanced emotions, the isolation paradox can be ruled out, as Lind does, by assuming $\lambda = 1$. Marglin's and my assumptions about people's concern for others $(\gamma = \alpha)$ differ from this, but if $\lambda = 0$ then, of course, the conditions for the existence of the isolation problem are the same as with $\gamma = \alpha$, no matter what emotional assumptions we make. While $\lambda = 1$ and $\lambda = 0$, represent two extreme cases, their positions are not symmetrical. In fact, for any value of λ in between these limits, i.e. from the open interval $]0, 1[$, the condition for the isolation paradox, with Lindian balanced emotions, will be exactly the same as with $\lambda = 0$, i.e. precisely the result we get from Marglin's and my assumptions.

Finally, the question of the future generation being, on the average, much richer than the present generation was studied as grounds for an objection that has been raised against the chances of the isolation paradox.[24] It was shown that a change in the average wealth of the future generation vis-à-vis that of the present generation, bringing about a change in α and γ in the same proportion, leave the possibility of the isolation paradox completely unchanged.

---

24. Tullock, *op. cit.*, 333–5; Harberger, *op. cit.*, Section 4. Harberger has a further argument which we have not discussed. 'The third argument (c), best reflected by Sen and Marglin, smacks of charity . . . . My reaction to this is simple: any individual who wants to help others, and to make sure that his contribution is not dissipated, can do so by selecting one or more people of the present generation to help' (pp. 14–15). This seems a good way of working off one's irrepressible urge towards charity, but surely this need not cure the mis-allocation in the rate of saving.

6
Terminal Capital and Optimum Savings

1 *The Fundamental Relations*

There are at least three political elements in the formulation of an optimum savings exercise in terms of maximizing the sum of utilities within a finite horizon, viz. (i) the choice of the utility function, (ii) the choice of the time horizon, and (iii) the choice of the terminal stock of capital. Of this the first problem is an inevitable part of any optimization exercise, but the latter two are the results of confining our attention to a finite time period. However, such finite programmes fit in more easily with the convenience of planning, and the question is not really one of a completely arbitrary break in the future, since the terminal stock of capital provides an adjustable link between the period within the horizon and the period beyond. It could even be argued that if problem (iii) is well solved, the arbitrariness of problem (ii) can be satisfactorily eliminated.

Much of this note is concerned with problem (iii). We shall assume that the problems (i) and (ii) have already been solved in a simple manner, so that the exercise has already been reduced to one of maximizing the sum of utilities given by a specified utility function, over a given time period T. The utility function depends only on consumption, $C(t)$, and is taken to be of the constant elasticity type, beyond a 'subsistence' consumption, $\bar{C}$.

$$U(t) = A \cdot [C(t) - \bar{C}]^{\alpha}. \tag{1}$$

An earlier version of this note was written in 1964 when the author was Visiting Professor of Economics at the University of California at Berkeley. I have benefited from the comments of Sukhamoy Chakravarty, Richard Goodwin, Jan Graaff, and Stephen Marglin. I am also very grateful to Maurice Dobb for clarifying some of the issues discussed in this note.

From C. H. Fenstein (ed.), *Socialism, Capitalism and Economic Growth*, Essays Presented to Maurice Dobb (Cambridge: Cambridge University Press, 1967), 40–53.

For a concave utility function with diminishing marginal utility, we assume $\alpha < 1$. The marginal utility is given by:

$$u(t) = \frac{dU(t)}{dC} = A \cdot \alpha \cdot [C(t) - \bar{C}]^{\alpha-1}. \tag{1a}$$

To simplify our calculations, we choose our units such that $(A \cdot \alpha)$ equals unity. There is no loss of generality involved here, and it is only a problem of normalization. Thus modified, the marginal utility can be taken to be:

$$u(t) = [C(t) - \bar{C}]^{\alpha-1}. \tag{1b}$$

We assume a constant output–capital ratio (b) so that the rate of accumulation is given by:

$$\dot{K}(t) = b \cdot K(t) - C(t), \tag{2}$$

The sum of utility over the period up to T, we call 'period welfare', or simply welfare, denoted by W.

$$W = \int_0^T U[C(t)] \cdot dt. \tag{3}$$

The problem is to maximize W, subject to the initial condition:

$$K(0) = K_0 \tag{4}$$

and a terminal stock, K_T, the decisions on which will be our primary concern, in what follows.

With $\bar{C}$ subsistence consumption, we can define a subsistence capital stock $(\bar{K})$, such that

$$\bar{K} = \frac{\bar{C}}{b}. \tag{5}$$

We can define over-subsistence capital stock, $S(t)$, as the capital stock over and above $\bar{K}$.

$$S(t) = K(t) - \bar{K}. \tag{6}$$

The terminal capital stock, K_T, can be specified in terms of the initial stock, as Chakravarty[1] does. Since he takes $\bar{C} = 0$, $K(t)$ can be expressed as simply an accumulated value of K_0 at the exponential rate (g) to be chosen. This is not convenient in our exercise, how-

1. S. Chakravarty, 'Optimal Savings with Finite Planning Horizon', *International Economic Review*, 3 (September 1972).

ever, since $\bar{C} \geqslant 0$, but we can use the same device for $S(T)$.

$$K_T = S(0) \cdot e^{gT} + \bar{K}. \tag{7}$$

We know of course, from (6), that

$$S(0) = K_0 - \bar{K}. \tag{6a}$$

Since over-subsistence capital cannot grow faster than at the rate b (corresponding to zero over-subsistence consumption), we require $g \leqslant b$.

Within these conditions, the optimal time path of capital can be obtained by solving the Euler–Lagrange equation, and checking that the second-order conditions are also satisfied.[2]

$$S(t) = A_1 \cdot e^{bt} + A_2 \cdot e^{bt/(1-\alpha)}. \tag{8}$$

The two constants, A_1 and A_2, are solved by using the initial and the terminal conditions, i.e. equations (4) and (7), taken with equation (6a). Then by using equation (2), and remembering that $\dot{K}(t) = \dot{S}(t)$, we obtain the following optimal path of consumption:

$$C(t) = \frac{S(0) \cdot \alpha \cdot b \cdot (e^{bT} - e^{gT})}{(1 - \alpha)(e^{bT/(1-\alpha)} - e^{bT})} \cdot e^{bt/(1-\alpha)} + \bar{C}. \tag{9}$$

The political difficulties in choosing K_T, or what comes to the same thing here, g, has been discussed extensively by Graaff.[3] We woud like to go into this problem, but before that we must examine a result of Chakravarty that 'the best consumption profiles are, in general, insensitive to changes in terminal capital stock within a wide range' (p. 342). Chakravarty obtains the result on the basis of some numerical examples. We shall instead try first to get an algebraic formula for 'sensitivity' and then apply his numerical values and other ones.

2   Sensitivity of Best Consumption Profiles to Variations in Terminal Capital

It is readily seen from equation (9) that the optimum consumption profiles all have an exponential component and a constant component. It is, naturally, the former component that is dependent on the assumption of the terminal capital stock. But it will also be noticed

2. See *ibid.*, p. 343. Note that the case $\alpha = 0$ is avoided, when we get multiple roots.
3. J. de V. Graaff, *Theoretical Welfare Economics* (Cambridge, 1957), Chapter VI.

that the exponential growth rate of over-subsistence consumption is given simply by $b/(1-\alpha)$, which is independent of g, i.e. of our terminal assumption. In fact writing $x(t)$ for over-subsistence consumption at time t, we can easily check that:[4]

$$x(t) = x(0) \cdot e^{bt/(1-\alpha)} \qquad (9a)$$

This means that an idea of the sensitivity of the whole path of $x(t)$ can be obtained by examining the sensitivity of $x(0)$ to the terminal assumption. We define a 'sensitivity indicator', η, by the following:

$$\eta = \left| \frac{dx(0)}{dg} \middle/ \frac{x(0)}{g} \right| \qquad (10)$$

We take the absolute value of the elasticity of $x(0)$ with respect to g, since we are interested in the magnitude of the elasticity and not in its sign, which, incidentally, will be always negative.

From (9), (9a) and (10), we get:

$$\eta = \frac{g \cdot T \cdot e^{gT}}{e^{bT} - e^{gT}}. \qquad (11)$$

Following Chakravarty,[5] we take $T = 20$, and $b = 0.33$. We try out the following ten values of g. The sensitivity is seen to be quite great for high values of g.[6] (See Table 6.1.)

Since Chakravarty took values of g within the closed range (0.05, 0.15), the sensitivity was very small. So his result is entirely correct. But since this low sensitivity result is not generally valid, i.e. is not independent of the numerical assumption, the question arises as to what is the relevant range for g. As higher values of g are taken, the sensitivity indicator rises abruptly, and with g approaching b, grows without bound.

How big a change is one from $g = 0.05$ to $g = 0.15$? It shifts the size of final over-subsistence capital from being 2.7 times the initial level to 20 times the initial level. But in the same period, over-subsistence consumption (in his model total consumption) grows about sixty thousand times, given by $e^{bT/(1-\alpha)}$, when $b = 0.33$, $T = 20$, $\alpha = 0.4$. If we treat this as total consumption, a shift of

---

4. This corresponds to the Ramsey result that marginal return to capital must equal the rate of fall of marginal utility, in an optimal path. See F. P. Ramsey, 'A Mathematical Theory of Saving', *Economic Journal*, 38 (December 1928).

5. Chakravarty, 'Optimal Savings with Finite Planning Horizon'.

6. Since this paper was written, a similar point has been made by A. Maneschi, in his 'Optimal Savings with Finite Planning Horizon: A Note', *International Economic Review*, 7 (January 1966). See also Chakravarty's 'Reply' in the same number.

TABLE 6.1   Terminal capital assumption (g) and the
sensitivity of over-subsistence consumption (η)

g	η	g	η
0.05	0.004	0.29	4.733
0.10	0.020	0.30	7.300
0.15	0.084	0.31	12.610
0.20	0.321	0.32	28.920
0.25	1.265	0.325	61.759

capital stock from 2.7 times to 20 times the initial level is not really
very big. If, instead, we assume the existence of a considerable subsistence level, the proportionate growth of *total* consumption will of
course be very much less; the phenomenally high rate of growth of
over-subsistence is coupled with starting at a level very near zero. But
in that case a shift from $g = 0.05$ to $g = 0.15$ does not change the
total terminal capital stock very much. Indeed assuming that 90 per
cent of the initial output represents subsistence requirement (as
seems to be the case in some underdeveloped countries), that shift
changes total capital stock from being 1.2 times the original value to
2.9 times that, which is a much narrower change.

Thus while Chakravarty's insensitivity result is entirely correct for
the range of values he confined his attention to, it does not eliminate
the need for facing Graaff's problem[7] of the determination of the
terminal capital stock. In the sections that follow, we concern ourselves with this question.

3   Definition and Use of a 'Terminal Margin'

What constitutes a 'proper' terminal stock? It is reasonable to argue
that if the stock $K(T)$ does not succeed in producing an output equal
to the terminal consumption $C(T)$, there is trouble immediately after
the period, for even at zero saving, the economy has to take on a
decline in the consumption level. This is in fact what does happen in
models of the kind discussed, since the optimality problem as posed
there does imply considerable 'eating up' of capital for consumption
purposes, in the last few moments. $K(T)$ can, however, be so selected

7. Graaff, *Theoretical Welfare Economics*, Chapter VI.

as to prevent this. In fact, we may go further and assume that $K(T)$ should be sufficient to produce enough output to invest a certain proportion of it, say λ, and still be left with $C(T)$ consumption as determined by the optimum path. We require that $1 > \lambda \geqslant 0$. In fact, $\lambda = 0$, corresponds to the first case of no investment.

We can call λ the 'terminal margin'. If $\lambda = 0.1$, this means that the terminal capital should be big enough to allow 10 per cent saving of the output in year T, and even after that there would be enough output left to meet the entire requirement of consumption as given by the optimal path for period T. The terminal margin being positive prevents the possibility of an immediate drop in consumption just beyond the horizon. The value judgement about how much of a margin over and above this should be left for the society at point T, is expressed pithily by the choice of a λ from the interval $(0, 1)$.

We now follow up the optimization problem in terms of such a margin. We retain, however, equations (8) and (9a), giving us the optimal growth rules for capital and consumption. As in the previous exercise:

$$K_0 - \bar{K} = S(0) = A_1 + A_2. \tag{12}$$

We know from (2), (8), and (12), when $\dot{S}(0)$ refers to the right-hand derivative of $S(t)$ with respect to time at $t = 0$:

$$x(0) = S(0) \cdot b - \dot{S}(0)$$
$$= A_2 \cdot b \cdot z \tag{13}$$

putting

$$z = \frac{\alpha}{\alpha - 1}. \tag{13a}$$

Since $\alpha < 1$, z is negative when $\alpha > 0$ and positive when $\alpha < 0$. The case $\alpha = 0$ is avoided (see footnote 2 above). From (13) and (9a), we have:

$$A_2 = \frac{x(T) \cdot e^{(b \cdot T)/(\alpha - 1)}}{b \cdot z} \tag{14}$$

In view of the postulated terminal condition:

$$x(T) = S(T) \cdot (1 - \lambda) \cdot b \tag{15}$$

From (6a), (8), (13), (14), and (15), the value of $x(0)$ is found to be:

$$x(0) = \frac{b \cdot z \cdot (1 - \lambda) \cdot e^{bzT}}{z + (1 - \lambda)(e^{bzT} - 1)} [K_0 - \bar{K}]. \tag{16}$$

Note that for $\lambda < 1$, $x(0) > 0$, no matter whether $z > 0$, or < 0. And this, coupled with (9), gives the optimum consumption profile:

$$C(t) = \bar{C} + x(0) \cdot e^{(b \cdot t)/(1-\alpha)} \tag{17}$$

The augmentation of the over-subsistence capital stock in this period is given by:

$$J = \frac{S(T)}{S(0)} = \frac{z \cdot e^{bT}}{z + (1-\lambda)(e^{bzT} - 1)}. \tag{18}$$

To put it in our old terms, we can convert the relation into an exponential one at the rate g:

$$J = e^{gT}. \tag{19}$$

Incidentally for our old values of $b = 0.33$, $\alpha = 0.4$, and putting the 'terminal margin' $\lambda = 0.1$, we get $g = 0.288$, and the corresponding value of sensitivity, η, is around 4.

The method of fixing the terminal stock through a 'terminal margin' may, in fact, be quite useful in practical decision making. The optimal time profile in our solution satisfies the condition of maximizing utility within the horizon, and ends up in a situation where the new level of consumption is (a) sustainable for $\lambda \geqslant 0$, and (b) further expandable with a leeway determined by the 'terminal margin' λ for $\lambda > 0$.

The method used here is a cross between Radner's Problems I and II,[8] for $\delta = 1$, and $T < \infty$. Radner's Problem I consists of maximizing total welfare within a horizon; and Problem II is the maximization of one-period welfare of the final stock at T. Here we have instead the problem posed as maximizing total welfare within the horizon subject to a boundary condition that makes the final stock exceed the requirement of the last period optimal consumption by a specific margin. The closest to our presentation is that of Goodwin,[9] in terms of maximizing total welfare within the horizon subject to having a specified terminal rate of growth. Indeed our presentation can be readily translated into his, though the method used here is probably simpler, and may allow us to see perhaps more clearly what issues are involved.[10]

---

8. R. Radner, *Optimal Growth in a Linear-Logarithmic Economy*, Center for Research in Management Science, University of California at Berkeley, Technical Report No. 18.

9. R. M. Goodwin, 'The Optimum Growth Path for an Underdeveloped Economy', *Economic Journal*, 71 (December 1961).

10. However, Goodwin in 'The Optimum Growth Path for an Underdeveloped Economy', bases his notion of welfare on individual utility and per capita consumption, and as such catches the impact of a changing population, which makes his analysis more interesting than

4 *Some Quantitative Exercises*

Before taking up some specific numerical values, we may introduce a measure of over-all growth achieved during the period T. J gives the growth rate of over-subsistence capital. We can define a corresponding growth-ratio of all capital, and call it the Over-all Growth Ratio.

$$G = \frac{S(T) + \bar{K}}{S(0) + \bar{K}} = \frac{J + m}{1 + m}, \qquad (20)$$

where m is the ratio of subsistence consumption to over-subsistence output in the initial period. If s is the share of subsistence consumption in initial output, we can check that:

$$m = \frac{s}{1 - s}. \qquad (21)$$

It is to be noted that in this model G is not specified from outside, but (given λ) is determined by the internal logic of utility maximization. It is, thus, a result of optimization in this model.

We take a time horizon of 20 years, a subsistence consumption ratio of 0.9, and the following set of numerical assumptions.[11]

$$b = \begin{bmatrix} 0.33 \\ 0.25 \end{bmatrix}, \quad \alpha = \begin{bmatrix} 0.4 \\ 0.1 \end{bmatrix}, \quad \text{and} \quad \lambda = \begin{bmatrix} 0.2 \\ 0.1 \\ 0.0 \end{bmatrix}.$$

The results are presented in Table 6.2.[12] The optimal growth ratio shows considerable variation, but even the lower ratios are relatively high. For example even if we take (i) $b = 0.25$ (i.e. a capital-output ratio of 4), (ii) $\alpha = 0.1$ (i.e. a 10 per cent increase in over-subsistence

---

ours, in many ways. See also S. Chakravarty and L. Lefeber, 'An Optimizing Planning Model', *Economic Weekly*, Annual Number (February 1965), for a terminal constraint in the shape of post-terminal rates of growth in a multi-sector model.

11. The assumption of $s = 0.9$ fits many underdeveloped countries but not the developed ones, unless subsistence is defined in some special way, e.g. in terms of habitual standard of living. However, this is not an especially limiting assumption here, for in any case the use of a constant capital-output ratio is not easily justifiable for a developed country. Even for the underdeveloped countries it may be a bad assumption as discussed in B. Horvat, 'The Optimum Rate of Investment', *Economic Journal*, 68 (December 1958); T. N. Srinivasan, 'Investment Criteria and Choice of Techniques of Production', *Yale Economic Essays*, 2 (1962); A. K. Sen, 'A Note on Tinbergen on the Optimum Rate of Saving', *Economic Journal*, 67 (December 1957); but see also J. Tinbergen, 'Optimum Savings and Utility Maximization Over Time', *Econometrica*, 28 (April 1960); and Goodwin, 'The Optimum Growth Path for an Underdeveloped Economy'.

12. Miss Edita Tan did the numerical computations.

TABLE 6.2   Optimal growth ratio with alternative numerical assumptions

Assumptions			Results		
b	α	λ	J	g	G
0.33	0.4	0.2	336.4	0.29	34.5
		0.1	315.0	0.29	32.4
		0	296.2	0.29	30.5
	0.1	0.2	155.0	0.25	16.4
		0.1	141.1	0.25	15.0
		0	129.4	0.24	13.8
0.25	0.4	0.2	69.2	0.21	7.8
		0.1	64.5	0.21	7.3
		0	60.7	0.21	7.0
	0.1	0.2	36.5	0.18	4.5
		0.1	33.3	0.18	4.2
		0	30.7	0.17	4.0

consumption increases utility by only 1 per cent), (iii) $\lambda = 0$ (i.e. we do not leave the people 20 years from now with any 'terminal margin'), even then the optimal growth ratio requires a four-fold expansion of the country's productive capital stock in 20 years. This is equivalent to a compound rate of growth of 7 per cent per period; though of course the optimal path of the capital stock is not an exponential one (see equation (8)).

5   Sensitivity to the Terminal Conditions

We noted earlier that while in some regions the optimal growth path was rather insensitive to the assumption of terminal capital, in other regions the sensitivity was quite high. As the value of g rose, the path became more and more sensitive. Now that the problem has been redefined in terms of a 'terminal margin' (λ), it is relevant to ask how the sensitivity aspects look in terms of the terminal margin. The problem is, however, not very well-defined. In the case of terminal capital as expressed by the equivalent compound accumulation rate (g), we considered the variation of the path in response to a given percentage change in g. But λ being itself defined as a percentage of income, its percentage variations do not give a very meaningful measure.

One consideration to pose is to continue to take the earlier definition of sensitivity (η) in terms of g, and to translate any λ into the corresponding g. Looking at Table 6.2 this way, we find that for terminal margins varying from 0 to 0.2, the value of g is fairly high almost throughout. That is, while the correspondence does depend on the capital–output ratio assumed and the elasticity of the utility function, for the values assumed here, g lies mostly in the 'sensitive' range (as can be seen by examining Table 6.1).

The above, however, is a somewhat different question from the one concerning the sensitivity of the optimal path to changes in the assumption of the terminal margin. One indicator of the latter is the variation in J, the over-all growth rate of over-subsistence capital, or in G, the overall growth ratio of total capital, with respect to variations in λ. Unlike in the previous exercise, J and G are not the assumptions of the exercise but their results, and as such the sensitivity of J and G to changes in λ is interesting. One of the remarkable aspects of Table 6.2 is the strikingly small size of the variation in J and G as the value of λ is raised from 0 per cent to as much as 20 per cent. Since the terminal margin is simply the saving rate in the terminal year, it is very likely to be contained within this region. However, even if we consider wider variations of λ within the entire region of 0 to 100 per cent, the variations in J and G are not very great. Table 6.3 gives the values of J and G as λ is raised from 0 to 1. As the elasticity of the utility function is changed from 0.1 to 0.4, the response becomes even smaller. Compared with the phenomenal

TABLE 6.3   Sensitivity of over-all growth to the terminal margin

	$\alpha = 0.1$		$\alpha = 0.4$	
λ	J	G	J	G
0.0	129.4	13.8	296.2	30.5
0.1	141.1	15.0	315.0	32.4
0.2	155.0	16.4	336.4	34.5
0.5	220.2	22.9	422.3	43.1
1.0	735.1	74.4	735.1	74.4

Assumptions: $T = 20, b = 0.33$.

scale of the growth possibility, it is interesting to note the relatively limited variation of J and G in the optimal path as λ is varied from one extreme of 0 to the other of 1.

We do not intend to go much further into the sensitivity question here. Obviously much depends on the precise numerical values and we have not given here anything more than some specific results in some specific regions that we find empirically relevant. Others might prefer to take different assumptions. But one relatively interesting aspect of the entire sensitivity question is worth emphasizing. The sensitivity of the optimal path to the terminal margin can be split into two questions, viz. (i) the sensitivity of the terminal capital stock (or of g) to the terminal margin, and (ii) the sensitivity of the optimal path to the terminal capital stock (or to g). Chakravarty discussed the latter question, and for his range of values found the response to be insensitive. By taking values outside this range, we found that the sensitivity was quite great. Furthermore, it is seen that to make economic sense, i.e. to avoid 'eating up' of capital, λ has to be specified to be non-negative,[13] and this puts g (for Chakravarty's quantitative assumptions) in the sensitive region rather than in the insensitive one.[14]

However, even in this region the sensitivity of type (i) is low, so that over-all sensitivity of the optimal path to the terminal margin, which depends on both (i) and (ii), may not be high. In Table 6.2 itself it can be seen that the three alternative values of g, varying the terminal margin (terminal saving rate) from 0 per cent to 20 per cent, changes the value of g remarkably little. The value of g is seen to vary greatly with changes in the assumption of the output-capital ratio and considerably with changes in the assumption about the utility function elasticity, but not with changes in the terminal margin. And this is found to be so for all the alternative combination of b and α considered here.

From these quantitative values, it becomes possible to argue the following. While the optimal path is sensitive to variations in the terminal capital in the relevant region, the terminal capital stock implied by the economically meaningful assumptions about the terminal margin is itself rather insensitive to the variations in the margin. Thus the sensitivity of the path to the terminal condition

13. Note that in this model $\lambda > 0$ is sufficient for there being no eating up of capital any time during the entire period up to the horizon if $1 > \alpha > 0$. See Section 7 below.

14. For all values of g considered by Chakravarty, viz. 0.05 to 0.15, we have $\lambda < 0$ for his assumptions of output–capital ratio ($b = 0.33$) and elasticity for the utility function ($\alpha = 0.4$), and indeed for all alternative values of b and α considered in Table 6.2. With $\lambda \geqslant 0$, g is higher and yields a higher value of sensitivity.

newly defined may not be very high even when the path is sensitive to the terminal capital stock as such. This lends support to Chakravarty's insight into the sensitivity question, once the terminal condition has been appropriately redefined.

6 Terminal Capital and Terminal Margin

The precise relationship between solving a finite-horizon, optimum savings problem with (a) a postulated terminal capital stock, and that with (b) the use of a postulated terminal margin as outlined here, is somewhat intricate, and some technicalities may be cleared up. Given the initial capital stock, problem (a) states: maximize W, subject to $K(T) = K_T$. Given the existence of an optimal solution to this problem and its uniqueness, both of which can be easily established given our assumptions, this will define a unique savings ratio $v(T)$ for the terminal point.[15] What is more important in this optimality-relationship is that not only is $v(T)$ a function of K_T, but the inverse function also exists, i.e. given a value of the terminal savings ratio $v(T)$ we can find out the corresponding K_T. Furthermore, the domain of the inverse function, i.e. of $K_T = f[v(T)]$, includes the closed interval $(0, 1)$, as is obvious from (18). Hence we can specify a given λ, between 0 and 1, and corresponding to it the proper value of K_T can be found, i.e. a K_T such that problem (a) when solved will yield an optimum solution with $v(T) = \lambda$.

We did not define problem (b) as: maximize W, subject to $v(T) = \lambda$. We defined it instead as: maximize W, subject to $K(T) = f(\lambda)$. Hence all the properties of optimum solutions of problem (a) are preserved in problem (b). The trick of stating the problem in terms of λ is simply to restrict the range of the terminal capital stock in terms of which the classical exercise of problem (a) can be carried out, without the danger of having an inevitable prospect of a drop in the level of consumption in the period beyond the horizon.

7 Monotonicity of Savings Rate and Non-negativity of Savings

One interesting feature of both problems (a) and (b) is that the savings rate $v(t)$ will be either monotonically decreasing, or mono-

15. We define $v(t)$ as the ratio of savings to over-subsistence income, i.e.

$$v(t) = \frac{\dot{S}(t)}{S(t) \cdot b}.$$

tonically increasing, or constant throughout the period. It is easy to check that by differentiating $v(t)$ with respect to time we get:

$$\dot{v}(t) = (A_1 \cdot A_2) \cdot H(b, \alpha, t), \tag{22}$$

where H is a function of b, α, and t, but is always positive for $\alpha < 1$, i.e. given diminishing marginal utility. So the sign of $\dot{v}(t)$ is independent of time.

From (12), (13), and (16), we obtain:

$$A_2 = \left[\frac{R}{1-R}\right] A_1, \tag{23}$$

where

$$R = \frac{(1-\lambda) e^{bzT}}{z + (1-\lambda)(e^{bzT} - 1)} \tag{24}$$

Now, for $1 > \alpha > 0$, we have $z < 0$, and $R < 0$. Thus A_1 and A_2 will have opposite signs, and $\dot{v}(t) < 0$, so that the savings rate will be monotonically decreasing. However, if the utility function is bounded on top, and $\alpha < 0$, then $1 > z > 0$, and $R > 0$. It is evident that: $\dot{v}(t) \{\lessgtr\} 0$, according as $R \{\lessgtr\} 1$, which is according to $\lambda \{\lessgtr\} 1/(1-\alpha)$. Thus if the terminal margin is chosen to be equal to $1/(1 - \alpha)$, the optimum profile of the savings ratio will be a stationary one. If the terminal margin is chosen to be lower, the savings rate will monotonically fall, and if higher, will monotonically rise. Since $(b \cdot \lambda)$ and $(b/(1 - \alpha))$ are respectively the postulated terminal rate of growth and the optimum rate of growth of over-subsistence consumption prior to the horizon, the critical values can also be stated in terms of these two magnitudes, making greater intuitive sense.

One important corollary of the monotonicity result is that if we take a utility function with $1 > \alpha > 0$, which is what we have done with our numerical illustrations, then the non-negativity of the terminal margin will automatically ensure positivity of the savings ratio throughout the period. Thus a separate non-negativity constraint on savings, if imposed,[16] will be redundant. Even when the utility function is bounded from the top provided the terminal margin λ is not above $(1/(1 - \alpha))$, the constraint will be redundant. Since the phenomenon of 'eating-up' of capital in these finite-horizon, one-commodity Ramsey-type models is rather disturbing, this result is important. Our method of posing the problem in terms of a postu-

---

16. Cf. Alan Manne, 'Numerical Experiments with a Finite Horizon Planning Model', *Indian Economic Review*, 2 (1967).

lated terminal margin also provides a method of eliminating this irritating feature of the simple optimum savings exercises.

Finally, we might comment on the relevance of a problem on terminal conditions raised by Diamond[17] and Cass.[18] With the possibility of free disposal, it makes obvious sense to pose problem (a) in terms of an inequality constraint on the terminal capital, i.e. as: maximize W, subject to $K(T) \geqslant K_T$. Since problem (b) is simply a suitably truncated problem (a), the same question will apply to our presentation also. It is easy to check, however, that with the possibility of 'eating up' capital, the value of period welfare W must be a *decreasing* function of K_T in the equality-constrained problem. Under these circumstances, the terminal condition even if imposed as a weak inequality, will bind as a strict equality. Hence nothing is lost here in defining the problem in terms of equality-constraints.

It might, however, look as if we have leaped from the frying pan to the fire, since the prospect of 'eating up' of capital with which we avoid the Diamond–Cass problem is itself very disturbing. However, our last result shows that even when the technical *possibility* of 'eating up' of capital exists, an *optimum* solution will not actually involve such an operation provided the terminal margin is chosen from the appropriate range.

8   *Choice of the Terminal Margin*

The problem of determination of the terminal capital stock is of course a political one. It includes the problem of determination of inter-generation distribution of consumption, various aspects of which have been discussed by Pigou, Dobb, Graaff, Baumol, Horvat, Eckstein, Sen, Marglin, and Feldstein,[19] among others. These problems cannot be eliminated. However, in this presentation, we have

17. P. A. Diamond, 'Optimal Growth on a Model of Srinivasan', *Yale Economic Essay*, 4 (Spring 1964).

18. D. Cass, 'Optimum Economic Growth in an Aggregative Model of Capital Accumulation: A Turnpike Theorem', Cowles Foundation Discussion Papers, No. 178.

19. A. C. Pigou, *Economics of Welfare* (London, 1932), pp. 24, 30; M. H. Dobb, *An Essay on Economic Growth and Planning* (London, 1960), Chapter 2; Graaff, *Theoretical Welfare Economics*; W. J. Baumol, *Welfare Economics and the Theory of the State* (Cambridge, Mass., 1952), Chapter 6; Horvat, 'The Optimum Rate of Investment'; Eckstein, 'Investment Criteria for Economic Development and the Theory of Intertemporal Welfare Economics', *Quarterly Journal of Economics*, 71 (February 1957); A. K. Sen, 'On Optimizing the Rate of Saving', *Economic Journal*, 71 (September 1961) [Essay 4 in this volume]; S. A. Marglin, 'The Social Rate of Discount and the Optimal Rate of Investment', *Quarterly Journal of Economics*, 77 (February 1963); M. S. Feldstein, 'The Social Time Preference Discount Rate in Cost–Benefit Analysis', *Economic Journal*, 74 (June 1964).

narrowed down the range of choice considerably by posing the problem in terms of the terminal margin λ, and by imposing the boundary conditions $1 > \lambda \geq 0$. This makes K_T dependent on optimal $C(T)$ and optimal $C(T)$ in its turn is of course dependent on K_T, so that the two problems have been simultaneously solved. The justification of the narrowing down of the range of choice of K_T is a value judgement that can be expected to be shared by most people, viz. that there should not be the necessity of a drop in the absolute level of consumption immediately beyond the horizon. (This requires $\lambda \geq 0$; the other boundary condition $\lambda < 1$ follows from the fact that terminal investment cannot exceed output.) The value judgement in question narrows down the field of choice considerably. Indeed the terminal capital stock is found to be not sensitive to the terminal margin for the empirical values considered.

If my hypothesis is right, i.e. if people would subscribe to the value judgement that the *necessity* of a future fall in consumption immediately beyond the horizon should be avoided, the problem of choice of terminal capital stock becomes considerably simpler. In fact for the numerical assumptions used in Table 6.2, the optimum values of G seem to be quite close to each other even when the terminal margin is varied from 0 to 20 per cent.

The method of optimization used here is a combination of Ramsey's rule about distribution of consumption *within* the horizon, and relating the terminal capital stock (for the period *beyond*) to the experience within the horizon. The latter relation is, however, not a unique one; but it rules out a variety of possible terminal stock assumptions (those that give $\lambda < 0$) by making use of a widely held value judgement. The problem of determining λ from the interval $(0, 1)$ however remains, and this is where the present paper merges with the literature (cited above) on the political questions behind the optimum rate of saving.

7

On Some Debates in Capital Theory

It is well known that the Venerable Subhuti had a conversation with Buddha on transcendental wisdom which was immortalized as the *Vajrachedikaprajñāpāramitā*, the so-called 'Diamond Sutra', translated into Chinese around AD 400 by Kumarajiva from Kucha (Eastern Turkestan); indeed this was the first printed book in the world. What has only very recently come to light is the fact that despite his virtuous life, Subhuti had some lapses, and was born again in this century. Since the lapses were moderately serious, Subhuti was reborn as an economist, and since he was what Buddha called 'a hair-splitting Brahmin' (see *Kassapa-Sihanada Sutta*), Subhuti was destined to specialize in capital theory. One day Subhuti was sighing in his study after reading Venerable Harcourt's survey and a hundred other books and papers on the subject, overwhelmed by the loftiness of the thoughts revealed in these works, when Buddha suddenly appeared, taking pity on his old acquaintance.

Subhuti promptly uncovered his right shoulder, knelt upon his right knee and raising his hands with palms joined, addressed Buddha thus: World-honoured One, have you come to help me out of this mess of measurement of capital?

Buddha said: Verily, I have come on a different purpose. To deflect you from your studies. Do not, O Subhuti, spend your life on a problem that is possibly trivial.

Subhuti said to Buddha: Trivial indeed, World-honoured One, from the standpoint of the 'Ultimate Principle of Reality'. But it is a

This paper has been written for Professor Amiya Kumar Dasgupta, a distinguished alumnus of the LSE, and is to be republished in the *Festschrift* in honour of him edited by Dr Ashok Mitra. [Later published, *Economic Theory and Planning* (London: Oxford University Press, 1974).] The paper was written when I was visiting the Jawaharlal Nehru University in New Delhi.

From *Economica*, 41 (August 1974), 328–35.

serious problem for economics which I have been fated to do in the great cycle of rebirth, and I must do my duty this time. Enlighten me, O Enlightened One.

Buddha said to Subhuti: Why do you want to measure capital, O Subhuti? What good will it do to you?

Subhuti replied: Despite early doubts I have lately become interested in using an aggregate production function. And I would like to have the rate of profit in the economy determined by the marginal product of capital. I know from some of the books I have read that the difficulty in this arises from having more than one capital good and the problem of measuring capital. O, how I wish that capital goods were homogeneous! Seeing you, World-honoured One, an idea occurs to me. Why don't you simply *make* all capital goods homogeneous? So many economists will be grateful to you for this, O Tathāgata.

Then Buddha said: As I have said many times, I am not a magician. I cannot do the impossible, and my admiration is great for those who can change reality at the stroke of a pen. But tell me, Subhuti, do you really believe that having only one homogeneous capital good will permit you to derive a rate of profit purely from the technical relationship between homogeneous capital and output?

Subhuti replied: Thus it is said in some venerable books.

Buddha said: Revere them, Subhuti, but trust them not. Suppose you do get the value of the marginal product of capital in terms of output of consumer goods. In what units will it be expressed? Physical units of additional consumer goods per unit of additional homogeneous capital. But the rate of profit is a pure number. Surely you will need something more in going from the first to the second to reflect the relative price of the capital good vis-à-vis the consumer good. But the equilibrium price of capital in units of consumer goods depends on the rate of profit used for discounting, and a variation of the rate of profit can involve a variation of the value of the same physical capital in units of consumer goods. This difficulty is not eliminated by having one homogeneous capital good.

Subhuti said: How does Venerable Solow do the whole thing so easily in his simple growth model? Has he then made a mistake, O Enlightened One? My heart aches badly.

Buddha replied: Forsake fear, Subhuti. Venerable Solow may make peculiar assumptions, but he never makes a mistake. He not only assumed a homogeneous capital good but simply one good in the economy, which eliminates the problem of the relative price of capital and consumer goods, which must be unity.

Subhuti asked: And Venerable Samuelson's model of surrogate production function? That does not assume one good in the economy, if I have followed it right.

Buddha replied: No, that belongs to a higher tradition. It eliminates the problem by assuming that the sectors producing the different goods have the same factor-intensity, i.e. the same ratio of physical capital to labour. This is essentially another way of eliminating the relative price problem. However, you must note, Subhuti, that the model accommodates heterogeneous capital goods also, and the problem of relative prices is carefully eliminated by the equal factor-intensity assumption.

Subhuti then spoke thus: I am worried by the equal factor-intensity assumption. Do we really require it, Enlighted One?

Buddha answered: No, it is sufficient but not necessary, in the sense that some rather special configurations of other things can almost accidentally yield a surrogate production function. But the closest we come to the heart of the matter is with Venerable Samuelson's assumption about factor intensities.

Subhuti spoke now in sorrow thus: But the equal factor-intensity assumption is not really very close to reality. Is there no method of getting the rate of profit as the partial derivative of some value of capital without going as far as Venerable Samuelson's assumptions?

Buddha replied: For special cases, certainly yes. For an economy in equilibrium growth with the rate of profit equal to the rate of growth, one can get the equality of the profit rate and the marginal product of capital value without much difficulty. But this covers only a particular situation.

Subhuti asked: Is there then no measure of capital value such that the rate of profit equals the marginal product of capital irrespective of the exact situation of the economy unless the Samuelsonian surrogate model holds?

Buddha said: There is indeed. Venerable Champernowne's chain index gives a measure of capital such that one can use it as an argument in the production function and such that the equilibrium rate of profit will equal the partial derivative of output with respect to capital at its appropriate chain index value. Of course, the neoclassical model is not fully restored since Venerable Champernowne's cunning trick lies in his skilful revaluation of capital, which may differ from the market value of capital.

Subhuti asked: Does this work always, World-honoured One?

Buddha said: No, but it demands less than the surrogate production function. However, if there are conditions that lead to multiple switching, i.e. a situation such that a technique that is more profitable than another at a high interest rate and less profitable at a lower interest rate could again become more profitable at a still lower interest rate, then, O Subhuti, the Champernowne index may not work, as Venerable Champernowne had pointed out in 1954 before the debate on multiple-switching erupted between Brahmins of different traditions.

Subhuti said: Verily, multiple-switching is a matter of great importance for the neoclassical aggregative model, I know that, O Enlightened One.

Buddha replied: Not quite, Subhuti. Because indices like Venerable Champernowne's index do not restore the neoclassical aggregative model, and to get it fully you need Venerable Samuelson's surrogate production function. And it is possible that while there may be no multiple switches, nevertheless Samuelson's assumptions may fail to be fulfilled. Furthermore, there are other assumptions in the neoclassical model that are at least as important and disturbing as the absence of multiple switches. For example that of an equilibrium; that of expectations that are always fulfilled; the stereotype of institutional assumptions on the distribution of income according to the so-called competitive demand and supply; and in some models that of malleability of past capital. In fact, despite the logical possibility of the existence of multiple-switching, there is little empirical evidence as to how common an occurrence it is in reality. It is, in fact, possible that it may yet turn out that far from being the most objectionable assumption in the neoclassical aggregative model, the assumption of the absence of multiple switching may be comparatively harmless in relation to the other assumptions, viewed from the empirical point of view.

Subhuti then asked: You puzzle me, Enlightened One. Why then has there been such a lot of interest in the multiple-switching debate? Why have so many pundits spent so much time on it?

Buddha said: There are possibly two reasons for this, as for most things. First, like Kurukshetra, Hastings or Waterloo, multiple-switching is famous as a battle ground. Here a group of Brahmins from the āshrama of Pundit Sraffa caught a group of Boston Brahmins boasting in the dark, and caused serious injury by throwing real numbers at them. People always enjoy battles, and verily that is why multiple-switching causes so much interest.

Subhuti asked: Is the lore of multiple-switching, then, just a war epic?

Buddha said: I said that there were two reasons for the fame of multiple-switching. I speak now of the second: listen carefully, O Subhuti. For the pure theorist empirical plausibility is often a relatively minor question. What engages him most is internal consistency. Since multiple-switching rules out an aggregate measure of capital – like that of Venerable Champernowne – that can be used as an argument in a neoclassical production function, and since the neoclassical model cannot analytically rule out the possibility of multiple-switching, a pure theorist would be excited by it, especially if he is constructing a purely analytical case against a class of neoclassical models. The practical problem of measurements is not the main thing in this debate.

Subhuti asked: But, World-honoured One, would the Brahmins of Pundit Sraffa's āshrama accept this? Why has Pundit Sraffa himself not written on this distinction, which – if correct – should be very important in understanding the motivation of his school?

Buddha replied: As you know, Pundit Sraffa finds it immoral to write more than one page per month, but on the banks of the Mediterranean in the Province of Corfu he gave an oral discourse on this as early as 1958, reported by Venerable Lutz and Hague (pp. 305–6). He spoke thus:

> One should emphasize the distinction between two types of measurement. First, there was the one in which the statisticians were mainly interested. Second, there was measurement in theory. The statistician's measurements were only approximate and provided a suitable field for work in solving index number problems. The theoretical measures required absolute precision. ... The work of J. B. Clark, Böhm-Bawerk and others was intended to produce pure definitions of capital, as required by their theories, not as a guide to actual measurement. If we found contradictions, then these pointed to defects in the theory, and an inability to define measures of capital accurately.

Subhuti said then: All right, I accept the motivation of Pundit Sraffa, and I am convinced that the neoclassical aggregate model as a piece of 'theory', in his sense, is a disaster. This is important for the disputes between different schools of theory, and I can see that this links up with Venerable Garegnani's analysis of the history of economic thought. But I am, in fact, also interested in actual measurement.

Buddha said: Many people from good families seem to be these days. The picture there is also a bit depressing as far as the neoclassical aggregate model is concerned. For example, Venerable Fisher's examination of this question from the point of view of econometric analysis and empirical predictions brings out the limitation of the neoclassical aggregate model especially when widely diverse industries are included. Note, Subhuti, that Venerable Fisher's motivation is quite different from that of Venerable Sraffa, and to quote the findings of the former as vindication of the position of the latter does not get one closer to enlightenment.

Subhuti then addressed Buddha in this way: O World-honoured One, these difficulties of the neoclassical aggregative approach fill me with profound depression. I shall tell you why this is so, Enlightened One. I devoted myself to development economics before I took to the path of capital theory. I had convinced myself that in some cheap labour economies like India and China it makes sense to recommend choosing relatively less capital-intensive techniques of production, but I now realize that this is not the enlightened way in view of the difficulties in the conception of capital as a factor of production. What sense can there be in talking of the ratio of capital to labour, or of capital to output? How naive have I been! I shall never again recommend choosing low capital-intensity in cheap-labour economies.

Buddha said: Why not, O Subhuti, why not? When you say you were recommending less capital-intensive techniques, you were suggesting specific technical alternatives over others. Perhaps recommending that in constructing an irrigational dam, the earth may be moved in a surplus-labour economy by men with baskets rather than by bulldozers. And other similar recommendations. The fact that you call the former a less capital-intensive technique, when recommending it, is strictly speaking quite incidental and does not affect the wisdom of your recommendation.

Subhuti then spoke thus: I see the point, World-honoured One. But surely this makes the whole thing completely *ad hoc*. We just say 'Choose this and this over that and that'. There is in this *ad hoc* approach no argument for preferring, in a surplus-labour economy, techniques that we recognize, in some real sense, to be less capital-intensive. It is not only that I had *called* these techniques less capital-intensive, but also I had arrived at the recommendation to choose them by a general argument in favour of using more labour and less capital. Such general arguments surely must be regarded as erroneous in view of what you have explained to me, Enlightened One.

Buddha replied: First of all, such general arguments are in fact quite doubtful, and one cannot choose between alternatives until one has looked into the details of each alternative. Secondly, the question of what constitutes cheap labour is itself a difficult one and the existence of surplus labour does not mean that it is costless, as has been argued by Venerable Dobb, among others. Thirdly – and for our purpose most importantly – in so far as your elementary reasoning indicates a general presumption in favour of techniques that can be called less capital-intensive, that general presumption is not much affected by the difficulties we discussed in capital theory.

Subhuti asked: How can that be, O World-honoured One? In view of the difficulties in the conception of capital that you have already opened your holy mouth on, surely it makes no sense whatever to talk of lower or higher capital intensity?

Buddha replied: That thought of yours is so complicated and involves so many different colours that you may well be born as a chameleon in your next incarnation. First, the fact that it may be unenlightened to hold that the rate of profit is determined by the marginal productivity of capital, need not in the least disturb the argument that at a given rate of profit, one technique may have a higher capital intensity than another. Second, when one recommends choosing less capital-intensive techniques in a surplus-labour economy, one is usually making a statement about investment and not about the existing capital stock. Therefore, the problem of *ex post* fixity versus malleability on which – as you point out in your humble Buddhist style – I have opened my holy mouth, is not relevant. I take it that you are not recommending that you scrap your already installed mechanized machinery and change them into baskets and such. Third, when one recommends a lower capital-intensity it is not a question of treating capital as one factor of production but of economizing on the use of the class of non-labour means of production vis-à-vis the use of labour, which is relatively abundant. Where is your commonsense, Subhuti?

Subhuti replied: In my incarnation as a modern economist I have learnt how deceptive commonsense can be. I prefer rigorous arguments. As you concede, the non-labour means of productions are heterogeneous. How can we talk about an overall capital intensity? Are there fixed relative prices among the different non-labour means of production? The debate on capital theory is not irrelevant to this question.

Buddha said: It is not, of course. But it may not make a difference when we are talking of sharp contrasts as we are doing when we recommend moving earth by hands and baskets rather than by bulldozers in building an irrigation project. We may not be absolutely certain of the correct relative price of baskets vis-à-vis bulldozers, but within the limits of variations that may be relevant the former may involve a lower capital intensity than the latter in each case. And when one is making a general recommendation in favour of less capital-intensive techniques in cheap-labour economies, one has in mind something of this kind. For less clear cases, one would, of course, need to do a detailed cost–benefit analysis, and comparison of overall capital intensity will not be the right way of going about it. But just because one cannot rank overall capital intensities in some cases, one should not rule out the rankings that one can do.

Subhuti said: I do not like unrigorous presentations. State precisely please, O Enlightened One.

Buddha said: Let $(q_1^1, \ldots, q_n^1)$ be the amounts of n types of capital good inputs needed per unit of output under technique 1 and $(q_1^2, \ldots, q_n^2)$ those under technique 2. We refer to them as vectors q^1 and q^2 respectively. The appropriate shadow prices may depend on many things and might not even be known with very great precision. They may even depend on the choice of q. Suppose the planner only knows that the price vectors p^1 and p^2 in the two cases would belong to some set π. Then we would be able to say that q^1 is more capital-intensive than q^2 if for *every* pair of price vectors p^1 and p^2 (not necessarily distinct) taken from π, we have:

$$p^1 q^1 > p^2 q^2$$

We know, of course, that for any π the ranking of the vectors of q will be a quasi-ordering, and satisfy some systematic properties, e.g. transitivity.

Subhuti said: Ah, I see now. Maybe I could say a few more things than I first thought. Both in positive and in normative spheres. To take an example from the former, I may be able to say the following, which I shall call Remark 1, to be rigorous. Remark 1: 'When there is persistent unemployment in a stagnant economy the redundant workers may take to employing themselves with tiny quantities of capital (say as shoeblacks or pedlars)'. Having said this, however, I feel a great relief in not finding Venerable Joan Robinson within earshot. She would have never forgiven me for referring to 'tiny quantities of capital'. Tell me Tathāgata, what will I do when I meet Veneral Joan Robinson and feel a compulsion to make a Remark like this?

Buddha said: That, first of all, is your problem. Second, be bold. And Third, why do you think Venerable Joan Robinson will object to your remark? She will not.

Subhuti said: She will of course. She does not like references to 'quantities of capital' – tiny or large. I shall surely run into her some day. How will I defend Remark 1, then? Tell me, O Enlightened One.

Buddha replied: She will know, of course, that Remark 1 is a quotation from pages 157–8 of her *Accumulation of Capital.* Curious that you should have had the same thought.

Subhuti spoke then: I am now tired, World-honoured One. What have I gained from studying all these debates on capital theory other than debunking the neoclassical use of capital as a factor of production and the determination of the rate of profit by the so-called marginal product of capital, which I did not really believe in any way in the first place?

Buddha said: Do not underestimate the value of the rarefied knowledge involved in capital theory. Do not judge an action by the fruit of it. As has been said: 'And do not think of the fruit of action. Fare forward'.

Subhuti asked: But, O Enlightened One, knowledge must lead to some real gain?

Buddha said: Do you remember what I told you 2,500 years ago in that park near Shravasti, when you asked me: 'In the attainment of the Consummation of Incomparable Enlightenment did Buddha make no acquisition whatsoever?'

Subhuti replied: I have forgotten, but here is A. F. Price's translation of the 'Diamond Sutra', and I notice on page 61 that you replied to my question thus: 'Just so, Subhuti. Through the Consummation of Incomparable Enlightenment I acquired not even the least thing: wherefore it is called "Consummation of Incomparable Enlightenment".'

Buddha said: Just so, Subhuti, just so.

References

Bliss, C. J. (1968): 'On putty-clay', *Review of Economic Studies*, **35**, 105-32.

Champernowne, D. (1954): 'The production function and the theory of capital', *Review of Economic Studies*, **21**, 112-35.

Dobb, M. H. (1960): *An Essay on Economic Growth and Planning* (London: Routledge).

Fisher, F. M. (1969): 'The existence of aggregate production functions', *Econometrica*, **37**, 553-77.

Garegnani, P. (1970): 'Heterogeneous capital, the production function and the theory of distribution', *Review of Economic Studies*, **37**, 407-36.

Harcourt, G. C. (1972): *Some Cambridge Controversies in the Theory of Capital* (Cambridge: University Press).

Lutz, F. A. and Hague, D. C. (1961): *The Theory of Capital* (London: Macmillan).

Levhari, D. (1965): 'A non-substitution theorem and switching of techniques', *Quarterly Journal of Economics*, **79**, 98-105.

Levhari, D. and Samuelson, P. A. (1966): 'The non-switching theorem is false', *Quarterly Journal of Economics*, **80**, 518-19.

McIntosh, J. (1972): 'Some notes on the surrogate production function', *Review of Economic Studies*, **39**, 505-10.

Pasinetti, L. (1966): 'Changes in the rate of profit and switching of techniques', *Quarterly Journal of Economics*, **80**, 503-17.

Price, A. F. (1955): *The Diamond Sutra* (London: The Buddhist Society).

Robinson, J. (1954): 'The production function and the theory of capital', *Review of Economic Studies*, **21**, 81-106.

—— (1956). *The Accumulation of Capital* (London: Macmillan).

Samuelson, P. A. (1962): 'Parable and realism in capital theory: the surrogate production function', *Review of Economic Studies*, **29**, 193-206.

Solow, R. M. (1956a): 'A contribution to the theory of economic growth', *Quarterly Journal of Economics*, **70**, 65-94.

—— (1956b): 'The production function and the theory of capital', *Review of Economic Studies*, **23**, 101-8.

—— (1957): 'Technical change and the aggregate production function', *Review of Economics and Statistics*, **39**, 312-20.

Sraffa, P. (1960): *Production of Commodities by Means of Commodities* (Cambridge: University Press).

Von Weizsäcker, C. C. (1971): 'Modern capital theory and the concept of exploitation'. Working Paper No. 2, Institute of Mathematical Economics, Bielefeld University.

8

Approaches to the Choice of Discount Rates for Social Benefit–Cost Analysis

In commenting on an earlier version of this paper, Bob Dorfman remarked to me that I had presented two papers concealed as one. He is, of course, quite right. The second paper begins with Section 5.

The first four sections deal with some standard issues in the choice of discount rates for social benefit–cost analysis. They closely relate to earlier debates on the subject, and involve developments on well-trodden grounds. These sections explore the relation of social vis-à-vis private rates of discount under assumptions of symmetry and asymmetry, and go on to discuss also the relation of social vis-à-vis market rates of discount, which is a distinct problem with which the former is sometimes confused. The relevant parameters in each case are identified and analysed (Sections 3 and 4).

In contrast, the last four sections attempt to reinterpret the problem in explicitly ethical terms, using the formal structure of 'social welfare functionals'. This permits the introduction and analysis of some important ethical issues that have tended to get obscured by rather mechanical formulations of the relation between private and social rates of discount. In this discussion the information relevant to the utilitarian approach is supplemented with that required for the 'Rawlsian' lexicographic maximin rule, but without necessarily accepting either utilitarianism or Rawls' 'Difference Principle' (Section 6). This combined information set also proves to be inadequate when issues of rights and liberty are analysed, requiring us

In revising the paper I have benefited from the helpful comments of Kenneth Arrow, Thomas Cotton, Robert Dorfman, Robert Lind, Talbot Page, Mark Sharefkin, and other participants. [The comments of Dorfman, Page and Sharefkin as discussants of my paper in the March 1977 conference at which my paper was presented, have also been published in the conference volume, edited by Lind, *Discounting for Time and Risk in Energy Policy*.]

From R. Lind (ed.), *Discounting for Time and Risk in Energy Policy* (Washington, DC: Resources for the Future, 1982), 325–53.

to go beyond what has been called 'welfarism' (Section 7). The relevance of these complex considerations for the choice of social discount rates in general and for discount rates for planning in particular is also discussed.

1   Interpretation

Controversies on the choice of the appropriate rate of discount often include ambiguities as to precisely what is being debated, and it may be useful to begin with some preliminary issues of interpretation. In general, the discount rate specifies the rate at which additional benefits in period $t + 1$ are converted into equivalent amounts of benefits in period t. The conversion takes the form of division by $(1 + r)$, when r is the rate of discount between these two periods. But clearly the discount rate between any two periods depends on:

(1) the measurement of 'benefits' (in particular, the units in which the benefits of each period are measured); and
(2) the concept of equivalence.

In a private profitability exercise in terms of discounted cash flows (a common exercise), the benefits have an obvious measure, namely, cash receipts (and payments). Not so in social benefit–cost analysis, no matter whether applied to public investment or to private investment evaluated from the point of view of public interest. Benefits or costs may occur *without* cash transactions (for example, skill formation, pollution, and other externalities). Even when the occurrence is accompanied by cash transactions, the social value of the benefits may not be reflected by the size of the cash transactions and may vary with a variety of factors, in particular with the commodities and persons involved in the transaction. Of course, the benefits in each period could be converted into units expressed in terms of cash, but the specification will depend on the interpretation of units of cash, for example, a dollar of commodity j going to person i may not be treated in the same way as a dollar of commodity h going to person g. It will be shown later (see Section 2) that some much-argued differences between social and private rates of discount arise entirely from differences in definition of units in which benefits are measured.

A relatively unambiguous, if austere, system of accounting is provided by the choice of the benefit unit in period t as a unit of a particular commodity j going to a particular person i in that year, x_{ij}^t. The units then are dated 'named goods' (see Hahn, 1971; Sen, 1976b). In the context of the exercises that will be undertaken in this paper, much use will be made of the specification of dating and naming, even though the intercommodity differences will typically receive less attention (see, however, Section 7).

Even in the context of aggregated units, differences exist in the literature. The discount rate (or 'discount factor') has been variously expressed in aggregate units of consumption (see Dasgupta, Marglin, and Sen, 1972), investment (see Little and Mirrlees, 1974), and 'utility' or 'felicity' (see Arrow and Kurz, 1970).

The other source of ambiguity is the conception of 'equivalence'. There are at least two alternative interpretations of equivalence, namely, in terms of (1) welfare and (2) possibility. In the first interpretation, a discount rate of r involves the judgement that one additional unit of benefit in year t would exactly compensate for the welfare loss of $(1 + r)$ units of benefit in year $t + 1$. The second interpretation involves the knowledge that one additional unit of benefit can be produced in year t by a minimal reduction of the benefit in year $t + 1$ by $(1 + r)$ units.

The difference between the two corresponds to what Hicks (1958) calls the 'utility interpretation' and the 'cost interpretation' of the social product, and each interpretation is possible without assuming anything about the other. Under certain general assumptions, it is necessary for social optimality that the welfare discount rates r_w equal the possibility rates of return r_p, respectively, but when these equalities do not hold, one would in general need both types of information for intertemporal decisions (see Marglin, 1963, 1976; Arrow and Kurz, 1970).

The information about welfare weights and production possiblities can be collapsed into a single term r if and only if the two happen to coincide, that is, $r_w = r_p$. If they do not, any averaging formula (see, for example, Harberger, 1968) must involve loss of relevant information (see Feldstein, 1972), since the same average can correspond to a large (in fact, uncountable) set of alternative combinations of welfare and possibility information (r_w, r_p).

In this paper, the term rate of *discount* will be reserved for the welfare interpretation, while rate of *return* will refer to the possibility interpretation. Further, unless otherwise stated, the unit of account will be consumption, typically that of a specified person at a specified point of time.

2   Private and Social Rates of Discount

The appropriateness of using the private rates of discount for social benefit–cost analysis was debated vigorously in the late 1950s and

1960s by such writers as Eckstein (1957), Sen (1957, 1961, 1967, 1968), Dobb (1960), Marglin (1963a, 1976), Feldstein (1964), Harberger (1964, 1968, 1973), Lind (1964), Tullock (1964), Usher (1964), Phelps (1965), Arrow (1966), and Baumol (1968a, 1968b). The case for using a social rate of discount lower than the private rate was argued on several grounds, of which the following received much of the attention:

(1) *The super-responsibility argument:* The government has responsibility not merely to the current generation but also to future generations (over and above the concern for future generations already reflected in the preferences of the present generation).

(2) *The dual-role argument:* The members of the present generation in their political or public role may be more concerned about the welfare of the future generations than they are in their day-to-day market activities.

(3) *The isolation argument:* Even with a *given* set of consistent preferences, members of the present generation may be willing to join in a collective contract of more savings by all, though unwilling to save more in isolation.

Although the first two arguments raise much deeper issues – concerned as they are with the nature of state and the integrity of human personality – it was the isolation argument (Sen, 1961; Marglin, 1963a) that caused most of the heated debate by, among others, Harberger (1964, 1973), Feldstein (1964), Lind (1964), Tullock (1964), Usher (1964), Phelps (1965), and Sen (1967). While a blow-by-blow account of the controversy will be devastatingly boring, the issue of interpretation discussed in the last section permits us to reassess the question in a somewhat different light.

When the private rates of discount differ among the individuals in the present generation, there will be, of course, nothing remarkable in the chosen social rate differing from any particular private rate, or even from all of them. But in the isolation argument such differences are not assumed, and all individuals are treated as identical (although of course the argument can be extended to the non-identical cases as well). Furthermore, the only principle of group aggregation used to arrive at a social rate of discount less than the private was the weak Pareto principle based on complete unanimity: if everyone in the present generation prefers x to y, then x must be judged to be socially superior to y for the present generation. This raises the fundamental question as to how social and private rates of discount can differ if the used concept of social preference is one of unanimous individual preference. Both must reflect exactly the same welfare valuations.

Indeed, no argument for differences between individual and social rates of discount in the *named good space* (or the named income space) emerges from the isolation argument. The argument runs thus. With a weight of unity on one's own consumption, each person attaches a weight β on a unit of consumption by others in the present generation, γ on a unit of consumption by his descendants in the future generation, and α on a unit of consumption by others in the future generation. It is assumed that β, γ, and α are all less than one. If a private act of saving today yields a point return that is enjoyed by the future generation and shared by one's descendants and others in the ratio λ to $(1 - \lambda)$, then the private rate of discount is taken to be:

$$\pi = \frac{1}{\lambda\gamma + (1 - \lambda)\alpha} - 1 \tag{1}$$

If, on the other hand, a collective saving contract of one additional unit of saving each by all n persons in the present generation yields a point return enjoyed by the future generation and shared by one's descendants and others in the ratio 1 to $(n - 1)$, then the social rate of discount is taken to be given by:

$$\rho = \frac{1 + (n - 1)\beta}{\gamma + (n - 1)\alpha} - 1 \tag{2}$$

There is clearly a family of values of λ, γ, and α/β that make the private rate of discount, π, and social rate of discount, ρ, equal. Lind (1964) identified the case in which $\lambda = 1$ and $\gamma = \alpha/\beta$, which, together, do just this. The interpretation of the condition $\lambda = 1$ is that one can capture for one's own descendants the *entire* return to one's private investment. The interpretation of the second condition is that one's relative weighting of reward to one's own descendants (γ) vis-à-vis that to oneself (1) is in exactly the same proportion as one's weighting of reward to others in the future generation (α) vis-à-vis that to others in the present generation (β).[1]

On the other hand, given $\gamma = \alpha/\beta$, if one fails to capture the entire reward for one's own descendants because of, say, income tax, inheritance tax, or job creation for people in the unemployment pool, then clearly $\rho < \pi$, and the social rate will fall short of the private rate of discount. Similarly, given $\lambda = 1$, if one's selfishness vis-à-vis others today is stronger than one's concern for one's descendants vis-à-vis

1. The same case was identified by Dennis Robertson in a personal communication to me, dated 4 April 1962, commenting on Sen (1961).

others in the future generation, then again the social rate will be lesss than the private rate. And, of course, a mixture of $\lambda < 1$ and $\gamma < \alpha/\beta$ will also have the same effect. Given the personal quality of selfishness that is not necessarily fully translated in the relative weights on one's descendants, and given the existence of taxes and unemployment, it is possibly reasonable to expect that the social rate will lie below the private rate.

So much for a quick recount. It is clear that the social and private rates here do not refer to the same units of benefits in the future and at present. The social rate refers to the weighting of an aggregate bundle of consumption at this moment vis-à-vis that of the future; the share of oneself in the present bundle is $1/n$ and so is the share of one's descendants in the future bundle. In contrast, the private rate refers to the weighting of a unit of one's own consumption today vis-à-vis an aggregate bundle in the future with a share λ of one's descendants in the latter. The difference does not lie in the private vis-à-vis social nature of the weighting, but in the *bundles* that are being weighted. Indeed, in terms of *named* consumption, the rates of discount are the same for all persons with an appropriate translation of one's identity and that of one's descendants. The social rate of discount is, in fact, a common *individual* rate of discount of equally distributed bundles of consumption for each generation.

This question of 'interpretation' of the two discount rates in the isolation problem also makes clear that it may be somewhat misleading to think of the problem as arising from externalities of consumption.[2] Of course, 'externalities' *are* involved in the sense that any concern for the consumption of people other than oneself and one's descendants is put under the broad heading of consumption externalities, and obviously the argument has much to do with such concerns. But whether or not there are externalities of consumption in this sense, private and social rates of discount in this exercise *may or may not* differ depending on how the units of rewards and sacrifices are defined. For example, even with externalities – no matter how strong – satisfying Lind's condition, $\gamma = \alpha/\beta$, the private and social rates must coincide if $\lambda = 1$. More important, even with no externalities of consumption at all, that is, with $\alpha = \beta = 0$, if $\lambda < 1$, the social rate of discount ρ will still be below the private rate π, as is readily checked from equations (1) and (2). The crucial question is *what* is being discounted vis-à-vis what, and not *whether* consumption externalities are present.

2. See the otherwise excellent contribution of Phelps (1965), which incidentally provides a good critical survey also of other arguments concerning possible divergence between private and social rates of discounts and returns.

3   *Private, Social, and Market Rates: The Symmetric Case*

The issue of composition of benefits is especially important in translating the lessons from this model of the isolation problem to the question of the relation between the market rate of interest and the appropriate rate of discount for social benefit–cost analysis of public and private investment (for example, investment in energy-related research and development). First, note that the 'private' rate of discount may not correspond to the market rate interest or profit. The market rate m refers to the part of the reward that goes to the investor or his heirs by the rules of property rights, and while the part of the benefits going to others through taxation is included in m, the part going to others through the creation of employment or through externalities of production is not. If m is the market rate and e the rate of reward to others through sources other than taxation and transfer, then it is $(m + e)$ that would be equated to the private rate of discount π, as defined in the previous exercise, interpreting λ as the share going to one's own descendants in the *total* consumption generated in the future. Thus:

$$m = \pi - e \tag{3}$$

where π is as defined in equation (1). Whenever e is positive, the market rate of interest will lie below the private rate of discount, and this opens up the possibility that the social rate of discount, even when below the private rate, might well exceed the market rate.

The social rate of discount will also depend on how the sacrifices and rewards are shared. In the symmetric case of identical individuals and identical sharing (as in the old isolation model), each person's relative weighting of the average unit of consumption sacrificed today vis-à-vis the average unit of consumption generated in the future will be given by the ratio of $1 + (n - 1)\beta$ to $\gamma + (n - 1)\alpha$, and the universally accepted social rate of discount ρ will be that expressed in equation (2). It is with this ρ that the market rate m must be compared.

Let A be the amount of total consumption generated in the future by the sacrifice of a unit of consumption today. It is the sharing of A that is in the proportions λ and $(1 - \lambda)$ when the investment is *privately* undertaken by a person, and in the ratio of 1 to $(n - 1)$ when it is undertaken by a *social* contract with equal sharing, as defined in the context of deriving (1) and (2). Let the proportion of A that is covered by the gross market return $(1 + m)$ be expressed as θ:[3]

$$1 + m = \theta A \tag{4}$$

Private investment is in equilibrium when

$$\frac{A}{1 + \pi} = 1 \tag{5}$$

Putting these relations together, it is clear that $m \{\gtreqless\} \rho$ according as $(1 + \pi)\theta \{\gtreqless\} 1 + \rho$; therefore from equations (1) and (2)

$$m \{\gtreqless\} \rho \text{ according as } \frac{\theta}{\lambda + (1 - \gamma)(\alpha/\gamma)} \{\gtreqless\} \frac{1 + (n - 1)\beta}{1 + (n - 1)(\alpha/\gamma)} \tag{6}$$

With Lind's assumption of 'balanced emotions', $\gamma = \alpha/\beta$, this reduces to

$$m \{\gtreqless\} \rho \text{ according as } \frac{\theta - \lambda}{1 - \lambda} \{\gtreqless\} \beta \tag{6*}$$

In using equation (6) or (6*), note must be taken of the restrictions that the various parameters must satisfy. They are: $1 \geqslant \theta \geqslant \lambda$; $1 > \beta$; $1 > \gamma$; and $1 > \alpha$. A few special cases are easy to identify.

Case 1: The condition $1 = \theta > \lambda$ implies that the social rate of discount must *lie below* the market rate of interest. This is the case in which the benefits accruing to others arise solely from taxation and other transfers, if any, out of the market return, and not from such things as externalities, or the employment of the otherwise unemployed.

Case 2: The condition $1 > \theta = \lambda$ implies that the social rate of discount must *exceed* the market rate of interest. This is the case in which *all* transfers to others take place through externalities, additional employment, and so forth, *outside* the market return rather than through taxation of, and transfers from, the market return.

Case 3: The condition $1 = \theta = \lambda$ implies that $\rho = \pi = m$. (This has to be checked from equation (6) rather than (6*) and from equations (4) and (5).) This was, in fact, the case discussed originally by Lind (1964), and there is no transfer to 'others' at all (that is, no taxation, no unemployed to be absorbed with benefit accruing to them, and no externalities).

---

3. Note that e defined earlier is given by $A(1 - \theta)$ and that A is $(1 + r)$ when r is the rate of return in consumption units (see Section 1).

Leaving out these special cases, the general relationship between the social rate of discount and the market rate of interest is given by equations (6) and (6*) subject to the restrictions mentioned above. To interpret equation (6*), note that $(1-\lambda)$ is the total proportionate share of others (that is, those other than one's own descendants) in the total future consumption generated A, while $(\theta - \lambda)$ is the part of the proportionate share going to others that comes from taxation (and other transfers, if any) out of the market return. Condition (6*) states that the social rate of discount will lie below the market rate of interest m if and only if the share going to others *through* taxation (and other transfers) out of the market return as a proportion of the total share going to them exceeds the *relative* weight that is put on the consumption of others (others today in comparison with oneself β, and others in the future in comparison with one's own descendants α/γ).

4   *Private, Social, and Market Rates with Asymmetries*

The comparisons of social and market rates were facilitated in the last section by the assumption of symmetry among the persons: (1) the members of the same generation were all identical in every way, including welfare characteristics and opulence, and (2) the social contract to save more involved equal participation by all members of the present generation. But both assumptions are quite limiting. Aside from personal differences among the people involved, some are rich and some are poor. Also investment programmes do not typically involve equal participation by all.

The absence of symmetry does, however, make the analysis much more complicated. In fact, even the definition of the social rate of discount becomes problematic once the reliance on the Pareto principle (to define 'social preference' in terms of unanimity) becomes unavailable. More demanding ethical principles now have to be invoked.

The social rate of discount to be used for benefit–cost analysis of a public investment, or of a private investment from the public point of view, will depend both on some *descriptive* features of the investment as well as on *evaluative* weights on benefits accruing to different people. The latter – no longer obtainable from unanimity – must presumably reflect some kind of a compromise over the views of different groups in the present generation. I shall have a little bit to say on the choice of these weights in Sections 5–7, but for the moment I simply take these weights as given. Let the present community be divided into k groups: $g = 1, \ldots, k$. Let the evaluative weight on each unit of current consumption of group g be β_g, and that on each unit of its 'future consumption' (that is, the consumption of its heirs) be α_g.

Regarding the descriptive features of this investment, the proportion of consumption benefit in the future that goes to group g (in fact, their heirs) is denoted by σ_g, and the proportion of current consumption sacrifice that falls on this group is σ_g'. Note that each σ_g and each σ_g' is non-negative, and

$$\sum_{g=1}^{k} \sigma_g = 1, \quad \text{and} \quad \sum_{g=1}^{k} \sigma_g' = 1$$

The social rate of discount ρ for this system of weighting is, clearly, given by the following equation.[4]

$$\rho = \frac{\displaystyle\sum_{g=1}^{k} \sigma_g' \beta_g}{\displaystyle\sum_{g=1}^{k} \sigma_g \alpha_g} - 1 \tag{7}$$

Consider now a private investment I^j undertaken by group j. Let the share of the additional future consumption accruing to each group g (in fact, to its heirs) be σ_g^j. The weight attached by group j to the future consumption of each group g is denoted by α_g^j. The weight on the current consumption of group g is β_g^j. The unit is taken to be the weight on one unit of *current* consumption of group j itself: $\beta_j^j = 1$.

The private rate of discount of group j for this investment is given by

$$\pi^j = \frac{1}{\displaystyle\sum_{g=1}^{k} \sigma_g^j \alpha_g^j} - 1 \tag{8}$$

The market rate of interest m is related to each private rate of discount π^j in the way specified by equations (4) and (5). Denoting

---

4. It can be easily checked that equation (7) reduces to equation (2) of the symmetric case if symmetric assumptions are added. With symmetric concerns for others and with $\sigma_g = \sigma_g' = 1/n$ for all g, each person j's evaluation of ρ is the same and is, in fact, that given by equation (2), when we put $\beta_j = 1$ (choice of unit), $\alpha_j = \gamma$, $\beta_g = \beta$ and $\alpha_g = \alpha$ for $g \neq j$ (choice of notation).

the relevant θ for the investment in question as θ^j yields

$$m = \theta^j(1 + \pi^j) - 1 \qquad (9)$$

Equations (8) and (9) together characterize, with the usual assumptions of smoothness, an equilibrium of divisible private investment for each group j. Thus the market interest rate m can be seen in terms of θ^j, $\{\sigma_g^j\}$ and $\{\alpha_g^j\}$ for any group j in an equilibrium of undertaken investment.

There is not a great deal that can be said about the relative magnitudes of private, social, and market rates without making more specific assumptions. Two assumptions of particular interest that we now explore are:

(1) The social weight on the consumption of each group g shifts in the same ratio γ as we move from the group to its descendants:

$$\alpha_g = \gamma\beta_g, \text{ for all } g \qquad (10)$$

(2) The private weight by group j on the consumption of each group g shifts in the same ratio γ as we move from the group g to its descendants:

$$\alpha_g^j = \gamma\beta_g^j, \text{ for all } j \text{ and } g \qquad (11)$$

If the relative opulence of the different groups does not change much over this period, then equation (10) may be a reasonable assumption under 'welfarism' (see Sections 5–7), but whether a similar argument can be constructed in particular non-welfaristic contexts as well is not clear. Assumption (11) is rather like Lind's (1964) case of 'balanced emotions', but most obviously involves restrictions on the stationarity of the *relative* opulence of different groups, since the weighting – as in Lind's case – is of consumption rather than of utility. The requirement that the *relative* rate of change is the *same* for social and private weights is also restrictive, even though this does not at all imply that the private weights of different persons must be close to each other, or close to the social weights.

Consider now the assumption that the sharing of consumption sacrifices and the sharing of consumption gains be in the same proportions for each group in the 'social' investment:

$$\sigma_g = \sigma_g', \text{ for each } g \qquad (12)$$

This could be regarded as an unreasonable assumption for public investment projects, since the relatively rich could be expected to bear a higher share of the costs than of the benefits in such projects. But whether this type of 'progressive' bias is typically the case even with public investments is far from clear. In any case, assumption (12) will be used tentatively, and the directional correction needed to incorporate the 'progressive' hypothesis will be analysed later.

The effect of assumptions (10) and (12) on the social rate of discount is a drastic simplification

$$\rho = \frac{1}{\gamma} - 1 \qquad (13)$$

The result is not surprising: what (12) does is to permit the incremental analysis to be done in terms of a 'composite' consumption bundle with an unchanging breakdown, and the characteristic of the same intertemporal relative movement (γ) of the social weights, embodied in assumption (10), reduces equation (7) to equation (13).

Given assumption (12), if assumption (10) is dropped and different relative rates of intertemporal changes in the evaluative weights are admitted, then equation (13) will hold only under the interpretation of γ standing for the $\sigma'_g \alpha_g$-weighted average of the group-specific intertemporal ratios $\{\gamma_g\}$ of the evaluative weights.

A more fundamental difference is made when assumption (12) is dropped since the composite-bundle approach is no longer usable. The 'progressive' case discussed earlier is particularly worth considering since such redistribution is a frequently articulated aspect of public investments of various types. On utilitarian or equity grounds (see Sections 5 and 6), the evaluative weights on the consumption of the richer groups can be taken to be less than those on the consumption of the poorer groups. The effect of this change is to raise the value of the denominator of the first term on the right-hand side of equation (7). Clearly, that must have the consequence of *lowering* the social rate of discount ρ.

Thus, it is easy to establish that when assumption (10) holds, but assumption (12) is dropped in favour of the 'progressive' assumption, then

$$\rho < \frac{1}{\gamma} - 1 \qquad (13^*)$$

In this sense, equation (13) gives an upper bound of the value of the social rate of discount.

When the dropping of (12) for the 'progressive' assumption is *combined with* the eschewing of (10), inequality (13*) can hold with γ interpreted as the $\sigma'_g \alpha_g$ = weighted average of the respective values of γ_g.

Turning now to the private rate of discount π^j for group j, it is given by the following equation in the presence of restriction (11).

$$\pi^j = \frac{1}{\sum\limits_{g=1}^{k} \sigma_g^j \beta_g^j} - 1. \tag{14}$$

Regarding the values of the weights β_g^j, we have already defined $\beta_g^g = 1$. Given the dominance of self-seeking over sympathy,[5] it may be reasonable to assume that for all $g \neq j$; $\beta_g^j < 1$. Thus unless $\sigma_g^j = 0$ for all $g \neq j$, the denominator of the first term on the right-hand side of equation (14) must fall short of γ. Thus, leaving out the case of no taxation, no external benefits, no employment creation, and so forth (corresponding to $\lambda = 1$ in the symmetric model in Sections 2 and 3), we must have

$$\pi^j > \frac{1}{\gamma} - 1. \tag{14*}$$

Thus, it would appear from statements (13), (13*), (14), and (14*) that under the specified assumptions the social rate of discount will tend to lie below the private rate of discount of each investing group j even in the asymmetric case.

But even with these assumptions, it is not certain that the social rate must lie below the *market* rate of interest m, since m itself lies below the private rate π^j whenever θ^j is less than unity (that is, when the share of 'others' in private investment comes partly from *outside* the market return — through externalities, job creation, and so forth). The assertion that the social rate of discount must be chosen to be lower than the market rate of interest must, therefore, be based on some additional assumption. One such assumption is, of course, that of $\theta^j = 1$, that is, the share of 'others' comes *entirely* from *within* the market return through taxation and other transfers. This will make the market rate equal the private rate of discount, thus exceeding the social discount rate to be used. An alternative set of assumptions that is sufficient for this purpose is a lack of concern for 'others': $\beta_g^j = 0$, for $g \neq j$, combined with *some part* of the share of others coming from *within* the market return: $\theta^j > \sigma_j^j$.

But these are very special assumptions, and there is little reason to be sure that the social rate must be pegged at a level below the *market* rate of interest, even when one is persuaded that the social rate does lie below the *private* rate of discount of the investing groups.

---

5. Note, however, that since the weighting is of consumption rather than utility, this will involve quite a strong dominance of self-seeking when one is much richer than some other groups.

5   Social Welfare Functions and Discounting

I turn now to the question of the determination of social weights. Let X be the set of alternative 'social states' including the current period, 0, and the next, 1. There are m people in the present generation (indexed $1, \ldots, m$), and $(n-m)$ in the next (indexed $m+1, \ldots, n$), making a community of a total of n people whose interests have to be considered. For any social state x in X, let x_i^0 stand for the consumption of person i in period 0 for $i = 1, \ldots, m$, and x_i^1 for the consumption of person i in period 1 for $i = m+1, \ldots, n$. Each individual i's personal welfare function W_i is defined over X, and while people live in exactly one period or the other, their personal welfare values may take note of any sympathy that people have for others, including for those living at another period.

Let R be any social ordering ('at least as good as') with P and I its asymmetric and symmetric factors, respectively. A *social welfare functional* (SWFL) is a functional relation that specifies exactly one social ordering R over X for any n-tuple of individual welfare functions (one for each person):

$$R = F(\{W_i\}) \tag{15}$$

The assumptions of measurability and interpersonal comparability of welfare are expressed through *invariance restrictions* on transformations of the n-tuples $\{W_i\}$ that preserve the welfare information, being 'permitted' transformations (see Sen, 1970, 1977a). For example, given 'ordinal' measurability of personal welfare and the complete absence of interpersonal comparability, if $\{W_i\}$ is transformed into $\{\hat{W}_i\}$ through the operation of any n-tuple of positive, monotonic transformations ϕ_i in the form: $\hat{W}_i = \phi_i(W_i)$ for all i, then $F(\{W_i\}) = F(\{\hat{W}_i\})$. This would make a social welfare functional SWFL a 'social welfare function' SWF in the sense of Arrow (1951). To take another example, if cardinal measurability is combined with full interpersonal comparability, then the invariance requirement is weakened exactly to the following: if $\{W_i\}$ is transformed into $\{\hat{W}_i\}$ through the operation of any positive, affine transformation ϕ in the form $\hat{W}_i = \phi(W_i)$ for all i, then $F(\{W_i\}) = F(\{\hat{W}_i\})$. Note that the change of the permitted type of individual transformations reflects a shift in the measurability assumption (from 'ordinal' to 'cardinal'), while the change from a distinct transformation ϕ_i for each person to one common transformation ϕ applied to all reflects a shift in the assumption of interpersonal comparability (from none to full).

Various other distinguished cases and continuums in between have been discussed elsewhere by Sen (1970, 1977a), Blackorby (1975), Fine (1975), d'Aspremont and Gevers (1977), Hammond (1977), Deschamps and Gevers (1978), Maskin (1979), and Roberts (1980a).

The relevant social rates of discount reflect a part of the content of a social ordering R. In particular, consider the choice between social state x including the social investment in question and social state y *without* it, and let this involve a reduction in the consumption in period 0 by one unit and an increase in the consumption in period 1 by $1 + q$ units. (The judgement on the relative social merits of x and y will not, in general, be independent of the interpersonal distributions of consumption gain and loss.) If xPy, then the social rate of discount relevant for this investment is less than q, and if yPx, then it exceeds q. If xIy, then the social rate of discount is exactly q.

The conditions that Arrow imposed on SWFs for his general possibility theorem correspond to the following conditions imposed on SWFLs.

Unrestricted domain (U): The domain of F includes all logically possible n-tuples of welfare functions $\{W_i\}$.

Weak Pareto principle (P): For any $\{W_i\}$, and any pair x, y, if $W_i(x) > W_i(y)$ for all i, then xPy.

Independence of irrelevant alternatives (I): For any two n-tuples $\{W_i\}$ and $\{\hat{W}_i\}$, if for some pair x, y: $W_i(x) = \hat{W}_i(x)$ and $W_i(y) = \hat{W}_i(y)$, for all i, then $xF(\{W_i\})y$ if and only if $xF(\{\hat{W}_i\})y$.

Non-dictatorship (D): There is no person i such that for any $\{W_i\}$ in the domain of F and any pair x, y, if $W_i(x) > W_i(y)$, then xPy.

Arrow's theorem translates in this framework into the proposition that there is no SWFL satisfying conditions U, P, I, and D and the invariance restriction for ordinal noncomparability.

The same impossibility holds even when the informational base is enriched to *cardinal* non-comparability with the invariance requirement covering $\{\hat{W}_i\}$ obtained from $\{W_i\}$ by an n-tuple of positive affine transformations ϕ_i (see Sen, 1970, Theorem 8*2). To gain any advantage with the imposed conditions, the informational base has to be enriched in the direction of introducing interpersonal comparability. The same applies to the determination of social rates of discount, which, as we have seen, is a problem embedded in the derivation of a SWFL.

If cardinal full comparability is admitted, a variety of rules can be used, and the Arrow conditions can also be strengthened in various ways.

Pareto indifference rule (P^o): For any $\{W_i\}$, and any pair x, y, if $W_i(x) = W_i(y)$ for all i, then xIy.

Strong Pareto principle (P^*): P^o holds, and also if for any $\{W_i\}$ and any pair x, y: $W_i(x) \geqslant W_i(y)$ for all i, and $W_i(x) > W_i(y)$ for some i, then xPy.

Anonymity (A): If $\{\hat{W}_i\}$ is a reordering of $\{W_i\}$, then $F(\{\hat{W}_i\}) = F(\{W_i\})$.

Strong neutrality (SN): For any two n-tuples $\{W_i\}$ and $\{\hat{W}_i\}$, if for social states x, y, a, b: $W_i(x) = \hat{W}_i(a)$ and $W_i(y) = \hat{W}_i(b)$ for all i, then $xF(\{W_i\}) y$ if and only if $aF(\{\hat{W}_i\}) b$.

It should be noted that strong Pareto principle (P^*), strong neutrality (*SN*), and anonymity (*A*) imply, respectively, Arrow's weak Pareto principle (*P*), independence of irrelevant alternatives (*I*), and non-dictatorship (*D*), but each is in fact a strict strengthening of the corresponding condition.

Among the class of SWFLs satisfying U, P^*, SN, and A, the utilitarian rule and Rawlsian lexicographic maximin rule (derived from Rawls' 'Difference Principle') have been much discussed.[6] Denote the jth worst off person in state x as $j(x)$, breaking ties when necessary in any arbitrary strict order.

Utilitarianism: xRy if and only if

$$\sum_{i=1}^{n} (W_i(x) - W_i(y)) \geqslant 0.$$

Rawlsian lexicographic maximin (leximin): xIy if and only if $W_{j(x)}(x) = W_{j(y)}(y)$ for all $j = 1, \ldots, n$. And xPy if and only if there is some r: $1 \leqslant r \leqslant n$, such that $W_{r(x)}(x) > W_{r(y)}(y)$, and for all $j < r$: $W_{j(x)}(x) = W_{j(y)}(y)$.

Utilitarianism and leximin can both be derived axiomatically starting from cardinal full comparability and U, P^*, I, and A by additional requirements (see Hammond, 1976; Strasnick, 1976; d'Aspremont and Gevers, 1977; Deschamps and Gevers, 1978; Gevers, 1979; Maskin, 1978, 1979; Roberts, 1980a, 1980b; Arrow, 1976; and Sen, 1977a). As the formulations of utilitarianism and

---

6. See Rawls (1971), Sen (1970, 1974b), Arrow (1973), Dasgupta (1974), Hammond (1976), Page (1977), and Phelps (1976), among many other contributors.

leximin make clear, the focus of the former is on gains and losses of personal welfare (without any concern about welfare levels as such), whereas the focus of the latter is on comparisons of welfare levels (without any concern about the exact sizes of welfare gains and losses). The dichotomy of ethical principles leads, therefore, to a dichotomy of information sets that are made 'inadmissible' in the sense of making the social ordering invariant with respect to information of that type (see Sen, 1973). A less wasteful and more sensitive social welfare approach should take note of *both* types of information sets, namely, welfare *levels* as well as welfare *gains and losses* (see Sen, 1974a, 1974b, 1977a).

In determining the social rate of discount relevant for a particular investment project through the formula given by equation (7), we need, of course, the factual information about the breakdown of consumption gains and losses, $\{\sigma_g\}$ and $\{\sigma_g'\}$, respectively. In addition we need the information on which the evaluative weights $\{\alpha_g\}$ and $\{\beta_g\}$ are to be based. For utilitarianism this information is supplied by the respective *marginal utilities* of consumption, while for leximin this information is provided by values of personal welfare *levels*. Indeed, for a suitably small investment project, the vector of marginal utilities W' and the vector of welfare levels W^* in the social state without the investment are adequate for determining the relative evaluative weights under the two approaches respectively. In what follows we shall be concerned with *both* W' and W^*.

Some of the underlying ethical conflicts may be easier to explain in terms of a model in which the current generation and the future generation are treated as two persons p and f, respectively, though there is not much difficulty in capturing the same conflicts also in terms of a more elaborate model. The social rate of discount can then be seen as a function of the two types of information specified:

$$\rho = D(W_p^*, W_f^*, W_p', W_f') \tag{16}$$

Let the respective partial derivatives − assuming differentiability − be D_p^*, D_f^*, D_p', and D_f'. What can we say about the signs of these derivatives? It is readily checked that under utilitarianism:

$$D_p' > 0, \ D_f' < 0, \ D_p^* = D_f^* = 0 \tag{17}$$

The Rawlsian approach is, of course, less sensitive since it gives absolute priority to the worse off, but the underlying ethical consideration is captured in a broader framework if − subject to $W_p' > 0$ and $W_f' > 0$ − we require that:

$$D_p^* < 0, \ D_f^* > 0 \tag{18}$$

Putting the two types of sensitivity together, we may require that:[7]

$$D_p^* < 0, \ D_f^* > 0, \ D_p' > 0, \ D_f' < 0 \qquad (19)$$

In the next section, equation (16) is explored subject to equation (19).

6 Welfare Levels and Differences: Directional Regularities

First, consider the impact of a higher growth between now and the future on the discount rate ρ. With an unchanged initial situation given by the welfare level W_p^* and marginal utility W_p', the result of the higher growth will be to raise the future welfare level W_f^* and to reduce the future marginal utility W_f', given strict concavity of the welfare function in the future. Since $D_f^* > 0$ and $D_f' < 0$ from (19), both the changes will induce the social discount rate ρ to rise. There is, thus, no ambiguity in this case about the direction of the movement of ρ, and the standard utilitarian result is reinforced.

Consider, next, an unchanged initial situation and unchanged growth rate between now and the future, but an increase of the degree of concavity of the shared welfare function relating personal welfare to own personal consumption: $W_i = W(C_i)$. Normalizing in such a way that W_p and W_p' remain unchanged, the result of such a uniform increase in concavity will be to reduce *both* W_f^* and W_f'. It follows from equation (19) that the decrease in W_f' will tend to reduce the social rate of discount; this is the standard utilitarian result. On the other hand, the decrease of W_f^* will have exactly the opposite effect. Thus the two influences will counteract each other, and the net result is no longer unambiguous.

The conflict can be illustrated in terms of the familiar utility function with a constant elasticity of marginal utility:

$$W_i = A + \frac{1}{\eta} (C_i)^\eta, \ \text{with} \ \eta < 1 \qquad (20)$$

Marginal utility of consumption is given by:

$$W_i' = (C_i)^{\eta - 1} \qquad (21)$$

A diminution of η, corresponding to a uniform increase in the degree of concavity, will reduce the welfare level as well as the marginal utility of consumption, for given C_i. Although the latter would shift

---

7. The class of rules satisfying these restrictions has a non-empty intersection with the class of rules based on adding strictly concave transformations of individual welfares (proposed by Mirrlees, 1971). But neither set is wholly contained in the other.

us in the direction of giving less weight to the future consumption on 'efficiency' grounds concerning the 'total' (the familiar utilitarian argument), the former would shift us in the direction of *raising* the weight on future consumption on grounds of 'equity' (the strength of one's claim being inversely related to one's relative prosperity). The net results will depend on the respective magnitude of the two effects, and that, of course, would depend on the particular specification of equation (16).

Therefore, the view that one does not become so much better off after all from an increased level of consumption cuts both ways. The constant-elasticity case is, of course, special in the sense that marginal and total utility are very closely related, and once a wider family of utility functions is considered, there is a greater scope for parametric variations in the relation between the marginal and the total.

Consider now a third type of variation, namely, that of a shift of the utility function over time. The impact on the discount rate ρ will depend on the nature of the shift, in particular on the respective influences on the welfare level and the marginal utility of consumption. For example, if the personal welfare function shifts in such a way that the marginal utility falls more sharply between now and the future while the rise of the overall welfare level is not changed, then clearly such a shift will kick up the social rate of discount. On the other hand, if the decline in marginal utility is not enhanced by the shift while the rise of welfare level is reduced, clearly ρ will be pulled down. An interesting case to consider in this conext is a fall of A over time in equation (20):

$$W_i^t = A(t) + \frac{1}{\eta}(C_i^t)^\eta, \quad \text{with} \quad \eta < 1, \quad \text{and} \quad \frac{dA(t)}{dt} < 0 \quad (22)$$

A faster rate of decline of $A(t)$ over time will have the effect of reducing W_f^*, keeping W_f' unchanged, and this will make the social discount rate ρ go down.

Is there a plausible interpretation of equation (22)? I would like to suggest two. First, increased pollution over time may cut down the general quality of life without necessarily affecting the marginal utility of consumption.[8] Even today the lack of fresh air in a city makes one feel that much worse off in general, but the usefulness of

---

8. See Dasgupta's (1971) use of a utility function of the form given by equation (22), interpreting the shift as arising from population 'congestion' (pp. 311–13). However, since his maximand is simply the sum total of individual utilities, the 'equity' consequences of this shift have no role in his model.

an additional unit of consumption may not be reduced (and may, in fact, even be increased if the consumer good in question is aimed at freshening the air or compensating for the ill effects of polluted air). If this characterization of increasing pollution is accepted, the result will be to make the discount rate less than otherwise, since the reduced welfare level will pull ρ down, while unchanged (and possibly enhanced) marginal utility of consumption will not counteract it (and will possibly reinforce it).

A second interpretation concerns the changing notion of the subsistence level. If $\eta < 0$, then the personal welfare function is bounded on top (as with Ramsey, 1928), but the value of $(1/\eta)(C_i^t)^\eta$ is negative for all consumption levels. If significance is attached not merely to marginal utility, but also to the value of the welfare level, then on A falls the task of pulling up the welfare schedule above the zero value for consumption levels exceeding a certain minimum, say $\bar{C}$ (see Figure 8.1). The value $\bar{C}$ of consumption level for which W_i is zero may be interpreted – not without reason – as the subsistence level. An increasing subsistence requirement over time is not contrary to the actual history of social ideas, and there may be good reason to think that in the future the concept of 'basic needs' will go on becoming more demanding. But this does not necessarily affect the notion of marginal utility of consumption. A downward shift of A, as in equation (22), will raise the subsistence level, pulling down total welfare values but without affecting the marginal utility schedule (see Figure 8.1).

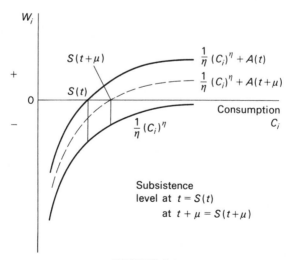

FIGURE 8.1

In choosing an appropriate social discount rate, therefore, one has to consider not merely the rate of growth of consumption, but also the relative roles of marginal utility vis-à-vis total welfare level, the nature and extent of concavity of the personal welfare function, as well as the characteristics of the shifts of the welfare function over time.

7   The Inadequacy of Welfarism

Utilitarianism, leximin, and the class of social welfare functionals satisfying condition (16) have the common feature of making the relative merits of the social states depend only on the personal welfare characteristics of the respective states. If any factor has to have an influence on the social ordering R, this can be only *through* its influence on the personal welfare vectors. Note that this is not a necessary characteristic of a social welfare functional, since that merely requires that the social ordering over X be a function of the n-tuple of individual welfare *functions* $\{W_i\}$.

Welfarism can be defined as making the social ordering of X depend only on the placing of each social state in the n-dimensional space of individual welfare values (ignoring the description of the states in other respects). If two states — however different — generate the same personal welfare values for each person, then under welfarism, they must be treated exactly in the same way.[9] Formally, this corresponds to the property of neutrality, which was defined in a strong form (incorporating independence of irrelevant alternatives) as condition SN in Section 4. The weaker version of 'neutrality', which characterizes welfarism, is the following (see also Arrow, 1963, p. 101).

Neutrality (N): If for some permutation function $\tau(\cdot)$ over X, $W_i(x) = \hat{W}_i(\tau(x))$ for all i and all x, and if $\hat{R}$ is the ordering of X obtained by replacing x by $\tau(x)$ in R for all x, then $R = F(\{W_i\})$ implies that $\hat{R} = F(\{\hat{W}_i\})$.

It can be shown that any SWFL satisfying unrestricted domain (U), independence (I), and the Pareto indifference rule (P^o) must satisfy strong neutrality SN (see d'Aspremont and Gevers, 1977; Sen,

---

9. Note, however, that while this is a characteristic of the Rawlsian lexicographic maximin rule as typically formulated in economic discussions, Rawls (1971) himself applied the difference principle to the problem of distribution of 'primary goods' only. Furthermore, Rawls' 'two principles' taken together depart substantially from welfarism because of the principle of liberty, which indeed has priority.

1977a).[10] Since *SN* implies neutrality, any approach that leads to a social welfare functional which fulfills U, P^o, and I must satisfy welfarism.

It is because of this result that in the axiomatic derivation of utilitarianism or leximin, neutrality does not have to be required as a condition on its own if U, I, and P^o (or, of course, P^*) are postulated. In fact, even in Arrow's own framework, neutrality is 'nearly' present, even though he held that 'the principle of neutrality is not intuitively basic' (Arrow, 1963, p. 101). Arrow combines conditions U and I with the weak Pareto principle P (dealing with unanimous strict preference) rather than the Pareto indifference rule P^o (dealing with unanimous indifference), and this leads to the neutrality of *winning* coalitions over all pairs of social states, but leaves open the question when the winning coalition is indifferent over a particular pair. (This is, in fact, the basic 'lemma' in Arrow's General Possibility theorem, the proof of the theorem being completed by the demonstration that the winning coalition must consist of only one person.)

How acceptable is welfarism and related forms of neutrality? We can readily note what it denies. First, it leaves out considerations of liberty defined in the form of a person's right to have his way in choices over *specific* pairs where the choice is thought to be legitimately his 'concern' only (see Sen, 1970, 1976a). Second, it leaves out 'rights' and 'claims' that arise from some particular action now or in the past (for example, in the concepts of 'value' and 'exploitation' in Marx (1887), or of 'entitlements' in Nozick (1974)). Third, it leaves out all judgements arising from concepts of 'desert', which — unlike 'needs' — cannot be readily captured in a welfaristic framework.

Are any of these considerations relevant to the choices involved in the social rate of discount? It is possible to argue that they may be. First, there is the question whether future generations have a *right* to enjoy natural resources that the present generation is depleting rapidly. Second, there is also the question whether the liberty of the future generations can be seen as being unacceptably compromised by certain activities of the present generation — failure to control pollution, for example.

One has to be careful to avoid double-counting. If the future generation's 'right' to the use of natural resources is related to their 'right' to have a decent standard of living, then this can — without undue strain — be accommodated within welfarism. On the other hand, if the right to natural resources is based on some innate concept

---

10. Guha (1972) and Blau (1976) have similar results for social decision functions (transforming each n-tuple of individual orderings to a quasi-transitive R). See also Blau and Deb (1977).

of 'entitlement', irrespective of whether the future generation is going to be well off, or badly off, then clearly this is an *additional* consideration. If so, the discount rate relevant to investments for better utilization of natural resources cannot be derived only from welfaristic considerations (W_p^*, W_f^*, W_p', W_f' and so on). The choice of evaluative weights has to reflect these rights as well.

It is fair to say that the recent increase in interest in 'entitlement theories' has not led to much discussion of this intergenerational issue. Many relevant questions have remained unanalysed. Are we free to blow natural resources as we like as long as we can justify it on grounds of our low welfare level, high marginal utility, and so forth, as compared with future generations? For example, even if our marginal utility from this resource use is greater than that of the future generation and even if we remain poorer in terms of welfare level than the future generation, can the future generation still legitimately claim that we are grabbing something to which we are not entitled (capitalizing on the arbitrary fact that we could get at the resources before the future generation could)? It is far from clear how one might go about answering these questions, but one can scarcely maintain that such questions simply do not arise. And the choice of social rates of discount for investments in the development of natural resources (including energy) is certainly not independent of these issues.

On the issue of pollution perhaps a bit more can be said. The analogy with torture is not absurd. While an isolated incident like Seveso can be an accident, the broad general development of pollution is typically the result of deliberate action. Lasting pollution is a kind of calculable oppression of the future generation. It may, therefore, be quite appropriate in this context to examine whether welfarism is adequate for a normative analysis of torture.

Let i be the 'inquisitor' and h the 'heretic'. I take it that it is unnecessary to specify who is in a position to torture whom. The social state t with torture will make h worse off and i better off than the social state s will without torture: $W_h(t) < W_h(s)$ and $W_i(t) > W_i(s)$. The utilitarian will be opposed to the torture if and only if $W_i(t) - W_i(s) < W_h(s) - W_h(t)$; that is, the torturer gains less than the tortured loses. Suppose this is not the case. The lexicographic maximin rule will be opposed to torture only if the minimal welfare level of the four possible 'positions' is that of being person h in social state t: $W_i(s) \geqslant W_h(t)$.[11] Suppose that is not the case either: the inquisitor suffers from depression, and he is worse off in the absence of torture

11. This is a necessary condition, becoming sufficient only if $\geqslant$ is replaced by $>$, or supplemented by $W_i(t) > W_h(s)$.

than the heretic is with torture: $W_i(s) < W_h(t)$. In fact, to make the welfaristic picture even more definitive on equity grounds, let us also assume that also $W_i(t) < W_h(t)$. So the miserable inquisitor is worse off than the resilient heretic whether or not the torture takes place, and his personal welfare gain from the torture is conceded to be greater than the welfare loss of the heretic.

Must we then support the torture? It is not easy to construct a welfaristic argument against torture in this case.[12] But it is legitimate to argue that the personal welfare data are inherently inadequate in deciding on an issue like this. We may wish to concede to person h his right to personal liberty, which cannot be violated on grounds of net gain of the utility sum or on grounds of the torturer being in general worse off. The choice is a particular one between t and s involving an act, namely, torture, and this descriptive feature of the social states has to be noted *directly*. Person h's right not to be tortured against his will cannot be captured in terms of arguments based on personal welfare information only. The same personal welfare numbers when holding for two social states t and s of *different* description (for example, t involving a tax on rich h for poor i's benefit, and s no such tax), may require us to judge the choice differently. This distinction violates neutrality and cannot be captured within welfarism.

If the similarity between torture and calculated pollution is accepted, then it can be argued that in deciding on social rates of discount for investment projects that have a bearing on pollution, the welfaristic models of Sections 5 and 6 (and in fact, virtually all models proposed so far in the literature) are quite inadequate. The evaluative weights considered in Sections 2–4 cannot be made functions *only* of personal welfare information, and the analysis requires supplementation by non-welfaristic considerations of liberty.

Suppose the investment project in question will eliminate some pollution that the present generation will otherwise impose on the future. Even if the future generation may be richer and may enjoy a higher welfare level, *and* even if its marginal utility from the consumption gain is accepted to be less than the marginal welfare loss of the present generation, this may still not be accepted to be decisive for rejecting the investment when the alternative implies long-term effects of environmental pollution. The avoidance of oppression of the future generations has to be given a value of its own.

---

12. Appeals to 'rule utilitarianism' and other non-act-evaluation arguments also raise problems that are well known; we can even make the situation quite unique. On this general question, see Sen (1979).

If, on the other hand, the investment project is itself a *polluting* one, then exactly the opposite kind of a case could possibly exist even when the investment seems justified on welfaristic grounds. The evaluation of investments and the choice of relevant social rates of discount cannot, therefore, be reduced simply to considerations involving personal welfare data relating to the present and the future.

These issues are relevant to the current controversy over investment in nuclear energy, particularly fast breeder reactors. These investments are not merely capital-intensive and sensitive to the discount rates. They also involve considerable risks of environmental pollution.[13] Despite safeguards against accidents, one cannot assume the probability of accidents to be zero; over time, accidents are difficult to rule out. The accidents that have occurred illustrate that not all possibilities are foreseen. In fact, in fast breeder reactors the possibility of the failure of normal control mechanisms opens up the eventuality of 'what is technically a nuclear explosion, though the growth of the chain reaction would be slow compared with that which occurs in a nuclear bomb and the energy released will be correspondingly less'. If the reactor containment fails to cope with such a contingency, 'then not only iodine and caesium, but substantial quantities of non-volatile fission products such as strontium, as well as plutonium, would be released' (Royal Commission on Environmental Pollution, 1976, pp. 46–7).

In addition to such accidents, the normal dangers of a plutonium economy are themselves quite worth considering, especially in the context of storage and reprocessing of radioactive wastes. There is also the not yet fully settled issue of the alleged special danger from 'hot' particles (see Tamplin and Cochran, 1976; Dolphin *et al.*, 1974; Lovins and Patterson, 1975; and UK Medical Research Council, 1975), which *if* true, will – according to some – 'effectively preclude the use of nuclear power' (Royal Commission on Environmental Pollution, 1976, p. 24).

The complexity of nuclear power issues arises from a variety of economic and ethical considerations. The returns from a nuclear energy programme in general and a programme of fast breeders in particular will, of course, depend on the alternative cost of energy production, for example, from sun, wind, and wave, and also from

13. One reason why a fast breeder programme is capital-intensive is that fast breeders require a large initial inventory of plutonium, specifically, four tons of plutonium per gigawatt (10^6 kilowatts) of electric output. To start a fast breeder of a given capacity, the required plutonium inventory would amount to seven years' output of a thermal Magnox reactor of equivalent output (see Royal Commission on Environmental Pollution, 1976, p. 46).

fusion. One cannot give an *a priori* judgement on any of these matters. But what is worth emphasizing in the context of the preceding discussion is that in addition to these relative cost considerations, there are issues in this choice involving 'welfaristic' questions of relative prosperity as well as 'non-welfaristic' factors involving rights of particular groups of people whose liberty may be violated by a calculated programme of nuclear energy development involving fast breeders. The cost-and-utility calculus cannot begin to convey the complexity of choices surrounding investment in nuclear power.

8   Concluding Remarks

We have investigated two departures from the utilitarian approach to the determination of social rates of discount. The first, concerned chiefly with 'equity', involves a systematic attempt to supplement considerations of marginal gains and losses of personal welfare by a concern about aggregate welfare levels (Section 5). Although the focus was not principally on the Rawlsian 'Difference Principle', the information set for maximin (concerned with welfare *levels*) was used to supplement the utilitarian information set (concerned with welfare *differences*). A general characterization of the respective influences permitted some directional conclusions to be drawn dealing with variations in the growth rate, in the pattern of concavity of personal welfare functions, and shifts in welfare functions due to growing pollution, changing conceptions of 'subsistence', and so forth (Section 6).

The other departure, involved chiefly with 'liberty', includes a rejection of 'welfarism', which judges social states exclusively by their personal welfare characteristics.[14] Related to an earlier argument that a concern for liberty requires us to go beyond welfarism (Sen, 1970, Chapter 6), the question of pollution was examined in the context of the liberty of future generations, and the need to go beyond personal welfare data was outlined (Section 7). Other possible 'rights' that may take us beyond welfarism (for example, the right to the use of natural resources) were touched on more briefly, noting some inherent ambiguities.

The format in which these ethical considerations were introduced is that of social welfare functionals (SWFL), which is an extension of

---

14. Note that a rejection of welfarism does not necessarily imply a rejection of the so-called end-state approach, or of 'consequentialism'. I have explored these issues in Sen (1979, 1982).

Arrow's (1951) framework of social welfare functions (Sections 5–7). The differences from Arrow consist of (i) a wider informational base of personal welfares admitted into the analysis, and (ii) the avoidance of elements of 'neutrality', which push us towards welfarism and which are logically implied by combining unrestricted domain (U) and independence of irrelevant alternatives (I) with any version of the Pareto principle. (Given U and I, Arrow's weak version P implies neutrality partially, while the strong Pareto principle P^* or even the Pareto indifference rule P^o implies it fully.)

While these ethical considerations enter the problem of evaluative weighting on which the determination of *social* rates of discount depends (Sections 3 and 4), the question has to be posed as to whether they do not equally enter the market determination of rates of interest through their influence on individual behaviour. The inadequacy of utilitarianism has no *necessary* implication regarding the inoptimality of the market interest structure.

However, it is unlikely that these ethical considerations play a sufficiently important role in people's market behaviour. First of all, they involve a fair amount of universalized moral analysis and deliberation about distant implications. Although I have tried to argue elsewhere (Sen, 1977b) that the assumption that people maximize their personal welfare in their actual behaviour is quite inadequate, the 'non-selfish' considerations have their own biases (concerning class, community, visibility and immediacy of effects, and so forth).

Second, the information on which the choice of social rates of discount is based (in the light of these ethical analyses) may not be widely available, and some of it may in fact require new investigation. The parsimonious informational structure on which the market operates (the adequacy of which under certain circumstances has been shown for the attainment of certain efficiency results, for example, Pareto optimality *or* being in the core) is in fact quite inadequate to sustain ethical analysis involving equity or liberty, or even utilitarianism.

Third, even if everyone had all the information and based their market actions on exactly the same ethical analyses as their political or public activities, the interpersonal weighting implicit in the market equilibria may be quite different from the weighting that is chosen for public decisions, or for social benefit–cost analysis. The problem is present whenever personal moralities differ even when all actions (including market actions) are assumed to be fully determined by the respective personal moralities.

Fourth, the interpersonal distributions of sacrifices and benefits are not the same in different types of investment. Indeed, the difference between private and social rates of discount under the 'isolation' argument can be reduced entirely to this contrast of 'composition' (Section 2). Even with the same evaluative weights on 'named goods' (or 'named consumption'), the private and social rates of discount will differ depending on the interpersonal compositions of present consumption sacrifices and future consumption gains in the two types of investment. (It was also shown that it is quite misleading to attribute this difference to externalities of consumption.) The market rates are based on a *third* type of composition, corresponding neither necessarily to the composition underlying the 'social' discount rate, nor necessarily to that implicit in the 'private' discount rate (Sections 3 and 4). Indeed, the conclusion that the social rate may lie below the private rate in the usual simple models did not, in fact, imply that the social rate must lie below the *market* rate, and different conclusions can emerge depending on the relevant parameters (see Sections 3 and 4).

There is, in fact, very little scope for avoiding a deliberate ethical exercise in choosing appropriate rates of discount for social benefit-cost analysis. The problem can be split into (1) investigation of compositions and (2) selection of evaluative weights on each element in the composite structure. The former category includes both the question of interpersonal composition of gains and losses (Sections 2-4) and the identification of those descriptive features (for example, generating or counteracting pollution, preserving natural resources) that may require us to go beyond welfarist considerations (Section 7). The relevance of the latter to investments in energy and related research and development can hardly be ignored.

The second category includes the use of utilitarian reasoning (based on identification of *gains and losses* of personal welfare), equity considerations (needing supplementation by considerations of personal welfare *levels*), and the analyses of the right to liberty and other rights that the future generations may be acknowledged to have (needing supplementation by non-welfare, descriptive information).

I do not doubt that different compromises can be reached about the relative importance to be attached to these various considerations. But the least we should require is that attention be paid to the competing claims of these different influences and that the *process* of choosing discount rates for social benefit-cost analysis be made more reasoned and more explicit. The search has to be more than an intellectual blindman's buff.

References

Arrow, K. J. (1951): *Social Choice and Individual Values* (New York: Wiley).

—— (1963): *Social Choice and Individual Values* (New York: Wiley), 2nd edn.

—— (1966): 'Discounting and Public Investment Criteria', in A. V. Kneese and S. C. Smith (eds), *Water Research* (Baltimore: Johns Hopkins University Press for Resources for the Future).

—— (1973): 'Some Ordinalist-Utilitarian Notes on Rawls' Theory of Justice', *Journal of Philosophy*, **70**.

—— (1976): 'Extended Sympathy and the Possibility of Social Choice', *American Economic Review*, **67**.

—— and Kurz, M. (1970): *Public Investment, the Rate of Return, and Optimal Fiscal Policy* (Baltimore: Johns Hopkins University Press for Resources for the Future).

Baumol, W. J. (1968a): 'On the Appropriate Discount Rate for Evaluation of Public Projects', in Hearings before the Subcommittee on Economy of Government of the Joint Economic Committee, US Congress (Washington: GPO).

—— (1968b): 'On the Social Rate of Discount', *American Economic Review*, **58**.

Blackorby, C. (1975): 'Degrees of Cardinality and Aggregate Partial Ordering', *Econometrica*, **43**.

Blau, J. H. (1976): 'Neutrality, Monotonicity and the Right of Veto: A Comment', *Econometrica*, **44**.

—— and Deb, R. (1977): 'Social Decision Functions and the Veto', *Econometrica*, **45**.

Dasgupta, P. (1971): 'On the Concept of Optimum Population', *Review of Economic Studies*, **38**.

—— (1974): 'On Some Alternative Criteria for Justice Between Generations', *Journal of Public Economics*, **3**.

——, Marglin, S. A. and Sen, A. K. (1972): *Guidelines for Project Evaluation*, UNIDO (New York: United Nations).

d'Aspremont, C. and Gevers, L. (1977): 'Equity and the Informational Basis of Collective Choice', *Review of Economic Studies*, **44**.

Deschamps, R. and Gevers, L. (1978): 'Leximin and Utilitarian Rules: A Joint Characterization', *Journal of Economic Theory*, **17**.

Dobb, M. H. (1960): *An Essay on Economic Growth and Planning* (London: Routledge).

Dolphin, G. W. *et al.* (1974): *Radiological Problems in the Protection of Persons Exposed to Plutonium* (United Kingdom: National Radiological Protection Board).

Eckstein, O. (1957): 'Investment Criteria for Economic Development and the Theory of Intertemporal Welfare Economics', *Quarterly Journal of Economics*, **71**.

Feldstein, M. S. (1964): 'The Social Time Preference Discount Rate in Cost-Benefit Analysis', *Economic Journal*, **74**.

—— (1972): 'The Inadequacy of Weighted Discount Rates', in R. Layard (ed.), *Cost-Benefit Analysis* (Harmondsworth and Baltimore: Penguin).

Fine, B. (1975): 'A Note on Interpersonal Comparisons and Comparability', *Econometrica*, **43**.

Gevers, L. (1979): 'On Interpersonal Comparability and Social Welfare Orderings', *Econometrica*, **47**.

Guha, A. S. (1972): 'Neutrality, Monotonicity and the Right of Veto', *Econometrica*, **40**.

Hahn, F. H. (1971): 'Equilibrium with Transaction Costs', *Econometrica*, **39**.

Hammond, P. J. (1976): 'Equity, Arrow's Conditions and Rawls' Difference Principle', *Econometrica*, **44**.

—— (1977): 'Dual Interpersonal Comparisons of Utility and the Welfare Economics of Income Distribution', *Journal of Public Economics*, **6**.

Harberger, A. C. (1964): 'Techniques of Project Appraisal', Universities National Bureau of Economic Research Conference on Economic Planning (27-28 November 1964).

—— (1968): 'On Measuring the Social Opportunity Cost of Public Funds', in *The Discount Rate in Public Investment Evaluation*, Report No. 17, Conference Proceedings from the Committee on the Economics of Water Resources Development of the Western Agricultural Economics Research Council (Denver, Colorado, 17-18 December 1968).

—— (1973): *Project Evaluation: Collected Papers* (Chicago: Markham).

Hicks, J. R. (1958): 'Measurement of Real Income', *Oxford Economic Papers*, **10**.

Lind, R. C. (1964): 'The Social Rate of Discount and the Optimal Rate of Investment: Further Comment', *Quarterly Journal of Economics*, **78**.

Little, I. M. D. and Mirrlees, J. A. (1974): *Project Appraisal and Planning for Developing Countries* (London: Hutchinson).

Lovins, A. B. and Patterson, W. C. (1975): 'Plutonium Particles: Some Like Them Hot', *Nature*, **254** (27 March), 278-80.

Marglin, S. A. (1963a): 'The Social Rate of Discount and the Optimal Rate of Investment', *Quarterly Journal of Investment*, **77**.

—— (1963b): 'The Opportunity Cost of Investment', *Quarterly Journal of Economics*, **77**.

—— (1976): *Value and Price in the Labour-Surplus Economy* (Oxford: Clarendon Press).

Marx, K. (1887): *Capital: A Critical Analysis of Capitalist Production*, vol. I (London: Sonnenschein; republished, Allen & Unwin, 1938).

Maskin, E. (1978): 'A Theorem on Utilitarianism', *Review of Economic Studies*, **45**.

—— (1979): 'Decision-Making Under Ignorance with Implications for Social Choice', *Theory and Decision*, **11**.

Medical Research Council (1975): *The Toxicity of Plutonium* (London: HMSO).

Mirrlees, J. A. (1971): 'An Exploration in the Theory of Optimal Income Taxation', *Review of Economic Studies*, **38**.

Nozick, R. (1974): *Anarchy, State and Utopia* (Oxford: Blackwell).

Page, T. (1977): *Conservation and Economic Efficiency* (Baltimore: Johns Hopkins University Press for Resources for the Future).

Phelps, E. S. (1965): *Fiscal Neutrality Toward Economic Growth* (New York: McGraw-Hill).

—— (1976): 'Recent Developments in Welfare Economics: Justice et Equité', Discussion Paper No. 75-7617, Economics Workshop, Columbia University. [Later published in M. D. Intriligator (ed.), *Frontiers of Quantitative Economics*, vol. 3 (Amsterdam: North-Holland, 1977), and in E. S. Phelps, *Studies in Macroeconomic Theory*, vol. 2, *Redistribution and Growth* (New York: Academic Press, 1980).]

Ramsey, F. P. (1928): 'A Mathematical Theory of Saving', *Economic Journal*, **38**.

Rawls, J. (1971): *A Theory of Justice* (Oxford: Clarendon Press).

Roberts, K. W. S. (1980a): 'Interpersonal Comparability and Social Choice Theory', *Review of Economic Studies*, **47**.

—— (1980b): 'Possibility Theorems with Interpersonally Comparable Welfare Levels', *Review of Economic Studies*, **47**.

Royal Commission on Environmental Pollution (1976): *Sixth Report* (London: HMSO).

Sen, A. K. (1957): 'A Note on Tinbergen on the Optimum Rate of Saving', *Economic Journal*, **67**.

—— (1960): *Choice of Techniques* (Oxford: Blackwell).

—— (1961): 'On Optimizing the Rate of Saving', *Economic Journal*, **71**. [Essay 4 in this volume.]

—— (1967): 'Isolation, Assurance and the Social Rate of Discount', *Quarterly Journal of Economics*, **81**. [Essay 5 in this volume.]

—— (1968): *Choice of Techniques* (Oxford: Blackwell), 3rd edn.

—— (1970): *Collective Choice and Social Welfare* (Edinburgh: Oliver & Boyd; San Francisco: Holden-Day). [Reprinted, Amsterdam: North-Holland, 1979.]

—— (1973): *On Economic Inequality* (Oxford: Clarendon Press; New York: Norton).

—— (1974a): 'Informational Bases of Alternative Welfare Approaches', *Journal of Public Economics*, **3**.

—— (1974b): 'Rawls vs. Bentham: An Axiomatic Examination of the Pure Distribution Problem', *Theory and Decision*, vol. 4; reprinted in N. Daniels (ed.), *Reading Rawls* (Oxford: Blackwell, 1975).

—— (1976a): 'Liberty, Unanimity and Rights', *Economica*, **43**. [Reprinted in *Choice, Welfare and Measurement* (Oxford: Blackwell, 1982).]

—— (1976b): 'Real National Income', *Review of Economic Studies*, **43**. [Reprinted in *Choice, Welfare and Measurement*.]

—— (1977a): 'On Weights and Measures: Informational Constraints in Social Welfare Analysis', Walras-Bowley Lecture, Econometric Society, *Econometrica*, **45**. [Reprinted in *Choice, Welfare and Measurement*.]

—— (1977b): 'Rational Fools: A Critique of the Behavioural Foundations of Economic Theory', *Philosophy and Public Affairs*, **6**. [Reprinted in *Choice, Welfare and Measurement*.]

—— (1979): 'Utilitarianism and Welfarism', *Journal of Philosophy*, **76**.

—— (1982): 'Rights and Agency', *Philosophy and Public Affairs*, **11**.

Strasnick, S. (1976). 'Social Choice Theory and the Derivation of Rawls' Difference Principle', *Journal of Philosophy*, **73**.

Tamplin, A. R. and Cochran, T. B. (1976): *Radiation Standards for Hot Particles*, petition to the Atomic Energy Commission and the Environmental Protection Agency (Washington: Natural Resources Defense Council).

Tullock, G. (1964): 'The Social Rate of Discount and the Optimal Rate of Investment: Comment', *Quarterly Journal of Economics*, **78**.

Usher, D. (1964): 'The Social Rate of Discount and the Optimal Rate of Investment: Comment', *Quarterly Journal of Economics*, **78**.

Part III

Shadow Pricing and Employment

9

Optimum Savings, Technical Choice and the Shadow Price of Labour

1 *Saving Optimality and Choice of Techniques*

The determination of the optimum *size* of total savings and that of the optimum *capital-intensity* of investment are interdependent problems. This interdependence provides the starting point of this book [*Choice of Techniques*].[1] In particular for some underdeveloped countries the choice of a more capital-intensive technique, through its effect on the distribution of income, can be expected to yield a higher proportion of reinvestment out of the income generated.[2] The choice between projects of different degrees of capital-intensity depends, thus, on the relative weights to be attached to investment vis-à-vis consumption.[3]

The relative weights to be attached to investment vis-à-vis consumption should normally vary with the relative share of investment in total income. When we are concerned with the determination of the degree of capital-intensity for the economy *as a whole*, we cannot treat the relative weight to be attached to investment vis-à-vis consumption to be invariant. In such an exercise, the degree of capital-intensity, the share of investment, and the relative weights on investment and consumption all have to be solved *together* as interdependent problems.[4]

The problem is, however, somewhat different when the object of the exercise is the determination of the capital-intensity of invest-

1. *Choice of Techniques* (Oxford: Blackwell, 1960), Chapter I.
2. *Ibid.*, Chapters II and V.
3. *Ibid.*, Chapter VIII.
4. *Ibid.*, Chapters II, III, VII, and VIII. See also Sen [24], Dobb [6], Eckstein [7], and Bagchi [2].

From *Choice of Techniques*, Third Edition, Oxford: Blackwell, 1968. This is the Introduction to the Third Edition of the book, xiii–xxix.

ment for a marginal project. In such an exercise of project selection, the ratio of total investment to total income may be hardly affected by the degree of capital-intensity chosen, since the project may represent a relatively small share of total production. In the exercise of project selection, therefore, it may often make sense to take the relative weight to be attached to investment vis-à-vis consumption as given, much as a perfectly competitive firm takes the prices as independent of its own actions.

If we attach equal weights on savings and consumption, the varying share of reinvestment out of the income generated (depending on the capital-intensity of investment) need not affect our valuation of the output. This will make the proportion of reinvestment out of the generated income irrelevant to the problem of choice of capital-intensity. While this is a common assumption in some of the more traditional presentations of the problem of choice of techniques, this book is based on the assumption that the proportion of reinvestment *is* relevant, and an extra weight has to be attached to the investible surplus generated. The question that must, therefore, be asked is: why should we *not* attach the same marginal weight on the part of the output reinvested as on the part consumed?

Indeed we *should* attach the same weight on each, *provided* the share of savings in the national income is already optimum, so that there is no net gain in a marginal shift from consumption to investment, or vice-versa. This is in fact the underlying assumption (usually implicit) in the traditional presentation of the problem of choice of techniques in project selection. If, however, we regard the proportion of national income invested to be *below* optimum, then at the margin a unit of investment must be regarded as more valuable than a unit of consumption. This calls for attaching an extra weight on the proportion of the generated income that is to be reinvested. The type of considerations outlined in this book becomes relevant for project selection in the context of an over-all sub-optimality of savings. In fact, it can be viewed as a 'Second Best' problem, viz., choosing the best technical combination for a project in a situation where some constraint keeps the over-all rate of investment below optimal. The question that we should now discuss concerns the reasons for making such an assumption of sub-optimality of total savings.

2   Interdependence, Constraints and Sub-optimal Savings

The question of the sub-optimality of the saving rate is somewhat different for a predominantly private enterprise economy compared with that for a fully socialist economy. In a predominantly private enterprise economy, the amount of savings is determined by a market mechanism. If people have a general concern for the well-being of the future generations whose welfare depends on the savings made today, this presents an 'externality' that in general would tend to make the market savings to be inoptimal, even in the weak Paretian sense.[5] Further, under a set of fairly reasonable assumptions,[6] the market savings rate is likely to be lower (rather than higher) than the 'optimal'. That is, people may be agreeable to sign a contract which forces everyone to save more, though individually they may not agree to raise their own savings unilaterally, given the savings of the others. This inoptimality of individualistic action is a standard problem in a class of a non-zero-sum games, and we referred to it elsewhere as the 'Isolation Paradox'.[7]

In the above discussion of the sub-optimality of the market rate of savings, the welfare criterion used is simply the Paretian ordering. Sometimes, the 'incompleteness' of the Paretian ordering may rule out this type of judgement, and then we may have to take recourse to some other criteria. One method may be that of majority decisions, when we may ask such questions as to whether a majority will be agreeable to support a contract forcing people to save more for the future. The method of majority decisions is, however, prone to inconsistencies,[8] but when certain 'similarities' in individual orderings exist, such inconsistencies may, in fact, never arise.[9] There are also other possible criteria for social welfare, e.g. the use of interpersonally comparable cardinal indicators of individual welfare, the advantages and difficulties of which are by now fairly well known.

What is more common in planning exercises is to work with a given social ordering, or a 'utility function' for the society as a whole[10] (i.e. a 'social welfare function' in the sense of Bergson and

---

5. See Baumol [3], Sen [25, 29], and Marglin [13].

6. See Marglin [13], Lind [12], and Sen [29].

7. Sen [25, 29]. One example is the two-person, zero-sum game known as the 'Prisoners' Dilemma'.

8. This is only a special case of the difficulties of the existence of a 'social welfare function' satisfying a set of reasonable conditions, discussed by Arrow [1].

9. See Arrow [1], Chapter VII, and Sen [26].

10. The expression 'utility function' is somewhat misleading, since 'utility' is also used in the more restricted sense of 'pleasure' as in the context of Benthamite philosophy. We use it here meaning any function that we wish to maximize. Incidentally, such a utility function may not exist, e.g. in the case of a 'lexicographic ordering' (see Debreu [5], pp. 72-3). The use of a utility function, even if 'ordinal', demands more than the use of simply a social ordering; its 'continuity' is crucial. Further, for some of the purposes for which the utility function is to be used, it has to be 'cardinal', in the sense of being unique up to a positive linear transformation, which is an even more demanding assumption.

Samuelson [23]), and not worry about how precisely it is derived from individual orderings. This 'utility function' presumably is one adopted by the planner. The arbitrary nature of the derivation of such utility function is somewhat disturbing,[11] and it has clearly authoritarian elements. But it simplifies the problem considerably,[12] and may provide a means of incorporating some weight on the welfare of the future generations as such in addition to the weight it might get via the present generation's general concern about the well-being of the future generations.[13]

Without going further into this complex question, we may simply assume that a utility function is taken by the planners. If the 'transformation' possibilities between present and future consumption yield a rate of return of r, with the rate of transformation being given by $(1 + r)$, we may compare this with the social rate of discount i, when the relevant rate of 'indifferent substitution' between today's consumption and that in the future is given by $(1 + i)$. If i and r are not equal, the savings rate is not optimal.[14]

If the utility function has time as such as one of its arguments, as will be the case when a 'pure time discount' is assumed, the value of i will also depend on the precise rate of pure time discount.[15] If no such pure time discount is used, and utility is simply a function of the level of consumption, then the social rate of discount will correspond purely to the diminishing marginal utility of consumption (see Chapter VIII [of *Choice of Techniques*]). The following formula can then be shown to hold:

$$i = m \, \frac{\dot{C}}{C}, \qquad (1.1)$$

where m is the absolute value of the elasticity of marginal utility with respect to consumption at the relevant portion, C the level of consumption, and $\dot{C}$ the absolute rate of growth of consumption over time.[16]

11. Chapter VIII [of *Choice of Techniques*], pp. 74–5.
12. It can also help the planner, as Mirrlees points out, in the preliminary exercise of having 'a dialogue with himself' on what is to be done: see Mirrlees [18].
13. See Sen [25] and Marglin [13].
14. Equality of r and i is a *necessary* condition for optimal accumulation, but is *sufficient* only under special assumptions.
15. Regarding some difficulties with the use of a 'pure' time discount, see Dobb [6], Chapter II.
16. We assume, of course, a smooth and well-behaved utility function. With $U = f(C)$, we can write:

$$m = -\frac{f''}{f'} C \qquad (2)$$

An unconstrained optimal path of growth requires that r and i be equal for every point of time. This equality represents a condition of optimum accumulation.[17] But in a predominantly private enterprise economy the path of total consumption may be largely given by the market mechanism, and the problem of choice of techniques for a marginal public project in such an economy may have to take the inequality of r and i as simply given, and assume an over-all inoptimality of the savings rate.

Even in a socialist economy there may be political limits to the variations in the savings rate,[18] so that it may not be possible to equate r and i. This is especially because the optimality of the savings rate often seems to require extraordinarily high rates of savings.[19] When the utility function assumed by the planner takes into account the interests of the future generations directly (in addition to the way it is reflected indirectly through the preferences of the present generation), there is nothing surprising in the existence of these constraints imposed by political factors. The present generation may well impose political limits on the extent to which their interests can be sacrificed for the welfare of the future generations.

When, however, the utility function is based only on the preferences of the present generation (including, of course, their concern for the future generations), it might appear that there could be no constraint that would keep the rate of saving below optimal in the case defined. Taking, for example, the 'Isolation Paradox', if indeed everyone agrees to signing a contract forcing all to save more for the

---

Since population grows over time, a somewhat different formulation of the utility function may be more sensible. *Per capita* utility may be related to *per capita* consumption (see Chapter VIII [of *Choice of Techniques*], p. 75). If the utility of the community at a given point of time is identified with the level of *per capita* utility, then the rate of discount corresponding to the maximization of the intertemporal aggregate of this utility is given by (n being population growth, and C per capita consumption):

$$i = n + m \left(\frac{\dot{C}}{C} - n \right) \tag{1.2}$$

If, however, the welfare of the community is identified with per capita utility *multiplied* by the size of the population, then the expression for the appropriate rate of discount is:

$$i = m \left(\frac{\dot{C}}{C} - n \right) \tag{1.3}$$

On this question, see Meade [17], and Marglin [16].

17. For example, Ramsey's celebrated 'rule' which equates the proportionate rate of fall of marginal utility to the rate of return on capital corresponds exactly to the equality of r and i. The same is true of other variational models of optimum accumulation, e.g. Goodwin [9], Chakravarty [4], Sen [28], which derive from Ramsey's model. See also Eckstein [7].

18. See Chapter V [of *Choice of Techniques*]. See also Dobb [6].

19. See, for example, Goodwin [9] and Chakravarty [4]. See, however, Mirrlees [19].

future generations,[20] what could prevent such a contract from actually coming into effect? And this process, it may be expected, should eliminate the sub-optimality of the rate of saving.

The picture is, however, not so simple, for there may be more than one contract that is Pareto-superior to no contract at all,[21] but not Pareto-superior to each other. This 'bargaining problem' does not arise with some of the games in terms of which the inoptimality of the market savings is illustrated (e.g. 'the Prisoners' Dilemma'), for in these games there tends to be a *unique* collective solution, Pareto-superior to the non-cooperative outcome.[22] But when a bargaining problem does exist thanks to a multiplicity of possible cooperative contracts, which is typically the case, the inoptimality of the non-cooperative outcome does not automatically show the way to the cooperative solution. Further, even if the planners may decide what is the 'right' solution to the bargaining problem, there may be difficulties in executing such a contract, for some individuals will be better off under some other contract. In fact, a conflict of interest of this kind between the members of the present generation may possibly rule out all but some of the mildest plans of raising the rate of saving. Thus political constraints that keep the savings rate sub-optimal can be expected *even when* our concept of optimality may not embrace anything other than the values of the present generation.

3   Programming and the Shadow Price of Labour

In an economy with surplus labour, the social opportunity cost of labour, in the sense of alternative marginal productivity, is nil,[23] and it is this consideration that prompted several economists to argue for choosing the most labour-intensive technique out of all the efficient ones, i.e. for preferring a more labour-intensive technique as long as the marginal product of labour is non-negative. This neat recommendation, however, gets disturbed if the over-all savings rate is sub-optimal, for then we must attach a higher weight to the part of the income that is reinvested compared with the part that is consumed,

20. See Appendix to Chapter VIII [of *Choice of Techniques*], pp. 79–80.
21. Sen [29]. This leads to a 'bargaining problem', on which see especially Nash [20].
22. Sen [29].
23. It is to be noted, however, that what we are concerned with is the possibility of the marginal product of labour measured in terms of *the number of men* being nil over a certain range, which does not require that the marginal product of *labour hours* be nil over a range (see Chapter I [of *Choice of Techniques*], pp. 3–5), or at all (Sen [27], pp. 429–32). The distinction is important for a peasant economy, a major source of labour for the growing 'advanced' sector.

and the division between consumption and savings depends on the division of income between wages and profits.[24] The marginal product of labour may be positive but less than the additional consumption generated by the extra wage payment, so that the positive impact on our objective function through greater output may be countered by a shift from investment to consumption, which makes a negative contribution given the lower weight on consumption.

From this line of reasoning it is easy to argue that labour is not costless even in an economy with surplus labour, if the volume of savings is sub-optimal. If, however, the savings are just right, and no extra weight is to be attached to investment vis-à-vis consumption, labour can be treated as costless, for at the margin consumption and investment are equally valuable.

The whole question turns on the relative weights to be attached to investment and savings, and this depends on the extent of sub-optimality (if any) of the savings rate, which in its turn depends on the welfare function chosen. One of the central results of this book, viz. that 'the difference between the ... schools of thought regarding the valuation of labour really boils down to a difference in objectives',[25] was derived from this line of reasoning.

To avoid confusion, however, we should clarify precisely what we mean by the cost of labour. Here it is taken as that magnitude to which the marginal product of labour at market prices is equated in choosing the optimum degree of labour-intensity. But this is not the only possible definition.

An alternative way of defining the cost of labour is to identify it as the 'shadow price' of labour obtainable from formulating the problem of resource allocation in this economy as an exercise in programming. The objective function W can be taken to be some concave function of the process selection vector x representing the intensity of each activity. The 'slack' (or excess supply) of each resource j is taken to be a concave function of x, viz. $f_j(x)$, given the total supply of resource j. With m types of resources, the set of $f_j(x)$ can be represented by $F(x)$. Also, with each choice of process intensities x, we generate certain purchasing power depending on the level of employment, wages, etc., and given the demand behaviours we can trace the minimum amount of consumer goods that must be produced to meet these demands. Let $E(x)$ represent the excess production vector standing for the difference between the actual production and these minimum output requirements. The choice variables consist of the elements of the vector x, which includes technological choice. The problem now is:

Maximize $\qquad\qquad W = W(x)$ $\qquad\qquad\qquad$ (3.1)

subject to

$$x \geqslant 0, \qquad\qquad\qquad (3.2)$$

$$F(x) \geqslant 0, \qquad\qquad\qquad (3.3)$$

and

$$E(x) \geqslant 0. \qquad\qquad\qquad (3.4)$$

This is an extremely general formulation, and the problem can be made more specific by further elaboration. If we take $W(x)$, $E(x)$ and $F(x)$ to be linear, this will be a problem of linear programming. Further, with the framework of linear activity analysis, we can get an output vector y linearly related to the activity vector, and then we can make W some function of y. In fact the relation between the choice of activities x and the value of the objective can be defined in a number of different ways, and the same is true of the constraints. Here we take a very general interpretation, and only assume that $W(x)$, $E(x)$ and $F(x)$ are all concave, but not necessarily strictly concave. This makes the problem one of concave programming, including the special case of linear programming.

Let x^* be an optimal solution to the problem, and let p^* and π^* be the optimal *dual* variables, corresponding respectively to the resource constraints and the demand constraints, with the saddle-point properties specified by the Kuhn–Tucker Theorem.[26] In the case of linear programming, p^* is interpretable simply as the set of shadow prices of the respective resources. Even in the more general case of concave programming, the *dual* variables specify the limits of marginal returns to the respective resources. Define $U(z)$ as the maximum value of $W(x)$ for a given resource supply vector z, subject to the constraints, remembering that $F(x)$ depends on the value of z, and can instead be written as $G(x, z)$ when z is a variable.

$$U(z) = \max_{x} W(x), \text{ subject to } G(x, z) \geqslant 0, E(x) \geqslant 0, \text{ and } x \geqslant 0 \quad (4)$$

26. See Karlin [11], theorem 7.1.1.

Consider z' another vector of the same resources such that z' and z are exactly the same except for some particular resource k being larger by one unit, i.e. $z'_j = z_j$, for all j except for $j = k$, and $z'_k = z_k + 1$. Now, $p^*_k(z)$ and $p^*_k(z')$ being the dual variables associated with resource k for the two problems one with resource supply z and another with resource supply z', it can be shown that:

$$p^*_k(z) \geqslant U(z') - U(z) \geqslant p^*_k(z') \tag{5}$$

That is the marginal return to a unit of resource k lies in the range defined by the dual variables corresponding to k, which indicates an obvious shadow price interpretation.

It can be demonstrated that the inner product of $E(x)$ and $F(x)$ with π^* and p^*, must be zero in the optimal solution:[27]

$$(\pi^*, E(x^*)) + (p^*, F(x^*)) = 0 \tag{6}$$

Since every p_j, π_i, f_i and E_i, must be non-negative, a strictly positive f_j must imply a zero p^*_j. But a strictly positive f_j implies that there is some excess ('slack') of resource j. So either a resource is fully employed, or its dual variable (corresponding to the shadow price) is nil.

There is nothing startling in this result, which is a standard one in concave programming, including the special case of linear programming. But how does it square with our result of the real labour cost varying with the objective function? This result (6) is quite independent of the exact specification of the objective function. We may attach more or less weight on investment, vis-à-vis consumption, but either there is full employment of labour, or its shadow price must be nil. Since we are concerned with a surplus labour economy, it might appear that we must treat labour to be costless, *no matter what objective function we choose.*

The contradiction, however, is purely terminological. If there is surplus labour even under optimal allocation, the marginal return to an additional unit of labour (given the constraints) must be zero. In this sense the shadow price of labour must indeed be nil. This does not, however, mean that the marginal product of labour is nil in the sense that no more output can be physically produced by using more labour, or in the sense that it is zero in terms of its market value. Marginal product can be given various interpretations. First, we may ask how much more of W can we produce given the resource requirement constraints, but not the demand constraints. In this problem, where the constraints (3.4) are ignored, the marginal return

27. See the proof of the Kuhn–Tucker theorem in Karlin [11], pp. 200–3.

to a unit of resource j may not be zero even when p_j^* as previously defined is nil. Second, $W(x)$ involves some valuation of the output, but it may not coincide with the market valuation of it. Taking y to be the output vector associated with the technological choice vector x, and q to be the vector of market prices, it is entirely possible that the inner product of q and y, viz. (q, y), may respond positively to an additional unit of resource j, even though $W(x)$ does not respond to it.

The last is an especially important distinction, because the sub-optimality of the savings rate implies that the relative prices of capital goods vis-à-vis consumer goods as reflected in the market are wrong. For example, in the special case of a perpetuity of constant return r per year and a constant social rate of discount of i, when i is less than r (see the last section), the 'true' value (measured in terms of today's consumption) of a unit of capital may exceed the nominal value of it by the proportion $((r/i) - 1)$.[28] Thus the marginal product of a unit of labour in terms of market value may be positive, even when the marginal return in terms of the objective W to be maximized is nil.

The difference can be best illustrated in terms of a simple model. Let us make the Ramsey-like assumption of a homogeneous good, the output of which we refer to as Q. Taking the capital stock as given, we take Q to be a well-behaved function of employment L, with the usual property of strictly diminishing marginal product. $Q(L)$ has in this case an inverse function. L is the amount of labour available. A part of the output is consumed, given by the propensities to consume of wage earners (c_1) and of the profit earners (c_2), the level of employment (L), and the wage rate (w). The rest can be saved (S), and on that part we put an extra weight λ over and above its weight of unity as a part of the aggregate output Q. Given the sub-optimality of savings, we take $\lambda > 0$. We assume further that $1 \geqslant c_1 \geqslant c_2 \geqslant 0$. The problem, to state it similarly to (3), is:

Maximize $\qquad\qquad V = Q + \lambda S,$ $\qquad\qquad\qquad$ (7.1)

subject to $\qquad\qquad L - Q^{-1}(Q) \geqslant 0,$ $\qquad\qquad\qquad$ (7.2)

and $\qquad\qquad Lw(1 - c_1) + (Q - Lw)(1 - c_2) - S \geqslant 0$ $\qquad$ (7.3)

It is obvious that with our assumptions, (7.3) will hold strictly, for $\lambda > 0$ will make it profitable to do this.

28. See Marglin [13] and [14].

The shadow price of labour, p_L, representing the marginal return of V to L, will equal:

$$p_L = \frac{\partial Q}{\partial L} + \lambda \frac{\partial S}{\partial L} \qquad (8)$$

If the constraint (7.2) is not binding, and there is surplus labour, then p_L is nil. This does not, however, mean that the labour intensity should be raised until the marginal product of labour $\partial Q/\partial L$ is zero, as under the criteria of Polak, Buchanan, Lewis, or Kahn, discussed in this book [*Choice of Techniques*] (see Chapter II). If we define the 'real cost of labour' w^* as that value to which the marginal product of labour is to be equated, the condition of optimum allocation is obtainable from (8) and by taking (7.3) as an equality:

$$w^* = \frac{\partial Q}{\partial L} = \left[\frac{(c_1 - c_2)\lambda}{1 + (1 - c_2)\lambda} \right] w \qquad (9)$$

This real cost of labour w^* is positive even when there is surplus labour, provided the over-all volume of savings is sub-optimal. When the sub-optimality is ruled out, and the problem does not correspond to one of the 'Second Best' type, we take $\lambda = 0$, and this yields:

$$w^* = 0 \qquad (9.1)$$

On the other extreme, when the premium is overwhelming, and λ is very large, then

$$w^* = \left[\frac{c_1 - c_2}{1 - c_2} \right] w \qquad (9.2)$$

In this special case with λ very large, if we assume further that the workers consume everything, i.e. $c_1 = 1$, we get:

$$w^* = w \qquad (9.3)$$

When, however, we assume that there is no difference in the propensities to consume of wage-earners and of the others, i.e. $c_1 = c_2$, then we have, in spite of any sub-optimality of the savings rate, and the positivity of λ, a zero real cost of labour:

$$w^* = 0 \qquad (9.4)$$

Thus the value of the real labour cost hinges on the savings functions of the two groups and on the sub-optimality (if any) of the savings rate. The Lewis–Polak–Buchanan–Kahn case[29] corresponds to

29. See [*Choice of Techniques*], pp. 15–16, 24–6, 51–2.

(9.1), with no extra weight on savings, which implicitly makes the assumption of no sub-optimality of overall savings. The Dobb–Galenson–Leibenstein case[30] corresponds to (9.3), when their objective is related only to growth[31] and thus to the volume of savings generated, with the further assumption of $c_1 = 1$. They also assume that $c_2 = 0$, but this has no impact on the real cost of labour w^*. If the assumption of $c_1 = 1$ is relaxed, we have the somewhat more general case of (9.2). The Bator view[32] that the fiscal machinery can alter the savings propensities freely, permits of the possibility of making $c_1 = c_2$, which yields (9.4). If it is completely variable for the economy as a whole, the sub-optimality of savings will disappear, and we shall get (9.1). In either case w^* is nil.

One object of this book was to provide a general framework in terms of which the variety of criteria presented in the literature could be easily interpreted. The different theories are shown to correspond to variations in the 'real cost of labour' w^*, which depending on the assumptions made may lie anywhere in the interval $(0, w)$, with (9.1) and (9.3) representing the two extreme cases. As has been shown in this section, this does not conflict at all with the 'shadow price' of labour (p_L) being nil (when surplus labour exists), defined as the optimal value of the dual variable corresponding to the labour supply constraint. The two ways of presenting the same problem can be readily translated into each other.

4   Savings and Technological Choice as Variational Problems

The concave programming formulation of the last section is not always the most convenient way of looking at this allocational problem. The problem of choice of techniques can also be posed as a dynamic problem. Unfortunately, the usual variational studies of problems of optimum allocation have tended to rule out problems of technological choice, or alternatively have tended to ignore any special link between savings and technological choice via the distribution of income.[33] However, Marglin [14] has provided a framework for a successful integration of these two aspects of economic planning.[34] It will be pointless to try to present here Marglin's main results, but the precise link between his variational formulation and

---

30. See [*Choice of Techniques*], pp. 16–17, 24–6, 51–2.
31. Galenson and Leibenstein [8] also discuss some other criteria.
32. See [*Choice of Techniques*], pp. 23, 24–6.
33. For example, Ramsey [22], Goodwin [9], Chakravarty [4], Sen [28].
34. See also Srinivasan [30], and Mirrlees [19], for other dynamic studies of the problem.

the concave programming framework of the last section is worth pointing out.

We use the following symbols: C = total consumption, K = total capital stock, Q = total output, l = employment per unit of capital, q = output per unit of capital, and U = utility (or welfare) at a given point of time, taken to be a function of C of that period, i.e. $U = U(C)$.[35] The function to be maximized is the intertemporal aggregate of U.[36] We retain the symbols w, c_1 and c_2 as used in the earlier section. $\dot{K}$ stands for investment, i.e. $\dot{K} = dK/dt$. With a constant-returns-to-scale production function, we get the following relations for output, savings, and consumption for the economy as a whole:

$$Q = Kq(l) \tag{10}$$

$$S = \dot{K} = K[q(l) - wl](1 - c_2) + Klw(1 - c_1) \tag{11}$$

$$C = Kq(l)c_2 + Klw(c_1 - c_2) \tag{12}$$

Taking K as the 'phase variable' and l (representing the technological choice) as the 'control variable', the following 'Hamiltonian' expression can be formulated:

$$H = U(C) + \psi\dot{K} \tag{13}$$
$$= U[Kq(l)c_2 + Klw(c_1 - c_2)]$$
$$+ \psi K[q(l) - wl](1 - c_2) + \psi Klw(1 - c_1)$$

ψ can be interpreted as the welfare price of capital investment and H the total welfare value of output in a given period. When Ω represents the control region, the optimal time sequence of technological choice will have to satisfy the following necessary condition given by

---

35. This assumption of the independence of this period's utility from the value of consumption in other periods is not very satisfactory (cf. Hicks [10], pp. 256-8). This is, however, not crucial to the problem being discussed here.

36. This aggregate can be carried out over a finite period, or over an infinite horizon. Since Marglin deals with the latter he follows Ramsey in assuming a utility function bounded from above, and treats the maximization of total utility as equivalent to the minimization of the integral of the difference between 'bliss' and total utility in each period. Marglin takes

$$U(0) = -\infty,$$

and

$$\lim_{C \to \infty} U(C) = 0,$$

with strict concavity throughout.

Pontryagin's 'Maximum Principle' for non-terminal points of time:[37]

$$H(\psi, K, l) = \sup_{l \in \Omega} H(\psi, K) \tag{14}$$

We may restrict l within the closed interval $(\underline{l}, \bar{l})$, where $\underline{l}$ is the value for which the marginal product of labour equals the wage rate, i.e. $q'(\underline{l}) = w$, and $\bar{l}$ is the value for which the wage bill just exhausts the total product, i.e. $q(\bar{l}) = \bar{l} \cdot w$.[38] These two limits correspond respectively to the Dobb–Galenson–Leibenstein solution and the Lewis–Polak–Buchanan–Kahn solution. If l lies in the interior of the region Ω,[39] we should then require:

$$\frac{\partial H}{\partial l} = 0 \tag{14.1}$$

The other necessary condition given by Pontryagin concerns the value of ψ, which yields:

$$\dot{\psi} = -\frac{\partial H}{\partial K} \tag{15}$$

From (13) and (14.1) we obtain:

$$\frac{U'(C)}{\psi} = \frac{w(c_1 - c_2) - q'(l)(1 - c_2)}{q'(l)c_2 + w(c_1 - c_2)} \tag{16}$$

Since ψ is the welfare price of investment and $U'(C)$ is the welfare value of consumption, the left-hand side of (16) corresponds to the society's marginal rate of indifferent substitution between consumption and investment. Since λ is the social 'premium' on investment vis-à-vis consumption, we can write:

$$1 + \lambda = \frac{\psi}{U'(C)} \tag{17}$$

It is easy to check that from (16) and (17) we can obtain the following value of the 'real cost of labour', w^*.

$$w^* = q'(l) = \frac{(c_1 - c_2)\lambda}{1 + (1 - c_2)\lambda} w.$$

37. Theorem 1 in Pontryagin [21], pp. 19–21; see also pp. 189–91.
38. Cf. Chapter II [of *Choice of Techniques*], pp. 19–21. In one other case we consider the upper limit of l is provided by the point where the marginal product of labour is nil, i.e. $q'(l) = 0$, shown by point E in diagram 2b. This possibility cannot arise with Marglin's analysis since the marginal product is assumed to be strictly positive throughout. Marglin's upper limit corresponds to our point T in diagram 2c and the case discussed on pp. 20–1.
39. Marglin shows that a set of assumptions of non-satiation and of continuity suffice to guarantee this. See Marglin [16], pp. 40–1.

This is precisely the same as that given by (9).[40] The relationship between the two ways of posing the problem is indeed a close one, and the concave programming formulation of the last section can be seen to fit well into the picture of finding an optimum path of technical choice over time, when λ is assigned its proper value derived form the variational exercise.

It is to be noted, however, that Marglin defines the 'shadow price' of labour differently both from the programming definition as well as from our definition of w^*. He defines it as that expression with which we should equate the marginal product of labour, not in terms of the market value (as we do), but taking into account the higher shadow price of that part of it which will be reinvested (taking the whole of the marginal output as going to the enterprise). Because of this definitional difference, Marglin's 'shadow price' of labour can even *exceed* the market wage w in some cases, whereas our w^* is contained in the interval $(0, w)$. Marglin's definition is in many ways more useful than ours, giving a corrected value of the marginal product of labour; though (on the other hand) in giving the decentralized project planner a simple rule to follow, viz. $q'(l) = w^*$ (i.e. to equate the market value of marginal product to the shadow wage), ours has some advantages also.

Analytically, however, the two rules are exactly equivalent. In fact, as we saw in the last section the *net* marginal return to labour in terms of the objective function must be nil in an optimum programme in a surplus labour situation, and in this programming sense the 'shadow price' of labour in a labour surplus economy is always zero. The difference between Marglin's and our definition of the shadow price of labour concerns merely the division between the 'benefit' and 'cost' items in the *net* return. In fact, denoting the shadow price of labour (p_L) in the sense of programming as $w^*(\text{I})$, that in our sense as $w^*(\text{II})$, and that in the sense of Marglin as $w^*(\text{III})$,[41] the following three *exactly equivalent* optimality conditions can be noted:

$$w^*(\text{I}) = \frac{\partial V}{\partial L} = \frac{\partial Q}{\partial L} + \lambda \left[w(c_2 - c_1) + \frac{\partial Q}{\partial L}(1 - c_2) \right] = 0 \ (18.1)$$

$$w^*(\text{II}) = \frac{\partial Q}{\partial L} = \left[\frac{(c_1 - c_2)\lambda}{1 + (1 - c_2)\lambda} \right] w \qquad (18.2)$$

40. Note that $q'(l) = \partial Q/\partial L$, thanks to the assumption of constant returns to scale.

41. Since Marglin takes $c_1 = 1$, and $c_2 = 0$, as simplifying assumptions, he gets $w^*(\text{III}) = \lambda \cdot w$. He also considers an alternative financing assumption, where the wage costs are financed by taxing the capitalists with a propensity to consume $c_2 > 0$; then he gets: $w^*(\text{III}) = (1 - c_2)\lambda \cdot w$. The general framework is that given by (18.3).

$$w^*(\text{III}) = \frac{\partial Q}{\partial L} \left[1 + (1 - c_2) \lambda \right] = (c_1 - c_2) \lambda w \qquad (18.3)$$

Which particular definition we use is entirely a matter of convenience, and makes no real difference.

References

[1] Arrow, K. J. *Social Choice and Individual Values* (New York: Wiley, 1963).

[2] Bagchi, A. K. 'The Choice of the Optimum Techniques', *Economic Journal*, 72 (September 1962).

[3] Baumol, W. J. *Welfare Economics and the Theory of the State* (Cambridge, Mass.: Harvard University Press, 1952).

[4] Chakravarty, S. 'Optimum Savings with Finite Planning Horizon', *International Economic Review*, 3 (September 1962).

[5] Debreu, G. *The Theory of Value* (London: Wiley, 1959).

[6] Dobb, M. H. *An Essay on Economic Growth and Planning* (London: Routledge, 1960).

[7] Eckstein, O. 'Investment Criteria for Economic Development and the Theory of Intertemporal Welfare Economics', *Quarterly Journal of Economics*, 71 (February 1957).

[8] Galenson, W. and Leibenstein, H. 'Investment Criteria, Productivity and Economic Development', *Quarterly Journal of Economics*, 69 (August 1955).

[9] Goodwin, R. M. 'The Optimum Growth Path for an Underdeveloped Economy', *Economic Journal*, 71 (December 1961).

[10] Hicks, J. R. *Capital and Growth* (Oxford: Clarendon Press, 1965).

[11] Karlin, S. *Mathematical Methods and Theory in Games, Programming, and Economics*, Volume I (Reading, Mass.: Addison-Wesley, 1959).

[12] Lind, R. C. 'The Social Rate of Discount and the Optimal Rate of Investment: Further Comment', *Quarterly Journal of Economics*, 78 (May 1964).

[13] Marglin, S. A. 'The Social Rate of Discount and the Optimal Rate of Investment', *Quarterly Journal of Economics*, 77 (February 1963).

[14] —— 'The Opportunity Costs of Public Investment', *Quarterly Journal of Economics*, 77 (May 1963).

[15] —— *Public Investment Criteria* (London: Allen & Unwin, 1967).

[16] —— *Industrial Development in the Labour-Surplus Economy*, mimeographed, January 1966. [Later published in a revised version as *Value and Price in the Labour-Surplus Economy* (Oxford: Clarendon Press, 1976).]

[17] Meade, J. E. *Trade and Welfare* (London: Oxford University Press, 1955).

[18] Mirrlees, J. 'Choice of Techniques', *Indian Economic Review*, August 1962.

[19] —— *Optimum Planning for a Dynamic Economy*, Ph.D. Thesis, University of Cambridge, 1963.

[20] Nash, J. F. 'The Bargaining Problem', *Econometrica*, **18** (1950).

[21] Pontryagin, L. S. *et al. The Mathematical Theory of Optimal Processes* (New York: Interscience, 1962).

[22] Ramsey, F. P. 'A Mathematical Theory of Saving', *Economic Journal*, **38** (December 1928).

[23] Samuelson, P. A. *Foundations of Economics* (Cambridge, Mass.: Harvard University Press, 1949).

[24] Sen, A. K. 'Some Notes on the Choice of Capital-Intensity in Development Planning', *Quarterly Journal of Economics*, **71** (November 1957).

[25] —— 'On Optimizing the Rate of Saving', *Economic Journal*, **71** (September 1961). [Essay 5 in this volume.]

[26] —— 'A Possibility Theorem on Majority Decisions', *Econometrica*, 34 (April 1966). [Reprinted in *Choice, Welfare and Measurement* (Oxford: Blackwell, 1982).]

[27] —— 'Peasants and Dualism with or without Surplus Labour', *Journal of Political Economy*, 74 (October 1966). [Essay 1 in this volume.]

[28] —— 'Terminal Capital and Optimal Savings', in C. H. Feinstein *et al.* (eds), *Capitalism, Socialism and Economic Growth: Essays in Honour of Maurice Dobb* (Cambridge: Cambridge University Press, 1967). [Essay 6 in this volume.]

[29] —— 'Isolation, Assurance and the Social Rate of Discount', *Quarterly Journal of Economics*, **81** (February 1967). [Essay 5 in this volume.]

[30] Srinivasan, T. N. 'Investment Criteria and Choice of Techniques of Production', *Yale Economic Essays*, **2** (October 1962).

[31] Webb, R. 'Sen on the Choice of Techniques', *Economic Record* (December 1963).

10

Control Areas and Accounting Prices: An Approach to Economic Evaluation

A prerequisite of a theory of planning is an identification of the nature of the State and of the government. The planner, to whom much of planning theory is addressed, is part of a political machinery and is constrained by a complex structure within which he has to operate. Successful planning requires an understanding of the constraints that in fact hold and clarity about precise areas on which the planners in question can exercise effective control. The limits of a planner's effective control depend on his position vis-a-vis the rest of the government as well as on the nature of the political, social and economic forces operating in the economy. This paper is concerned with an analysis of some aspects of these interrelationships in the specific context of project appraisal and benefit–cost evaluation.

In Section 1 the problem is posed. In Section 2, the OECD *Manual of Industrial Project Analysis*, prepared by Professors Little and Mirrlees [12], is critically examined in the light of the approach outlined in Section 1. In Section 3 the approach is illustrated in the specific context of fixing a shadow price of labour in benefit–cost analysis.

1 Spheres of Influence and Control Variables

For any planning agent the act of planning may be viewed as an exercise in maximizing an objective function subject to certain constraints. In the absence of non-convexities it is relatively easy to

This is based on a seminar given at Nuffield College, Oxford, in the Summer Term of 1969–70. For useful discussions I am grateful to Partha Dasgupta, Al Harberger, Ian Little, Stephen Marglin, James Mirrlees and Maurice Scott.

From *Economic Journal*, 82 (March 1972, Supplement), 486–501.

translate the problem into a framework of shadow prices. Corresponding to the maximizing 'primal' problem one could define a 'dual' problem involving the minimization of a function where there will be one shadow price (acting as a value-weight) corresponding to each constraint in the original problem. All this is straightforward and mechanical and there is not really very much to argue about. The interesting questions arise with the *selection* of the objective function and the constraints.

If $W(x)$ is the objective to be maximized through the selection of choice variables in the form of a vector x subject to a set of m constraints, $F_i(x) \leqslant R_i$, for $i = 1, \ldots, m$, then the dual related to any particular constraint F_i will correspond to the additional amount of maximized W that would be generated by relaxing the constraint by one unit, i.e. by raising R_i by a unit. Thus, the dual p_i corresponding to F_i can be viewed as the marginal impact of R_i on W, the objective, and if R_i is the amount of a given resource then p_i is the marginal contribution of R_i to W (not necessarily corresponding to the marginal product in terms of market evaluation). It may be convenient to view p_i as the shadow price of resource i. Since the value of p_i is essentially dependent on the objective function $W(x)$ and on the other constraints, the shadow price of any resource clearly depends on the values of the planner reflected in the objective function W and on his reading of the economic and other constraints that bind his planning decisions.

Consider now a project evaluator. What does he assume about other agents involved in the operation of the economy, e.g. the private sector (if any), the households and the other government agencies? Presumably, in so far as he can influence the private sector and households directly or indirectly he builds that fact into his description of the exercise, but except for this the operation of the private sector and households will constrain his exercise. He may express this either in the form of specific constraints or in the form of implicit relations embodied in other constraints or even in the objective function. The actual form may not be very important but the inclusion of these elements is, of course, a crucial aspect of realistic planning. In principle, the position outlined above may be fairly widely accepted, though I would argue later that the implications of this position are frequently overlooked.

What about the relation between the project evaluator and other planning agents and how does his role fit in with the rest of the government apparatus? This question has several facets, one of which is the problem of coordination, teamwork, decentralization and related issues. This basket of problems has been discussed quite a bit in the literature and will not be pursued here.[1] Another facet is the problem of conflict between the interests of the different government agencies. This is particularly important for a federal country since the relation between the State governments and the centre may be extremely complex. But even between different agencies of the Central government there could be considerable conflict of interests, e.g. between the road authorities and the nationalized railways, to take a narrow example, or between the department of revenue and the public enterprises, to take a broader one. Whenever such conflicts are present a question arises about the appropriate assumption regarding other agencies of the government in the formulation of the planning exercise by any particular agency.

A third facet is the question of the impact not of government policy on the private business sector but of the private business sector on government policy. The control variables are affected by such influences but they are often not affected in a uniform way. For example, a public sector project evaluator may think that certain taxes cannot be imposed because of political opposition, but somewhat similar results could be achieved through variations in the pricing and production policy of the public sector.

In a very broad sense taxes, tariffs, quotas, licences, prices and outputs of the public sector are all control variables for the government as a whole. But they are each constrained within certain ranges by administrative, political and social considerations. For a project evaluator, therefore, it is important to know which variables are within his control and to what extent, and in this respect a feeling of oneness with the totality of the government may not be very useful. This aspect of the problem has been frequently lost sight of because of the concentration in the planning models on a mythical hero called 'the Planner', and unitarianism is indeed a dominant faith in the theory of economic planning.

2　The Use of World Prices

A distinguishing feature of the Little–Mirrlees *Manual* (henceforth, LMM) is its advocacy of the use of world prices in the evaluation of commodities. For 'traded' goods produced in the economy the evaluation is at the import price (c.i.f.) or the export price (f.o.b.) depending on whether it would potentially replace imports or be

---

1. I have tried to discuss the relation of this range of issues to the exercise of project evaluation (Sen [22]).

available for exports; and a traded good used up is valued at the import price if its source (direct or indirect) is imports and at the export price if it comes from cutting out potential exports. When opportunities of trade are present these values reflect the opportunity costs and benefits. The non-traded goods are also related to trade indirectly since they may be domestically produced by traded goods, and the non-tradeables involved in their production can be traced further back to tradeables. 'Following the chain of production around one must end at commodities that are exported or substituted for imports.'[2]

This is not the place to discuss or evaluate the nuances of the LMM. Problems such as imperfections of international markets are taken into account by replacing import and export prices by corresponding marginal cost and marginal revenue considerations. Externalities are somewhat soft-pedalled partly on the ground that there is 'little chance, anyway, of measuring many of these supposed external economies',[3] and also because a discussion of the main types of externalities generally emphasized makes the authors 'feel that differences in those external effects, which are not in any case allowed for in our type of cost–benefit analysis, will seldom make a significant difference'.[4] These and other considerations may be important in practical decisions but I do not want to discuss them here. These problems are essentially factual in nature and can only be resolved by detailed empirical work.

The crucial question lies in deciding on what is to be regarded as a 'traded' good. The LMM proposes two criteria, viz. '(a) goods which are actually imported or exported (or very close substitutes are actually imported or exported)', and '(b) goods which would be exported or imported if the country had followed policies which resulted in an optimum industrial development'.[5] It is the second category that relates closely to the question we raised in Section 1 of this paper.

Suppose it appears that project A would be a worthwhile investment if a certain raw material R needed for it were to be imported but not if R were to be manufactured domestically (assuming that R is not economically produced in the economy). 'Optimal industrial development' requires that R be not manufactured in the economy but be imported. Suppose the project evaluator examining project A finds that the country's trade policies are not 'sensible', and R would

2. Little and Mirrlees [12], p. 93.
3. Little and Mirrlees [12], p. 37.
4. Little and Mirrlees [12], p. 219.
5. Little and Mirrlees [12], p. 92.

in fact be manufactured, no matter what he does. It does not seem right, in these circumstances, to recommend that project A be undertaken on the ground that 'if the countries had followed policies which resulted in an optimal industrial development' then R would not in fact have been domestically produced; the question is whether or not R will be domestically produced *in fact.*

The question at issue here is the theory of government underlying the planning model of the LMM. Little and Mirrlees explain their approach thus:

> Sometimes, our guess about whether a commodity will be imported or not may be almost a value judgment: we think that a sensible government would plan to import some, so we assume that it will do so. Of course, if one of our assumptions required government action in order to be fulfilled, this should be drawn to the attention of the appropriate authorities.[6]

The judgment would readily become a fact if the appropriate authorities would do the 'sensible' thing whenever their attention is drawn to such action. There is no logical problem in this approach; the only question is: *Is this a good theory of government action?*

One could doubt that this is a good theory on one of many grounds.[7] Some people may doubt whether governments typically do think sensibly. Often enough, evidences of sensible thinking, if present, would appear to be very well concealed. But more importantly, something more than 'sensible thinking' is involved in all this, and it is necessary to examine the pressures that operate on the government. There would certainly be some interest groups involved, e.g. those who would like to produce good R under the protection of a quota, or an enhanced tariff, or some other restriction. By choosing project A and thus creating a domestic demand for R (or by augmenting the demand that existed earlier) one is opening up this whole range of issues involving protection and domestic production. If the project evaluator thinks that the pressures for domestic production of good R will be successfully crushed by the government agencies responsible for policies on tariff, quota, etc., it will certainly be fair to choose project A. But what if the project evaluator thinks that it is very likely that if project A is chosen then there will be irresistible pressure for domestic production of good R inside the economy? Similarly, what

---

6. Little and Mirrlees [12], p. 106.
7. See also Sen [21] and Dasgupta [3]. Further, Dasgupta, P. and Stiglitz, J. 'Benefit-Cost Analysis and Trade Policies', mimeographed, 1971, forthcoming in the *Journal of Political Economy.* [Published later in volume 81, 1973.]

should the project evaluator do if he finds that there already exists a quota restriction on the import of good R so that the additional demand for R will be met by domestic production unless the trade policies are changed, and he does not believe that they will change because of political pressures in favour of the continuation of these policies? It is not a question of *knowing* what is the 'sensible' policy in related fields but of being able to *ensure* that these policies will in fact be chosen. This would depend on one's reading of the nature of the State and of the government and on one's analysis of the influences that affect government action. And on this should depend the appropriate set of accounting prices for cost–benefit analysis.

It is possible to argue that if one uniform assumption has to be made about the actions to be undertaken by other government agencies, then the LMM assumption is as good as any. It may well be better to assume that the actions taken by the other agencies will be all 'sensible' in the sense defined rather than be 'distorted' in a uniform way in all spheres of decision taking. But there is, in fact, no very compelling reason for confining oneself artificially to assumptions of such heroic uniformity. The correct assumption may vary from country to country and from case to case, and may also alter over time, since the projects sometimes have a long life and the political and social influences on the tax and trade policies may change during the lifetime of the project. What the LMM approach seems to me to do is to assume implicitly that either the project evaluator is very *powerful* so that he can ensure that the rest of the government machinery will accept his decisions in other fields as well (and the political acceptance of 'sensible' tax, tariff and quota policies is ensured), or that he is very *stupid* so that he cannot be trusted to make a realistic appraisal of the likely policies and should be better advised to assume a role of uniform simplicity.

3   *Cost of Labour in Project Analysis*

This section will be concerned with the valuation of labour cost and will be divided into six subsections. In 3.1 a general expression for the social cost of labour will be suggested, and in 3.2 some of the other formulae will be compared and contrasted with the one proposed here. In the subsequent subsections the problem of evaluation of specific value weights will be discussed in the line of the general questions raised earlier in the paper.

3.1   *Social cost of labour: an expression*

Let w be the wage rate of the kind of labour with which we are concerned and let these labourers be drawn from a peasant economy. The reduction of output in the peasant economy as a consequence of someone being withdrawn from there is m, and the value of income which the person thus drawn away would have received had he stayed on in the rural area may be y. If there is surplus labour, we have $m = 0$, but y is, of course, positive. Even when m is positive and there is no surplus labour it will often be the case that $y > m$ since the marginal product of a labourer may be considerably less than the average income per person. When the peasant in question moves away as a labourer in the urban area, his income goes up from y to w, and those remaining behind experience an increase in income equal to $(y - m)$. However as a consequence of the departure of one member of the family those remaining behind may also work harder, and the value of more sweat is a relevant constituent of the social cost of labour. Let z^1 and z^2 be the increase in work effort respectively for the peasant family and for the person who moves to the project in question.[8]

A part of the respective increases in income may be saved, and we may assume that the proportions saved out of the marginal earnings of the peasant family and of the migrant worker are respectively s^1 and s^2. The proportion of project profits that are saved[9] may be denoted s^3. The marginal impact on project profits of the employment of one more man is given by $(q - w)$, where q is the relevant marginal product. Thus the total impact on the different groups can be summarized as shown in Table 10.1. Taking v^{ij} to be the relevant marginal weight for the jth item in the ith row in the social welfare function W, we obtain the following expression for the change in social welfare as a consequence of the employment of one more person in the project.

$$U = v^{11}(y - m) + v^{12}(y - m)s^1 + v^{13}z^1 + v^{21}(w - y)$$
$$+ v^{22}(w - y)s^2 + v^{23}z^2 + v^{31}(q - w) + v^{32}(q - w)s^3$$

$$(1)$$

If there is no other restriction on the use of labour, the optimal policy would be to expand the labour force as long as U is positive,

---

8. If project work is more or less backbreaking than peasant farming an adjustment for this may be included in z^2.

9. It is conventional to assume that $s^3 = 1$ if it is a public project. But there are problems of group consumption for project employees and they may be tied to project profits.

TABLE 10.1

Category	1. Increase in income	2. Increase in savings	3. Increase in efforts
1. Peasant family	$y - m$	$(y - m) s^1$	z^1
2. Labourer migrating	$w - y$	$(w - y) s^2$	z^2
3. Project	$q - w$	$(q - w) s^3$	

and making the usual divisibility assumptions the optimal position will be characterized by $U = 0$.

U is in one sense the social cost of labour, and indeed the shadow price of labour in this sense must be zero since there is no binding constraint on labour in addition to the relations that have already been fed into the expression of social welfare. However, the shadow price is frequently used in the sense of *that* value of labour which, if equated to the marginal product of labour, will give the optimal allocation of labour.[10] In this sense the shadow price of labour (w^*) is the value of q for $U = 0$. This is readily obtained from (1).

$$w^* = [w\{(v^{31} - v^{21}) + (v^{32} s^3 - v^{22} s^2)\} - y\{(v^{11} - v^{21})$$
$$+ (v^{12} s^1 - v^{22} s^2)\} + m(v^{11} + v^{12} s^1)$$
$$- (v^{13} z^1 + v^{23} s^2)]/(v^{31} + v^{32} s^3) \qquad (2)$$

3.2 Some other expressions

In the basic model in my *Choice of Techniques* (Sen [19]), henceforth COT, I made the following assumptions which are here translated into the terminology used in subsection 3.1 above:

(i) all current consumption is equally valuable, i.e. $v^{11} = v^{21} = v^{31}$;

(ii) all saving is equally valuable and marginally more valuable than consumption, i.e. $v^{12} = v^{22} = v^{32} = \lambda > 0$;[11]

(iii) marginal disutility of efforts are negligible, i.e. $v^{13} = v^{23} = 0$;

(iv) the peasant economy has surplus labour, i.e. $m = 0$;

(v) the savings propensity of the workers and peasants are equal at the margin, and less than that out of project profits, i.e. $s^1 = s^2 < s^3$.

10. See Sen [19]; Little and Mirrlees [12]; Stern [23].
11. q is a 'premium' since savings get a weight anyway as part of income.

Taking consumption as the numeraire, i.e. putting $v^{11} = 1$, we can obtain from (2):

$$w^* = w\lambda(s^3 - s^2)/(1 + \lambda s^3) \qquad (3.1)$$

Certain distinguished cases may be commented on. First, in the Polak–Buchanan–Kahn–Tinbergen criterion the shadow price of labour is taken to be zero in a surplus labour economy. This follows from taking consumption and savings to be equally valuable at the margin, i.e. $\lambda = 0$.

$$w^* = 0 \qquad (3.2)$$

The case associated with the names of Dobb [5] and Galenson and Leibenstein [7] corresponds to the assumption that the growth rate should be maximized, which amounts to maximizing the savings rate with no weight on consumption, i.e. taking λ to be infinitely large, and this leads to:

$$w^* = w(s^3 - s^2)/s^3 \qquad (3.3)$$

With the further assumption of no savings out of wages, i.e. $s^2 = 0$, we get:

$$w^* = w \qquad (3.3^*)$$

The case of using taxes in a manner such that the savings propensities of the different classes are equated, as put forward by Bator [1], will lead to (3.2), as is readily checked by putting $s^3 = s^2$ in (3.1).

The LMM takes a set of assumptions that are equivalent to (i)–(iii) and (v) above, but omits the assumption (iv) of surplus labour, and in addition assumes:

(vi) $s^1 = s^2 = 0$;
(vii) $s^3 = 1$.

This yields from (3) the following expression:[12]

$$w^* = (w\lambda + m)/(1 + \lambda) \qquad (3.4)$$

The following aspects of the problem will now be discussed:

(a) the premium on investment, i.e. λ being positive:
(b) the question of distributional weights, reflected in v^{11}, v^{21}, v^{31}, etc.;
(c) the valuation of efforts, i.e. the choice of v^{13} and v^{23}; and

---

12. See Little and Mirrlees [12], p. 167. Their formula is the same as (3.4) but for notational differences.

(d) the question of the relation between the intake of labour into the project and the outflow of labour out of the peasant economy.

These are not the only problems that deserve comment, but they do seem to be related closely to the general issues raised in the earlier sections of the paper.

3.3 *Premium on investment*

The question of whether λ should be positive depends on whether at the margin investment is regarded as more important than consumption. It is assumed to be so in the COT as well as in the LMM. The underlying assumption is one of sub-optimality of savings. The question is why should such an assumption be made?

The tendency for market savings to be below optimal has been argued from various points of view. One reason is the presence of an externality in the form of members of the present generation having some concern for the well-being of the future generations which is, therefore, like a public good in the Samuelsonian sense. Another reason is the presence of a tax system which makes the private after-tax rate of return lower than the social rate of return to investment. In the underdeveloped countries with surplus labour it can also be argued that the private rate of return falls short of the social since wages are a cost for the individual investor whereas the social opportunity cost of labour may be much lower so that the market underestimates the rate of return. There are other possible arguments and Phelps [17] has provided a critical survey of the literature.

All these, however, amount merely to demonstrating that the level of market-determined savings may be sub-optimal. But this is not a good enough reason for taking λ to be positive, because that would require us to assume that savings are sub-optimal *even after* any possible government policy that could be used to change the rate of saving. If the savings as given by the market are too low, why not raise their level through taxation, subsidies, deficit spending, etc., to make it optimal and then proceed to do the project selection exercise without having to bother about raising the rate of savings through project evaluation itself? This is precisely where the argument relates to the main question with which this paper is concerned. We have to look at the relevant constraints that restrict the planners.

The project evaluator may find the savings rate to be sub-optimal for one of two different reasons. First, his judgements about the relative importance of present consumption vis-a-vis future consumption may be different from that of the planners in charge of taxes and other policies that influence the national rate of savings. He may wish to attach a higher weight on savings than that which is reflected in the government policy concerned with macroeconomic planning. Second, the planners in charge of taxes etc., may themselves regard the savings level to be sub-optimal but be unable to set it right through taxes etc., because of political constraints on taxation and other instruments.

In putting an extra weight on savings in the determination of the shadow price of labour one is essentially exploring the possibility of raising the savings rate through project selection and the choice of capital-intensity of investment.[13] It raises the question as to whether such a means of savings generation can be utilized when there are constraints that prevent the savings rate from being raised through more taxes. In one case savings are raised by income being taxed away and in the other savings are raised by choosing a lower level of employment in the project design thereby reducing disposable wage income and cutting down consumption. I have tried to discuss elsewhere the mechanism as well as the plausibility of using choice of techniques as a means of raising savings (Sen [19], Chapter 5), so that I shall not go into the problem further here. I would only point out that the question rests on two propositions, viz. (i) the project evaluator finds the savings rate to be sub-optimal which implies more than finding that the *market-determined* savings rate is sub-optimal since the possibility of government action (through taxes etc.) is present, and (ii) the project evaluator believes that the political or other constraints that rule out raising savings through taxes would not rule out raising savings indirectly through an employment policy. The whole problem turns on the precise reading of the area of control for the project evaluator.

3.4   *Income distributional considerations*

Should there be differences in the weights attached to different kinds of income on grounds of distribution? In expressions (1) and (2) this will take the form of v^{11}, v^{21} and v^{31} being not necessarily equal, and similarly v^{12}, v^{22} and v^{32} being different. The simplicity of expressions

---

13. The problem of optimal development in an economy with constraints on taxation and savings and with a wage-gap (i.e. in a dual economy) is, of course, a complex one, and the precise determination of q must be posed as a variational problem involving intertemporal optimality. On this question see Marglin [15], Dixit [4], Lefeber [9], Stern [23], and Newbery [16].

(3.1)–(3.4) arose partly from neglecting these differences. What could be said in defence of such a procedure?

The most common argument is that income distributional changes are best brought about by taxes and subsidies and other general policy measures and not by affecting project designs. If lump-sum transfers were permitted then the force of this argument is obvious, but in an important paper it has been demonstrated by Diamond and Mirrlees [2] that, even in the absence of the possibility of lump-sum transfers, social welfare maximization requires that production efficiency be preserved, given some assumptions, including constant returns to scale. If the incomes of two factors of production are valued differently in making production decisions it could conceivably violate production efficiency. The rate of substitution between the factors in the production process to be decided on may then be different from that in the rest of the economy, and this will amount to production inefficiency.

Once again the question turns on the possibilities of taxation. While Diamond and Mirrlees [2] do not necessarily assume the availability of any taxes other than commodity taxes, they do assume that there are no constraints on the quantum of such taxes, e.g. there will be no political difficulty in having a tax rate of, say, 1000 per cent on some commodity if the optimization exercise requires this. This may or may not be a good assumption, but what is our concern here is to note that the question relates once again to the identification of political and other influences on the operation of the government machinery; and also that the result depends on the ability to tax *all* commodities if necessary. There is a clear link here with the problem discussed in the last section. If wages could be taxed and the rise in income of the peasant family could also be taxed, then the question of using employment policy as a vehicle of savings adjustment will diminish in importance; COT, LMM, and other frameworks do imply a certain inability to tax all commodities (including labour). It may in fact turn out that this is not a limiting constraint for the problem of income distribution, but the question will have to be posed in the context of commodity taxes *with* some constraints even in that sphere and not in terms of a model where any tax rate on any commodity is possible.

In addition to this aspect of the problem viewed from the angle of the totality of the planning set-up, there is, of course, also the problem of the project evaluator being constrained by the operation of the tax system on which he may not have more than a small amount of control. *Given* the tax system he might feel the necessity to violate efficiency by introducing income distributional considerations even though he might have preferred to do the adjustment through changing the tax system rather than affecting the project selection. The question relates again to the identification of areas of control.

This problem may also arise in the context of locational planning. In many developing countries an important constituent of planning is the regional allocation of investment. To take an illustration from India, in spite of the higher rate of return (in the absence of distributional considerations) from investment in fertilizers to be used in wet land vis-à-vis that from investment in irrigation in the dry areas, the appropriateness of the policy of emphasizing fertilizers and ignoring irrigation is open to question on distributional grounds. The problem would disappear if inter-regional transfers could be arranged so that more income might be generated through an appropriate production policy and the distribution to be looked after through transfers. But the question of inter-state transfers in a federal country like India has important political limits and the choice of agricultural policy must, therefore, depend on a reading of the areas of control.

Another set of illustrations from India relates directly to the question of social cost of labour for projects. Given the limitations of regional transfers there are considerable social pressures on the location of big industrial projects, and this seems to have been an important consideration in a number of locational decisions. The inoptimality of it has been well discussed by Manne [13] and others. The question does, however, depend on the constraints that bind. By attaching a higher weight on the income of workers from the backward regions it is possible to alter substantially the benefit–cost balance sheet. But there remains the question of the control that the project evaluator can, in fact, exercise on the actual choice of manpower for projects. It is not uncommon for a project evaluator to decide to locate a project in a backward region on grounds of income distribution, and then for project managers to recruit labour from outside. When project selection is guided by one set of shadow prices and the performance of the project manager judged by profits in the commercial sense at market prices, this can easily happen. In some of the major industrial projects in India local labour has not really been much absorbed; project managers have seen considerable advantage from the point of view of 'performance' in using labour from areas with earlier industrial experience. However, from the point of view of the project evaluator the ranking may be in descending order: (1) project A in the backward region with the use of local labour, (2) project A in a non-backward region closer to the traditional sources of supply of industrial labour, and (3) project A in the backward region with importation of labour from traditional sources. If the area of control of the project evaluator extends to the location of the project but not to the exact recruitment policy, the use of shadow prices with distributional weights may conceivably make the situation worse from every point of view than ignoring distribution altogether. This complex range of issues is involved in the choice of appropriate weights and much depends on a clear perception of the exact sphere of the project evaluator's influence.

3.5   *Valuation of sweat*

Neither the COT model nor the LMM model attaches any value to greater effort on the part of the peasant family in cultivation after the departure of the labourer for the project. In the COT model it is assumed that the disutility of labour up to a point is zero, and this feature produces a surplus labour in that model.

A similar assumption about no disutility of labour may have been implicitly made by Little and Mirrlees [12] since the 'plausible simplified utility function' for the labouring community as presented in the 'Appendix for Professional Economists' takes individual utility to be a function only of individual income without any account of efforts. But if this is really so then there clearly must be surplus labour in the peasant economy, since the marginal rate of substitution between income and leisure will be constant at zero; and constancy (at zero or not) is known to be the necessary and sufficient condition for the existence of surplus labour (Sen [20]). However, surplus labour is not assumed in the LMM model, and unlike in the COT model the value of m (alternative marginal product of a labourer) is not assumed to be zero.

It would, thus, appear that in the LMM model the peasants do dislike more work in the relevant region but this dislike is not to be reflected in the social objective function. That is, the peasant's attitude to work is accepted in the LMM model as a constraint that binds the planner but not as an element that directly enters the objective function.

If, on the other hand, it is assumed that if the peasants dislike more sweat then it must be reflected in the social objective function, then the problem will require reformulation. The positivity of m will imply that v^{13} must be positive. It should also be added that even if m is zero, i.e. even if there is surplus labour, it does not follow that v^{13} should not be positive. Surplus labour will exist whenever the marginal rate of substitution between income and leisure is constant in the relevant region and this rate need not necessarily be zero. Thus the existence of surplus labour may still require a positive shadow price of labour even in the absence of a premium on investment, i.e. even if $\lambda = 0$. The movement of labour from the peasant economy may not reduce the output there since those who remain behind may work harder, but then the enhanced effort of the remaining members requires some valuation in the planning exercise.† In this view the peasants' attitude to work will be treated not merely as a constraint but also as a constituent of social welfare measure.

3.6   *Control of migration*

The point has been raised that when there is a wage differential between a protected urban labour market and the average earning in the rural sector from which the labourers come, there will be a tendency for more people to move than the number of jobs created.[14] Migration from the rural to the urban sector may equate the expected value of earnings in the urban area with that in the rural area, and if w is the urban wage rate, p the probability of employment in the urban area and m the level of rural marginal product, then the migration will be up to the point that would guarantee:

$$pw = m \qquad (4)$$

Further, if the probability of employment p equals the proportion of urban labour force that is employed, then the migration equilibrium will exactly equate the wage rate of the employed people to the alternative marginal product sacrificed in the rural sector as a consequence of the movement of labour. For every employed man with w wage rate there will be $1/p$ men in the urban labour pool (including the employed and the unemployed), and m/p will be the amount of output sacrificed in the rural sector. And thanks to (4), w must equal m/p.

Thus in the absence of considerations of savings premium, income distribution and effort variation, the market wage rate will be the appropriate shadow wage rate for project evaluation in spite of the existence of dualism and the wage-gap, i.e. in spite of $w > m$. There is much force in this argument. Professor A. C. Harberger, who is responsible for this form of the argument, has also extended it to the case where the migrant labourers may not maximize the expected

---

† [On this question, see Carl Hamilton, 'On the Social Cost of Individuals' Extra Effort', *Journal of Development Studies*, **13** (1977).]

14. See Todaro [25] and Harris and Todaro [26].

value of earnings.[15] Suppose they are risk averse and pw exceeds m at equilibrium; it could still be argued that they regard the probability p of w income to be equivalent to the certainty of m, so that for project choice w is still the right measure of labour cost if social welfare must be based on the individual's measure of expected utility. There is scope for dispute in this, since it is arguable that social welfare should be based not on the *expected* utility of the labour force (all of whom had probability p of getting a job) but on the *realized ex post* utility of all of them (making a distinction between those who got the job and those who did not). And when pw is not equated to m by expected utility calculus it will make a difference whether *ex ante* expected utility (Neumann–Morgenstern type) or *ex post* realized utility (certainty type) is taken.

There is also the question as to whether the migrant regards m or y as the value of income that he is sacrificing by moving. His income while in the peasant economy was y and his marginal product m, which might or might not have been zero depending on whether surplus labour existed or not. If he acts from the point of maximizing *family welfare* then m is the cost that he should consider, but if he wants to maximize his personal welfare then the relevant cost is y. The equilibrium condition will then be:

$$pw = y \tag{5}$$

In explaining the gap between the urban wage rate and the marginal product of labour in the rural sector, it has often been suggested that the migrant views his loss in terms of his income rather than in terms of the income of the previously joint family, and it is even possible to take a model[16] where $w = y > m$. This type of personal motivation will, of course, reduce the incidence of urban unemployment as a device of marginal equilibrium, and in the case where $w = y$, the problem will disappear altogether. Also, the correctness of the thesis that the market wage rate is the right wage rate even in the presence of a gap between w and m depends on these considerations.

4   Concluding Remarks

One of the most complex aspects of the exercise of project appraisal is the precise identification of the project evaluator's areas of control. This will affect the nature of the exercise that he has to solve and the

15. Presented in a seminar in Nuffield College, Oxford, in May 1970. [Later published in a revised version as 'On Measuring the Social Opportunity Cost of Labour', *International Labour Review*, **103** (1971).]

16. See Lewis [10]. See also Jorgenson [8].

shadow prices that will be relevant for his evaluation. Much of the paper was concerned with demonstrating how variations in the assumptions about areas of control will radically alter the nature of the appropriate shadow prices.

The important approach to project evaluation developed by Professors Little and Mirrlees was studied in this context. The procedure of using world prices for project evaluation was critically examined and it was argued that that procedure required a rather extraordinary assumption about the project evaluator's areas of control.

The relation between the project evaluator's control areas and the appropriate shadow prices was illustrated in terms of the question of labour cost. The relevance of a premium on savings over consumption, weights based on income distributional considerations, valuation of efforts by the peasant family and the labourers, and the impact of employment creation on migration, were analysed in this context. The determination of the appropriate shadow price of labour is impossible without a clear understanding of the extent of influence that the planner exercises over the relevant variables in each category. There was an attempt in the paper to relate differences among schools of thought on the accounting price of labour to differences in assumptions (often implicit) about the areas of control and the motivation of the relevant economic agents.

References

[1] Bator, F. 'On Capital Productivity, Input Allocation and Growth', *Quarterly Journal of Economics*, **71** (1957).

[2] Diamond, P. and Mirrlees, J. 'Optimal Taxation and Public Production: I and II', *American Economic Review*, **60** (1971).

[3] Dasgupta, P. 'Two Approaches to Project Evaluation', *Industrialization and Productivity* (1970).

[4] Dixit, A. K. 'Optimal Development in the Labour-Surplus Economy', *Review of Economic Studies*, **35** (1968).

[5] Dobb, M. H. *An Essay on Economic Growth and Planning* (London: Routledge, 1960).

[6] Eckstein, O. 'Investment Criteria for Economic Development and the Theory of Intertemporal Welfare Economics', *Quarterly Journal of Economics*, **71** (1957).

[7] Galenson, W. and Leibenstein, H. 'Investment Criteria, Productivity and Economic Development', *Quarterly Journal of Economics*, **69** (1955).

[8] Jorgenson, D. W. 'The Development of a Dual Economy', *Economic Journal*, **71** (1961).

[9] Lefeber, L. 'Planning in a Surplus Labour Economy', *American Economic Review*, 58 (1968).

[10] Lewis, W. A. 'Economic Development with Unlimited Supplies of Labour', *The Manchester School*, 22 (1954).

[11] Little, I. M. D. 'Public Sector Project Evaluation in Relation to Indian Development', in Bhuleshkar, A. V. (ed.), *Indian Economic Thought and Development* (Bombay, 1968).

[12] —— and Mirrlees, J. A. *Manual of Industrial Project Analysis in Developing Countries*, Vol. II (Paris: OECD, 1969).

[13] Manne, A. S. *Investment for Capacity Expansion: Size, Location and Time-Phasing* (London: Allen & Unwin, 1967).

[14] Marglin, S. A. *Public Investment Criteria* (London: Allen & Unwin, 1967).

[15] —— 'Industrial Development in the Labour-Surplus Economy', mimeographed (1966). [Later published in a revised version as *Value and Price in the Labour-Surplus Economy* (Oxford: Clarendon Press, 1976).

[16] Newbery, D. 'The Choice of Techniques in a Dual Economy', Cowles Foundation Discussion Paper, No. 278. [Later published in a revised version as 'Public Policy in a Dual Economy', *Economic Journal*, 82 (1972).]

[17] Phelps, E. S. *Fiscal Neutrality Toward Economic Growth*, Chapter 4, reproduced in Sen, A. K. *Growth Economics* (London: Penguin, 1970).

[18] Sen, A. K. 'Some Notes on the Choice of Capital-Intensity in Development Planning', *Quarterly Journal of Economics*, 71 (1957).

[19] —— *Choice of Techniques* (Oxford: Blackwell, 1960: 3rd edn, 1968).

[20] —— 'Peasants and Dualism With or Without Surplus Labour', *Journal of Political Economy*, 74 (1966). [Essay 1 in this volume.]

[21] —— 'The Role of Policy-Makers in Project Formulation and Evaluation', *Industrialization and Productivity*, Bulletin 13 (1969).

[22] —— 'Interrelations between Project, Sectoral and Aggregate Planning', *United Nations Economic Bulletin for Asia and for the Far East*, 21 (June/September 1970).

[23] Stern, N. H. 'Optimum Development in a Dual Economy', *Review of Economic Studies*, 39 (1972).

[24] Tinbergen, J. *The Design of Development* (Baltimore: Johns Hopkins Press, 1958).

[25] Todaro, M. P. 'A Model of Labor Migration and Urban Employment in Less Developed Countries', *American Economic Review*, 59 (1969).

[26] Todaro, M. P. and Harris, J. R. 'Migration, Unemployment and Development: A Two-Sector Analysis', *American Economic Review*, 60 (1970).

[27] UNIDO *Guidelines for Project Evaluation*, mimeographed (1970), authored by Dasgupta, P., Marglin, S. A. and Sen, A. K. [Later published by United Nations, New York, 1972.]

11

Employment, Institutions and Technology: Some Policy Issues

This note comments on some of the important issues involved in using technological choice as an instrument of employment policy in developing countries.[1] It will not, of course, be possible in this short paper to go into a thorough analysis of each of the issues, or to illustrate them with concrete examples, for both of which the reader is referred to the monograph,[2] but it is possible to discuss the direction in which answers to these questions may be sought and also to outline some features of a general approach for tackling the problems involved.

1   The Concept of Employment

At the risk of oversimplification we can distinguish between three different aspects of employment:

(i) the *income* aspect: employment gives an income to the employed;
(ii) the *production* aspect: employment yields an output;
(iii) the *recognition* aspect: employment gives a person the recognition of being engaged in something worth while.

It may look as if we have listed them in order of increasing complexity and this probably is the case.

---

1. This paper is based largely on my monograph, *Employment Policy and Technological Choice*, referred to below as Sen (1975). That monograph was prepared in 1973 for the ILO World Employment Programme.
2. Most of the detailed illustrations come from India, though empirical materials are drawn from other countries as well.

From *International Labour Review*, 112 (July 1975), 45–73.

Consider the recognition aspect first. Employment can be a factor in self-esteem and indeed in esteem by others. Much, of course, depends on the class one comes from. To a member of 'the leisured class' the fact that one does not work for one's living may be, in fact, a source of pride, but for those who have to work for a living, lack of 'employment' is not only a denial of income, it can also be a source of shame. In the same way, if a person is forced by unemployment to take a job that he thinks is not appropriate for him, or not commensurate with his training, he may continue to feel unfulfilled and indeed may not even regard himself as 'employed'. The phenomenon of people having a job but nevertheless regarding themselves as 'unemployed' is a common one and has been observed in different countries. In assessing whether a person is employed or not, clearly his own views on the subject have to be given some weight since it is a question of having not only a gainful occupation but also one which satisfies some of the minimal expectations of the jobseeker.

The question is of a certain amount of practical interest. The ILO Mission to Sri Lanka (then Ceylon) discussed cases 'where people said they were "unemployed" when they meant that they did not have a regular job offering security and some sort of steady income'.[3] The Mission went on, legitimately, to conclude: 'To the extent that respondents thought in these terms and interviewers did not probe very deeply, the data on the numbers shown as openly unemployed may be somewhat overstated.' On the other hand, the question remains whether joblessness is the best way of viewing unemployment, and through its emphasis of 'matching employment opportunities and expectations' the Mission was, in fact, forced to view employment in a wider perspective.

The question of recognition can influence one's choice of jobs, if such a choice should arise. For example, a marked preference for working for oneself rather than for others may partly relate to this problem of recognition both in terms of status as well as in terms of one's reaction to being ordered around. M. I. Finley has argued that the absence of wage employment in ancient Greece was related to this question: 'What we rarely find is the free wage labourer, for such a man was "under the restraint of another", in Aristotle's phrase, and even the poorest Greek avoided that position if he possibly could.'[4] Marxian discussions of 'alienation' also relate closely to this question. So do the recent discussions on the 'dualism' of the labour market in the developing countries – in particular the reluctance of peasants

3. ILO (1971, p. 26).
4. Finley (1959).

to accept wage employment elsewhere unless the wages are relatively high.[5]

A specific aspect of this question is the position of women. While women have not always followed Benjamin Franklin's advice to Catherine Ray: 'Go constantly to Meeting – or church – till you get a good Husband – then stay at home, and nurse the Children, and live like a Christian',[6] women's ability – and indeed their inclination – to accept outside employment have usually been severely constrained. On the other hand, the jobs done by women within the home have typically not been regarded as 'employment' at all, and the story of the man marrying his cook and thereby reducing both the national income as well as the employed workforce has rarely been viewed as an economic scandal.

In contrast with the recognition aspect, the production aspect of employment is less psychological and deals with the output produced. The theory of 'disguised unemployment' has been concerned with the number of people who can be removed from the traditional sector (usually peasant agriculture) without affecting the output level there. Consider the following example, involving a peasant family of four working members with a small plot of land – providing enough productive work for two full-time workers but no more. Each of the four working members works half time (or with half the 'intensity' of effort), and when one of them leaves for the town, the others work that much harder leaving the total labour effort and total output unchanged.[7] Was this man 'unemployed'? He was certainly working and earning something, and conceivably he also valued being in the family enterprise. Clearly he was *not* 'unemployed' in every sense, but this is thought to be a case of 'disguised unemployment' in the sense of the family output being unaffected by his departure.

The income aspect of employment, in contrast, can be altogether divórced from the production aspect, though usually the two are related. If a government wants to increase the income of a certain group of people, or of a certain region, one of the most effective means is by expanding employment. Keynes thought of paying people to dig holes and fill them up in order to expand effective demand in a situation of unemployment, and similar policies may also be relevant for redistributing income between regions or communities even when the total output is unresponsive to an expansion of effec-

---

5. See, for example, Visaria (1970).

6. *The Autobiography of Benjamin Franklin*, selected and arranged by C. van Doren (New York: Pocket Books, 1940), p. 254.

7. For the assumptions necessary and sufficient for this to happen, see Sen (1966) and (1973, Chapter 4).

tive demand.[8] Employment has often been thought of as an effective means of income distribution. While the same function can be served simply by paying doles or subsidies, the political difficulties involved may well be considerable.

The income aspect of employment is concerned with that part of one's income which is received on condition that one works. If one enjoys a share of the joint family income whether one works or not, then that share is, obviously, not covered by the income aspect of employment. The focus of the income aspect of employment should, therefore, be on this question of conditionality, and not just on whether the income level is high or low.[9]

In the case of self-employment, the income aspect is not easy to separate from the production aspect. A family farm's income comes from its production and contributing to the latter expands the former as well. But what about the individual? Or the nuclear family as it breaks away from a joint family in the process of migrating to the town? The identification no longer holds. Even though the nuclear family might not have been making any net contribution to the joint family output, as in the example discussed earlier in this section, it was receiving a share of the joint family income and was in fact living on it. While the contribution to net output might have been zero or very small, the amount of income enjoyed was more than that.

It could, however, be asked whether the income enjoyed was related in any way to the work done rather than being a 'social' requirement for a joint family. There would typically be a clear relation. One would usually have precious little chance of enjoying a share of the joint family income if one refused to take part in the family work. Thus, even though the departure of this man (or this nuclear family) might leave the total joint family output unchanged, so that from the production point of view he (or it) would have been in 'disguised unemployment', nevertheless from the income point of view the man (or the working members in the nuclear family) might have been 'employed'.[10]

To avoid possible confusion I should comment on the distinction between the income approach to unemployment as developed here and the view that 'an adequate level of employment must be defined in terms of its capacity to provide minimum living to the popula-

8. See Chopra (1972).

9. Contrast ILO (1972, p. 1).

10. This has some relation to the discrepancy between the low estimates of unemployment in rural India according to the standard measures (see Government of India, 1970) and the high estimates obtained by using the production approach, e.g. by Mehra (1966). See Sen (1975, Appendix A).

tions'.[11] The ILO Mission to Kenya took an approach to unemployment similar to the latter, and indeed put 'the greatest emphasis on ... the poverty level of returns from work'.[12] This criterion of unemployment – essentially as a matter of inadequate income – has cropped up in other works as well.[13]

As a criterion for the existence of a social problem, inadequate income is of obvious relevance. The question is whether it is best viewed as a criterion of *unemployment* as such. There is a good case for keeping the concepts of poverty and unemployment distinct, without of course assuming them to be independent of each other. Employment is an important means of generating and distributing income, but a person can be rich yet unemployed if he has other sources of income and also a person can work very hard indeed and still be very poor. Poverty is a function of technology and productivity, ownership of means of production, and social arrangements for production and distribution. To identify unemployment with poverty seems to impoverish both notions since they relate to two quite different categories of thought. Further, it can also suggest erroneous policy measures in seeking extra work for a person who is already working very hard but is poor.

In contrast, the income approach used here is concerned not with checking whether a person's income is high or low, but with the extent to which it is conditional on the work he performs. From this point of view, a member of a joint family working on the family farm is to be regarded as unemployed if he would continue to receive economic support even if he did not work on that farm, but is to be regarded as employed if his emoluments would cease if he stopped working there. In the determination of the supply price of labour for work elsewhere, the precise institutional arrangements for income sharing are most important.

This distinction is also of some importance in assessing the extent of surplus labour at the peak agricultural seasons. It is quite common for labourers engaged in other activities, e.g. services and industries, to migrate to their family farms during the busy weeks.[14] This may mean that without their labour the agricultural output would be

11. Dandekar and Rath (1971).
12. ILO (1972), p. 1.
13. See Raj Krishna's (1973) illuminating study of the alternative approaches to the estimation of unemployment in India. Contrast, however, the 'income approach' to unemployment presented here (and extensively analysed in Sen, 1975), which is quite different from one based on poverty as such.
14. Doubts about the existence of 'disguised unemployment' are frequently based on this observation.

lower, but not necessarily. Working is not merely a method of producing output, it is also a way of establishing one's rights to a share in the family income from a joint farm. It is, therefore, possible to overestimate the workforce requirement during the peak seasons if we consider only the actual numbers sharing in the activities in those periods, sometimes leaving other work to do this. One has to take into account the institution set-up and the principles of income-sharing that are in use in peasant communities.[15] Measures of unemployment as seen from the production point of view and from the income point of view can differ sharply, and they have very different bearings on economic policy making.

2   Production Modes, Institutional Structure and Labour Utilization

As discussed in the last section, the concept of employment has several different aspects and the relationship between them depends on the precise institutional structure for production and distribution, which varies considerably in developing economies. In studying the effectiveness of labour utilization, the modes of production and distribution again assume some prominence. Some of the relevant contrasts can be brought out in terms of an extremely simple model.

Let x be the amount of labour time supplied by a typical labourer and n the number of such persons. Hence the total amount of labour time L is given by:

$$L = nx. \tag{1}$$

Given the non-labour resource base, output Q is assumed to depend simply on L, increasing at a diminishing rate as more and more labour is applied:

$$Q = f(L), \text{ with } f' > 0 \text{ and } f'' < 0. \tag{2}$$

Note that f' stands for the marginal product of labour, and the lower its value the higher is the corresponding total output Q.

The effort involved in working is a function of the amount of labour, and to simplify the picture it is assumed that the required

---

15. The fact that sometimes male labourers moving to the towns in order to work as domestic servants or in industry leave their nuclear family behind with the rest of the joint family does tend to put them under a straightforward obligation to come and help in the peak farming activities. The relation between economic support and work obligations is a particularly complex one in the traditional agrarian societies.

compensation for an additional unit of work is constant, measured in units of output:[16]

$$S(x) = zx. \tag{3}$$

The work equilibrium will therefore be characterized by the condition of equating z with the gain from an additional unit of work. It is assumed that of the additional output produced by such work the labourer gets a proportionate share of α, with α lying between 0 and 1. The person values a unit of output going to others at h per unit (in terms of units of output enjoyed by himself).[17] Typically, h also will lie between 0 and 1. If the person is completely 'alienated' from others, then $h = 0$. If he puts the same weight on his own income as on the income of the others involved, then $h = 1$.

The work equilibrium will be given by the equality of the cost of an additional unit of labour (i.e. z) to the reward from it. The direct reward of the person providing the effort is $\alpha f'$, while $(1 - \alpha) f'$ goes to others and this he values at $h(1 - \alpha) f'$. Hence:[18]

$$z = [\alpha + (1 - \alpha) h] f'. \tag{4}$$

As was noted before, in view of (2), the lower the value of f', the higher is the total output produced:

$$Q = G(f'), \text{ with } G \text{ diminishing.} \tag{5}$$

Putting (4) and (5) together, we obtain:

$$Q = G(z/[\alpha + (1 - \alpha) h]), \text{ with } G \text{ diminishing.} \tag{6}$$

We conclude that output and employment will be larger if:

 (i) α (own share) is larger
 (ii) h (concern for others) is larger
(iii) z (labour cost) is smaller.

This shockingly simple framework is, however, broad enough to permit a preliminary sorting out of issues for the different modes of employment on a comparative basis. However, there are variations

---

16. This is an oversimplification; for a more general model see Sen (1975, Section 3.3); also Sen (1966).

17. The value of h would depend not only on one's 'concern' for others' welfare but also on their respective income levels; if one is richer than others, h could even exceed 1. For an analysis of the underlying behaviour assumptions see Sen (1966, 1966a). See also Hymer and Resnick (1969), Wellisz (1968), W. C. Robinson (1969, 1971), Jorgenson and Lau (1969), and Zarembka (1972).

18. There must be some 'boundary conditions' on the total amount of labour that can be supplied by a typical person, i.e. $x \leqslant x^*$, and there is no guarantee that (4) would hold for $x \leqslant x^*$. See Sen (1975, Section 3.3).

TABLE 11.1

Category	Parameter	Family system	Extended family system	Wage employment	Co-operative system
Own share	α	High	Medium	High?	Low
Concern	h	High	Medium	Low	Medium?
Labour cost advantage	$1/z$	High	High	Low	High?
Technology	β	Low	Medium	High	High

Note: We take the inverse of z rather than z itself, so that 'high' means a positive influence rather than a negative one.

in technological parameters also, especially related to the possibilities of utilizing technologies that require a larger scale of operation. The production function that is suitable for a large wage-based factory enterprise might not be available to a small household production unit. This is not very easy to integrate into the framework outlined here and we shall do it — shamefully naïvely — through a 'technology parameter' β. The object of the exercise is to be able to catch the relative advantages of the different modes in terms of output production and when a mode lends itself to larger-scale operation we shall reflect this advantage through a higher value of the multiplicative parameter β (always positive) applied to f:

$$Q = \beta f(L), \tag{7}$$

and

$$Q = G(z/\beta[\alpha + (1-\alpha)h]), \text{ with } G \text{ diminishing.} \tag{8}$$

In Table 11.1 a rough schematic structure for the four influences (α, h, z and β) is considered for four modes of labour use, viz. 'family system', 'extended family system', 'wage employment' and 'cooperative system'; these are, of course, only very rough stereotypes.

As far as α (own share) is concerned, it is obviously high for the family system since a family is a small unit and each worker will get back a high share of his contribution to output.[19] This share will be less for an extended family since α may correspond roughly to $1/n$, where n is the number of people involved, which will be larger for the extended family. For a cooperative run on a larger scale, α will

19. For share-cropping and other feudal systems in agriculture, α will be smaller.

tend to be smaller still, if the distribution system in the cooperative is geared towards some family-type criterion. A cooperative that is run on the basis of payments according to work rather than on some criterion of needs may approximate 'wage employment' in essential respects and should be put in that category.[20]

As far as wage employment itself is concerned, if the marginal productivity theory of wages held, α should equal 1, but the weaknesses of that theory are well known. In any case, if the market is not competitive and there are monopolistic elements in the product market or monopsonistic features in the labour market, the wage earner will get less than his marginal product even according to neoclassical theory.

Coming now to h (concern for others' income), members of the same family are likely to have much concern for each other, so that h should be high. This may be less so for the extended family and still less for a large cooperative, even though that will depend very much on the values and social consciousness of the society in question. Under the capitalist wage system it may be expected that the wage earner's interest in the welfare of the capitalist, who takes away a part of his product, will be rather slight.

As far as z (labour cost) is concerned, one of the common features of models of the 'dual' economy is the relatively low level of the supply price of labour in the family system (and this should also apply to the extended family as well as to a cooperative organized in a community-centred way) as opposed to capitalist wage employment.[21] The capitalist is deterred from choosing relatively labour-intensive techniques by the level of the wage rate he has to pay. But the height of the wage rate may reflect institutional constraints and the labour cost calculations of the family enterprise may be completely different. To what extent this cost advantage will apply to a cooperative enterprise as well will depend on how alienated the members of the cooperative feel from the management and from each other. At one extreme is the case of the cooperative being one big family and at the other is the case in which members treat their work simply as a source of income. The value of z will depend on the appropriate assumption.

Each system seems to have some advantages and also some disadvantages. All of them survive today in different parts of the world – sometimes even side by side. Wherever the technological advantages of large scale are particularly important, e.g. in modern manufacturing,

20. There are, however, some special problems with cooperative payment according to work as well, on which see Ward (1958, 1971), Domar (1966) and Sen (1966a, 1975).
21. See Sen (1966).

the family system and the extended family system tend to die out. They survive in areas where the technological advantages of scale are not too great (especially when scale is reckoned in terms of the size of the workforce), whereas traditional values reinforce the preference for working for oneself or for the family, e.g. in agriculture.[22]

The case of the non-wage cooperative mode involves the most challenging questions of organization of employment and production. In principle it can combine the technological advantages of a wage system with the cost advantages of a family-type mode, with a high technology parameter β and a low labour cost z. While the share α may be low, given a socially oriented motivation a high value of h can compensate for it, as should be obvious from (6) or (8).[23] Not surprisingly in countries making major efforts in the direction of non-wage cooperative production, such as China, much emphasis has been placed on a cultural reorientation of behaviour and a complete revision of work motivation.[24] The opportunities for effective utilization of economic resources depend not merely on technological and institutional considerations (e.g. β and α), but also on the social psychology of the people (affecting z and h).

3   Employment, Income Distribution and Consumption

In the last section employment was considered from the point of view of output generation. Shifting our attention now from the production aspect to the income aspect, it becomes essential to examine the relation of employment to income distribution, which is indeed an important policy. There are very few methods of distributing income that are thought to be as effective as offering employment. It is worth inquiring why this should be so.

The question can be asked whether the aim of giving income to economically depressed groups could not be better served by simply paying these people subsidies. To concentrate on the income approach only, we leave out of this picture the recognition aspect; people may in fact prefer to receive income for work rather than be on the dole, but let us not go into this question here. So we now have a case of

22. For a comparison of data from 28 different countries and their interpretation in the light of the analytical model proposed here see Sen (1975, Chapter 3).

23. In the extreme case where $h = 1$, the value of Q is completely independent of α. The higher the value of h, the lower the sensitivity of Q to α.

24. See Hoffmann (1967), J. Robinson (1969) and Riskin (1973) for illuminating analyses of the experiments on work motivation in China. See also Ishikawa (1973) for an important general study of choice of technology in China.

employment that has no consequence for production and that has no recognition aspect. Under these circumstances, it could well be asked: why make the poor work rather than simply hand them subsidies?

Two types of issues seem to be relevant in answering this question, and each involves more than economics. First, a widespread system of pure subsidies in a developing economy may be difficult to run because of the possibilities of corruption involved in it. By relating payment to employment, these possibilities may be substantially reduced since the records are easier to check and fictitious payments by corrupt officials easier to eliminate. Second, if the subsidy mechanism is not broad enough to cover everyone owing either to a lack of funds or to the limitation of the administrative machinery, there is a serious problem of selection of beneficiaries for special favour. By offering people jobs rather than pure subsidies, the government may be less exposed to charges of arbitrary discrimination, and indeed it is possible to discriminate in favour of those who need support most and are ready to work for it. This type of administrative and political consideration may provide the rationale of employment schemes for the purpose of income redistribution, such as the one with the somewhat distinguished name 'Crash Scheme for Rural Employment', launched in India in 1971.[25]

There is, however, a problem of feasibility even in the case of the employment method of redistributing income. Suppose n jobs are to be offered at w wage rate. If only n people wish to work at that wage rate, then clearly there is no problem of selection, though in that case the question can be raised as to whether the wage rate is enough of a hidden income subsidy. If, on the other hand, more than n people try to get these jobs, the question of selection and therefore of arbitrary discrimination would crop up again.[26] So would the possibility of corruption and bribery. Employment may not, therefore, be as fine a method of income redistribution as it is sometimes made out to be. The crux of the matter is that the whole purpose of pure redistribution is to give something free, and given that fact — no matter how the process is administered — it will tend to generate pressures influencing the officials involved in the give-away. Whether the employment mechanism minimizes these problems more than the other vehicles of redistribution is still an open question. A detailed examination of the feasibility constraints is essential.

Turning now to the other side of the coin, it is important to recognize that since employment generates income and purchasing

25. For a detailed examination see Sen (1975, Appendix B).
26. In the Indian experiment this seems to have been a serious problem (Sen, 1975, Appendix B).

power, the feasibility of employment creation is also constrained by the availability of the consumer goods the demand for which will expand with employment. This has a significant bearing on employment policy. One of the commonest problems of employment policy is to choose between two alternatives, one of which, say alternative A, produces more output but yields less employment than alternative B, all other resources being equal. Should B be chosen, despite its lower productivity, if employment is regarded as an important goal? No doubt such an argument can be made out, but it is not necessarily an easy one to defend. B is, of course, technically inefficient, but this need not in itself be a sufficient reason for rejecting it.[27] The important question is: what determines the aggregate level of employment? Does the level of employment in one enterprise influence that in others?

If more employment is sought, we have to ask why it is not possible simply to hire more people in some public sector project such as road building? It can be argued that the main difficulty here lies in the need for consumer goods to meet the additional demand arising from the additional wages bill. When more people are hired, more wages will be paid out, thereby creating more effective demand. In a situation of Keynesian unemployment, this would, of course, lead to more supply, but not so in the developing economy given the fact that typically, in such an economy, output is restricted by resources and organization rather than by effective demand.[28] Thus the extra demand arising from the additional wages bill will simply have to be met from some reallocation of the existing output, e.g. through inflationary readjustments, which may have considerable political and economic repercussions, and can also involve reduction of employment elsewhere.

It is this fact which casts serious doubts on the view that aggregate employment can be easily raised at the cost of reducing output of consumer goods. If in the choice posed earlier, alternative B is chosen, yielding more employment and less output, the opportunity of creating employment elsewhere will be less because of the reduction of output.[29] In fact at the risk of oversimplification, the total opportunity of wage employment $\hat{E}$ can be viewed as being given by

27. If employment is a desirable goal in itself, B can be 'superior' from the social point of view despite technical inefficiency.

28. See Das-Gupta (1954, 1956), and Rao (1956).

29. The argument is immediate if the output in question is of goods consumed by the wage earners. If the product consists of capital goods, a similar argument exists through the possibility of shifting resources between the production of capital goods and that of consumer goods. The same holds for the case of consumer goods of other kinds.

the available supply of wage goods M and the real wage rate w, assuming that all wages are consumed:

$$\hat{E} = \frac{M}{w}. \tag{9}$$

A reduction in output would tend to reduce M, so that even if direct employment in this project is larger, its over-all impact on total employment can be negative.[30]

This type of consideration has an important bearing on the framework in which employment policy may be discussed. Important contributions have been made in recent years by analysing the generation of 'indirect employment' through input–output relationships. The creation of demand for related goods can be taken to expand employment through their labour content.[31] If this is interpreted as a model of *determination* of total employment (direct plus indirect), there are obvious problems, since what the process really implies is the creation of a market demand for labour.[32] In a completely free enterprise economy this may be the way employment is determined, but if there is employment planning by the government, the real bottleneck to employment expansion will be in the supply of wage goods rather than on the demand side, which the government can in any case alter through public sector projects if wage goods are available. The framework of analysis in terms of direct and indirect employment is useful in exploring the creation of market demand for labour, but to interpret it as a process of determination of employment would be a hang-over from the Keynesian model of demand bottleneck.

A government pursuing the employment objective seriously should always be able to make up the gap between the employment opportunity as given by (9) and the existing demand for labour. The distinction is important when doing project evaluation in terms of the employment objective, because the question does arise whether to take credit for the 'indirect employment' to be generated by the project through the demand for related goods and thus through the derived demand for labour. The answer really depends on the government's own policy. If it merely maintains law and order, and does

---

30. If alternative B involves a lower real wage, that fact will tend to work in the opposite direction, but it need not fully cancel out the greater employment potential of the larger output of A. However, the picture is simplest when there is a uniform wage rate, as is assumed in (9).

31. See, for example, Hazari and Krishnamurty (1970), and Gaiha (1972).

32. In this sense it is an extension of the older concept of the 'employment multiplier' (Keynes, 1936).

not pursue any employment policy, then it may make sense to count in the 'indirect employment', since demand may also be a bottleneck. If, however, the government does try to expand employment subject to the constraint given by (9), it can always make up for any demand gap, so that (9) will be the binding constraint. Employment will then depend simply on the supply of wage goods.

This analysis is based on the use of the wage system at a given real wage rate. The advantages of lower real cost of labour for certain modes of production and employment have been discussed earlier. One way of breaking through the barrier of (9) is to use a non-wage system of employment generation, e.g. through cooperative work projects in which the reward for extra work comes only later in the form of greater output for the cooperative and the community. This is essentially a method of extending the advantages of a non-wage family system[33] to operations of larger scale.

4 *Dualism*

In the controversial field of economic development one of the few areas of agreement is on the existence of multiple labour markets in many developing countries. Wage gaps are a common feature of such different models of growth as those of Lewis (1954) and Fei and Ranis (1964) on the one hand, and those of Jorgenson (1961) and Zarembka (1972) on the other; and there are also the models of Marglin (1966), Dixit (1968), Hornby (1968), Newbery (1972), and Stern (1972), to mention just a few.

In the case of the wage system the gaps are readily noticeable in terms of differences in the wage rates for the same kind of labour in different labour markets. However, when one contrasts a wage-based labour market with labour use under a non-wage system, one has to be careful about defining real labour costs appropriately. For 'self-employed labour' or 'unpaid family labour' the appropriate cost of labour is given by the rate of substitution between output and non-work that is acceptable to the labourer.[34] If a self-employed person accepts two units of output as making it just worth his while to put

---

33. There have been some attempts to use this strategy in China, and whether (9) would be binding or not would depend on the possibility of expanding employment outside the wage system. The question of appropriate work motivation is crucial for the possibility of exploring this avenue.

34. If the non-wage labourer simply obeys the commands of the head of the family enterprise, then the valuation has to be that of the head in question.

in an additional unit of work, then 2 is the relevant 'real labour cost' expressed in terms of output.

One has to be careful in interpreting the 'real labour cost' since the substitution in question is not that between the person's labour and his *own share* of output, but that between the former and the *entire* output produced by that unit of his labour. For example, if he gets one half of the output contribution he makes and regards two units of output, of which he gets one unit, to be just adequate compensation for his work, then the real labour cost is 2 and not 1. In terms of the model outlined earlier, the real labour cost j is given not by z but by:

$$j = z/[\alpha + (1 - \alpha) h].\qquad(10)$$

Only with a homogeneous family unit — typically a nuclear family rather than a joint family — when one's 'own share' is the whole ($\alpha = 1$), or when concern is total ($h = 1$), could we have the special result:[35]

$$j = z.\qquad(11)$$

In general it is j and not z that has to be compared with the ruling market wage w since j and w would play identical roles in decisions on labour allocation.

While the formula given by (10) involves psychological factors, estimating j on the basis of observed choices need not bring in these factors explicitly. In such an exercise of estimation one would have to check precisely at what point the labourer in question stops putting in additional units of labour and to see the implied value of j from it in terms of production possibilities. The value of (10) lies not in this estimation, but in understanding the underlying process and in interpreting the estimates.

The problem of estimation is simpler for wage-based labour markets in which the operating wage rates can be easily observed. However, there is need for caution in interpreting the wage rate as the real labour cost in any market in which imperfections exist. For example, if labour is available at a given wage rate w but the output thus produced is sold in an imperfect product market, then the profit-maximizing capitalist would apply labour to the point such that the wage rate w is equated to the marginal revenue product.[36]

---

35. Cf. Sen (1966).

36. That is: $w = pf'(L)\{1 - (1/e)\}$, where e is the elasticity of demand for the product of this firm and p the price of it. In units of output the 'real labour cost' j would then be not w but: $j = w/\{1 - (1/e)\}$. Similar corrections would have to be made if there were monopsonistic elements in the labour market. See J. Robinson (1933).

Needless to say that if the output of the non-wage unit is sold in an imperfect product market, then a similar correction would have to be made in the formula given by (10) as well. Frequently, this would not be needed since the peasant family units typically tend to sell their product in a market with innumerable sellers, e.g. in peasant agriculture, but there can be exceptions, as in the case of family-based production units making specialized handicrafts in which each producer may enjoy a substantial share of the market.[37]

The dualism of labour markets can have a number of different causes, which it is necessary to distinguish clearly. They include:

(1) *Labourers' job preferences:* The labourer in question could actually prefer to be in one sector rather than in another, e.g. working in peasant agriculture rather than in wage employment in the town.

(2) *Indivisibilities in labour supply:* A labourer could prefer to work half time in his farm and half time in a factory but he may not be able to do this given the physical problems of location and the organizational problems of the factory system. To take up a job in the factory he may have to leave his farm altogether or at least for long stretches of time, and the same may be true of accepting a job in, say, an irrigation project. High transport costs, as well as the monetary and psychological costs of settling in, may persuade the labourer to stick to his farm unless the reward elsewhere is very high. But settled in his own farm the supply price of labour z and the real cost of labour j for hours (or days) of effort may be comparatively low.

(3) *Loss of share of family income:* A movement away from one's farm may involve the loss of one's share of the family income. In terms of orthodox economic theory it is possible to split the earnings of the peasant into two parts – one being the reward for labour and the other that for being a joint owner of family resources, in particular the plot of land. But there is a kind of labour theory of value which tends to influence the distributional principles in a peasant society, and the possibility of the ex-peasant working in the town but nevertheless cashing in the 'implicit rent' on his share of the land is usually rather remote. The peasant in question may have an economic incentive not to move even when his marginal contribution to the family income is negligible or low.[38] What wage he will accept

---

37. It may also sometimes be the case that essentially identical labour is sold at different prices because of artificial distinctions. A typical example of this is the Indian phenomenon of using highly educated labour in jobs that do not at all require that type of education. On this see Blaug, Layard and Woodhall (1969), and Sen (1971).

38. See Sen (1975, Appendices A and B).

as minimal compensation will depend partly on his concern for the welfare of the joint family compared with that for his own welfare (or the welfare of the nuclear family).

(4) *Labour legislation and union pressure:* In many countries there is labour legislation specifying a minimum wage for employment in the organized sector, and even if the number of people seeking such jobs far exceeds the number of jobs available, still the wage rate does not decline. The same result is sometimes achieved by unionized labour through wage bargaining. This provides a straightforward institutional explanation of the wage gap between organized and unorganized sectors.[39]

(5) *Employers' incentives for paying high wages:* The employer is, under certain circumstances, better off paying wages higher than the minimum at which he can recruit labour, partly to reduce the costs of rapid labour turnover, partly to avoid discontent and potential labour strife, but also because higher wages may have a direct impact on labour productivity through better nutrition and greater ability to work hard.[40]

The consequences of the dual labour markets depend on the cause of the phenomenon. For example, if the wage gap arises from labour legislation or union pressure (cause 4), or from the employers' incentives for paying high wages (cause 5), then not only will there be different wages in different markets, but labourers from the low-labour-cost sector will be available in substantial numbers to move to the high-wage sector. The high wages will be restrained from falling by legislation, or union action, or the employers' expected profit calculations, but many people will be looking for jobs and will be ready to work even at somewhat *lower* wages. If, however, the explanation is labourers' job preferences (cause 1), or indivisibilities in labour supply (cause 2), or loss of share of family income (cause 3), the wage gap will be a reflection of labour supply constraints, and there will not be a mass of people hanging around in readiness to wok at lower wages.[41]

The wage gap under causes 4 and 5 leads to rather complicated decision problems for the potential wage labourer. If he gets a job

39. Bhalla (1970) argues that it may not be in the interest of the class of labourers as a whole to bid down wages since people benefit from income transfers from their high-wage-earning relatives. This implies some 'tacit collusion'.

40. On the last see Leibenstein (1957), Mazumdar (1959) and Galenson and Pyatt (1964).

41. There may, however, be a large 'reserve army of labour' available for work *at* the ruling wage rate given by the subsistence level in one version of cause 3; see Marx (1887); also Lewis (1954).

at the ruling wage, he will clearly prefer it to working in the family-based production unit. On the other hand, he prefers his current work to unemployment. Given such a ranking it can be argued that he will be indifferent between the certainty of his job in the family system and a given probability mixture of getting a high-wage job in the organized sector and being unemployed.[42] This crucial probability ρ^* of getting a high-wage job is given by (12) in which $U(w)$ stands for his utility from employment in the high-wage sector, $U(y)$ for that from his current family-enterprise employment, and $U(0)$ for that from unemployment, with $U(w)$ larger than $U(y)$ and $U(y)$ larger than $U(0)$:

$$U(y) = \rho^* U(w) + (1 - \rho^*) U(0). \tag{12}$$

Obviously, ρ^* will lie between 0 and 1. A rather simpler version of this approach has been presented by Harris and Todaro (1969), in which the calculation is done not in terms of utility but directly in terms of incomes. If y is the income of the person in the unorganized sector and w that in the high-wage sector, with w larger than y, then the person is assumed to be indifferent between the certainty of getting y and probability ρ^* of getting w and $(1 - \rho^*)$ of getting nothing when:[43]

$$\rho^* = \frac{y}{w}. \tag{13}$$

If the subjective probability ρ of getting high-wage employment in the town is greater than ρ^*, then this person moves to town; if less, he does not. If ρ exceeds ρ^*, then more and more people crowd into the towns, thereby raising the incidence of unemployment and reducing the proportion of the workforce that is employed there until their subjective probability of employment ρ comes down to ρ^*. The opposite happens if we start from ρ less than ρ^*, and the equilibrium given by $\rho = \rho^*$ is stable according to this adjustment process.

This is a theory of the determination of the subjective probability ρ of finding a job. More has, however, been read into it, and a model of the determination of the urban unemployment ratio has been based on it. By assuming that the subjective probability of employ-

42. This is not an analytic requirement and there is obviously no mathematical reason why such a probability must exist. However, it seems to be a reasonable behaviouristic postulate and implies essentially a continuity assumption. On this see von Neumann and Morgenstern (1947).

43. This corresponds to (12) if utility is a linear function of income. Choosing the origin arbitrarily as $U(0) = 0$, we get $U(w) = w$ and $U(y) = y$ through appropriate choice of units.

ment in this high-wage sector is equal to the ratio of the employed to the total workforce in that location, the condition of subjective equilibrium given by (13) has been converted into a theory of the determination of the *actual* ratio of the employed to the workforce.[44]

One consequence of making this translation and of interpreting (13) thus, is to make the market wage rate equal the opportunity cost of labour. For every person in employment there has to be $(1/\rho^*)$ people in the urban workforce and thus the alternative earnings forgone are (y/ρ^*), which by virtue of (13) exactly equal w. What the market pays the labourer equals, on this interpretation, the corrected opportunity cost of his employment. The Invisible Hand strikes again!

There are, however, several difficulties with this analysis. First, the workers in question need not have the behavioural characteristics implied by (12), i.e. may not be expected utility maximizers. In matters of 'life and death' such as these decisions involve, affecting one's entire economic existence, the assumption of expected utility maximization is recognized to be quite restrictive. Second, even if they do follow (12), they may not follow (13), which requires them to maximize expected *income* and not expected utility, which rules out diminishing marginal utility with increasing income. Third – and perhaps more important – the people in question may not think of the possibility of employment in terms of a given probability of getting a job *independent of time* but in terms of a definite period of *waiting* after which they can expect to be employed. Studies of unemployment in several developing countries[45] have indicated that the way the labour market adjusts to variations of excess supply is mainly through a variation of the length of time a person has to wait before he gets his first job. On this interpretation, the way to bring the excess labour supply situation into the individual's rational calculations is through a discounting of future higher incomes and not through a probability weight independent of time. Various intermediate possibilities can also be considered.[46]

44. See Todaro (1966) and Harris and Todaro (1969). See also Harberger (1971), pp. 568–72. Stiglitz (1972) provides an alternative set of assumptions that also lead to induced unemployment just offsetting the gap between the wage rate and the opportunity cost of labour in a model in which the government directly controls the urban employment level and the ratio of urban unemployment, or equivalently directly controls the urban employment level and the urban wage rate.

45. See Blaug, Layard and Woodhall (1969), ILO (1971, 1972). See also Sen (1975, Appendix A), on the average lag between registration in Indian employment exchanges and the first call.

46. See Anand (1971).

Finally, even if people do think exclusively in terms of expected probability of employment, as given by (13), they may not identify their subjective probability of employment with the actual ratio of the employed to the workforce, and it is only under this very special interpretation that the Invisible Hand could grab the prize.[47]

5   Dualism and Resource Allocation

While in the last section the wage gap was defined in fairly general terms, the focus of our attention was on rural–urban differences. There are, however, important problems that arise from dual labour markets *within* the agricultural sector itself. The total amount of labour L applied in a family farm and the output Q produced in the farm can be seen to be determined by the 'real labour cost' j:

$$L = E(j), \tag{14}$$

and

$$Q = G(j). \tag{15}$$

Both E and G are strictly diminishing functions of the real labour cost.[48] For wage-based farms with the same production possibilities, (14) and (15) give the relevant relationships if j is replaced by the wage rate w.

The essence of dualism lies in the simple fact that:

$$w > j. \tag{16}$$

It follows from the fact that E and G are strictly diminishing functions of j that:

$$E(w) < E(j), \tag{17}$$

and

$$G(w) < G(j). \tag{18}$$

That is, the family farmers could yield a higher value of labour and output per acre than the wage-based farms. It has been argued[49] that

47. Note also that even if this theory of urban unemployment were accepted, this would equate the wage rate w only to the private income interpretation of the opportunity cost of labour from the traditional sector. The latter can diverge from the 'production aspect' of the opportunity cost when the 'implicit rent' from his share of the joint ownership of land is lost to the migrant as he moves.

48. The real labour cost j is given by $z/[\alpha + (1 - \alpha)h]$, and $E(j) = f^{-1}(G(j))$.

49. Sen (1962, 1964). There has been a vigorous controversy on the subject which is reviewed in Sen (1975, Appendix C).

(17) and (18) explain why smaller farms in India tend to have higher productivity per acre than larger ones, since the dependence on hired labour tends to go up as farms of larger size groups are considered.

A special case of (18) has been much discussed in the context of the 'relative efficiency' of peasant agriculture and capitalist farming.[50] Taking the real labour cost of 'overpopulated' peasant economies to be zero ($j = 0$), we get:

$$G(w) < G(0). \tag{18.1}$$

In view of the seasonal nature of agriculture, this argument needs to be somewhat extended.[51] Consider two seasons, in one of which there is a wage gap, viz. $j_1 < w_1$, while there is none in the other, viz. $j_2 = w_2$. If complete complementarity is assumed so that labour is used in fixed proportions (say, in the ratio $b : 1$), the effective cost of a composite unit of labour in the family farm would be $(bj_1 + j_2)$ and that in the wage-based farm $(bw_1 + w_2)$. It follows immediately from the strictly diminishing nature of the E and G functions that:

$$E(bj_1 + j_2) > E(bw_1 + w_2), \tag{19}$$

and

$$G(bj_1 + j_2) > G(bw_1 + w_2). \tag{20}$$

That is, the employment level and the output volume per acre in the family farm would be higher than in the wage-employment farm.

It is obvious that this result can be easily extended to a model of many seasons, and the directional results will hold as long as there is a wage gap in *at least* one season. Furthermore, it is not necessary that labour in different seasons be perfectly complementary. If we assume that a greater use of labour in one season increases the productivity of labour in other seasons,[52] the result will hold good.

Incidentally, in some models of labour allocation it has been argued that if the seasonality of the production process is taken into account, then surplus labour cannot exist. Perhaps the most interesting of these models is that of Stiglitz (1969). As he puts it, 'we have proved that, provided leisure is a superior good and labour supplied at harvest and planting times and at other times of the year are complementary, output must fall as labour migrates to the urban sector: labourers cannot be in surplus'.[53] Explaining the difference between his results and those in Sen (1966), Stiglitz says:

50. See Bauer (1948), and Georgescu-Roegen (1960).
51. Cf. Sen (1966).
52. That is, the 'cross-partials' are non-negative.
53. Stiglitz (1969, p. 11).

This result can be contrasted with that of Sen (1966). He argues that agricultural output will remain unchanged as labour leaves the agricultural sector if and only if there is constant marginal utility of leisure and income (so the indifference curves are straight lines). The reason for the divergence between our results and his is his strong assumption that L^1 and L^2 (labour supplied at different periods of the year) are perfect substitutes. Even if we allow L^1 and L^2 to be substitutes, but not perfect substitutes, his results will not obtain.

This, if correct, is a very serious criticism of the model of surplus labour since we do know with certainty that labour applied in different seasons is not perfectly substitutable. We cannot replace a day's work at harvest time by a day's work at sowing time, or by a day's work when the crop is quietly growing in the fields while the cultivator is resting his limbs without having much to do. But is the criticism correct? I would argue that Stiglitz gets his result precisely because of an additional assumption brought in by him without much fanfare.

The crucial difference rests in Stiglitz's assumption that, in at least one of the seasons of the year, each person is already doing the maximum amount of work that he *possibly* can, and this combined with the fact that labour applications in different seasons are not perfect substitutes immediately produces the no-surplus-labour consequences. Stiglitz explains his assumption thus:

> For simplicity, we shall divide the year into two periods, planting and harvesting, during which labourers are assumed to be fully utilized (i.e. *work the maximum that is possible at those times*), and the other times of the year, during which the supply of labour (hours worked per week) by each labourer is determined so as to maximize utility.[54]

No wonder that this model produces the result that 'labourers cannot be in surplus', since it begins by assuming that there is no slack whatsoever in one season, which, combined with the perfectly reasonable assumption that labour in other seasons cannot fully substitute for busy season labour, must yield the no-surplus-labour result! Surplus labour can exist with any degree of substitutability between labour in different seasons.[55]

Coming back to dualism, it is worth mentioning that (17) and (18) apply to wage gaps caused by 'labourers' job preferences', 'loss of

54. Stiglitz (1969, p. 3); italics added.
55. See Sen (1975, Chapters 4 and 8), for a fuller discussion.

share of family income', or 'labour legislation and union pressure', but not necessarily to 'employers' incentives for paying high wages'. In the last case the relevance of (17) and (18) will depend on the precise reasons behind the employers' higher wage offers. If the motivation is higher productivity (say, due to the influence of improved nutrition), the effective labour cost may not be higher even when wages are greater. The relationships discussed here hold only for differences in effective real labour cost after correction for productivity differences.

Dualism has consequences for various other aspects of resource allocation. One such is the choice of appropriate age of the machinery. Consider two sectors A and B of an economy such that sector A has a higher wage and a lower interest rate. (We can think of A as 'advanced' and B as 'backward'.) The relative prices of old and new machines that would be equilibrating from the point of view of profits in sector A would not offer the same rates of profit in sector B, and this provides a case for trade in second-hand machinery.

Take the simplest case first. Let the gross profits (quasi-rents) of a machine with a fixed life be P per year in both sectors A and B. But the interest rate is lower in sector A, i.e. $r_a < r_b$. The equilibrium price of the machine one year before the end of its life in sectors A and B will be respectively $P/(1 + r_a)$ and $P/(1 + r_b)$, and the corresponding prices two years before its end will be $\{P/(1 + r_a)\} + \{P/(1 + r_a)^2\}$ and $\{P/(1 + r_b)\} + \{P/(1 + r_b)^2\}$ respectively. The price ratios of the one-year-left machine to the two-years-left machine in sectors A and B are respectively:

$$\rho_a = (1 + r_a)/(2 + r_a), \tag{21}$$

and

$$\rho_b = (1 + r_b)/(2 + r_b). \tag{22}$$

Since $r_b > r_a > 0$, it is clear that:

$$\rho_b > \rho_a. \tag{23}$$

Thus an older machine is a relatively better investment for the high-interest backward sector B. The argument can be easily generalized for all periods of time. If the new and old machines all sell in the advanced sector A at relative prices such that they are equally profitable investments in sector A, then in the absence of transport costs an investor in sector B will always find it more profitable to buy an older machine rather than anything of newer vintage.

Of course, it is likely that sector B will have not merely a higher interest rate but also a higher gross profit P since the wage rate there is lower. Will the above argument be affected if we take P_a and P_b as the respective quasi-rents and assume that $P_a < P_b$? The answer is: not at all. In fact, ρ_a and ρ_b given by (21) and (22) are completely independent of P_a and P_b. The relative advantage in favour of older machinery, i.e. (23), holds even though the lower-wage sector may have a higher gross profit per machine in sector B and not merely a higher interest rate.[56]

Export of second-hand machinery from countries with high wages and low interest to those with lower wages and higher interest does, of course, take place on a substantial scale. A factor that acts against this is the cost of transport, which is larger if machinery has to be frequently replaced and imported. Also, in countries with import controls and licensing the industrialist may feel more inclined to import a new machine that will last for a long time rather than one which will have to be replaced very soon, thereby requiring a new licence. The latter issue is, however, usually inoperative for transfers between sectors *within* a country, and the transport costs will also be typically lower than those for inter-country transfers. Such inter-sectoral transfers have been observed on a very large scale in Japan as well as in India. The dualism characterized by differential capital and labour costs not only affect the extent of mechanization of different sectors but also influences systematically the optimal age structure of capital goods in use.

6   Cost–Benefit Evaluation and Shadow Pricing

The institutional, technological and psychological aspects touched on in the earlier sections have important implications for cost–benefit analysis of the employment aspect of alternative policies. It is not the purpose of this section to discuss the methods of cost–benefit analysis and the derivation of shadow prices presented and discussed in some detail in Sen (1975), but to comment on some alternative definitions of shadow prices, each used extensively in the literature.

There are, in fact, several alternative definitions of shadow prices and they coincide only under specific (and sometimes very restrictive) assumptions. Four approaches are particularly worth distinguishing:

56. Cf. Sen (1962a). The model can be extended in several directions to take account of labour input variation with age and of technical progress related to vintage; see Smith (1976).

(1) Shadow prices as the contribution to social welfare (i.e. whatever is being maximized by the planner) of having one more
unit of the good or resource in question.
(2) Shadow prices in the technical sense of the 'dual' corresponding
to the constraint of the resource in question in the maximizing
programming (primal) problem.
(3) Shadow prices as the accounting prices which if used for profit
maximization lead to the choice of the social-welfare-maximizing
combination of policies.
(4) Shadow prices as the prices that would equate demand in a competitive market to the competitive supply.

Under some assumptions (1) and (2) correspond to each other
closely (see Sen, 1968), so that the technical concept of the shadow
price as the 'dual' is perhaps best interpreted in terms of the incremental contribution to social welfare made by an additional unit of
labour. In some senses (3) coincides with this too, but there are some
tactical problems which have been responsible for a certain confusion; these relate to not using shadow prices uniformly but using
uncorrected market prices for a few items. For example, consider the
following problem. In an economy with surplus labour, the project
selector is trying to choose the appropriate labour intensity to
maximize a weighted sum of immediate consumption and reinvest-
able savings valued higher than corresponding units of consumption
at market prices.[57] If q is the market value of the additional output
generated by one more unit of employment and w the additional
wage, the net gain in social welfare from an additional unit of
employment is given by:

$$N = w + (q - w) p^I, \qquad (24)$$

where p^I is the weight on savings (greater than unity with consumption as the unit of account) and where all wages are consumed and all
profits saved.[58] Given surplus labour, social welfare will be maximized
by going to the point where N is zero, i.e. q falls so much that not
only is $(q - w)$ negative but $w = (w - q) p^I$. The contribution of an
additional unit of labour to social welfare will then be zero and the
appropriate shadow price in sense (1), and also in sense (2), will be
nil as well. But if the project selector decides to refer to the shadow
price as that labour cost to which the additional *market-valued* productivity of labour should be equated to get to $N = 0$, then clearly

57. See Sen (1960), Marglin (1966), Little and Mirrlees (1968), Dasgupta, Marglin and
Sen (1972).
58. For more general models see Sen (1968, 1975).

this 'shadow price' equals $q = w(p^I - 1)/p^I$. Similar 'terminological' problems abound in the literature of resource allocation and require careful treatment.

Turning now to sense (4), the assumptions needed to make it coincide with (1) and (2) are very restrictive indeed. This use of 'shadow' or 'accounting' prices is, therefore, particularly abundant in pitfalls. In his pioneering exercise in using 'accounting prices' for development planning, Tinbergen (1958) took this approach:

> They [accounting prices] are the prices at which supply is just sufficient to satisfy demand; they represent the value of the marginal product to be obtained with their aid, since projects showing no surplus above the cost, at accounting prices, of the factors used, will be on the margin between acceptance and rejection.[59]

This conception is, obviously, close to the notion of shadow prices as a guide to decentralized decision-taking, since perfect competition is a method of decentralized resource allocation. But the difference between the two approaches is quite substantial. The existence of competitive equilibrium would guarantee only Pareto optimality (and that under certain specific circumstances),[60] and an arbitrary competitive equilibrium need not at all correspond to the maximization of the objectives of planning, even if those objectives include Pareto optimality.[61]

This concentration on the competitive market led Tinbergen into an unduly narrow framework of accounting prices and also made him come out with a rather limited set of reasons for which accounting prices should differ from the market prices.

> In other words, there are two reasons why market prices do not truly reflect 'intrinsic values'. First, the realization of the investment pattern will itself influence these values, but only after some time, since investment processes are essentially time-consuming. Secondly, there do exist, in underdeveloped countries especially, a number of 'fundamental disequilibria'.[62]

This leaves out divergences of accounting prices from market prices arising from the planning objectives being different from whatever it is that the particular competitive mechanism may achieve when in

59. Tinbergen (1958, p. 40).

60. See Koopmans (1957, Essay 1).

61. Further, certain circumstances may rule out the achievement of Pareto optimality through the competitive mechanism, but not decentralized procedures in general.

62. Tinbergen (1958, p. 39).

equilibrium. Some of the more important reasons for the divergence between market prices and accounting prices may have nothing whatsoever to do with either of the two reasons suggested by Tinbergen and may relate instead to income distributional judgements, existence of certain types of non-market interdependences between the individuals and groups,[63] and so on.

It should be noticed that while the difference between approaches (1), (2) and (3) to shadow pricing is one of presentation and there is no real conflict between them, the same does not hold for the differences between approach (4) and the earlier three. The prices that would equate demand and supply under the competitive mechanism in a given economic environment may indeed have nothing very much to do with the shadow prices in terms of the other definitions.

7 Partial Ignorance and Policy Making

One of the difficulties of using a very broad framework of analysis involving institutional, technological, psychological and political factors is the near-certainty that its practical application will be extremely difficult. Methodologically, one is faced with the choice between using an uncomplicated model which will be easy to apply, but which will miss many important dimensions of employment policy and technological choice, and using a more comprehensive model which will be difficult to apply.

It is worth emphasizing in this context that the exercise of systematic economic evaluation should not be viewed as an all-or-nothing game. In some circumstances one may know for certain that the relevant shadow prices lie within a certain range but be unsure of their precise level. It is this type of constraint that has led to the increasing use of sensitivity analysis in project evaluation.[64] However, sensitivity analysis only shows precisely which shadow prices have to be estimated very accurately and which can be assessed somewhat more loosely. It is, in fact, possible to go beyond that and to define rigorously the decisions that can be made with confidence in a state of partial ignorance and those that cannot. Formally, it is possible to think of social preference as a quasi-ordering rather than as a complete ordering. A quasi-ordering may lack completeness, that is, it is possible that a policy x may be thought to be neither better than,

---

63. Some types of 'externalities' would rule out the existence of shadow prices in the sense of the dual, but not all.

64. See Dasgupta, Marglin and Sen (1972); also Datta–Chaudhuri and Sen (1970).

nor worse than, nor indifferent to, say policy y, while x and z and also y and z are easily comparable. This type of framework has been used in other problems of policy making and planning,[65] and it can be applied to employment policy as well.

Let r_i be a set of consequences of hiring one more person and let v_i be the appropriate shadow price (in sense 1) of element r_i. Then the impact on social welfare of an additional unit of employment is given by:

$$w^* = \sum_i r_i v_i. \tag{25}$$

One may, however, be uncertain of the precise values of r_i and v_i and know only that they lie within the sets R_i and V_i respectively. Considering all possible combinations of these values we can easily define the price range H in which the shadow price of labour w^* will lie.[66] In evaluating any project one can then use not one combination of shadow prices but a set of combinations, and it can be easily checked that this will mean that the ranking of projects will be a quasi-ordering, which will be transitive, but not necessarily complete. That is, if project A is judged superior to B, and B to C, then project A will also be judged superior to project C, and the consistency condition of transitivity will be met. However, cases *can* arise in which two projects cannot be ranked against each other. Such incompleteness of ranking is, however, not a real deficiency, since it only reflects the extent of partial ignorance characterizing the choice problem. Arbitrary choices between them may have to be made, but the approach outlined here would simply define precisely which choices are arbitrary and which can be made with confidence even in the given state of partial ignorance.

The alternative to this would be to leave out a whole set of questions which we have been discussing here (and in Sen, 1975) and which, I would argue, make employment an important goal and employment policy a serious exercise. While the complexity of institutional, behavioural, technological and political features does make many of the choices difficult, there is no way in which one can

---

65. On its use for income distributional judgements and policies see Sen (1975). For a more general analysis see also Sen (1970, Chapters 7, 7*, 9 and 9*).

66. That is, H is given by:

$$\left[\operatorname*{Inf}_{\substack{v_i \in V_i \\ r_i \in R_i}} \sum_i v_i r_i, \; \operatorname*{Sup}_{\substack{v_i \in V_i \\ r_i \in R_i}} \sum_i v_i r_i \right].$$

escape this difficulty without shutting one's eyes to significant aspects of technological choice and employment policy. A quasi-ordering derived in the way described would reflect our ability to say something though not everything, whereas the requirement of a complete ordering is a compulsion to express an opinion on every choice that can arise. Happily, silence and babbling are not the only possible approaches to employment planning.

References

Anand, S. (1971): 'Rural–urban Migration in India: An Econometric Study' (mimeographed).

Bauer, P. T. (1948): *The Rubber Industry* (London: Longmans).

Bhalla, A. S. (1970): 'The Role of Services in Employment Expansion', in *International Labour Review*, May.

Blaug, M., Layard, R. and Woodhall, M. (1969): *The Causes of Graduate Unemployment in India* (London: Allen Lane The Penguin Press).

Chopra, K. R. (1972): *Dualism and Investment Patterns* (Bombay: Tata McGraw-Hill).

Dandekar, V. M. and Rath, N. (1971): *Poverty in India* (Poona: Indian School of Political Economy).

Das-Gupta, A. K. (1954): 'Keynesian Economics and Underdeveloped Countries', *Economic Weekly* (Bombay), 26 January, reprinted in Das-Gupta (1965).

—— (1956): 'Disguised Unemployment and Economic Development', *Economic Weekly* (Bombay), 25 August, reprinted in Das-Gupta (1965).

—— (1965): *Planning and Economic Growth* (London: Allen & Unwin).

Dasgupta, P., Marglin, S. and Sen, A. (1972): *Guidelines for Project Evaluation*, UNIDO (New York: United Nations).

Datta-Chaudhuri, M. and Sen, A. K. (1970): 'Durgapur Fertilizer Project: An Economic Evaluation', *Indian Economic Review*, 5.

Dixit, A. K. (1968): 'Optimal Development in the Labour-Surplus Economy', *Review of Economic Studies*, 35.

Domar, E. D. (1966): 'The Soviet Collective Farm as a Producer Cooperative', *American Economic Review*, 56.

Fei, J. C. H. and Ranis, G. (1964): *Development of the Labor Surplus Economy: Theory and Policy* (Homewood, Illinois: Irwin).

Finley, M. I. (1959): 'The Greeks and their Slaves', in *The Listener*, 10 September.

Gaiha, R. (1972): 'An Input-Output Analysis of Labour Productivity in the Indian Economy' (Delhi: Institute of Economic Growth; mimeographed).

Galenson, W. and Pyatt, G. (1964): *The Quality of Labour and Economic Development in Certain Countries* (Geneva: ILO).

Georgescu-Roegen, N. (1960): 'Economic Theory and Agrarian Reforms', *Oxford Economic Papers*, 12.

Government of India (1970): *Report of the Committee of Experts on Unemployment Estimates* (New Delhi).

Harberger, A. C. (1971): 'On Measuring the Social Opportunity Cost of Labour', *International Labour Review*, June.

Harris, J. R. and Todaro, M. P. (1969): 'Wages, Industrial Employment and Labour Productivity: the Kenyan Experience', *Eastern Africa Economic Review*, 1.

Hazari, B. and Krishnamurty, J. (1970): 'Employment Implications of India's Industrialization: Analysis in an Input–Output Framework', *Review of Economics and Statistics*, 52.

Hoffmann, C. (1967): *Work Incentive Practices and Policies in the People's Republic of China, 1953-1965* (Albany, New York: State University of New York Press).

Hornby, J. M. (1968): 'Investment and Trade Policy in the Dual Economy', *Economic Journal*, 78.

Hymer, S. and Resnick, S. (1969): 'A Model of an Agrarian Economy with Nonagricultural Activities', *American Economic Review*, 59.

ILO (1970): *Towards Full Employment. A Programme for Colombia* (Geneva).

—— (1971): *Matching Employment Opportunities and Expectations. A Programme of Action for Ceylon* (Geneva).

—— (1971a): *Concepts of Labour Force Underutilisation* (Geneva).

—— (1972): *Employment, Incomes and Equality. A Strategy for Increasing Productive Employment in Kenya* (Geneva).

—— (1973): *Employment and Income Policies for Iran* (Geneva).

Ishikawa, S. (1973): 'A Note on Choice of Technology in China', *Journal of Development Studies*, 9.

Jorgenson, D. W. (1961): 'The Development of a Dual Economy', *Economic Journal*, 71.

—— and Lau, L. J. (1969): *An Economic Theory of Agricultural Household Behaviour*, paper presented to the Fourth Far Eastern Meeting of the Econometric Society, Tokyo.

Keynes, J. M. (1936): *The General Theory of Employment, Interest and Money* (London: Macmillan).

Koopmans, T. C. (1957): *Three Essays on the State of Economic Science* (New York: McGraw-Hill).

Leibenstein, H. (1957): 'The Theory of Underemployment in Backward Economies', *Journal of Political Economy*, 65.

Lewis, W. A. (1954): Economic Development with Unlimited Supplies of Labour', *Manchester School*, 22.

Little, I. M. D. and Mirrlees, J. A. (1968): *Manual of Industrial Project Analysis in Developing Countries*, Vol. II: *Social Cost Benefit Analysis* (Paris: OECD).

Marglin, S. A. (1966): 'Industrial Development in the Labor Surplus Economy' (Harvard University; mimeographed); later published as *Value and Price in the Labour-Surplus Economy* (Oxford: Clarendon Press, 1976).

Marx, K. (1887): *Capital: A Critical Analysis of Capitalist Production*, Vol. I, edited by F. Engels (London: Sonnenschein).

Mazumdar, D. (1959): 'Marginal Productivity Theory of Wages and Disguised Unemployment', *Review of Economic Studies*, 26.

Mehra, S. (1966): 'Surplus Labour in Indian Agriculture', *Indian Economic Review*, 1.

Newbery, D. M. G. (1972): 'Public Policy in the Dual Economy', *Economic Journal*, 82.

Raj Krishna (1973): 'Unemployment in India', *Economic and Political Weekly*, 8, 3 March.

Rao, V. K. R. V. (1956): 'Investment, Employment and the Multiplier', in V. B. Singh (ed.), *Keynesian Economics* (Delhi: People's Publishing House).

Riskin, C. (1973): 'Maoism and Motivation: A Discussion of Work Motivation in China', in *Bulletin of Concerned Asian Scholars*.

Robinson, J. (1933): *The Economics of Imperfect Competition* (London: Macmillan).

—— (1969): *The Cultural Revolution in China* (Harmondsworth: Penguin).

Robinson, W. C. (1969): 'Types of Disguised Rural Unemployment and Some Policy Implications', *Oxford Economic Papers*, 21.

—— (1971): 'The Economics of Work Sharing in Peasant Agriculture', *Economic Development and Cultural Change*, 20.

Sen, A. K. (1960): *Choice of Techniques* (Oxford: Blackwell). Also Sen (1968): 'Introduction to Third Edition' [Essay 8 in this volume.]

—— (1962): 'An Aspect of Indian Agriculture', *Economic Weekly*, Annual number, 14.

—— (1962a): 'On the Usefulness of Used Machines', *Review of Economics and Statistics*, 44.

—— (1964): 'Size of Holdings and Productivity', *Economic Weekly*, Annual number, 16.

—— (1966): 'Peasants and Dualism with or without Surplus Labour', *Journal of Political Economy*, 74. [Essay 1 in this volume.]

—— (1966a): 'Labour Allocation in a Cooperative Enterprise', in *Review of Economic Studies*, 33. [Essay 2 in this volume.]

—— (1971): 'Aspects of Indian Education', in P. Chaudhuri (ed.): *Aspects of Indian Economic Development* (London: Allen & Unwin).

—— (1973): *On Economic Inequality* (Oxford: Clarendon Press).

—— (1975): *Employment Policy and Technological Choice* (Geneva: ILO, 1973). Published as *Employment, Technology and Development* (Oxford: Clarendon Press, 1975).

Smith, M. A. M. (1976): 'Wage Differentials and Trade in Second Hand Machines', *Journal of International Economics*, 6.

Stern, N. H. (1972): 'Optimum Development in a Dual Economy', *Review of Economic Studies*, 39.

Stiglitz, J. A. (1969): 'Rural–Urban Migration, Surplus Labour, and the Relationship between Urban and Rural Wages', *Eastern Africa Economic Review*, 1.

—— (1972): 'Alternative Theories of Wage Determination and Unemployment in LDCs: I. The Labor Turnover Model', Cowles Foundation Discussion Paper No. 335, Yale University, New Haven, Connecticut. An abridged version appeared in *Quarterly Journal of Economics*, 88 (1974).

Tinbergen, J. (1958): *The Design of Development* (Baltimore: Johns Hopkins Press).

Todaro, M. P. (1969). 'A Model of Labor Migration and Urban Unemployment in Less Developed Countries', *American Economic Review*, **59**.

Visaria, P. (1970): 'The Farmers' Preference for Work on Family Farms', in Government of India (1970).

von Neumann, J. and Morgenstern, O. (1947): *Theory of Games and Economic Behavior* (Princeton: University Press).

Ward, B. (1958): 'The Firm in Illyria: Market Syndicalism', *American Economic Review*, **48**.

—— (1971): 'Organization and Cooperative Economics: Some Approaches', in A. Eckstein (ed.), *Comparison of Economic Systems* (Berkeley: University of California Press).

Wellisz, S. (1968): 'Dual Economies, Disguised Unemployment and the Unlimited Supply of Labour', *Economica*, **35**.

Zarembka, P. (1972): *Toward a Theory of Economic Development* (San Francisco: Holden-Day).

Part IV

Morals and Mores

12

Ethical Issues in Income Distribution: National and International

There is an old Jewish story about why British Jews have been less successful than Jews in America. They all left from Russia in a ship holding tickets to New York. When the ship stopped to refuel in Liverpool, the stupid ones got off.

I have, I fear, got off at 'ethical issues, etc.'. It may well be that in view of that choice, this is indeed what I deserve, but it is not clear that I can at all deliver. While delivery here does not require one to assert, with John of Gaunt: 'methinks I am a prophet new inspired', even the limited task of sorting out the complex issues involved is not an easy one. There will be gaps and rough corners; but no further apologies.

In Section 1 there is an attempt to discuss the main moral principles involved – these are general and do not deal *only* with income distribution. Applications to income-distributional problems are systematized in Section 2. That discussion will not, however, bring in national boundaries, these will raise their heads – ugly or not – in Section 3. Concluding remarks are made in Section 4.

1   The Principles Involved

1.1   Utilitarianism factorized

Utilitarianism provides a convenient point of departure in examining moral issues. Utilitarianism can be factorized into the following constituent parts.

Paper presented at the Saltsjöbaden Symposium on the Past and Prospects of the Economic World Order, arranged by the Institute for International Economic Studies, University of Stockholm, August 1978.

From S. Grassman and E. Lundberg (eds), *The World Economic Order: Past and Prospects* (London: Macmillan, 1981), 464–94.

(1) *Consequentialism:* The rightness of actions — and (more generally) of the choice of all control variables — must be judged
entirely by the goodness of the consequent state of affairs.[1]
(2) *Welfarism:* The goodness of states of affairs must be judged
entirely by the goodness of the set of individual utilities in the
respective states of affairs.[2]
(3) *Sum-ranking:* The goodness of any set of individual utilities must
be judged entirely by their sum total.[3]

Each of these features has much appeal and has received many
defences. But they remain eminently controversial, and rival theories
of morality have argued for the replacement of one or more of these
features. A number of such rivals are considered next, with comments
on how they differ from the axioms underlying utilitarianism.

1.2   Maximin and leximin

In the 'maximin' approach, the axiom of sum-ranking is replaced by
the requirement that the goodness of any set of individual utilities
must be judged entirely by the value of its least member, that is, by
the utility level of the worst-off individual. This theory is identified
with John Rawls' (1971) 'difference principle', and it certainly came
to prominence in that context, even though this interpretation of the
'difference principle' is strictly speaking apocryphal. While Rawls
motivated his difference principle in terms of individual utilities and
seemed to be pointing towards the maximin criterion, in fact he
defined the principle formally not in terms of utilities at all but
through an index of 'primary goods'.[4] This approach will be discussed
in the next subsection, but the maximin approach — whether Rawlsian
or not — has some claim to be considered on its own as an appealing
moral approach, taking a particular view of 'economic justice'.

Furthermore, it can be made consistent with the strong Pareto
principle — and other dominance-based criteria such as Suppes'
(1966) 'grading principles' — by being defined in the lexicographic
form (see Sen, 1970). In this form, if the worst-off utility levels
happen to be the same in a pairwise comparison, then the pair can be

1. Various versions of utilitarianism, such as act utilitarianism, rule utilitarianism, motive
utilitarianism, differ on the nature of the control variable chosen for the consequentialist
exercise.
2. In the collective choice literature, the condition of 'neutrality' or 'strong neutrality'
is close to this (see Sen, 1977b).
3. If population is a variable, then there is need for further specification as to whether
the maximand should be the simple sum ('classical utilitarianism'), or the sum per head
('average utilitarianism').
4. See Rawls (1975) for clarification of a possible ambiguity.

ranked by the utility level of the second worst off; if they too tie, then by the utility level of the third worst off; and so on.[5] This 'leximin' approach, like maximin, satisfies welfarism, and can be combined with consequentialism,[6] but violates sum-ranking.

1.3 The difference principle

In John Rawls' (1971, 1975) version of 'a Kantian concept of morality', moral judgements of states of affairs take particular note of the conditions of the most deprived group of persons, deprivation being defined in terms of the availability of 'primary goods', or 'things it is supposed a rational man wants whatever else he wants' (Rawls, 1971, p. 92). Despite the 'priority' given by Rawls to liberty, this difference principle is central to the Rawlsian notion of justice.

Since the list of primary goods is diverse (one list by Rawls includes 'rights, liberties and opportunities, income and wealth, and the social basis of self-respect'), to identify the least advantaged is – to put it mildly – a non-trivial task, and requires the construction of an over-all index of vectors of different goods. Such a construction poses daunting problems, unless there are strong similarities of tastes and quasi-homotheticity of shared preferences.[7] But nevertheless the exercise may be relatively easier than operating on utilities, and avoid difficulties of identifying the efficiency of different persons as 'pleasure machines'.[8]

But the contrast of the 'primary goods' version of the difference principle and utility-based leximin (or maximin) lies not merely – or even primarily – in these tactical advantages, but in the different basis of moral judgement. In leximin, a person's claim to more goods arises from his being worse off in terms of welfare, whereas in the pure Rawlsian version it originates in his having less primary goods than others. The latter avoids what many find the morally unattractive possibility of having to give a lot more income to people with

5. It is this leximin criterion that has recently been axiomatized elegantly by Hammond (1976), Strasnick (1976), d'Aspremont and Gevers (1977), Deschamps and Gevers (1978), and others. On related issues, see Arrow (1977), Roberts (1980) and Maskin (1978).

6. The use of consequentialism is implicitly – but very firmly – present in the applications of maximin and leximin to public finance and other policy issues; see Atkinson (1973), Phelps (1973), Dasgupta (1974), Meade (1976), Calvo (1978), Phelps and Riley (1978), among others.

7. See Gorman (1975) and Muellbauer (1976).

8. Some of the difficulties of utility theory in its 'static, descriptive interpretation' (see Kornai, 1971, Chapters 10 and 11) will, however, apply also to the Rawlsian use of primary goods index. But not all of them apply, especially since the index may not be based on the revealed preference interpretation of actual behaviour. In making effective use of leximin (or maximin) also, there is a good case for going beyond the crude framework of revealed preference and modern utility theory (see Sen, 1977a).

expensive tastes (for example, to 'gourmets' – who are unhappy in the absence of culinary extravaganza), and Rawls has emphasized the importance of recognizing a person's responsibility for his own ends.

On the other hand, this Rawlsian version of the difference principle is insensitive to special needs, such as, of the disabled, the old, or the ill. Having the same supply of primary goods leaves them clearly worse off, and the difference may not be due to anything for which they can be held responsible. Rawls (1975, p. 96) may be right that 'problems of special health care and how to treat the mentally defective' and other 'hard cases' can 'distract our moral perception by leading us to think of people distant from us whose fate rouses pity and anxiety', but our moral approach must deal with these cases as well.† Such handicaps may not be very rare either, since neither illness nor old age are unusual predicaments of human beings.

Differences of needs can also arise from climatic conditions (such as clothing, shelter, food), urbanization (such as transport, pollution effects), work performed (such as calories or other nutrients), or even body size (such as food and clothing). To judge advantage in terms of availability of primary goods only leads to the loss of these important parameters. Thus Rawls' own version of the difference principle seems to have serious difficulties. Its possibly superior ability to handle the man with the expensive taste (through justice by neglect) is achieved at a high cost.

1.4   *Equity, needs and powers*

Utilitarianism is sensitive to *total* benefits of different persons; the difference principle, leximin or maximin is not. On the other hand, the latter is sensitive to interpersonal utility *distribution*, which utilitarianism is not. It is tempting to combine total-sensitivity with distribution-sensitivity. Various equity criteria have tried to do this by incorporating considerations of distributive justice without forcing the extremism of leximin or maximin or the difference principle.[9] The Weak Equity Axiom (henceforth WEA) requires that if person 1 is worse off than person 2 whenever both have the same income, then in dividing a given total of income among a group

---

† [This statement, it is now clear to me, misrepresents Rawls' position; he is arguing for postponing the question of need difference, not for ignoring it altogether.]

9. This extremism comes out sharply in cases in which the interest of the worse-off person goes against that of everybody else, possibly millions or billions. Curiously enough it can be shown that the 2-person version of leximin (such that the worse-off person receives priority when all persons other than two are indifferent) logically entails leximin *in general* within the framework of social welfare functionals with unrestricted domain and independence of irrelevant alternatives (see Theorem 8, Sen, 1977b).

including persons 1 and 2, the best division must give more income to person 1 than to 2.[10]

Utilitarianism will often violate WEA, but leximin always satisfies it.[11] While WEA was motivated by Rawlsian arguments against utilitarianism, Rawls' own version of the difference principle can violate WEA. This is because the difference operates on the availability of primary goods as the indicator of advantage and is, therefore, unable to notice differences arising from other sources, in particular differences in needs. The appeal of WEA is certainly not unconditional, but in cases of obvious variation of recognized primary needs arising from, say, the person being a cripple or having a backbreaking load of work (see Sen, 1973, pp. 16–19), WEA would reflect a moral intuition shared by many. On the other hand, in the case of the man who plunges into depression when deprived of champagne and caviar, WEA may not be all that attractive.

It is possible to consider a modification of WEA which will capture the rationale of Rawls' focus on 'primary goods' as opposed to utility, and at the same time avoid the pitfall of identifying everyone's needs irrespective of work load, location, physical fitness, climatic conditions, etc. It is possible to concentrate neither on *utility* as such, nor on the availability of primary *goods*, but on the realization of certain primary *powers* (or 'basic abilities'), for example, the power to fulfil one's nutritional requirements or the necessities of clothing and shelter, or the ability to move about. The cripple's entitlement to more income arises in this view neither from his low utility level, nor from any lower availability of primary goods, but from the deprivation of his ability to move about unless he happens to have more income or more specialized goods (for example, vehicles for the disabled) at his command. Similarly, the greater needs of a higher work load lead to a greater entitlement not on the basis of utility deprivation as such but the deprivation of the power to meet the necessary calorie requirements *if* one had the same intake of food that would meet the calorie requirements of someone working much less.[12] The modified version of WEA would require that a person

10. Proposed in Sen (1973). A requirement very similar to this was used much earlier by Ragnar Bentzel in his Inaugural Lecture at Uppsala University dealing with social insurance against being born an idiot.

11. Indeed, Hammond's (1976) axiomatization of leximin is based on a generalized and more demanding version of WEA. See also d'Aspremont and Gevers (1977) and Deschamps and Gevers (1978).

12. The generalization involved in moving from primary goods to primary powers involves going beyond the framework of 'characteristics' explored by Gorman (1956), Lancaster (1966) and others. The 'characteristics' (for example, calories) are properties of goods on their own (for example, of bread) and not of the relationship of people to goods (for example, the power to meet one's calorie requirements).

whose primary powers (or basic abilities) are less for the same level of income is entitled to get more income.

This general framework of judging advantage in terms neither of utilities nor of primary goods but in terms of primary powers has, of course, many problems of its own. There is the difficult problem of arriving at an index of primary power fulfilment since different types of powers are involved. (It is a problem comparable to Rawls' problem of getting an index of the availability of primary goods.) There is also the complicated issue of what powers count as primary (for example, why not the power to satisfy the requirements of one's cultivated palate?), and philistinism is not a negligible danger.[13] I have tried to go into these issues elsewhere (Sen, 1978a), and will not attempt here a facile answer to rather profound problems. Instead, I shall merely claim that the approach of primary powers provides an alternative framework for considerations of equity, distinct both from the framework of utilities and from that of availabilities of primary goods, but also note *each* of these three approaches has many problems.

1.5   *Personal liberty and rights*

Utilitarianism involves consequentialism, welfarism, and sum-ranking. Leximin or maximin relaxes sum-ranking, but sticks to welfarism and is consistent with consequentialism. Rawls' difference principle based on primary goods, and equity principles based on primary powers, drop welfarism also, but remain consistent with consequentialism. I turn now to right-based moralities that focus on such issues as personal liberty, and these frequently involve the rejection of consequentialism as well.

Under the consequentialist approach, actions, obligations and rights must be judged ultimately in terms of the 'outcome morality', that is, morality involved in judging states of affairs. But it is possible to defend a person's rights not in terms of the goodness of its consequences, but on the grounds that these rights have intrinsic moral acceptability irrespective of the consequences of the exercise of these rights. Many libertarians and proponents of other right-based moralities take a non-consequentialist route to these morals. 'Rights',

---

13. Cf. Marx's (1844) warning about 'crude communism' and 'levelling-down proceeding from *preconceived* minimum'. 'How little this annulment of private property is really an appropriation is in fact proved by the abstract negation of the entire world of culture and civilisation, the regression to the *unnatural* simplicity of the *poor* and crude man who has few needs and who has not only failed to go beyond private property, but has not yet even reached it' (p. 95).

argues Nozick (1974, p. 166), 'do not determine the position of an alternative or the relative position of two alternatives in a social ordering; they operate upon a social ordering to constrain the choice it can yield'. Severing the discipline of consequentialism permits firm acceptance of rights in judgements of actions, for example, in rejecting interference in what Hayek (1960, p. 140) calls a person's 'protected sphere'.

An alternative way of dealing with liberty and other rights in the moral structure is to incorporate them in the outcome morality itself, judging the outcomes in terms of whether people get their entitlements as specified by a system of rights. The 'social ordering' of outcomes then incorporates attitudes towards the fulfilment or violation of rights, and the actions can then be judged taking note of rights even within a consequentialist framework. Outcome morality formulations of liberty and rights (see Sen (1970, 1976b, 1978a), Gibbard (1974), Blau (1975), Farrell (1976), Suzumura (1978), among others) will violate welfarism, but may or may not be combined with full consequentialism.[14]

These formulations may, however, conflict with the Pareto principle, even when the rights are internally compatible with each other, and there are consistency problems for the 'Paretian libertarian' (see Sen, 1970, 1976b). While many economists seem to respond to any violation of the Pareto principle as if motherhood is under cruel attack, Paretianism is essentially a weak version of welfarism. Considerations of liberty and rights, which militate against an exclusive concern with utility values, can go against relying exclusively on utility magnitudes even in the Paretian special case ('everyone has more utility, ask no further questions'), and this becomes clear when *interpair* consistency of judgements is considered.

The alternative of leaving considerations of liberty and rights completely out of the outcome morality and using a vigorously non-consequentialist framework has problems of its own. First, there is the difficulty that an outcome involving gross violation of rights (such as, a person being roughed up by a gang of sadists) may have to be described as a good *outcome* (for example, under utilitarian outcome morality when the aggregate utility gain of the gang exceeds

14. Obviously for the outcome morality to have any muscle at all in judging actions, actions must be judged taking note of goodness of outcomes. But whether the moral structure will be *fully* consequentialist or not will depend on whether this is *all* that is taken into account. There can be alternative definitions of what counts as 'consequent' states of affairs, for example, whether the actions themselves could count as part of the states generated by them; this would be the case under a broad view of consequentialism. But even with such a broad view, consequentialism is not a trivial issue (on which see Williams, 1973, pp. 82-93).

the utility loss of the solitary victim), even though the *action* of roughing up is taken to be unacceptable in view of the right of the victim not to be tortured. Apart from severely restricting the nature of moral judgements made, this makes it difficult to accommodate person 1's moral involvement when person 2 is roughed up by a strong-armed person, 3.[15] Second, by keeping considerations of liberty and rights outside outcome morality, and by downgrading the role of outcome morality to a lexicographically inferior position, this approach makes it difficult to accommodate 'tradeoffs' between competing moral claims,[16] involving those considerations that are incorporated in the outcome evaluation (for example, utility aggregates and distribution) and those that come in as constraints on actions (for example, rights and liberties). The weighing and balancing of conflicting consequences within an outcome morality provides a more flexible format than a hierarchy of priorities and constraints.

1.6   *Entitlement theories: labour and property rights*

The labour theory of value can be interpreted in many different ways, for example, descriptive, predictive or evaluative,[17] and while the descriptive interpretation can be thought to be the primary one, the evaluative interpretation has been important in social criticism using such Marxian concepts as 'exploitation'. In this approach welfarism is rejected, and the entitlements are related not to utilities but to labour contributions (or to corrected labour contributions in terms of 'socially necessary labour'). In a limited form the concept of labour entitlements also find expression in such demands as 'equal pay for equal work'. On a much wider canvas it lends critical weight to the diagnosis of 'unequal exchange' in international economic relations (see Emmanuel, 1972).

While labour rights have a wide moral appeal, property rights have also had much support for nearly three hundred years (see Locke, 1690). Recently Robert Nozick (1974) has provided an elegantly worked out entitlement theory covering property rights. He defines principles of justice in *acquisition* and *transfer*; a person acquiring holdings in accordance with these principles are entitled to them, and no one is entitled to a holding except by repeated applications of these two principles. The principles are so constructed that a person is not only entitled to what he himself produces with his own

---

15. I have tried to discuss this problem in Sen (1978a). [Partly published in 'Rights and Agency', *Philosophy and Public Affairs*, 11 (1982).]
   16. Cf. Hart's 1973 far-reaching critique of Rawls' position on the 'priority' of liberty.
   17. See Sen (1978b).

labour, but also to what is produced by resources owned by him and what he can acquire by free exchange of what he legitimately holds. Holdings also legitimately pass from one person to another through inheritance or gift. This structure of entitlements differs sharply from the labour-based entitlement system chiefly in three respects: (a) assigning to the owners of non-labour productive resources the fruits of owning those resources; (b) accepting free exchange as just irrespective of the inequality in the distribution of means of production; and (c) accepting the legitimacy of inheritance (and gift).[18]

Most of the criticisms of these entitlement theories – whether of labour entitlements (and 'exploitation') or of property rights (and Nozick's structure) – have emphasized the arbitrariness of the chosen 'principles'.[19] In so far as the ethical framework is one of moral intuition, the question has to be whether these principles capture these moral intuitions deeply enough, or whether they build on immediate prejudices, which will be rejected on reflection. More structured tests will be used by those who choose a non-intuitionist framework, for example, by making use of the discipline of the language of morals (see Hare, 1976), or by attributing unique ethical relevance to acceptability in a hypothetical 'original position' with primordial equality without anyone knowing who is going to be who (see Rawls, 1971; and Harsanyi, 1977).

It is perhaps worth remarking that while Marx made considerable use of the notion of exploitation and undoubtedly gave it evaluative relevance, he also expressed scepticism about the moral depth of labour entitlements (see particularly Marx, 1844, 1875). Giving ultimate priority to distribution 'according to needs', he describes claims arising from labour as residing within 'the narrow horizon of bourgeois rights', viewing persons 'only as workers, and nothing more is seen in them, everything else being ignored' (Marx, 1875, pp. 22–3).

1.7 Agent-relative action moralities

The special sense of responsibility that a person feels for his or her family or friends may influence his moral judgements. If that influence affects his judgements of goodness of outcomes, it may be argued that this partiality is a violation of the requirement of 'universalizability' which has characterized much of ethical theory at

18. While Nozick's moral structure is not consequentialism it is possible to construct a consequentialist variant of it incorporating the principles of justice directly in a non-Paretian outcome morality (see Sen, 1978a).

19. For critiques of Nozick on these lines, see – among many other contributions – Nagel (1975) and Scanlon (1978).

least since Kant (1785). While such partiality in judging states of affairs may be thought to be a moral weakness, the case is somewhat less clear when it comes to judging actions, since actions are agent-specific in a manner that states of affairs are not. A person conceding that the outcome in which he gives a toy to a child he meets in the street may be a better outcome than the one resulting from his giving this toy to his own child, may nevertheless argue that it is right that he should give the toy to his own child for he owes a special duty to his own child. He could universalize this judgement by arguing that anyone in his circumstances should do the same. If this line is taken, then the morality in question has to be non-consequentialist, since agent-relativity would have to be introduced in evaluating actions but not outcomes.†

Agent relativity is one of the most complex issues in ethics. It is tempting to argue that the moral appeal of agent relativity is 'instrumental'. It is a rule which, if widely followed, might well serve non-agent-relative goals, even utilitarian ones. If agent-relative decisions are justified on these lines, that is, as fulfilling non-agent-relative goals, then the moral approach can satisfy consequentialism, properly defined, to take note of appropriate rules (rather than acts) as 'control' variables.

Whether this captures all there is to capture in the moral appeal of agent-relative evaluation of actions is, however, less clear.[20] Arguments for taking a non-instrumental view of agent-relativity can be strong (see Williams, 1973). The vision of the good society of hard men doing agent-independent calculations not responding to demands of love and affection except instrumentally is perhaps also slightly depressing. Agent-relative duties can also be based on ties other than those of kinship and affection, and can even reflect economic or political relations, for example, what one citizen owes to another. I shall call this general class of agent-relative obligations as 'relational obligations'.

---

† [This statement, I now think is wrong. It is possible, and arguably sensible, to make the evaluation of 'outcomes', or states of affairs, relative to the *position* of the evaluator in the states of the affairs, in cases in which agent-relativity of action judgements make sense. See my 'Evaluator Relativity and Consequential Evaluation', *Philosophy and Public Affairs*, 12 (1983).]

20. Since duty relations can be mirror images of rights, a non-consequentialist structure of rights vis-à-vis others will involve an agent-relative structure of duties. (On these relationships, see Kanger (1971, 1972) and Lindahl (1977).) If you have a non-consequentialist right irrespective of outcome that I do something for you (such as, feed you or work for you), then I have an agent-relative duty to do that thing for you, irrespective of outcome. This type of agent-relative duties relates closely to the issues discussed earlier, in the context of possible non-consequentialist formulations of rights.

Agent-relative duties can also be based on past events, leading to a sense of 'duty owed'. In Tolstoy's *Resurrection*, when Katyusha is wrongly sentenced to Siberia, and Nekhlyudov, who was in the jury, recognizes the girl as the one whom he had seduced leading to an abortive pregnancy and then abandoned, his response is unequivocal: 'Of course, it's a strange and striking coincidence, and it is absolutely necessary to do all in my power to lighten her fate, and to do it as soon as possible'.[21] I shall refer to this type of agent-relativity arising from events that have taken place as 'event obligation'.

2 *Distributional Conflicts*

2.1 *Moral claims to income*

In what does the force of a person's moral claim to income rest? The answer would clearly depend on the moral approach chosen. On the basis of the principles discussed in the last section, at least the following different sources are potentially relevant:

(1) High marginal utility of personal income, for example, under utilitarianism (Section 1.1).
(2) Low total personal utility, for example, under leximin or maximin (Section 1.2).
(3) Low personal availability of primary goods, for example, under Rawlsian difference principle (Section 1.3).
(4) Low primary powers of the person, for example, under need-based equity axioms (Section 1.4).
(5) Violation of personal liberty consequent on denial of income to the person, for example, under libertarian principles (Section 1.5).
(6) High labour contribution (or necessary labour contribution) to production, for example, under labour entitlement theories (Section 1.6).
(7) High entitlement under acknowledged principles of justice in acquisition and transfer, for example, under Nozick's entitlement theories (Section 1.6).
(8) High relational obligation or event obligation of others vis-à-vis this person on matters of income, for example, under agent-relative action moralities (Section 1.7).

There is, of course, nothing contradictory in accepting more than one source of moral claim. Indeed, value judgements in this area

21. L. Tolstoy, *Resurrection*, English translation by L. Maude (Progressive Publishers, Moscow, 1972), p. 117.

typically tend to be 'non-compulsive' (see Sen, 1967), even though purist systems like utilitarianism or entitlement theories demand unqualified adherence. When more than one moral claim is accepted and there are several non-compulsive principles competing for attention, we have a complex moral structure. Since moral complexity, in this sense, is a commonly observed phenomenon, it is necessary to discuss how such complexities may be resolved. This question is taken up in the next two subsections.

2.2   Weighting and partial ordering

Faced with conflicts between different criteria, a common approach is to go by dominance, that is, make only those judgements that satisfy *all* the criteria. Dominance is a widely used approach in economics, for example, in 'efficiency' calculations based on vector dominance over commodity bundles, or in 'Pareto optimality' discussions based on vector dominance over interpersonal utility bundles. The approach can be more widely used without bringing in real numbers and vectors, and it is easy to establish that when one considers a group of criteria each yielding a complete ordering of a set, then the dominance ranking based on their intersection will be a partial ordering of that set, satisfying the property of transitivity fully.[22] For example, different criteria for outcome morality can be used to generate a dominance partial ordering of states of affairs, and then using consequentialism, the combinations of control variables can be partially ordered correspondingly, leading to some guidance to policy, even though not a complete determination of all policy choices. If a non-consequentialist approach is chosen, the different criteria can be applied directly or indirectly, to the control variables (that is, with or without invoking their consequences), and then the dominance partial ordering of controls can be identified from that.

Sometimes the partial ordering based on dominance may be quite extensive, and may be able to give much guidance to policy. In other cases, it may yield very little. Indeed, if two criteria yield two complete orderings that conflict with each other over every ranking, then the dominance partial ranking will yield nothing whatever (still

---

22. See Sen (1973), pp. 72-4. The dominance ranking will be a partial ordering even when the criteria themselves yield partial (rather than complete) orderings. The dominance partial ordering can be defined either *narrowly* to cover only those rankings that are strictly endorsed by all criteria, or *broadly* to cover those rankings that are strictly endorsed ('better than') by some criterion and weakly endorsed ('at least as good as') by all criteria.

radiating the glory of transitivity, but – alas – in vacuum). Something like this is, in fact, a very real possibility in dealing with distribution of income by invoking as diverse a set of criteria as we listed in Section 2.1. In the field of income distribution much moral complacency is, I imagine, based on the failure of dominance reasoning to yield much.

An alternative is to go beyond the dominance reasoning by specifying a weighting procedure for different criteria. The weighting can be in the lexicographic form with no tradeoffs, for example, criterion 7 used first, and then criterion 1 'if there are any choices left to make',[23] and so on. Or else, tradeoffs may be specified, even though often such tradeoff mappings have to be very complex given the nature of the criteria in question. It is possible to specify tradeoff *ranges*, if there are difficulties in choosing clear-cut values, and such ranges would typically yield partial orderings more extensive than the dominance ranking but less pervasive than a complete ordering.[24] The narrower the range of tradeoffs specified, the more extensive, in general, will be the derived partial ordering. There is a real conflict here between arbitrary articulation (making the ranges very narrow) and indecisive judgements (keeping them very wide).

2.3   *Partial information and permissive dominance*

So far nothing has been said about informational limitation that may make it difficult to apply one or more of the criteria in question. But moral arguments are often based on informational limitation that rule out the use of one criterion or another. Lionel Robbins' (1938) attack on utilitarianism based on the alleged absence of interpersonally comparable utility information is a well-known example. The informational limitation can be intrinsic (for example, in Robbins' claim about the impossibility of making factual statements about interpersonal comparisons of utility[25]), or it can be case-specific (for example, not knowing how well off a recipient of charity might be).

The dominance reasoning discussed in the last section proceeded on the 'affirmative' basis of asserting only those rankings that are endorsed by all the criteria. If instead one proceeds on the 'permissive' basis of asserting those rankings that are affirmed by some criteria

23. Nozick (1974, p. 166). Nozick is specific on the one-step lexicographic priority of entitlement judgements on action over judgements derived from other criteria involved in the social ordering of states of affairs, but does not go on to outline a full lexicographic structure.
    24. See Sen (1970, Chapter 7*), Blackorby (1975), Fine (1975), Basu (1976).
    25. For a critique of this claim, see Little (1957).

and not contradicted by any,[26] then the silence induced by informational lacunae can help to make the dominance partial ordering more extensive. This approach is very often taken in practical moral decisions when one proceeds on the basis of an established case for some action and none established against, possibly due to informational limitation.

The point can be illustrated by considering the problem of a person who is asked by three boys to arbitrate who should get a flute (made of bamboo) about which the boys are quarrelling. Consider first three alternative scenarios. In the first case, it is known that boy A plays the flute well and with very great pleasure, while boys B and C are less musical. It is clear to the arbitrator that A will get more happiness out of the flute than the other two. The arbitrator knows nothing else about the three boys, and decides to give the flute to A, in conformity with utilitarianism. In the second case, the arbitrator knows that boy B is much more deprived than the other two and has very few toys and other sources of pleasure and that he is generally much less happy than the other two. Nothing else is known about the boys, including who plays the flute well; the arbitrator decides, in this case, to give the flute to B on grounds of leximin or difference principle. In the third case, the arbitrator gathers that boy C made the flute with his own labour starting from a bamboo belonging to no one, while the others not only did not contribute anything to this effort, but wanted to take the flute away from him. She knows nothing else about the boys, for example, who is how well off, or who enjoys playing the flute more. In this case, the arbitrator decides to give the flute to C because of his labour, or as part of an entitlement structure incorporating the right to what one has produced, or on libertarian grounds (see, for example, Nozick, 1974).

In each case the arbitrator may feel that an unambiguously correct decision has been made. On the other hand, the three sets of information on which the three different decisions are based happen to be consistent with each other. It can be the case that boy A will get more joy out of the flute, boy B is most deprived, and boy C in fact did make the flute. What makes the decision unambiguous in *each* case for an arbitrator having a complex moral structure involving the

---

26. Contrasted with the 'broad' version of the affirmative dominance ranking (see footnote 22 above), the permissive dominance ranking is more extensive in treating 'incompleteness' in the same way as 'indifference'. An alternative is ranked above another in the permissive dominance ranking if it is higher according to some criterion and not lower (covering both asserted indifference as well as no assertion at all) according to any.

principle cited is the dual characteristic of the *presence* of some information *and* the *absence* of others.[27]

2.4 Instrumental justifications and incentives

So far we have been concerned only with a person's moral claim to income. But a person can be rightly given more income not only on grounds that he has a moral claim to have it, but also on grounds that giving more income would have the consequence of serving some other goal, for example, produce more income and make others happier. This type of 'instrumental' justification is quite important in income distributional policy, and indeed the whole of the incentive literature depends crucially on such instrumental reasoning.

Consider, for example, the case for wage differential in favour of the more productive. Though they are frequently confused, it is possible to make a clear distinction between entitlement arguments based on acknowledged rights and arguments based on instrumental considerations. The distinction is brought out by considering cases in which one of the two arguments cannot operate while the other still will. If productive workers remain just as productive irrespective of what they are paid, then the incentive argument for paying them more does not hold, whereas the entitlement argument, if accepted, will still apply.[28]

On the other hand, if conspicuously high payment to the Joneses does not increase their own productivity much but increases remarkably the productivity of others in their effort to keep up with the aforementioned Joneses, and if the Joneses cannot freely secure contracts with high payment for their labour, then the case for such high payment to Joneses must be based on instrumental grounds of incentives rather than on entitlement arguments based on either personal productivity or free contract. The two types of argument are quite distinct, even though they are typically not distinguished

27. The role of information in moral judgements raises many related issues, which I have tried to analyse elsewhere – Sen (1967, 1977c, 1978a).

28. It was indeed this case that Marx (1875, p. 23) considered in his vision of the good society in the 'higher phase' of socialism, 'after labour has become not only a means of life but life's prime want; after the productive forces have also increased with the all-round development of the individual, and all the springs of cooperative wealth flow more abundantly'. Marx's rejection of differentials based on work and productivity in this case – crossing 'the narrow horizon of bourgeois right' based on labour – shows that his support for payment according to labour in early socialism was largely based on instrumental grounds rather than on entitlement reasoning.

in 'the why and wherefore of differentials': 'a differential is defended because it is right and proper'.[29]

Similarly, the entitlement argument for rewards to ownership of non-labour resources (as in Nozick, 1974) must not be confused with the instrumental argument for such rewards (as in Friedman, 1962). In the first case the rewards reflect rights that are not to be violated irrespective of consequences, while in the second case they are justified on the basis of the consequences of these rights within the structure of competitive capitalism. Someone arguing against these rewards would have to take quite different routes depending on which of these two justifications he happens to be currently disputing.

3   International Issues

3.1   The rich and the poor

The ethics of international income distribution have been much discussed recently in the context of proposals for the so-called 'New International Economic Order'. Two simple approaches to this thorny issue are so common that it may be just as well to get them out of the way.

The first approach is based on treating rich and poor nations as if they are rich and poor *persons*, and the moral case for income transfers from the rich to the poor nations is usually then based on some kind of a welfarist and consequentialist argument, such as, poor nations have a higher marginal utility of income (the utilitarian argument), or the poor nations have a lower total utility per head (the leximin argument). The question of distribution within each country does not arise in this formulation.

I shall call this approach the 'fiction of all nations throbbing as symbolic individuals in existence' -- 'fantasie' for short. The literature demanding New International Economic Order does show a touch of 'fantasie', and as Richard Cooper (1977, p. 355) has noted, 'much recent discussion on transfer of resources falls uncritically into the practice of what I would call anthropomorphising nations, of treating nations as though they are individuals and extrapolating to them on the basis of average per capita income the various ethical arguments that have been developed to apply to individuals'.

The question of distribution within each country is certainly an important consideration, and treating nations as persons is to lose

---

29. Phelps-Brown (1962, p. 147). Phelps-Brown argues that 'it may even be that instead of opinions about what is fair having shaped the pay structure, it is the structure that has shaped the opinions' (p. 151).

this perspective altogether (see Sen, 1976a, 1976c). This is particularly limiting in the context of policy questions that arise in negotiations for a new economic order, since there is some evidence that 'the international bargaining process now under way, to the extent it results in fairer shares for the South, serves to strengthen Southern élites who in the main have little autonomy form antiequity class forces at home' (Fishlow *et al.*, 1978, p. 199). Given the 'power realities' of the prevailing political system in the developing countries, it may indeed be 'touchingly naive not to anticipate the failure of asset distribution policies or the appropriation by the rich of a dis-proportionate share of the benefits of public investment' (Bardhan, 1974, p. 261).

So much for one of the two simple approaches; I turn now to the other. The other is a conservative belief that the population of each country is entitled to what it happens to have currently, and while a change needs justification, the *status quo* does not. I shall call this approach that of 'entitlement valid for all substance I own now' — 'evasion' for short. If demands for a new international order often reflect 'fantasie', the resistance to it in rich countries frequently reveals 'evasion'. In its stronger form 'evasion' leads to a hard-nosed dismissal of humanitarian arguments for transfer to, or a better deal for, the poor countries. In its milder form, the morality of such transfers or better deals are dismissed *unless* the case for them is 'clearly' or 'unequivocally' established. Given the difficulty of tracing cause-and-effect relations in the field of international policy, such clarity or unambiguity is often absent, and then even the milder version of 'evasion' leads to inaction, if not complacency.

The moral basis of 'evasion' may be thought to rest on some entitlement theory, for example, that of Nozick (1974). But in order to establish this, one would have to show that the existing holdings were derived exclusively from the 'principles of justice in acquisition and transfer' (Section 1.6). Given the acknowledged lack of free and competitive exchange in the trade between nations, and given the documented records of colonial economic relations, this would be, to put it mildly, no mean task. While Nozick's entitlement theory is not inimical to inequality as such, it is exacting in its own way.

3.2 *Consequential reasoning*

Among the three principles into which utilitarianism was factorized (Section 1.1), consequentialism had the role of disciplining the assessment of actions, institutions, etc., by confining the assessment to the evaluation of the consequent states of affairs generated by those actions, institutions, etc. In judging intercountry transfers, or changes in the institutional features of international relations, the consequentialist approach will require that the relevant effects of these policies on states of affairs be identified as much as possible. The criterion of what effects are relevant will, of course, depend on the outcome morality chosen.

With the utilitarian outcome morality, the consequences that have to be pursued are the utility gains or losses incurred by people in different countries. While the ultimate focus has to be on utility, and not on other descriptive features, such as incomes, prices, distributional parameters, etc., it is quite natural that non-utility features may be studied either as 'intermediate products' in the causal chain from policies to utilities, or as 'surrogates' for utilities themselves. There are many tactical issues involved in this, but the main strategic one is to focus on *utility gains and losses*. In contrast, the leximin approach will lead to a strategic focus on *utility levels* as such, that is, not on whether there is a great deal of utility gain, but whether the gains go to the people who are relatively worse off in utility terms. These 'welfarist' approaches are, however, united in not giving more than a tactical role to non-utility consequences.

In contrast, the Rawlsian version of the difference principle will concentrate on the availability of primary goods not as surrogates to utility, but as the relevant focus in itself. Similarly, equity principles based on primary powers will have a non-utility focus. In the context of international policies, the difference introduced by concentrating on primary *powers* as opposed to primary *goods* (Section 1.4) is rather significant. Calorie and nutritional requirements as well as needs of clothing and shelter vary with climatic conditions. Social developments like urbanization bring about additional needs, and thus a lowering of primary powers given the same availability of primary goods. These differences have to be seriously dealt with in moral judgements of international distribution of incomes, and a person in the rich country with a higher real income than a person in a poor country must not automatically be taken to be more advantaged.[30] Even after such adjustments the moral case for international redistributions based on equity considerations is likely to be quite strong, and there is little merit in spoiling a legitimate moral argument by arbitrary overstatement based on overlooking relevant differences.

30. This consideration is quite distinct from (and, in a sense, additional to) the point that real income differences are often less acute than nominal money income contrasts, because of differences in the price structure (see, for example, Usher, 1969).

In applying consequentialist reasoning to policy issues the task consists essentially of (a) determining the outcome morality to be used, and (b) identifying the consequences of alternative policies on factors relevant to the chosen outcome morality. In a universalized consequentialist moral structure, the population of the world has to be viewed together, and the outcome morality chosen has, in principle, to be applied to the world population as a whole. (Needless to say actual moral debates must be based on less exacting exercises in view of practical difficulties, but the general approach is the one against which practical shortcuts have to be judged.) The approach leads to the rejection not merely of the make-believe world of 'fantasie' and the unreasoned prejudice of 'evasion', but also of the tradition of viewing 'social welfare' *separately* for each country in nationalist terms.[31] The differences in circumstances depending on the country of one's residence must, of course, be reflected as part of the relevant data, not because social welfare is best thought of in national terms, but because consideration of social welfare in the world context requires one to be alive to these relevant distinctions. More than the mechanics of such calculations, there is in this a shift in the entire *outlook* to international policy affecting the way of viewing these problems; the mechanics are merely reflections of this fundamental departure.

3.3 Agent-relativity and obligations

The universalized consequentialist approaches discussed in the last section can, of course, be rejected if an agent-relative action morality is chosen (Section 1.7), asserting that the government of each country has an obligation to pursue the interests of its own members only (or pursuing these interests *more* than the interests of non-members). It is necessary in this context to make a distinction between an *instrumental* justification of such agent-relativity as opposed to a justification of it in terms of its own intrinsic merits. In the instrumental case, the argument has to be that a system in which each government is responsible for its own members is an optimum feasible system for pursuing world welfare in terms of the chosen outcome morality. Support for such a position may be based on, say, the role of effective control in apportioning responsibility,

---

31. If the outcome morality satisfies certain conditions of 'separability' (see Gorman, 1975), it may be legitimate to think of world welfare as a function of national welfares, even when national welfares are of no intrinsic interest in themselves. But the assumptions are exacting, and even when fulfilled, give rather limited status to national welfares (based on 'representation' possibilities).

or on the need for delineating spheres of obligation in line with informational availability. Assessment of such arguments will require complex cause-and-effect studies.

On the other hand, if a non-instrumental justification is sought, it would have to be argued that irrespective of the consequences of such nationalist focus on world affairs, it is right that each national government should confine itself to such a focus. This would then be treated as a fundamental 'relational obligation'.

As was mentioned earlier such relational obligations are difficult to assess, even when the relations involved have the simplicity of family ties. But it is also worth noting that consideration of 'event obligations' (Section 1.7) may require a somewhat different focus. While Harry Johnson (1977, p. 360) refers to the 'largely mythological view of past relations between advanced and less developed countries as "imperialism"', imperialism is hardly a unicorn.[32] For the rich countries of today to sink into the complacency of a nation-focused morality will leave something to be desired even *within* the structure of agent-relative moral reasoning.

There is also some evidence to indicate that the narrowness of the focus of relational obligations is not independent of the nature of the morality that is used within the focus. Erik Lundberg (1977, p. 370) has noted that the 'egalitarian spirit', once 'established *inside* a country like Sweden', seems to have had the effect 'in a very half-hearted way to extend beyond its boundaries'. There seem to exist forces of 'disequilibrium' even *within* these moral structures. This perhaps does bring out the *ad hoc* nature of these agent-relative moralities – based on a narrow national focus – which tend to dominate policy discussions today.

3.4   *Rights and entitlements*

It may be useful to distinguish between two types of obligations which might act as barriers to taxing the rich countries to benefit the poor ones. One, which was discussed in the last section, is the question of the relational obligation of taxing authorities of a rich country to serve the interests of the members of that country. The second, essentially unrelated to this, concerns the right of people not to be taxed, and the freedom to enjoy what one has legitimately come to hold. As was argued in Section 3.1 (in the context of examining the

---

32. For examples of various arguments leading to a very different diagnosis from Johnson's, see Frank (1967), Magdoff (1969), Sunkel (1973), Amin (1974), Diaz-Alejandro (1978), and Fishlow (1978).

approach that was called 'evasion'), it is difficult to find justification within the 'entitlement theories' for the exact inequalities that we happen to observe today. This does not, however, imply that the entitlement theories will not argue for any restriction whatever to redistributions, but only that the restrictions will not take the form of blanket prohibitions.

In so far as entitlement theories like those of Nozick will impose restrictions to redistribution, it is important to be clear whether one accepts such entitlements or not. Resistance to such acceptance will come not only from need-based or welfarist moralities (such as utilitarianism or leximin), but also from *rival* entitlement theories and also theories giving different views of desert. Even ignoring such austere views of desert as Hamlet's: 'use every man after his desert, and who shall escape whipping?', there are entitlement theories focusing on other sources of right, in particular labour (Section 1.6). For example, what is an application of 'the principle of justice in acquisition' for Nozick (1974) is patently 'unequal exchange' for Emmanuel (1972).[33]

Other concepts of rights discussed in Section I of the paper include the right to a minimal amount of primary goods (Section 1.3), and that to a minimum amount of primary powers (Section 1.4). While the force of Nozick's entitlement system is in the direction of morally accepting the outcome of inequalities, the force of labour-based rights as well as that of need-based rights would be usually in the opposite direction. It is, I think, a mistake to presume that a right-based morality must typically be conservative, in contrast with, say, utilitarianism.

3.5   Consequences and asymmetry

As was discussed earlier, rights and entitlements can be incorporated in the outcome morality itself rather than being kept out of it for application only in judgements of action. This would have the effect of expanding the scope of a consequentialist framework very substantially. This is particularly important since explicitly or implicitly various right-based considerations do enter people's moral values.

But the importance of studying consequences need not be based on the acceptance of consequentialism, since a denial of consequentialism is a denial of the *sufficiency* of consequences for moral judgements, not of their *necessity*. There are, in fact, very few moral

33. See also Amin (1974).

theories that are fully consequence-independent. The necessity to check the *actual* consequences of international policies, thus, goes well beyond the rejection of 'fantasie' or 'evasion' (Section 3.1).

In the context of the relevance of studying consequences, Richard Cooper (1977, p. 355) has referred to an important difficulty.

> Not to ask questions about these linkages would be morally obtuse. Yet to ask them involves peering inside the national shell, an activity that many developing countries view as a gross and unwarranted infringement of their national sovereignty. The current mood among developing countries resists strongly the notion that donor nations have a legitimate interest, much less (on the above argument) a moral obligation, to inquire closely into the use of resource transfers to be sure that their ethically based objectives are being served. A clear impass thus results.

The problem arises partly from the *asymmetry* in the position of the donor and recipient countries, in the sense that it is the 'national shell' of the recipient country that has to be 'peered inside' according to the quoted position, without the necessity of such a peering exercise the other way.

But is there a moral case for such an asymmetry? If the correctness of a policy would depend upon *all* its consequences, clearly there is the need for checking the consequence of such policies on donor nations *as well as* on recipient countries. Indeed, the donor country has no more a 'legitimate interest' or 'moral obligation' to peer inside the national shell of the recipient country than the recipient country has to peer inside the national shell of the donor country. As far as the judgement of outcomes is concerned, the moral requirement is direction neutral.

It can, of course, be argued that the asymmetry is legitimate since it is the disposition of the wealth of the donor countries that is being discussed. In practical terms, possession is indeed nine points of the law, but to argue that a corresponding *moral* asymmetry also exists will require some type of an entitlement reasoning, which is missing. Such a moral assertion can, of course, be easily made, for example, in the form of what was called 'evasion', but a moral defence is less straightforward (Section 3.4).

It may, however, be argued that the asymmetry arises from the fact that it is the donor country that is taking the *action* of transfer, and is thus peculiarly responsible. But, in fact, the actions will typically take the form of bilateral or multilateral agreements, and they are not just the actions of the donor country. (The belief that he who pays the piper should call the tune, is not based on the idea that the *action* is only that of the payer and not of the piper, but on the notion that the payer has an *entitlement* based on the money he is offering.)

Nor can it be argued that the consequences on the donor countries are obvious in a manner that consequences on recipient countries are not. In fact, the effects of international policies on national economies can be very complicated indeed. Consider Richard Cooper's argument (1977, p. 356) that

> if we are to justify transfers on ethical grounds, then, it must be on the basis of knowledge that via one mechanism or another the transferred resources will benefit those residents of the recipient countries who are clearly worse off than the worst-off 'taxed' (including taxes levied implicitly through commodity prices) residents of the donor countries.

The wording might suggest implicit use of leximin or the difference principle as the relevant 'ethical grounds' (ignoring, for example, *how much* is gained or lost), but that is clearly not the intention of Cooper's remark; leximin if chosen is presumably chosen for illustration. What is more important in the current context is the asymmetry that would arise in comparing the *actual* gain in the recipient country with the *maximal* loss that the donor country can potentially sustain, that is, the loss to the worst-off taxed resident. It is quite legitimate for someone from the recipient country to ask: is the *actual* effect of an additional unit of transfer in the donor country to increase the 'tax' on the *worst-off* 'taxed' resident in that country?[34] The moral search for consequences has to be even-handed.[35] The recipient country has no worse a case, on consequentialist reasoning, for 'peering inside' the donor country to decide how much aid it should demand, than the donor country has for 'peering inside' the recipient country to decide how much aid it should offer.

3.6 *Information and Consequences*

Richard Cooper is certainly right in emphasizing the necessity of examining consequences; the need to universalize his recommendation does not detract from the merit of his criticism of consequence-

---

34. Or: is the *actual* effect of avoiding an international transfer to bring relief to the *poorest* 'taxed' resident?

35. Commenting on this paper, Richard Cooper has explained to me, in a private communication, that this was indeed what he wanted: 'I may have worded my sentence clumsily, but its intent is to compare the *actual* gain with the *actual* loss'.

independent policy prescriptions. The critique applies not merely to intergovernment transfers, but also to international agreements on schemes such as 'brain-drain taxation'.

The consequences to be examined are not merely of immediate effects on income distribution (important though they are), but also the overall effects on the respective societies. To tax Picasso, the drained brain, to pay General Franco, ruling poor Spain, need not have been morally blissful. To dissociate the analysis of consequences from political considerations is to leave the consequential analysis seriously deficient, and morality can hardly be based on half-blindness. Such justice, to borrow a phrase from Arthur Miller, 'would freeze beer'.

Partial information on consequences can have the effect of producing 'permissive dominance' in a pluralist morality (Section 2.2). It is common to acknowledge the relevance of multiplicity of claims, and if some important ones are snuffed out by the absence of information, others – maybe less important ones – could dominate. For someone of a strongly conservative bent and somewhat attracted by 'evasion', the lack of definitive information as to who would benefit from transfers could lead to complacency about inaction. For apolitical income-redistributors, lack of information on precisely who would gain given the political mechanism, or how the political mechanism itself might be affected, could lead to simplistic policy analyses, not far removed from 'fantasie'. The sensitivity of moral judgements to information may be very great indeed.

Information also has an important role in changing people's focus from agent-relative moralities based on a narrow, nationalist conception of relational obligation. One may, with some justice, deny responsibility for inaction about matters the existence of which one does not know. In a small way, even the limited publicity given by OXFAM or UNICEF to human suffering, and to the relatively low cost of removal of some of these sufferings, has the effect of making many people face responsibilities which they would not have otherwise acknowledged. The role of information in the ethics of international income distribution can hardly be overemphasized.

4   Concluding Remarks

There will be no attempt to summarize the arguments presented in this paper, but some general remarks will be made to put the discussion in perspective.

(1) Utilitarianism is an amalgam of (a) consequentialism, (b) welfarism, and (c) sum-ranking (Section 1.1). Each of these characteristics can be and has been criticized, and can be eschewed, severally or jointly. For example, leximin violates sum-ranking but is welfarist and consequentialist (Section 1.2); Rawls' difference principle is not even welfarist, but can be combined with consequentialism; agent-relative moralities based on relational obligation violate consequentialism, but not necessarily the other two characteristics (Section 1.3).

(2) The moral claim to income can be seen as arising from many different factors (Section 2.1). For example (a) high marginal utility (utilitarianism), (b) low total utility (leximin), (c) low availability of primary goods (differences principle), (d) low primary powers (need-based equity principles), (e) labour contribution (labour entitlement theories), (f) holdings justified by principles of acquisition and transfer (Nozick's entitlement theory), (g) consistency with personal liberty (libertarian principles), and (h) relational obligations or event obligations (agent-relative moralities).

(3) When moral considerations conflict, one has to go either by dominance, yielding partial orderings, or by supplementation through weighting, or through no-tradeoff (lexicographic) priorities. If dominance is considered in the 'permissive' rather than the 'affirmative' form, the scope of the generated partial ordering may be very substantially expanded in a situation of incomplete information (Sections 2.2–2.3), a fact of some considerable relevance for judgements of international income distribution (Section 3.6).

(4) It may be instrumentally right that a person receives a particular income even when he has no moral claim to it, *if* the consequence of his having that income is a greater fulfilment of some other goal. Incentive arguments for inequality rest on such reasoning, and must be distinguished from arguments based on entitlement or desert (Section 2.4).

(5) While Rawls' formation of the difference principle in terms of primary goods rather than utility avoids some of the difficulties of a utility-based equity criterion (such as, leximin), it is exposed to difficulties of another kind (Section 1.3). Both these types of problems are avoided in an approach based on 'primary powers', which is a version of a need-based approach, but it too has problems of its own (Section 1.4). The differences between these alternative need-based approaches are acutely relevant in judging international distributions of income, because of systematic variation of needs.

(6) Considerations of rights can enter moral judgements in various contexts (such as, in judging outcomes or actions), and in various

forms (such as labour entitlements, libertarian rights, or entitlements based on rules of acquisition and transfer). There are some advantages in incorporating them in the outcome morality in a consequence-dependent framework rather than only in judgements of action in a consequence-independent framework, even though this may require an eschewal of the unqualified acceptance of the Pareto principle (Section 1.5).

(7) Entitlement theories conflict not only with non-entitlement theories, but also with each other (Section 1.6), and these conflicts are of considerable importance in judging the morality of inter-national inequalities (Section 3.4).

(8) The relevance of identifying consequences is not confined merely to consequentialist theories, and may be very great even for non-consequentialist approaches, since they need not be consequence-independent. In assessing consequences, certain asymmetries between the need to 'peer inside' donor and recipient countries may appear natural, but as it happens these alleged asymmetries have little moral force (Section 3.5).

(9) While nation-focused, agent-relativity can have complex instru-mental justification, there seems to be some considerable *ad hocism* in treating this to be valuable in itself. Relational obligations can also conflict with event obligations based on historical considerations (Section 3.3).

(10) The importance of the role of information in moral judge-ments on international distribution can hardly be overemphasized. Informational limitation restricts or distorts consequential judge-ments, encourages arbitrary agent-relativity, and even provides 'permissive' justification for the make-belief reasoning of 'fantasie' and the unreasoned prejudice of 'evasion' (Section 3.6), despite the crippling limitation of both these approaches (Section 3.1).

This paper was aimed at sorting out ethical issues in distributional judgement, and not at achieving a unique moral resolution. Apart from the complexity of the moral concepts involved, their abundance is really rather remarkable. There is also some evidence that the moralities people adopt often vary – in a most un-Kantian way – with their own position. This makes a moral consensus on these issues particularly difficult. I end with some discouraging words which Shakespeare put on the lips of Philip the Bastard, and only hope – but not expect – that he got it wrong:

Well, whiles I am a beggar, I will rail,
And say there is no sin but to be rich;
And being rich, my virtue then shall be
To say that there is no vice but beggary.

References

Amin, S. (1974): *Accumulation in a World Scale* (New York: Monthly Review Press).

Arrow, K. J. (1977): 'Extended Sympathy and the Possibility of Social Chance', *American Economic Review*, **67**.

Atkinson, A. B. (1973): 'How Progressive Should Income Tax Be?', in M. Parkin (ed.), *Essays in Modern Economics* (London: Longmans, 1973).

Bardhan, P. (1974): 'Redistribution with Growth: Some Country Experiences: India', in Chenery *et al*. (1974).

Basu, K. (1976): 'Revealed Preference of Governments: Concept, Analysis, Evaluation' (London School of Economics Ph.D dissertation). [Later published, *Revealed Preference of Government* (Cambridge: Cambridge University Press, 1980).]

Bhagwati, J. N. (ed.) (1977): *The New International Economic Order: The North-South Debate* (Cambridge, Mass.: MIT Press).

Blackorby, C. (1975): 'Degrees of Cardinality and Aggregate Partial Ordering', *Econometrica*, **43**.

Blau, J. H. (1975): 'Liberal Values and Independence', *Review of Economic Studies*, **42**.

Calvo, G. (1978): 'Some Notes on Time Inconsistency and Rawls' Maximin Criterion', *Review of Economic Studies*, **45**.

Chenery, H., Ahluwalia, M. S., Bell, C. L. G., Duloy, J. H. and Jolly, R. (1974): *Redistribution with Growth* (London: Oxford University Press).

Cooper, R. N. (1977): 'Panel Discussion on the New International Economic Order', in Bhagwati (ed.) (1977).

Dasgupta, P. (1974). 'Some Alternative Criteria for Justice between Generations', *Journal of Public Economics*, **3**.

D'Aspremont, C. and Gevers, L. (1977): 'Equity and Informational Basis of Collective Choice', *Review of Economic Studies*, **46**.

Deschamps, R. and Gevers, L. (1978): 'Leximin and Utilitarian Rules: A Joint Characterization', *Journal of Economic Theory*, **17**.

Diaz-Alejandro, C. F. (1978): 'Delinking North and South: Unshackled or Unhinged?', in Fishlow *et al*. (1978).

Emmanuel, A. (1972): *Unequal Exchange: A Study of the Imperialism of Trade* (New York: Monthly Review Press, and London: NLB).

Farrell, M. J. (1976): 'Liberalism in the Theory of Social Choice', *Review of Economic Studies*, **43**.

Fine, B. (1975): 'A Note on "Interpersonal Comparisons and Partial Comparability"', *Econometrica*, **43**.

Fishlow, A. (1978): 'A New International Order: What Kind?' in Fishlow *et al*. (1978).

——, Diaz-Alejandro, C. F., Fagen, R. R. and Hansen, R. D. (1978): *Rich and Poor Nations in the World Economy* (New York: McGraw-Hill).

Frank, A. G. (1967): *Capitalism and Underdevelopment in Latin America* (New York: Monthly Review Press).

Friedman, M. (1962): *Capitalism and Freedom* (Chicago: Chicago University Press).

Gibbard, A. (1974): 'A Pareto-Consistent Libertarian Claim', *Journal of Economic Theory*, **7**.

Gorman, W. M. (1956): 'The Demand for Related Goods', *Journal Paper J 3129* (Iowa Agricultural Experimental Station, Ames, Iowa).

—— (1975): 'Tricks with Utility Functions', in M. Artis and A. R. Nobay (eds), *Essays in Economic Analysis* (Cambridge: Cambridge University Press).

Hammond, P. J. (1976): 'Equity, Arrow's Conditions and Rawls' Difference Principle', *Econometrica*, **44**.

Hare, R. M. (1976): 'Ethical Theory and Utilitarianism', in H. D. Lewis (ed.), *Contemporary British Philosophy* (London: Allen and Unwin).

Harsanyi, J. C. (1977): 'Morality and the Theory of Rational Behaviour', *Social Research*, **44**.

Hart, H. L. A. (1973): Rawls on Liberty and Its Priority', *University of Chicago Law Review*, **40**; reprinted in N. Daniels (ed.), *Reading Rawls* (Oxford: Blackwell, 1975).

Hayek, F. A. (1960): *The Constitution of Liberty* (London: Routledge).

Johnson, H. G. (1977): 'Panel Discussion on the New International Economic Order', in Bhagwati (ed.).

Kanger, S. (1971): 'New Foundations for Ethical Theory', in R. Hilpinen (ed.), *Deontic Logic: Introductory and Systematic Readings* (Dordrecht: Reidel).

—— (1972): 'Law and Logic', *Theoria*, **38**.

Kant, I. (1907): *Grundlegung zur Metaphysik der Sitten*, 1785. English translation by T. K. Abbott, *Fundamental Principles of the Metaphysics of Ethics*, 3rd edn (London: Longmans).

Kornai, J. (1971): *Anti-Equilibrium* (Amsterdam: North-Holland).

Lancaster, K. J. (1966): 'A New Approach to Consumer Theory', *Journal of Political Economy*, **74**.

Lindahl, L. (1977): *Position and Change: A Study in Law and Logic* (Dordrecht: Reidel).

Little, I. M. D. (1957): *A Critique of Welfare Economics* (Oxford: Clarendon Press).

Locke, J. (1967): *Two Treatises on Government*, 1690 (P. Laslett, ed.), 2nd edn (Cambridge: Cambridge University Press).

Lundberg, E. (1977): 'Panel Discussion on the New International Economic Order', in Bhagwati (ed.) (1977).

Magdoff, H. (1969): *The Age of Imperialism* (New York: Monthly Review Press).

Marx, K. (1844): *Economic and Philosophic Manuscripts of 1844*, English translation (Moscow: Progress Publishers, 1977).

—— (1875): *Critique of the Gotha Programme*, English translation in K. Marx and F. Engels, *Selected Works*, vol. II (Moscow: Foreign Language Publishing House, 1951).

Maskin, E. (1978): 'A Theorem on Utilitarianism', *Review of Economic Studies*, **45**.

Meade, J. E. (1976): *The Just Economy* (London: Allen & Unwin).

Mirrlees, J. A. (1971): 'An Exploration in the Theory of Optimal Income Taxation', *Review of Economic Studies*, **38**.

Muellbauer, J. (1976): 'Community Preferences and the Representative Consumer', *Econometrica*, **44**.

Nagel, T. (1975): 'Libertarianism without Foundations', *Yale Law Review*, **85**.

Nozick, R. (1974): *Anarchy, State and Utopia* (Oxford: Blackwell).

Phelps, E. S. (ed.) (1973): *Economic Justice* (Harmondsworth: Penguin).

—— and Riley, J. G. (1978): 'Rawlsian Growth: Dynamic Programming for Capital and Wealth for Intergeneration "Maximin" Justice', *Review of Economic Studies*, **45**.

Phelps-Brown, E. H. (1962): *The Economics of Labour* (New Haven, Conn.: Yale University Press).

Rawls, J. (1971): *A Theory of Justice* (Cambridge, Mass.: Harvard University Press, and Oxford: Clarendon Press).

—— (1975): 'A Kantian Conception of Equality', *Cambridge Review* (February).

Robbins, L. (1938): Interpersonal Comparisons of Utility', *Economic Journal*, **48**.

Roberts, K. (1980): 'Interpersonal Comparability and Social Choice Theory', *Review of Economic Studies*, **47**.

Scanlon, T. (1978): 'Rights, Goals and Fairness', forthcoming in S. Hampshire (ed.), *Public and Private Morality* (Cambridge: Cambridge University Press).

Scitovsky, T. (1976): *The Joyless Economy* (London and New York: Oxford University Press).

Sen, A. K. (1967): 'The Nature and Classes of Prescriptive Judgments', *Philosophical Quarterly*, **17**.

—— (1970): *Collective Choice and Social Welfare* (San Francisco: Holden-Day, and Edinburgh: Oliver and Boyd; distribution taken over by North-Holland, Amsterdam).

—— (1973): *On Economic Inequality* (Oxford: Clarendon Press, and New York: Norton).

—— (1976a): 'Real National Income', *Review of Economic Studies*, **43**. [Reprinted in *Choice, Welfare and Measurement* (Oxford: Blackwell, 1982).]

—— (1976b): 'Liberty, Unanimity and Rights', *Economica*, **43**. [Reprinted in *Choice, Welfare and Measurement*.]

—— (1976c): 'Poverty: An Ordinal Approach to Measurements', *Econometrica*, **44**. [Reprinted in *Choice, Welfare and Measurement*.]

—— (1977a): 'Rational Fools: A Critique of the Behaviour Foundations of Economic Theory', *Philosophy and Public Affairs*, **6**. [Reprinted in *Choice, Welfare and Measurement*.]

—— (1977b): 'On Weights and Measures: Informational Constraints in Social Welfare Analysis', *Econometrica*, **45**. [Reprinted in *Choice, Welfare and Measurement*.]

—— (1977c): 'Informational Analysis of Moral Principles', presented at the Thyssen Philosophy Group meeting (September 1977). [Published in Ross Harrison (ed.), *Rational Action* (Cambridge: Cambridge University Press, 1979).]

—— (1978a): 'Welfare and Rights', text of Hägerström Lectures given at Uppsala University. [Parts of the manuscript published as 'Rights and Agency', *Philosophy and Public Affairs*, **11** (1982).]

—— (1978b): 'On the Labour Theory of Value: Some Methodological Issues', *Cambridge Journal of Economics*, 2.

Strasnick, S. (1976): 'Social Choice Theory and the Derivation of Rawls' Difference Principle', *Journal of Philosophy*.

Sunkel, O. (1973): 'Transnational Capital and National Disintegration in Latin America', *Social and Economic Studies*.

Suppes, P. (1966): 'Some Formal Models of Grading Principles', *Synthese*, **6**; reprinted in his *Studies in the Methodology and Foundations of Science* (Dordrecht: Reidel, 1969).

Suzumura, K (1978): 'On the Consistency of Libertarian Claims', *Review of Economic Studies*, **45**.

Usher, D. (1969): *The Price Mechanism and the Meaning of National Income Statistics* (Oxford: Clarendon Press).

Williams, B. (1973): 'A Critique of Utilitarianism', in J. J. C. Smart and B. Williams, *Utilitarianism: For and Against* (Cambridge: Cambridge University Press).

13

Rights and Capabilities

1 *Overlooking*

In his *Principles of Psychology*, William James has remarked: 'The art of being wise is the art of knowing what to overlook'. I like the remark not just because it wisely overlooks so many other aspects of wisdom, but also because assessing what is overlooked does indeed seem to be quite a good way of judging what is being asserted. For example, the various approaches to moral judgements can plausibly be examined in terms of what the approaches respectively leave out. The dog that does not bark provides the clue.

Take utilitarianism. In insisting on justification of actions, rules, institutions, etc., in terms of their effects on human happiness and suffering, the Benthamite tradition overlooks the claims of such hallowed sentiments as national glory and pride. This overlooking clearly must have introduced a breath of fresh air in the debates on public policy in Bentham's time. Indeed, the need for that air is not altogether lost in the present-day world either, not even in the more sophisticated countries, as the nature of public reaction to the recent Falklands crisis clearly demonstrated in Britain. Bentham's insistence on judging choices in terms of effects on human beings has become neither obsolete, nor irrelevant, in the modern world.[1]

1. Samuel Brittan has made this point forcefully in 'Two Cheers for Utilitarianism', in his *The Role and Limits of Government: Essays in Political Economy* (London: Temple Smith, 1983).

This paper draws much on my James Lecture at the New York Institute for the Humanities in November 1982 and my Boutwood Lectures at Corpus Christi College, Cambridge, in November 1983. For helpful comments on an earlier draft I am most grateful to John Bennett, John Broome, Ronald Dworkin, Isaac Levi and Tom Nagel. I also had the privilege of having several interesting and illuminating discussions with John Mackie on the subject matter of this paper during 1980–81.

From T. Honderich (ed.), *Ethics and Objectivity* (London: Routledge, forthcoming).

On the other hand the list of 'overlooked' items under the utilitarian approach is by no means confined only to such objects as national pride or glory, and blind prejudice or bloated sanctimony. Indeed, it is not quite correct to say that utilitarianism judges choices in terms of their effects on human beings, since it in fact judges them by the effects exclusively on one limited aspect of human beings, to wit, their utilities – just their pleasures and pains and over-all desires.[2] It has been argued, with a good deal of justice, that utilitarianism is not really interested in persons as such, and that a person is viewed by a utilitarian as nothing other than the *place* in which that valuable thing called happiness takes place. It does not ultimately matter how this happiness happens, what causes it, what goes with it, and whether it is shared by many or grabbed by a few. All that really matters is the total amount of this 'marvellous' thing: happiness or desire-fulfilment.

In fact, utilitarianism is unable to distinguish even between different types of pleasures and pains, or different types of desires, when the valuation is performed. This was, of course, one of John Stuart Mill's difficulties, though like his other complaints against utilitarianism, this too figured in the unlikely form of an indirect defence of the utilitarian outlook. In fact, utilitarianism has to face the problem of heterogeneity of utilities even in the distinction between pleasure and pain, since pain can hardly be seen as negative pleasure. Dr Johnson's well-known remark: 'Marriage has many pains, but celibacy has no pleasures',[3] would have – I imagine – prompted the purest utilitarian to check whether the *net* sum was positive or negative without wasting further time.

The limitation of utilitarianism arising from its overlooking everything other than total utility – aggregated over different types of utilities and different persons – has been much discussed in the recent literature.[4] There is, however, one particular aspect of this limitation which has received much less attention than, I believe, is due. The most blatant forms of inequalities and exploitations survive

2. See especially John Rawls, *A Theory of Justice* (Cambridge, Mass.: Harvard University Press, and Oxford: Clarendon Press, 1971), and 'Social Unity and Primary Goods', in Amartya Sen and Bernard Williams (eds), *Utilitarianism and Beyond* (Cambridge: Cambridge University Press, 1982).

3. *Rasselas*, Chapter 26.

4. For a recent collection of papers presenting arguments on different sides and of different types, see Sen and Williams (eds), *Utilitarianism and Beyond*. The editors' own assessment is presented there in the 'Introduction' to the volume. See also J. J. C. Smart and B. A. O. Williams, *Utilitarianism: For and Against* (Cambridge: Cambridge University Press, 1973), and A. K. Sen, 'Utilitarianism and Welfarism', *Journal of Philosophy*, 76 (1979).

in the world through making allies out of the deprived and the exploited. The underdog learns to bear the burden so well that he or she overlooks the burden itself. Discontent is replaced by acceptance, hopeless rebellion by conformist quiet, and — most relevantly in the present context — suffering and anger by cheerful endurance. As people learn to adjust to the existing horrors by the sheer necessity of uneventful survival, the horrors look less terrible in the metric of utilities.[5]

Let me illustrate the point with an example. In 1944 — the year after the Great Bengal Famine — a survey was carried out by the All-India Institute of Hygiene and Public Health in Singur, near Calcutta.[6] Among the categories of people surveyed in this immediate post-famine year there were many widows and widowers. I should add that the condition of women in India outside elite groups — and of widows in particular — is generally recognized to be nothing short of scandalous, and the position of women in terms of nutrition tends to be particularly bad. But how did the different groups respond to the questionnaire? As many as 48.5 per cent of widow*ers* — men that is — confided that they were 'ill' or in 'indifferent' health. The proportion of widows, on the other hand, in that dual category was just 2.5 per cent. The picture becomes even more interesting if we look at the answers to the question as to whether one was in indifferent health, leaving out the question about being definitely ill, for which of course there are more objective standards. In the more subjective category of being in 'indifferent' health, we find 45.6 per cent of the widowers. And what about the widows? It is reported that the answer is 0 per cent! Quiet acceptance of deprivation and bad fate affects the scale of dissatisfaction generated, and the utilitarian calculus gives sanctity to that distortion. This is especially so in *interpersonal* comparisons. If one has to get away from this mental-reaction view of deprivation that utilitarianism has made common, then one must look at deprivation in terms of some other metric. I shall presently argue that the metric of capabilities to function is a sensible one to choose, using information regarding who can in fact *do* what, and not just the way people *desire or react to*

---

5. I have tried to discuss this problem, in the specific context of sex discrimination in the distribution of food and medical facilities, in my 'Family and Food: Sex-bias in Poverty', essay 15 in this volume. The general question of adjustment of wants and desires in the light of feasibilities has been well discussed by Jon Elster, 'Sour Grapes — Utilitarianism and the Genesis of Wants', in Sen and Williams (eds), *Utilitarianism and Beyond*.

6. See R. B. Lal and S. C. Seal, *General Health Survey, Singur Health Centre, 1944* (Calcutta, All-India Institute of Hygiene and Public Health, 1949).

their ability or disability to do these things. But I have other approaches to consider before I get there.

2   Rights and Entitlements

It has been argued that a rights-based moral approach has many advantages.[7] In particular, it may be able to do a better job of dealing with deprivation than the utility-based approaches can. A person has some moral rights, and to be denied them is to be deprived of something valuable. But this starting point may be seen as begging a question: *why* do people have rights? Indeed, *do* they have moral rights? Whether this is at all a plausible point to begin has been forcefully disputed in recent years, despite the long history of morally appealing to natural rights, or human rights, or some other similar concept.

I raise this question here not because I intend to discuss it, but because I do not. The question of foundation is a very difficult one to resolve, and it is not very clear what would count as providing an adequate foundation of a substantive moral theory. There is, in fact, some evidence of arbitrary distinction when it comes to evaluation of particular moral theories. Some who find no difficulty at all in intrinsically valuing 'utility', or 'interests' of individuals, or some idea of 'equal treatment', find it intolerably arbitrary to begin with an assertion of rights. But any moral theory would have to begin with some primitive diagnosis of value (even if it is a procedural one in terms of some mythical primordial state), and the real question is whether the acknowledgement of rights cannot play that primitive role. The question is not meant as a rhetorical one. I accept fully that one has to dig for foundation,[8] but there is a substantial issue involved in deciding where to stop digging.

The issue also depends on what kind of activity we take moral evaluation to be.[9] I shall not have the opportunity of pursuing these deeper questions in this paper.

Rights can take very many different forms. In terms of actual legal rights against the state, they sometimes take the form of a substantive claim to, say, minimal health care, unemployment benefit,

---

7. See particularly John Mackie, 'Can There Be a Right-based Moral Theory', *Midwest Studies in Philosophy*, 3 (1978).

8. See T. N. Scanlon, 'Contractualism and Utilitarianism', in Sen and Williams (eds), *Utilitarianism and Beyond*.

9. See Thomas Nagel, 'The Limits of Objectivity', in S. McMurrin (ed.), *Tanner Lectures on Human Values* (Cambridge: Cambridge University Press, 1980).

poverty relief, etc. But such specific legal rights are typically not justified in terms of their intrinsic importance, but on some instrumental grounds, e.g. the belief that they lead to a happier community. I shall have more to say on this question presently. But I first take up the approach that is more common in moral theories of rights and which takes a strongly *procedural* form.

In this form, rights do not specify directly what a person may or may not have, but specify the rules that have to be followed to make his or her actual holdings and actions legitimate. For example, the rights may take the form of specifying rules of ownership and transfer, and the results of these rules are accepted precisely because they have resulted from obeying the right rules, not because the results judged as outcomes are in themselves good, which they may or may not be. In his justly famous book, *Anarchy, State and Utopia*,[10] Robert Nozick argued against any 'patterning' of outcomes. Such 'patterning' would – as it were – over-determine the system, since the rules that are accepted would lead to some outcomes and not others, and respecting these procedures does require the acceptance of whatever outcomes happen to emerge.

I believe this consequence-independent way of seeing rights is fundamentally defective.[11] Take a theory of entitlements based on a set of rights of 'ownership, transfer and rectification'. In this system a set of holdings of different people are judged to be just (or not just) by looking at past history, and not by checking the consequences of that set of holdings. But what if the consequences are recognizably terrible? I shall be self-indulgent enough at this point to refer to some empirical findings in a work on famines I did recently. In a book called *Poverty and Famines: An Essay on Entitlement and Deprivation*,[12] I have presented evidence to indicate that in many large famines in the recent past, in which millions of people have died, there was no over-all decline in food availability at all, and the famines occurred precisely because of shifts in entitlements resulting from exercises of rights that are perfectly legitimate. The legitimacy referred to here is, of course, of the legal type rather than that of being supported by a given moral system, but as it happens the moral system of ownership, transfer and rectification outlined by Nozick is, in many respects, quite close to such a legal system of property rights and market exchange.

10. R. Nozick, *Anarchy, State and Utopia* (New York: Basic Books, and Oxford: Basil Blackwell, 1974).
11. See my 'Rights and Agency', *Philosophy and Public Affairs*, 11 (1982).
12. *Poverty and Famines: An Essay on Entitlement and Deprivation* (Oxford: Clarendon Press, and New York: Oxford University Press, 1981).

I do not wish to spend any time in discussing whether or not famines can plausibly occur with a system of rights of the kind morally defended in various ethical theories, including Nozick's. I believe the answer is straightforwardly yes, since for many people the only resource that they legitimately possess, viz. their labour-power, may well turn out to be unsaleable in the market, giving the persons no command over food. The question I am asking is this: if results such as starvation and famines were to occur, would the distribution of holdings still be morally acceptable despite their disastrous consequences? There is something deeply implausible in the affirmative answer. Why should it be the case that rules of owner-ship, etc., should have such absolute priority over life-and-death questions?

It is, of course, possible to claim that only in these extreme cases should the entitlements based on rights of ownership and transfer be compromised, but not otherwise. Indeed, Nozick keeps the question open as to whether 'catastrophic moral horrors' can provide a ground for justly violating rights. But once it is admitted that consequences can be important in judging what rights we do or do not morally have, surely the door is quite open for taking a less narrow view of rights, rejecting assessment by procedures only. The bad consequences may, of course, be less disastrous in some other cases, but the extent of violation of procedural rights to avoid the bad consequences could be weaker *too*. Once trade-offs based on consequential evaluation are accepted, there is no obvious stopping place for a theory that was set up on a purely procedural approach.

Many authors in recent years have argued against what is often called 'consequentialism' — judging choices (say between actions, or between rules, or between institutions) exclusively in terms of conse-quent states of affairs. I believe some of these attacks may exaggerate difficulties with consequentialism since they do not take full note of the extent of freedom that consequentialism permits if the states of affairs are seen more completely than many traditional theories allow, e.g. if non-utility features in the states of affairs are taken seriously (against the tradition of utilitarian concern with utility information only).[13] Nevertheless, it is not implausible to argue that even with as rich a view of states of affairs as is possible, conse-quentialism will still be quite seriously inadequate. But that debate, viz. 'consequentialism or not', must not be confused with the debate

13. I have tried to discuss this question in my 'Rights and Agency', *Philosophy and Public Affairs*, 11 (1982), and 'Evaluator Relativity and Consequential Evaluation', *Philosophy and Public Affairs*, 12 (1983).

'consequence-sensitivity or not'. A substantive moral theory can be non-consequentialist but consequence-sensitive. Consequent states of affairs may not be the *only* things that matter, but they can nevertheless *matter*. Since it is implausible – indeed I believe incredible – to claim that consequences in the form of life or death, starvation or nourishment, indeed pleasure or pain, are intrinsically matters of moral indifference, or have only very weak intrinsic moral relevance, it is not easy to see why history-based rules of procedure should be so invulnerable to the facts of their consequences.

The procedural view of rights have typically taken what may be called a 'negative' form, corresponding somewhat to the well-known distinction between negative and positive freedoms. This affinity might at first sight appear to be a bit puzzling. If we are asserting the moral legitimacy of certain procedures, e.g. of ownership and exchange, why is it not just as much a positive assertion that we do have these rights, as it is a negative assertion that others must not stop us from enjoying these rights? But the negative assertion in this view has a practical content that the positive assertion lacks. The rights in question are not concerned with my actual capability of doing this or that, but my freedom to do them without let or hindrance. It binds others negatively – they must not interfere – but they are under no obligation to help me to exercise these rights.

This begs a difficult – and a very old – question. Why is it important that I should not be stopped from doing something and – at the same time – unimportant whether or not I can in fact do that thing? I shall have something to say on that presently, but before that I ask a more limited question. Suppose we are concerned only with negative freedom, to wit, that people *should not be stopped by others* from doing what they have a right to do (e.g. to move about freely). Should we see the ability to exercise these negative rights as good things that should be supported, or do we take the constraint view of negative freedom and just assert that one should not oneself interfere in these rights of others? If the former, i.e. if the violation of negative freedom counts as a bad consequence which is to be avoided, consequential reasoning can justify – indeed require – many *positive* actions in pursuit of *negative* freedom, e.g. that one should stop A from stopping B from moving about freely.

Indeed, *valuing* negative freedom *must* have some positive implications. If I see that negative freedom is valuable, and I hear that you are about to be molested by someone, and I can stop him or her from doing that, then I should certainly be under some obligation to consider doing that stopping. It is not adequate for me to resist molesting you; it is necessary that I value the things I can *do* to stop others from molesting you. I would fail to *value negative freedom* if I were to refuse to consider what I could do in defence of negative freedom.

In fact, the positive implications of negative freedom can go further. Suppose I can stop A from molesting B by using C's telephone, in his absence, and suppose I also know that C would not have permitted me to use his telephone for this purpose had he been around. Should I violate C's negative freedom not to have me enter his room and use his personal telephone against his wishes, to stop the violation of the negative freedom of B not to be beaten up by A? I would say – unless there is something important not captured by the description of the story – the answer must be yes. But that implies that it must be sometimes right to violate deliberately someone's negative freedom to bring about the prevention of a more serious violation of the negative freedom of someone else.

There is no tension in all this if we are allowed to assess or qualify rights – including negative freedoms – using consequence-sensitive analysis. The benefits in the form of stopping serious violations of negative freedoms can be seen as far outweighing the costs in the form of less serious violations of negative freedom. Such a 'cost–benefit analysis' may not be decisive except for the full consequentialist, but even non-consequentialists could accept a good deal of consequence-sensitivity in an otherwise deontological perspective. But consequence-sensitive evaluation with trade-offs is, of course, precisely what the constraint view of rights and negative freedom rules out. That view seems to me to be deeply defective. If freedom is important, it may *well be* valuable. If freedom *is* valuable, it may have some consequential relevance to the choice of actions. The old idea that vigilance – eternal or not – may indeed be important for liberty is not so easily dismissible.[14]

Thus, even if negative freedoms were all we valued, there would still be a strong case for having consequence-sensitive evaluation of negative freedoms, and for accepting contingently some *positive* obligation to protect negative freedoms. But – to move on – why should our concern stop only at protecting negative freedoms rather than be involved with what people can actually do? Should one be under an obligation to save the person who has been *pushed* into the river but not the person who has *fallen* into it? In deciding whether one is under an obligation to help a starving person, should one say 'yes' if the person has been robbed (with his negative freedom

---

14. On this see my 'Liberty as Control: An Appraisal', *Midwest Studies in Philosophy*, 7 (1982), and 'Liberty and Social Choice', *Journal of Philosophy*, 80 (1983).

being violated), but remain free to say 'no' if he has been fired from his job, or has lost his land to the moneylender, or has suffered from flooding or drought (without any violation of negative freedom)?

I shall not pursue this question further here. But I would like to investigate some interesting questions that arise once positive freedoms are accepted as valuable and when some obligation to support such freedom is given an important place in our moral thinking. How should these freedoms be characterized? Should they be seen as inputs to other — more fundamental — goals, e.g. the creation of a better society from the utilitarian point of view? Should they be seen as collateral benefits arising from the application of some deeper theory of justice, e.g. John Rawls' difference principle involving a just distribution of what he calls primary goods? I will, in fact, dispute these possible diagnoses, but before that I would try to outline a characterization of positive freedoms in the form of capabilities of persons.

3 Capabilities

Consider a good, e.g. rice. The utilitarian will be concerned with the fact that the good in question creates utility through its consumption. And indeed, so it does. But that is not the only thing it does. It can also give the person nutrition. *Owning* some rice gives the person the *capability* of meeting some of his or her nutritional requirements.

In modern consumer theory in economics, the nature of the goods has been seen in terms of their 'characteristics', and authors such as Terence Gorman and Kelvin Lancaster have done much to explore the view of goods as bundles of characteristics.[15] Rice has nutrition-giving characteristics, but other characteristics as well, e.g. satisfying hunger, providing stimulation, meeting social conventions, offering the opportunity of getting together, etc.[16] Not all of these characteristics are easy to pursue through the use of market data, and in that context economic analysis has tended to concentrate on a more restricted view of characteristics. But in this paper I am not really concerned with characteristics as such, but wish to go beyond that to what I have been calling capabilities. A characteristic — as used in consumer theory — is a feature of a good, whereas a capability is a

15. W. M. Gorman, 'The Demand for Related Goods', *Journal Paper J3129*, Iowa Experiment Station, Ames, Iowa, 1956; K. J. Lancaster, 'A New Approach to Consumer Theory', *Journal of Political Economy*, 74 (1966).

16. See Mary Douglas and B. Isherwood, *The World of Goods* (New York: Basic Books, 1979). See also T. Scitovsky, *The Joyless Economy* (Oxford: Oxford University Press, 1976).

feature of a person in relation to goods. Having some rice gives me the capability of functioning in a particular way, e.g. without nutritional deficiencies of particular types. The capability to function is the thing that comes closest to the notion of positive freedom, and if freedom is valued then capability itself can serve as an object of value and moral importance.

Four different notions need distinction in this context. There is the notion of a *good* (in this case, rice); that of a *characteristic* of a good (e.g. giving calories and nutrition); that of *functioning* of a person (in this case, living without calorie deficiency); that of *utility* (in this case, the pleasure or desire-fulfilment from the functioning in question, or from some other functioning related to the characteristics of rice). The entitlement theorists such as Nozick would be concerned with none of these directly, but would accept whatever holdings of goods by different persons follow from rules that are seen as legitimate or just. Utilitarianism – or more generally any utility-based moral theory – would concentrate on the last item of the four, and this is related to the view that the only thing of intrinsic value is utility. Egalitarians concerned with income distribution will come close to worrying about the distribution of goods, and will focus on the first item. The Rawlsian focus on primary goods (including incomes) in the context of the difference principle again relates to the category of goods in this four-fold classification, though – as I shall argue presently – there are also other elements in the Rawlsian perspective.

Focusing on the third item – the functioning of a person – has advantages that are both unique and important.[17] In fact, the natural interpretation of the traditional view of positive freedoms is in terms of capabilities to function. They specify what a person can or cannot do, *or* can or cannot be. These freedoms are not primarily concerned with what goods or income or resources people have. Nor with precisely how much pleasure or desire-fulfilment people get out of these activities (or from the ability to do these activities). The category of capabilities is the natural candidate for reflecting the idea of freedom to do. This is not to say that there are no ambiguities in this correspondence. Indeed, there are ambiguities, and I will discuss some of these later, but nevertheless the category of capabilities does come close to being able to reflect freedom in the positive sense.

17. See my 'Equality of What?' in S. McMurrin (ed.), *Tanner Lectures on Human Values* (Cambridge: Cambridge University Press, and Salt Lake City: University of Utah Press, 1980); reprinted in my *Choice, Welfare and Measurement* (Oxford: Basil Blackwell, and Cambridge, Mass.: MIT Press, 1982). In the latter volume, see also 'Introduction', pp. 30–1.

The distinctions involved in the four-fold classification are obvious enough, but they are sometimes confused, and perhaps the contrast between characteristics and functioning is worth a further remark. Characteristics represent, of course, an abstraction from goods, but they relate to goods rather than to persons. Functionings are, however, personal features; they tell us what a person is doing. Capability to function reflects what a person *can* do. Of course, characteristics of goods owned by a person do *relate* to the capabilities of persons, because a person achieves these capabilities through the use of those goods, among other things, but still capabilities of persons are quite different from the characteristics of goods possessed. Valuing one has *implications* on favouring the other, but valuing one is *not the same thing* as valuing the other.

If, for example, we value a person's ability to function without nutritional deficiency, we would tend to favour, up to a point, arrangements in which the person in question has more food with those nutritional characteristics, but that is not the same thing as valuing the possession of that food as such. If, say, some disease makes the person unable to achieve the capability of avoiding nutritional deficiency even with an amount of the food that would suffice for others, then the fact that he does possess that amount of the food (or has the resources to possess it) and command its characteristics, would not outweigh the loss of capability. If we value capabilities, then that is what we do value, and the possession of goods with the corresponding characteristics is instrumentally and contingently valued only to the extent that it helps in the achievement of the thing that we do value, viz. capabilities.

All this would not be worth spelling out in such painful detail but for the fact that despite the obvious relevance of capabilities of persons, various moral explorers have decided to pitch their tents on grounds other than capabilities. I turn now to an examination of some of those other positions.

4 *Utility*

The class of 'welfarist' moral theories includes utilitarianism. But what distinguished the class is not the fact that utilities are summed up to reflect the goodness of a state of affairs, but that utilities are regarded as adequate information for judging states of affairs. Furthermore, in the case of moral theories that are *both* welfarist and consequentialist, all choices of actions, rules, motives, institutions, etc., can also be judged in terms of the utility information only, regarding the consequent states of affairs. An example of a moral theory that is welfarist (i.e. utility-based, in this sense), without being utilitarian, is the theory that has been much explored in welfare economics under the influence of Rawls' writings and which is called, by stretching a point, 'Rawlsian'. This takes the form of judging the goodness of a state of affairs in terms of the utility level of the worst-off individual in that society in that state, and economists such as Phelps and Atkinson, among others,[18] have done much to explore the implications of such an approach.

There are two distinct reasons why any welfarist theory must be inadequate in dealing with freedom. First, freedom is concerned with what one *can* do, and not just with what one does do. Second, freedom is concerned with what one can *do*, and not just with what utility that doing leads to. Taking the latter question first, a welfarist distributional system determines what one should get on the basis of the psychological reactions in the form of pleasures and pains, or anticipations in the form of desires. Utilitarians reward *high marginal utility*, i.e. high psychological response to rewards; the so-called 'Rawlsians' of the welfarist variety, on the other hand, respond to *low total utility*, i.e. low over-all psychological state of happiness. These different uses of utility information may take us in different directions, but all welfarist theories agree that if two persons have identical utility features then they must have the same claims to a share of a given total. But suppose one of them is really much more deprived in terms of what he can do, e.g. he is blind or disabled in some other way, and his utility features match that of the other only because he has a much more cheerful and resilient temperament. The fact of his disadvantage should then play no part in the welfarist calculus, but it remains true to say that he has less capabilities since he cannot do many things that the other can do. Is the fact of this disadvantaged person's cheerfulness, or easier desire fulfilment, adequate ground for him to be given no special resource to help combat that disadvantage? Does a cheerful blind person because of his buoyancy forgo the help that he could otherwise claim from the society? We need not drown the information about a person's disadvantages in the loud noise of utilities, as welfarists would do. A person, as we argued before, is more than the location of utilities, and it does matter what kind of a deal he is getting.

The other issue concerns the special attention that freedom has to pay to the *possibilities* open to a person as opposed to the particu-

18. See E. S. Phelps (ed.), *Economic Justice* (Harmondsworth: Penguin, 1973); A. B. Atkinson, *Social Justice and Public Policy* (Brighton: Wheatsheaf, 1983).

lar one he or she happens to choose. It could be the case that an illiterate person, had he been literate, would have still chosen not to read anything, and it certainly could be the case that his or her utility would not have been any different had he been literate. For the welfarist such an illiterate person need not be seen as deprived, but from the point of view of freedom, notwithstanding the congruence on the utility space, the positions of the literate and the illiterate persons are not the same. One can do many things that the other cannot, and this fact is not rendered irrelevant by the other fact that they happen to choose to do the same things and get the same utility in the case under discussion.

This last point should not be taken to imply that it is being asserted that it does not morally matter at all whether a person himself values some capability or not, and whether he chooses to use that capability. Far from it. This is partly because freedom is not the only moral consideration that a freedom-inclusive moral system might support. Even if something is irrelevant to freedom, it could be morally important in such a plural system because of the other value elements in that system. But more immediately, freedom itself is not insensitive to what a person values. The index of capabilities can be sensitive to the strength of desires without converting everything into the metric of desires. The welfarist picture drops out everything other than desires. A non-welfarist over-all index of capabilities may not drop out desires and may well be sensitive to the strength of desires *without ignoring* other influences on the indexing.[19]

5   Primary Goods

I turn now to the Rawlsian approach as reflected in his difference principle. In this view a person's advantage is judged by an index of primary goods, including income. This differs from the welfarist approach in refusing to accept the hegemony of the metric of desires or pleasures. While this is achieved at the cost of having to devise an alternative system of weighting of different primary goods, the task of weighting is — explicitly or implicitly — an essential one in any moral theory of this kind. But it is important to check first whether the holding of primary goods is a good guide to a person's advantage.

On the reasoning presented earlier, if what we value is freedom, then primary goods can be valued only instrumentally *and* very

19. The problems of indexing capabilities, I have discussed elsewhere, in my 1982 Hennipman Lecture, given at Amsterdam University; *Commodities and Capabilities*, to be published by North-Holland.

contingently. If someone has a physical handicap, it is quite possible that income may do less for him or her than it does for another, and other primary goods — similarly — may have variable importance. These are not just special cases, as Rawls has been somewhat inclined to think.[20] Depending on our size and body metabolism, our need for food varies between community and community, and within a community, between person to person, and the resulting difference can be enormous in the context of a poor country. When it comes to rich countries, the income requirements of various social goals such as taking part in the life of the community or having self-respect may vary depending on a variety of circumstances. The correspondence between 'primary goods' and what may be called 'primary capabilities' is not that of a tight mapping that operates independently of persons or communities.[21]

There are, however, good reasons to think that Rawls himself — contrary to what his own theory formally states — is really after something like capabilities. He motivates the focus on primary goods by discussing what the primary goods enable people to do. It is only because of his assumption — often implicit — that the same mapping of primary goods to capabilities holds for all, that he can sensibly concentrate on primary goods rather than on the corresponding capabilities. Once that untenable assumption about the same mapping is dropped, the natural response should be to come back to the motivating concern with capabilities.[22]

Rawls' ambiguity on this subject is caught very well by his vacillation between taking 'self-respect' as a primary good, on the one hand, and 'the social bases of self-respect', or simply 'the bases of self-respect', as the primary good dealing with this feature. Sometimes he moves from one to the other within one page.[23] Self-respect is, of course, just an outcome, and by extension it can refer to the ability to achieve this particular functioning of a person. On the other hand, social *bases* of self-respect — like income — are only means to the end of that functioning. Rawls is more consistent in his list of primary goods when he talks about the 'social bases' or 'bases'

20. J. Rawls, 'A Kantian Concept of Equality', *Cambridge Review*, February 1975.

21. See my 'Equality of What?'. These issues are central to comparisons of standard of living. I have tried to go into this question, among others, in 'The Living Standard', forthcoming in *Oxford Economic Papers*.

22. See my 'Equality of What?'. Incidentally, in that paper, I had in fact, unwittingly, somewhat misstated Rawls' own position, and this has been clarified in my *Choice, Welfare and Measurement* (1982), pp. 365–6. Also see Rawls' response to this point in his recent paper 'Social Unity and Primary Goods', in Sen and Williams (eds), *Utilitarianism and Beyond*, pp. 168–9.

23. Rawls, *A Theory of Justice*, p. 62.

of self-respect, along with other primary goods such as 'rights, liberties and opportunities, income and wealth'. But he seems, in fact, to be closer to his real concern when he talks about the 'primary good of self-respect'.

6 Resources

I turn now to a different − though not unrelated − ground on which to base moral analysis, to wit, the resources of persons. The case for equality of resources has been persuasively developed recently by Ronald Dworkin.[24] Much of his argument is concerned with what equality of resource might really mean, and Dworkin argues that the idea involves both the operation of an economic (in fact competitive) market and the assumption − strongly counterfactual − of the existence of some insurance markets covering differences of abilities and productive power to make the equality of resources a persuasive moral criterion.

In this context Dworkin considers the focus on capabilities advocated by this author in an earlier paper (my Tanner Lecture 'Equality of What?').[25] He notes that 'people's powers are indeed resources, because these are used, together with material resources, in making something valuable out of one's life'.[26] This comes close to taking explicit note of capabilities in defining the resources themselves, and it could be argued that this way of seeing resources would lead to a congruence of the requirements of equality of capabilities and that of equality of resources. This raises an interesting issue, but as it happens, while Dworkin sees the taking of counterfactual insurance against handicaps as part and parcel of his characterization of the good society, he argues against bringing in handicaps into the idea of equality of resources as such. This is partly because these personal resources are not transferable, but also because of two 'practical and theoretical inadequacies'. First, Dworkin argues that for effective use of the idea of compensating for mental or physical handicaps, we require 'some standard of "normal" powers to serve as the benchmark for compensation', and this does not exist. Second, he notes that 'no amount of initial compensation could make someone born blind or mentally incompetent equal in physical or mental resources with someone taken to be "normal" in these ways'.[27]

24. Ronald Dworkin, 'Equality of Resources', *Philosophy and Public Affairs*, 10 (1981).
25. See footnote 17 above.
26. Dworkin, *op. cit.*, p. 300.
27. *Ibid.*, p. 300.

The first of these arguments seems to suffer from the unjustified belief that the equality of capabilities – and the equality of resources derived from that – cannot make sense without some idea of normal levels of capabilities. Why so? The case for equality of capabilities is no more dependent on the idea of 'normal capabilities' than the case for equality of resources of other kinds is dependent on the idea of 'normal resources' such as 'normal income'. The latter would be absurd, since the notion of normal income varies from society to society. The former is absurd for much the same reason. But neither compromises the possibility and indeed the importance of thinking in terms of equality of either kind. The notion of normality is not central to *comparing* capabilities, and to *ranking* them as 'more' or 'less' in interpersonal contrasts. Indeed, the idea of normality is quite unnecessary for such binary comparisons.

The second argument – related to the impossibility of full compensation of the handicapped person such as the blind – rests on the implicit beliefs that one cannot talk about the value of equality, if it is not feasible, and one cannot recommend a move towards equality if absolute equality cannot be achieved. Both presumptions are open to questioning. Many ideals are known to be unachievable without being useless for that reason. Indeed, very few egalitarians of any kind – Babeuf or Marx not excluded – had thought that absolute equality of the kind they advocated would be really achievable.

Further, since equality of capabilities in the aggregate sense is based on some kind of an over-all *index* of capabilities, it may indeed be possible to achieve full equality even without giving sight to the blind, or making the deaf hear all. Finally, even when full equality is not achievable, a move towards it may be possible. 'More equality' is not an empty slogan, and the best need not be made the enemy of the good.

But Dworkin is certainly right that personal physical and mental qualities are not resources in the sense in which ordinary material resources are, and they cannot be 'manipulated or transferred' in the way material resources can be. More importantly, there does not seem to be any real advantage in translating the valuation of capabilities into an equivalent notion of the valuation of resources and getting an idea of equality of resources that is thoroughly parasitical on the idea of equality of capabilities. But in all these recognitions, there is no argument for rejecting the value of capabilities as such, nor the moral claim of equality of capabilities to be the right general concept of equality, and Dworkin presents no such argument. Thus, in an important way, the rather limited notion of equality of resources, which overlooks the interpersonal differences in the mapping from resources to capabilities, remains undefended.

Indeed, to see the interpersonal variations of the mapping from resources to capabilities as due only to handicaps of some people is to underestimate the general nature of the problem. As was already mentioned, depending on our body size, metabolism, temperament, social conditions, etc., the translation of resources into the ability to do things does vary substantially from person to person and from community to community, and to ignore that is to miss out on an important general dimension of moral concern.

7   Concluding Remarks

In this paper I have outlined and defended an interpretation of positive freedoms. The interpretation sees freedoms in the form of particular capabilities. While a moral argument need not require that the various capabilities be converted into an aggregate measure, some arguments will need this, and that requires the use of some procedure of indexation. The problem is similar to that of constructing an index of primary goods as needed by John Rawls, but it is in some ways easier to handle.

Capabilities are – as I have argued – directly valuable in a way that the possession of primary goods cannot be, since they evidently are means to some more human ends. Judgements of relative import-ance are, thus, less contingent and less remote in the case of capabili-ties as opposed to primary goods. Nevertheless, there are difficulties in such indexation. I have not discussed that issue in this paper, though I have tried to do this elsewhere.[28]

I have argued against the utilitarian – and more generally welfarist – moral focus as well as against the focus of Rawlsian difference principle and Dworkin's notion of equality of resources. The Rawlsian and Dworkinian notions are moves in the right direction, but they seem to me to be generally deficient as moral criteria, and in particu-lar take inadequate note of the ideas behind positive freedom.

I have also argued against the consequence-insensitive ways of characterizing moral rights and entitlements, as put forward by Robert Nozick and others. Valuing negative freedoms in the form of constraints on action is, I have tried to show, a fundamentally

28. In my Hennipman Lecture (1982), *Commodities and Capabilities* (North-Holland, forthcoming).

defective moral perspective. If, on the other hand, preserving negative freedom is seen as valuable, then some positive action recommendations follow from this consequentially. In addition to arguing that negative freedoms have positive implications, I have also argued against confining attention to negative freedoms only.

Concern with positive freedoms leads directly to valuing people's capabilities and instrumentally to valuing things that enhance these capabilities. The notion of capabilities relates closely to the functioning of a person. This has to be contrasted with the ownership of goods, the characteristics of goods owned, and the utilities generated.

14

Poor, Relatively Speaking

1 Introduction

When on 6 January 1941, amidst the roar of the guns of the Second World War, President Roosevelt announced that 'in the future days ... we look forward to a world founded upon four essential freedoms', including 'freedom from want', he was voicing what was soon to become one of the major themes of the post-war era. While the elimination of poverty all over the world has become a much-discussed international issue, it is in the richer countries that an immediate eradication seemed possible. That battle was joined soon enough after the war in those affluent countries, and the ending of poverty has been a major issue in their policy discussions.

There are, however, great uncertainties about the appropriate way of conceptualizing poverty in the richer countries, and some questions have been repeatedly posed. Should the focus be on 'absolute' poverty or 'relative' poverty? Should poverty be estimated with a cut-off line that reflects a level below which people are − in some sense − 'absolutely impoverished', or a level that reflects standards of living 'common to that country' in particular? These questions − it will be presently argued − do not bring out the real issues clearly enough. However, a consensus seems to have emerged in favour of taking a 'relative' view of poverty in the rich countries. Wilfred Beckerman and Stephen Clark put it this way in their important recent study of poverty and social security in Britain since 1961: 'we have measured poverty in terms of a "relative" poverty

Revised version of a Geary Lecture given on 6 September 1982, at the Economic and Social Research Institute, Dublin, Ireland. For helpful comments I am most grateful to Wilfred Beckerman, Graciela Chichilnisky, Theo Cooper, Jan Graaff, Kieran A. Kennedy, Paul Seabright, Peter Townsend and Dorothy Wedderburn.

From *Oxford Economic Papers*, 35 (July 1983), 153−69.

line, which is generally accepted as being the relevant concept for advanced countries'.[1]

There is indeed much merit in this 'relative' view. Especially against the simplistic absolute conceptualization of poverty, the relative view has represented an entirely welcome change. However, I shall argue that ultimately poverty must be seen to be primarily an absolute notion, even though the specification of the absolute levels has to be done quite differently from the way it used to be done in the older tradition. More importantly, the contrast between the absolute and the relative features has often been confused, and I shall argue that a more general question about ascertaining the absolute standard of living lies at the root of the difficulty. In particular, it will be claimed that *absolute* deprivation in terms of a person's *capabilities* relates to *relative* deprivation in terms of commodities, incomes and resources.

That is going to be my main theme, but before I get to that general issue, I ought to make clear the sense in which I believe that even the narrow focus on relative poverty has been valuable in the recent discussions on poverty. In the post-war years there was a premature optimism about the elimination of poverty in rich countries based on calculations using poverty lines derived from nutritional and other requirements of the kind used by Seebohm Rowntree in his famous poverty studies of York in 1899 and 1936, or by Charles Booth in his nineteenth century study of poverty in London. The post-war estimates using these given standards yielded a very comforting picture of the way things had improved over the years, and indeed in terms of old standards, the picture certainly looked greatly more favourable than in the darker pre-war days. For example, the third York survey of 1951, following Rowntree's earlier ones, indicated that using the same standard, the proportion of working class population in poverty appeared to have fallen from 31 per cent at the time of the last survey in 1936 to less than 3 per cent in the new survey of 1951.[2] This was partly the result of general economic growth and a high level of employment, but also the consequence of various welfare legislations following the Beveridge Report of 1942, covering family allowances, national insurance, national assistance and national health service. Deducting public transfers would have made the poverty ratio higher than 22 per cent rather than less than 3 per cent. The changed situation – despite some statistical problems – was indeed genuine, but it was much too

1. Beckerman and Clark (1982).
2. Rowntree and Lavers (1951, p. 40).

slender a basis on which to declare victory in the war against poverty. While the Labour government did go to the electorate in 1950 with the emphatic claim in its Manifesto that 'destitution has been banished', and that the government has 'ensured full employment and fair shares of the necessities of life',[3] there was little real reason to be smug about eradication of poverty in Britain. There were lots of people who were in misery and clearly deprived of what they saw (as I shall presently argue, *rightly*) as necessities of life, and the battle against poverty was far from over.

It is in this context that the change of emphasis in the academic literature from an absolutist to a relativist notion of poverty took place, and it has the immediate effect of debunking the smug claims based on inadequate absolute standards. But instead of the attack taking the form of disputing the claim that the old absolute standards were relative still, it took the investigation entirely in the relativist direction, and there it has remained through these years. The relativist response to the smugness was effective and important. Using what he regarded as the orthodox or conventional poverty line fixed at a level 40 per cent higher than the basic National Assistance scale, plus rent, Peter Townsend (1962) showed that as many as one in seven Britons were in poverty in 1960. Other important questions were also raised, e.g. by Dorothy Wedderburn (1962), and more detailed and comprehensive estimates soon followed, and the poverty battle was seen as wide open.[4] While I shall question the conceptualization underlying this change, I certainly would not dispute the value of the relativist contribution in opening up the question of how poverty lines should be determined, as well as in preventing a premature declaration of victory by the old absolutist school.

2   A Thoroughgoing Relativity?

Peter Townsend, who − along with other authors such as Gary Runciman − has made pioneering and far-reaching contributions to the relativist view of poverty puts the case thus:

> Any rigorous conceptualisation of the social determination of need dissolves the idea of 'absolute' need. And a thorough-going relativity applies to time as well as place. The necessities of life are not fixed. They are continuously being adapted and

3. Quoted by David Bull (1971, p. 13).
4. See especially Abel-Smith and Townsend (1965) and Atkinson (1970b).

augmented as changes take place in a society and in its products. Increasing stratification and a developing division of labour, as well as the growth of powerful new organisations, create, as well as reconstitute, 'need'. Certainly no standard of sufficiency could be revised only to take account of changes in prices, for that would ignore changes in the goods and services consumed as well as new obligations and expectations placed on members of the community. Lacking an alternate criterion, the best assumption would be to relate sufficiency to the average rise (or fall) in real incomes.[5]

The last remark – that the best assumption would be to relate sufficiency to 'the average rise (or fall) in real incomes' – is obviously *ad hoc*. But the more general argument is undoubtedly quite persuasive. However, I think this line of reasoning suffers from two quite general defects. First, *absoluteness* of needs is not the same thing as their *fixity over time*. The relativist approach sees deprivation in terms of a person or a household being able to achieve *less than what others* in that society do, and this relativity is not to be confused with *variation over time*. So the fact that 'the necessities of life are not fixed' is neither here nor there, as far as the competing claims of the absolutist and relativist views are concerned. Even under an absolutist approach, the poverty line will be a function of *some* variables, and there is no *a priori* reason why these variables might not change over time.

The second problem is perhaps a more difficult one to sort out. There is a difference between achieving *relatively less than others*, and achieving *absolutely less because of falling behind others*. This general distinction, which I think is quite crucial to this debate, can be illustrated with a different type of interdependence altogether – that discussed by Fred Hirsch (1976) in analysing 'positional goods'. Your ability to enjoy an uncrowded beach may depend on your knowing about that beach when others do not, so that *the absolute* advantage you will enjoy – being on an uncrowded beach – will depend on your *relative* position – knowing something that others do not. You want to have that information, but this is not because you particularly want to do *relatively better than or as well as others*, but you want to do *absolutely well*, and that in this case requires that you must have some differential advantage in information. So your absolute achievement – not merely your relative success – may depend on your relative position in some other space. In examining

5. Townsend (1979b, pp. 17-18). See also his major study of poverty in the UK, Townsend (1979a).

the absolutist *vs.* the relativist approach it is important to be clear about the space we are talking about. Lumping together needs, commodities, etc., does not help to discriminate between the different approaches, and one of the items in our agenda has to be a closer examination of the relationship between these different spaces.

Before I come to that, let me consider a different approach to the relativist view – this one occurring in the important study of 'poverty and progress in Britain' between 1953 and 1973 by Fiegehen, Lansley and Smith. They put the question thus:

> In part the renewed concern with 'want' reflected generally increased prosperity and the feeling that the standard of living which society guaranteed should be raised accordingly. This led to 'relative' concepts of poverty, by which the extent of poverty is judged not by some absolute historically defined standard of living, but in relation to contemporary standards. By such a moving criterion poverty is obviously more likely to persist, since there will always be certain sections of society that are badly off in the sense that they receive below-average incomes. Thus renewed interest in poverty stemmed to a considerable extent from a recognition that it is incumbent on society to assist the *relatively* deprived.[6]

One consequence of taking this type of rigidly relativist view is that poverty cannot – simply cannot – be eliminated, and an anti-poverty programme can never really be quite successful. As Fiegehen, Lansley and Smith note, there will always be certain sections of society that are badly off in relative terms. That particular feature can be changed if the relative approach is differently characterized, e.g., checking the number below 60 per cent of median income (the answer *can* be zero). But it remains difficult to judge, in any purely relative view, how successful an anti-poverty programme is, and to rank the relative merits of different strategies, since gains shared by all tend to get discounted. It also has the implication that a general decline in prosperity with lots of additional people in misery – say due to a severe recession or depression – need not show up as a sharp increase in poverty since the relative picture need not change. It is clear that somewhere in the process of refining the concept of poverty from what is viewed as the crudities of Charles Booth's or Seebohm Rowntree's old-fashioned criteria, we have been

---

6. Fiegehen, Lansley and Smith (1977, pp. 2–3).

made to abandon here an essential characteristic of poverty, replacing it with some imperfect representation of *inequality* as such.

That poverty should in fact be viewed straightforwardly as an issue of inequality has, in fact, been argued by several authors. The American sociologists Miller and Roby have put their position thus:

> Casting the issue of poverty in terms of stratification leads to regarding poverty as an issue of inequality. In this approach, we move away from efforts to measure poverty lines with pseudo-scientific accuracy. Instead, we look at the nature and size of the differences between the bottom 20 or 10 per cent and the rest of the society.[7]

I have tried to argue elsewhere (Sen (1981), Chapter 2) that this view is based on a confusion. A sharp fall in general prosperity causing widespread starvation and hardship must be seen by any acceptable criterion of poverty as an intensification of poverty. But the stated view of poverty 'as an issue of inequality' can easily miss this if the *relative* distribution is unchanged and there is no change in 'the differences between the bottom 20 or 10 per cent and the rest of the society'. For example, recognizing starvation as poverty is scarcely a matter of 'pseudo-scientific accuracy'!

It can, however, be argued that such sharp declines are most unlikely in rich countries, and we can forget those possibilities. But that empirical point does nothing to preserve the basic adequacy of a conceptualization of poverty which should be able to deal with a wide variety of counter-factual circumstances. Furthermore, it is not clear that such declines cannot really take place in rich countries. A measure of poverty should have been able to reflect the Dutch 'hunger winter'[8] of 1944–45, when widespread starvation was acute. And it must not fail to notice the collapse that would surely visit Britain if Mrs Thatcher's quest for a 'leaner and fitter' British economy goes on much longer. The tendency of many of these measures to look plausible in situations of growth, ignoring the possibility of contraction, betrays the timing of the birth of these measures in the balmy sixties, when the only possible direction seemed forward.

---

7. Miller and Roby (1971). See also Miller, Rein, Roby and Cross (1967). Contrast Townsend's (1979a) rejection of the identification of poverty with inequality (p. 57).

8. This famine was indeed spread very widely across the Dutch population, thereby making the relative extents of deprivation quite muddled; see Aykroyd (1974) and Stein, Susser, Saenger and Marolla (1975).

3 *The Policy Definition*

While one could easily reject a *fully* relativized view of poverty, making poverty just 'an issue of inequality', it is possible to adopt a *primarily* relativized view without running into quite the same problems. The poverty line that has been most commonly used in recent studies of British poverty is the one given by the Official Supplementary Benefit scale,[9] and this scale has been consistently revised with attention being paid to the average level of British income. In fact, the scale has been revised upwards faster than the average income growth, and the poverty line in real terms did in fact double between July 1948 and November 1975.[10] Using this poverty line, adjusted for cost-of-living changes on a month to month basis, Beckerman and Clark (1982) have estimated that the number of persons in poverty in Britain went *up* by about 59 per cent between 1961–63 and 1974–76 (p. 3). This rise is not entirely due to the upward revision of the poverty line, and another important factor is the demographic change associated with an increase in the number of pensioners in the British population, but the upward trend of the poverty line is certainly a major influence in this direction.[11]

This practice of using the Supplementary Benefit scale as the poverty line is open to some obvious problems of its own. Not the least of this is the perversity whereby an increase in the attempt by the State to deal with poverty and low incomes by raising the Supplementary Benefit scale will tend to increase rather than diminish the measured level of poverty, by raising the poverty line. In this view, *helping* more is read as more help being *needed*. The most effective strategy for the government to adopt to reduce the number of the 'poor', under this approach, is to *cut*, rather than *raise*, the level of assistance through Supplementary Benefits. This can scarcely be right.

Identifying the poverty line with the Supplementary Benefit scale belongs to a more general tradition, which the United States

9. See, for example, Atkinson (1970b), Bull (1971), Fiegehen *et al.* (1977), Berthoud and Brown with Cooper (1981), and Beckerman and Clark (1982).

10. Beckerman and Clark (1982, p. 4).

11. Beckerman and Clark (1982, pp. 3–4). A big factor in this increase in the Beckerman–Clark calculation is their procedure of adjusting the poverty line for cost-of-living increase every month in between the official adjustments of the Supplementary Benefit scale, so that those whose incomes were raised exactly to the Supplementary Benefit level through that scheme would shortly appear as being *below* the Beckerman–Clark poverty line as a result of the monthly adjustments.

President's Commission on Income Maintenance in 1969 called the 'policy definition' of poverty.[12] It is a level of income that is seen as something 'the society feels some responsibility for providing to all persons'. This approach too is, I believe, fundamentally flawed.[13] The problem is that the level of benefits is determined by a variety of considerations going well beyond reflecting the cut-off point of identified poverty. For one thing, it reflects what is feasible. But the fact that the elimination of some specific deprivation – even of starvation – might be seen, given particular circumstances, as unfeasible does not change the fact of that deprivation. Inescapable poverty is still poverty. Furthermore, the decisions regarding State assistance will reflect – aside from feasibility considerations – other pressures, e.g., pulls and pushes of politically important groups, policy objectives *other than* poverty removal (such as reduction of inequality). Attempts to read the poverty line from the assistance level are riddled with pitfalls. If Mrs Thatcher decides today that the country 'cannot afford' the present level of Supplementary Benefits and the scale must be cut, that decision in itself will not reduce poverty in Britain (through lowering the poverty line below which people count as poor).

4   *The Absolutist Core*

Neither the various relativist views, nor seeing poverty as 'an issue in inequality', nor using the so-called 'policy definition', can therefore serve as an adequate theoretical basis for conceptualizing poverty. There is, I would argue, an irreducible absolutist core in the idea of poverty. One element of that absolutist core is obvious enough, though the modern literature on the subject often does its best to ignore it. If there is starvation and hunger, then – no matter what the *relative* picture looks like – there clearly is poverty. In this sense the relative picture – if relevant – has to take a back seat behind the possibly dominating absolutist consideration. While it might be thought that this type of poverty – involving malnutrition or hunger – is simply irrelevant to the richer countries, that is empirically far from clear, even though the frequency of this type of deprivation is certainly much less in these countries.

Even when we shift our attention from hunger and look at other aspects of living standard, the absolutist aspect of poverty does not

12. US President's Commission on Income Maintenance (1969, p. 8).
13. Sen (1981, pp. 17-21).

disappear. The fact that some people have a lower standard of living than others is certainly proof of inequality, but by itself it cannot be a proof of poverty unless we know something more about the standard of living that these people do in fact enjoy. It would be absurd to call someone poor just because he had the means to buy only one Cadillac a day when others in that community could buy two of these cars each day. The absolute considerations cannot be inconsequential for conceptualizing poverty.

The temptation to think of poverty as being altogether relative arises partly from the fact that the *absolute* satisfaction of some of the needs might depend on a person's *relative* position vis-à-vis others in much the same way as − in the case discussed earlier − the absolute advantage of a person to enjoy a lonely beach may depend upon his relative advantage in the space of knowledge regarding the existence and access to such beaches. The point was very well caught by Adam Smith when he was discussing the concept of necessaries in *The Wealth of Nations*:

> By necessaries I understand not only the commodities which are indispensably necessary for the support of life, but what ever the custom of the country renders it indecent for creditable people, even the lowest order, to be without.... Custom... has rendered leather shoes a necessary of life in England. The poorest creditable person of either sex would be ashamed to appear in public without them.[14]

In this view to be able to avoid shame, an eighteenth-century Englishman has to have leather shoes. It may be true that this situation has come to pass precisely because the typical members of that community happen to possess leather shoes, but the person in question needs leather shoes not so much to be *less ashamed* than others − that relative question is not even posed by Adam Smith − but simply not to be ashamed, which as an achievement is an absolute one.

5   Capabilities Contrasted with Commodities, Characteristics and Utilities

At this stage of this discussion I would like to take up a somewhat more general question, viz., that of the right focus for assessing standard of living. In my Tanner Lecture (given at Stanford Uni-

14. Smith (1776, pp. 351–2).

versity in 1979) and my Hennipman Lectures (given at the University of Amsterdam in 1982), I have tried to argue that the right focus is neither commodities, nor characteristics (in the sense of Gorman and Lancaster), nor utility, but something that may be called a person's capability.[15] The contrasts may be brought out by an illustration. Take a bicycle. It is, of course, a commodity. It has several characteristics, and let us concentrate on one particular characteristic, viz., transportation. Having a bike gives a person the ability to move about in a certain way that he may not be able to do without the bike. So the transportation *characteristic* of the bike gives the person the *capability* of moving in a certain way. That capability may give the person utility or happiness if he seeks such movement or finds it pleasurable. So there is, as it were, a *sequence* from a commodity (in this case a bike), to characteristics (in this case, transportation), to capability to function (in this case, the ability to move), to utility (in this case, pleasure from moving).

It can be argued that it is the third category — that of capability to function — that comes closest to the notion of standard of living. The commodity ownership or availability itself is not the right focus since it does not tell us what the person can, in fact, do. I may not be able to use the bike if — say — I happen to be handicapped. Having the bike — or something else with that characteristic — may provide the basis for a contribution to the standard of living, but it is not in itself a constituent part of that standard. On the other hand, while utility reflects the use of the bike, it does not concentrate on the use itself, but on the mental reaction to that use. If I am of a cheerful disposition and enjoy life even without being able to move around, because I succeed in having my heart leap up every time I behold a rainbow in the sky, I am no doubt a happy person, but it does not follow that I have a high standard of living. A grumbling rich man may well be less happy than a contented peasant, but he does have a higher standard of living than that peasant; the comparison of standard of living is not a comparison of utilities. So the constituent part of the standard of living is not the good, nor its characteristics, but the ability to do various things by using that good or those characteristics, and it is that ability rather than the mental reaction to that ability in the form of happiness that, in this view, reflects the standard of living.

---

15. Sen (1980, 1982b). Also Sen (1982a, Introduction, pp. 30–1).

6 Absolute Capabilities and Relative Commodity Requirements

If this thesis of the capability focus of standard of living is accepted (and I believe the case for it is quite strong), then several other things follow. One of them happens to be some sorting out of the absolute-relative disputation in the conceptualization of poverty. At the risk of oversimplification, I would like to say that poverty is an absolute notion in the space of capabilities but very often it will take a relative form in the space of commodities or characteristics.

Let us return to Adam Smith. The capability to which he was referring was the one of avoiding shame from the inability to meet the demands of convention.[16] The commodity needed for it, in a particular illustration that Smith considered, happened to be a pair of leather shoes. As we consider richer and richer commodities, the commodity requirement of the same capability — avoiding this type of shame — increases. As Adam Smith (1776) noted, 'the Greeks and Romans lived . . . very comfortably though they had no linen', but 'in the present time, through the greater part of Europe, a creditable day-labourer would be ashamed to appear in public without a linen shirt' (pp. 351-2). In the commodity space, therefore, escape from poverty in the form of avoiding shame requires a varying collection of commodities — and it is this collection and the resources needed for it that happen to be relative vis-à-vis the situations of others. But on the space of the capabilities themselves — the direct constituent of the standard of living — escape from poverty has an absolute requirement, to wit, avoidance of this type of shame. Not so much having equal shame as others, but just not being ashamed, absolutely.

If we view the problem of conceptualizing poverty in this light, then there is no conflict between the irreducible absolutist element in the notion of poverty (related to capabilities and the standard of living) and the 'thoroughgoing relativity' to which Peter Townsend refers, if the latter is interpreted as applying to commodities and

16. This particular capability, emphasized by Adam Smith, clearly has a strong psychological component in a way that other capabilities that have been thought to be basic may not have, e.g. the ability to be well nourished or to move about freely or to be adequately sheltered (see Sen, 1980). The contrast between capability and utility may, in some ways, be less sharp in the case of capabilities involving psychology, even though it would be impossible to catch the various psychological dimensions within the undifferentiated metric of utility (no matter whether defined in terms of pleasure and pain, or choice, or desire fulfilment). In fact, the capability of being happy can be seen as just one particular capability, and utility — shorn of its claim to unique relevance — can be given some room *within* the general approach of capabilities. These issues have been further discussed in Sen (1982b).

resources. If Townsend puts his finger wrong, this happens when he points towards the untenability of the idea of absolute needs. Of course, needs too can vary between one society and another, but the cases that are typically discussed in this context involve a different bundle of commodities and a higher real value of resources fulfilling the *same* general needs. When Townsend estimates the resources required for being able to 'participate in the activities of the community', he is in fact estimating the varying resource requirements of fulfilling the same absolute need.

In a poor community the resources or commodities needed to participate in the standard activities of the community might be very little indeed. In such a community the perception of poverty is primarily concerned with the commodity requirements of fulfilling nutritional needs and perhaps some needs of being clothed, sheltered and free from disease. This is the world of Charles Booth or Seebohm Rowntree in nineteenth-century or early twentieth-century London or York, and that of poverty estimation today, say, in India. The more physical needs tend to dominate over the needs of communal participation, on which Townsend focuses, at this less affluent stage both because the nutritional and other physical needs would tend to have a more prominent place in the standard-of-living estimation and also because the requirements of participation are rather easily fulfilled. For a richer community, however, the nutritional and other physical requirements (such as clothing as protection from climatic conditions) are typically already met, and the needs of communal participation – while absolutely no different in the space of capabilities – will have a much higher demand in the space of commodities and that of resources. Relative deprivation, in this case, is nothing other than a relative failure in the commodity space – or resource space – having the effect of an absolute deprivation in the capability space.

The varying commodity requirements of meeting the same absolute need applies not merely to avoiding shame from failing to meet conventional requirements, and to being able to participate in the activities of the community, but also to a number of other needs. It has been pointed out by Theo Cooper in a regrettably unpublished paper (Cooper, 1972) that in West Europe or North America a child might not be able to follow his school programme unless the child happens to have access to a television. If this is in fact the case, then the child without a television in Britain or in Ireland would be clearly worse off – have a lower standard of living – in this respect than a child, say, in Tanzania without a television. It is not so much that the British or the Irish child has a brand new need, but that to meet the same need as the Tanzanian child – the need to be educated – the British or the Irish child must have more commodities. Of course, the British child might fulfil the need better than the Tanzanian with the help of the television – I am not expressing a view on this – but the fact remains that the television is a necessity for the British child for school education in a way it is not for the Tanzanian child.

Similarly, in a society in which most families own cars, public transport services might be poor, so that a carless family in such a society might be *absolutely poor* in a way it might not have been in a poorer society. To take another example, widespread ownership of refrigerators and freezers in a community might affect the structure of food retailing, thereby making it more difficult in such a society to make do without having these facilities oneself.

It is, of course, not my point that there is no difference in the standards of living of rich and poor countries. There are enormous differences in the fulfilment of some of the most basic capabilities, e.g. to meet nutritional requirements, to escape avoidable disease, to be sheltered, to be clothed, to be able to travel, and to be educated. But whereas the commodity requirements of these capability fulfilments are not tremendously variable between one community and another, such variability is enormous in the case of other capabilities. The capability to live without shame emphasized by Adam Smith, that of being able to participate in the activities of the community discussed by Peter Townsend, that of having self-respect discussed by John Rawls,[17] are examples of capabilities with extremely variable resource requirements.[18] And as it happens the resource requirements typically go up in these cases with the average prosperity of the nation, so that the relativist view acquires plausibility despite the absolutist basis of the concept of poverty in terms of capabilities and deprivation.

It is perhaps worth remarking that this type of *derived* relativism does not run into the difficulties noted earlier with thoroughgoing relativity of the kind associated with seeing poverty as 'an issue of inequality'. When the Dutch in the hunger winter of 1944–45 found themselves suddenly in much reduced circumstances, their commodity requirements of capability fulfilments did not go down immediately to reduce the bite of poverty, as under the rigidly relativist account. While the commodity requirements are sensitive

17. Rawls (1971, pp. 440-6).
18. Education is perhaps an intermediate case, where the resource variability is important but perhaps not as extreme as with some of these other capabilities related to social psychology.

to the opulence and the affluence of the community in general, this relationship is neither one of instant adjustment, nor is it a straightforward one to be captured simply by looking at the average income, or even the current Lorenz curve of income distribution. Response to communal standards is a more complex process than that.

7   Primary Goods and Varying Requirements between and within Communities

I should also remark on a point of some general philosophical interest related to this way of viewing personal advantage and social poverty. The philosophical underpinning of the recent poverty literature has been helped enormously by John Rawls' far-reaching analysis of social justice. One respect in which Rawls differs sharply from the utility-based theories, e.g. utilitarianism, is his focus on what he calls 'primary goods' rather than on utility in judging a person's advantage. Our focus on capability differs *both* from the utilitarian concern with just mental reactions and from the Rawlsian concern with primary goods as such, though the approach of capabilities is much influenced by Rawls' moral analysis. Making comparisons in the capability space is quite different from doing that either in the utility space (as done by utilitarians), or in the space of commodities or primary goods (even when this is done very broadly, as Rawls does). In this view the variables to focus on consist of such factors as *meeting* nutritional requirements rather than either the pleasure from meeting those requirements (as under utilitarianism), or the *income* or *food* needed to meet those requirements (as in the Rawlsian approach). Similarly, the capability approach focuses on meeting the need of self-respect rather than *either* the pleasure from having self-respect, *or* what Rawls calls 'the social basis of self respect'.[19] The capability approach differs from the traditional utility-based analysis as strongly as the Rawlsian approach does, but it continues to concentrate on human beings – their capabilities in this case – rather than moving with Rawls to incomes, goods and characteristics.[20] Rawls himself motivated his focus on primary goods, using arguments that rely on the importance of capabilities.

19. Rawls (1971, pp. 60-5). Note, however, that Rawls vacillates between taking 'the *bases* of self-respect' as a primary good (this is consistent with taking income as a primary good), and referring to 'self-respect' itself as a primary good, which is closer to our concern with capabilities.

20. I have discussed this contrast more extensively in Sen (1980, 1982a: 30-1, 1982b). See also Rawls (1982, pp. 168-9).

What the capability approach does is to make that basis explicit and then it goes on to acknowledge the enormous variability that exists in the commodity requirements of capability fulfilment. In this sense, the capability approach can be seen as one possible *extension* of the Rawlsian perspective.

The extension makes a substantial practical difference not merely because the commodity requirements of capability fulfilment vary between one community and another, or one country and another, but also because there are differences *within* a given country or community in the mapping from commodities to capabilities. In a country with various racial groups, even the food requirements of nutritional fulfilment may vary a great deal from one group to another.[21] For example, in India the people in the state of Kerala have both the lowest level of average calorie intake in the country and the highest level of longevity and high nutritional fulfilment. While part of the difference is certainly due to distributional considerations and the availability of back-up medical services, the physiological differences in the calorie requirements of the Malayali in Kerala compared with, say, the larger Punjabi, is also a factor.

This type of *intra*-country or *intra*-community difference can be very important even in rich countries and even those with a basically homogeneous population. This is because of other variations, e.g. that of age. Of particular relevance in this context is the fact that a high proportion of those who are recognized as poor in the richer countries are also old or disabled in some way.[22] Inability to earn an adequate income often reflects a physical disadvantage of some kind, and this disadvantage is not irrelevant to the conversion of goods into capabilities. While the nutritional requirements may not increase with age or disability − may even decrease somewhat − the resource requirements of − say − movement, or of participation in the activities of the community, may be considerably larger for older or disabled people. The focus on absolute capabilities brings out the importance of these *intra*-community variations in the commodity space, going well beyond the *inter*-community variations emphasized in the typical relativist literature.

While it might not be easy to take full note of such intra-community variations in practical studies of poverty, it is important to have conceptual clarity on this question and to seek more sensitive practical measures in the long run. I should think the direction in

21. This is in addition to inter-individual and inter-temporal variations emphasized by Sukhatme (1977), Srinivasan (1979), and others. See also Scrimshaw (1977).
22. See Wedderburn (1961) and Atkinson (1970b).

which to go would be that of some kind of an efficiency-adjusted level of income with 'income' units reflecting command over capabilities rather than over commodities. This will be, I do not doubt, quite a rewarding field of research.

8 *Aggregate Poverty Measures and Relativities*

Even when incomes are not thus adjusted within a given country or community, conceptualization of poverty does, of course, involve more than just fixing a poverty line. I have so far said nothing at all on that question, and I should now briefly turn to it. The predicaments of people below the poverty line are not by any means homogeneous even when their respective abilities to convert commodities into capabilities are identical, since they differ from each other in the size of their respective shortfalls of income from the poverty line. Traditionally, poverty measurement has tried to make do with operating on two aggregate magnitudes, viz., the head-count ratio (i.e. the proportion of population below the poverty line) and the income-gap ratio (i.e. the average income shortfall of all the poor taken together as a proportion of the poverty line itself, or alternatively as a proportion of the mean income of the community). But it is easy to show that these two magnitudes taken together cannot capture poverty adequately since any sensible measure of poverty must be sensitive also to the distribution of that income shortfall among the poor. Bearing this in mind, several of us in recent years have tried to propose various distribution-sensitive measures of poverty.

The one I proposed in *Econometrica* of 1976 is based on an axiomatic structure that gets numerical weights from ordinal information regarding relative incomes much in the same way as Borda − in his theory of voting − obtained his rank-order method by converting ranks into weights. With such an axiomatization, and a chosen procedure of normalization, it can be shown that one gets a measure of poverty P that depends on three parameters, viz., the headcount ratio H, the income-gap ratio I as a proportion of the poverty line and the Gini coefficient G of the distribution of income among the poor:[23]

$$P = H[I + (1 - I)G]$$

23. Sen (1976a, Theorem 1). An earlier version, with slight axiomatic variations, was presented in Sen (1973).

Equivalently, this measure P can be expressed as a function of the head-count ratio H, the poverty line π, and the equally distributed equivalent income e^g of the poor (as defined by Kolm, 1969 and Atkinson, 1970a) using the Gini social evaluation function,[24]

$$P = H(\pi - e^g)/\pi$$

A generalization of this measure, proposed by Blackorby and Donaldson (1980) replaces the equally distributed equivalent income e^g based on the specific Gini social evaluation function by any member e of equally distributed equivalent incomes for a whole class of such social evaluation functions:

$$P = H(\pi - e)/\pi$$

Other variations have also been proposed by such authors as Kakwani; Takayama; Hamada and Takayama; Anand; Osmani; Thon; Szal; Fields; Pyatt; Clark, Hemming and Ulph; Foster; Foster, Greer and Thorbecke; Chakravarty; Foster and Shorrocks; and others.[25]

I do not propose to discuss here the various properties of these different variants. But there is one slightly contrary property that is worth a comment because it links up with the absolute–relative question with which this lecture has been concerned. In presenting my measure in *Econometrica* 1976, I expressed some support for the view that the poverty measure must satisfy an adapted version of the so-called Pigou–Dalton condition of transfer, to wit, any transfer of income to a poor person from a person who is richer must reduce the recorded poverty level. This axiom was not used in deriving my measure P, and indeed as I noted the following year in *Econometrica*, it is possible for the measure P to violate this Pigou–Dalton condition, albeit in rather rare circumstances.[26] It turns out that all the variants of this measure mentioned above – with a few exceptions involving other unattractive characteristics – can also violate the Pigou–Dalton condition.[27] For the violation result to hold it is necessary – though not sufficient – that the transfer from the rich person should make him fall from above to below the poverty line as a consequence of the transfer. Is this violation of the Pigou–Dalton transfer condition a disturbing characteristic?

24. On the Gini social evaluation function, see Sen (1974, 1976b) and Hammond (1978). On related issues, see Graaff (1977), Kakwani (1980) and Roberts (1980).
25. Many of these variations are discussed in Sen (1981, Chapter 3 and Appendix C), and in Sen (1982a, Introduction, pp. 31–6).
26. Sen (1977, p. 77).
27. Sen (1981, Appendix C).

The Pigou–Dalton condition is certainly an appealing one as a requirement of a measure of *inequality*, and this is indeed how it has been used by Kolm (1969) and Atkinson (1970a), and how it has been related to the property of *S*-concavity in a paper on economic inequality by Dasgupta, Starrett and myself.[28] But does this make sense for a measure of poverty as opposed to inequality? If one takes the thoroughgoing relativist view that poverty is nothing other than 'an issue in equality', as Miller and Roby put it, then clearly the Pigou–Dalton axiom must be unexceptionable as a restriction on permissible poverty measures.[29] But if the absolutist view is taken, then the poverty line is not just a reflection of some relative characteristic of the distributional statistics, but represents a line with some absolute justification of its own. For example, in the capability view, the poverty line may be defined to represent the level at which a person can not only meet nutritional requirements, etc., but also achieve adequate participation in communal activities (as characterized by Townsend) and be free from public shame from failure to satisfy conventions (as discussed by Adam Smith). In this case if a transfer drags a person from above to below that threshold while reducing the income gap of a poorer person, it is not obvious that the overall poverty measure must invariably be expected to decline. The poverty line has some absolute significance and to cross it is a change of some importance. Thus, the absolutist approach to conceptualizing poverty – even though it involves a relativist reflection in the commodity space – will tend to reject the invariable insistence on the Pigou–Dalton condition of transfer when such a transfer changes the number of people below the poverty line.

There is a weaker version of the transfer axiom, which I called the Weak Transfer Axiom,[30] which insists on the Pigou–Dalton condition being invariably satisfied whenever the transfer to the poor person from the richer person does not change the number below the poverty line, and this of course is fully consistent with the absolutist approach, and is indeed satisfied by the measure P and most of its variants.†

9 Concluding Remarks

I end with a few concluding statements. First, I have argued that despite the emerging unanimity in favour of taking a relative as

† [The recent literature on the measurement of poverty has been illuminatingly surveyed and assessed by James E. Foster, 'On Economic Poverty: A Survey of Aggregate Measures', forthcoming in *Advances in Econometrics*, Vol. III (JAI Press).]

28. Dasgupta, Sen and Starrett (1973). See also Rothschild and Stiglitz (1973).

29. This will, of course, not be the case when there are efficiency differences in converting resources into capability, as discussed above.

30. See Sen (1977, p. 77), and also Sen (1981, p. 186).

opposed to an absolute view of poverty, there is a good case for an absolutist approach. The dispute on absolute vs. relative conceptualization of poverty can be better resolved by being more explicit on the particular space (e.g. commodities, incomes or capabilities) in which the concept is to be based.

Second, I have outlined the case for using an absolute approach to poverty related to the notion of *capability*. Capabilities differ both from commodities and characteristics, on the one hand, and utilities, on the other. The capability approach shares with John Rawls the rejection of the utilitarian obsession with one type of mental reaction, but differs from Rawls' concentration on primary goods by focusing on capabilities of human beings rather than characteristics of goods they possess.

Third, an absolute approach in the space of capabilities translates into a relative approach in the space of commodities, resources and incomes in dealing with some important capabilities, such as avoiding shame from failure to meet social conventions, participating in social activities, and retaining self-respect.

Fourth, since poverty removal is not the only object of social policy and inequality removal has a status of its own, taking an absolutist view of poverty must not be confused with being indifferent to inequality as such. While poverty may be seen as a failure to reach some absolute level of capability, the issue of inequality of capabilities is an important one – on its own right – for public policy.[31]

Fifth, while the inter-country and inter-community differences have been much discussed in the context of conceptualizing poverty, the differences *within* a country and *within* a community need much more attention because of interpersonal variations in converting commodities into capabilities. This is particularly important since poverty is often associated with handicaps due to disability or age. This problem could perhaps be handled by using efficiency-income units reflecting command over capabilities rather than command over goods and services.

Finally, I have argued that the reasonableness of various axioms that aggregative measures of poverty may or may not be asked to satisfy depend (sometimes in an unobvious – certainly unexplored – way) on whether fundamentally a relative or an absolute approach is being adopted. This has practical implications on the choice of statistical measures to be used. It is important to know whether the poor, relatively speaking, are in some deeper sense absolutely deprived. It makes a difference.

31. See Sen (1980, 1982b).

References

Abel-Smith, B. and Townsend, P. (1965): *The Poor and the Poorest* (London: Bell).

Atkinson, A. B. (1970a): 'On the Measurement of Inequality', *Journal of Economic Theory*, 2.

—— (1970b): *Poverty in Britain and the Reform of Social Security* (Cambridge: Cambridge University Press).

Aykroyd, W. R. (1974): *The Conquest of Famine* (London: Chatto and Windus).

Beckerman, W. and Clark, S. (1982): *Poverty and Social Security in Britain Since 1961* (Oxford: Oxford University Press).

Berthoud, R. and Brown, J. C. with Cooper, S. (1981): *Poverty and the Development of Anti-Poverty Policy in the UK* (London: Heinemann).

Blackorby, C. and Donaldson, D. (1980): 'Ethical Indices for the Measurement of Poverty', *Econometrica*, 48.

Bull, D. (ed.) (1971): *Family Poverty* (London: Duckworth).

Cooper, T. C. (1971): 'Poverty', unpublished note, St Hugh's College, Oxford.

Dasgupta, P., Sen, A. and Starrett, D. (1973): 'Notes on the Measurement of Inequality', *Journal of Economic Theory*, 6.

Fiegehen, G. C., Lansley, P. S. and Smith, A. D. (1977): *Poverty and Progress in Britain 1953–73* (Cambridge: Cambridge University Press).

Graaff, J. de V. (1977): 'Equity and Efficiency as Components of General Welfare', *South African Journal of Economics*, 45.

Hammond, P. J. (1978): 'Economic Welfare with Rank Order Price Weighting', *Review of Economic Studies*, 45.

Hirsch, F. (1976): *Social Limits to Growth* (Cambridge, Mass.: Harvard University Press).

Kakwani, N. (1980): *Income, Inequality and Poverty* (New York: Oxford University Press).

Kolm, Ch. S. (1969): 'The Optimal Production of Social Justice', in Margolis, J. and Guitton, H. (eds), *Public Economics* (London: Macmillan).

Miller, S. M., Rein, M., Roby, P. and Cross, B. (1967): 'Poverty, Inequality and Conflict', *Annals of the American Academy of Political Science*.

Miller, S. M. and Roby, P. (1971): 'Poverty: Changing Social Stratification', in Townsend, P. (ed.), *The Concept of Poverty* (London: Heinemann).

Rawls, J. (1971): *A Theory of Justice* (Cambridge, Mass.: Harvard University Press, and Oxford: Clarendon Press).

—— (1982): 'Social Unity and Primary Goods', in Sen, A. and Williams, B. (eds), *Utilitarianism and Beyond* (Cambridge: Cambridge University Press).

Roberts, K. (1980): 'Price Independent Welfare Prescriptions', *Journal of Public Economics*, 13.

Rothschild, M. and Stiglitz, J. E. (1973): 'Some Further Results in the Measurement of Inequality', *Journal of Economic Theory*, 6.

Rowntree, Seebohm B. and Lavers, G. R. (1951): *Poverty and the Welfare State* (London: Longmans).

Scrimshaw, N. S. (1977): 'Effect of Infection on Nutrition Requirements', *American Journal of Clinical Nutrition*, **30**.

Sen, A. K. (1973): 'Poverty, Inequality and Unemployment: Some Conceptual Issues in Measurement', *Economic and Political Weekly*, **8**.

—— (1974): 'Informational Bases of Alternative Welfare Approaches: Aggregation and Income Distribution', *Journal of Public Economics*, **4**.

—— (1976a): 'Poverty: An Ordinal Approach to Measurement', *Econometrica*, **44**; reprinted in Sen (1982a).

—— (1976b): 'Real National Income', *Review of Economic Studies*, **43**; reprinted in Sen (1982a).

—— (1977): 'Social Choice Theory: A Re-Examination', *Econometrica*, **45**; reprinted in Sen (1982a).

—— (1980): 'Equality of What?' in McMurrin, S. (ed.), *The Tanner Lectures on Human Values* (Cambridge: Cambridge University Press); reprinted in Sen (1982a).

—— (1981): *Poverty and Famines: An Essay on Entitlement and Deprivation* (Oxford: Clarendon Press).

—— (1982a): *Choice, Welfare and Measurement* (Oxford: Blackwell, and Cambridge, Mass.: MIT Press).

—— (1982b): *Commodities and Capabilities*, Hennipman Lecture given on 22 April 1982; to be published by North-Holland, Amsterdam.

Smith, Adam (1776): *An Inquiry into the Nature and Causes of the Wealth of Nations* (Everyman Edition: London: Home University Library).

Srinivasan, T. N. (1979): 'Malnutrition: Some Measurement and Policy Issues', mimeographed, World Bank, Washington, DC.

Stein, Z., Susser, M., Saenger, G. and Marolla, F. (1975): *Famine and Human Development: The Dutch Hunger Winter of 1944-1945* (London: Oxford University Press).

Sukhatme, P. V. (1977): *Nutrition and Poverty* (New Delhi: Indian Agricultural Research Institute).

Townsend, P. (1962): 'The Meaning of Poverty', *British Journal of Sociology*, **8**.

—— (1979a): *Poverty in the United Kingdom* (London: Allen Lane and Penguin Books).

—— (1979b): 'The Development of Research on Poverty', in Department of Health and Social Security, *Social Security Research: The Definition and Measurement of Poverty* (London: HMSO).

US President's Commission on Income Maintenance (1969): *Poverty amid Plenty* (Washington, DC: US Government Printing Office).

Wedderburn, Dorothy (1961): *The Aged in the Welfare State* (London: Bell).

—— (1962): 'Poverty in Britain Today – The Evidence', *Sociological Review*, **10**.

15

Family and Food: Sex Bias in Poverty

The food consumption of a person depends among other things, on (1) the power of the family to command food, and (2) the division of food within the family. The former variable I have tried to examine in an earlier series of studies (Sen, 1976, 1977a, 1981a, 1981b), concentrating particularly – though not exclusively – on famines and acute starvation. The studies used what was called 'the entitlement approach', focusing on ways and means through which a family can acquire bundles of commodities, making use of the legal, economic, social and political opportunities faced by the family. Starvation was seen in this context as resulting from a failure of entitlement.

Entitlements of families do not, however, determine what a particular member of the family can eat. The division of food within the family can be a variable of importance of its own. Governed by mores, conventions and other factors, there may be various patterns of distribution within the family. It is with this problem of division of food within the family that this paper is concerned. It concentrates on the elementary question of the presence or absence of sex-bias in the distribution of food within the family. There is no attempt at causal analysis here, though I have tried to go into that question elsewhere.[1]

I am grateful for support from the Leverhulme Trust, which provided me with the invaluable research assistance of Ms Jocelyn Kynch. I have also received help and advice from Professor P. Bardhan, Professor N. S. Deodhar, Professor B. N. Ghosh, Dr Ashok Mitra, Dr G. C. Pine, Dr Sukumar Sinha and Professor T. N. Srinivasan. The paper was written in 1981 for a projected volume of essays to be edited by P. Bardhan and T. N. Srinivasan, which is to be called *Rural Poverty in South Asia*. I have made a few small alterations to reflect the passage of time since the paper was written, including referring to some work that has been done following this paper.

1. Sen (1983a, 1983b), Kynch and Sen (1983) and Sen and Sengupta (1983). These studies have followed up some issues raised in this paper.

A slightly revised version of a paper written in 1981 for P. Bardhan and T. N. Srinivasan (eds), *Rural Poverty in South Asia*, which is still (I understand) forthcoming.

The regional concentration of this paper is on Bengal, more specifically on West Bengal in India, even though I shall have some things to say also about the other part of Bengal, viz. Bangladesh. But despite this relatively narrow regional focus, the main analysis may possibly be of some relevance in understanding poverty and malnutrition in the Third World in general. It also has implications for economic theory related to welfare economics, normative statistics, household economics and planning.

1   Intra-family Disparities

There is a good deal of evidence from all over the world that food is often distributed very unequally within the family – with a distinct sex bias (against the female) and also an age bias (against the children). Such biases have been observed even in the richer countries,[2] but the picture of discrimination is, of course, much sharper and more widespread in the poorer Third World economies. Evidences of sex bias and age bias in the distribution of food within the family are indeed plentiful (see the survey of den Hartog, 1973, and Schofield, 1975), and come from different parts of the world, including Africa,[3] Asia[4] and Latin America.[5]

However, many of the more striking case studies are of the anecdotal variety, so that it is difficult to decide how much weight to attach to them. Also, the information is very often 'directional' (e.g. noting that women get less) rather than quantitative (e.g. how much less?). Given the nature of the comparison, hard, quantitative information is indeed difficult to get. Who eats how much in a family is a part of the private life of a family, and there is little possibility of an observer coming and measuring precisely what is happening, without affecting the phenomenon to be observed.

Nevertheless, there have been several careful studies, and two in particular related to Bangladesh deserve special attention. The Institute of Nutrition and Food Science of the University of Dacca

2. See, for example, Ritchie (1963) on the food consumption behaviour of Scottish mining families during the last World War, and that of US mining families during the depression of the thirties. See also Spring Rice (1939).

3. See, for example, Thomson (1954), Nicol (1959), Davey (1962a, 1962b), McFie (1967), Bohdal, Gibbs and Simmons (1968), University of Ibadan (1970), Crawford and Thorbecke (1980).

4. Postmus and Van Veen (1949), Mathur, Wahi, Shrivastava and Gahlaut (1961), Blankhart (1967), Government of Pakistan (1970), Institute of Nutrition and Food Science, Dacca (1977), D'Souza and Chen (1980) and Chen, Huq and D'Souza (1980).

5. Flores, Garcia, Florez and Lara (1964), Foster (1966), Flores, Menchu, Lara and Guzman (1970).

TABLE 15.1   Calorie and protein intake by age and sex in Matlab, Bangladesh
(June–August 1978)

| Age (years) | Calories | | | Protein (grams) | | |
	Male	Female	Female shortfall (−) (percentage)	Male	Female	Female shortfall (−) (percentage)
0–4	809	694	−14	23.0	20.2	−12
5–14	1590	1430	−10	50.9	41.6	−18
15–44	2700	2099	−22	73.6	58.8	−20
45+	2630	1634	−38	71.8	46.9	−35
Total	1927	1599	−17	55.0	45.5	−17

Source: Chen, Huq and D'Souza (1980).

did a sample survey during 1975–76 of 60 households each from 12 locations in rural Bangladesh.[6] Chen, Huq and D'Souza (1980) also did a study, in 1978, of intra-family food allocation in 135 families residing in four villages in Matlab Thana in Bangladesh.[7]

Table 15.1 presents the results of the Chen, Huq and D'Souza study. In every age group the female members seem to consume less calories and less protein than the male members, with an overall shortfall of 17 per cent in each of these two nutrients. The disparity is particularly large for later age groups with the 45+ having a 38 per cent calorie shortfall and a 35 per cent protein shortfall.

Table 15.2 presents the results of the survey by the Institute of Nutrition and Food Science of Dacca University. The age classification is finer, even though there is no sex classification for children (under 10). The sex bias is seen in every age group for both calories and proteins, with the disparity reaching its peak for the oldest group, viz. 70+. The next highest contrast comes in the adolescent

6. From a total of about 5000 'census circles' in the 1974 Bangladesh census, 160 were selected at random. These 160 circles, each containing 10–14 villages, were then arranged into four groups 'according to the four major administrative divisions of the country' (Chittagong, Dacca, Rajshahi and Khulna). Then three census circles were selected in each of these divisions by a sampling method based on the total population of the census circles. Then from each of these census circles a single village was selected at random. A total of 12 'locations' was thus obtained, and 60 households were studied in each location.

7. The families were selected 'purposefully' using the criteria of households (a) having one or more children under 5 years, (b) being accessible for practical organization of dietary observation, and (c) grouped according to landownership ('landless', 'marginal' and 'surplus').

TABLE 15.2 Calorie and protein intake by age and sex in rural Bangladesh (1975-76)

Age (years)	Calories			Protein (grams)		
	Male	Female	Female shortfall (−) (percentage)	Male	Female	Female shortfall (−) (percentage)
10-12	1989	1780	−11	56.6	52.7	−7
13-15	2239	1919	−14	61.2	53.9	−12
16-19	3049	2110	−31	83.3	55.8	−33
20-39	2962	2437	−18	82.0	66.6	−19
40-49	2866	2272	−21	79.8	65.3	−18
50-59	2702	2193	−19	78.2	60.3	−23
60-69	2564	2088	−19	72.7	58.1	−20
70+	2617	1463	−44	72.4	40.9	−44

Source: Institute of Nutrition and Food Science, Dacca (1977).

years of 16-19. It is not, of course, possible to compare the exact age patterns of disparity in the reported results of the two surveys, since the age classifications are quite different in the two studies.

These tables are, however, far from compelling in establishing that there exists any clear sex bias in Bangladesh rural consumption of food. The difficulty rests not just in possible doubts about the representative nature of the two samples, but also in the fact that the so-called 'requirements' of food may be different for males and females. Indeed, the Institute study postulates food requirements that have the effect of showing that typically men are *more* deprived compared with women in terms of the relation of food intake vis-à-vis 'requirements'. This is shown in Table 15.3. The female intake shortfall is, in every case other than that for children between 10 and 12 years of age, less than the 'requirement' gap.[8] Indeed, from these Institute figures it would look as if the females have no deficit compared with requirements after the age of 15, and even before 15 their deficits − substantial as they are − are equal to or less than that of males. In fact, throughout the age range between

8. The nutritional 'deficit' of the children is marked. The average calorie intakes of children of age groups 1-3, 4-6 and 7-9 years are respectively 630 ('requirement' 1360), 1172 ('requirement' 1830) and 1497 ('requirement' 2190). The disproportionately high mortality rates of children in Bangladesh has been analysed by McIntosh, Nasim and Satchell (1981).

TABLE 15.3   Calorie intake vis-à-vis alleged requirement by age and sex in rural Bangladesh (1975–76)

Age (years)	Male			Female			Female 'requirement' gap (−) (percentage)	Female intake shortfall (−) (percentage)
	Intake	'Requirement'	Percentage 'deficit' (−) or 'excess' (+)	Intake	'Requirement'	Percentage 'deficit' (−) or 'excess' (+)		
10–12	1989	2600	−24	1780	2350	−24	−10	−11
13–15	2239	2753	−19	1919	2224	−14	−19	−14
16–19	3049	3040	0	2110	2066	+2	−32	−31
20–39	2962	3122	−5	2437	1988	+23	−36	−18
40–49	2866	2831	+1	2272	1870	+21	−34	−21
50–59	2702	2554	+6	2193	1771	+24	−31	−19
60–69	2569	2270	+13	2088	1574	+33	−31	−19
70+	2617	1987	+32	1463	1378	+6	−31	−44

Source: Institute of Nutrition and Food Science, Dacca (1977).

20 and 69 the women seem to have intakes greatly in excess of their 'requirements'. Men do far less well, and the tables seem to be turned.

The nutritional requirement figures used in these Institute estimates have distinguished lineage, viz. the recommendations of FAO/WHO Expert Committee (1973).[9] But distinction is a different virtue from accuracy, and there are by now a great many doubts about the whole basis of nutritional requirement calculations.[10] There seems to be a substantial amount of interpersonal variability, and even for a given person much variation over time. Also possibilities of 'multiple equilibria' of energy intake and use – at various levels of consumption – seem to exist. Furthermore, there are good reasons to dispute the assumptions about the energy use of activities performed by women, which are not as 'sedentary' as calorie calculations tend to assume.[11] Also the extra nutrition requirements of the pregnant women and lactating mothers require fuller acknowledgement.

Finally, there is a great danger of circular reasoning in linking calorie 'requirements' to physical characteristics, since energy 'requirements' are calculated by multiplying the body weight by 'energy requirement per kg body weight',[12] related to the activity level, while the person's body weight as well as his or her activity level does depend crucially on the energy intake of the person.[13] Calorie deficiency can, up to a point, justify itself!

Chen, Huq and D'Souza (1980) carry out rather different corrections – though also based on body weight and activity level – and come to the general conclusion that 'for all age groups, male : female intake to requirement ratios are at near parity, although marked male predominance persists among the young children', though they also warn that 'these adjustments are illustrative rather than precise' (p. 10). In fact, it is very doubtful that given the theoretical problems and practical obscurities, the comparison of intake-requirement ratios throws much light on the relative positions of men and women in the division of food within the family.

It may be more useful to look at the actual consequences of food disparity rather than trying to compare the intake disparity with

9. See also WHO (1974).

10. See, for example, Sukhatme (1977, 1978), Scrimshaw (1977), Srinivasan (1977, 1979); also Davidson, Passmore, Brock and Truswell (1979).

11. Chen, Huq and D'Souza (1980) blame 'faulty national statistics on women's work and lack of quantitative information on the energy demands of household and home-based work' (p. 10). See also Farouk and Ali (1977).

12. Institute of Nutrition and Food Science, Dacca (1977, p. 31).

13. On the complex relationships between work and food, see Bliss and Stern (1978).

the 'requirement' disparity. This pushes us in the direction of anthropometric comparisons and also towards contrasting morbidity and mortality related to nutritional deficiency. There is indeed some evidence of greater incidence of malnutrition among female children than male children in rural Bangladesh.[14] There is some evidence also of excess female mortality among children, and a suggestion that ' "excess" female mortality was consistently higher during the food shortage years 1974–75 vis-à-vis 1975–77'.[15]

2 Floods and Undernutrition: Rural West Bengal 1978–79

There were damaging floods in West Bengal during August–October 1978, affecting 30,000 square kilometres, with a population of 15 million, of whom – it is estimated – that 3.5 million lost their livelihood because of crop destruction and reduction of employment.[16] There was quite an extensive and efficient flood relief programme carried out by the state government. In connection with that work an extensive survey was carried out in 1979 of all the children registered in four child-care centres – selected at random – in each 'block', choosing five blocks out of 30,[17] also by random method.

Undernutrition of the children was studied in terms of 'weight for age', following the conventional standard adopted by the Indian Academy of Pediatrics, classifying the children into four groups, viz, 'normal', and suffering respectively from Grades I, II and III undernutrition.[18] Using these data, Table 15.4 has been constructed, partitioning the children into three groups: (1) Grade III (severe undernutrition), (2) Grades III and II (substantial to severe undernutrition), (3) Grades III, II and I (moderate, substantial or severe undernutrition), and (4) normal. The children are classified into these categories for each 12-month age group (i.e. 0–12, 13–24, etc.). Total number of observations in each age group is also recorded in Table 15.4.

The picture that emerges from this is one of uniformly larger incidence of undernutrition among female children compared with the male. There is only one exception to it, viz. age group 61–72

14. See Table 7.7 in Institute of Nutrition and Food Science, Dacca (1977).
15. Chen, Huq and D'Souza (1980, p. 9).
16. See UNICEF (1981).
17. The combined population of the 30 blocks is 4.2 million.
18. These standards were determined in the Hyderabad meeting of the Nutrition Subcommittee of the Indian Academy of Pediatrics in 1972.

TABLE 15.4 Extent of 1979 malnutrition among children in five rural blocks affected by 1978 floods in West Bengal (percentage of respective age and sex group)

| | Age in months | | | | | | | | | | | | | |
| | 0–12 | | 13–24 | | 25–36 | | 37–48 | | 49–60 | | 61–72 | | Total | |
Grades of malnutrition	male	female	male	female	male	female	male	female	male	female	male	female	male	female
Grade III	7.1	11.3	18.2	26.2	9.4	16.6	6.0	10.5	6.5	7.6	4.1	10.3	9.2	14.6
Grades III and II	21.4	27.8	42.2	56.5	35.7	48.2	29.6	47.4	30.8	37.2	18.9	41.0	31.8	44.6
Grades III, II and I	59.5	75.2	87.0	89.3	79.0	84.6	70.8	74.2	69.8	73.1	67.6	66.7	73.9	79.4
Normal	40.5	24.8	13.0	10.7	21.0	15.4	29.2	25.8	30.2	26.9	32.4	33.3	26.1	20.6
Total (number)	126	133	192	168	224	247	216	190	169	145	74	39	1001	922

Source: Based on data presented in UNICEF (1980) sample Survey Report.

months, in the aggregate category of Grades III, II and I undernutrition, and the gap there is slight (67.6 per cent for males vis-à-vis
66.7 per cent for females). In every other comparison − 17 in all −
the level of undernutrition of girls exceeds − often by far − that of
boys of comparable age. Indeed, even for the age group 61–72
months the incidence of severe (Grade III) undernutrition is much
greater for females (10.3 per cent vis-à-vis 4.1 per cent for males) and
the same contrast holds for substantial to severe (Grades III and II)
undernutrition (41.0 per cent vis-à-vis 18.9 per cent for males). The
figures are also represented in diagrammatic form in Figure 15.1 for
visual comparison.

It should be remarked that these comparisons do not suffer from
some of the difficulties noted in the last section concerning food-
intake studies. They deal with *results* of food-intake rather than
with the quantities of food-intake itself, and the doubtful concept
of 'food requirement' does not have to be invoked. In Section 4 the
contrast between the two approaches will be taken up at a more
general level.

On the other hand, it should be noted that the comparisons refer
to a distress situation − one following severe flooding and coinciding
with unusual economic deprivation. In fact, a relatively small survey
of rural households from *all parts* of West Bengal, carried out earlier
in 1978, indicated a markedly greater incidence of undernutrition
(in terms of weight for age) among boys vis-à-vis girls in the 1–5
year age group.[19] Indeed, in terms of the alleged normally superior
performance of girls, the substantially greater incidence of undernutrition among girls in a situation of economic distress is particularly striking.

3   Differential Morbidity: Calcutta 1976–78

The Calcutta Metropolitan Development Authority carried out
surveys of health and socioeconomic conditions in greater Calcutta
during 1976–78. The findings can be used for comparison of male
and female morbidity in Calcutta and its immediate vicinity. This is
a large settlement, with 3.31 million people living in Calcutta proper,

---

19. See National Institute of Nutrition, Hyderabad (1979, Tables 24 and 25). The better
performance of girls holds for every one of the ten Indian States that were covered, except
for Madhya Pradesh, for one category ('severe') malnutrition. However, the samples are
small, e.g. in West Bengal only 518 children were surveyed from the whole state (in contrast
with 1923 children from only 30 blocks in flood-affected districts in West Bengal in the
1979 UNICEF survey).

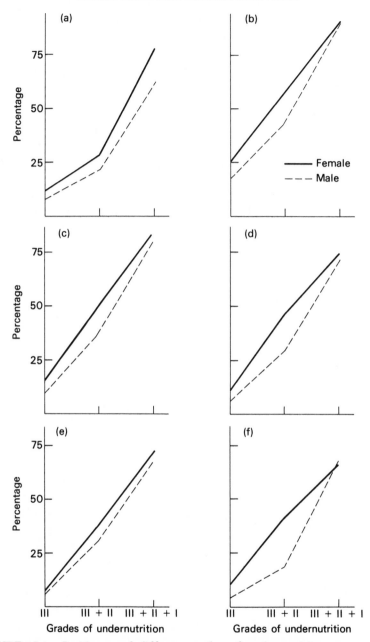

FIGURE 15.1 *Incidence of different grades of undernutrition among rural children in flood-affected West Bengal, 1979, by age (see Table 15.4): (a) 0–12 months, (b) 13–24 months, (c) 25–36 months, (d) 37–48 months, (e) 49–60 months, (f) 61–72 months*

1.28 million in the adjacent town of Howrah, 1.01 million people in the town of Hooghly and 4.72 million in other adjacent towns and villages, forming a total urban complex of 10.33 million people (in early 1978). Greater Calcutta has the reputation of being noticeably the poorest large city in the world.

The survey, which was conducted in collaboration with the Indian Statistical Institute and the Department of Health of the Government of West Bengal, was based on a stratified multi-stage sampling scheme. Altogether 4728 households were surveyed out of an estimated total of 2.19 million households, representing 0.22 per cent coverage.

While undernutrition data were not directly covered, morbidity information was gathered and analysed. Table 15.5 presents comparative morbidity incidence of males and females in different parts of greater Calcutta, classified according to age groups. Three general categories were used, viz. 'well', 'indifferent' and 'ill'. Table 15.5 (and Figure 15.2) present percentages of ill people in each category, as well as percentages of people who were either ill or in indifferent health.

These categorized data – based on interviewing – have some obvious defects, but the survey was carefully done, and it is interesting to see the picture that emerges from them for the poorest city of the world. The pattern is a mixed one, but there is a higher level of female morbidity compared with male morbidity in most regions except for the very young (14 and below).[20]

There are also data for the slum-dwellers in Calcutta. Table 15.6 presents the figures for two types of 'bustees' – the 'unimproved' and the 'improved' (with certain amenities provided). With very few exceptions, female morbidity in terms of both categories (viz. 'ill' and 'ill or indifferent') emerge as being appreciably higher than male morbidity in each age group.

It is not, of course, by any means obvious that morbidity is primarily the result of malnutrition. But malnutrition is one of the factors in morbidity, and the pattern of deprivation in food may well go together with other types of deprivation. In any case, for what it is worth, the morbidity picture – possibly providing some indirect evidence of nutritional disparity – gives some reason to expect discrimination against the female, though the pattern here is not at all as clear as the pattern of malnutrition among the children in the flood-affected regions of rural West Bengal (Section 2 above).

20. It is worth noting here that there is very often a tendency towards under-reporting of female morbidity. See Sen (1982).

TABLE 15.5 Incidence of poor health conditions of usual male and female residents of the CMDA area (percentage of each age-sex group)

	Health	Age in years last birthday											
		14 and below		15–25		26–45		46–60		61 and above		All ages	
		male	female	male	female	male	female	male	female	male	female	male	female
(a) North Calcutta	ill	1	1	1	1	0	1	1	2	8	9	1.0	1.7
	ill and indifferent	37	35	16	25	15	38	38	56	63	68	25.9	37.3
(b) Central Calcutta	ill	2	3	2	4	1	3	5	6	4	14	2.0	3.8
	ill and indifferent	31	29	15	33	23	39	39	50	67	68	27.1	36.7
(c) South Calcutta	ill	2	3	1	1	2	3	1	2	4	7	1.6	2.7
	ill and indifferent	20	21	5	13	13	31	15	44	50	62	14.8	27.0
(d) Total Calcutta	ill	1	3	2	2	1	2	3	4	4	8	1.6	2.8
	ill and indifferent	30	30	13	25	18	37	32	47	58	67	23.6	34.4
(e) Howrah and municipal towns	ill	3	2	2	1	1	2	3	2	6	5	2.0	2.0
	ill and indifferent	35	34	23	33	23	47	47	57	78	73	31.4	41.0
(f) Other towns and villages	ill	2	1	1	0	1	2	2	0	15	8	1.9	1.5
	ill and indifferent	20	20	13	15	14	35	32	47	65	64	19.9	27.0
(g) Total CMDA area	ill	2	2	2	1	1	2	3	2	5	9	1.9	2.2
	ill and indifferent	29	28	18	26	19	40	39	49	64	70	26.1	34.7

Source: CMDA (1980). The columns for 'all ages' are based on Table 71 of the general report, while the other columns are derived from Table 202 of Part III of 'Tables with Notes'. The latter are reconstructed from an overall percentage breakdown, and to avoid spurious precision, are recorded only as percentage whole numbers.

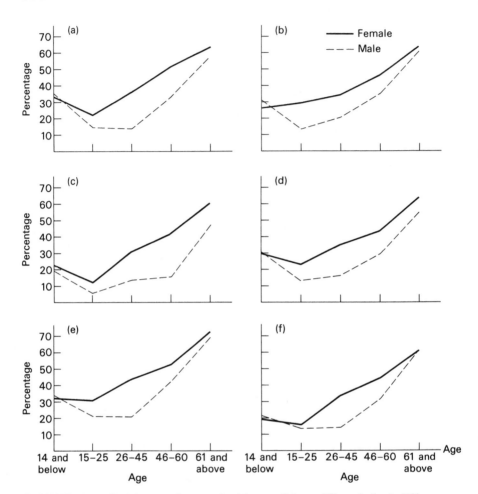

FIGURE 15.2 *Incidence of poor health conditions (ill and in indifferent health) in the CMDA area by district: (a) North Calcutta, (b) Central Calcutta, (c) South Calcutta, (d) Calcutta (total), (e) Howrah and municipal towns, (f) Other towns and villages in the CMDA area*

Finally, the figures relating to the slums have the advantage of concentrating on an economically deprived group. The over-all figures for the normal residents of greater Calcutta, presented in Table 15.5, aggregate over a very wide range of income groups. This is a source of some possible bias, since sex distribution might well be related to the income level, particularly in view of the large number of migrant (often out-of-state) male labourers who work in Calcutta

TABLE 15.6 Incidence of poor health conditions of usual male and female residents in the improved and unimproved bustees in CMDA (percentage of each age-sex group)

		14 and below		15-25		26-45		46-60		61 and above		All ages	
Health		*male*	*female*	*male*	*female*	*male*	*female*	*male*	*female*	*male*	*female*	*male*	*female*
Improved bustees	ill	3	5	–	–	1	3	–	3	–	18	1.4	4.0
	ill and indifferent	22	27	17	18	24	56	40	67	44	53	24.4	38.6
Unimproved bustees	ill	1	1	2	1	–	4	6	3	–	–	1.1	1.6
	ill and indifferent	36	38	13	21	21	52	37	61	65	80	27.5	41.1

Age in years last birthday

Source: The columns for 'all ages' are based on Table LI of Seal *et al.* (1981). The other columns are derived from Table 202 of Part III of 'Tables with Notes' of CMDA (1980), and being reconstructed from an over-all percentage breakdown, are recorded only as percentage whole numbers, to avoid spurious precision. Dash (–) stands for zero or negligible.

TABLE 15.7 Incidence of poor health conditions of usual male and female residents of the CMDA area by per capita household expenditure groups (percentage of each sex-expenditure group)

| | Per capita monthly expenditure group (Rupees per month) | | | | | | | |
| | 0–54 | | 55–128 | | 129 and above | | Total | |
	male	female	male	female	male	female	male	female
Ill	2.4	2.5	1.8	2.2	1.6	2.0	1.9	2.2
Ill and indifferent	30.6	34.6	26.5	37.1	21.7	28.4	26.0	34.7

Source: Table 73 of the general report of CMDA (1980).

and have their families back in the village. The CMDA data do, however, cover monthly household expenditures per capita of the households surveyed. Table 15.7 presents the picture for the different expenditure groups (see also Figure 15.3). As is to be expected, the incidence of illness typically goes down with rise in household per capita expenditure – a rough index of economic prosperity – but the females have consistently greater morbidity in *each* expenditure group.

4 Implications for Economic Analysis and Policy

The existence of substantial intra-family disparities would have serious implication on economic analyses of many different types. The family is often the decision-making unit for work and consumption. If these decisions are based on systematic discrimination between different members of the family it becomes difficult to relate these decisions to individual welfare.[21]

This particular problem is typically avoided in traditional economic theory by one of three possible devices. One is simply to abstract from the family, and carry on the analysis as if each individual takes decisions on 'his' own, and this is the typical structure of, say, the theoretical literature on 'general equilibrium'. The model works neatly enough, but that is not the way the world is, in fact, organized.

21. This adds to the dichotomy between choice and welfare that exists even without considering the problem of intra-family distribution. On that general dichotomy, see Sen (1977b).

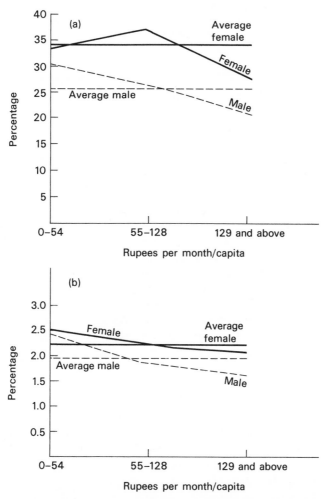

FIGURE 15.3 *Incidence of poor health conditions in the CMDA area by expenditure group (see Table 15.7): (a) Ill and in indifferent health, (b) Ill only*

The second approach is to ignore the individual altogether, and to take the family as the unit of analysis — of decisions, of actions, and even of welfare. In terms of economic behaviour this may or may not be close to the reality, but even if it is, it raises the deep question as to whether the well-being of individuals can be ignored in making social welfare judgements or in comparing standards of living, and whether economic policy should be geared only to the conception of family well-being that the decision-takers in the family could be seen as pursuing. If that family-based conception permits disparities (e.g. putting lower weight on the undernourishment of the children or of women), should that be the basis of social assessment and public policy? I believe to ask this question is to answer it. It would be very odd indeed if the family head's view of family welfare were all that mattered for public judgement and social policy.

The third approach is to *assume* complete harmony within the family, with the well-being of every member of the family being equally served by the family decisions. In this approach everyone shares the same level of well-being, and it does not matter whether we look at the average level (in the Benthamite way), or at the minimal level (in a Rawlsian way), since they give the same answer. This is an empirical assumption, and if true, it avoids many practical difficulties. The trouble is that as an empirical assumption, it is very difficult to justify. Indeed, the evidence on the sharp disparities within the family, discussed in this paper, would seem to militate against the assumption.

While these are the traditional assumptions — though usually made implicitly — there is a fourth approach that is worth considering, and which has received some support recently. It can be argued that the notion of 'individual welfare' itself is a non-viable concept in societies in which the family is dominant. There might be, it is argued, no way of specifying the welfare of the individual in contrast with that of the family.[22] This fourth view has some similarity with the second, except that individual welfare is not so much *ignored* as taken to be a *non-sustainable* concept in this context.

It is important to distinguish between two different views that may be associated with this approach. First, it may be argued that individual welfare cannot be taken to be independent of the welfare of the rest of the family.[23] This is convincing enough, but it need not really make the concept of individual welfare non-sustainable, since it only rejects the *independent* conception of that welfare. *Separateness* of individual welfare has to be distinguished from the *independence* of individual welfare. Individual welfares may be interdependent but distinct.

Second, it might be argued that the *introspective* notion of individual welfare may be itself unsustainable, since that is not how members of the family do introspect. Certainly, for some members

22. Cf. Das and Nicholas (1981).
23. Cf. '. . . in the important area of food, nutrition and health, it would be a gross oversimplification to define an individual's welfare as his state of satisfaction from the goods and services that he receives from his environment' (Das and Nicholas, 1981, p. 26).

of the family – such as infants and children – the introspective notion is problematic or useless; but for others it seems a bit difficult to claim that a member of the family would not be able to attach any meaning to the notion of his or her individual welfare as it appears to him or her. The issue is not whether the person poses this question to himself or herself as a regular introspective activity, but whether he or she is able to understand and answer such a question if it were posed. The traditional acceptance of deep inequalities within the family – against women in particular – does indeed thrive on not asking some of these questions that appear to be 'divisive', but that is *not* because such questions cannot, *if posed*, be understood or answered.

It is, of course, possible to argue that the introspective concept of individual welfare – while perfectly sustainable – is not an adequate basis for discussions on social welfare, standard of living and economic policy. Indeed, I have tried to argue in that direction elsewhere, showing the limitation of the traditional notion of 'utility' as a basis of judgement and action.[24] In particular, there are good grounds for arguing that a person's capability failure may well be judged not on the metric of how upset he is about it, but by the *extent* of the capability failure itself. If a person is unable to get the nourishment he or she needs, or unable to lead a normal life due to some handicap, that failure – on this view – is itself important, and not made important only because he or she incurs dissatisfaction or disutility from that failure.

If the focus is on the deprivation of *personal capabilities*, then inequalities within the family have an importance of their own, no matter what view we take of the sustainability of the notion of individual welfare in cultures in which the family plays a dominant role. There is no escape from the grave tragedy of the disproportionate undernourishment of children (or sharper undernourishment of the *female* children in distress situations, as discussed in Section 2), or the unusual morbidity of women (as discussed in Section 3). The problem has to be distinguished from the deprivation of goods as such since the 'capability approach' is concerned with what goods can do to human beings.[25] Thus, undernourishment and

24. Sen (1977c, 1979, 1980). [See also Essays 13 and 20 in this volume.]
25. The 'capability approach' (Sen, 1980) can be seen as an extension of Rawls' (1971) focus on 'primary goods'. Rawls motivates his concern with primary goods by showing their relevance to what people are able to do. While he postpones the question of interpersonal variation in the transformation of primary goods into capabilities, the capability approach takes explicit note of that. For nutrition and health such variations are, of course, inescapable. [See Essays 13 and 20 in this volume.]

morbidity – not to mention mortality – provide a better focus than food-intake itself (see Section 1).

If disparities within the family are not ruled out of court with one assumption or another, the implications for economic analysis and policy are truly monumental. This is not the occasion to go into a full-fledged analysis of the different implications, but some may be briefly referred to as examples.

First, in terms of policy, the problem of malnutrition and hunger can no longer be seen only as a matter of entitlement of the family, depending on the family's earning power and market command, and requires analysis of the division of entitlements *within* the family.[26] The issue of social values, including what 'divisive' questions are or are not posed (as discussed earlier), becomes a central one, in this context.

Second, the gap between decisions of family heads and the well-being – introspective or not – of individual members of the family makes market data that much more difficult to interpret in terms of need satisfaction. The market demands would, at least, reflect the relative importance of different items as seen by the decision-takers ('revealed preference' cannot go beyond that, even if it can go so far as that).[27] This calls into question not merely the traditional efficiency or optimality results related to the market mechanism (for market socialism[28] as well as for competitive capitalism),[29] it also has far-reaching implications for public policy and planning using market information.[30]

Third, the evaluation of standard of living is usually done on the basis of market data. While the problems arising from different sizes and compositions of families are often neglected, there have been a number of important contributions recently to correct for variations of size and composition through the use of 'equivalence scales'.[31]

26. This is not to deny the importance of entitlement of families in the causal analysis of starvation and undernourishment, both in famine and non-famine situations (see Sen, 1981a, 1981b). But the analysis has to be carried beyond that, especially in catching the specific pattern of deprivation. In Sen (1984) there is an attempt to extend the entitlement analysis to divisions *within* the family interconnected with entitlements *of* families.

27. See Samuelson (1947).

28. See Lange (1936, 1938) and Lerner (1944).

29. See Arrow (1951), Debreu (1959) and Arrow and Hahn (1971).

30. It is, of course, quite possible that the favouring of the male children (see Section 2) reflects hard-headed calculation by the family heads regarding the greater future earning power of the male children. Devotees of the 'invisible hand' would no doubt see its benign presence in these distressing facts. But even if this were the only reason for the disparity, which I doubt, it would still be legitimate to distinguish between the returns to the family heads (e.g. through support in old age) and the return to *all* members of the family (*including*, of course, the family heads).

31. See especially Deaton and Muellbauer (1980, Chapter 8), who also discuss the earlier literature.

But these scales operate on a notion of 'family welfare' that is reflected by the maximand of the family's market behaviour. For reasons already discussed the procedure is not easy to justify.

Much of economic analysis proceeds on the basis of linking decision-taking with individual well-being. Disparities within the family strike at the root of this relationship.

References

Arrow, K. J. (1951): 'An Extension of the Basic Theorems of Classical Welfare Economics', in J. Neyman (ed.), *Proceedings of the Second Berkeley Symposium on Mathematical Statistics and Probability* (Berkeley: University of California Press).

—— and Hahn, F. H. (1971): *General Competitive Analysis* (Edinburgh: Oliver & Boyd; reprinted by North-Holland: Amsterdam).

Bardhan, P. (1974): 'On Life and Death Questions', *Economic and Political Weekly*, **9**, Special Number.

Blankhart, D. N. (1967): 'Individual Intake of Food in Young Children in Relation to Malnutrition and Night Blindness', *Tropical and Geographical Medicine*, **19**.

Bliss, C. and Stern, N. H. (1978): 'Productivity, Wages and Nutrition', Parts I and II, *Journal of Development Economics*, **5**, 4.

Bohdal, M., Gibbs, N. E. and Simmons, W. K. (1968): 'Nutrition Survey and Campaign Against Malnutrition in Kenya', mimeographed, report to the Ministry of Health of Kenya on the WHO/FAO UNICEF 1964–1968 assisted project.

CMDA (1980): 'Health and Socio-Economic Survey of Calcutta Metropolitan Development Area', Calcutta: I.S.I. and Calcutta Metropolitan Development Authority.

Chen, L. C., Huq, E. and D'Souza, S. (1980): 'A Study of Sex-Biased Behaviour in the Intra-Family Allocation of Food and the Utilization of Health Care Services in Rural Bangladesh', International Centre for Diarrhoeal Disease Research, Bangladesh and Department of Population Sciences, Harvard School of Public Health.

Crawford, L. and Thorbecke, E. (1980): 'The Analysis of Food Poverty: An Illustration from Kenya', *Pakistan Development Review*, **19**.

Das, V. and Nicholas, R. (1981): ' "Welfare" and "Well-Being" in South Asian Societies', mimeographed, ACLS–SSRC Joint Committee on South Asia, SSRC, New York.

Davey, P. L. H. (1962a): 'Report on the National Nutrition Survey', mimeographed, Food and Nutrition Board, Accra.

—— (1962b): 'A Summary of Conclusions and Recommendations of the National Surveys of 1961 and 1962', mimeographed, Food and Nutrition Board, Accra.

Davidson, S., Passmore, R., Brock, J. F. and Truswell, A. S. (1979): *Human Nutrition and Dietetics*, 7th edn (Edinburgh: Churchill Livingstone).

Deaton, A. and Muellbauer, J. (1980): *Economic and Consumer Behaviour* (Cambridge: Cambridge University Press).

Debreu, G. (1959): *The Theory of Value* (New York: Wiley).

den Hartog, A. P. (1973): 'Unequal Distribution of Food Within the Household', *FAO Newsletter*, **10**, 4 (October-December).

D'Souza, S. and Chen, L. C. (1980): 'Sex Biases of Mortality Differentials in Rural Bangladesh', mimeographed, International Centre for Diarrhoeal Disease Research, Dacca, Bangladesh.

FAO/WHO Expert Committee (1973): *Energy and Protein Requirements.* (Rome: Food and Agriculture Organization of the United Nations).

Farouk and Ali, N. (1977): *The Hardworking Poor (A survey of how people use their time in Bangladesh)* (Dacca: Bureau of Economic Research, University of Dacca).

Flores, M., Garcia, B., Florez, Z. and Lara, M. Y. (1964): 'Annual Patterns of Family and Children's Diet in Three Guatemalan Indian Communities', *British Journal of Nutrition*, **18**, 281-93.

—— Menchu, M. T., Lara, M. Y. and Guzman, M. A. (1970): 'Relación entre la ingesta de calorías y nutrientes en preescolares y la disponibilidad de alimentos en la familia', *Archivos Latino-Americanos de Nutricion*, **20** (1), 41-58.

Foster, G. M. (1966): *Social Anthropology and Nutrition of the preschool child, especially as related to Latin America* (Washington, DC: National Academy of Sciences, National Research Council, Publication 1282).

Government of Pakistan (1970): *Nutrition Survey of West Pakistan – Ministry of Health Labour and Family Planning February 1965-November 1966* (Islamabad: Government of Pakistan).

Institute of Nutrition and Food Science, Dacca (1977): *Nutrition Survey of Rural Bangladesh 1975-76* (Dacca: University of Dacca).

Kynch, J. and Sen, A. K. (1983): 'Indian Women: Well-being and Survival', *Cambridge Journal of Economics*, **7**.

Lange, O. (1936): 'On the Economic Theory of Socialism', *Review of Economic Studies*, **4** (1936-37).

—— (1938): 'The Foundations of Welfare Economics', *Econometrica*, **10**.

Lerner, A. P. (1944): *The Economics of Control* (London: Macmillan).

Mathur, K. S., Wahi, P. N., Shrivastava, S. K. and Gahlaut, D. S. (1961): 'Diet in Western Uttar Pradesh', *Journal of Indian Medical Association*, **37** (2), 58-63.

McFie, I. (1967): 'Nutrient Intakes of Urban Dwellers in Lagos, Nigeria', *British Journal of Nutrition*, **21**, 257-68.

McIntosh, J., Nasim, A. and Satchell, S. (1981): 'Differential Mortality in Rural Bangladesh', mimeographed, University of Essex. Presented at the Development Studies Association 1981 Annual Conference.

Miller, B. (1981): *The Endangered Sex: Neglect of Female Children in Rural North India* (Ithaca, NY: Cornell University Press).

Mitra, A. (1980): *Implications of Declining Sex Ratio in India's Population* (Bombay: Allied Publishers).

National Institute of Nutrition, Hyderabad (1979): 'National Nutrition Monitoring Bureau Report for the Year 1978', mimeographed.

Nicol, B. M. (1959): 'The Calorie Requirements of Nigerian Peasant Farmers', *British Journal of Nutrition*, 13, 293-306.

Postmus, S. and Van Veen, A. G. (1949): 'Dietary Surveys in Java and East Indonesia (II)', *Chron. Nat.*, 105 (11), 261-8.

Rawls, J. (1971): *A Theory of Justice* (Cambridge, Mass.: Harvard University Press).

Registrar General of India (1980): *Survey of Infant and Child Mortality, 1979: A Preliminary Report* (New Delhi: Office of the Registrar General of India).

Ritchie, J. A. S. (1963): *Teaching Better Nutrition*, FAO Nutritional Studies, 6 (Rome: FAO).

Samuelson, P. A. (1947): *Foundations of Economic Analysis* (Cambridge, Mass.: Harvard University Press).

Schofield, S. (1975): *Village Nutrition Studies: An Annotated Bibliography*, Institute of Development Studies, University of Sussex.

Scrimshaw, N. S. (1977): 'Effect of Infection on Nutrient Requirements', *American Journal of Clinical Nutrition*, 30, 1536-44.

Seal, S. C., Bhattacharjee, B., Roy, J. and Rao, R. (1981): 'Comparative Study of Improved and Unimproved Bustees', mimeographed, Calcutta Metropolitan Development Authority.

Sen, A. K. (1976): 'Females as Failures of Exchange Entitlements', *Economic and Political Weekly*, 11, 31-33, Special Number.

—— (1977a): 'Starvation and Exchange Entitlements: A General Approach and its Application to the Great Bengal Famine', *Cambridge Journal of Economics*, 1, 33-59.

—— (1977b): 'Rational Fools: A Critique of the Behavioural Foundations of Economic Theory', *Philosophy and Public Affairs*, 6, 317-44; reprinted in F. Hahn and M. Hollis (eds), *Philosophy and Economic Theory* (Oxford: Oxford University Press), and my *Choice, Welfare and Measurement* (Oxford: Blackwell, 1982).

—— (1977c): 'On Weights and Measures: Informational Constraints in Social Welfare Analysis', *Econometrica*, 45, 1539-72, reprinted in *Choice, Welfare and Measurement*.

—— (1979): 'Personal Utilities and Public Judgments: Or What's Wrong with Welfare Economics?', *Economic Journal*, 89, 537-58; reprinted in *Choice, Welfare and Measurement*.

—— (1980): 'Equality of What?', in S. McMurrin (ed.), *Tanner Lectures on Human Values* (Cambridge: Cambridge University Press); reprinted in *Choice, Welfare and Measurement*.

—— (1981a): *Poverty and Famines: An Essay on Entitlements and Deprivation* (Oxford: Clarendon Press).

—— (1981b): 'Ingredients of Famine Analysis: Availability and Entitlements', *Quarterly Journal of Economics*, 95, 433-64; Essay 18 in this volume.

—— (1982): 'Food Battles: Conflicts in the Access to Food', Coromandel Lecture, 12 December 1982, New Delhi.

—— (1983): 'Economics and the Family', *Asian Development Review*, 1 [Essay 16 in this volume].

—— (1984): 'Women, Technology and Sexual Divisions', Working Paper, Technology Division, UNCTAD, Geneva.

—— and Sengupta, S. (1983): 'Malnutrition of Rural Children and the Sex Bias', *Economic and Political Weekly*, 18, Annual Number.

Spring Rice, M. (1939): *Working-Class Wives: Their Health and Condition* (Harmondsworth: Penguin).

Srinivasan, T. N. (1977): 'Development, Poverty and Basic Human Needs: Some Issues', *Food Research Institute Studies*, 16.

—— (1979): 'Malnutrition: Some Measurement and Policy Issues', mimeographed, World Bank, Washington, DC.

Sukhatme, P. V. (1977): *Nutrition and Poverty* (New Delhi: Indian Agricultural Research Institute).

—— (1978): 'Assessment of Adequacy of Diets at Different Income Levels', *Economic and Political Weekly*, 13, Special Number.

Thomson, B. P. (1954): 'Two Studies in African Nutrition', Lusaka: Rhodes Livingstone papers, No. 24.

UNICEF (1981): *A Sample Survey Report on the Health and Nutrition Status of Children Covered by the Mother and Child Care Programme under the UNICEF Assisted Food Rehabilitation Programme in West Bengal (First Assessment 1979)* (Calcutta: UNICEF).

University of Ibadan (1970): *Technical Report on the Nutrition Survey, Oje District, Ibadan Town* (Nigeria: Food Science and Applied Nutrition Unit, University of Ibadan).

Visaria, P. (1961): *The Sex Ratio of the Population of India*, Monograph 10, Census of India 1961 (New Delhi: Office of the Registrar General of India).

WHO (1974): *Handbook of Human Nutrition Requirement* (Geneva: World Health Organisation).

16

Economics and the Family

The family is a remarkable institution. And a complex one. Indeed, so complex that much of economic theory proceeds as if no such thing exists. In the standard theory of prices and equilibrium (the most elegant version of which is to be found in the theory of general equilibrium[1]), individuals and firms are visible, but definitely no families. The individual owns resources, sells them, earns an income, buys goods and services, and has utilities. The firm buys resources, makes commodities, sells them, makes profits, and gives incomes to individual owners. So the story runs, with no family in sight − and children neither heard nor seen.

1   Theory and Practice

Does this omission matter? It need not. Not every misdescription is serious, and any description must pick and choose. There are indeed many problems for which introducing the family as an economic unit will not alter the main results in any significant way. But a number of important results of price theory do depend crucially on each consumer deciding for himself what to buy and consume, subject to his budget constraint. Indeed, the model of utility maximization in consumer equilibrium thoroughly depends on it. So does the alleged Pareto optimality and economic efficiency of competitive equilibrium. One person deciding for another weakens those links.

For helpful comments on an earlier version of the paper, I am most grateful to Sudhir Anand, John Muellbauer and Seiji Naya.

1. G. Debreu, A Theory of Value (New York: Wiley, 1959); and K. J. Arrow and F. Hahn, General Competitive Analysis (Edinburgh: Oliver & Boyd, 1971; reprinted by North-Holland, Amsterdam).

From Asian Development Review, 1 (1983), 14-26.

And the links are also strained severely by the problem of dividing consumer goods, housework, etc., among various members of the household. These important allocations work *outside* the price mechanism. Family members do not share commodities and work through market transactions within the household.

The theoretical problems involved in incorporating the family into standard economic theory may not worry the 'practical economists' who run the government departments, planning commissions and international institutions that make policies in real life. They may feel less vulnerable. Theories are known to be unrealistic. Practice must not take them too seriously.

However, so much of practical economics (including the rationale of many actual policies) rests *implicitly* on economic theory that the sense of invulnerability is somewhat illusory. Policies are based on beliefs about what the market does or does not do, what the prices stand for, what the national income statistics reflect, what the unemployment data reveal, etc., and these things, in turn, depend implicitly on an enormous body of economic theory. There is no uncrossable Maginot Line protecting economic practice from the difficulties in economic theory.

I do not wish to suggest that the problems involving the role of the family are the most difficult ones that traditional economic theory faces. Or that they are the most damaging ones for policymaking and practical economics. Many difficulties for theory and practice have been noted in the standard literature, and a comparative assessment of difficulties or damages is neither particularly easy nor especially worthwhile. There are, in fact, very powerful grounds for scepticism about the practical lessons that are often taken to have been learned from, say, price theory, and there are difficulties of the most fundamental kind that have nothing whatsoever to do with the existence of families. For example, Hahn has pointed out just how seriously misleading it is to assess economic policies with the implicit assumption − regrettably much too common − that the economy jumps from one general competitive equilibrium to another.[2] The 'practical economist' often attaches more value − implicitly but firmly − to the simpler, but highly qualified, results of economic theory than the theorists themselves may wish to do.

There are very important difficulties also with the assumption of so-called 'rational' behaviour, including consistent self-seeking, on which so much of standard economic theory relies. This seems to

2. F. Hahn, 'Reflections on the Invisible Hand', *Lloyds Bank Review*, 144 (1982).

depart substantially from the patterns and norms of actual behaviour.[3] Further, the presence of indivisibilities, externalities, public goods, etc., raises a whole host of problems, which economic theory has long accepted as important, but the implications of which are far from fully reflected in the working of standard theory, or in policy discussions and practical debates. These problems – and many others – stand, even without making economic theory go the family way.

2 Special Assumptions?

Nevertheless, the existence of families and the part they play in the working of the economy also raise important and difficult issues for economic theory and policy. Indeed, as already discussed, they threaten some of the basic results and views.

Can the traditional 'lessons' of price theory and market equilibrium be preserved, or at least neatly adapted without much loss, by making some special assumptions about how the family functions? The answer is, yes, but the assumptions are quite strong and far-fetched. Three alternative ways of doing this may be briefly discussed to explain what is involved.

2.1 The glued-together family

One approach is to ignore individuals altogether and to take the family as the unit in terms of which economic decisions are taken and economic processes function. This can make sense only if families do typically act in this way and if the individuals have no individuality whatsoever. There are, then, no individual decisions, individual utility, etc., but only family decisions, family welfare, etc., and the traditional theory is simply reinterpreted in terms of families wherever and whenever individuals figured previously.

This model of 'the glued-together family' is nothing if not neat. But neatness is a different virtue from realism or relevance. The all-embracing integration needed for this is severe. Indeed, it boggles the mind to think of behaviour without bringing in persons at all. The family does not think – the members of the family do, and the

3. See J. Kornai, Anti-Equilibrium (Amsterdam: North-Holland, 1971); A. K. Sen, 'Behaviour and the Concept of Preference', Economica, 40 (1973); T. Scitovsky, The Joyless Economy (Oxford Oxford University Press, 1976); A. O. Hirschman, Shifting Involvements: Private and Public Action (Princeton: Princeton University Press, 1982); H. Margolis, Selfishness, Altruism and Rationality (Cambridge: Cambridge University Press, 1982); and G. Akerlof, 'Loyalty Filters', American Economic Review, 73 (1983).

anthropomorphic view of the family can be adequate for perception and choice only under very severe assumptions of congruence. Furthermore, from the point of view of welfare economics and public policy, having no notion of personal well-being – only of family welfare – raises some disturbing questions. Living and dying, illness and health, and joys and sufferings happen to persons, and welfare economics can scarcely ignore these personal conditions.

2.2   The super-trader family

The second route, best explored by Gary Becker[4] involves, in some ways, going to the other extreme. Under what Becker calls 'the economic approach' (somewhat unfairly to economics, I think), individuals are assumed to be relentlessly pursuing their individual utilities, and in doing this they enter into trades at implicit prices resulting in marriages and the working of the family. While the individual utilities can include concern for others (this is an important departure from standard behavioural assumptions), the process of utility maximization is carried out uncompromisingly – without constraints or propriety, norm or convention. The relationship between different members of such a 'super-trader family' takes the form of 'as if' market transactions at implicit prices.[5]

Becker claims a long heritage for his approach:

> The economic approach has been refined during the last two hundred years. It now assumes that individuals maximize their utility from basic preferences that do not change rapidly over time, and that the behavior of different individuals is coordinated by explicit and implicit markets.[6]

Refined it may have been over the last 200 years, but despite that, the approach does remain rather crude. Conceptualizing marriage as 'a two-person firm with either member being the "entrepreneur" who "hires" the other' and 'receives residual "profits"'[7] can perhaps be said to be a rather simple view of a very complex relationship.

---

4. G. Becker, *A Treatise on the Family* (Cambridge, Mass.: Harvard University Press, 1981).

5. It should be noted that the issue of consumption and welfare of children remains outside this trading format, since they are not parties to 'as if' market contracts but are, nevertheless, affected by them.

6. Becker, *op. cit.*, p. ix.

7. G. Becker, 'A Theory of Marriage', in T. W. Schultz (ed.), *Economics of the Family* (Chicago: University of Chicago Press, 1974). There are also a number of other interesting contributions in this volume.

It is, of course, not the case that there is no insight whatsoever to be gained from this way of seeing family relationships. Trading transactions may well figure among other features of the family. Further, as Bernard Shaw had remarked, 'Like fingerprints, all marriages are different'. The Beckerian view of marriages may quite possibly provide a nice clue to important aspects of many marriages. What Becker does is to convert a wisecrack into a theory of all marriages and all family relations. What would have been a witty and insightful aphorism thus becomes a rather odd general theory.

In the Beckerian world, market transactions take place within the family in an imagined way at imagined prices and imagined wages (with demand and supply in balance as under a Walrasian *tâtonnement*). A robust implicit-price equilibrium is seen as quickly emerging. The difficulties in this analytically powerful representation does not arise only from the oddities of the behavioural assumptions within the family,[8] but also from the requirement that the enormous demands of a market equilibrium process can somehow be fully met without any actual prices, trades, and adjustment procedures. Actual market transactions work on the basis of a great complex of institutions for trading, negotiations, contract-making, and enforcement of contracts. To expect market-like equilibria without markets is to assume that such institutions are, in fact, *redundant*.

2.3   *The Despotic Family*

A third approach is to assume that a despotic head of the family takes all decisions and others just obey. The family behaviour would then be just a reflection of the head's choice function, and family welfare – in terms of revealed preference – would then have to be seen as the maximand implicit in the head's choice function. There are insights to be gained from this model too, but it is difficult to assume that in actual societies family heads do typically have such complete command over all economic actions of everyone in the family. Further, even if the head did have such complete command, it would be absurd to think that his view of the welfare of the family should be the only view that counts in welfare analysis (e.g. in specifying Pareto optimality). The 'subordinated' and 'subjugated' mem-

8. Such maximizing behaviour without constraints of norms and duty, and other non-preference influences on choice, may not be a sensible assumption even outside the family, but it is hardly credible inside it. [See my 'Rational Fools: A Critique of the Behavioural Foundation of Economic Theory', *Philosophy and Public Affairs*, 6 (1977), reprinted in *Choice, Welfare and Measurement* (Oxford: Blackwell, 1982). Especially the contrast between 'sympathy' and 'commitment'.]

bers of the family might well obey orders, but why should it be assumed that their views about their own welfare and about the family's welfare should have no status? Indeed, the rapidly growing literature on the position of women often accepts – indeed asserts – a variant of the descriptive view of the despotic family without, of course, seeing family welfare in terms of the despot's objective function.[9]

So none of these three special assumptions offer a good way of retaining the old results (or traditional views) of price theory and market allocations. They offer interesting insights, which may be useful in particular problems, but they do not save us from the necessity to think afresh about the whole question of family economics and its implications for the traditional theory of prices and allocation.

3　Cooperative Conflicts

Where do we go from here? How can we retain the results and views of traditional price theory and market equilibrium? I address the second question first. We *need not* retain those results and views! At least need not retain them with the level of generality that requires us to extinguish contrary cases. If, for example, the biases of family allocation lead to allocational errors, well, we ought to recognize them, and look for their implications, rather than trying to deny their existence.

The first question is harder to deal with. What type of family economics do we need? I do not really know the answer, but I shall make a few remarks on the direction in which we may possibly go.

First, there has to be a clearer analysis of the existence of both cooperative and conflicting elements in family relations. Formally, the structure of the problem is similar to what Nash, the mathematician, had called 'the bargaining problem'.[10] I should explain that

9. See, for example, A. H. Amsden (ed.), *The Economics of Women and Work* (Harmondsworth: Penguin Books, 1980); and M. Evans (ed.), *The Women Question: Readings on the Subordination of Women* (London: Fontana, 1982). [Oddly enough, Becker's approach – market-directed as it is – can be so formulated that the outcome takes the form of falling in line with the preferences of the family 'head' who is taken to be 'altruistic'. As Becker puts it in *A Treatise on the Family*: 'In my approach the "optimal reallocation" results from altruism and voluntary contributions, and the "group preference function" is identical to that of the altruistic head, even when he does not have sovereign powers' (p. 192).]

10. J. F. Nash, 'The Bargaining Problem', *Econometrica*, 18 (1950). For applications to different aspects of family economics, see M. Manser and M. Brown, 'Marriage and Household Decision-Making: A Bargaining Analysis', *International Economic Review*, 21 (1980);

Nash was not assuming that some actual bargaining must be involved in such cases, and perhaps in some ways, Nash's term was not sufficiently general for the class of problems he formalized. The essence of the problem is that there are many cooperative outcomes – beneficial to all the parties compared with non-cooperation – but the different parties have strictly conflicting interests in the choice among the set of efficient cooperative arrangements. So the problem is one of 'cooperative conflict'.

Second, the bargaining problem of finding a particular cooperative solution, yielding a particular distribution of benefits, will be sensitive to various parameters, including the respective powers of the different members of the family, given, for example, by the nature of the 'fall-back' positions if there should be a breakdown. If, for example, men have typically better bargaining power, related to better outside job opportunities (possibly connected with inequalities of education or training, or with sexist discrimination in the job market), then that would lead to a correspondingly more favourable cooperative outcome for the men. Further, such differential advantage may feed on themselves. A better deal for the male in one period may, *inter alia*, include a better role in the division of labour with better training and more profitable job experience, and these may lead to a better placing in the next period's bargaining problem. Certain 'traditional' arrangements may emerge, e.g. women doing housework and being able to take up outside work *only if* it is additional. These inequalities may solidify over time.

The acceptance of the bargaining perspective in the fixing of household arrangements (i.e. who does what work and gets what goods and services) does not, of course, deny that feelings such as love, affection and concern, may also play important parts in the choice of the arrangements. The parameters of the bargaining problem can include many complex ones. It does, however, deny that rather than thinking of all this as a firmly non-market procedure, the intrafamily allocation of work and commodities should be seen in terms of an 'as if' market with implicit prices (as suggested by Becker). The two approaches are fundamentally different ways of

and A. K. Sen, 'Cooperative Conflicts: Technology and the Position of Women', mimeographed, All Souls College, Oxford, 1983. [See also S. Clemhout and H. Y. Wan, Jr., 'Symmetric Marriage, Household Decision Making and Impact on Fertility', Working Paper 152, Cornell University, 1979, M. B. McElroy and M. J. Horney, 'Nash-Bargained Household Decisions: Toward a Generalization of the Theory of Demand', *International Economic Review*, 22 (1981); S. C. Rochford, 'Nash-Bargained Household Decision-Making in a Peasant Economy', mimeographed, 1981; R. A. Pollock, 'A Transaction Cost Approach to Families and Households', mimeographed, University of Pennsylvania, 1983, See also 'Introduction', Section 4.2, above, pp. 28–30].

seeing intrahousehold allocation, and they will often lead to very different results.

Third, the predictive aspect of the case of despotic families can, in fact, be seen as a special case of the bargaining-problem view. In that special case, the outcome involves dominance by one party, viz. the head of the family. To note this does not, of course, imply any acceptance of the *normative* features of such a model (or support for family-less welfare analysis related to traditional price theory and market economics). In fact, seeing family economics as a bargaining problem with cooperative conflicts leaves the normative question open.

4 Capabilities and Comparisons

Fourth, I have tried to argue elsewhere that there is a good case for judging individual well-being, neither in terms of commodities consumed nor in terms of the mental metric of utilities, but in terms of the 'capabilities' of persons.[11] This is the perspective of 'freedom' in the *positive* sense: who can *do* what, rather than who has what bundle of *commodities*, or who gets how much *utility*. This is not the occasion to go into that general question, but if the capabilities perspective is accepted, then family well-being can sensibly be seen as some function of what positive freedoms the different members of the family can enjoy.

The capabilities that can be achieved will, of course, vary with economic prosperity and the extent of economic development. For example, the capability to be free from hunger and to meet nutritional needs is widely relevant in judging well-being in a poor country, though typically not so in a rich country, in which this capability is usually unproblematic (except for specially deprived groups). In judging the relative positions of different members of the family, the perspective of capabilities can provide a useful line of vision.

Fifth, the capabilities perspective can be used for children too, particularly in poor economies, in which hunger, malnutrition, illiteracy, preventable morbidity, etc., happen to be quite common. While the comparison of relative utilities of adults and children often does not make much sense, it is possible to attach some importance to relative frequencies of cases of, say, undernourishment and nutri-

---

11. A. K. Sen, *Choice, Welfare and Measurement* (Oxford: Blackwell, 1982), pp. 29–31, 353–69.

tion-related diseases. More immediately, this perspective can be very helpful in checking sex discrimination applied to children.[12]

Sixth, in analysing family allocations, both the immediate-benefit aspect and the investment aspect of personal consumption have to be considered. For example, in looking after children, there is obviously a concern for the well-being of the child, including immediate well-being. But this can be combined with long-run considerations of survival of the child and, related to it, the chances of the adult members of the family getting support in old age. For example, in a 'despotic family' in a very poor country, this investment aspect may even be a reason for sex discrimination among the children because of the greater likelihood — real or perceived — of getting support in old age from male progeny rather than female progeny.[13]

5   Equivalence Scales

While this odd collection of remarks is meant as no more than outlining some required aspects of an approach to family economics, the requirements are, in fact, quite demanding. Many approaches to family economics would have to be re-examined.

The distinguished and, in many ways, extremely useful literature on 'equivalence scales' in dealing with the evaluation of family consumption is one of them.[14] The method of 'equivalence scales', which goes back to Engel, sees the consumption vector of the entire family as a point in an integrated indifference map. It assumes, explicitly or by implication, either a 'glued-together family', or a 'despotic family' (taking the despot's indifference map), or a family in which an egalitarian distribution equates the level of well-being of each member. Since the first two approaches have already been discussed (rather unflatteringly), it may make sense to concentrate on the third possibility, viz. that of intra-family equality. Under that assumption, family well-being can, without much problem, be identified with the

12. A. K. Sen, 'Family and Food: Sex-Bias in Poverty', mimeographed, 1981 [Essay 15 in this volume]; and J. Kynch and A. K. Sen, 'Indian Women: Well-being and Survival', *Cambridge Journal of Economics*, 7 (1983).

13. P. Bardhan, 'Little Girls and Death in India', *Economic and Political Weekly*, 17 (Bombay, 1982); and B. Miller, *The Endangered Sex: Neglect of Female Children in Rural North India* (Ithaca, NY: Cornell University Press, 1981). [See also M. R. Rosenzweig and T. P. Schultz, 'Market Opportunities, Genetic Endowments, and Intrafamily Resource Distribution: Child Survival in Rural India', *American Economic Review*, 72 (1982).]

14. The approach and the underlying main issues are discussed excellently by A. Deaton and J. Muellbauer, *Economics and Consumer Behaviour* (Cambridge: Cambridge University Press, 1980).

well-being of *any* member of the family, since they all enjoy the same level of well-being. This property is useful in the reasoning underlying 'equivalence scales'. If the amounts of specialized goods that the adults consume give us a good clue as to the level of well-being of each adult (following an approach suggested by Rothbarth), then the same indicator can be used as a guide to the well-being of the children *as well*, since they share the same level of well-being. Hence, the quantities of 'adult' goods per adult in the family can serve as the basis of judging everyone's well-being *in* the family, and thus the well-being *of* the family.[15]

The rub lies, of course, in the assumption of equality of levels of well-being. If the levels differ from person to person in the same household, then it will not be possible to use this approach without substantial modification. The idea of 'equivalence' in 'equivalence scales' refers to the same level of family well-being. This becomes a complex idea if and when, on the one hand, we do not have a 'glued-together' family, or a 'despotic' one (or do have such a despotic family but do not accept the despot's objective function as giving the right concept of equivalence), and on the other, we do not accept that the levels of well-being of all the family members must be equal through some process of intra-family equalization. A much more articulate family welfare function would then be needed to relate the collection of unequated levels of well-being of family members to an aggregate measure for the family as a whole. This will, of course, involve a 'mini social choice problem'. While that may raise difficulties of its own, the problem cannot be avoided in the absence of one of the simplifying assumptions already examined. The approach of 'equivalence scales' would have to be integrated more fully with intra-family allocation, on the one hand, and theories of aggregation of unequal well-beings, on the other.

6   Sex Inequalities

The possibility of differences in well-being between different members of the family is not just a theoretical curiosum. There is, in fact, very extensive evidence of systematic differences between the positions of men and women in poor countries and, indeed, even in the rich ones. In the rich countries, the biases against women seem to have typically taken the form of less education, less satisfactory jobs, less decision-making power, more boring and repetitive work,

15. A. Deaton, 'Three Essays on a Sri Lanka Household Survey', *LSMS Working Paper* (Washington, DC: World Bank, 1981).

etc., which imply differences of capabilities related to certain important aspects of living. However, these disadvantages have not resulted
in giving women a lower capability to live a long life. In fact, the
typical expectation of life at birth in the richer countries is longer for
women than for men, and though this difference in favour of women
may be ultimately traced to biological features, social factors may
have a role too. One result of these sustained differences in the
mortality rates is that the ratio of women to men in the richer
countries is substantially higher than unity – around 1.05 in Europe
and North America. The relative advantage of women in longevity
does not, of course, reduce the importance of the serious failures of
capability that women suffer in other spheres even in rich countries.

However, when it comes to the poorer countries, even the basic
capabilities of survival and sustenance often show an anti-female bias.
The ratio of females to males in the population of much of Asia is
substantially below unity in contrast with the European and North
American figure of 1.05. It is, in fact, only 0.96 in East Asia (including the People's Republic of China) and in Southwest Asia, and as
low as 0.93 in South Asia (including India).[16] While the mortality
disadvantages of the female in some of the poorer countries are
being countered, there is still a long way to go.

7   Indian Case Studies

The low female–male ratio in the Indian population and the lower
life expectancy of women in India are matched by evidence of serious
extra deprivation of women in terms of other basic capabilities. I
have presented the results of some empirical studies on this subject
elsewhere, including in some joint works with Jocelyn Kynch and
Sunil Sengupta.[17] Here I shall refer to some of the results very briefly.

There was evidence of greater morbidity of women vis-à-vis men
in a comparative study of the population of Calcutta as a whole and
specifically of the population of slums of Calcutta as well. While the
level of health tends to improve with income, the differential of men
vis-à-vis women seems to be maintained – even expanded.[18]

The use of medical facilities in Bombay, which was the subject
of another study, indicated a clear bias in favour of the male, judging

16. United Nations, *Demographic Yearbook 1981* (New York: United Nations).
17. Sen, 'Family and Food: Sex Bias in Poverty'; Kynch and Sen, 'Indian Women: Well-
being and Survival'; and A. K. Sen and S. Sengupta, 'Malnutrition of Rural Children and the
Sex Bias', *Economic and Political Weekly*, 18 (Bombay, 1983), Annual Number.
18. Sen, 'Family and Food: Sex Bias in Poverty'.

hospital use in terms of the ratio of hospital treatment to deaths (in the hospitals and also in the city in general).[19] Remarkably enough, this anti-female bias applies also to the use of hospital facilities by children – girls have consistently a lower hospital utilization ratio than boys. Biases in nutrition and health care against the female child vis-à-vis the male child had been observed earlier in rural North India,[20] but the existence of such a bias in Bombay, which is justly regarded as the most progressive city in India, indicates how hard it may be to get rid of the entrenched anti-female bias. While the bias against adult females seems to have diminished over the years, that against girls vis-à-vis boys does not seem to have substantially changed.[21]

8   Land Reform and Direct Feeding Programmes

Interestingly enough, the picture regarding sex bias in the nutrition of children can vary between one village and another within a very short distance. In a study of children below five years of age in two villages in the Birbhum district of West Bengal in India that Sunil Sengupta and I did during January–March 1983,[22] we found a sharp sex bias against girls in one of the villages (Kuchli) and a very mild one (statistically not very significant) in the other village (Sahajapur), only ten kilometres away from the first. Causal analysis of possible determining factors indicated the relevance of various distinguishing parameters. One of the contrasts that is particularly important from the point of view of policy is the difference between the form of public intervention in the two villages. In Kuchli the land reform policy has been much more successful, resulting in the fact that only 18 per cent of the children now belong to landless families, as opposed to 60 per cent in Sahajapur. The general level of nutrition of children is correspondingly higher in Kuchli, but at the same time the extent of sex bias is, as already stated, also very much sharper in Kuchli. In fact, the nutritional position of girls in the two villages is roughly the same, and both the higher *average* level of nutrition and the greater sex *differential* in Kuchli are largely the result of the same difference, to wit, a higher level of nutrition of boys in Kuchli than in Sahajapur. It is tempting to argue from this that economic improvement seems to have benefited the male child in a way that it has not helped the female child.

19. Kynch and Sen, 'Indian Women: Well-being and Survival'.
20. Bardhan, 'Little Girls and Death in India'; and Miller, *The Endangered Sex*.
21. Kynch and Sen, 'Indian Women: Well-being and Survival'.
22. Sen and Sengupta, 'Malnutrition of Rural Children and the Sex Bias'.

However, other differences are also involved. As far as public policy is concerned, there is a programme of direct nutritional intervention in Sahajapur, covering the so-called 'scheduled tribes' who constitute a little over a third of the population of that village, all among the poorer section. There is no such programme in Kuchli. It is interesting that despite much greater landlessness in Sahajapur, the scheduled tribe children – boys and girls together – in Sahajapur do marginally better than the same communal group in Kuchli, and the difference must be largely due to the feeding programme. But more importantly, the extent of *sex bias* is greatly reduced in the intervened population. This is not, of course, surprising, since the public feeding takes place on the street, and there is no sex bias in the distribution of food in this way, in contrast with feeding at home. Since direct feeding programmes have been recently subjected to a good deal of criticism in public policy debates in developing countries, their positive role in the present context is particularly worth noting.

The contrast raises an interesting question about the planning of family well-being. If the kind of difference we found between these two villages were to be more widely observed, then the case for public intervention in feeding would be strong. Despite the fact that land reform obviously provides a more sustained basis of general prosperity, its failure to provide a square deal to the girls arises from the biases *within* the family allocational process, through which the effects of land reform work. Direct nutritional intervention, on the other hand, reduces the role of family heads and other adult family members in the division of food, and this can have the effect of reducing the bias against girls.

9 *International Perspectives*

It would be a mistake to build too much on the insecure foundations of a few case studies. But there is enough here to raise some disturbing questions. Other studies elsewhere in the developing world have provided evidence of sex bias in the distribution of food and health facilities within the family, and on nutrition and related morbidities.[23] It appears that the extent of sex bias in the intra-family

23. See, for example, A. P. den Hartog, 'Unequal Distribution of Food Within the Household', *FAO Newsletter*, 10 (October–December, 1973); S. Schofield, *Village Nutrition Studies* (Brighton: Institute of Development Studies, 1974); and L. C. Chen, E. Huq and S. D'Souza, 'A Study of Sex-biased Behaviour in the Intra-Family Allocation of Food and the Utilization of Health Care Services in Rural Bangladesh' (Cambridge, Mass.: Harvard School of Public Health, mimeographed, 1980).

division of even the most basic means of survival, such as food and medical attention, may well be very substantial.

There is a methodological problem in judging sex bias in food division that is worth a comment. The point has been made that while women very often consume substantially less food than men in poor families in developing countries, typically the 'requirements' of women (of, say, calories) are also much lower. In fact, it has been often suggested that despite consuming less food, women satisfy a higher percentage of their nutritional requirement than men do.[24]

Specification of so-called 'requirements' of calories and other nutrients may have rather little scientific basis, because of such factors as interpersonal variations in metabolic rates, the role of parasitic diseases in affecting the absorption of food, and the existence of multiple equilibria for the same person.[25] Furthermore, the commonly used requirement figures seem to have built into them some systematic biases. In the widely used 'requirement' figures specified by the distinguished FAO/WHO Expert Committee,[26] the energy used in housework is assumed to be quite low, since housework is treated as a sedentary activity. One wonders where such delectable housework was observed. Perhaps in a gadget-filled Manhattan apartment, preparing quietly for the twenty-first century.

The requirement-intake comparisons also suffer from the serious problem of getting accurate information on the food intake of each individual member of the family. Obviously, food-purchase data — the mainstay of 'equivalence scale' analysis — are not adequate for this. Family members have to be observed eating, and — more than that — the food partaken would have to be weighed in the process of its journey from the plate to the mouth. (There is, as it were, a weighing trip 'twixt the cup and the lip.) I suppose a family with true grit will be able to take all this without any effect on the consumption behaviour to be observed, but the weaker ones may go under. So the actual intake figures may well be no more reliable than the alleged 'requirement' figures, and the blind shall lead the blind.

24. Such remarks have frequently appeared in development literature. One example, in which this claim is supported by a detailed comparison of 'intake' figures with 'requirement' assumptions, is to be found in: Institute of Nutrition and Food Science, *Nutrition Survey of Rural Bangladesh 1975-6* (Dacca: University of Dacca, 1977).

25. See N. S. Scrimshaw, 'Effect of Infection of Nutrition Requirements', *American Journal of Clinical Nutrition*, 30 (1977); P. V. Sukhatme, *Nutrition and Poverty* (New Delhi: Indian Agricultural Research Institute, 1977); S. Davidson, R. Passmore, J. E. Brock and A. S. Truswell, *Human Nutrition and Dietetics* (Edinburgh: Churchill Livingstone, 1979); and T. N. Srinivasan, 'Malnutrition: Some Measurement and Policy Issues', *Journal of Development Economics*, 8 (1981).

26. FAO/WHO Expert Committee, *Energy and Protein Requirements* (Rome: Food and Agriculture Organization, 1973).

All this is, in fact, quite the wrong way of going about the problem. If nutrition is what we are concerned with, then nutrition it is we must observe. We have to look not at food intakes, but at signs of undernourishment. There are several clinically significant tests of undernourishment. That is surely the direction in which to go. The empirical results on comparative nutrition that were reported earlier were based on direct nutritional observations rather than on 'requirement' and 'intakes'.

10 Illiteracy and Schooling

Although sex bias in nutritional matters goes to the very root of family life, there are other features of sex bias in the developing world that also deserve serious attention. One of them is the remarkable survival of female illiteracy in many parts of the world even when big strides have been made in overcoming male illiteracy. One way of seeing the continuation of sex bias in this field is to compare the 'enrolment ratio' of male and female children in primary schools.[27] For the 'low-income countries', as defined by the latest *World Development Report*, taking them altogether, the male enrolment ratio is fully 31 per cent higher than the female enrolment ratio in the last year reported (1980). In the People's Republic of China, where the enrolment ratios are in fact higher than unity (presumably because of schooling of students other than in the primary school age group), the sex difference is less but present, with the male ratio being 14 per cent higher than the female. In India it is 48 per cent higher. For the low-income countries other than the People's Republic of China and India, the male ratio exceeds the female by as much as 51 per cent. The differences are truly startling in some cases. The male enrolment ratio is higher than the female ratio by a 100 per cent in Guinea, 115 per cent in Benin, 138 per cent in Nepal, 168 per cent in Chad, 170 per cent in Pakistan, and a solid 390 per cent in Afghanistan.[28]

In fact, all over Asia and Africa, girls are getting consistently less schooling than boys, and whatever the family heads are trying to achieve, it is not educational equality between one child and another. Smaller differences, and in a few cases the absence of it, can be observed among the poorer countries only when there is a determined public policy to deal with the sex differences in primary schooling,

27. The figures give the ratio of total enrolment in primary schools to the population in primary school age, for boys and girls, respectively.
28. World Bank, *World Development Report 1983* (New York: Oxford University Press, 1983), pp. 196-7.

e.g. in the People's Republic of China, Sri Lanka, Viet Nam, Tanzania and Kenya.

There is another systematic pattern, a regional one. Throughout Southeast Asia, the differences are much smaller, e.g. Indonesia (12 per cent), Burma (7 per cent), Philippines (3 per cent), and Malaysia (3 per cent). I should also mention here that countries in Southeast Asia stand out among the Asian countries even in terms of female–male ratio in the total population. Unlike in South Asia (including India), Southwest Asia and East Asia (including the People's Republic of China), the female–male ratio in the Southeast Asian population is greater than unity (1.01 to be specific). Clearly, the influences of regional cultures and societies can be quite substantial in matters of sex bias. Whether there are easily identifiable economic bases for these contrasts is certainly worth studying. Greater female participation in outside work may be a factor, as it seems to be in distinguishing South India from North India, and possibly Africa from much of Asia.[29]

11 Concluding Remarks

Traditional models of price theory and market behaviour are silent on the family. When that silence is broken, the old results and views turn out to be very insecure. While they can be preserved by some special – and typically far-fetched – assumptions, that is hardly the way to face real challenges. We have to break fresh ground and resist the temptation to try to assimilate the problems of family economics mechanically into some already existing framework, such as competitive market theory.

I have outlined some general characteristics that we may try to incorporate in developing a more satisfactory approach to family economics. The format of cooperative conflicts (illustrated by the so-called 'bargaining problem') helps to capture one aspect of family relations between adults. Other features were pointed out, and I shall not try here to summarize the points made. But one issue that emerges clearly is the need to recognize inequalities, possibly substantial, within the household. That recognition threatens some of the more convenient techniques of family economic analysis, includ-

29. See E. Boserup, *Women's Role in Economic Development* (London: Allen & Unwin, 1970); Bardhan, 'Little Girls and Death in India'; and Miller, *The Endangered Sex*. Note, in this context, that the ratio of females to males in population is higher than unity in Africa (1.02), in contrast with much of Asia.

ing the use of 'equivalence scales', which has to be correspondingly modified and adapted. That is a price to pay for realism and relevance, and the difficulties have to be dealt with by a fuller treatment of intra-family allocation and family well-being.

Evidence of inequalities within the family is widespread across the world, but in the poorer countries sex bias can be very strong even in such elementary matters as survival, nutrition, health and literacy. While there are regional differences, the contrasts also relate to political systems and public policy.

The case for going against family allocation through public policy (e.g. direct feeding programmes for children) raises some deep issues as to how interventionist the state should be. There is great reluctance to enter into an area of action that has traditionally been thought to be the preserve of the family heads. That reluctance is easy to understand and respect, but it is possible that the reluctance is at least partly based on certain hypotheses about the nature of family decisions that may simply not be accurate.

Once families are brought into economic analysis explicitly, a variety of questions of economic theory and policy emerge irresistibly. They have the disquieting role of disputing the traditional treatments of resource allocation, public economics, welfare theory, and normative measurement. They also challenge the traditional wisdom on the division of labour between the state and the family.

In answering the policy questions, we may decide to take a radical line or a conservative one. But we have to face these deep-seated problems. They are there, and cannot be wished away.

Part V
Goods and Well-being

17

The Welfare Basis of Real Income Comparisons

1 The Problem: 'So Clear, So Palpable'?

In presenting his estimates of 'la richesse territoriale de France', Antoine Lavoisier (1791) pointed out that the object of such estimation is to furnish 'a veritable thermometer of national prosperity'.[1] That certainly has provided the motivation behind much work on national income estimation and comparison. Lavoisier was an optimist, and he felt that there need be little room for dispute if the problem were correctly posed and pursued:

> A work of this nature will contain in a few pages the whole science of political economy; or, rather, it would do away with the further need for this science; because the results will become so clear, so palpable, the different questions that could be raised would be so easily solved, that there would no longer be any differences of opinion.[2]

Economic theories, however, have proved to be less combustible than 'phlogiston', and alternative claimants to the right method of using national income as a thermometer of national prosperity seem to survive side by side remarkably easily. This paper is concerned

For extremely helpful and admirably detailed comments on an earlier draft of this paper, I am most grateful to Jan Graaff and John Muellbauer. I have also benefited much from suggestions made by Moses Abramovitz, Charles Blackorby, Terence Gorman, Mark Perlman, Robert Pollak, Roger Ransom and Tibor Scitovsky, and would like to take this opportunity of thanking them.

1. The translation used for this quotation and the one that follows is from Studenski (1958, p. 71).
2. Ibid.

From *Journal of Economic Literature*, 17 (March 1979), 1–45.

with critically surveying alternative approaches to comparisons of real income from the welfare point of view. Section 2 is devoted to real *personal* income and Section 3 to real *national* income.

One reason why alternative approaches to real national income theory do not crowd each other out is that the perception of national welfare depends on the value judgements used for conceptualizing the aggregate welfare of the nation. These judgements are very often not stated sharply enough, and there is, I believe, much scope for clarification here. Concepts used in recent developments in collective choice theory can be used to clarify these distinctions, which are often implicitly assumed rather than explicitly stated.

A second version why different theories exist side by side is that they aim at answering rather different questions. One fundamental distinction deals with the contrast between comparisons of welfare as opposed to comparisons of production possibilities,[3] since the real income method can be used for either purpose. Thus the data one would seek and the techniques of analysis one would use would differ depending on the exercise in question. This paper is concerned with real income as a guide to welfare rather than to production possibility as such, but the two motivations will be compared in Section 3.2.

Another distinction relates to the contrast between (i) comparing two *alternative* situations for the same person (or the same group of persons) at a given point of time, and (ii) comparing the *actual* situations of two different persons (or groups), or of the same person (or group) at two different points of time. While much of real income *theory* has been concerned with the former, practical real income comparisons (e.g. international contrasts) clearly must deal also with the latter. But that exercise again can be given several alternative interpretations, which are pursued in Section 2.3 for real *personal* income and in Section 3.11 for real *national* income.

A third reason relates to the choice of prices used for weighting. The essence of the real income procedure is to compare vectors of quantities at *constant* prices. If the prices to be used are taken to be those ruling in the market, then the measures in question are simply *given* to us by the institution of the market, and the only issue is to ascertain what the use of these measures imply. This approach, which I shall call the 'institutional approach', is sharply presented by Hicks (1958, p. 126):

3. The distinction was first clarified by John Hicks (1940). Unlike in neoclassical 'general equilibrium theory', which requires prices to reflect both 'utility' and 'cost', in the standard 'real income theory' one needs one *or* the other.

Our problem is not one of the kind of measure to use, for we have no choice about that; it is a problem of the meaning which we can give to the measures which we have to employ.

If in contrast, the 'prices' chosen for the constant-price comparisons are not the institutionally given prices, but obtained in line with one's conceptual requirements by doctoring the institutional prices appropriately or by rejecting them altogether, then the approach will be called 'conceptual' as opposed to 'institutional'.

Both approaches have obvious limitations. The 'institutional' approach may require postulating particular theories regarding the real world, e.g. the market price ratios equal each person's marginal rate of indifferent substitution (cf. Hicks, 1940), or 'optimal re-allocations of income can be assumed to keep the ethical worth of each person's marginal dollar equal' (cf. Paul Samuelson, 1950, p. 29; 1956, p. 21). It is not typically asserted that these assumptions are indeed correct; instead the investigation just explores the conclusions that could be drawn *if* they were correct. Naturally, the results are not more interesting than the realism of the assumptions permit, and this *can* be rather small in some cases. On the other hand, the 'conceptual' approach has to bridge the gap from the other side by trying to construct statistics that may have the chosen conceptual interpretation, and this act is, of course, much more debatable than simply *observing* certain market data.[4]

Finally, a very fundamental difficulty of the welfare approach to real national income arises from the fact that none of the standard theories of social welfare permit it to be conceived of as a function of the vector of commodities irrespective of distribution, whereas the standard procedures of real income comparison require us to compare such commodity vectors from the point of view of social welfare. This leads *either* to imaginary exercises (*as if* distribution did not matter) *or* to very specific distributional assumptions being made – explicitly or by implication. The results depend much on the assumptions chosen.

The format for national income comparisons that will be used in this paper is a more general one, proposed in Sen (1976a), where the same commodity going to two different persons is treated as two different 'goods', so that the specification of the goods vector inevitably involves specification of the distribution as well. This

4. Cf. James Mirrlees: 'Undeniably, it is awkward to want an economic statistic that is not defined by standard procedures applied to observable data: the 'objectivity' of statistics appear to be compromised. But there is no way out. Either one has a (relatively) meaningless figure, or one employs economic expertise and guesswork in the construction of the statistics' (1969).

makes it more plausible to think of social welfare as a function of the vector of 'goods' thus defined, permitting a more direct analysis. But perhaps more importantly for this *survey* paper, this procedure helps to clarify the nature and effects of the various distributional assumptions underlying different real national income theories.

Section 2 of the paper is devoted to comparisons of *personal* real income. The problem is of interest on its own and also gets some reflected glory from those theories of real *national* income that treat the nation as if it were a person. Section 3 is concerned with real *national* income theory. These two parts, divided into many sections (each dealing with a particular aspect of the respective problems), form the bulk of the paper. Section 4 gathers together some concluding observations.[5]

2   Real Personal Income

2.1   Revealed preference versus convexity

Pure real income theory is concerned with using constant-price comparisons of different commodity bundles to rank them. While welfare conclusions can be drawn from such comparisons, the nature of the deduction depends on the interpretation of the constant prices. As argued in Section 1, the prices can be given at least two alternative types of interpretation.

In the institutional sense prices can be taken to represent actual opportunities of market transactions, and the 'chosen' position can be declared to be 'superior' to the available opportunities that were not chosen. This 'revealed preference' approach can be used to make personal welfare judgements based on constant-price comparisons of real income (see Samuelson, 1947; and Little, 1950; 1957, pp. 40–1). Underlying this *revealed preference* approach is the notion of *optimality* of actual choice from the point of view of the welfare of the person making the choice.

This approach can be contrasted with another that uses constant-price comparisons, not to identify what alternatives were available,

---

5. Some important problems of real income comparison will not be pursued in this paper. One such problem is the question of the valuation of capital goods (on which see among others, Samuelson (1961), Stephen Marglin (1976), Martin Weitzman (1976) and Dan Usher (1976)). In fact, the topic of this paper is more appropriately described as 'real consumption' rather than 'real income' (a statement that would apply to a good deal of what is typically called 'real income theory'). Another excluded problem is that of quality variation of goods (on which see Zvi Griliches (1971) and John Muellbauer (1974c), among other recent contributions). Also, the difficulties of actually gathering market price and quantity data − no mean problem − will not be pursued here.

but as indicators of a set of bundles that clearly must be inferior to the specified bundle *x* *if* the prices used are the ones that reflect relative weights on the different commodities (around *x*) and *if* the preferences can be taken to be convex. If at weights that are locally relevant for a bundle *x* an alternative bundle *y* is shown to have a lower aggregate value than *x*, then the assumption of convex indifference surfaces permits the inference that *x* is superior to *y* (see Jan de V. Graaff, 1957, pp. 162–3). The crucial notion underlying this approach is *convexity*.

These two alternative approaches are often not distinguished sufficiently clearly in the literature and are indeed sometimes treated as identical. The reason for this lies perhaps in the fact that the two approaches do lead to the same result under special assumptions that are frequently used in the standard theory of consumer behaviour. In Figure 17.1, *x* is the chosen bundle, and the market price ratio is given by the slope of *AB*. The locally relevant rate of indifference substitution at *x* is given by the slope of the indifference curve through *x*, and on the assumption of the consumer's choice being optimal from the point of view of his own welfare, the market price ratio given by the slope of *AB* is also taken to be the slope of the indifference curve through *x*.

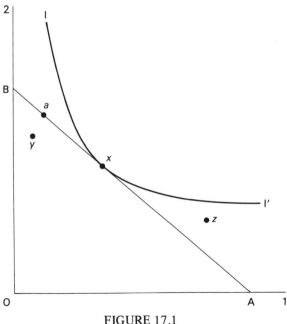

FIGURE 17.1

On the basis of the *revealed preference approach*, it can be asserted that x is superior to y, since y was within the available set (satisfying the budget constraint) when x was chosen. No assumption of convexity of preference has, in fact, been made in this deduction.[6] On the basis of the *convexity* approach, it can be asserted that x is superior to y, since the line AB is tangential to the indifference curve through x, so that all the points on or above the indifference curve lie on one side of AB, while y lies on the other side; and y must therefore be inferior to x. In this deduction, no use is made of the information regarding the bundles that are available when x was chosen, and the interpretation of AB is that of a tangent to the indifference curve through x rather than that of the budget line.

While these two deductions follow quite different logical courses, it so happens that in the standard theory with self-seeking consumer optimality under convex preferences and competitive buying, not much is lost in not distinguishing between them, since both lead to exactly the same results. But the assumptions can, of course, be readily altered to precipitate a dichotomy between the two approaches. In Figure 17.2, the consumer faces a noncompetitive market and the available set is given by the region OCD, even though the market exchange ratio when x is purchased is represented by the slope of AB.[7] It is now no longer deducible on the basis of 'optimality' alone that y is indeed inferior to x, and the revealed preference approach is no longer identical with constant-price real income comparison. But if the indifference curve through x to which AB is tangential is taken to be convex to the origin, then it is still assertible that y is inferior to x. Indeed, for this deduction AB need not have the interpretation of the market exchange ratio but of the tangent to the indifference curve through x (more generally, that of a hyperplane through x bounding from below[8] the set of points that are at least as good as x). In this case, the constant-price real-income method depends not on the foundations of revealed preference theory, but on those of convex preferences, using as prices the locally relevant weights at x.

6. Strictly speaking, in the absence of assuming a *strict* ordering, revealed preference theory should only assert here that x is at least as good as y, and help *can* be sought from the assumption of strict convexity of the indifference curve (i.e. strict convexity of the 'at least as good' region) to show that y is strictly inferior, since exactly one point from the highest indifference curve will then be available. But even this use of convexity can be dispensed with by using transitivity and the assumption of 'strict monotonicity' (i.e. the more the merrier), so that y is seen to be strictly worse than some point a on the budget line AB, when a itself is at most as good as x, since x was chosen when a was available.

7. Cf., Tapas Majumdar (1969).

8. To make sure that x is a non-interior point of the set of bundles that are at least as good as x, strict monotonicity may be assumed.

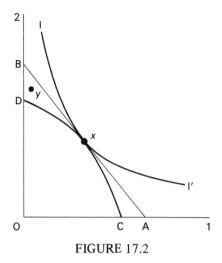

FIGURE 17.2

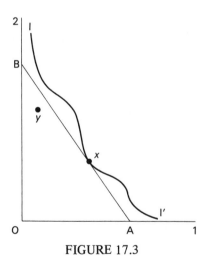

FIGURE 17.3

On the other hand, in Figure 17.3, the indifference curves are not convex to the origin, and the convexity approach cannot be used. But under competitive buying with self-seeking-consumer optimality, it is still assertible that x is superior to y using the revealed preference approach.[9]

9. Subject to the condition of strict monotonicity: see footnote 6.

And of course, when we can neither assume convex preference, nor competitive buying and optimality, then y cannot be shown to be inferior to x, even though x is valued higher than y at market exchange rates ruling around x. Indeed, y can then, in fact, be superior to x, as in Figure 17.4.

The two approaches to constant-price real-income comparison as a basis for welfare judgement are, thus, quite different. Even when they yield the same result, they do so out of coincidence arising from special assumptions. (In Figure 17.1, AB happens to be *both* a lower bound of the set of points on or above the indifference curve through x *and* a lower bound of the set of points that were *not* available when x was chosen.) And they may well give very different results, with one approach yielding a clear ranking, while the other yields nothing whatsoever. The distinction becomes particularly important when we move to the welfare basis of national – as opposed to personal – income comparisons with some approaches using both optimality and convex preferences (see for example, Samuelson, 1950, pp. 28–9; 1956; and Graaff, 1957, pp. 162–3), some using first-best or second-best optimality but not convex preferences (see, for example, Mirrlees, 1969) and some using convex preferences but not optimality (see, for example, Sen, 1976a).

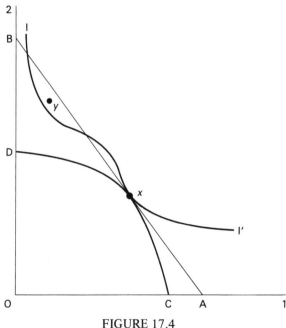

FIGURE 17.4

2.2   The economic quantity index: a contrast

Can the real income method rank *any* two bundles? In terms of both the approaches discussed in the last section, the answer is clearly no. The commodity bundle z in Figure 17.1 happens, in fact, to be inferior to x, but this is not demonstrable by the real income method using price and quantity data for x and z.[10] In terms of the 'optimality' approach, z is not, in fact, available when x is chosen, so that x is not revealed preferred to z, even though it is, in fact, superior to z. Similarly, in terms of the 'convexity' approach, at the locally relevant weights for x, x happens to be valued *less* than z, even though z is inferior to x. The real income procedure under both interpretations only separate out a set of some bundles that are definitely inferior (area OAB in Figure 17.1), but cannot split up the remainder into points superior to x, inferior to x, and indifferent to x, respectively.

In contrast with pure real income theory, the approach of 'economic quantity index' provides completeness and goes much further. Many of the recent results in the field of economic quantity indexing (including duality relations with price indexing) can be found in Paul A. Samuelson and Subramanian Swamy (1974), providing some new results and a helpful survey of the literature on this subject.[11] To construct a set of economic quantity indexes, the

10. Price and quantity data relating to choices other than x and z might permit ranking x and z on the basis of the 'transitive closure' of the revealed preference relation. (If x^1 is revealed preferred to x^2, x^2 to $x^3, \ldots, x^{n-1}$ to x^n, then x^1 is preferred to x^n according to the 'transitive closure' of the revealed preference relation.) Such extensions are discussed in Section 2.4.

11. The theory of economic quantity indexes relates very closely to that of economic price indexes (not astonishingly). The literature on economic indexes – price and quantity – is distressingly vast. In this paper there will be occasion to go into only a few limited aspects of this literature, since – as argued in the text – the pure theory of real income is motivationally quite different from the theory of economic indexes. However, to whet the appetite of the true seeker of knowledge, I include a 'short' bibliography of developments since Irving Fisher (1922). A. A. Konüs (1924), Gottfried Haberler (1927), Hans Staehle (1935), Wassily Leontief (1936), Ragnar Frisch (1936), John Hicks (1939; 1956; 1958), Paul Samuelson (1947; 1950; 1974a and b), Melville J. Ulmer (1949), Hendrick Houthakker (1950), Jean Ville (1952), R. G. D. Allen (1953; 1963; 1975), Herman Wold (1953), William M. Gorman (1953; 1956; 1976), S. Malmquist (1953), Milton Gilbert and Irving B. Kravis (1954), Jerome L. Nicholson (1955), Sidney Afriat (1956; 1972; 1976; 1977), Richard Stone (1956), Geer Stuvel (1957), Lionel McKenzie (1957), Robin Marris (1958), Irma Adelman (1958), Kali Banerjee (1961), A. P. Barten (1964), S. Swamy (1965; 1970), Henri Theil (1967), Richard Ruggles (1967), Wilfred Beckerman (1968), Franklin Fisher and Karl Shell (1968; 1972), Dan Usher (1968; 1976), R. W. Shephard (1953), John S. Chipman *et al.* (1971), Zvi Griliches (1971), Robert Pollak (1971; 1975a; 1977), Arnold Harberger (1971), John Muellbauer (1972; 1974a and b; 1976; 1977), Dale Jorgenson and Lawrence Lau (1975), W. E. Diewert (1976a and b), W. Eichhorn (1976), Y. O. Vartia (1976), K. Sato (1976), Lau (1977a and b), Charles Blackorby and R. Robert Russell

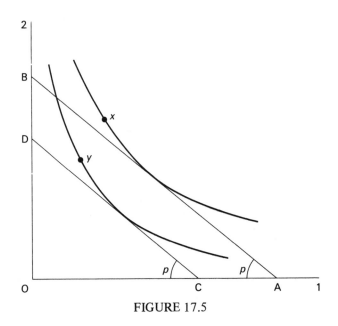

FIGURE 17.5

indifference map of the person in question is used and, in addition, a set of prices is specified. The 'economic quantity index' of bundle x vis-à-vis bundle y is the ratio of the minimum expenditures needed to reach respectively the welfare levels of x and y at the given prices p. They are not necessarily the costs of buying x or y, but the costs of the least expensive bundles that put the person on the same indifference curves as x and y, respectively.

In Figure 17.5, the specified price ratio is given by the angle p, with the vertical axis representing the commodity in units of which expenditures are measured (it makes no difference which axis is chosen given the constant price ratio). The index of x vis-à-vis y is given by the ratio of OB to OD. While this indexing depends on the set of relative prices chosen, it will be independent of this set if and only if preferences are homothetic, income elasticity of each good being unitary. (The indifference curves then will be, as it were, symmetric blow ups – or blow downs – of each other.) This same condition is needed to make the economic price indexes independent

(1978), Angus Deaton (1979), Blackorby, Daniel Primont, and Russell (1977), W. Eichhorn *et al.* (1978) and M. Fuss and Daniel McFadden (1978). The last three contain most of the main results, though the enthusiast for the blow-by-blow account must not be thus deflected.

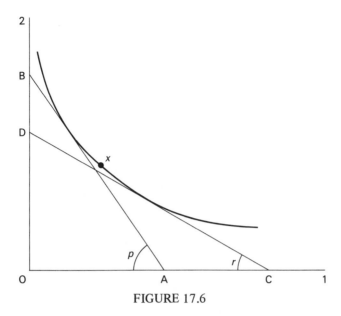

FIGURE 17.6

of the specified quantity bundle: the price index of p vis-à-vis r (see Figure 17.6) being defined as the ratio of minimum costs in the two price situations, respectively, of reaching the welfare level specified by a given quantity bundle. In Figure 17.6, the price index of p vis-à-vis r is OB/OD for the specified commodity bundle x (or any other bundle on the same indifference curve). If the preferences are homothetic with unitary income elasticity, then the price indexes come out the same no matter which quantity bundle is specified, must as the quantity indexes come out the same no matter which relative prices are specified.

In order to construct the 'economic quantity index' (or the 'economic price index') we need to know the indifference map (at least the relevant indifference curves). Informationally, therefore, this exercise is much more demanding than the exercises of real income comparisons discussed in the last section, which I shall call the 'pure' real income exercise. Indeed, while it might look super-ficially that the two exercises are doing similar jobs, viz. constructing indexes of prosperity, they are, in fact, addressed to totally different problems. The pure real income exercise is addressed to finding out which situation – whether x or y – is better, given rather limited information dealing with prices in the two situations interpreted either as market prices (institutional) or as locally relevant weights (conceptual). Some additional *qualitative* assumptions are added to this, e.g. optimality of actual choices, competitive markets, or convex preferences. But it is never presumed that the indifference map is known. Indeed if the indifference map were *known*, the exercise of whether x was better than y could be resolved straight away without any further ado. In contrast, the exercise of constructing the economic quantity index is *based* on the indifference map. It can, therefore, scarcely be addressed to the same problem.

What then *is* the problem to which the economic quantity index is, in fact, addressed? One answer to this question seems to be that it – combined with the economic price index – responds to Irving Fisher's (1922) quest for index numbers with certain ideal properties reflecting characteristics of a single good's quantity or price. Ragnar Frisch (1930) had shown, in a classic paper, that such indexes do not in general exist when the number of goods is two or more. Whereas the economic price and quantity index numbers seem to satisfy – what Samuelson and Swamy (1974) call – 'the spirit of all Fisher's criteria' in the case in which preferences are homothetic with unitary income elasticities of demand.[12] Samuelson and Swamy point out that 'this seeming contradiction with Frisch is possible because the price and quantity variables are not here allowed to be ... independent variables, but rather are constrained to satisfy the observable demand functions which optimize well-being' (1974, p. 566). This certainly is so, but notice also that these 'economic' indexes cannot be constructed without knowledge of the person's indifference map, so that the informational *basis* of index numbering has been entirely changed from the basis used by Irving Fisher.

Indeed, 'observable demand functions which optimize well-being' is a blanket phrase that covers both actually observed choices as well as 'counterfactuals' dealing with what expenditure level *would have* made the optimized choice lie on the same indifference surface as another specified bundle. In Figure 17.7, x and y are two observed choices at prices p and r respectively. To construct the economic quantity index of one in terms of the other at some specified prices, we have to go beyond these observed choices, *even if* the prices specified happen to be p or r. For example, to index x in terms of y at prices p, the 'counterfactual' equilibrium at y' would have to be located, putting the person on the same indifference curve as y at prices p and expenditure level OF, yielding the index number OB/OF. Conceptually, there is, of course, nothing illegitimate about this

12. See also Swamy (1965).

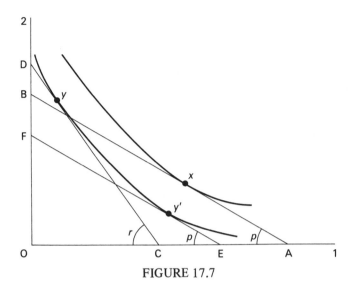

FIGURE 17.7

operation, but clearly the information requirement for constructing indexes has been radically expanded by this reformulation, going well beyond the ruling prices and quantities on which the class of indexes such as Paasche, or Laspeyres, or Fisher's 'ideal' index is based.

It is, however, possible to show that the conventional measures provide 'bounds' within which the 'economic' indexes must lie. If x^0 and x^1 are chosen respectively at prices p^0 and p^1, with welfare-optimizing behaviour under competitive conditions, then the economic index of x^1 in terms of x^0 at prices p^0 – denoted $e(x^1, x^0; p^0)$ – must be no larger than the Laspeyres quantity index $\lambda(x^1, x^0)$, while $e(x^1, x^0; p^1)$, i.e. the economic index at p^1 prices, must be no smaller than the Paasche quantity index $\pi(x^1, x^0)$:

$$e(x^1, x^0; p^0) \leqslant \lambda(x^1, x^0) \qquad (1)$$

$$e(x^1, x^0; p^1) \geqslant \pi(x^1, x^0) \qquad (2)$$

Obviously, when the economic indexes are *independent* of the price vectors, i.e. in the homethetic case, the price-independent economic quantity index $e(x^1, x^0)$ must lie *between* the Paasche and Laspeyres indexes:

$$\pi(x^1, x^0) \leqslant e(x^1, x^0) \qquad (3)$$
$$\leqslant \lambda(x^1, x^0)$$

Samuelson and Swamy also provide an approximation theorem to the effect that any symmetric mean of the Laspeyres and Paasche indexes will approximate the true index number up to the third order in accuracy, in the homothetic special case (1974, p. 582). This is clearly an interesting result. It should, however, be noted that the result concerns closeness of *index values* rather than of the *graphs of orderings* generated by them, and the gap between approximation of indexes and approximation of welfare orderings can be met only by *additional* restrictions.

It is worth remarking that the limit results (1)–(3) have no greater value for ranking a pair of bundles x^0 and x^1 than can be done by direct reasoning in the tradition of 'pure' real income theory without introducing the notion of an 'economic' index. Consider the points x, y and z in Figure 17.1, with x chosen at prices p. Interpreting x as x^1 and p as p^1 makes the Paasche index $\pi(x, y)$ of x vis-à-vis y greater than unity, and since the Paasche index is a lower bound of the 'economic quantity index' $e(x^1, x^0. p^1)$ (see equation (2)), clearly x is superior to y. (The conclusion can also be derived, alternatively, again in terms of 'economic quantity index', by taking x as x^0 and p as p^0, noting that the Laspeyres index − less than unity − is an *upper* bound to the economic index $e(x^1, x^0; p^0)$, using equation (1).) But that conclusion was derived *anyway* on the basis of the 'pure' real income theory in Section 2.1. On the other hand, it is not possible to rank x and z on the basis of these limit results any more than it was possible to do so without introducing the apparatus of economic indexes. With x as x^1 and z as x^0, the Paasche index of x vis-à-vis z will be less than unity, and the Laspeyres index − if the prices for the choice of z were shown − would be greater than unity, permitting no ranking of x vis-à-vis z, even when homotheticity is assumed. *These limits* of the economic index only reassert what we knew already.[13]

This is, of course, not to deny the conceptual merit of having the 'economic quantity index' and seeing the other indexes as 'erroneous' in some way or other. But the 'erroneous' indexes such as Laspeyres and Paasche need not lead to any actual errors as long as they are used to generate a *partial* ordering (as discussed in Section 2.1) based on partitioning the set of bundles into 'inferior' and 'undecided' subsets.

The 'economic' index becomes of practical − as opposed to purely conceptual − value if we happen to have access to the person's

13. The limits can, of course, be narrowed if additional structural assumptions are made about the nature of the underlying preference. For an illuminating account of the problem of the limits of the economic *price* index, see Afriat (1977).

indifference map, however estimated. The fact that this permits a *complete* welfare ordering of all bundles is, of course, trivial, since that is what we are starting with in the shape of the indifference map.[14] But the quantitative values of the index numbers can be seen to be of significance. It reduces a vector to a scalar measure and permits one to interpret and easily communicate the 'quantity' involved in a vector of commodities as a simple real number. The transformation of a commodity vector into a utility number can then be split up into two intuitively interpretable steps: (i) going from a commodity vector to a 'quantity' real number, and (ii) going from a 'quantity' real number to a utility real number. This split up has much merit from the point of view of understanding, analysing, and communicating, and aside from direct use, it provides the way to other useful presentations, e.g. splitting up expenditure changes into changes of a quantity index and a price index (as in Muellbauer, 1974a).

The motivation of the economic quantity is, thus, quite different from that of the pure real income theory, even though the economic quantity index has superficially the same form as the use of constant-price weighted values. It is also worth noting in this context that for the purpose for which the economic quantity index is sought, this price weighting form can, in fact, be dispensed with if one were to follow Malmquist (1953) in indexing commodity vectors in terms of the distance from the origin of the indifference curve to which it belongs, measured along a specified 'ray', i.e. for specified ratios of commodities. Vectors x and y belonging to indifference curves I and I' in Figure 17.8 would then be indexed in the ratio OA to OB if α were taken as the specified commodity ratio (and, thus, OC the specified 'ray').[15] The indexing will be independent of the 'ray' specified if and only if the preferences are homothetic, and in that special case the 'distance function' indexes will also coincide with the standard economic indexes for any specified price vector.

It is important to recognize that compared with the pure real income theory, economic quantity indexes – whether based on constant-price cost functions or constant-ratio distant functions – not only demand more information (viz. knowledge of the indifference map), but also deliver more (viz. not just an ordering but

14. Note that the ordering implicit in an economic *price* index is not, however, just a repetition of the ordering from which we start, since it utilizes orderings of the *commodity bundles* to get orderings of *price vectors*.

15. Deaton (1979) provides a thorough and illuminating exploration of the distance-based approach to indexing. See also Gerard Debreu (1951), Hicks (1958), Shephard (1953), Pollak (1971), Diewert (1976a and b), Blackorby and Russell (1978), Blackorby and D. Donaldson (1978), G. Hanoch (1978) and McFadden (1978).

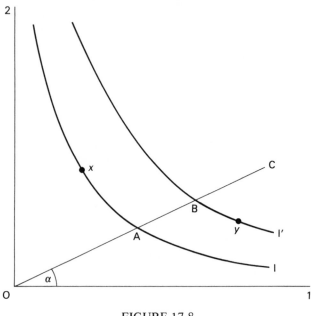

FIGURE 17.8

a ratio-scale real-numbered measure of quantities). Samuelson and Swamy rightly note this, but in the process seem to introduce fresh ambiguities (1974, p. 568):

> The fundamental point about an economic quantity index, which is too little stressed by writers, Leontief and Afriat being exceptions, is that it must itself be a cardinal indicator of ordinal utility.

What precisely *is* a 'cardinal indicator or ordinal utility'? It isn't obvious how an ordinal utility can have a cardinal index that captures it exactly. But there must be at least two underlying questions here: (1) Does the invariance property of the index correspond to that of 'cardinality', viz. uniqueness up to a positive affine transformation? (2) Is 'cardinality' – or whatever property of invariance the index is seen to satisfy – a property of it as an indicator of *utility*?

On the first question, note that the indexing of commodity bundles ordered by an indifference map is simply *unique* given the price vector *p*. If the units in which prices or quantities are measured are changed, this would still preserve all the ratios, so that the index system is measured in the 'ratio scale'. That is, the uniqueness is up to a homogeneous linear transformation, and the restriction is not, in fact, cardinal. If it is nevertheless called 'cardinal', this must be because it does satisfy the uniqueness properties of cardinality *plus* some more. I guess there need be no great harm in calling any measure satisfying a restriction more demanding than cardinality as 'cardinal', but it may be noted that for exactly similar reasons, such a measure could be called 'ordinal' as well, since it also satisfies the uniqueness properties of ordinality *plus* some more!

For homothetic preferences, this property of having ratios that are invariant is maintained even when the price vector p is changed and the relative prices can vary. So the economic index is a *ratio-scale* measure *both* (i) with given relative prices, as well as (ii) independently of the price vector in the homothetic case.

The second question is a more important one. In what sense does the index provide a cardinal or a ratio-scale indicator of *utility*? Note that with a given price vector p (and independently of prices in the homothetic case), any ordering of the commodity bundles in the form of an indifference map can be translated into only one particular ratio-scale index system. A variation of one's intensities of pleasure or welfare cannot, therefore, find any reflection in this numbering system as long as the ordering remains unchanged. It is obvious, therefore, that the index can hardly be treated as a ratio-scale (or cardinal) measure of *utility* as such. Indeed, an attempt to interpret two equal differences in the index values of the economic quantity index as representing equal differences of utility will be quite illegitimate.

This last point is a rather serious one for the interpretation of real income indexes in the context of welfare. In Section 2.1 there was no attempt to go beyond treating the indicators as having only ordinal significance. If the ratio-scale invariance of the economic quantity index could have been given the interpretation of a 'ratio-scale' measure of utility, then much more could have been read into these figures. In particular, even percentage growth rates – a common application of real income measures – would have had a clear welfare interpretation, which these rates do not have under the 'ordinal' interpretation (or for that matter – under the 'cardinal' interpretation of the measure, because of the arbitrary origin). But, as we have just seen, such a 'ratio-scale' (or, for that matter, 'cardinal') interpretation of the index as an indicator of utility is quite unacceptable, and the economic quantity index does not really take us beyond an ordinal measure as far as *welfare* is concerned.

2.3 *Comprehensive and situational comparisons*

The discussion so far has not distinguished between contrasting *alternatives* for a given person at a given point of time and comparing different actual *situations* (e.g. successive positions). The former is entirely legitimate for a theory of rational choice (or of planning), since such a theory has to deal with evaluating a set of alternatives *only one* of which – at most – will occur. In contrast, a theory of comparison of real incomes has to take note of the fact that the situations to be dealt with are *all* actual situations, and the occurrence of one does not negate the occurrence of the others. Whether the argument involves my well-being today vis-à-vis that of a year earlier, or my real income today vis-à-vis yours today, or the real income per head of France vis-à-vis Germany, the reference is to actual situations (faced by different persons or at different points of time). It is for this reason that a rational-choice or a planning-theory approach to real income comparisons must be fundamentally incomplete.

While real income comparisons are concerned with comparisons of actual situations, these comparisons can be interpreted in two different ways. The distinction refers to that between statements of the type: (A) 'I am better off this year than I was last year', and those of the type: (B) 'I am better off this year than I would have been if I had last year's commodity bundle this year', or 'I would have been better off last year if I had this year's commodity bundle rather than the one I actually had'. The former compares the welfares actually generated including the effect of any shift in the welfare characteristics of the person between the two periods, while the latter compares the situations in terms of a given welfare mapping (relating one welfare value to each commodity bundle). I shall call the first 'comprehensive comparisons' (the contrasts being combination of differences in welfare characteristics of the persons and the situations in which they find themselves) and the second 'situational comparisons' (the contrasts being exclusively confined to the situations in which they find themselves).

The distinction is sometimes discussed in terms of 'constant' or 'variable' *tastes*, but as Fisher and Shell note, 'the man's efficiency as a pleasure machine may have changed without changing his tastes' (1972, p. 3).[16] This is an important distinction since a person's indifference map may remain unchanged while the welfare levels associated with each curve may have changed substantially.

---

16. This problem was discussed extensively in the PhD thesis of Herbert Gintis (1969).

To illustrate the point, consider a manic-depressive person, who was manic in year 0 when he had commodity bundle x^0, and depressive in year 1 when his bundle was x^1. Assume further that his indifference map is the same in both years, and that both in year 0 and year 1, he would have been better off with x^1 than with x^0. But this does not guarantee that he was better off *in year 1* with x^1 (depressive as he then was) than he had been *in year 0* with x^0. Neither the consistency of situational comparisons in terms of each year's tastes, nor the constancy of the indifference map, permit us to make comprehensive comparisons based on that map. Only if it is further asserted that the welfare characteristics of the person have not changed (i.e. no change in the person's efficiency as a pleasure-machine and no change in sources of joy that are not captured by the commodity bundles), will it be possible to translate immediately 'situational comparisons' into 'comprehensive comparisons'.[17]

That something more than indifference maps is involved in comprehensive comparisons was seen much earlier by Jan Graaff (1957), but in the tradition of the day, he immediately proceeded to interpret this in terms of the distinction between 'ordinal' and 'cardinal' utility.

Let us suppose that it is W^* on the basis of the first year's tastes, and W^{**} on the basis of the second year's. There are now two distinct possibilities. If the ethical beliefs defining the W's are such that they have *cardinal* significance, we can say that welfare has increased whenever $W_2^{**} > W_1^*$. But if the W's have only *ordinal* significance, we can do no more than compare the two years first on the basis of the one's tastes, and then on the basis of the other's. It may easily happen that $W_2^{**} > W_1^{**}$ and $W_2^* < W_1^*$, so that we have an ambiguity. This is one of the few instances I have been able to discover where a cardinal social welfare function has advantages over an ordinal one.[18]

Graaff saw clearly the inadequacy of basing what we are calling 'comprehensive comparisons' on *ordinal* 'situational comparisons', but the same difficulty exists even if the welfare measures used for

17. However, the constancy of welfare characteristics is not always necessary to *infer* 'comprehensive comparisons' from 'situational comparisons'. For example, in the case cited above in which both in year 0 and in year 1 the bundle x^1 is regarded as better than the bundle x^0, if it is further known that the person had uniformly *more favourable* welfare characteristics in year 1 than in year 0, then it could be deduced that he was better off in year 1 than in year 0.

18. Graaff (1957, pp. 157–8). Graaff's dicussion is about 'social' as opposed to 'personal' welfare, but the considerations are exactly similar.

situational comparisons are cardinal. If W^* and W^{**} emerge from two welfare functions respectively, each cardinal, there is still no way of saying whether W^* is less than or more than W^{**}. On the other hand, if W^* and W^{**} emerge from the *same* welfare function (unchanged welfare characteristics) then even if that welfare function is ordinal, we can still rank W^* and W^{**} perfectly clearly. Thus the problem would arise not from ordinality as such, but from the lack of interperiod comparability.[19] (There is an analogy here with the tendency to blame the absence of cardinality for frustrating results in interpersonal aggregation, e.g. see the otherwise excellent note of Murray Kemp and Yew-Kwang Ng (1977), when the real culprit would seem to be the lack of interpersonal comparability; see Sen (1977a).)

Situational comparisons are rather difficult to define in the context of comparisons of real *national* income as opposed to real *personal* income, and this problem will be discussed in Section 3.11. Sticking for the moment to comparisons of personal incomes as guides to personal welfare comparisons, note that constancy of tastes is not necessary for situational comparisons. Since the comparison is made in terms of the welfare characteristics (*including* tastes) of one *specified* period, e.g. statements of the type of (B) above, there is no need to assume that the tastes do not change between one period and the next.

Thus, constancy of tastes is *unnecessary* for direct situational comparisons, and it is *insufficient* for translating situational comparisons into comprehensive comparisons. The dividing line does not fall on the constancy of the preference map in either exercise.

2.4   *The use of transitivity*

Constancy of tastes does, however, have a role in generating a partial ordering out of a set of partial rankings. The real income method leads to a partial ranking of the commodity bundles in each judgement, e.g. x is preferred to bundles within the triangle OAB in Figure 17.1. Note that when more than one choice are combined together, the result need not be transitive, even when the indifference map has remained unchanged and displays transitivity. In Figure 17.9, x can be demonstrated to be better than y by the real income method (either through revealed preference or through con-

---

19. Note also that the ambiguity exists not merely when '$W_2^{**} > W_1^{**}$ and $W_2^* < W_1^*$', but also when $W_2^{**} > W_1^{**}$, and $W_2^* > W_1^*$, since it still does not permit us to say anything about the ranking of W_2^{**} vis-à-vis W_1^*.

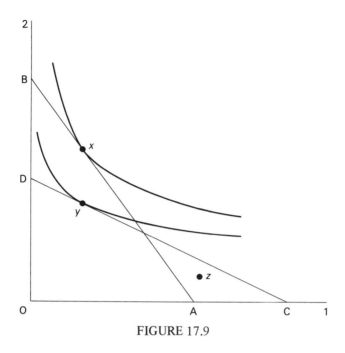

FIGURE 17.9

vexity as discussed in Section 2.1), and y is similarly demonstrably better than z. But it is not possible to demonstrate by the same method that x is better than z.

If, however, constancy of tastes can be assumed in the sense of an unchanged consistent indifference map, then it would be legitimate to conclude that x is better than z. This is because the demonstrations that x is better than y and that y is better than z indicate parts of the underlying consistent preference, and it is then legitimate to conclude that x must be better than z in terms of that underlying pattern. Under these circumstances, one is entitled to accept the 'transitive closure' of the partial rankings based on comparisons of actual situations: if x^1 is demonstrated to be better than x^2, x^2 than $x^3, \ldots, x^{n-1}$ than x^n, then it can be accepted that x^1 is better than x^n. This yields a strict partial ordering (transitive and asymmetric).

Notice that this approach uses both (i) the assumption of constancy of tastes, as well as (ii) that of consistent underlying preferences. The consistency conditions can also be stated from the observational point of view, i.e. directly in terms of consistency of observed choices. Houthakker (1950) stated this in the form of a condition of 'semi-transitivity', which is essentially a requirement of the *absence* of strict cycles of revealed preference, such as x^1 shown better than x^2, x^2 shown better than $x^3, \ldots, x^{n-1}$ shown better than x^n, and x^n shown better than x^1. The consistency conditions can be stated in somewhat different forms, but the important anaytical point to note is that the absence of observed inconsistency over *all* conceivable choice situations under competitive buying will hold if and only if the underlying preference pattern is itself consistent (i.e. in the words of Afriat (1977), 'revealed consistency is equivalent to general consistency').[20] This is, of course, based on the further assumption of constant tastes (i.e. assumption (i) above), and also that the choices are made optimally in a competitive market (see Section 2.1 above).

Two warnings about the use of this approach are, however, in order. First, the derived relationship (i.e. the 'transitive closure') is usable only for *situational* comparisons, even when tastes are constant. Deducing *comprehensive* comparisons out of them will remain a *non sequitur* for reasons discussed in the last section. Second, while the absence of revealed inconsistency when every *conceivable* choice situation has been faced may be proof of the absence of any inconsistency in the underlying preference pattern (assumed constant), nothing of the sort is, of course, implied when no revealed inconsistency shows up in the subset of *actual* choices that happen to have occurred. Nor does the absence of revealed inconsistency in these choices establish that tastes have not changed *even if* it is assumed *a priori* that any underlying preference pattern must be a consistent ordering. Thus, in terms of any actually observed sequence of choices, the assumptions of constancy and consistency of tastes must remain open to doubt. (Methodologically, it is possible to construct a justification of this approach on the ground that the hypothesis *is* falsifiable, and it can be legitimately accepted until it is falsified. The force of this defence is somewhat reduced by the fact that the observed choices typically are a tiny fraction – could be of measure zero – of the total set of choices that are possible.)

The assumption of constancy of tastes is indeed quite a strong one, especially when the observed situations are separated a great deal in time. There is, however, a genuine dilemma here, since taking observations for very short periods very close to each other is exposed to the other danger of taking as taste change what may be nothing other than a taste for variety (e.g. beef one day and lamb on another) embedded in stable long-run tastes. When real income

20. For the main results in this area, see Afriat (1976; 1977).

comparisons are made for choices over one year at a time (as is often the case), it may be more legitimate to expect that the search for variety is fulfilled *within* each year's choices, but then the other problem becomes serious, since the assumption of constancy of tastes for observations involving many years will tend to be quite a dubious one.

There is also the problem arising from people learning from experience.[21] The use of transitive closures to obtain partial orderings as representing underlying preferences gets into quite considerable difficulty once 'endogenous tastes' are considered.

Problems of taste variations arise not merely in intertemporal comparisons but also in making situational comparisons involving different persons (or nations). It is, thus, easy to have considerable sympathy with Irving Fisher's reluctance to use transitivity 'to compare Egypt and Norway *via* Georgia' on the ground that the comparison between Egypt and Norway is 'none of Georgia's business' (1922, p. 272). One may, therefore, be inclined to register a mild protest at Samuelson and Swamy's off-hand dismissal of Fisher's reluctance to use Georgia to compare Egypt with Norway: 'This simply throws away the transitivity of indifference and has been led astray by Fisher's unwarranted belief that only fixed-weights lead to circular tests being satisfied' (Samuelson and Swamy, 1974, p. 576).[22] That view about circular tests is certainly unwarranted, but the real income or cost of living in Egypt or Norway does remain 'none of Georgia's business', unless there are good reasons to think that Georgia's tastes are similar to those of Egypt or Norway.[23]

It is certainly true that if we refuse to make the assumption of constancy of tastes, the real income judgements would have to be confined only to *direct* partial rankings, partitioning the bundles into two subjects vis-à-vis any actually chosen bundles, viz. a set of definitely worse bundles and a set of bundles that could be better, worse or indifferent (see Section 2.1). This might be a great deal less than what can be said by taking 'transitive closures' based on the assumption of constant, consistent tastes. But even these direct partial rankings do permit many real income judgements to be made.

21. For discussions of this issue and some results, see Gorman (1967), Pollak (1970; 1976; 1978), Carl Christian von Weizsacker (1971), János Kornai (1971, chs 10 and 11), Gintis (1974) and Wulf Gaertner (1974), among a number of other contributions.

22. Both Fisher's observation as well as Samuelson and Swamy's comment deal with construction of *price* indexes rather than that of indexes of *quantity*, or of real income. But the issues are quite similar in the two exercises.

23. There remains, of course, the different issue as to whether there are such things as Georgia's tastes, since Georgia isn't a person but a state. This issue is taken up in Section 3 of this paper.

And saying less with conviction is not always inferior to saying more with great doubts. There is indeed a real choice here, and one that must be explicitly faced: the choice between *scope* and *reliability* is an important one not merely for personal income comparisons but also for comparisons of real national income, as will be seen in Section 3 of this paper.

2.5   *Market prices and consumption benefits*

Under the 'conceptual' approach, the price vector used for weighting has the interpretation of local indifferent substitution rates at the point of observation. In the usual real income exercise these local substitution rates are identified with the market prices. This identification can be questioned from various points of view.

Before discussing these problems, it is perhaps worth clearing up an issue involving consumer's surplus that frequently emerges in this context. As Tibor Scitovsky notes:

> When the market value of goods and services is used as an estimate of the value people put on the satisfaction they get from consuming them, it must be recognized as being always an *underestimate*. The consumer gets more satisfaction out of anything he buys than out of the money he pays for it, otherwise he would not buy it. That additional satisfaction is his consumer's surplus whose value cannot be estimated, although it can be gauged by finding out what he would pay, if necessary, for continued access to a particular good at its present price rather than go without it altogether.[24]

While this does indicate an underestimation error if the value of real income is taken as a measure of satisfaction as such, no such error is, of course, involved in using the real income method to generate a partial ordering (as in Section 2.1 and subsequently). The consumer's surplus is related to the extent of the curvature of the indifference curves, and the partial rankings were identified simply on the assumption that the indifference curves were convex (with unspecified curvatures). Indeed, the partial ranking related to substitution rates locally relevant for any bundle x partitions all bundles simply into 'inferior' ones and 'undecided' ones, and that is all that is used; it is the further divisions of the latter subset into 'inferior', 'indifferent' and 'superior' bundles that depend on the curvatures in question. Thus the difficulty, while a real one for treating con-

---

24. Scitovsky (1976, p. 85); italics added. See also Robert D. Willig (1976).

sumption values as quantitative indicators of welfare (with which Scitovsky is concerned in this context (1976)), does not affect at all the real income method for welfare judgements based on convexity.

But the other issues with which Scitovsky is concerned in this contribution, viz. those relating to the motivation underlying consumer choice, and to sources of happiness other than goods purchased in markets, are of central relevance to the real income method based on market prices. Scitovsky — and also others (e.g. Kornai, 1971; Harvey Leibenstein, 1976; Fred Hirsch, 1976 and A. E. Andersson, 1977) — have recently argued against various aspects of the rather crude psychology underlying the assumption that personal rates of indifferent substitution equal market price ratios. The motivation underlying choice is believed to be a great deal more complex than can be captured under the assumption of maximization of personal satisfaction.

This type of difficulty has, in fact, more serious consequences for the 'revealed preference' approach to real income comparisons than for the 'convexity' approach as such. The revealed preference interpretation has to rest squarely on the supposition that the chosen position is the best one (or, at least, *a* best one) for the chooser, among the ones available to him. If one rejects the proposition that a person's choices must reflect the maximization of personal welfare,[25] then the 'revealed preference' approach is simply unusable. On the other hand, all it does against the 'convexity' approach is to bar the use of market prices as the locally relevant substitution rates. One can 'correct' these market prices to take into account the considerations in question. Or even proceed entirely on the basis of questionnaire rather than observing market choices (see Richard Easterlin, 1974; Julian Simon, 1974; Scitovsky, 1976, ch. 7; Bernard van Praag, 1971; van Praag and Arie Kapteyn, 1973 and others). The informational economy in permitting a global partial ordering on the basis of local substitution information holds whether or not these substitution rates are obtained from market prices, as long as the convexity of the preference structure is accepted. The 'conceptual' approach to real income comparisons permits considerable freedom about how the 'bridge' might best be built to use the convexity properties coupled with local preference information.

The same applies to sources of satisfaction other than goods bought in the market. These sources obviously don't have market

---

25. Various alternative interpretations of this proposition are possible, and each raises difficulties of its own; see Sen (1977b).

prices, but if the person's welfare-based preference,[26] including these sources of satisfaction, is convex, then constant-weight real-income comparisons can be made in exactly the same way as with marketed commodities. The only difference would lie in not having ready-made prices that could be taken as local substitution rates (with whatever justification!), but having to construct such prices out of other – rather indirect – information. That such exercises can be done with imagination and skill has been amply demonstrated by such works as William Nordhaus and James Tobin (1972) and M. Shinohara *et al.* (1973). It is, however, possible to argue that these works attach too much importance to the exact numerical values of the vectors of goods at local substitution rates, rather than using these values to precipitate a partial ordering, which is, in fact, the extent of legitimacy of the welfare judgement, as discussed above.[27] (The concern with exact quantitative values partly reflects interest in estimating growth rates, on which there tends to be much public curiosity.) The same techniques could, of course, also be used to isolate partial rankings in line with real income theory.[28]

If, however, the assumption of convexity is itself found unacceptable, then the real income approach based on it must obviously be rejected. Indeed, if this rejection is combined with the acceptance of the proposition that a person's choices *do* maximize his personal welfare and the choices are subject to linear budget constraints, then the real income approach based on revealed preference will be the one to use. (Note, though, it can hardly provide a good basis for valuing non-marketed goods.)

These alternative possibilities exist only because – as discussed in Section 2.1 – the 'revealed preference' approach and the 'convexity' approach provide essentially two *independent* ways of using the real income method, and either can survive without the other. It is, of course, also possible that neither 'revealed preference' nor 'convexity' would be acceptable assumptions in the context of consumer choice. If that is indeed the case, then – I fear – there will be little use for the theory of real income comparison in making personal welfare judgements.

26. Preference can be given either a choice interpretation, or a welfare interpretation, either of which can be made definitional, but not both simultaneously (see Sen, 1977b). Here the welfare interpretation is intended.

27. That is, real income theory based on convexity (rather than linearity) has to be concerned mainly with partitioning the commodity space into 'worse' and 'undecided' subsets through a hyperplane rather than concentrating on the value of the hyperplane *itself*.

28. There is, of course, also the further problem of interpersonal aggregation, since these estimates are meant to deal with national rather than personal incomes. See Section 3.

3 Real National Income

3.1 The nation as a person

While the discussion in Section 2 was explicitly concerned with *personal* real income comparisons, much the same framework is very often used for comparisons of real national income as well. The nation is then treated as if it were a person with a given indifference map defined over the national commodity bundles. This is sometimes stated explicitly, e.g. in Hicks' exposition of 'classical theory' (Hicks, 1958), or 'base theory', which 'neglects differences among consumers' (Hicks, 1974, pp. 9–10). Some other approaches to national income theory don't spell the assumption out, but make ready sense only under such an implicit assumption. For example, the interesting recent debates on the appropriate exchange rates to be used for international comparison of real national income seem to treat the nation as a person in this sense (see, for example, Usher, 1968; Paul David, 1972; 1973; Bela Balassa, 1973; 1974; and Samuelson, 1974a).[29] Indeed, several of the developments in the theory of real personal income have taken place in the context of national income comparisons, and the two problems are often lumped together.

The nation is not, of course, a person, so that a theory of *national* income in the lines of Section 2 above must be acknowledged to be a bit romantic. That it certainly is, but the treatment of the nation as a person does not have to be based on sharing John Milton's complex vision of 'a noble and puissant nation rousing herself like a strong man after sleep, and shaking her invincible locks'. It is sufficient to assume that the nation consists of many people who happen to be identical in every respect, each enjoying the national mean commodity bundle,[30] and sharing identical welfare characteristics. This is, of course, still very romantic, but it is a popular romance and indeed for a preliminary analysis it does have some obvious merits. But there would not have been much of a theory of real national income had the subject ended with this personal view of the nation.

29. The traditional empirical studies of international comparisons (e.g. Simon Kuznets (1948), Gilbert and Kravis (1954), Wilfred Beckerman and Robert Bacon (1966), Kravis, Alan Heston and Robert Summers (1978a and b)) make good use of this assumption.

30. Note, however, that the mean consumption basket may include 'contradictions', e.g. medicines that raise blood pressure and those that reduce it. The assumption that some integrated person actually consumes the national mean commodity bundle is indeed a difficult supposition. That all of them do that is obviously more so.

3.2 *Production possibilities and real output comparison*

The distinction between the welfare approach and the production possibility approach to real income comparisons was one of the main points of Hicks' (1940) classic paper. It is important to note that they operate independently of each other, the welfare interpretation being based on the use of indifferent substitution surfaces and the production interpretation on the use of transformation surfaces. For neither approach is it necessary to assume that the marginal conditions of optimality prevail in the form of the substitution rates equalling the corresponding transformation rates; nor is it necessary to require the convexity of *both* substitution and transformation surfaces.[31]

In production possibility comparison, which is sometimes called 'real output comparison', the question that is being asked is of this type: in the production situation in which x was in fact produced, would it have been within the nation's production possibility to have produced instead an alternative bundle of goods y? Or, to put it as Fisher and Shell do (1972, p. 53):

In effect, in each comparison we are asking whether the production system that produced x^A would have to be expanded, contracted, or left unchanged to produce x^B.

Let $x\,Q\,y$ stand for the statement that a system that can generate x can also generate y. It is assumed that the relation Q is an ordering (transitive, reflexive and complete). Assuming free disposal, if x includes more of some commodity and no less of any compared with y, then clearly $x\,Q\,y$. A system can be described as being 'just able' to produce x, if it is capable of producing x but not any bundle that contains more of some commodity and no less of any compared with x. Let $Q(x)$ be defined as the set of all alternative bundles that can be produced by a system that is 'just able' to produce x. Given 'completeness' in the form that for any pair x, y, either $x\,Q\,y$, or $y\,Q\,x$ (or both), and 'convexity' in the form that $Q(x)$ for each x is convex, it is possible to use the constant-price real-income method to try to compare any two bundles x and y on the basis of local transforma-

31. The import of the dichotomy pointed out by Hicks was absorbed rather slowly in the literature. While Hicks felt able to express satisfaction in 1958 that his distinction 'appears to have stood up quite well to the fire of controversy' (1958, p. 125), the Samuelson–Graaff approach to comparing social welfare based on convex indifferent substitution surfaces – proposed by Samuelson (1950) and corrected by Graaff (1957) – carried the excess baggage of assuming that 'diminishing returns prevail and prices equal marginal costs' (Graaff, 1957, p. 162).

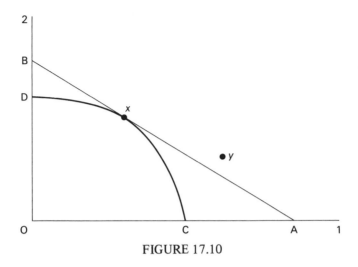

FIGURE 17.10

tion information even without knowing the entire production possibility map given by the relation Q. The approach is exactly analogous to that of constant-price real-income comparison using the convexity approach to precipitate a partial ordering of welfare, based on local substitution information (see Section 2.1).

In Figure 17.10, x is produced by a particular production system. The feasible bundles given by set $Q(x)$ are represented by the area $OCxD$. This is convex, and thus through x there goes a straight line AB such that all the feasible bundles lie below this line.[32] If y lies above that line, then clearly y could not have been produced when x was produced. Since the local transformation rates will give the slope of such a line, all that need be checked is whether at these relative prices y represents a higher value than x. That is, if p represents the transformation rates around x, then under the assumptions specified, $px < py$ implies that y could not have been produced when x was produced.

It is easily seen that the entire analysis proceeds on the basis of a given Q, i.e. a given production possibility map. If x and y represent production with two different states of technical knowledge, then it is likely that the production possibility maps are different in the

32. If more than two commodities were considered, the partitioning would be done not by a line AB but by a hyperplane. The existence of such a hyperplane is guaranteed by x being a non-interior point of a convex region.

two cases. This is exactly comparable to the problem of taste change discussed in the context of the 'dual' problem of using the real-income approach to make situational comparisons of welfare (see Section 2).[33]

However, given the other assumption, viz. completeness of each ordering Q, monotonicity (including free disposal), and convexity, a situational comparison can be made from the vantage of each production system. If x^0 and x^1 are produced in two different situations when the local transformation rates are p^0 and p^1, respectively, it is still possible to say that: (i) if $p^0x^0 < p^0x^1$, then x^1 could not have been produced when x^0 was produced, and (ii) if $p^1x^1 < p^1x^0$, then x^0 could not have been produced when x^1 was produced.

These relations could be interpreted in terms of the usual Laspeyres and Paasche indexes, provided the local transformation rates are reflected by the prices used for weighting. The interpretation of prices are, thus, different now from that in the welfare exercise; they are indicators of local transformation rates as opposed to local substitution rates. Correspondingly, the focus may shift from consumer prices (including commodity taxes) to producer prices (excluding commodity taxes) in making comparisons of types (i) and (ii) above.[34]

It can be argued that the use of the convexity approach to 'real output' comparison is more difficult than its use in situational comparisons of welfare because convexity is less plausible for production relations (because of the prevalence of increasing returns to scale) than it is for preference relations. Furthermore, the assumption of 'completeness' of the production possibility relation Q may be more open to doubt. On the other hand, given the importance of the

33. Similarly, just as there was a contrast between 'taste' changes and shifts in 'welfare characteristics' in the welfare exercise, there is a contrast here between changes in the production possibility map and shifts in production characteristics. In fact, technical progress could leave the map completely unchanged but at the same time reduce the resource requirement of each production possibility frontier. This leads to undecidability on whether or not the resource-base has expanded when one had only the production possibility map to go by, just comparable to the undecidability about 'comprehensive' welfare judgements based on comparisons with an unchanged indifference map (see Section 2.3 above). However, the question of resource-base expansion is perhaps less innately interesting than that of welfare comparison, and – more importantly – it is decidable by *direct* observation in a manner that the welfare comparison is not.

34. Notice also that there is a change in the way of using indexes in the two exercises. For production possiblity comparison, a rise in the Laspeyres index and a fall in the Paasche index are significant (see (i) and (ii) above), while for welfare comparison, a rise in the Paasche index and a fall in the Laspeyres index are the relevant bases of judgement (see Sections 2.1 and 2.2 above).

distributional question for social welfare judgements, it may be more difficult to justify the interpretation of market prices as the locally relevant social rates of indifferent substitution than the interpretation of producer prices (net of taxes) as giving the locally relevant social rates of transformation. So both are problematic, but for rather different reasons.

3.3 Named goods and social welfare

I turn now to the problem of welfare interpretation of real national income. A major difficulty in viewing national income in terms of social welfare arises from the importance of distribution in our conceptions of social welfare. Even when the amount of every commodity that is available for enjoyment by the nation as a whole has been specified through a commodity vector x, we are still not in a position to associate a social welfare value W to x, since W will not be independent of the distribution of x among the persons in the nation.

There is, however, a way of specifying the distribution entirely through the vector of goods itself by redefining a 'good' as a particular commodity going to a particular person, e.g. 'named good' ij is commodity j going to person i.[35] A shirt going to person i will then be treated as a different good from a shirt − otherwise identical − going to person g, and the weights ('prices') given to the goods can reflect distributional considerations among other concerns. For example, for a given distribution of commodities over the persons, if i is very rich and g very poor, it is possible to attach a higher weight on the named good $(g, shirt)$ than on the named good $(i, shirt)$, locally for that distribution. While this type of named-good weighting may look rather complex and somewhat over-ambitious for practical purposes, it is, in fact, eminently usable. The usefulness of the approach rests partly in clarifying conceptual issues in the theory of real national income (see Sections 3.4–3.8), but also in its empirical applicability to actual comparisons (see Sections 3.9 and 3.10).

Let y be any vector of named goods with mn components when there are m commodities and n persons. It is not unreasonable to think of social welfare as a function of the named good vector y: $W = W(y)$. If, furthermore, social preference is taken to be convex

---

35. See Sen (1976a). The term 'named good' is due to Frank Hahn (1971). Note that a named good vector gives exactly the same information as a 'commodity matrix' as defined by Franklin Fisher (1956), or an 'allocation' as defined by Chipman and Moore (1976).

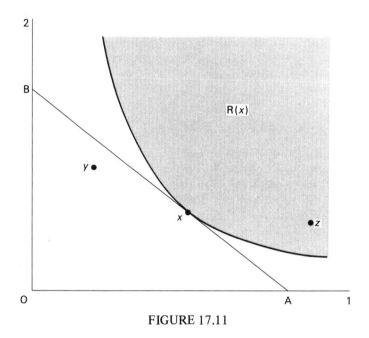

FIGURE 17.11

over the set of bundles of named goods,[36] which again need not be a very unreasonable assumption, then the entire real income logic based on 'convexity', as expounded in Section 2, can be immediately applied to real national income comparisons for social welfare judgements.

In Figure 17.11 the two axes represent two named goods.[37] For any named good bundle x, we can consider the set $R(x)$ of bundles that are at least as good as x. Given a Bergson–Samuelson social welfare function representing the value judgements to be used for evaluating social welfare, there is no difficulty in identifying $R(x)$. In addition, if it is assumed that the social preference is strictly monotonic (the more the merrier) and convex (roughly, having non-increasing marginal rates of substitution), then x can be seen as lying on the border of a concave region $R(x)$. The 'basic theorem of constant-weight comparisons' now states that there are weights p

36. That is, if $W(.)$ is a quasi-concave function.
37. The two-dimensional nature of the diagram is a bit limiting for representing bundles of named goods, since that permits only one commodity if there are two persons. But the diagram is for illustration only, and there is no difficulty in applying the analysis to the more general case of m goods and n persons.

such that any bundle y that has a lower total value py than px must be strictly inferior to x according to the social ordering. All bundles y with a value py less than px will lie below the line AB (with its slope given by p), while all bundles z that are at least as good as x will lie above that line.[38] Given the completeness of the social ranking, py being less than px must, thus, imply that y is strictly inferior to x. This is just an application of the logic of convexity underlying real income comparisons (see Section 2.1) to the case of the named good bundles, and the technique consists in using constant-price comparisons to precipitate a partial ordering.[39]

The weights p can be thought of as 'prices' used for weighting, and any such p will be called a price-support vector for x. But these are not prices – neither necessarily nor typically – in the institutional sense. They reflect the relative importance of the different named goods at the point x according to the given Bergson–Samuelson social welfare function. There can, of course, be more than one such price vector for any x, as can be readily imagined by considering a kink at the border of $R(x)$ at x. The important point is that there is *at least* one such price support vector, and that is, of course, adequate for the use of constant-price real-income comparisons to generate a global ranking on the basis of locally relevant weights.

There are, I think, at least four major problems that this approach has to face. First, is it at all sensible to think of a social welfare ordering of named good vectors? Underlying this question is the more elementary question: Isn't any Bergson–Samuelson social welfare function to be used for the exercise of social ranking open to impossibility results of the type derived by Arrow (1951)? However, as argued elsewhere (Sen, 1977a), the Arrow-type impossibility results and the corresponding impossibility theorems for the Bergson–Samuelson social welfare functions *both* arise essentially from the severe informational limitations that are imposed, viz. ruling out the use of non-utility information about social states in ranking them ('welfarism')[40] while making the utility information

38. In the general case, the 'dividing line' will be a hyperplane.

39. The method applied to any subset of bundles yields a partial ranking that is acyclic, but not necessarily transitive, because of incompleteness. The relation can be made transitive by taking its finite closure (Sen, 1976a, pp. 20-1). The finite closure of any subset of direct rankings will be a partial ordering.

40. Welfarism makes social welfare a function of the vector of personal utilities only. It is a version of the condition of 'neutrality over alternative social states', and has the effect of constraining the social choice exercise in very narrow lines (see Sen, 1977a). On various properties of social choice related to neutrality conditions, see Arrow (1951; 1963), Sen (1970; 1977a), Ashok Guha (1972), Claude d'Aspremont and Louis Gevers (1977), Douglas Blair (1976) and Julian Blau and Donald Brown (1978), among other contributions. 'Welfarism' is not directly assumed by Arrow (1951), but it is *implied* – so far as *strict* indivi-

remarkably poor (given by interpersonally non-comparable individual orderings).[41] There are some exercises for which such a limited-information framework is indeed appropriate, but the judgement of economic well-being of nations is hardly one of them. The procedure has to be, in general, informationally more demanding (and not just to avoid impossibility results). In the framework used in the named goods approach, there is, of course, no ban on using non-utility information (e.g. judgements about the relative social worth of goods going to people with different conditions of material prosperity being based on their commodity holdings as opposed to suppositions about their utility levels). Nor is there a ban on using utility information in richer forms (e.g. making certain systematic suppositions about people's relative utility levels).

However, even without any existence problems about social welfare functions, it may be asked whether it is sensible to think of social welfare being a function of named good vectors as such. A good deal of relevant information is not captured by the specification of named goods bundles, e.g. 'historical' information used in approaches to social judgements as diverse as those of Karl Marx (1887) and Robert Nozick (1974). Even the utility information finds no direct place in named good vectors. If other information is thought to be relevant for the judgement of social welfare, then under this approach they have to be brought in through the specification of the social welfare function $W(.)$ defined on the set of named good vectors. There is, in principle, no great problem in this, but to load the choice of the functional form of $W(.)$ in this way does raise some practical difficulties.

Second, for public goods the concept of named goods does raise a characterization problem. 'Person i's shirt' is clear enough, but 'person i's public park' isn't an easy concept. In order to make sense, the named goods would have to be defined in this context in terms of the services of public goods enjoyed by particular persons, e.g. 'person i's walk in the park'. There are some really complex issues here. For example, the appropriate valuation of an entitlement (e.g. the right to walk in a park) that one never exercises is far from a trivial issue.

---

dual and social orderings are concerned — by his set of axioms (see Sen, 1977a). A social welfare function satisfying 'welfarism' is sometimes called an 'individualistic' function — a somewhat odd expression, since the utility of a person is hardly the *only* expression of his individuality.

41. A great many positive possibility theorems in collective choice theory have been proved recently with richer informational basis. For some examples, see Sen (1974; 1977a), Peter Hammond (1976a), d'Aspremont and Gevers (1977), Robert Deschamps and Gevers (1978), Eric Maskin (1978) and Kevin Roberts (1980).

Third, the assumption of convex preferences is limiting. While it may be less so than the assumption of convex *production* relations, which is frequently assumed in the literature but not needed for the exercise under examination, there are examples of non-convexities that apply to social welfare judgements as well (e.g. increasing importance of nutrition as the food availability is raised from levels of starvation death to survival).

Fourth, the problem of actually obtaining locally relevant social weights (and giving an empirical basis to this approach) remains. This problem will be taken up further in Sections 3.9 and 3.10, and it will be argued that there are indeed practical methods of doing this. But it is worth mentioning here that even if the named-goods approach had no immediate empirical application, which is not the case, it might still be useful as a format for critically analysing the existing approaches to real national income evaluation. Indeed, it is this format that will be used in the next few sections to analyse various theories that have been proposed in the literature.

3.4 *Real income and compensation*

One way of avoiding the complexity arising from the distributional question was proposed in a pioneering paper by Nicholas Kaldor (1939) and further developed by Hicks (1939; 1940) and Scitovsky (1941; 1942). The 'compensation tests' deal with what was called 'potential welfare', based on social welfare potentials implicit in a situation, including all possible redistributions.

Consider two bundles x^0 and x^1 of commodities distributed among the persons in specified ways leading to named good vectors q^0 and q^1 respectively. If there exists no redistribution of the bundle x^0 among these persons that would make everybody as well off as each is under q^1, then — according to a definition used by Hicks (1940) — q^1 represents a higher 'real income' than q^0. Notice that this definition is not distribution-neutral, and indeed q^1 having a higher real income than q^0 does not imply that the same must hold for every distribution of x^1. (The actual distribution of x^0 – given by q^0 – does not matter in this proposition, since all distributions of x^0 are compared with the particular distribution of x^1 given by q^1.) In the language of compensation, this means that in a change from q^1 to q^0, the gainers would not be able to compensate the losers and still remain at least as well off as at q^1.

Given the assumptions of competitive equilibrium of consumers at fixed prices, strictly convex and continuous individual preferences, no consumption externalities, non-satiation, and unchanged tastes,

Hicks showed that $p^1 x^1 > p^1 x^0$ implies that q^1 has a higher real income than q^0 in the sense defined above (1940).[42] Thus the real income method is used here to arrive at a weak welfare conclusion relevant for a community rather than a person.

Interesting as the result is, there are two rather different limitations of this approach. First, there is the problem of consistency, since it is perfectly possible for q^1 to have a higher real income than q^0 *and* for q^0 to have a higher real income than q^1, in this sense. Even when such inconsistencies do not occur, intransitivities can. Much discussed in the context of the 'compensation tests' (see Scitovsky, 1941; Samuelson, 1950; Baumol, 1952; Gorman, 1955; Ian Little, 1950, 1957; Graaff, 1957 and E. J. Mishan, 1960), these consistency problems can be avoided only by rather special assumptions. In particular, when individual preferences are homothetic and identical, then a rise in income at base and current year prices must imply that 'potential welfare' has increased in the sense that gainers can compensate the losers and still retain some gain (see Chipman and Moore, 1973a).[43]

The second difficulty is, in fact, more elementary. In what sense is a rise of 'potential welfare' of interest to *actual* welfare comparisons? Even if gainers *could* overcompensate the losers, why is that an improvement? It might be thought that the answer depends on whether compensations are *actually* paid or not. But there is a problem in *either* case.

If compensation is *not* paid, then the situation with greater *potential* welfare can be judged to be in fact worse, *if* more weight is attached to the losers' loss than to the gainers' gain. The particular example, viz. the repeal of the Corn Laws in Britain that motivated the formulation of compensation tests, involved losses for landlords but gains for the rest (see Roy Harrod, 1938 and Kaldor, 1939). The fact that landlords don't typically receive much sympathy may have played a psychological part in making unpaid compensation more acceptable. But the losers can just as easily be the poorest of the poor. Or, the most deserving according to any criterion of desert that we might wish to specify. A change that leaves them losers, though potentially compensatable, may not be an improvement in any obvious sense.

42. Not all these assumptions were explicitly specified by Hicks (1940), but were intended to be fulfilled, as is clear from the argument to establish the theorem. See also Charles Kennedy (1954) and Chipman and Moore (1971).

43. Chipman and Moore (1973a) show that identical, homothetic preference is also, in a sense, 'necessary' (and not merely 'sufficient') for the result. This is the minimal sufficiency condition for the class of such qualitative restrictions.

If, on the other hand, compensation *is* actually paid, then *after* the act of compensation, everyone is at least as well off as before and someone is strictly better off. That being the case, the situation is a welfare improvement on straightforward Paretian grounds. But then no compensation tests are needed, since the Pareto criterion itself is sufficient! Thus it would seem that compensation tests are either unconvincing (when compensations are not actually made) or redundant (when they are).[44] Real income analysis based on the compensation criteria remains, consequently, a rather futile approach (even though the compensation criteria continue to receive some patronage in cost–benefit analysis and in international trade theory).

3.5   *The assumption of optimal distribution*

The problem of real national income evaluation in the special case in which optimal lump-sum redistribution of income is made was investigated by Samuelson (1950; 1956). Under these circumstances, a consistent map of social indifference curves in the shape of 'Bergson frontiers' – each frontier representing a given level of social welfare – can be obtained over the 'anonymous' commodity vectors (see also Graaff, 1957). If the social indifference curves are convex, then the real-income approach to welfare judgements can be applied to national income comparisons directly in the same way as to personal real income. Samuelson and Graaff use this for national income evaluation at market prices, which involves the additional assumptions that (i) the social welfare function respects the Pareto-principle, (ii) the buyers are all price-takers in a competitive market, (iii) each person's welfare depends only on what he purchases, and (iv) each buyer is 'rational' in the peculiar sense, common in economic theory, that his choice function is 'binary' and the binary relation revealed by his choice in his welfare ordering.[45]

In the format of the 'named good' vectors, this case can be translated into two propositions regarding the price vector p to be used for weighting.

AXIOM X (EFFICIENT EXCHANGE). For each named good vector y, there is a price-support vector p such that for all persons i and all

---

44. This does not, of course, contradict Hicks' belief that 'the route' by which compensation tests were arrived at 'has clarified ideas: and it has thrown light on what can be done, can usefully be done, in practical cases' (1974, p. 15). Hicks provides a reflective assessment of what 'new welfare economics' aimed at doing and what it achieved. For an assessment in a totally different spirit, see Chipman and Moore (1973b) on the 'end of new welfare economics'; see also Kotaro Suzumura (1977).

45. While these assumptions will not be further examined here, see Section 2.5 above dealing with real *personal* income comparisons for criticisms of (iii) and (iv).

commodities j and h: $p_{ij}/p_{ih} = m_j/m_h$ where m_j and m_h are the market prices of j and h respectively.

AXIOM D (OPTIMAL DISTRIBUTION). For each named good vector y, a price-support vector p satisfying Axiom X, also satisfies for all persons i and g and all commodities j: $p_{ij} = p_{gj}$.

Axiom X makes the ratio of the market prices of any two commodities the relevant social rate of indifferent substitution between these two commodities going to any given person. Axiom D makes the same commodity going to any two persons equally valuable from the social point of view at the margin. While both assumptions are criticizable, it can be argued that Axiom D is by far the more objectionable of the two. Its rationale rests on Samuelson's assumption that optimal lump-sum redistributions 'keep the ethical worth of each person's marginal dollar equal' (Samuelson, 1956, p. 21). Samuelson calls this the 'economics of a good society' (1956, p. 22) – and a very good society it is, though alas not a very real one. If the use of real national income calculations has to await the emergence of such a society, then we clearly have time on our hands.

Pollak has characterized a society with such full optimality as a 'maximizing society' (1977). This sense of maximization should be contrasted with the sense in which Mirrlees (1969) poses the problem of 'national income in an imperfect economy', in which the government does its best subject to the constraints it faces, which rules out achieving full optimality through lump-sum transfers. Mirrlees specifically considers the case discussed in the commodity taxation model of Peter Diamond and Mirrlees (1971) in which commodity taxes and subsidies can be used freely, but not necessarily other policies. It transpires that in the model specified, productive efficiency is still a necessary condition of social welfare maximization subject to constraints. If this is accepted, then for *small changes* the appropriate relative weights on the different commodities are given by the marginal rates of transformation.

The Mirrlees approach to national income evaluation aims, thus, at basing marginal welfare judgement on transformation rates, making the assumption of constrained optimality.[46] It differs from the Samuelson approach based on optimal distribution through lump-sum taxes (so that Axiom D cannot be invoked). It also differs from the use of transformation rates to make judgements about production possibility as in Section 3.2, since Mirrlees is concerned with

---

46. Mirrlees assumes convexity of production possibility but not of social welfare frontiers.

welfare judgements (reading welfare significance into transformation rates by virtue of the need for productive efficiency under constrained optimization by the government). However, it fits more easily into planning theory than into the theory of national income because the focus is on marginal changes only. The possibility, in this context, of using these locally relevant weights for precipitating a global partial ordering through the use of convexity (as elaborated in Section 2) remains open.

3.6 The assumption of constant distribution

In the Samuelson approach, discussed in the last section, the evaluation of named good vectors was converted into a problem of weighting 'anonymous' goods through the assumption of optimal distribution of commodities over the persons. An alternative possibility is to attempt this translation through the assumption of *constant* distribution. Can this be done?

In the named good context a natural interpretation of constant distribution is that of 'the same percentage distribution of each commodity' over the different persons in the named good vectors to be compared (see Sen, 1976a, p. 23),[47] and this does lead to valid use of constant-price real-income comparison with 'anonymous' commodities. The result is not surprising. Given the same percentage distribution over the persons and the usual additive framework, the appropriate ratio of weights w_j/w_h on two goods j and h is given by:

$$w_j/w_h = \sum_{i=1}^{n} p_{ij} d_{ij} \Big/ \sum_{i=1}^{n} p_{ih} d_{ih} \tag{4}$$

where d_{ij} and d_{ih} are the proportionate shares of person i in the total availability of goods j and h respectively, and where p_{ij} and p_{ih} are the weights ('prices') of named goods ij and ih respectively in a price-support vector p.

This simply notes the possibility of applying constant-price comparisons to anonymous commodity vectors, but the 'price' w_j used for weighting the commodities need not be the market prices, even when Axiom D is accepted. This is because two commodities may be distributed among the persons quite differently. That possibility can be eliminated if it is assumed that everyone happens to have the *same* set of 'homothetic' preferences. Then clearly the percentage share of the total amount of any commodity j going to

---

47. This is equivalent to the named good vectors having the same 'distribution matrix' in the sense of Fisher (1956).

any person i must be exactly the same as the percentage of the total amount of any other commodity h going to the same person i, i.e. $d_{ij} = d_{ih}$. And since by virtue of Axiom D each p_{ij} can be seen as the product of market price m_j with some parameter related to the person i, i.e. $p_{ij} = v(i)m_j$, it is clear from (4) that the ratio of the 'anonymous' commodity weights must be given by the market price ratio.

It is easily checked that under the assumption of the same homothetic preferences shared by all, the requirement of 'constant distribution' need not be specified in terms of *commodity* distributions, and it is sufficient to assume that the distribution of *income* remains constant. This still permits the use of market prices as the appropriate weights for the commodities.

But the assumption of the same homothetic preference shared by all is an important one. Though it is not correct to assert the necessity – in addition to sufficiency – of this condition, i.e. to say that *only* under the assumption of the same homothetic preferences shared by all would the market prices be the right weights to use for comparing bundles with the same distribution, it is, in fact, true that if the individual preferences are all homothetic then they also must be identical for this result to hold (see Chipman and Moore, 1976).

3.7 The representative consumer and the social cost of living

The case of constant distribution is a rather special one. Can this be dispensed with while retaining the advantage of being able to deal with commodities anonymously? It is not unnatural in this context to inquire into the conditions that permit interpersonal aggregation in terms of *market* behaviour. In a classic paper, Gorman (1953) established the result that if the marginal propensities to consume for any good are the same across consumers and the same irrespective of income (provided income is higher than a certain level), then the market behaviour of a community of consumers can be represented by a set of community preferences (provided everyone has 'sufficiently' high income).[48] Gorman's requirement for preference – sometimes called 'quasi-homotheticity' – is less strict than homotheticity. It requires *linear* expenditure paths (relating income to each commodity purchased), but these paths need not go through the origins as under homotheticity; contrast Figure 17.12 with Figure 17.13. However, the requirement of everyone having a

48. See also Houthakker (1953), Gorman (1968; 1976), Chipman (1974), Muellbauer (1975; 1976), Pollak (1977) and Blackorby, Primont and Russell (1977).

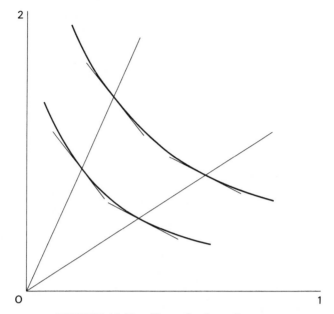

FIGURE 17.12 *Homothetic preferences*

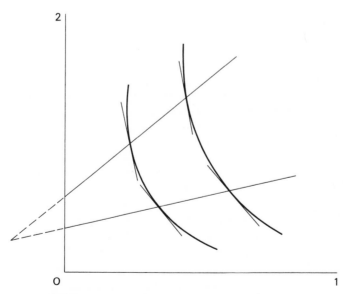

FIGURE 17.13 *Quasi-homothetic preferences*

'sufficiently large' income, which guarantees that we don't have zero consumption of any good by anyone, is itself somewhat limiting. If we want to avoid that, then the assumption of homotheticity is a natural one to make (despite the overkill).

Note, however, that given homothetic preferences identical for all, or given quasi-homothetic preferences with identical slopes for all and sufficiently high incomes for all, the market behaviour of a *group* of consumers can be treated as if it were that of one consumer with one consistent set of indifference curves.[49] It is tempting to ask: Can we not apply the real income analysis to such a 'community preference field'?

The answer is that we can do this, but the results need not have any welfare significance. The purpose of the 'community preferences' of the 'representative consumer' is to be able to explain or predict market behaviour, and that is all there is to it.[50] By the assumption of the *same* marginal propensity of *all* consumers to consume any good, market demand is made essentially independent of the *distribution* of income. While this renders distribution of income irrelevant for explaining or predicting market *behaviour*, it does not, of course, make distribution irrelevant for *social welfare*! Thus the aggregation achieved by identical homotheticity or quasi-homotheticity does not permit us to base social welfare judgements on real income comparisons of anonymous commodity vectors. Of course, we can leave out this problem if we assume that the distribution of income remains constant (as we saw in the last section), but that is a very special assumption. While for the purpose of studying market behaviour that assumption can be dropped still retaining the aggregation over the consumers, the same clearly does not hold for making social welfare judgements.

While welfare judgements based on real income comparisons of anonymous commodities are not derivable from the assumptions that lead to a 'representative consumer', there is some gain for the concept of 'social cost of living'. It may be recalled that the 'economic price index' for two price vectors was defined – see Section 2.2 – in terms of the ratio of least-cost expenditure needed at these two respective price situations to attain a given level of personal welfare (i.e. a given indifference curve). The cost was not of the actual bundle but of the 'counterfactual' least-cost bundle. If a similar definition is chosen for the social cost of living, then we would define it as the ratio of least-cost expenditures needed at these

49. These conditions can be somewhat relaxed, on which see Muellbauer (1976).
50. See also Muellbauer (1976).

two price situations to attain a given level of social welfare. Pollak (1971) has investigated this problem involving 'counterfactuals'.[51] Given certain assumptions, the social cost of living in this sense does indeed turn out to be the cost of living of the representative consumer.

This coincidence follows essentially from the freedom to choose named good vectors that the definition of 'social cost of living' permits. Just as in the case of the personal 'economic' price index it was assumed that the person can choose any commodity bundle within his budget (with no further restrictions) and thus the best one can be considered, it is assumed *for the purpose* of calculating the 'social cost of living' that distribution is an entirely controllable policy variable and the best one can be taken. The result is precipitated by the combination of (i) the independence of market behaviour from distribution (e.g. by identical homothetic preferences) and (ii) the freedom to choose distributions from the welfare point of view to calculate the least-cost method of achieving a specified level of social welfare. It is not assumed – as in the Samuelson case of optimized distribution (what Pollak calls the 'maximizing society') – that the *actual* distribution is accepted by the evaluator as optimum, but the definition of the 'social cost of living' requires the evaluator to calculate what the least-cost expenditure *would have been* if he had the freedom to choose the distribution optimally.

This concentration on 'counter-factuals' is a characteristic that the 'social cost of living' shares with the 'economic' price and quantity indexes for a given *person* (see Section 2.2). But, of course, in the *social* as opposed to the *personal* case, this requires considering not merely the optimal allocation over commodities for each person, but also optimal interpersonal distribution. In interpreting the 'social cost of living', the demanding nature of this assumption has to be borne in mind.

3.8   *The use of supplementary distributional judgements*

In all the cases of social welfare judgements based on real national income discussed above, something or other special has been assumed about the nature of distribution, viz. either it is assumed to be actually *optimal*, as in Samuelson (1950; 1956) (see Section 3.5), or assumed to be *optimizable* for doing the indexation, as in Pollak (1977) (see Section 3.7), or assumed *constant*, as in Chipman and

51. See also Scitovsky's motivational discussion (1941).

Moore (1976) (see Section 3.6). When such an assumption has not been made, no proper social welfare implications have emerged, e.g. in the analysis of 'potential welfare', which implies little about actual welfare (see Section 3.4), or in the use of the representative consumer's market 'preference', which implies nothing at all about social welfare, unless some *additional* distributional assumptions are made (see Section 3.7).

Is it not possible to *supplement* the 'real national income' analysis by some explicit distributional judgements? The question was investigated by Ian Little (1950; 1963) and a partial answer was found. Translated into the 'named good' format, a named good vector x is called 'distributionally' superior to another y if and only if some interpersonal redistribution of y yields a redistributed named good vector y^* such that: (i) y^* is Pareto-comparable to x and (ii) y^* is regarded as better than y from the point of view of social welfare.[52] That is, if some redistribution of y taking the situation within the Pareto-comparable region of x is regarded as a social improvement, then x is 'distributionally' better than y.

This 'distributional' criterion can be now used to supplement the 'potential welfare' judgements based on real income comparisons. Using the Hicksian theorem that a rise in real income in a move from y to x at final year prices would imply that no redistribution of y could be Pareto superior to x (see Section 3.4), an overall welfare comparison between x and y could be made under these circumstances. Since the redistribution of y in the shape of y^* is Pareto-comparable to x, but – given the real national income inequality – y^* is not Pareto-superior to x, then clearly y^* is Pareto-inferior or Pareto-indifferent to x. But y^* has already been judged to be socially better than y. Clearly then, x is socially better than y. The deduction uses only the *transitivity* of the social welfare relation coupled with assuming that the relation incorporates the Pareto principle.

Notice that the 'distributional' comparisons between x and y include factors other than what are purely distributional in the usual sense, and Little's approach is not based on a dichotomy between 'size' considerations on one side and 'distributional' considerations on the other. But if such judgements can be made, they can surely be used to supplement constant-price real-national-income comparisons to arrive at overall social welfare judgements.

52. The criterion can be readily extended to permit y^* to be any named good vector attainable by varying production as well as distribution starting from y, given the set of resources. This 'broader' interpretation of the Little criterion for 'distributional' improvement requires a corresponding reformulation of the real-national-income component in his 'double' criterion. See Little ([1950] 1957, ch. 6), Sen (1963) and Ng (1971; 1979).

Aside from some persistent misunderstandings of the content of Little's criterion, the main criticism of it has been based on questioning whether it is any easier to compare y vis-à-vis y^* than it is to compare y with x 'quite directly' (Graaff, 1957, p. 89). The argument rests on the usefulness of having 'intermediate' points to facilitate comparison. While the present author finds such intermediate points helpful in thinking about moral judgements, he is aware that some people[53] are enviably endowed with complete social orderings neatly packed up in their mind and have no need for contemplating intermediate points to sort out complex issues of judgements.[54]

In the Little approach, the real-national-income comparison provides only one part of a 'double' criterion, supplemented by 'distributional' judgements in the sense specified. The possibility of weaving in the distributional judgement into the real income evaluation itself, dispensing with the use of intermediate points, was examined in Section 3.3 and is further explored in the next section.

3.9   Named good valuation and the example of rank-order weighting

As discussed in Section 3.3, given the convexity of social preference over the named good bundles, the 'basic theorem of constant-weight comparisons' permits the use of constant-price weighting to make social welfare judgements. The interesting issues arise with the interpretation of the 'prices' p and with devising ways of obtaining them. As mentioned earlier, these are not institutional prices, but reflect the value judgements used to evaluate named good bundles, including any distributional judgements that we may wish to incorporate. They should reflect the relative importance attached to additional amounts of the various named goods when the availability and distribution of commodities is given by x, and they are in this sense the 'locally relevant weights' at x. The essence of the convexity-based approach to real-income evaluation is to be able to use the locally relevant weights to get a global partial ordering. If local weights can be decided upon, global conclusions will emerge from them.

For the evaluation of real national income it is important that the value judgements in terms of which the locally relevant weights are to be derived should be (i) clearly statable, (ii) empirically usable,

<hr>

53. See Kennedy's (1963) forceful rebuttal of Sen's (1963) timid defence of the usefulness of Little's criterion.

54. For examples of other uses of intermediate points, inspired by Little's criterion, see Mishan (1960), Ng (1971), Chipman and Moore (1973b) and Sen (1976a, pp. 23–4).

and (iii) have broad acceptability. The standard practice of evaluating national income at prices that happen to rule in the market has obvious merits in terms of clarity of statement as well as empirical usability. On the other hand, in ignoring distributional questions altogether, its claim to being accepted as a guide to social welfare is severely compromised. This raises the question as to whether it is possible to modify the market-price framework in such a way that distributional judgements are reflected in the choice of locally relevant weights (and thus in the global partial orderings generated by them), without losing altogether the firmness, clarity, and empirical tractability of the use of market prices for evaluation.

In the usual national income computation market prices have two rather different roles in the context of social welfare evaluation. One role is (a) the weighting of *different commodities* going to the *same person*, and the other is (b) the weighting of the *same commodity* going to *different persons*. In terms of the welfare interpretation under the Samuelson–Graaff approach (see Section 3.5 above), explicitly or implicitly Axiom X (efficient exchange) legitimizes the first and Axiom D (optimal distribution) legitimizes the second. Concern with distribution and the acceptance of the inoptimality of the actual distribution would lead to a rejection of Axiom D, but this need not have any effect on Axiom X as such.

It is indeed possible to replace Axiom D by some alternative procedure for distributional judgement and still retain some use for the market prices because of their relevance – given Axiom X – for weighting different named goods going to the *same* person. While the general approach of named-good based evaluation was the main focus in Sen (1976a), it explored in some detail a particular procedure for obtaining locally relevant weights by combining Axiom X with some explicit distributional judgements (Section 8 in that paper). The distributional judgements were based on the axiom of 'rank order weighting', which can be shown to be implicit in the welfare interpretation of the Gini coefficient of inequality (Sen, 1974, Theorems T.3 and T.4).[55] The results could be used for actual empirical exercises, and were, in fact, applied to comparisons of regional disparities of income in India with available data (Sen, 1976a, Appendix).

The motivation behind 'rank order weighting' can be explained by inquiring into the reasons for the unacceptability of Axiom D (optimal distribution). Under Axiom D, each commodity gets the

---

55. See also Sen (1976b), Koichi Hamada and Noriyuki Takayama (1977), Kakwani (1978) and Takayama (1979). Also, S. R. Osmani (1978).

same weight no matter to whom it accrues, e.g. an additional loaf of bread for the hungry gets exactly the same weight as a loaf going to the very rich. From here the transition to rank order weighting can be made in two steps. First, instead of a uniform weight on the same commodity irrespective of the person to whom it accrues, it may be required that the poorer a person is, the higher should be the weight on any commodity he purchases compared with the weight on the same commodity going to a richer person. That is, if $r(i)$ is a person's rank in the scale of total income comparisons (i.e. for the kth richest person i: $r(i) = k$), then a named good accruing to person i should have a higher weight than the same commodity going to some person g whenever $r(i) > r(g)$. If this is to be combined with the use of Axiom E (dealing with *intra*-personal weighting), then a simple way of achieving this is to choose a weighting system:

$$p_{ij} = m_i f(r(i)) \qquad (5)$$

when m_j is the market price of commodity j, and f is an increasing function.

The second step makes the weighting more specific. A simple increasing function $f(.)$ is the identity function, so that $f(r) = r$ itself. Applied to (5), this yields the system of rank-order weighting.

AXIOM R (RANK ORDER WEIGHTING).   Any named good vector x has a price-support vector p such that for all persons i and all commodities j:

$$p_{ij} = Am_j r(i) \qquad (6)$$

with $A > 0$ a constant.

Let $e(x)$ and $e(y)$ be the per capita money values of the commodity bundles in the named good vectors x and y respectively both evaluated at market prices associated with x. And let $G(x)$ and $G(y)$ be the Gini coefficients of the personal distributions of money incomes at x and y respectively, evaluated at the same prices. It can now be shown (see Sen, 1976a, Theorem T.12) that given Axiom R: if $e(x)(1 - G(x)) > e(y)(1 - G(y))$, then x is socially better than y. Thus, the standard real income comparisons corrected by the values of the respective Gini coefficients at constant prices yields the partition into 'inferior' and 'undecided' subsets that we have been seeking under the real-income method.

Axiom R is, however, quite a demanding requirement. While the distributional weighting based on rank orders has some appeal, it is possible to bring in distributional considerations in many other ways (see Section 3.10). Furthermore, the use of Axiom X (efficient exchange) implicit in Axiom R is also rather limiting. Even the restricted role given to market prices in this way pays little attention to the complexity of consumer behaviour and difficulties in interpreting market prices as the relevant marginal weights on different commodities going to the *same* person.[56]

There is another limitation arising from the same quarter. Axiom R with this limited use of market prices will be consistent with a welfarist framework (i.e. with social welfare being taken to be a function of the vector of individual utilities only) if and only if everyone has the same homothetic preference map, or everyone has the same quasi-homothetic preference map along with everyone's income being 'sufficiently high' (see Hammond, 1978). While welfarism was not postulated in the framework proposed in Sen (1976a), nevertheless to be *forced* to reject it bindingly *is* indeed a limitation. The trouble arises essentially from trying to make use of market prices in an aggregate evaluation: under Axiom R market prices are used for solving one aspect of the weighting problem, even though the distributional considerations lead to a rejection of market prices as weights for commodities going to *different* persons. If the merits of using market prices to reflect the relative values of different goods going to the same person are considered to be serious enough and one incorporates this use in the form of Axiom R, then one has to pay the price of restricting the nature of individual preference maps *or* rejecting welfarism bindingly (and not merely permissively). There remains a difficult choice here even after the distributional weighting implicit in market prices has been rejected (as is done by Axiom R).

3.10 *National income and an 'efficiency-quality' factorization*

The formula $e(1 - G)$ representing the value of the named good vector at appropriate prices in line with Axiom R can be interpreted as having two components, viz. e standing for the 'size' of the national income and $(1 - G)$ for its 'distributional acceptability'. This aggregate split up is a *consequence* of Axiom R, and it cannot, in general, be presupposed that such a break-up will be always possible.

Recently, Graaff (1977) and Muellbauer (1977) have explored the general problem of achieving a split up between 'efficiency' and 'equity'. I shall follow here Graaff's method. Define the degree of

---

56. See the discussion in Section 2.5 above and such critiques of the traditional interpretation of market behaviour as Scitovsky (1976) and Leibenstein (1976).

economic efficiency ϵ as the smallest fraction of the potentially producible outputs of commodities with which every person can be kept at their existing level of well-being. That is, if it is possible to produce an output mix such that by appropriately distributing 75 per cent of each output each person can be kept at their current level of well-being, then the current economic efficiency is no more than 75 per cent. If 75 per cent turns out to be the minimal ratio that has to be used to do this feat, considering all potentially producible bundles, then 75 per cent is indeed the value of ϵ.

While ϵ refers to the possibility of keeping everyone at his current level of welfare, ϵ_0 is defined by Graaff to correspond to the possibility of keeping society overall at the current level of welfare, even if some individuals are better off and some worse off compared with now. That is, if ϵ_0 is 65 per cent, this means that it is possible to produce a bundle of commodities such that by appropriately distributing 65 per cent of it (of each commodity) the society can be made altogether just as well off as it is now. (Note that while ϵ relates to the so-called 'Scitovsky frontier', ϵ_0 corresponds to the 'Bergson frontier'.) Graaff suggests that if everyone agrees on the nature of the appropriate social welfare function – in the Bergson–Samuelson sense – then ϵ_0 can, in fact, be treated as an indicator of social welfare. With given production possibilities, this suggestion is quite appropriate, since a higher level of social welfare would then require a higher minimal ratio ϵ_0 of retention to match the current level. Graaff treats ϵ as an indicator of 'efficiency', and the ratio ϵ_0/ϵ as an indicator of the degree of 'equity' η. Social welfare is then seen as the product of measures of 'efficiency' and 'equity' thus defined: $W = \epsilon\eta$.

Graaff proves that with identical homothetic preference maps for all persons, if an economy is exchange-efficient, has no public goods, and has fixed hours of work, then the proportionate change in the degree of efficiency is adequately reflected, for small changes, by the proportionate change in the value of national income evaluated at current prices (held constant). This is supplemented by the proportionate change in the 'equity' parameter η to arrive at the overall proportionate change.[57]

57. In fact, Graaff goes on to weight the equity parameter by a factor σ as an index of social agreement, varying between 0 and 1, with the general welfare function being defined as: $W = \epsilon\eta^\sigma$. This yields:

$$\frac{dW}{W} = \frac{d\epsilon}{\epsilon} + \sigma\frac{d\eta}{\eta} \qquad (7)$$

It is the component $d\epsilon/\epsilon$ that corresponds to the proportionate change in real national income at market price.

For making a practically usable correction of the real national income through the equity parameter η, the social welfare function would have to be specified. Graaff considers various alternative possibilities by postulating different characterizations of η, including $(1 - G)$ – discussed in the last section[58] – and some measure of the extent of 'non-envy' (in the tradition established by Duncan Foley (1967), Allen Feldman and Alan Kirman (1974), Hal Varian (1974) and others).

Graaff also establishes a clear relation between changes in real national income at prices actually prevailing in the market and the defined degree of efficiency: assuming identical homothetic preference maps.[59] Note that the derivation of the result uses the equality of market price ratios *both* with individual indifferent substitution rates and with production transformation rates,[60] and this prevents an easy translation of the local complete ordering into a global partial ordering.

3.11 *Situational comparisons for national income*

The discussion on real national income in the preceding sections has been based on pretending that the object is to evaluate *alternative* named good vectors that a given society would enjoy at a given point of time. But – as argued in Section 2.3 – while this is a legitimate assumption in decision theory, it is quite inappropriate for comparisons of real income. Such a comparison has to take note of the fact that the situations in question have occurred at different points of time or have been related to different people. The contrast between 'comprehensive' comparisons and 'situational' comparisons was discussed in this context (Section 2.3). Comprehensive comparisons – complicated enough in the case of *personal* real income – are immensely more so for real national income: we have to compare the welfare characteristics of two whole nations, or the same nation at two periods. What about situational comparisons?

Situational comparisons are difficult to *define* in the context of two nations. While A. C. Pigou (1920) had no difficulty in seeing that real national income contrasts would involve counter-factuals, e.g. 'if the German population with German tastes were given the national dividend of England ...' (pp. 52–3), he did not discuss what would be the description of the German population being given the

---

58. Graaff's reasoning in favour of the indicator $(1 - G)$ is close to the analysis presented by Graham Pyatt (1976) in terms of pairwise differences.

59. This holds for small changes. See, however, Muellbauer (1977).

60. The exercises discussed earlier typically used one or the other, but not both.

national dividend of England. One group of n persons can be placed in the position of another group of n persons in $n!$ different ways. And the problem of placing a group of n persons in the position of m persons (with $m \neq n$) *is* rather challenging. Of course, the problem would not arise if the comparison is restricted to treating each nation as one person enjoying the mean commodity bundle (as in Section 3.1), but that hardly does justice to comparisons of real *national* income.

The problem of correspondence in placing one group in the position of another *equi-numbered* group may be taken up first. The real income statement, say, that the Germans would be worse off if they were in the situation of the English, could be interpreted in at least three different ways (assuming that the Germans are exactly as numerous as the English, with n people each):

(1) There *exists* some way of assigning the n commodity baskets of the Englishmen to the n Germans such that the German community with its actual baskets is judged to be better off (the *existential approach*).

(2) For a *specified* way of assigning the n English baskets to the n Germans (e.g. the ith richest in Germany getting the basket of the ith richest in England), the German community is judged to be better off with its actual baskets (the *distinguished approach*).

(3) For *every* way of assigning the n English baskets to the n Germans, the German community is judged to be better off with its actual baskets (the *universal approach*).

These approaches have been listed in the increasing order of demandingness, and they can lead to quite different results (see Sen, 1976a). They will, of course, all coincide if all individuals in a given society are assumed to have the same utility function and if they are treated symmetrically in a 'welfarist' social welfare function.

The problem of unequal numbers is, in some sense, more baffling: it is not at all clear how n Germans may be assigned m English baskets when n and m differ. One way of handling this is to consider an m-fold replica of the German society (with m persons of identical utility functions, consumption basket, etc., in place of each) and similarly an n-fold replica of the English society. After such hypothetical replication, both the enlarged communities would have mn members, and any of the three alternative approaches of correspondence for equi-numbered communities can then be used. The result can be reasonably assumed to apply to the *standard* of welfare – the welfare version of the standard of living – of the two actual communities, since it is quite natural to require that replication should not change the standard of welfare of a community. While such hypothetical replication may appear to be complicated – and certainly leads to *very* large hypothetical communities – given the acceptance of the axiom regarding replication, the operation is not, in fact, very complicated. And it is easy to translate the results for equi-numbered communities (e.g. the one involving rank-order weighting) to comparisons of societies of unequal size. It is in this form that the rank-order weighting system has been used in Sen (1976a, Appendix) to compare inter-state disparities of welfare standards in India using the approach of real national income comparisons applied to vectors of named goods.

4 *Concluding Remarks*

No attempt will be made to summarize the main arguments of this article, for a lot of ground has been covered in this survey paper. However, a few remarks may help to put the discussion into perspective.

(1) The theories of revealed preference and that of convex preferences provide two *alternative* avenues to welfare judgement based on real income evaluation (Section 2.1). The two approaches are often identified, and indeed for some models of reality they do coincide. But they are essentially two *different* routes to generating partial rankings of welfare. The revealed preference approach concentrates on what was rejected, and the presumption of canny self-seeking permits this to be used to identify a partial ranking. The approach based on convex preference concentrates on the substitution rates that are locally relevant and the presumption of convexity permits this to be used for deriving a global partial ranking. Both approaches have substantial limitations, but rather different ones (Section 2.5).

(2) While the economic quantity index is an indicator of real income in some sense, it is not addressed to the problem of making welfare judgements based on limited price and quantity information (Section 2.2). Its role in identifying the welfare ordering is redundant (since it is derived from such an ordering), and to use it as a 'cardinal indicator of ordinal utility' – to quote Samuelson and Swamy (1974) – makes little sense.

(3) Unlike in decision theory, real income comparisons are not concerned just with *alternatives*, only one of which – at most – would occur. It deals with *actual* situations of two persons (or

communities), or of the same person (or community) at two different points of time. This raises important problems of interpretation of welfare judgements based on real income comparisons. There are basically two different types of comparisons, viz. 'situational' (the same person with same welfare characteristics in two different situations) and 'comprehensive' (different persons with different welfare characteristics facing different situations). Constancy of tastes between the persons or over time is not a relevant dividing line, being *unnecessary* for the former, and *insufficient* for the latter (Section 2.3). That assumption does, however, have its role in permitting the use of 'transitive closures' to 'construct' preferences, though the practical limitations of this exercise are considerable (Section 2.4).

(4) Personal real income theory translates readily into the theory of real national income if the nation is viewed as a person (Section 3.1), which is not of course outrageously realistic. The convexity approach can be applied also to generating partial rankings of production possibility and of real national products (Section 3.2). But this answers a different question from that of welfare judgement, unless some assumption of planning optimality is made leading to technical efficiency as a necessary part of social welfare maximization, permitting marginal welfare judgements to be based on weighting at transformation rates, as in the Mirrlees (1969) formulation (Section 3.5).

(5) The 'compensation tests' approach permits the use of real national income comparisons to make judgements on 'potential welfare'. Problems of consistency of such judgements are, however, quite serious, and in terms of welfare relevance they are exposed to the danger of being *either* unacceptable, *or* redundant (Section 3.4).

(6) The general framework for evaluation of social welfare used in this paper makes social welfare a function of the named good vector treating the same commodity going to two different persons as two different goods. The real income approach based on convexity can be easily extended to this framework to derive partial social welfare rankings (Section 3.3).

(7) Within this general framework, special assumptions can be seen to lead to the possibility of using real income comparisons at market prices for making social welfare judgements. Perhaps the most difficult problem in this arises from the treatment of distribution between persons, and this is typically handled by making some very special assumptions; viz. *optimal* distribution (Section 3.5), or *constant* distribution with identical homothetic preferences (Section 3.6).

(8) The conditions that guarantee the treatment of the market in terms of a representative consumer and permit the existence of consistent 'community preference fields' do not by themselves give any clear welfare value to real national income comparisons at constant market prices, and supplementation by distributional assumptions is necessary. While the 'social cost of living' does have welfare significance, its interpretation involves the assumption of controllability of distribution and counterfactual optimality, for the purpose of doing the indexing (Section 3.7).

(9) An alternative to making special distributional assumptions is to supplement real national income comparisons with 'distributional' judgements. One approach to this – developed by Little (1950) – while modest, is quite useful (Section 3.8). Another approach, explored recently by Graaff (1977) and also Muellbauer (1977), is more ambitious. It permits the treatment of real national income as an indicator of efficiency, and the efficiency indicator can be multiplicatively combined with an equity parameter (Section 3.10).

(10) The general approach of valuing named good vectors and generating partial orderings of social welfare through real national income can be used for various alternative systems of social welfare functions. One illustration explored in Sen (1976a), does this through a system of rank-order weighting, which corrects the market prices for commodities into person-specific named good prices based on the relative incomes of the persons in question. The method is fairly easy to apply within the structure of available statistics, and has been used for making interregional contrasts of real income in India (Section 3.9).

(11) Situational comparisons for *national* (as opposed to personal) income are difficult to define, and formulations frequently used involve considerable ambiguity. It is, however, possible to sort out clearly the *alternative* meanings of a nation being better off with its own named good vector than the named good vector of another nation, and welfare judgements can be explored in each context (Section 3.11).

The real income theorist is typically not unsympathetic to the view expressed in 'Burnt Norton' that:

Human kind
Cannot bear very much reality.[61]

That view is not in dispute: simplification *is* a coveted virtue of real income measures. But humankind can be made to bear a bit more

61. T. S. Eliot, *Four Quartets* London, Faber, 1944), p. 8.

reality than the real national income theory has traditionally tried to do. There is also something to choose among different types of simplifications that may be used to make the problem tractable. The time has certainly come when such politically absurd assumptions as distribution being optimal should cease to provide the background to comparisons of real national income. It is a small demand but with rather large implications, and I have tried to discuss the ways in which it might be met. Much, of course, remains to be done.

References

Adelman, Irma (1958): 'A New Approach to the Construction of Index Numbers', *Review of Economics and Statistics*, **40**, 240-99.

Afriat, Sidney N. (1956): 'The Theory of Index Numbers', mimeographed, Department of Applied Economics, Cambridge University.

—— (1972): 'The Theory of International Comparisons of Real Income and Prices', in Daly, D. J. (ed.), *International Comparisons of Prices and Output*, (New York: National Bureau of Economic Research), pp. 13-69.

—— (1976): *Combinatorial Theory of Demand* (London: Input-Output Publishing).

—— (1977): *The Price Index* (Cambridge: Cambridge University Press).

Allen, R. G. D. (1953): 'Index Numbers of Volume and Price', in Allen, R. G. D. and Ely, J. Edward (eds), *International Trade Statistics* (New York: Wiley), pp. 186-211.

—— (1963): 'Price Index Numbers', *International Statistical Review*, **31**, 281-301.

—— (1975): *Index Numbers in Theory and Practice* (London: Macmillan).

Andersson, A. E. (1971): 'Merit Goods and Micro-economic Dependence', mimeographed.

Arrow, Kenneth J. (1951): *Social Choice and Individual Values* (New York: Wiley); 2nd edn, 1963.

d'Aspremont, Claude and Gevers, Louis (1977): 'Equity and the Informational Basis of Collective Choice', *Review of Economic Studies*, **44** (2), 199-209.

Balassa, Bela (1973): 'Just How Misleading are Official Exchange Rate Conversions? A Comment', *Economic Journal*, **83** (332), 1258-67.

—— (1974): 'The Rule of Four-Ninths: A Rejoinder', *Economic Journal*, **84** (335), 609-14.

Banerjee, Kali S. (1961): 'A Unified Statistical Approach to the Index Number Problem', *Econometrica*, **29**, 591-601.

—— (1963): 'Best Linear Unbiased Index Numbers and Index Numbers Obtained through a Factorial Approach', *Econometrica*, **31**, 712-18.

Barten, A. P. (1964): 'Family Composition, Prices and Expenditure Patterns', in Hart, P. E., Mills, G. and Whitaker, J. K. (eds), *Econometric Analysis for National Economic Planning*, Colston Papers, University of Bristol, no. 16 (London: Butterworths), pp. 277-92.

Baumol, William J. (1952): *Welfare Economics and the Theory of the State* (Cambridge, Mass.: Harvard University Press); 2nd edn, 1965.

Beckerman, Wilfred (1968): *An Introduction to National Income Analysis* (London: Weidenfeld and Nicolson).

—— and Bacon, Robert (1966): 'International Comparisons of Income Levels: A Suggested New Measure', *Economic Journal*, 76, 519-36.

Blackorby, Charles and Donaldson, David (1978): 'Measures of Relative Equality and Their Meaning in Terms of Social Welfare', *Journal of Economic Theory*, 18 (1), 59-80.

——, Primont, Daniel and Russell, R. Robert (1977): *Duality, Separability and Functional Structure: Theory and Economic Applications* (New York: American Elsevier).

—— and Russell, R. Robert (1978): 'Indices and Subindices of the Cost of Living and the Standard of Living', *International Economic Review*, 19 (1), 229-40.

Blair, Douglas H. (1976): 'Neutrality and Independence Conditions in Social Choice Theory', mimeographed.

Blau, Julian H. and Brown, Donald J. (1978): 'The Structure of Neutral Monotonic Social Functions', Cowles Foundation Discussion Paper no. 485 (March).

Bös, Dieter (1978): 'Cost of Living Indices and Public Pricing', *Economica*, 45 (177), 59-69.

Chipman, John S. (1974): 'Homothetic Preferences and Aggregation', *Journal of Economic Theory*, 8 (1), 26-38.

—— and Moore, James C. (1971): 'The Compensation Principle in Welfare Economics', in Zarley, Arvid M. and Moore, James C. (eds), *Papers in Quantitative Economics*, vol. 2 (Lawrence: University Press of Kansas), pp. 1-77.

—— and Moore, James C. (1973a): 'Aggregate Demand, Real National Income, and the Compensation Principle', *International Economic Review*, 14 (1), 153-81.

—— and Moore, James C. (1973b): *The End of New Welfare Economics*, Technical Report no. 102, Economic Series (Stanford, Calif.: Institute for Mathematical Studies in the Social Sciences, Stanford University). [See the later paper by Chipman and Moore, 'On Social Welfare Functions and Aggregation Preferences', *Journal of Economic Theory*, 21 (1979).]

—— and Moore, James C. (1976): 'Real National Income with Homothetic Preferences and a Fixed Distribution of Income', mimeographed. [Later published in *Econometrica*, 48 (1980).]

—— et al. (eds) (1971): *Preferences, Utility and Demand: A Minnesota Symposium* (New York: Harcourt).

David, Paul A. (1972): 'Just How Misleading are Official Exchange Rate Conversions?' *Economic Journal*, 82 (327), 979-90.

—— (1973): '[Just How Misleading are Official Exchange Rate Conversions]: A Reply to Professor Balassa', *Economic Journal*, 83 (332), 1267-76.

Deaton, Angus (1979): 'The Distance Function in Consumer Behaviour with Applications to Index Numbers and Optimal Taxation', *Review of Economic Studies*, 46, 391-405.

Debreu, Gerard (1951): 'The Coefficient of Resource Utilization', *Econometrica*, **19**, 283-92.

Deschamps, Robert and Gevers, Louis (1978): 'Leximin and Utilitarian Rules: A Joint Characterization', *Journal of Economic Theory*, **17** (2), 143-63.

Diamond, Peter A. and Mirrlees, James A. (1971): 'Optimal Taxation and Public Production', *American Economic Review*, **61** (3), 8-27; 261-78.

Diewert, W. E. (1976a): 'Harberger's Welfare Indicator and Revealed Preference Theory', *American Economic Review*, **66** (1), 153-52.

—— (1976b): 'Exact and Superlative Index Numbers', *Journal of Econometrics*, **4** (2), 115-46.

Easterlin, Richard A. (1974): 'Does Economic Growth Improve the Human Lot? Some Empirical Evidence', in David, Paul A and Reder, Melvin W. (eds), *Nations and Households in Economic Growth: Essays in Honor of Moses Abramovitz* (New York: Academic Press), pp. 89-125.

Eichhorn, W. (1976): 'Fisher's Tests Revisited', *Econometrica*, **44** (2), 247-56.

—— *et al.* (1978): *Theory and Applications of Economic Indices* (Wurzburg).

Feldman, Allen M. and Kirman, Alan (1974): 'Fairness and Envy', *American Economic Review*, **64** (6), 995-1005.

Fisher, Franklin M. (1956): 'Income Distribution, Value Judgements and Welfare', *Quarterly Journal of Economics*, **70**, 380-424.

—— and Shell, Karl (1968): 'Tastes and Quality Change in the Pure Theory of the True Cost-of-Living Index', in Wolfe, J. N. (ed.), *Value, Capital and Growth: Papers in Honour of Sir John Hicks* (Edinburgh: Edinburgh University Press), pp. 97-139.

—— and Shell, Karl (1972): *The Economic Theory of Price Indices* (New York: Academic Press).

Fisher, Irving (1922): *The Making of Index Numbers* (Boston: Houghton Mifflin).

Foley, Duncan K. (1967): 'Resource Allocation and the Public Sector', *Yale Economic Essays*, **7** (1), 45-98.

Frisch, Ragnar (1930): 'Necessary and Sufficient Conditions regarding the Form of an Index Number which shall Meet Certain of Fisher's Tests', *Journal of American Statistical Association*, **25** (172), 397-406.

—— (1934): 'Annual Survey of General Economic Theory: The Problem of Index Numbers', *Econometrica*, **4**, 1-38.

Fuss, M. and McFadden, Daniel (eds) (1978): *Production Economics: A Dual Approach to Theory and Applications* (Amsterdam: North-Holland).

Gaertner, Wulf (1974): 'A Dynamic Model of Interdependent Consumer Behavior', *Zeitschrift für Nationalökonomie*, **34** (3-4), 327-44.

Gilbert, Milton and Kravis, Irving B. (1954): *An International Comparison of National Products and the Purchasing Power of Currencies* (Paris: OECD).

Gintis, Herbert M. (1969): 'Alienation and Power: Towards a Radical Welfare Economics', PhD dissertation, Harvard University.

—— (1974): 'Welfare Criteria with Endogenous Preferences: The Economics of Education', *International Economic Review*, **15** (2), 415-30.

Gorman, William M. (1953): 'Community Preference Fields', *Econometrica*, **21**, 63-80.

—— (1955): 'The Intransitivity of Certain Criteria Used in Welfare Economics', *Oxford Economic Papers*, 7, 25–35.

—— (1956): 'The Demand for Related Goods', Journal Paper J3129, Iowa Experimental Station, Ames, Iowa.

—— (1959): 'Are Social Indifference Curves Convex?' *Quarterly Journal of Economics*, 73, 485–96.

—— (1967): 'Tastes, Habits and Choices', *International Economic Review*, 8 (2), 218–22.

—— (1968): 'The Structure of Utility Functions', *Review of Economic Studies*, 35 (4), 367–90.

—— (1976): 'Tricks with Utility Functions', in Artis, Michael J. and Nobay, A. R. (eds), *Essays in Economic Analysis* (Cambridge: Cambridge University Press), pp. 211–43.

Graaff, Jan de V. (1957): *Theoretical Welfare Economics* (Cambridge: Cambridge University Press).

—— (1977): 'Equity and Efficiency as Components of the General Welfare', *South African Journal of Economics*, 45 (4), 362–75.

Griliches, Zvi (1971): *Price Indexes and Quality Change: Studies in New Methods of Measurement* (Cambridge, Mass.: Harvard University Press).

Guha, Ashok S. (1972): 'Neutrality, Monotonicity and the Right of Veto', *Econometrica*, 40 (5), 821–26.

Haberler, Gottfried (1927): *Der Sinn der Indexzahlen* (Tübingen: Mohr).

Hahn, Frank H. (1971): 'Equilibrium with Transaction Costs', *Econometrica*, 39 (3), 417–39.

Hamada, Koichi and Takayama, Noriyuki (1977): 'Measures of Poverty and their Policy Implications', mimeographed, presented at the 41st Congress of International Statistical Institute at New Delhi, December.

Hammond, Peter J. (1976a): 'Equity, Arrow's Conditions and Rawls' Difference Principle', *Econometrica*, 44 (4), 793–804.

—— (1976b): 'Endogenous Tastes and Stable Long-Run Choice', *Journal of Economic Theory*, 13 (2), 329–40.

—— (1978): 'Economic Welfare with Rank Order Price Weighting', *Review of Economic Studies*, 45 (2), 381–4.

Hanoch, G. (1978): 'Generation of New Production Function through Duality', in Fuss and McFadden (eds), 1978.

Harberger, Arnold C. (1971): 'Three Basic Postulates for Applied Welfare Economics: An Interpretive Essay', *Journal of Economic Literature*, 9 (3), 785–97.

Harrod, Roy F. (1938): 'Scope and Method of Economics', *Economic Journal*, 48, 383–412.

Harsanyi, John C. (1955): 'Cardinal Welfare, Individualistic Ethics and Interpersonal Comparisons of Utility', *Journal of Political Economy*, 63, 309–21.

Hicks, John R. (1939): 'The Foundations of Welfare Economics', *Economic Journal*, 49, 696–712.

—— (1940): 'The Valuation of Social Income', *Economica*, 7, 104–24.

—— (1956): *A Revision of Demand Theory* (Oxford: Clarendon Press).

—— (1958): 'The Measurement of Real Income', *Oxford Economic Papers*, **10**, 125-62.

—— (1974): 'Preference and Welfare', in Mitra, Ashok (ed.) *Economic Theory and Planning: Essays in Honour of A. K. Das Gupta* (Delhi: Oxford University Press), pp. 3-16.

Hirsch, Fred (1976): *Social Limits to Growth* (Cambridge, Mass.: Harvard University Press).

Houthakker, Hendrik S. (1950): 'Revealed Preference and the Utility Function', *Economica*, **17** (2), 159-74.

—— (1953): 'La Forme des Courbes d'Engel', *Cahiers du Seminaire d'Econometrie*, **2**, 59-66.

Jorgenson, Dale W. and Lau, Lawrence J. (1975): 'The Structure of Consumer Preferences', *Annals of Economic and Social Measurement*, **4** (1), 49-101.

Kakwani, Nanak (1978): *Income Distribution: Methods of Analysis and Applications* (New York: Oxford University Press).

Kaldor, Nicholas (1939): 'Welfare Propositions of Economics and Interpersonal Comparisons of Utility', *Economic Journal*, **49**, 549-52.

Kemp, Murray C. and Ng, Yew-Kwang (1977): 'More on Social Welfare Functions: The Incompatibility of Individualism and Ordinalism', *Economica*, **44** (173), 89-90.

Kennedy, Charles (1954): 'An Alternative Proof of a Theorem in Welfare Economics', *Oxford Economic Papers*, **6**, 98-9.

—— (1963): 'Two Comments [on Welfare Criteria]: II', *Economic Journal*, **73** (4), 780-81.

Konüs, A. A. (1924): 'The Problem of the True Index of the Cost of Living', *Institute of Economic Conjuncture Economic Bulletin*, nos. 9-10 (Moscow).

Kornai, János (1971): *Anti-equilibrium* (Amsterdam: North-Holland).

Kravis, Irving B., Heston, Alan W. and Summers, Robert (1978a): *International Comparisons of Real Product and Purchasing Power* (Baltimore: Johns Hopkins University Press).

—— Heston, Alan W. and Summers, Robert (1978b): 'Real GDP *per capita* for more than One Hundred Countries', *Economic Journal*, **88** (2), 215-42.

Kuznets, Simon (1948): 'On the Valuation of Social Income: Reflections on Professor Hicks' Article', *Economica*, **15**, 1-16; 116-31.

—— (1966): *Modern Economic Growth: Rate, Structure and Spread* (New Haven: Yale University Press).

Lancaster, Kelvin J. (1966): 'A New Approach to Consumer Theory', *Journal of Political Economy*, **74**, 132-57.

Lau, L. J. (1977a): *Existence Conditions for Aggregate Demand Functions: The Case of a Single Index*, Technical Paper no. 248, Economic Series (Stanford, Calif.: Stanford Institute for Mathematical Studies in the Social Sciences).

—— (1977b): *Existence Conditions for Aggregate Demand Functions: The Case of Multiple Indexes*, Technical Report no. 249, Economic Series (Stanford, Calif.: Stanford Institute for Mathematical Studies in the Social Sciences).

Lavoisier, Antoine (1791): *De la Richesse territoriale du royaume de France* (Paris).

Leibenstein, Harvey (1976): *Beyond Economic Man: A New Foundation for Microeconomics* (Cambridge, Mass.: Harvard University Press).

Leontief, Wassily W. (1936): 'Composite Commodities and the Problem of Index Numbers', *Econometrica*, **4**, 39-59.

Little, I. M. D. (1950): *A Critique of Welfare Economics* (Oxford: Clarendon Press); 2nd edn, 1957.

—— (1963): 'Two Comments [on Welfare Economics]: I', *Economic Journal*, **73**, 778-9.

Majumdar, Tapas (1969): 'Revealed Preference and the Demand Theorem in a Not-Necessarily Competitive Market', *Quarterly Journal of Economics*, **83** (1), 167-70.

Malmquist, S. (1953): 'Index Numbers and Indifference Surfaces', *Trabajos de Estadistica*, **4**, 209-42.

Marglin, Stephen A. (1976): *Value and Price in the Labour-Surplus Economy* (Oxford: Oxford University Press).

Marris, Robin (1958): *Economic Arithmetic* (London: Macmillan).

Marx, Karl (1887): *Capital: A Critical Analysis of Capitalist Production*, vol. 1 (London: S. Sonnenschein, Lowrey).

Maskin, Eric (1978): 'A Theorem on Utilitarianism', *Review of Economic Studies*, **45** (1), 93-6.

McFadden, Daniel (1978): 'Cost, Revenue and Profit Functions', in Fuss and McFadden (eds), 1978.

McKenzie, Lionel W. (1957): 'Demand Theory without a Utility Index', *Review of Economic Studies*, **24**, 185-9.

Mirrlees, James A. (1969): 'The Evaluation of National Income and an Imperfect Economy', *Pakistan Development Review*, **9** (1), 1-13.

Mishan, Ezra J. (1960): 'A Survey of Welfare Economics: 1939-1959', *Economic Journal*, **70**, 197-256.

Muellbauer, John (1972): 'The Theory of True Input Price Indices', mimeographed, Warwick Economic Research Paper no. 17, revised April.

—— (1974a): 'Inequality Measures, Prices and Household Composition', *Review of Economic Studies*, **41** (4), 493-504.

—— (1974b): 'The Political Economy of Price Indices', Birkbeck Discussion Paper in Economics no. 22, March.

—— (1974c): 'Household Production Theory, Quality and the "Hedonic Technique"', *American Economic Review*, **64** (6), 977-94.

—— (1975): 'Aggregation, Income Distribution and Consumer Demand', *Review of Economic Studies*, **42** (4), 525-43.

—— (1976): 'Community Preferences and the Representative Consumer', *Econometrica*, **44** (5), 979-99.

—— (1977): 'Distributional Aspects of Price Comparisons', Birkbeck Discussion Paper no. 53 (April).

Ng, Yew-Kwang (1971): 'Little's Welfare Criterion under the Equality Assumptions', *Economic Record*, **47** (120), 579-83.

—— (1975): 'Bentham or Bergson? Finite Sensibility, Utility Functions and Social Welfare Functions', *Review of Economic Studies*, **42** (4), 545-69.

—— (1979): *Welfare Economics* (London: Macmillan).

Nicholson, Jerome L. (1955): 'National Income at Factor Cost and Market Prices', *Economic Journal*, 65, 216-24.

Nordhaus, William and Tobin, James (1972): 'Is Growth Obsolete?' in National Bureau of Economic Research, *Economic Growth: Fiftieth Anniversary Colloquium V* (New York: NBER), pp. 1-80.

Nozick, Robert (1974): *Anarchy, State and Utopia* (Oxford: Blackwell; New York: Basic Books).

Osmani, S. R. (1978): 'Economic Inequality and Group Welfare: Theory and Application to Bangladesh', PhD dissertation, London University. [Later published, Oxford: Clarendon Press, 1982.]

Pigou, A. C. (1920): *Economics of Welfare*, 4th edn (London: Macmillan); 4th edn 1932.

Pollak, Robert A. (1970): 'Habit Formation and Dynamic Demand Functions', Part I, *Journal of Political Economy*, 78 (4), 745-63.

—— (1971): 'The Theory of Cost of Living Index', Research Discussion Paper no. 11, Office of Prices and Living Conditions, US Bureau of Labor Statistics (June).

—— (1975a): 'Subindexes of the Cost of Living Index', *International Economic Review*, 16 (1), 135-50.

—— (1975b): 'The Intertemporal Cost of Living Index', *Annals of Economic Social Measurement*, 4 (1), 179-95.

—— (1976): 'Habit Formation and Longrun Utility Functions', *Journal of Economic Theory*, 13 (2), 272-97.

—— (1977): 'The Social Cost of Living Index', Working Paper no. 70, Office of Prices and Living Conditions, US Bureau of Labor Statistics (July).

—— (1978): 'Endogenous Tastes in Demand and Welfare Analysis', *American Economic Review*, 68 (2), 374-9.

Portes, Richard (1977): 'The Control of Inflation: Lessons from East European Experience', *Economica*, 44 (174), 109-29.

van Praag, Bernard M. S. (1971): 'The Welfare Function of Income in Belgium: An Empirical Investigation', *European Economic Review*, 2 (3), 337-69.

—— and Kapteyn, Arie (1973): 'Further Evidence on the Individual Welfare Function of Income: An Empirical Investigation in the Netherlands', *European Economic Review*, 4 (1), 33-62.

Pyatt, Graham (1976): 'On the Interpretation and Disaggregation of Gini Co-efficients', *Economic Journal*, 86 (342), 243-55.

Rawls, John (1971): *A Theory of Justice* (Cambridge, Mass.: Harvard University Press, Belknap Press).

Roberts, Kevin W. S. (1980): 'Interpersonal Comparability and Social Choice Theory', *Review of Economic Studies*, 47.

Ruggles, Richard (1967): 'Price Indexes and International Price Comparisons', in *Ten Economic Studies in the Tradition of Irving Fisher* (New York: Wiley), pp. 171-205.

Samuelson, Paul A. (1947): *Foundations of Economic Analysis* (Cambridge, Mass.: Harvard University Press).

—— (1950): 'Evaluation of Real National Income', *Oxford Economic Papers*, 2, 1-29.

—— (1956): 'Social Indifference Curves', *Quarterly Journal of Economics*, **70**, 1-22.

—— (1961): 'The Evaluation of "Social Income": Capital Formation and Wealth', in Lutz, F. A. and Hague, D. C. (eds), *The Theory of Capital* (London: Macmillan), pp. 32-57.

—— (1974a): 'Analytical Notes on International Real-Income Measures', *Economic Journal*, **84** (335), 595-608.

—— (1974b): 'Remembrances of Frisch', *European Economic Review*, **5** (1), 7-23.

—— and Swamy, Subramanian (1974): 'Invariant Economic Index Numbers and Canonical Duality: Survey and Synthesis', *American Economic Review*, **64** (4), 566-93.

Sato, Kazuo (1976): 'The Ideal Log-Change Index Number', *Review of Economics and Statistics*, **58** (2), 223-8.

Scitovsky, Tibor (1941): 'A Note on Welfare Propositions in Economics', *Review of Economic Studies*, **9**, 77-88.

—— (1942): 'A Reconsideration of the Theory of Tariffs', *Review of Economic Studies*, **9** (2), 89-110.

—— (1976): *The Joyless Economy: An Inquiry into Human Satisfaction and Consumer Dissatisfaction* (London: Oxford University Press).

Sen, Amartya K. (1963): 'Distribution, Transitivity and Little's Welfare Criteria', *Economic Journal*, **73**, 771-8.

—— (1978): *Collective Choice and Social Welfare* (Edinburgh: Oliver & Boyd; San Francisco: Holden-Day). [Reprinted Amsterdam: North-Holland, 1979.]

—— (1974): 'Informational Bases of Alternative Welfare Approaches: Aggregation and Income Distribution', *Journal of Public Economics*, **3** (4), 387-403.

—— (1976a): 'Real National Income', *Review of Economic Studies*, **43** (1), 19-39. [Reprinted in Sen, 1982.]

—— (1976b): 'Poverty: An Ordinal Approach to Measurement', *Econometrica*, **44** (2), 219-31. [Reprinted in Sen, 1982.]

—— (1977a): 'On Weights and Measures: Informational Constraints in Social Welfare Analysis', *Econometrica*, **45** (7), 1539-72. [Reprinted in Sen, 1982.]

—— (1977b): 'Rational Fools: A Critique of the Behavioural Foundations of Economic Theory', *Philosophy and Public Affairs*, **6**. [Reprinted in Sen, 1982.]

—— (1982): *Choice, Welfare and Measurement* (Oxford: Basil Blackwell).

Shephard, Ronald W. (1953): *Cost and Production Functions* (Princeton: Princeton University Press).

Shinohara, M. *et al.* (1973): *Measuring Net National Welfare of Japan* (Measurement Committee, Economic Council of Japan).

Simon, Julian L. (1974): 'Interpersonal Welfare Comparisons Can Be Made — and Used for Redistribution Decisions', *Kyklos*, **27** (1), 63-98.

Staehle, Hans (1935): 'A Development of the Economic Theory of Price Index Numbers', *Review of Economic Studies*, **2**, 163-88.

Stone, Richard (1956): *Quantity and Price Indexes in National Accounts* (Paris: OECD).

Studenski, P. (1958): *The Income of Nations*, parts One and Two (New York: New York University Press).

Stuvel, Geer (1957): 'A New Index Number Formula', *Econometrica*, **25** (1), 123-31.

Suzumura, Kotaro (1977): 'Compensation Principle as a Collective Choice Mechanism: An Evaluation', mimeographed, Kyoto University.

Swamy, Subramanian (1965): 'Consistency of Fisher's Tests', *Econometrica*, **33**, 619-23.

—— (1970): 'On Samuelson's Conjecture', *Indian Economic Review*, **5**.

Takayama, Noriyuki (1979): 'Poverty, Income Inequality and their Measures: Professor Sen's Axiomatic Approach Reconsidered', *Econometrica*, **47**.

Theil, Henri (1967): *Economics and Information Theory* (Chicago: Rand McNally).

Ulmer, Melville J. (1949): *The Economic Theory of Cost of Living Index Numbers* (New York: Columbia University Press).

Usher, Dan (1968): *The Price Mechanism and the Meaning of National Income Statistics* (Oxford: Clarendon Press).

—— (1976): 'The Measurement of Real Income', *Review of Income and Wealth*, **22** (4), 305-29.

Varian, Hal R. (1974): 'Equity, Envy, Efficiency', *Journal of Economic Theory*, **9** (1), 63-91.

Vartia, Y. O. (1976): *Relative Changes and Index Numbers* (Helsinki: Research Institute of the Finnish Economy).

Ville, Jean (1952): 'The Existence Conditions of a Total Utility Function', *Review of Economic Studies*, **19** (2), 123-28.

Wald, Abraham (1939): 'A New Formula for the Index of Cost of Living', *Econometrica*, **7**, 319-31.

Weitzman, Martin L. (1976): 'On the Welfare Significance of National Product in a Dynamic Economy', *Quarterly Journal of Economics*, **90** (1), 156-62.

von Weizsacker, Carl Christian (1971): 'Notes on Endogenous Changes of Tastes', *Journal of Economic Theory*, **3** (4), 345-72.

Willig, Robert D. (1976): 'Consumers' Surplus without Apology', *American Economic Review*, **66** (4), 589-97.

Wold, Herman (1953): *Demand Analysis: A Study in Econometrics* (New York: Wiley).

18

Ingredients of Famine Analysis:
Availability and Entitlements

The main purpose of the paper is to develop an approach to famine
analysis and to examine its implications. The entitlement approach,
which contrasts with the more usual food availability approach,
concentrates on the ability of people to command food through the
legal means available in that society (including the use of production
possibilities, trade opportunities, entitlements vis-à-vis the state,
etc.). The main line of analysis is presented in Section 2, relating
endowment vectors to sets of alternative commodity entitlements
through an exchange entitlement mapping. Application to famine
analysis is discussed in general terms in Section 3, including limitations of the approach, while entitlement failures are broadly categorized in Section 4. Then the approach is applied to studying three
actual famines: the Bengal famine of 1943 (Section 5), the Ethiopian
famine of 1973 in Wollo (Section 6), and the Bangladesh famine of
1974 (Section 7). While data scarcity constrains some of the analysis,
some firm conclusions do emerge. The limitations of the food availability approach – its cluelessness – come out sharply. Some general
remarks on famine analysis are made in the concluding section.

1 The Availability Approach

Famines have received a good deal of attention recently, partly
because they have continued to occur despite mid-twentieth-century

This paper was completed during the author's visit to Cornell University in September-
October 1979. For helpful comments, I am most grateful to M. Alamgir, John Flemming,
Keith Griffin, Judith Heyer, Jay Kynch, Mukul Majumdar, Felix Paukert, Debraj Ray,
Jaroslav Vanek, Henry Wan, Jr., and to the referees of *The Quarterly Journal of Economics*.
The paper draws heavily on my forthcoming book, Sen (1981) [since published].

From *Quarterly Journal of Economics*, 95 (August 1981), 433-64.

prosperity,[1] but also because much fear seems to be entertained currently about a coming 'world food crisis'.[2] It has even been suggested that 'the biggest famine in history has just begun' (Dumont, 1975, p. 29).

The traditional approach to famines looks for a decline in food availability: 'a sudden, sharp reduction in the food supply in any particular geographic locale has usually resulted in widespread hunger and famine' (Brown and Eckholm, 1974, p. 25). This approach of food availability decline (FAD approach for short) has some superficial plausibility, since it seems natural to sense a shortage of food when people die as a result of not having food. The FAD approach also fits in well with Malthusian long-run analysis of increased mortality as food supply falls relative to the size of the population.[3]

However, starvation is a matter of some people not *having* enough food to eat, and not a matter of there *being* not enough food to eat.[4] While the latter can be a cause of the former, it is clearly one of many possible influences. The next section is devoted to developing a different approach to starvation and famines based on the notion of entitlement.

2   The Entitlement Approach

Ownership of food is one of the most primitive property rights, and in each society there are rules governing this right. The entitlement approach concentrates on each person's entitlements to commodity bundles including food, and views starvation as resulting from a failure to be entitled to any bundle with enough food.[5]

---

1. Important examples of recent famines include the Great Bengal Famine of 1943, the Biafra famine in Nigeria of 1968, the Ethiopian famines of 1973–74, famine in the Sahel countries in the early seventies, the Bangladesh famine of 1974, and famines in Kampuchea and in East Africa in recent years.

2. See Ehrlich and Ehrlich (1972), Brown and Eckholm (1974), Aziz (1975), among many other contributions. See also Johnson (1975) and Sinha (1976) for general analyses of the available information.

3. Robert Malthus himself provided a closely reasoned short-run analysis of famines in Malthus (1800), following his long-run analysis of population growth in Malthus (1798).

4. The distinction corresponds to that between 'goods' and 'named goods', which is central to the welfare-based evaluation of national income (see Sen, 1976b). See also Hahn (1971) for a different use of the contrast, which can be related to Hicks' (1946) notion of 'dated goods'.

5. It may be worth mentioning that the use of 'entitlement' here is descriptive rather than normative, and the entitlement approach presented here must not be confused with Nozick's (1974) moral theory of the same name. Some of the normative issues are discussed in Sen (1977a).

In a fully directed economy, each person i may simply get a particular commodity bundle that is assigned to him. To a limited extent, this happens in most economies, e.g. to residents of old people's homes or of mental hospitals. Typically, however, there is a menu – possibly wide – to choose from. E_i is the entitlement set of person i in a given society, in a given situation, and it consists of a set of vectors of alternative commodity bundles, any one of which the person can decide to have.[6] In an economy with private ownership and exchange in the form of trade (exchange with others) and production (exchange with nature), E_i can be characterized as depending on two parameters: the endowment vector x and an exchange entitlement mapping $E_i(\cdot)$, which specifies the set of commodity bundles any one of which person i can choose to have through 'exchange' (trade and production).[7]

I have examined elsewhere the formal characterization of entitlement relations and their use (see Sen, 1981, Chapters 1, 5, 10, and Appendices A and B). It should be noted here that the exchange entitlement mapping, or E-mapping for short, will, in general, depend on the legal, political, economic and social characteristics of the society in question and the person i's position in it. Perhaps the simplest case in terms of traditional economic theory is one in which the endowment vector can be exchanged in the market at fixed relative prices into any bundle costing no more, and here the *value* of the exchange entitlement mapping will be a traditional 'budget set'.

Bringing in production ('exchange with nature') will make the E-mapping depend on production opportunities as well as trade possibilities of resources and products. It will also involve legal rights to apportioning the produce, e.g. the capitalist rule of the 'entrepreneur' owning the produce. Sometimes the social conventions governing these rights can be very complex indeed, e.g. those governing the rights of migrant members of peasant families to a share of the peasant output (Sen, 1975, 1981).

Social security provisions are also reflected in the E-mapping; e.g. the right to unemployment benefits if one fails to find a job, or the right to income supplementation if one's income would otherwise fall below a certain specified level. And so are employment guarantees when they exist – as they do in some socialist economies – giving one the right to sell one's labour power to the government at

---

6. Formally, E_i can be seen as a subset of the nonnegative orthant X of n-dimensional real space (given n commodities).

7. $E_i(\cdot)$ is a function from X to the power set of X, the set of all subsets of X:

$$E_i: X \to 2^X, \quad \text{with } x \in E_i(x), \quad \text{for all } x \in X. \tag{1}$$

a minimum price. E-mappings will also depend on provisions of taxation.

Person i will have to starve if given his endowment x_i and the exchange entitlement mapping $E_i(\cdot)$, no element of $E_i(x_i)$ contains enough food. The 'starvation set' S_i of endowment vectors consists of those commodity vectors z such that he cannot meet his food requirements through exchange, starting from z (i.e. the exchange entitlement set $E_i(z)$ contains no vectors satisfying his minimum food requirements).[8]

In standard models of general equilibrium for capitalist economies,[9] it is assumed *in effect* that everyone's endowment vector lies outside the starvation set, and in this way the problem of survival is eliminated. As Koopmans (1957) puts it: 'they assume that each consumer can, if necessary, survive on the basis of the resources he holds and the direct use of his own labour, without engaging in exchange, and still have something to spare of some type of labour which is sure to meet with a positive price in any equilibrium' (p. 59). The advantages of such an assumption for general equilibrium models are clear enough, but it is not the case that, say, barbers, or shoemakers, or goldsmiths, or general labourers, or even doctors or lawyers, can survive without trading. The problem that is thus eliminated by assumption in these general equilibrium models is precisely the one that is central to a theory of starvation and famines.

The 'survival problem' for general equilibrium models calls for a solution not in terms of a clever assumption that eliminates it irrespective of realism, but for a reflection of the real guarantees that actually prevent starvation deaths in advanced capitalist economies. This involves bringing in social security provisions, which precisely play this role, and there need be no great difficulty in incorporating such transfers in the formulation of a general equilibrium model with the state providing minimum entitlement transfers.

The real problem is not one of convenience of analysis but of *actual* existence of such entitlement guarantees, and starvation and famines can flourish in different parts of the world precisely because of the absence of such guarantees.

8. The set of commodity vectors, each of which satisfies person i's minimum food requirement, is denoted $F_i \subseteq X$. Person i will be forced to starve because of unfavourable entitlement relations if and only if he is not entitled to any member of F_i, given his endowment vector and his exchange entitlement mapping:

$$E_i(x_i) \cap F_i = \phi; \tag{2}$$

The 'starvation set' S_i is given by:

$$S_i = \{z \mid z \in X \text{ and } E_i(z) \cap F_i = \phi\}. \tag{3}$$

9. See Debreu (1959) and Arrow and Hahn (1971).

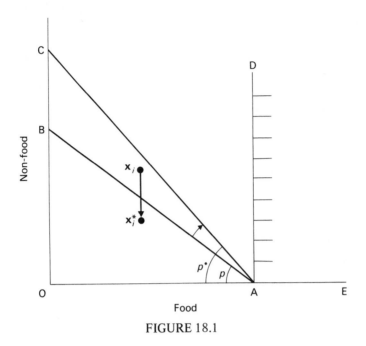

FIGURE 18.1

3   *Famines as Entitlement Failures*

Person i can be plunged into starvation *either* through a fall in the endowment vector x_i, *or* through an unfavourable shift in the exchange entitlement mapping $E_i(\cdot)$.[10] The distinction is illustrated in Figure 18.1 in terms of the simple case of pure trade involving only two commodities, namely, food and non-food. The exchange entitlement mapping is taken to assume the simple linear form of constant price exchange. With a price ratio p, and a minimum food requirement OA, the starvation set S_i is given by the region OAB. If the endowment vector is x_i, the person is in a position to avoid starvation. This ability can fail either (i) through a lower endowment vector, e.g. x_i^*, *or* (ii) through a less favourable exchange entitlement mapping, e.g. that given by p^*, which would make the starvation set OAC.

10. Note that this account, if taken as a real shift over time, involves a more short-run view of exchange possibilities than in the classic Arrow–Debreu formulation with present contracting of all future transactions.

It is easy to see that starvation can develop for a certain group of people as its endowment vector collapses, and there are indeed many accounts of such endowment declines on the part of sections of the poor rural population in many developing countries through alienation of land, sale of livestock, etc., and of consequent hardship.[11] Shifts in exchange entitlement mappings are rather less palpable, and more difficult to trace, but starvation can also develop with unchanged asset ownership through movements of exchange entitlement *mapping*. This will be impossible only if the endowment vector was itself an element of F_i, e.g. in Figure 18.1, if it belonged to the region DAE.

Before proceeding to the use of the entitlement approach, a few of the limitations may be briefly noted. First, there can be ambiguities in the specification of entitlements. Even in capitalist market economies, entitlements may not be well defined in the absence of a unique and reachable Walrasian market-clearing equilibrium,[12] and in pre-capitalist formations, there can be a good deal of vagueness on property rights and related matters.[13] In many cases the appropriate characterization of entitlements may pose problems, and in some cases it may well be best characterized in the form of 'fuzzy' sets and related structures – taking precise note of the vagueness involved.[14] In empirical studies of actual famines the question of precision is compromised by data problems as well, and the focus here will not be on characterizing entitlements with pretended exactitude, but on studying shifts in some of the main *ingredients* of entitlements. Big shifts in such ingredients can be decisive in outlining entitlement failures, even when there is some 'fuzziness' in the entitlement relations.

Second, while entitlement relations concentrate on rights within the given legal structure in that society, some transfers involve violation of these rights, e.g. looting or brigandry. When such extra-entitlement transfers are important, the entitlement approach to famines will be defective. On the other hand, many, though not all, recent famines seem to have taken place in rather orderly societies

11. See, for example, Griffin and Khan (1976) and Riffin (1978).
12. See Hicks (1946) and Arrow and Hahn (1971).
13. There is also the critique by Dworkin (1977) of 'legal positivism' disputing the view of law as a set of 'rules', and emphasizing the role of 'principles, policies, and other sorts of standards' (p. 27), which are, of course, inherently more ambiguous. See also Summers (1978).
14. A similar problem arises from the ambiguity of values in economic planning, requiring 'range' – rather than 'point' – specification of shadow prices, leading to *partial* orders (see Sen, 1975).

without anything 'illegal' about the process leading to starvation. In fact, in guarding ownership rights against the demands of the hungry, the legal forces uphold entitlements, e.g. in the Bengal famine of 1943 the people who died in front of well-stocked food shops protected by the state[15] were denied food because of lack of legal entitlement and not because of their entitlements being violated.

Third, people's actual food consumption may fall below their entitlements for a variety of other reasons, e.g. ignorance, fixed food habits, or apathy.[16] In concentrating on entitlements, something of the total reality is obviously neglected in our approach, and the question is how important these ignored elements happen to be and how much of a difference is made by this neglect.

Finally, the entitlement approach focuses on starvation, which has to be distinguished from famine mortality, since many of the famine deaths – in some cases *most* of them – are caused by epidemics, which have patterns of their own.[17] The epidemics are, of course, induced partly by starvation, but also by other famine characteristics, such as population movement and breakdown of sanitary facilities, adding to the force of contagion.

4   *Direct and Trade Entitlement Failures*

Consider occupation group j, characterized as having commodity j to sell or directly consume. Let q_j be the amount of commodity j each member of group j can sell or consume, and let the price of commodity j be p_j. The price of food per unit is p_f. Let F_j be the maximum food entitlement of group j. Clearly, $F_j = q_j p_j / p_f = q_j e_j$, when e_j is occupation j's food exchange rate (p_j / p_f).

Commodity j may or may not be a *produced* commodity. The commodity that a labourer has to sell is labour power, and it is his means of survival just as commodities in the shape of baskets and jute are the means of survival of the basket-maker and the jute-grower, respectively. In general, it may be necessary to associate several different commodities, rather than one, with the same occupation, but there is not much difficulty in redefining q_j and p_j as vectors (with $q_j p_j$ as an inner product and e_j a weighted ratio).

15. See Ghosh (1944) and also Government of India (1945).

16. Also people sometimes *choose* to starve rather than to sell their productive assets (see Jodha, 1975, for some evidence of this in Indian famines), and this issue can be accommodated in the entitlement approach only in a relatively long-run formulation (taking note of future entitlements). There is also some tendency for asset markets to collapse in famine situations, making the reward from asset sales rather puny.

17. See Sen (1980) for a study of the pattern of mortality in the Great Bengal Famine.

A special case arises when the occupation consists of being a producer of food, say, rice, which is also what members of that occupation live on. In this case $p_j = p_f$, and $e_f = 1$, with $F_f = q_f$. Given the selective nature of calamities such as floods and droughts, affecting one food-producing group but not another, it will sometimes be convenient to take the group f to be a *specific part* of that occupation category.

It is worth emphasizing that this drastically simple modelling of reality makes sense only in helping us to focus on some important parameters of famine analysis; it does not compete with the more general structure sketched in Sections 2 and 3. Furthermore, these simplifications will be grossly misleading in some contexts, e.g. in analysing entitlements in an industrialized economy, because of the importance of raw materials, intermediate products, asset holdings, etc. Even in applying this type of structure to analyse *rural* famines in developing countries, care is needed to insure that the distortions are not too great.

For any group j to start starving *because of* an entitlement failure, F_j must decline, since it represents the *maximum* food entitlement. F_j can fall either because one has produced less food for own consumption, or because one can obtain less food through trade exchanging one's commodity for food. The former will be called a 'direct entitlement failure', and the latter a 'trade entitlement failure'. The former will arise when q_f falls for some food-producing subgroup, while the latter can occur either because of a fall in e_j, or because of a fall in q_j, for a group that sells its commodity to buy food. Such a fall in q_j can occur either due to an autonomous production decline (e.g. a cash crop being destroyed by a drought), or due to insufficiency of demand (e.g. a labourer being involuntarily unemployed, or a basket-maker cutting down the output as the demand for baskets slackens).

It is, in fact, possible for a group to suffer *both* direct entitlement failure as well as trade entitlement failure, since the group may produce a commodity that is both directly consumed as well as exchanged for some other food. For example, the Ethiopian or Sahelian pastoral nomad both eats the animal products directly and also sells animals to buy food grains (thereby making a net gain in calories), on which he is habitually dependent.[18] Similarly, the Bengali fisherman does consume some fish, though for his survival he is dependent on grain-calories, which he obtains at a favourable rate by selling fish — a luxury food for most Bengalis.

18. See Chapters 7 and 8 in Sen (1981).

In the next sections the following famines are briefly examined in the light of the framework presented in the preceding sections: the Bengal Famine of 1943; the Ethiopian famine in Wollo province in 1973; and the Bangladesh famine of 1974. They draw on fuller studies,[19] but the intention here is to put them in a comparative perspective, using the ingredients of famine analysis presented here. There will be attempts to answer the following questions in each case:

(1) Was there a substantial food availability decline compared with normal supply?
(2) To which occupation groups did the famine victims chiefly belong?
(3) Did these groups suffer from substantial entitlement declines, and if so, what were the characteristics of these entitlement failures (e.g. endowment loss *versus* unfavourable shifts in exchange entitlement mappings, direct entitlement failures versus trade entitlement failures)?

5   The Great Bengal Famine of 1943

The Bengal famine of 1943 was characterized by an acute period of starvation during May to October of 1943. The death rate stayed up for several years because of epidemics that the famine unleashed. The contemporary official estimate of excess death due to the famine was 1.5 million in a population of around 60 million (see Government of India, 1945, pp. 119–20). However, use of later data, including reverse-survival estimates based on the 1951 census, indicates that 3 million was closer to the mark (see Sen, 1980). The famine was mostly a rural phenomenon, affecting every district in rural Bengal,[20] but Calcutta saw the famine mainly in the form of masses of rural destitutes trekking into the city and dying on the streets (see Das, 1949).

Was there a substantial food availability decline compared with normal supply? The official Famine Inquiry Commission, which produced an admirably detailed report, thought so, and diagnosed that the primary cause of the famine was 'a serious shortage in the total supply of rice available for consumption in Bengal'.[21] This FAD

19. See Sen (1980), which also examines other cases of famines, e.g. those in Sahel countries in the seventies and the starvation of nomads in the Ogaden region of Ethiopia in 1974.
20. See the *Census of Pakistan 1951* and the *Census of India 1951*.
21. Government of India (1945, p. 77).

TABLE 18.1   Food availability in Bengal, 1940-43 (base: 1941 value = 100)

Year	Index of rice output	Index of rice supply	Index of foodgrains available	Index of foodgrains availability per capita
1940	125	124	122	123
1941	100	100	100	100
1942	141	135	131	130
1943	113	112	111	109

Source: Sen (1977b, Table 2).

explanation would have seemed plausible, since there were several factors working negatively on the supply of rice, which is the staple food of the Bengali, and on the supply of foodgrains in general. To wit: (i) a cyclone in October 1942 had affected, in some areas, the main crop (*aman*) of rice to be harvested in December 1942; (ii) import of rice from Burma into India had been disrupted by the Japanese occupation of Burma; (iii) London persistently turned down requests from New Delhi of shipping allocation for importing grains into India; (iv) interprovince movements of grain were largely prohibited except through intergovernmental agreements that did not get organized until after the famine; and (v) a cunning British policy of 'rice denial' to the oncoming Japanese led to removal of rice stocks from three coastal districts in Bengal in 1942 (without causing much anxiety to the Japanese, since they failed, for other reasons, to show up).

Nevertheless, a careful tally of food availability in Bengal does not fit with the FAD explanation of the famine. Table 18.1 presents the results of food supply calculation, taking into account local production and trade, choosing – wherever the data permit – an assumption as unfavourable to 1943 as possible. Current availability of food grains was at least 11 per cent higher in 1943 than in 1941, when there was nothing remotely like a famine. Even in per capita terms the current availability was 9 per cent higher in 1943.[22]

22. For the details of the estimation procedure, see Sen (1977b). Since figures on carry-over of stocks do not exist, two-year and three-year moving averages were also considered. The three-year moving average ending in 1943 is just marginally lower than that ending in 1941, while the two-year moving average ending in 1943 is higher than any since 1939-40 (see Table 2 in Sen, 1977b). Splitting up the availability during 1943 to take note of trade flow variations during the year does not alter the picture substantially either (see Sen, 1977b, pp. 40-1). See also Alamgir (1980) and Sen (1981, Chapter 6).

TABLE 18.2   Destitution indices for rural occupation groups during the Bengal famine

Occupation groups	Index A	Index B
Fishermen	9.6	10.5
Transport	6.0	6.9
Agricultural labour	4.6	6.1
Other productive occupations	4.6	4.6
Non-agricultural labours	3.7	4.5
Craft	3.8	4.3
Trade	2.2	2.6
Professions and services	2.1	2.5
Non-cultivating owners	1.6	2.4
Part peasant, part labour	1.4	2.0
Peasants and sharecroppers	1.3	1.4

Source: Sen (1977b, Tables 9 and 10). Index A is the 'transition' percentage to 'living on charity'; it represents the percentage of January-1943-population of each occupation group responding in 1944 that they were 'living on charity'. Index B is the sum of destitution Index A and the 'transition' percentage to 'husking paddy' – a classic destitution occupation.

I turn now to the second question: who were the famine victims? There is overwhelming evidence that the famine victims came almost exclusively from the rural population.[23] Hardly any came from Calcutta, even if Sir Manilal Nanavati might have exaggerated the contrast in his claim that 'in the end not a single man died of starvation from the population of Greater Calcutta, while millions in rural areas starved and suffered' (Government of India, 1945, p. 102). Within the rural areas, a picture of relative destitution can be constructed from the sample survey carried out in the famine stricken areas of Bengal by Mahalanobis, Mukherjea, and Ghosh (1946). Using these data, inter-occupation transition matrices can be constructed reflecting changes over the famine period (see Tables 9 and 10 in Sen, 1977b). They include, inter alia, relative frequencies of destitution of different rural occupation groups, using two indicators: (A) transition percentage to 'living on charity', and (B) transition percentage to 'living on charity' or 'husking paddy' – a typical destitution occupation with easy entry. The destitution indicators are presented in Table 18.2.

23. See Government of India (1945), Ghosh (1944), Mahalanobis, Mukherjea, and Ghosh (1946), Das (1949), and Mukerji (1965).

The *most* affected groups in this list of rural occupations were fishermen, transporters, and agricultural labourers in that order, followed by 'other productive occupations', non-agricultural labour, and crafts. In absolute number by far the largest groups of destitutes came from the class of agricultural labourers (see Mahalanobis, Mukherjea, and Ghosh, 1946). The surveys of the destitutes who trekked into Calcutta also confirm this (see Das, 1949), and so do other rural surveys dealing with destitution as well as occupation-specific mortality (see especially Mukerji, 1965).

The *least* affected group among the rural occupations was that of peasants and sharecroppers, as can be seen from Table 18.2. Other studies again broadly confirm this.[24]

Information about entitlements is very limited. However, Table 18.3 presents indices of rice exchange rate e_j for some of the occupations from data contemporarily collected in the Birbhum district near Bolpur. The occupation classification in these statistics is rather different from the categorization used by Mahalanobis and his colleagues, except for agricultural labour and fishermen. But the rice exchange rates of barbers and bamboo craftsmen are also relevant, and those of peasants and sharecroppers growing rice can, of course, be put as unity on analytical grounds (as discussed in Section 4). Table 18.3 presents these rice exchange rates, defined as the amount of common grade rice that could be bought with one unit of the occupational commodity. They are indexed (a) with the December-1942-value as 100 (to indicate absolute changes), and (b) with the same-month-1942-value as 100 (to filter out seasonal patterns).

The contrast between the obvious stationarity of e_j for rice-cultivating peasants and sharecroppers and the devastatingly steep decline of e_j for agricultural labourers, fishermen, and other groups is striking.[25] This was mainly the result of rice price rise, with prices of other commodities and rural wages falling behind.

There was little information about quantities q_j, except the un-quantified, but reported to be large, decline in the amounts of fish caught and river transportation because the government's 'boat denial' policy was carried out in 1942.[26] That policy, like the 'rice denial' policy, was also aimed at the elusive Japanese, and took the

24. For example, in the villages surveyed by Mukerji (1965), peasant and sharecroppers were the least affected with the exception of landlords and office employees. See also Bhatia (1967).

25. A qualification is worth mentioning here. There is evidence that some peasants and sharecroppers had sold off their stock shortly after the harvest (often to repay loans), and had to buy back grains for consumption later in the year, and would have suffered from the high retail price of foodgrains.

26. See Government of India (1945, pp. 26–7); also Ghosh (1944).

TABLE 18.3 Indices of rice-exchange rate e_j of rural occupations during the Bengal famine: Birbhum District around Bolpur (Base: (a) December 1942 values; (b) same month 1942 values)

Month	Agricultural labourers		Fishermen		Barbers		Bamboo craftsmen		Rice-cultivating peasants and sharecroppers	
	(a)	(b)	(a)	(b)	(a)	(b)	(a)	(b)	(a)	(b)
1941										
December	152	152	119	119	179	179	118	118	100	100
1942										
December	100	100	100	100	100	100	100	100	100	100
1943										
January	106	n.a.	77	68	93	48	100	75	100	100
February	114	n.a.	85	75	100	52	115	77	100	100
March	67	n.a.	55	48	66	34	81	45	100	100
April	55	n.a.	40	39	48	31	71	41	100	100
May	36	n.a.	32	36	32	24	51	32	100	100
June	39	n.a.	46	30	34	22	56	30	100	100
July	41	n.a.	45	31	34	23	55	31	100	100
August	47	n.a.	44	34	34	26	52	34	100	100
September	58	43	67	43	50	32	78	46	100	100
October	58	68	60	60	45	45	67	62	100	100
November	73	126	95	118	57	71	86	106	100	100
December	120	120	126	126	75	75	106	106	100	100

Source: Sen (1977b, Tables 4 and 5). Rice price is that of grade no. 2 rice. Agricultural wages are those of unskilled, male, agricultural labourers (daily rate). Other occupations are represented by the following commodities respectively: *pona* fish (fishermen); haircut (barbers); bamboo umbrellas (bamboo craftsmen); grade no. 2 rice (rice-cultivating peasants and share-croppers).

form of destroying or removing boats capable of carrying ten passengers or more in a vast area of river-based Bengal; it did not touch the Japanese, but played havoc with river transport (widespread in river-based Bengal), and fishing. These quantity losses were reflections of endowment loss, compounding, at least in the case of fishermen, the decline in exchange entitlement mapping resulting from a fall in the rice exchange rate.

What happened to entitlements of the Calcutta population, which escaped the famine raging all around it? While there was a little decline of real wages (see Palekar, 1962), the Calcutta population was effectively insulated from the steep rise in foodgrains prices by subsidized rice being made available through a system of rationing covering more than a million employees and their dependents, and also through a network of 'controlled' shops for regular residents of Calcutta. Virtually the whole of the Calcutta population was kept supplied with foodgrains at prices far below those ruling elsewhere (and indeed also below those existing in Calcutta for purchase outside rationing and control). There is little doubt that the government was successful in its policy of keeping the Calcutta population well fed, based on the belief that 'the maintenance of essential food supplies to the industrial area of Calcutta must be ranked on a very high priority among the government's wartime obligation' (Government of India, 1945, p. 30). And indeed, war efforts were not disrupted in Calcutta.

It is not part of my programme here to investigate the causation of the change of food prices and declines in rice exchange rates of rural occupation groups. I have tried to go into this question elsewhere (Sen, 1977b, pp. 49–55), even though the explanations are speculative, and data limitations make any kind of proper testing virtually impossible. The main factors to emerge are as follows: (i) the importance of demand expansion connected with war-related military, industrial, and construction activities along with a massive increase in effective demand and money supply through 1942 and 1943, (ii) speculative withdrawal of rice in 1943 caused partly by panic after early reports of starvation, but also by the extreme profitability of holding rice even under the assumption of stationary expectation (rice prices nearly doubled in 1943, the year preceding the famine) and a relatively low money rate of interest (well below 10 per cent); (iii) uneven distribution of the demand for labour reflecting the uneven impact of war-related activities, leaving most rural labour out of the activity boom; (iv) institutional sluggishness of the rural wage mechanism used to largely stationary rice prices in the quarter of a century preceding 1942; and (v) 'derived destitution' through collapse of demand for commodities other than food grains (such as craft products, rural services, fish and other luxury food, etc.) as the purchases of these commodities fell into destitution.[27]

The pattern of destitution suggests that the failure of entitlements, which was widespread and massive, was mainly *trade* entitlement failure rather than *direct* entitlement failure. Evidence of *endowment* loss was found for fishermen and rural transporters, but evidence of collapse of *exchange entitlement mapping* is much more widespread.

The rise in rice prices, which played a crucial part in this, does *not* seem to have been the result of an availability failure. There is, in fact, very little evidence for availability failure in the famine year. Indeed, rice prices had also nearly doubled in the year *preceding* the famine, i.e. in 1942, a year in which food availability per capita reached a record level (30 per cent higher than in the preceding year).[28] The clue lies on the demand side, and the entitlement failures associated with the Bengal famine seem to relate to the powerful, but uneven, expansionary forces working on the economy of Bengal. The Bengal famine was indeed a boom famine.

6　*The Wollo Famine of 1973*

The 1973–74 famines in Ethiopia were associated with droughts. The main – *kremt* – rains in mid-1972 failed in parts of Ethiopia particularly in the northeast, and this was followed by a failure of the spring – *belg* – rains in early 1973. The famine that gripped Ethiopia in 1973 was centred on the province of Wollo. While the *kremt* rains of 1973 were good in the northeast, a new drought situation developed further south. When the famine of 1974 raged over the province of Harerghe, the northeastern famine had substantially ended. So Ethiopia experienced two rather distinct famines during 1973 and 1974, though the former was by far the larger episode, and it is with the former that this section is concerned.[29]

The mortality estimates for the Ethiopian famines vary between 50 000 and 200 000 in a population of about 27 million.[30] Most of the deaths took place in 1973, in Wollo. Starvation reached its peak in Wollo around August of 1973.[31]

27. See also Sen (1981, Chapter 6 and Appendix B).
28. The entitlement decline of many of the occupation groups had already started in 1942, especially of agricultural labour (see Sen, 1977b, Tables 4 and 5).
29. For an analysis of the Harerghe famine and a more detailed account of the Wollo famine, see Sen (1981, Chapter 7).
30. See Rivers, Holt, Seaman, and Bowden (1976) and Gebre-Medhin and Vahlquist (1977).
31. See Holt and Seaman (1976, p. 4) and Seaman and Holt (1975).

Was there a substantial food availability decline in Ethiopia in 1973 compared with normal availability? Data on this are difficult to obtain, and furthermore, the heterogeneity of types of food consumed makes over-all indicators difficult to define (unlike in Bengal). The Food and Agricultural Organization of the United Nations does, however, present estimates of food availability per head in terms of calories consumed in the *FAO Production Yearbooks*. The 1973 availability figure, while just a bit lower than that of the preceding year, is hardly lower than for the 1961–65 period, and a good deal higher than the figures for 1964–69 and 1970.[32] On this basis there is no reason to read a food availability decline for Ethiopia as a whole in the famine year 1973. (For a more detailed account see Sen, 1981, Chapter 7.)

Should the FAD analysis relate to the Ethiopian food availability or to that in Wollo? It is, of course, always possible to make a FAD explanation work by choosing units sufficiently small, since some people dying of famine must mean that food was not 'available' to *them*! However, Wollo is a big province, and given reported transport difficulties, may *deserve* to be considered on its own. I shall later take up the complex issue involved in the choice of focus for FAD, but will turn first to the food production and supply situation in Wollo.

Food production did fall quite drastically in the province of Wollo. As far as the main crop is concerned, dependent on the *kremt* rains of 1972, 90 per cent of the districts had 'below normal' production, with more than half of them 'substantially below normal', according to a Ministry of Agriculture survey. No exact production figures have been reliably estimated for Wollo, but a big food production decline in Wollo seems indisputable (Hussein, 1976).

Was there a substantial movement of food into the deficit province of Wollo from the rest of Ethiopia? While there was some movement, no exact figures exist, but it appears that the movement was not very substantial during the famine year. Indeed, there is a record of movement of food *out of* Wollo into Addis Ababa and Asmera through the famine period (see Holt and Seaman, 1976). This would indicate that while food availability did fall in Wollo, something more than food availability had also fallen.

Who were the famine victims? While there is evidence that the pastoral population, especially of the *Afar* community, was among

32. For a more detailed analysis (and examination of data consistency), see Sen (1981, Chapter 7). The calorie estimates were interrupted in the Yearbooks for 1972 to 1975, but the 1976 Yearbook presents the figures for 1972 and 1973. 1971 is the only missing year, covered neither in the 1971 Yearbook, nor in the 1976 Yearbook.

the first to face acute problems (Holt and Seaman, 1976, p. 3), and had a high proportional destitution rate (Hussein, 1976, p. 19),[33] most of the destitutes came from agricultural backgrounds. Indeed, it appears that 'relief-centre populations were mainly made up of members of the farming peoples of principally low-land areas which are many times more densely populated than the Afar region'.[34] While there were some urban-origin people in the relief camps,[35] the bulk of the destitutes came from a farming background – a majority from the three *awrajas* (subregions) of Raya and Kobo, Yeju, and Ambassel,[36] belonging to the eastern lowlands of Wollo, severely affected by the failure of the *kremt* rains of 1972.

What about entitlements? For food-growing farmers consuming the food grown, the food exchange rate e_j is trivially unity. Thus, the production failure translates *directly* into an entitlement failure. The farming population faced starvation, since their own food output was insufficient and they did not have the ability to *buy* food from others, as food output is also their source of income.

It is the last point that provides a clue to the relative absence of food movement into Wollo from elsewhere in Ethiopia. For the farmers i in the region affected by drought, the collapse of the food entitlement F_f is a *direct* entitlement crisis related to a fall in q_f, without the overall food availability and markets making much difference (see Section 4).[37]

This explanation could be challenged by arguing that food did not get to the famine-affected people in Wollo because of transportation difficulties, and not because of the lack of purchasing power. Indeed, the roads inside Wollo are few and bad, and a large number of complaints were heard about them in discussions on the famine. If bad roads rather than lack of purchasing power prevented food from getting to the famine victims, then one must treat the province of Wollo rather than the country of Ethiopia as the right

33. The *Afar* pastoralist suffered not only from drought but also from the loss of some of the best grazing ground, just before the drought, due to encroachment from commercial agriculture (see Bondestam, 1974; Flood, 1976; and Hussein, 1976). A similar conflict with commercial agriculture seems to have played a prominent part in the famine in the Sahel countries (see Comité Information Sahel, 1974; Meillassoux, 1974, 1975; and Copans, 1975). Sen (1981) takes up some of the issues raised.

34. Holt and Seaman (1976, p. 3). See also Gebre-Medhin *et al.* (1974), and Belete *et al.* (1977).

35. These included daily male labourers and women in various service occupations: domestic service, water-carrying, beer-selling, and prostitution.

36. See Belete *et al.* (1977, Tables I and II).

37. A farmer owning land and livestock can, of course, sell these endowments. But many farmers did not possess saleable land; land and livestock prices were severely depressed; and there was also much endowment loss in the form of livestock death.

focus for a FAD analysis, and must then give food availability decline an important role in the famine. Can this hypothesis be rejected?

There is indeed strong evidence against the hypothesis of transport limitation. First, while roads are few and bad in much of Wollo, two highways run through it, and the main north–south Ethiopian highway linking Addis Ababa and Asmera runs right through the area most affected by the famine (see Holt and Seaman, 1976, and Belete *et al.*, 1977). Indeed, much of the early information about the famine came from travellers being stopped on this highway to ask for food (see Holt and Seaman, 1976). Nearly all the relief camps that were eventually set up were located near the highway, not merely because of easy access for supplies coming in, but also because of the high intensity of destitution in that region (see Belete *et al.*, 1977). Underdeveloped roads would not explain the starvation in these famine-affected regions.

Second, as mentioned earlier, there was some movement of food *out of* Wollo through the famine period. This was not very large in volume, but it did provide some support for the market entitlement view rather than the transport-limitation view of food shortage in Wollo.

Third, despite the disastrous failure of food output, food prices did not go up very much in Wollo. When in October 1973 Holt and Seaman started collection of food prices in the hardest hit district of Raya and Kobo, which had more than a tenth of its population in relief camps by May–June 1974,[38] they found that food prices were within 15 per cent of the pre-drought levels (Holt and Seaman, 1976, p. 5).

Food prices in Dessie, the main grain market in Wollo, also rose relatively little. Taking the average prices of 1970–72 as the 'pre-famine' levels, prices in the famine year 1973 were, on the whole, remarkably close to pre-famine levels: somewhat higher for some (e.g. teff, millett), and somewhat lower for others (e.g. wheat, sorghum, barley, maize).[39] People starved to death without there being a substantial rise in food prices. In terms of entitlement approach, there is, of course, no puzzle in this. Since the farmers' food entitlement is a *direct* entitlement (without going through the

38. See Belete *et al.* (1977, Tables I and II).

39. See Sen (1981, Table 7.4). These prices, collected by the National Bank of Ethiopia and the Ethiopian Grain Agency, relate to the Ethiopian calendar. So 1973 corresponds to September 1972 to September 1973. While it begins a bit early (and no time breakdown could be obtained), it avoids the period of very late 1973 in which relief supplies started coming into Wollo in some volume. Also, the main crop failure was clear by September 1972, the *kremt* rains having already failed. I am grateful to Julius Holt for giving me these unpublished official data.

market), a collapse of it can operate without a rise in market prices. On the other hand, the transport-limitation view would have suggested a substantial increase in prices because of the excess demand arising from supply limitation.[40]

The transport-limitation view is, therefore, not easy to defend. Insofar as the starving people in Wollo could draw on food from the rest of Ethiopia *if* they had the market power to pull food into Wollo, the appropriate unit for a FAD analysis has to be Ethiopia rather than Wollo. Food did not move into Wollo in sufficient amount (and some moved out), not so much because the roads did not permit such movements, but because the Wollo residents lacked the market command.

Finally, while the entitlement failure of the Wollo farmer was a *direct* entitlement failure, this led to *trade* entitlement failures of other groups. Farm servants and dependents were dismissed. The usual food sales to urban markets were reduced, and demands for urban goods and services were cut, leading to 'derived destitution' there. The multiplier process would lead to other destitutions as a consequence. The composition of the relief centre population confirms such indirect entitlement failures.[41] If the Bengal famine had the character of a *boom* famine, the Wollo famine certainly looks more like a contraction-based *slump* famine.

7   The Bangladesh Famine of 1974

The Bangladesh famine of 1974 is associated with floods that came during June to September of 1974 on an inflated Brahmaputra river. Reports of famine could be heard not much after the flooding began, though the official declaration of the famine did not come until late September. Some relief centres (*langarkhanas*) providing cooked food came into operation under private initiative in early September, and massively under government auspices in early October. At one stage nearly 6000 langarkhanas were providing relief to 4.35 million people – more than 6 per cent of the total population of the country. By November the crisis seemed to be passing, and the langarkhanas were shut down by the end of November.

Mortality estimates vary widely. The official figure of deaths due to the famine is 26 000. Other estimates suggest that in the Rangpur

40. The Wollo grain prices in 1973 remained in the neighbourhood of – typically only a little higher than – those ruling in Addis Ababa despite the starvation in Wollo, according to Ethiopian Grain Agency data.

41. See Gebre-Medhin *et al.* (1974), Holt and Seaman (1976), and Belete *et al.* (1977). See also other accounts of destitution, e.g. Hussein (1976) and Wood (1976).

TABLE 18.4   Foodgrains output and availability in Bangladesh, 1971-75
(base: 1971 value = 100)

Year	Index of per capita rice output (a)	Index of per capita foodgrains availability (b)	Calories per capita (c)
1971	100	100	
1972	90	103	1900
1973	95	103	1913
1974	105	107	2023
1975	99	100	

Source: (a) and (b) calculated from Alamgir (1980); (c) is obtained from *FAO Production Year book 1976.*

district alone '80 to 100 thousand persons died of starvation and malnutrition in 2-3 months' (Haque *et al.*, 1976, p. 43). Another estimate suggests an excess-death figure of around one million during August 1974 and February 1975, and a further half a million in the year following (Alamgir, 1980).

Was there a substantial food availability decline? There were factors contributing to this. The floods did wipe out a part of the standing *aus* crop of rice, which is harvested in July and August, and also washed away rice seedlings being transplanted for the principal *aman* crop, harvested around December. Importing was proving difficult due to dollar shortage (see Islam, 1977), and food aid from the United States was in serious jeopardy because of the US objection to Bangladesh's export of jute to Cuba, until Bangladesh agreed to stop further export (see McHenry and Bird, 1977; also Sobhan, 1979).

But *did* the food availability in Bangladesh decline in the famine year? Table 18.4 provides the indices of rice production as well as of per capita availability of rice and total foodgrains. Far from being a bad availability year, it seems that 1974 was the year of peak availability in the first half of the decade. A similar picture emerges from the estimates of calorie consumption.[42] It is difficult to defend a FAD explanation of the Bangladesh famine of 1974.

42. The rice *output* figure for 1974 in the *FAO Production Yearbook* is low because it *includes* the December 1974 harvest and *excludes* the December 1973 harvest. The production figures given in Table 18.4 here are based on Alamgir's (1980) estimation that rightly identifies the output relevant for 1974 as including the crop harvested in December 1973, and not that harvested in December 1974, which is consumed over the *next* year. The same method was used in estimating output of foodgrains in Bengal during the Bengal famine of 1943 in Section 5 above, and in Sen (1977b).

Who were the famine victims? The survey of langarkhana destitutes carried out by the Bangladesh Institute of Development Studies permits us to give an answer to the question in terms of rather broad categories. It appears that the destitutes were almost entirely from the rural areas. The breakdown among broad rural occupation groups is given in Table 18.5. The biggest occupation group among the langarkhana destitutes was that of 'farmers' (38.7 per cent), followed by agricultural labourers (24.1 per cent) and other labourers (20.4 per cent). Farmers are also the most numerous occupation group in Bangladesh, and if we look at the relative *intensity* of destitution (see Table 18.5), it would appear that rural labourers as a group had a much higher rate of destitution than the farmers – in fact, about three times as high. Incidentally, if we put the rural labourers together rather than splitting them into agricultural and non-agricultural (there is easy movement between the two groups), then they are also the most numerous occupational group of destitution in terms of absolute numbers.

The study by the Bangladesh Institute separated out three districts as 'famine districts' namely, Rangpur, Mymensingh, and Sylhet, because of incidence of destitution and effects of the flood as revealed by the survey. The langarkhana data support this diagnosis, and these three are certainly among the top four districts (Rangur, Mymensingh, Dinajpur, and Sylhet) in terms of proportions of their

TABLE 18.5   Occupational distribution and intensity of destitution in Bangladesh, 1974

Occupation	Percentage of total langarkhana population (a)		Percentage of Bangladesh rural households by major sources of income (b)	Destitution intensity (a)/(b)
Farmers		38.7	58.6	0.66
Agricultural labourers	24.1			
Other rural labourers	20.4			
Total rural labourers		44.5	23.7	1.88
Others		16.8	17.7	0.95
Total		100.0	100.0	1.00

Source: (a) and (b) obtained from the results of sample surveys by the Bangladesh Institute of Development Studies, reported by Alamgir (1980).

TABLE 18.6   Interdistrict variations of foodgrains availability and change
(Bangladesh, 1974)

District	Foodgrains availability per head (oz/day)	Percentage change of foodgrains availability between 1973 and 1974	Percentage change of rice production between 1973 and 1974
Dinajpur	25.1	+23.0	+32.1
Mymensingh	22.8	+10.7	+22.3
Sylhet	22.1	+ 3.3	+10.3
Bogra	20.8	+ 7.8	+25.8
Rangpur	20.1	+ 9.8	+17.1
Chittagong	19.7	+ 7.1	+12.6
Noakali	16.7	− 6.2	+ 6.5
Jessore	16.3	+11.6	+24.6
Khulna	16.2	+17.4	+42.2
Barisal	16.0	−14.0	− 9.6
Rajshahi	15.8	+ 1.3	+ 6.4
Patuakhali	15.7	−34.9	−33.0
Tangail	15.3	+ 4.1	+22.0
Comilla	14.9	− 7.5	+ 3.9
Chittagong Hill Tracts	14.4	− 2.7	+38.8
Dacca	13.8	− 4.8	+ 8.0
Faridpur	13.5	+12.5	+20.1
Kushtia	12.8	+ 6.7	+22.8
Pabna	10.8	+ 3.8	+12.4

Source: Alamgir (1980).

respective total population who lived on langarkhanas (respectively, 17 per cent, 12 per cent, 9 per cent, and 8 per cent). In the case of the fourth, Dinajpur, it appears that a considerable proportion of the local destitutes really 'came from the adjoining district of Rangpur' (Alamgir, 1980).

How did these three 'famine districts' fare in terms of food availability change? Estimates relating to this have been presented in Table 18.6. Rice production in all three districts *went up* substantially. So did food availability per head. Furthermore, in terms of absolute foodgrains availability per head, these three famine districts were among the *best supplied* five districts in a list of nineteen!

What about entitlements, especially of rural labour? Table 18.7 presents the indices of rice-exchange for rural labour for each month in 1974 with two alternative bases: namely, (a) December 1973 as

TABLE 18.7 Indices of rice-exchange rate e_j of rural labour during the Bangladesh famine, 1974 (base: (a) December-1973 values; (b) same-month-1973 values)

Month	Rural wage rate		Price of rice		Index value of rice-exchange rate e_j for 1974 month	
	1973	1974	1973	1974	(a)	(b)
January	4.78	6.22	72.37	92.11	86	102
February	4.91	6.36	76.68	98.93	82	100
March	5.14	7.17	83.84	117.33	78	100
April	5.35	8.22	96.49	136.98	77	108
May	5.47	8.72	96.29	135.68	82	113
June	5.83	8.26	91.11	139.04	76	93
July	6.02	8.61	87.06	141.78	78	88
August	5.81	8.82	85.92	171.25	66	76
September	5.72	8.80	89.47	212.80	53	65
October	5.85	8.64	94.11	251.78	44	55
November	6.00	8.39	89.65	213.73	50	59
December	6.32	8.70	80.90	188.98	59	59

Source: Calculations based on data compiled by the Bangladesh Institute of Development Studies, reported in Alamgir *et al.* (1977), Tables 3.3 and 4.3.

100; and (b) the same month in 1973 as 100. The decline of the e_j indices in the months just preceding the famine and through the famine months is very sharp indeed. The fall is a bit less if we use the same-month-previous-year base, which does something to eliminate the seasonal drop, but even there the fall is large. At the peak of the famine the fall is 35 to 45 per cent compared with the same month in the previous year, for a group of people already close to subsistence.

The sharpest decline comes just after the floods started, and Table 18.8 presents the fall of the rice-exchange rate of rural labour during June to October. There was no such decline in the preceding year (see Table 18.7), and data for earlier years also show no substantial seasonal fall over these months.

The decline in the rice-exchange rate of rural labour for the districts are also presented in Table 18.8. The three most affected districts in terms of precipitate decline of the rice-exchange rate are Mymensingh (70 per cent), Rangpur (58 per cent) and Sylhet (58 per cent) — precisely the three 'famine districts'.[43]

43. For more detailed analyses of the interdistrict pattern of entitlement decline and destitution, see Alamgir (1980) and Sen (1981, Chapter 9).

TABLE 18.8   Decline of rice-exchange rate of rural labour in Bangladesh
between June and October 1974

Area	Wage rate in October 1974 with June 1974 value as 100	Rice price in October 1974 with June 1974 value as 100	Percentage decline in e_i for rural labour between June and October 1974
Bangladesh	104.6	181.1	42.2
Mymensingh	69.0	225.9	69.5
Rangpur	80.0	190.3	58.0
Sylhet	100.0	236.0	57.6
Noakhali	100.0	209.8	52.3
Barisal	87.0	177.3	50.9
Chittagong Hill Tracts	100.0	201.3	50.3
Tangail	106.3	211.4	49.7
Pabna	100.0	172.3	42.0
Chittagong	100.0	170.5	41.3
Patuakhali	100.0	167.9	40.4
Dacca	118.9	192.6	38.3
Khulna	96.2	153.9	37.5
Bogra	100.0	158.2	36.8
Dinajpur	114.3	179.1	36.2
Comilla	135.7	205.0	33.8
Jessore	108.3	155.0	30.1
Kushtia	112.0	151.4	26.0
Rajshahi	123.1	156.4	21.3
Faridpur	158.3	164.5	3.8

Basis: Calculated from Tables 3.3 and 4.3 of Alamgir et al. (1977), pp. 57-8 and 92.

What led to this severe exchange entitlement decline? The main factor would appear to be the rise in rice prices, but it is worth noting that in two of the three 'famine districts', viz. in Rangpur and Mymensingh, even the money wages fell, respectively, by 20 per cent and 31 per cent (Table 18.8). The floods certainly did reduce employment in those areas in which crops or seedlings got washed away cutting down the scope for fruitful work.[44] While the floods did not reduce the over-all aus crop in Bangladesh, and could not reduce per capita food availability in any of the 'famine districts' (given the relatively large aman harvest in the preceding November–January); nevertheless, the labour market during the aus harvesting and aman transplanting was clearly disrupted, particularly in the 'famine districts'. The reduced *aman* harvest of November–January 1974–75 did not, of course, affect food availability in Bangladesh until *after* the famine was over, but its impact was *immediately* felt in the labour market since wage employment was curtailed straight away.

But the rise in *rice* prices cannot be explained in terms of labour market disruption, and the question arises as to why rice prices rose so fast just after the floods hit. Anticipation of the coming shortage, seeing the effects of the flood, would have been a possible immediate reason, and there was clearly some speculative rise (see Alamgir, 1980). But inflationary forces operating on the rice market had started pushing rice prices up very sharply much before the floods hit. This had been going on throughout the early seventies (see Faaland and Parkinson, 1976; and Islam, 1977). But the rise in the early months (January–April) of 1974 was particularly severe, and there was about a 50 per cent rise between January and April in 1974.[45] In this inflationary development the floods that came in June and later could hardly have played a role.

Thus, while floods were associated with the Bangladesh famine and played the part of disrupting the labour market as well as leading to some loss of crops by farmers and consequent destitution,[46] the forces that wreaked havoc must be traced in part to *macroeconomic* factors operating on the economy of Bangladesh. The floods seemed to have made it impossible for some deprived groups, especially rural labourers, to keep up with the expansionary forces pushing food prices up in the economy (see Sen, 1981, Chapter 9).

While the *explanation* of the entitlement shifts of the victim groups must remain somewhat speculative, the *facts* of the entitlement shifts are clear enough. It is also established that whatever might have caused these shifts, a substantial decline in food availability could not have played this part, for the simple reason that such a decline did not occur. It occurred neither for Bangladesh as a whole, nor for the 'famine districts' within Bangladesh.

---

44. See Rahman (1974). Also Alamgir (1978, 1980).

45. There is a seasonal element in this too, but the rise was much sharper in 1974.

46. The langarkhana destitutes came mostly from the class of landless labourers or the little-landowning peasantry. Of the langarkhana destitutes surveyed, 81 per cent owned no land or less than $\frac{1}{2}$ an acre compared with 26 per cent for the average rural population of Bangladesh. Ninety-nine per cent of destitutes owned less than $2\frac{1}{2}$ acres if they owned any land at all, compared with 65 per cent of the average rural Bangladeshi population. The tendency toward land alienation had been strong in Bangladesh in the preceding years to the famine (see, especially, Rahman, 1974; Khan, 1977; Abdullah, 1976; and Adnan and Rahman, 1978), and this endowment loss over the years would have made a larger population vulnerable to the famine that took place.

8   Concluding Remarks

This paper has been concerned with presenting the entitlement approach to famine analysis. The theoretical structure was outlined with critical discussion in Sections 2–4, and then the approach was used for analysing three recent famines in Sections 5–7. The entitlement approach analyses famines as economic disasters, not as just food crises. The empirical studies bring out several distinct ways in which famines can develop, defying the stereotyped uniformity of food availability decline (FAD). While famine victims share a common predicament, the economic forces leading to that predicament can be very different indeed.

Table 18.9 presents a comparative picture of a few aspects of the four famines studied, though it misses out many other contrasts discussed in detail in Sections 5–7. (Other famines have been similarly scrutinized in Sen, 1981.)

That famines can take place without a substantial food availability decline is of interest mainly because of the hold that the food availability approach has on the usual famine analysis.[47] It has also led to disastrous policy failures in the past.[48] The entitlement approach concentrates instead on the ability of different sections of the population to establish command over food using the entitlement relations operating in that society depending on its legal, economic, political, and social characteristics.

I end with five general observations. First, the entitlements approach provides a general framework for analysing famines rather than one particular hypothesis about their causation. There is, of course, a very *general* hypothesis underlying the approach, which is subject to empirical testing. It will be violated if famine starvation is shown to arise not from entitlement failure but either from choice characteristics (e.g. people refusing to eat unfamiliar food that they are in a position to buy),[49] or from non-entitlement transfers (e.g.

47. In addition to explicit use of the FAD approach, very often it is implicitly employed in separating out the total food supply per head as the strategic variable to look at.

48. The failure to *anticipate* the Bengal famine, which killed about three million people (Section 5) and indeed the inability even to *recognize* it when it came, can be traced largely to the government's overriding concern with aggregate food availability statistics (see Sen, 1977b, Section 7).

49. Cf. 'Now, the people of Bengal are traditionally rice eaters and they would not change their eating habits; they literally starved to death in front of shops and mobile units where wheat was available' (Moraes, 1975, p. 40). There is, however, little evidence in favour of this account of the Bengal famine; see Ghosh (1944), Government of India (1945), and Das (1949) on people's willingness to eat anything during the famine. The explanation of people dying in front of well-stocked shops has to be sought elsewhere.

TABLE 18.9 Comparative analysis of three famines

Which famine?	Was there a food availability collapse?	Which occupation group provided the largest number of famine victims?	Did that group suffer substantial endowment loss?	Did that group suffer exchange entitlement shifts?	Did that group suffer direct entitlement failure?	Did that group suffer trade entitlement failure?	What was the general economic climate?
Bengal famine 1943	No	Rural labour	No	Yes	No	Yes	Boom
Ethiopian famine (Wollo) 1973	No	Farmer	A little, yes	Yes	Yes	No	Slump
Bangladesh famine 1974	No	Rural labour	Earlier, yes	Yes	No	Yes	Mixed

looting).[50] But the main interest in the approach does not, I think, lie in checking *whether* most famines are related to entitlement failures, which I believe would be found to be the case, but to characterize the *nature* and *causes* of the entitlement failures where such failures occur. The contrast between different types of entitlement failures is important in understanding the precise causation of famines and in devising famine policies: anticipation, relief, and prevention.

Second, it is perhaps of a certain amount of interest that famines can arise in overall *boom* conditions (as in Bengal 1943) as well as in *slump* conditions (as in Ethiopia 1973). Slump famines may appear to be less contrary to the 'common sense' about famines, but it is quite possible for such a slump to involve contraction of outputs *other than* those of food (e.g. of cash crops). Boom famines might seem particularly counterintuitive, but as discussed, famines can take place with increased output in general and of food in particular if the command system (e.g. market pull) shifts against some particular group. In this relative shift the process of the boom itself may play a major part if the boom takes the form of uneven expansion (e.g. favouring the urban population and leaving the rural labourers relatively behind). In the fight for market command over food, one group can suffer precisely from another group's prosperity, with the Devil taking the hindmost.[51]

Third, it is important to distinguish between decline of food availability and that of direct entitlement to food. The former is concerned with how much total food there is in the economy in question, while the latter deals with each foodgrower's output of food that he is entitled to consume directly. In a peasant economy a crop failure would reduce both food availability as well as direct entitlement to food of the peasants. But insofar as the peasant typically lives on his

---

50. Such non-entitlement transfers have played a part in some famines of the past. As an example, see Walter Mallory's (1926) account of the 1925 famine in Szechwan: 'The Kweichow troops invaded southern Szechwan and after some fighting were driven out. When they left they took with them all available beasts of burden, loaded with grain. The Szechwan troops who replaced them brought very little in the way of supplies and forthwith appropriated the remainder of the food reserves of the district – leading the population, who had no interest in either side, to starve' (pp. 78-9).

51. When the fast progressing groups are themselves poor, the development of the famine may be accompanied by a reduction in the number of people below some general 'poverty line', leading to a recorded reduction of poverty as it is conventionally measured, i.e. in terms of head-count ratio. The problem is somewhat less acute with distribution-sensitive measures of poverty, as proposed in Sen (1976a). See also variants of such measures discussed in Sen (1973, 1979), Anand (1977), Hamada and Takayama (1978), Osmani (1978), Takayama (1979), Thon (1979), Kakwani (1980a, 1980b), Blackorby and Donaldson (1980), Chakravarty (1980), and Pyatt (1980).

own-grown food and has little ability to sell and buy additional food from the market anyway, the immediate reason for his starvation would be his direct entitlement failure rather than a decline in food availability in the market. Indeed, if his own crop fails, while those of others do not, the total supply may be large while he starves. Similarly, if his crop is large while those of others go down, he may still be able to do quite well despite the fall in total supply. The analytical contrast is important even though the two phenomena may happen simultaneously in a general crop failure. While such a crop failure may superficially look like just a crisis of food availability, something more than availability is involved. This is important to recognize also from the policy point of view, since just moving food into such an area will not help the affected population, and what is required is the generation of food entitlement.

Fourth, entitlement shifts also explain why the world has seen so many cases of 'food countermovement', with food moving *out of* the famine area, rather than into it. The famine-affected region may lose out in market competition with people from other areas, and it may thus lose a part of even the food supply that it has. Some food countermovement was found in the case of the Wollo famine (Section 6). The classic case of food countermovement is, of course, the Irish famine of the 1840s, and as Woodham-Smith puts it: 'In the long and troubled history of England and Ireland no issue has provoked so much anger or so embittered relations between two countries as the indisputable fact that huge quantities of food were exported from Ireland to England through the period when people of Ireland were dying of starvation' (Woodham-Smith, 1975, p. 70). This is not the occasion to comment on the shortsightedness of British policy in Ireland, but to note that market forces would tend to encourage precisely such food movements when failure of purchasing ability outweighs availability decline.[52]

Finally, the focus on entitlement has the effect of emphasizing legal rights (see Section 3). Other relevant factors, e.g. market forces, can be seen as operating through such a system of legal relations (ownership rights, contractual obligations, legal exchanges, etc.). The law stands between food availability and food entitlement, and famine deaths can reflect legality with a vengeance.

---

52. In China, British refusal to agree to a ban of rice exports from famine-affected Hunan was one of the causes of a popular uprising in 1906, and later a similar thing was involved in the famous Changsha rice riot of 1910; see Esherick (1976). There is also evidence of food movement from Bangladesh to India during the Bangladesh famine, though the magnitude of such movements is a matter of controversy (see Alamgir, 1980; Ambirajan, 1978; and Rashid, 1980).

References

Abdullah, A. A. (1976): 'Land Reforms and Agrarian Change in Bangladesh', *Bangladesh Development Studies*, **4**.

Adnan, S. and Rahman, H. Z. (1978): 'Peasant Classes and Land Mobility: Structural Reproduction and Change in Rural Bangladesh', Working Paper No. 9, Village Study Groups, Dacca.

Alamgir, M. (1978): *Bangladesh: A Case of Below Poverty Level Equilibrium Trap* (Dacca: Bangladesh Institute of Development Studies).

—— (1980): *Famine in South Asia – Political Economy of Mass Starvation in Bangladesh* (Cambridge, Mass.: Oelgeschlager Gunn and Hain).

—— *et al.* (1977): *Famine 1974: Political Economy of Mass Starvation in Bangladesh, A Statistical Annex* (Dacca: Bangladesh Institute of Development Studies).

Ambirajan, N. (1978): *Classical Political Economy and British Policy in India* (Cambridge: University Press).

Anand, S. (1977): 'Aspects of Poverty in Malaysia', *Review of Income and Wealth*, **23**.

Arrow, K. J. and Hahn, F. H. (1971): *General Competitive Analysis* (Edinburgh: Oliver & Boyd; distribution taken over by North-Holland, Amsterdam).

Aziz, S. (ed.) (1975): *Hunger: Politics and Markets: The Real Issues in the Food Crisis* (New York: University Press).

Bardhan, P. K. and Srinivasan, T. N. (eds) (1974): *Poverty and Income Distribution in India* (Calcutta: Statistical Publishing Society).

Belete, S., Gebre-Medhin, M., Hailemariam, B., Maffi, M., Vahlquist, B. and Wolde-Gabriel, Z. (1976): 'Study of the Shelter Population in the Wollo Region', *Environment and Child Health* (Feb. 1977), 15-22, republished from *Courrier*, **26**.

Bhatia, B. M. (1967): *Famines in India 1860-1965*, 2nd edn (Bombay: Asia).

Blackorby, C. and Donaldson, D. (1980): 'Ethical Indices for the Measurement of Poverty', *Econometrica*, **48**, 1053-60.

Bondestam, L. (1974): 'People and Capitalism in the North-East Lowlands of Ethiopia', *Journal of Modern African Studies*, **12**, 423-39.

Brown, L. R. and Eckholm, E. P. (1974): *By Bread Alone* (Oxford: Pergamon Press).

Chakravarty, S. R. (1980): 'New Indices for the Measurement of Poverty', Indian Statistical Institute, Calcutta, mimeo.

Comité Information Sahel (1974): *Qui Se Nourrit de la famine en Afrique?* (Paris: Maspero).

Copans, J. (1975): *Sécheresses et Famines du Sahel* (Paris: Maspero).

Das, T. (1949): *Bengal Famine (1943)* (Calcutta: University of Calcutta).

Debreu, G. (1959): *The Theory of Value* (New York: Wiley).

Dumont, R. (1975): 'The Biggest Famine in History Has Just Begun', in Aziz (1975).

Dworkin, R. (1977). *Taking Rights Seriously* (London: Duckworth).

Ehrlich, P. R. and Ehrlich, A. H. (1972): *Population, Resources, Environment: Issues in Human Ecology* (San Francisco: Freeman).

Esherick, J. W. (1976): *Reform and Revolution in China* (Berkeley, CA: University of California Press).

Faaland, J. and Parkinson, J. R. (1976): *Bangladesh: The Test Case of Development* (London: Hurst).

Flood, G. (1976): 'Nomadism and Its Future: the Afar', in Hussein (1976).

Gebre-Medhin, M. *et al.* (1974): *Profile of Wollo under Famine* (Addis Ababa: Ethiopian Nutrition Institute, 24/74).

—— and Vahlquist, B. (1977): 'Famine in Ethiopia — The Period 1963-75', *Nutrition Reviews*, **35**, 194-202.

Ghosh, K. C. (1944): *Famines in Bengal 1770-1943* (Calcutta: Indian Associated Publishing).

Government of India (1945): *Famine Inquiry Commission: Report on Bengal* (New Delhi: Government of India).

Griffin, K. (1976): *Land Concentration and Rural Poverty* (London: Macmillan).

—— (1978). *International Inequality and National Poverty* (London: Macmillan).

—— and Khan, A. R. (eds) (1976): *Poverty and Landlessness in Rural Asia* (Geneva: ILO).

Hahn, F. (1971): 'Equilibrium with Transaction Costs', *Econometrica*, **39**.

Hamada, K. and Takayama, N. (1978): 'Censored Income Distribution and the Measurement of Poverty', *Bulletin of the International Statistical Institute*, **47**.

Haque, W., Mehta, N., Rahman, A. and Wignaraja, P. (1975): *Towards a Theory of Rural Development* (Bangkok: UN Asian Development Institute).

Hicks, J. R. (1946): *Value and Capital*, 2nd edn (Oxford: Clarendon Press).

Holt, J. and Seaman, J. (1976): 'The Scope of the Drought', in Hussein (1976).

Hussein, A. M. (ed.) (1976): *Rehab: Drought and Famine in Ethiopia* (London: International African Institute).

Islam, N. (1977): *Development Planning in Bangladesh: A Study in Political Economy* (London: Hurst).

Jodha, N. S. (1975): 'Famine and Famine Policies: Some Empirical Evidence', *Economic and Political Weekly*, **10** (11 October).

Johnson, D. Gale (1975): *World Food Problems and Prospects* (Washington, DC: American Enterprise Institute for Policy Research).

Kakwani, N. (1980a): *Income Distribution: Methods of Analysis and Applications* (New York: Oxford University Press).

—— (1980b): 'On a Class of Poverty Measures', *Econometrica*, **48**, 437-46.

Khan, A. R. (1977): 'Poverty, and Inequality in Rural Bangladesh', in Griffin and Khan (1977).

Koopmans, T. C. (1957): *Three Essays on the State of the Economic Science* (New York: McGraw-Hill).

Mahalanobis, P. C., Muherjea, R. and Ghosh, A. (1946): 'A Sample Survey of After-Effects of the Bengal Famine of 1943', *Sankhya*, **7**, Part IV (16).

Mallory, W. H. (1926): *China: Land of Famine* (New York: American Geographical Society).

Malthus, T. R. (1798): *Essay on the Principle of Population as it Affects the Future Improvement of Society*.

—— (1800): *An Investigation of the Cause of the Present High Price of Provisions*.

McHenry, D. F. and Bird, K. (1977): 'Food Bungle in Bangladesh', *Foreign Policy*, No. 27 (Summer).

Meillassoux, C. (1974): 'Development or Exploitation: Is the Sahel Famine Good for Business?', *Review of African Political Economy*, 1.

—— (1975): *Femme, Greniers, et Capitaux* (Paris: Maspero).

Miller, D. S. and Holt, J. F. J. (1975): 'The Ethiopian Famine', *Proceedings of the Nutritional Society*, 34, 167-72.

Moraes, D. (1975): 'The Dimensions of the Problem: Comment', in Aziz (1975).

Mukerji, K. (1965): *Agriculture, Famine and Rehabilitation in South Asia* (Santiniketan: Visva-Bharati).

Nozick, R. (1974): *Anarchy, State and Utopia* (Oxford: Blackwell).

Osmani, S. R. (1978): *Economic Inequality and Group Welfare: Theory and Application to Bangladesh*, mimeo. [Later published; Oxford: Clarendon Press, 1982.]

Palekar, S. A. (1962): *Real Wages in India 1939-1950* (Bombay: International Book House).

Pyatt, G. (1980): 'Poverty and Welfare Measures Based on the Lorenz Curve', Development Research Center, World Bank, Washington, DC, mimeo.

Rahman, Anisur (1974): 'The Famine', mimeographed, Dacca University.

Rashid, S. (1980): 'The Policy of Laissez-faire during Scarcities', *Economic Journal*, 90.

Rivers, J. P. W., Holt, J. F. J., Seaman, J. A. and Bowden, M. R. (1976): 'Lessons for Epidemiology from the Ethiopian Famines', *Annales de la Société Belge de Médecine Tropicale*, 56, 345-57.

Seaman, J. and Holt, J. (1975). 'The Ethiopian Famine of 1973-74, 1. Wollo Province', *Proceedings of the Nutritional Society*, 34.

Sen, A. K. (1973). 'Poverty, Inequality and Unemployment: Some Conceptual Issues in Measurement', *Economic and Political Weekly*, 8; reprinted in Bardhan and Srinivasan (1974).

—— (1975): *Employment, Technology and Development* (Oxford: Clarendon Press).

—— (1976a): 'Poverty: An Ordinal Approach to Measurement', *Econometrica*, 44, 219-32. [Reprinted in my *Choice, Welfare and Measurement* (Oxford: Blackwell, 1982).]

—— (1976b): 'Real National Income', *Review of Economic Studies*, 43, 19-39. [Reprinted in *Choice, Welfare and Measurement*, 1982.]

—— (1977a): 'On Weights and Measures: Informational Constraints in Social Welfare Analysis', *Econometrica*, 45, 1539-72. [Reprinted in *Choice, Welfare and Measurement*, 1982.]

—— (1977b): 'Starvation and Exchange Entitlements: A General Approach and its Application to the Great Bengal Famine', *Cambridge Journal of Economics*, 1, 33-59.

—— (1979): 'Issues in the Measurement of Poverty', *Scandinavian Journal of Economics*, **81**, 285-307.

—— (1980): 'Famine Mortality: A Study of the Bengal Famine of 1943', in Hobsbawn *et al.*, *Peasants in History: Essays in Memory of Daniel Thorner* (Calcutta: Oxford University Press).

—— (1981): *Poverty and Famines* (Oxford: Clarendon Press).

Sinha, R. (1976): *Food and Poverty* (London: Croom Helm).

Sobhan, R. (1979): 'Politics of Food and Famine in Bangladesh', *Economic and Political Weekly*, **14**.

Summers, R. S. (1978): 'Two Types of Substantive Reasons: The Core of a Theory of Common-Law Justification', *Cornell Law Review*, **63**, 707-88.

Takayama, N. (1979): 'Poverty, Income Inequality and Their Measures', *Econometrica*, **47**, 747-60.

Thon, D. (1979): 'On Measuring Poverty', *Review of Income and Wealth*, **25**.

Wood, A. P. (1976): 'Farmers' Response to Drought in Ethiopia', in Hussein (1976).

Woodham-Smith, C. (1975). *The Great Hunger: Ireland 1845-9* (London: New English Library; earlier edition, Hamish Hamilton, 1962).

19

Development: Which Way Now?

1 *The Promise and the Default*

'Development economics is a comparatively young area of inquiry. It was born just about a generation ago, as a subdiscipline of economics, with a number of other social sciences looking on both skeptically and jealously from a distance.'[1] So writes Albert Hirschman, but the essay that begins so cheerfully turns out to be really an obituary of development economics – no longer the envy of the other social sciences. In this illuminating essay, aptly called 'The Rise and Decline of Development Economics', Hirschman puts his main thesis thus:

> our subdiscipline had achieved its considerable lustre and excitement through the implicit idea that it could slay the dragon of backwardness virtually by itself or, at least, that its contribution to this task was central. We now know that this is not so.[2]

The would-be dragon-slayer seems to have stumbled on his sword.

There is some plausibility in this diagnosis, but is it really true that development economics has no central role to play in the conquest of underdevelopment and economic backwardness? More specifically, were the original themes in terms of which the subject was launched really so far from being true or useful? I shall argue that the obituary may be premature, the original themes – while

Presidential Address of the Development Studies Association given in Dublin on 23 September 1982. In preparing the final version of the paper, I have benefited from the comments of Louis Emmerij, Albert Hirschman, Seth Masters, Carl Riskin, Hans Singer, and the editorial referees of the *Economic Journal,* and from the discussions following my DSA address, and also that following a talk I gave on a related theme at the Institute of Social Studies in the Hague on 11 October 1982.

1. Essay 1 in Hirschman (1981).
2. Hirschman (1981, p. 23).

From *Economic Journal*, 93 (December 1983), 745–62.

severely incomplete in coverage – did not point entirely in the wrong direction, and the discipline of development economics does have a central role to play in the field of economic growth in developing countries. But I shall also argue that the problematique underlying the approach of traditional development economics is, in some important ways, quite limited, and has not – and could not have – brought us to an adequate understanding of economic development. Later on, I shall take up the question as to the direction in which we may try to go instead.

There is a methodological problem in identifying a subject – or a subdiscipline as Hirschman calls it – with a given body of beliefs and themes rather than with a collection of subject matters and problems to be tackled. But Hirschman is certainly right in pointing towards the thematic similarities of the overwhelming majority of contributions in development economics. While some development economists such as Peter Bauer and Theodore Schultz have not been party to this thematic congruence, they have also stood outside the mainstream of what may be called standard development economics, as indeed the title of Peter Bauer's justly famous book, *Dissent on Development*,[3] indicates. The subdiscipline began with a set of favourite themes and the main approaches to the subject have been much moulded by these motifs. Clearly, the subject cannot live or die depending just on the success or failure of these themes, but the main approaches would need radical reformulation if these themes were shown to be fundamentally erroneous or misguided.

Hirschman identifies two major ideas with which development economics came into being, namely 'rural underemployment' (including so-called 'disguised unemployment') and 'late industrialization'. The former idea led naturally to a focus on utilization of under-employed manpower and to acceleration of capital accumulation. The latter called for an activist state and for planning to overcome the disadvantages of lateness through what Hirschman calls 'a deliberate, intensive, guided effort'. The subject expended a lot of time in developing 'new rationales... for protection, planning, and indus-trialization itself'.[4]

While there have been differences in assertion and emphasis *within* the mainstream of the subdiscipline, it is fair to say that in terms of policy the following have been among the major strategic themes pursued ever since the beginning of the subject: (1) industrial-ization, (2) rapid capital accumulation, (3) mobilization of under-

3. Bauer (1971). See also Schultz (1964) and Bauer (1981). For a forceful critical account without breaking from traditional development economics, see Little (1982).
4. Hirschman (1981, pp. 10–11).

employed manpower, and (4) planning and an economically active state.[5] There are, of course, many other common themes, e.g. emphasis on skill formation, but they have not typically been as much subjected to criticism as these other themes, and there is thus much to be said for concentrating on these four.

These themes (especially the need for planning, but also the deliberate fostering of industrialization and capital accumulation and the acceptance of the possibility of surplus labour) are closely linked to criticisms of the traditional neoclassical models as applied to developing countries. Hirschman calls this eschewal of 'universal' use of neoclassical economics the rejection of 'mono-economics'. Monoeconomics sounds perhaps a little like a disease that one could catch if not careful. I shall avoid the term, though some would no doubt have thought it quite appropriate to characterize universal neoclassical economics as a contagious affliction.

It was argued by development economists that neoclassical economics did not apply terribly well to underdeveloped countries. This need not have caused great astonishment, since neoclassical economics did not apply terribly well anywhere else. However, the role of the state and the need for planning and deliberate public action seemed stronger in underdeveloped countries, and the departure from traditional neoclassical models was, in many ways, more radical.

The discrediting of traditional development economics that has lately taken place, and to which Hirschman made reference, is undoubtedly partly due to the resurgence of neoclassical economics in recent years. As Hirschman (1981) rightly notes, 'the claim of development economics to stand as a separate body of economic analysis and policy derived intellectual legitimacy and nurture from the prior success and parallel features of the Keynesian Revolution' (p. 7). The neoclassical resurgence against Keynesian economics was to some extent paralleled by the neoclassical recovery in the field of economic development. The market, it was argued, has the many virtues that standard neoclassical analysis has done so much to analyse, and state intervention could be harmful in just the way suggested by that perspective.

The neoclassical resurgence has drawn much sustenance from the success of some countries and the failure of others. The high performance of economies like South Korea, Taiwan, Hong Kong and Singapore — based on markets and profits and trade — has been seen as bringing Adam Smith back to life. On the other hand, the low performance of a great many countries in Asia, Africa and Latin

5. See Rosenstein-Rodan (1943), Mandelbaum (1945), Dobb (1951), Datta (1952), Singer (1952), Nurkse (1953) and Lewis (1954, 1955).

America has been cited as proof that it does not pay the government to mess about much with the market mechanism. Recently, doubts raised about the record of China, and the vocal desire of the Chinese leadership to make greater use of material incentives, have been interpreted as proof that even a powerful socialist regime cannot break the basic principles on which the market mechanism is founded.

The attack on state activism and planning has been combined with criticism of some of the other features of traditional development economics. It has been argued that enterprise is the real bottleneck, not capital, so that to emphasize capital accumulation and the creation of surplus – as was done for example by Maurice Dobb (1951, 1960) and Paul Baran (1957) – was to climb the wrong tree. The charge of misallocation of resources has been levelled also against industrialization, especially for the domestic market. Hirschman (1981) notes: 'By itself this critique was highly predictable and might not have carried more weight than warnings against industrialization emanating from essentially the same camp ten, or twenty, or fifty years earlier.' But – as he goes on to say – the effectiveness of this critique was now greater for various reasons, including the fact that 'some of the early advocates of industrialization had now themselves become its sharpest critics' (p. 18). Hirschman refers in this context to some 'neo-Marxist' writings and the views of some members of the so-called 'dependency' school. Certainly, the particular pattern of industrial expansion in Latin America provides many examples of exploitative relations with the metropolitan countries, particularly the United States of America, and the internal effects were often quite terrible in terms of fostering economic inequality and social distortion. But to move from there to a rejection of industrialization as such is indeed a long jump.

I should explain that Hirschman, from whom I have been quoting extensively, does not in many cases endorse these attacks on the policy strategies of traditional development economics. But he provides excellent analyses of the arguments figuring in the attacks. I believe Hirschman is more hesitant in his defence of traditional development economics than he need have been, but his own reasons for rejecting that tradition – to which he himself has of course contributed much[6] – rests primarily on the argument that development economics has tended to be contemptuous of underdeveloped countries, albeit this contempt has taken a 'sophisticated form'. These countries have been 'expected to perform like wind-up toys and "lumber through" the various stages of development single-

6. See particularly Hirschman (1958, 1970).

mindedly'. As Hirschman (1981) puts it, 'these countries were perceived to have only *interests* and *no passions*' (p. 24).[7]

I believe this diagnosis has much truth in it. But I also believe that, contemptuous and simplistic though development economics might have been in this respect, the main themes that were associated with the origin of development economics, and have given it its distinctive character, are not rejectable for that reason. I shall argue that they address common problems, which survive despite the particular passions.

2 Traditional Themes in the Light of Recent Experiences

Growth is not the same thing as development and the difference between the two has been brought out by a number of recent contributions to development economics.[8] I shall take up the complex question of the content of economic development presently (in Sections 3–5 below). But it can scarcely be denied that economic growth is one aspect of the process of economic development. And it happens to be the aspect on which traditional development economics – rightly or wrongly – has concentrated. In this section I do not assess the merits of that concentration (on which more later), but examine the appropriateness of the traditional themes, given that concentration. Dealing specifically with economic growth as it is commonly defined, the strategic relevance of these themes is examined in the light of recent experiences. How do these theories – formulated and present mainly in the forties and fifties – fare in the light of the experiences of the sixties and seventies?

The World Development Report 1982 (henceforth *WDR*) presents comparative growth data for the period 1960–80 for 'low-income economies' and 'middle-income economies', with a dividing line at US$410 in 1980. Leaving out small countries (using a cut-off line of 10 million people) and excluding the OPEC countries which have had rather special economic circumstances during the seventies, we have 14 countries in the low-income category for which data on economic growth (GNP or GDP) are given in *WDR*. Correspondingly, there are 18 such countries in the middle-income category. Table 19.1 presents these data. For three of the low-income countries, namely China, Bangladesh and Afghanistan, the GNP growth figures

---

7. For the conceptual framework underlying the distinction, see Hirschman (1977).
8. See, for example, Streeten (1981). See also Grant (1978), Morris (1979) and Streeten *et al.* (1981).

TABLE 19.1

Country	GNP per head		1980 gross domestic investment (% of GDP)	1980 share of industry in GDP (%)
	1980 Value ($)	1960-80 Growth (%)		
Low-income				
Bangladesh	130	1.3*	17	13
Ethiopia	140	1.4	10	16
Nepal	140	0.2	14	13
Burma	170	1.2	24	13
Afghanistan	–	0.9*	14	–
Zaire	220	0.2	11	23
Mozambique	230	−0.1	10	16
India	240	1.4	23	26
Sri Lanka	270	2.4	36	30
Tanzania	280	1.9	22	13
China	290	3.7*	31	47
Pakistan	300	2.8	18	25
Uganda	300	−0.7	3	6
Sudan	410	−0.2	12	14
Middle-income				
Ghana	420	−1.0	5	21
Kenya	420	2.7	22	21
Egypt	580	3.4	31	35
Thailand	670	4.7	27	29
Philippines	690	2.8	30	37
Morocco	900	2.5	21	32
Peru	930	1.1	16	45
Colombia	1180	3.0	25	30
Turkey	1470	3.6	27	30
S. Korea	1520	7.0	31	41
Malaysia	1620	4.3	29	37
Brazil	2050	5.1	22	37
Mexico	2090	2.6	28	38
Chile	2150	1.6	18	37
South Africa	2300	2.3	29	53
Romania	2340	8.6	34	64
Argentina	2390	2.2	–	–
Yugoslavia	2620	5.4	35	43

Source: World Development Report 1982, Tables 1-5. The countries included are all the ones within the 'Low-income' and 'Middle-income' categories, other than those with less than 10 million population, members of OPEC, and countries without GNP or GDP growth figures. Asterisked growth rates are based on GDP growth figures per head (Tables 2 and 17).

are not given in *WDR* and they have been approximately identified with GDP growth. In interpreting the results, this has to be borne in mind, and only those conclusions can be safely drawn which would be unaffected by variations of these estimates within a wide range.

The fourteen low-income economies vary in terms of growth rate of GNP *per capita* during 1960–80 from *minus* 0.7% in Uganda to 3.7% in China. The top three countries in terms of economic growth are China (3.7%), Pakistan (2.8%) and Sri Lanka (2.4%). (Note that China's pre-eminent position would be unaffected even if the approximated growth figure is substantially cut.) In the middle-income group, the growth performance again varies a great deal, ranging from *minus* 1.0% for Ghana to 8.6% for Romania. The top three countries in terms of economic growth are Romania (8.6%), South Korea (7.0%) and Yugoslavia (5.4%).

How do these high-performance countries compare with others in the respective groups in terms of the parameters associated with the main theses of traditional development economics? Take capital accumulation first. Of the three top growth-performers, two also have the highest share of gross domestic investment in GDP, namely Sri Lanka with 36% and China with 31%. Pakistan comes lower, though it does fall in the top half of the class of fourteen countries.

Turning now to the middle-income countries, the top three countries in terms of growth are also the top three countries in terms of capital accumulation, namely Yugoslavia with 35%, Romania with 34%, and South Korea with 31%. Thus, if there is anything to be learned from the experience of these successful growers regarding the importance of capital accumulation, it is certainly not a lesson that runs counter to the traditional wisdom of development economics.

It might, however, be argued that to get a more convincing picture one should look also at failures and not merely at successes. I don't think the cases are quite symmetrical, since a failure can be due to some special 'bottleneck' even when all other factors are favourable. Nevertheless, it is not useless to examine the cases of failure as well, especially with respect to capital accumulation, since it has been seen in traditional development economics to be such a *general* force towards economic growth.

The three worst performers in the low-income category in terms of growth rate are, respectively, Uganda with *minus* 0.7%, Sudan with *minus* 0.2%, and Mozambique with *minus* 0.1%. In terms of capital accumulation, Uganda's rank is also the worst there, with only 3% of GDP invested. Mozambique is the second lowest investor, and Sudan the fifth lowest.

What about growth failures in the middle-income countries? The worst performers in terms of growth rate are Ghana with *minus* 1%,

Peru with 1.1%, and Chile with 1.6%. As it happens these countries are also respectively the lowest, the second lowest and the third lowest accumulators of capital in the category of the middle-income countries.

So both in terms of cases of success and those of failure, the traditional wisdom of development economics is scarcely contradicted by these international comparisons. Quite the contrary.

Hans Singer (1952) in his paper entitled 'The Mechanics of Economic Development', published thirty years ago, seems to be almost talking about today's worst case of growth failure in the combined category of low-income and middle-income countries, namely Ghana. Using the Harrod–Domar model with an assumed capital–output ratio, Singer argues that a country with 6% savings and a population growth rate of 1.25% will be a 'stationary economy'. While Ghana has managed an investment and savings ratio of just below 6% (5% to be exact) it has had a population growth between 2.4 and 3.0% during these decades as opposed to Singer's assumption of 1.25%. Rather than being stationary, Ghana has accordingly slipped back, going down at about 1% a year. The Harrod–Domar model is an over-simplification, of course, but the insight obtained from such reasoning is not altogether without merit.

I turn now to the theme of industrialization. In the category of low-income countries, the top performers – China, Pakistan and Sri Lanka – happen to be among the four countries with the highest share of industries in GDP. In the middle-income group, the top growers – Romania, South Korea and Yugoslavia – are among the top five countries in terms of the share of industries in GDP.[9]

The picture at the other end, i.e. for countries with growth failures, is certainly less neat than at the top end in this case, or at either end in the case of capital accumulation. It is, however, certainly true that Uganda, which occupies the bottom position in the low-income category in terms of growth rate, also has the bottom position in terms of the share of industries, and similarly Ghana, with the lowest record of growth in the middle-income group, also has the lowest share of industries in that group. But the positions of second and third lowest are not quite so telling. In the low-income category, low-performing Sudan and Mozambique have middling industrial ratios. In the middle-income group, the second-lowest growth performer, Peru, has the third *highest* ratio of industries in that group, though the third-lowest growth performer, Chile, has a middling industrial

9. An additional one in this case is South Africa, and its industrial share is high mainly because mining is included in that figure. In fact, if we look only at manufacturing, South Africa falls below the others.

ratio. The picture is, thus, a bit more muddled at the lower end of growth performance.[10]

Altogether, so far as growth is concerned, it is not easy to deny the importance of capital accumulation or of industrialization in a poor pre-industrial country. Turning to the thesis of underemployment and the role of labour mobilization, there have been several powerful attempts at disestablishing the thesis of 'disguised unemployment', e.g. by Theodore Schultz (1964), but they have not been altogether successful.[11] Furthermore, what is really at issue is the crucial role of labour mobilization and use, and not whether the opportunity cost of labour is exactly zero.[12] It is worth noting, in this context, that the high growth performers in both groups have distinguished records of labour-using economic growth, and some (e.g. China and South Korea) have quite outstanding achievements in this area. While they have very different political systems, their respective successes in labour mobilization have been specially studied and praised.[13]

The question of planning and state activism is a field in which comparative quantitative data is particularly difficult to find. But some qualitative information is of relevance. Of the three top growing economies in the low-income group, one – China – is obviously not without an active state. While Pakistan is in no way a paradigmatic example of determined state planning, it has been frequently cited as a good example of what harm government meddling can do.[14] The third – Sri Lanka – has been recently studied a great deal precisely because of its active government intervention in a number of different fields, including health, education and food consumption.

In the middle-income group, of the three top performers, Romania and Yugoslavia clearly do have a good deal of planning. The third – South Korea – has had an economic system in which the market mechanism has been driven hard by an active government in a planned way. Trying to interpret the South Korean economic experience as a triumph of unguided market mechanism, as is sometimes

10. The rank correlation coefficient between *per capita* growth and the share of gross domestic investment in GDP is 0.72 for middle-income countries, 0.75 for low-income countries and 0.82 for the two groups put together. On the other hand, the rank correlation coefficient between *per capita* growth and the share of industries is only 0.22 for middle-income countries, even though it is 0.59 for the low-income countries and 0.68 for the two groups put together.

11. My own views on this are presented in Sen (1975). See also Sen (1967) and the exchange with Schultz following that in the same number of the *Economic Journal*.

12. See Marglin (1976, Chapter 2). Also Sen (1975, Chapters 4 and 6). See also Fei and Ranis (1964).

13. See Little (1982). See also the important study of Ishikawa (1981), which discusses the empirical role of labour absorption in different Asian economies.

14. For example, Little *et al.* (1971).

done, is not easy to sustain. I have discussed this question elsewhere,[15] and I shall not spend any time on it here. I should only add that, aside from having a powerful influence over the direction of investment through control of financial institutions (including nationalized banks), the government of South Korea fostered an export-oriented growth on the secure foundations of more than a decade of intensive import substitution, based on trade restrictions, to build up an industrial base. Imports of a great many items are still prohibited or restricted. The pattern of South Korean economic expansion has been carefully planned by a powerful government. If this is a free market, then Walras' auctioneer can surely be seen as going around with a government white paper in one hand and a whip in the other.

The point is not so much that the government is powerful in the high-growth developing countries. It is powerful in nearly *every* developing country. The issue concerns the systematic involvement of the state in the *economic* sphere, and the pursuit of *planned* economic development. The carefully planned government action in, say, China or Sri Lanka or South Korea or Romania, contrasts – on the whole strongly – with the economic role of the government in such countries as Uganda or Sudan or Chile or Argentina or Ghana.

This examination of the main theses of traditional development economics has been too brief and tentative, and certainly there is no question of claiming anything like definitiveness in the findings. But, in so far as anything has emerged, it has not gone in the direction of debunking traditional development economics; just the contrary.

Before I move on to develop some criticisms of my own, I should make one last defensive remark about traditional development economics. The general policy prescriptions and strategies in this tradition have to be judged in terms of the climate of opinion and the over-all factual situation prevailing at the time these theories were formulated. Development economics was born at a time when government involvement in deliberately fostering economic growth in general, and industrialization in particular, was very rare, and when the typical rates of capital accumulation were quite low. That situation has changed in many respects, and, while that may suggest the need to emphasize different issues, it does not in any way invalidate the wisdom of the strategies then suggested.

The point can be brought out with an example. In the 1952 paper of Hans Singer from which I have already quoted, one of the conclusions that Singer emphasized is the need to raise the then existing rate of saving. He argued, with some assumptions about production

---

15. Sen (1981b), and the literature cited there, especially Datta-Chaudhuri (1979).

conditions, that to achieve even a 2% rate of *per capita* growth, with a population growing at 1.25% per year, 'a rate of net savings of $16\frac{1}{4}$% is necessary', and that 'this rate of saving is about three times the rate actually observed in underdeveloped countries' (Singer, 1952, pp. 397–8). The current average rate of saving is no longer a third of that figure, but substantially *higher* than the figure. The weighted average ratio of gross domestic saving for low-income developing countries is estimated to be about 22%, and that for middle-income developing countries about 25%; and, even after deducting for depreciation, Singer's target has certainly been exceeded. And, even with a faster growth of population than Singer anticipated, the weighted average of GDP growth rates *per capita* has been about $2\frac{1}{2}$% per year for low-income countries and more than 3% per year for middle-income countries over the seventies.[16]

The point of policy interest now is that, despite these *average* achievements, the performances of different countries are highly divergent. There is still much relevance in the broad policy themes which traditional development economics has emphasized. The strategies have to be adapted to the particular conditions and to national and international circumstances, but the time to bury traditional development economics has not yet arrived.

3 *Fast Growth and Slow Social Change*

I believe the real limitations of traditional development economics arose not from the choice of means to the end of economic growth, but in the insufficient recognition that economic growth was no more than a means to some other objectives. The point is not the same as saying that growth does not matter. It may matter a great deal, but, if it does, this is because of some associated benefits that are realized in the process of economic growth.

It is important to note in this context that the same level of achievement in life expectancy, literacy, health, higher education, etc. can be seen in countries with widely varying income per capita. To take just one example, consider Brazil, Mexico, South Korea, China and Sri Lanka.[17]

---

16. See Tables 2, 5 and 17 of the *World Development Report 1982*.

17. Taken from *World Development Report 1982*, Table 1. The 1982 Chinese census indicates a higher expectation of life – around 69 years. The Sri Lankan figure of 66 years relates to 1971, and the current life expectancy is probably significantly higher.

TABLE 19.2

Country	Life expectancy at birth, 1980 (years)	GNP per head, 1980 (US dollars)
Brazil	63	2050
China	64	290
Mexico	65	2090
South Korea	65	1520
Sri Lanka	66	270

China and Sri Lanka, with less than a seventh of GNP per head in Brazil or Mexico, have similar life expectancy figures to the two richer countries. South Korea, with its magnificent and much-eulogised growth record, has not yet overtaken China or Sri Lanka in the field of longevity, despite being now more than five times richer in terms of *per capita* GNP. If the government of a poor developing country is keen to raise the level of health and the expectation of life, then it would be pretty daft to try to achieve this through raising its income per head, rather than going directly for these objectives through public policy and social change, as China and Sri Lanka have both done.

Not merely is it the case that economic growth is a means rather than an end, it is also the case that for some important ends it is not a very efficient means either. In an earlier paper (Sen, 1981b) it was shown that had Sri Lanka been a typical developing country, trying to achieve its high level of life expectancy not through direct public action, but primarily through growth (in the same way as typical developing countries do), then it would have taken Sri Lanka – depending on assumptions – somewhere between 58 years and 152 years to get where it already now happens to be.[18] It might well be the case that 'money answereth all things', but the answer certainly comes slowly.

4   *Entitlements and Capabilities*

Perhaps the most important thematic deficiency of traditional development economics is its concentration on national product,

18. See Sen (1981b, pp. 303–6). See also Jayawardena (1974), Marga Institute (1974), Isenman (1978), Alailima (1982), Gwatkin (1979).

aggregate income and total supply of particular goods rather than on 'entitlements' of people and the 'capabilities' these entitlements generate. Ultimately, the process of economic development has to be concerned with what people can or cannot do, e.g. whether they can live long, escape avoidable morbidity, be well nourished, be able to read and write and communicate, take part in literary and scientific pursuits, and so forth. It has to do, in Marx's words, with 'replacing the domination of circumstances and chance over individuals by the domination of individuals over chance and circumstances'.[19]

Entitlement refers to the set of alternative commodity bundles that a person can command in a society using the totality of rights and opportunities that he or she faces. Entitlements are relatively simple to characterize in a purely market economy. If a person can, say, earn $200 by selling his labour power and other saleable objects he has or can produce, then his entitlements refer to the set of all commodity bundles costing no more than $200. He can buy any such bundle, but no more than that, and the limit is set by his ownership ('endowment') and his exchange possibilities ('exchange entitlement'), the two together determining his over-all entitlement.[20] On the basis of this entitlement, a person can acquire some capabilities, i.e. the ability to do this or that (e.g. be well nourished), and fail to acquire some other capabilities. The process of economic development can be seen as a process of expanding the capabilities of people. Given the functional relation between entitlements of persons over goods and their capabilities, a useful – though derivative – characterization of economic development is in terms of expansion of entitlements.[21]

19. Marx and Engels (1846); English translation taken from McLellan (1977, p. 190).

20. The notion of 'entitlements' is explored in Sen (1981a). It is worth emphasizing here, to avoid misunderstandings that seem to have occurred in some discussions of the concept, that (1) 'exchange entitlement' is only a *part* of the entitlement picture and is incomplete without an account of ownership or endowment, and (2) 'exchange entitlement' includes not merely trade and market exchange but also the use of production possibilities (i.e. 'exchange with nature').

21. Capabilities, entitlements and utilities differ from each other. I have tried to argue elsewhere that 'capabilities' provide the right basis for judging the advantages of a person in many problems of evaluation – a role that cannot be taken over either by utility or by an index of commodities (Sen, 1982a, pp. 29–38, 353–69). When we are concerned with such notions as the well-being of a person, or standard of living, or freedom in the positive sense, we need the concept of capabilities. We have to be concerned with what a person can do, and this is not the same thing as how much pleasure or desire fulfilment he gets from these activities ('utility'), nor what commodity bundles he can command ('entitlements'). Ultimately, therefore we have to go not merely beyond the calculus of national product and aggregate real income, but also that of entitlements over commodity bundles viewed on their own. The focus on capabilities differs also from concentration on the mental metric of utilities, and this contrast is similar to the general one between pleasure, on the one hand, and positive freedom, on the other. The particular role of entitlements is *through* its effects

For most of humanity, about the only commodity a person has to sell is labour power, so that the person's entitlements depend crucially on his or her ability to find a job, the wage rate for that job, and the prices of commodities that he or she wishes to buy. The problems of starvation, hunger and famines in the world could be better analysed through the concept of entitlement than through the use of the traditional variables of food supply and population size. The intention here is not, of course, to argue that the supply of goods – food in this case – is irrelevant to hunger and starvation, which would be absurd, but that the supply is just one influence among many; and, in so far as supply is important, it is so precisely because it affects the entitlements of the people involved, typically through prices. Ultimately, we are concerned with what people can or cannot do, and this links directly with their 'entitlements' rather than with over-all supplies and outputs in the economy.[22]

The failure to see the importance of entitlements has been responsible for millions of people dying in famines. Famines may not be at all anticipated in situations of good or moderate over-all levels of supply, but, notwithstanding that supply situation, acute starvation can hit suddenly and widely because of failures of the entitlement systems, operating through ownership and exchange. For example, in the Bangladesh famine of 1974, a very large number died in a year when food availability per head was at a peak – higher than in any other year between 1971 and 1975. The floods that affected agriculture did ultimately – much later than the famine – reduce the food output, but its first and immediate impact was on the rural labourers who lost jobs in planting and transplanting rice, and started starving long before the main crop that was affected was to be harvested. The problem was made worse by forces of inflation in the economy, reducing the purchasing power especially of rural labourers, who did not have the economic muscle to raise their money wages correspondingly.[23]

Entitlements may not operate only through market processes. In a socialist economy entitlements will depend on what the families can

on capabilities. It is a role that has substantial and far-reaching importance, but it remains derivative on capabilities. On these general issues, see Sen (1982a,d, 1983) and Kynch and Sen (1983).

22. See Sen (1981a,b), Arrow (1982), Desai (1983).

23. See Sen (1981a, Chapter 9). Other examples of famines due to entitlement failure without a significant – indeed any – reduction of overall food availability can be found in Chapter 6 (the Great Bengal Famine of 1943) and Chapter 7 (the Ethiopian famine of 1973–4); see also Chapter 7 (the Sahelian famines of the 1970s). On related matters, see also Sen (1976, 1977), Ghose (1979), Alamgir (1978, 1980), Chattopadhyay (1981), Oughton (1982), Ravallion (1983). See also Parikh and Rabar (1981) and Srinivasan (1982). Also the special number of *Development*, Aziz (1982).

get from the state through the established system of command. Even in a non-socialist economy, the existence of social security – when present – makes the entitlements go substantially beyond the operation of market forces.

A major failing of traditional development economics has been its tendency to concentrate on supply of goods rather than on ownership and entitlement. The focus on growth is only one reflection of this. Extreme concentration on the ratio of food supply to population is another example of the same defective vision.[24] Recently the focus has shifted somewhat from growth of *total incomes* to the *distribution of incomes*. This may look like a move in the right direction, and indeed it is. But I would argue that 'income' itself provides an inadequate basis for analysing a person's entitlements. Income gives the means of buying things. It expresses buying power in terms of some scalar magnitude – given by one real number. Even if there are no schools in the village and no hospitals nearby, the income of the villager can still be increased by adding to his purchasing power over the goods that are available in the market. But this rise in income may not be able to deal at all adequately with his entitlement to education or medical treatment, since the rise in income as such guarantees no such thing.

In general, one real number reflecting some aggregate measure of market power can scarcely represent so complex a notion as entitlement. The power of the market force depends on relative prices and, as the price of some good rises, the hold of income on the corresponding entitlement weakens. With non-marketability, it slips altogether. In the extreme case, the entitlement to live, say, in a malaria-free environment is not a matter of purchase with income in any significant way.

In dealing with starvation and hunger, the focus on incomes – though defective – is not entirely disastrous. And of course it is a good deal better than the focus on total food output and population size. The weighting system of real income and cost-of-living pays sufficient attention to food in a poor community to make real income a moderately good 'proxy' for entitlement to food in most cases.[25] But when it comes to health, or education, or social equality,

24. On this and related issues, see Aziz (1975), Taylor (1975), Griffin (1978), Sinha and Drabek (1978), Spitz (1978), Lappé and Collins (1979), George and Paige (1982), Rao (1982).

25. However, the index of real income will continue to differ from the index of food entitlement since the price deflators will not be the same, though the two will often move together. A problem of a different sort arises from *intra*-family differences in food consumption (e.g. through 'sex-bias'), as a result of which both the real income and the food entitlement of the family may be rather deceptive indicators of nutritional situations and particular

or self-respect, or freedom from social harassment, income is miles off the target.

5   *Political Complexities*

To move from concentrating on growth to supplementing that with an account of income distribution is basically an inadequate response to what is at issue. It is also, in effect, an attempt to refuse to come to terms with the complexity of entitlement relations. The metric of income, as already discussed, is much too crude. Indeed, entitlements related even to purely economic matters, e.g. that to food, may actually require us to go beyond the narrow limits of economics altogether.

Take the case of famine relief. A hungry, destitute person will be *entitled* to some free food *if* there is a relief system offering that. Whether, in fact, a starving person will have such an entitlement will depend on whether such a public relief operation will actually be launched. The provision of public relief is partly a matter of political and social pressure. Food is, as it were, 'purchased' in this context not with income but with political pressure. The Irish in the 1840s did not have the necessary political power. Nor did the Bengalis in the Great Bengal Famine of 1943. Nor the Ethiopians in Wollo in the famine of 1973. On the other hand, there are plenty of examples in the world in which timely public policy has averted an oncoming famine completely.

The operation of political forces affecting entitlements is far from simple. For example, with the present political system in India, it is almost impossible for a famine to take place. The pressure of newspapers and diverse political parties make it imperative for the government in power to organize swift relief. It has to act to retain credibility. No matter how and where famine threatens – whether with a flood or a drought, whether in Bihar in 1967–68, in Maharashtra in 1971–73, or in West Bengal in 1978 – an obligatory policy response prevents the famine actually occurring.

On the other hand, there is no such relief for the third of the Indian rural population who go to bed hungry every night and who lead a life ravaged by regular deprivation. The quiet presence of non-acute, endemic hunger leads to no newspaper turmoil, no political agitation, no riots in the Indian parliament. The system takes it in its stride.[26]

---

members of the family. On this issue, see Bardhan (1974), Sen (1981c), Kynch and Sen (1983) and Sen and Sengupta (1983).

26. See Sen (1982b, c).

The position in China is almost exactly the opposite of this. On the one hand, the political commitment of the system ensures a general concern with eradicating regular malnutrition and hunger through more equal access to means of livelihood, and through entitlements vis-à-vis the state; and China's achievements in this respect have been quite remarkable. In a normal year, the Chinese poor are much better fed than the Indian poor. The expectation of life in China is between 66 and 69 years in comparison with India's miserable 52 years. On the other hand, if there is a political and economic crisis that confuses the regime and makes it pursue disastrous policies with confident dogmatism, then it cannot be forced to change its policies by crusading newspapers or by effective pressure from opposing political groups.

It is, in fact, now quite clear that in China during 1959–61 there were deaths on a very large scale due to famine conditions. The extent of the disaster has only recently become evident, even though there are still many uncertainties regarding the exact estimation of extra mortality.[27] Important mortality data were released in 1980 by Professor Zhu Zhengzhi of Beijing University,[28] indicating that the death rate rose from about 10.8 per thousand in 1957 to an average of 16.58 per thousand per year during 1958–61. This yields a figure of extra mortality of 14–16 million in China in the famine-affected years – a very large figure indeed. It is, in fact, very much larger than the extra mortality (calculated in the same way) even in the Great Bengal Famine of 1943 (namely about 3 million),[29] the largest famine in India in this century.

In 1981 the noted economist Sun Yefang released some further mortality data,[30] referring to 'the high price in blood' of the economic policy pursued at that time. He reported that the death rate per thousand had risen to as high as 25.4 in 1960, indicating an extra mortality of 9 million in that year alone. His figures for the four years also yields a total of around 15 million extra deaths during the Chinese famine of 1959–61.[31] Others have suggested even higher mortality.[32]

27. See Aird (1982, pp. 277–8).
28. Zhu Zhengzhi (1980, pp. 54–5). These data have been analysed by Coale (1981). See also Bernstein (1983b).
29. See Sen (1981a, Appendix D). In both cases the death rate immediately preceding the famine-affected year is taken as the bench mark in comparison with which the 'extra' mortality in famine-affected years are calculated.
30. Sun Yefang (1981) and People's Republic of China (1981).
31. See Bernstein (1983a, b).
32. See Bernstein's (1983b) account of the literature. See also Aird (1980). For a description of the intensity of the famine in a particular commune (the Liyuan Commune in Anhui province), see Research Group of the Fen Yang County Communist Party Com-

These are truly staggering figures. Even if we take a level quite a bit below the lower limit of the estimates, the sudden extra mortality caused by the famine[33] would still be on a scale that is difficult to match even in pre-independent India (and there has of course been no famine in India since independence).

Is it purely accidental that a famine – indeed one on an enormous scale – could take place in China while none has occurred in post-independent India? The contrast is particularly odd when viewed in the context of the undoubted fact that China has been very much more successful than India in eliminating regular malnutrition. There may well be an accidental element in the comparative records on famines, but as already noted (on p. 500), on a number of occasions potentially large famines have been prevented in India through quick, extensive and decisive government intervention. Reports on deaths from hunger reach the government and the public quickly and dramatically through active newspapers, and are taken up vigorously by parties not in power. Faced with a threatening famine, any government wishing to stay in office in India is forced to abandon or modify its on-going economic policy, and meet the situation with swift public action, e.g. redistribution of food within the country, imports from abroad, and widespread relief arrangements (including food for work programmes).

Policy failures in China during the famine years (and the Great Leap Forward period), which have been much discussed in China only recently, relate not merely to factors that dramatically reduced output, but also to distributional issues, e.g. inter-regional balances, and the draconian procurement policy that was apparently pursued relentlessly despite lower agricultural output.[34] Whatever the particular policy errors, the government in power was not forced to re-examine them, nor required to face harrowing newspaper reports and troublesome

---

mittee (1983). 'The commune's population of 5,730 people in 1957 had dropped to 2,870 people in 1961. More than half died of starvation [*e si*] or fled the area. . . . In 1955, the Houwang production team was a model elementary cooperative. The village had twenty-eight families, a total of 154 people . . . fifty-nine people starved to death [*e si*], and the survivors fled the area' (p. 36).

33. The number of deaths due to a famine must not be confused with the number actually dying of starvation, since most people who die in a famine tend to die from other causes (particularly from disease endemic in the region) to which they become more susceptible due to undernutrition, and also due to breakdown of sanitary arrangements, exposure due to wandering, eating non-eatables, and other developments associated with famines. See Sen (1981a, pp. 203–16).

34. See Bernstein (1983b), who also argues that the harsh procurement policies in China did not have the ideologically 'anti-peasant' character that similar policies in the USSR did during 1932–3, but reflected 'erroneous' reading of the level of output and of the economic situation.

opposition parties. The contrast may not, therefore, be purely accidental.

In an interesting and important speech given in 1962 – just after the famine – Chairman Mao made the following remarks to a conference of 7000 cadres from different levels: 'If there is no democracy, if ideas are not coming from the masses, it is impossible to establish a good line, good general and specific policies and methods. . . . Without democracy, you have no understanding of what is happening down below; the situation will be unclear; you will be unable to collect sufficient opinions from all sides; there can be no communication between top and bottom; top-level organs of leadership will depend on one-sided and incorrect material to decide issues, thus you will find it difficult to avoid being subjectivist; it will be impossible to achieve unity of understanding and unity of action, and impossible to achieve true centralism.'[35] Ralph Miliband (1977), who has provided an illuminating and far-reaching analysis of the issue of democracy in capitalist and socialist societies from a Marxist perspective, points out that Mao's 'argument for "democracy" is primarily a "functional" one' (pp. 149–50), and argues that this is an inadequate basis for understanding the need for 'socialist democracy'.[36] That more general question certainly does remain, but it is worth emphasizing that even the purely 'functional' role of democracy can be very crucial to matters of life and death, as the Chinese experiences of the famine of 1959–61 bring out.[37]

Finally, it is important to note that the protection that the Indian poor get from the active news distribution system and powerful opposition parties has very severe limits. The deprivation has to be dramatic to be 'newsworthy' and politically exploitable (see Sen, 1982c). The Indian political system may prevent famines but, unlike the Chinese system, it seems unable to deal effectively with endemic malnutrition. In a normal year when things are running smoothly both in India and China, the Indian poor is in a much more deprived general state than his or her Chinese counterpart.[38]

35. Mao Zedong (1974, p. 164).
36. Miliband goes on to argue: 'Much may be claimed for the Chinese experience. But what cannot be claimed for it, on the evidence, is that it has really begun to create the institutional basis for the kind of socialist democracy that would effectively reduce the distance between those who determine policy and those on whose behalf it is determined' (p. 151).
37. The Soviet famines of the 1930s and the Kampuchean famine of more recent years provide further evidence of penalties of this lacuna.
38. The crude death rate in China in 1980 was reported to be 8 per thousand in contrast with India's 14 (*World Development Report 1982*, Table 18, p. 144). Only in famine situations did the reported death rate in China (e.g. 25.4 reported in 1960) exceed that in India.

6   Concluding Remarks

I shall not try to summarize the main points of the paper, but I will make a few concluding remarks to put the discussion in perspective.

First, traditional development economics has not been particularly unsuccessful in identifying the factors that lead to economic growth in developing countries. In the field of causation of growth, there is much life left in traditional analyses (Section 2).

Secondly, traditional development economics has been less successful in characterizing economic development, which involves expansion of people's capabilities. For this, economic growth is only a means and often not a very efficient means either (Section 3).

Thirdly, because of close links between entitlements and capabilities, focusing on entitlements – what commodity bundles a person can command – provides a helpful format for characterizing economic development. Supplementing data on GNP *per capita* by income distributional information is quite inadequate to meet the challenge of development analysis (Section 4).

Fourthly, famines and starvation can be more sensibly analysed in terms of entitlement failures than in terms of the usual approach focusing on food output per unit of population. A famine can easily occur even in a good food supply situation, through the collapse of entitlements of particular classes or occupation groups (Section 4).

Fifthly, a study of entitlements has to go beyond purely economic factors and take into account political arrangements (including pressure groups and news distribution systems) that affect people's actual ability to command commodities, including food. These influences may be very complex and may also involve apparently perplexing contrasts, e.g. between (1) India's better record than China's in avoiding famines, and (2) India's total failure to deal with endemic malnutrition and morbidity in the way China has been able to do (Section 5). Whether the disparate advantages of the contrasting systems can be effectively combined is a challenging issue of political economy that requires attention. Much is at stake.

References

Aird, J. (1980): 'Reconstruction of an official data model of the population of of China', US Department of Commerce, Bureau of Census, 15 May.

—— (1982): 'Population studies and population policy in China', *Population and Development Review*, 8, 267–97.

Alailima, P. J. (1982): 'National policies and programmes of social development in Sri Lanka', mimeographed, Colombo.

Alamgir, M. (1978): *Bangladesh: A Case of Below Poverty Level Equilibrium Trap* (Dhaka: Bangladesh Institute of Development Studies).

—— (1980): *Famine in South Asia – Political Economy of Mass Starvation in Bangladesh* (Cambridge, Mass.: Oelgeschlager, Gunn and Hain).

Arrow, K. J. (1982): 'Why people go hungry', *New York Review of Books*, **29** (July 15), 24-6.

Aziz, S. (1975) (ed.): *Hunger, Politics and Markets: The Real Issues in the Food Crisis* (New York: NYU Press).

—— (1982) (ed.): 'The fight against world hunger'. Special number of *Development*, 1982: **4**.

Baran, P. A. (1957): *Political Economy of Growth* (New York: Monthly Review Press).

Bardhan, P. (1974): 'On life and death questions', *Economic and Political Weekly*, **9**, 1293-1304.

Bauer, P. (1971): *Dissent on Development*, London (Weidenfeld and Nicolson).

—— (1981): *Equality, the Third World, and Economic Delusion* (Cambridge, Mass.: Harvard University Press).

Bernstein, T. P. (1983a): 'Starving to death in China', *New York Review of Books*, **30** (6 June) 36-8.

—— (1983b): 'Hunger and the state: grain procurements during the Great Leap Forward; with a Soviet perspective', mimeographed, East Asia Center, Columbia University.

Chattopadhyay, B. (1981): 'Notes towards an understanding of the Bengal famine of 1943', *Cressida*, **1**.

Coale, A. J. (1981): 'Population trends, population policy, and population studies in China', *Population and Development Review*, **7**, 85-97.

Datta, B. (1952): *Economics of Industrialization* (Calcutta: World Press).

Datta-Chaudhuri, M. K. (1979): 'Industrialization and foreign trade: an analysis based on the development experience of the Republic of Korea and the Philippines', ILO Working Paper WP II-4, ARTEP, ILO, Bangkok.

Desai, M. J. (1983): 'A general theory of poverty', mimeographed, London School of Economics, to be published in *Indian Economic Review*.

Dobb, M. H. (1951): *Some Aspects of Economic Development* (Delhi: Delhi School of Economics).

—— (1960): *An Essay on Economic Growth and Planning* (London: Routledge).

Fei, J. C. H. and Ranis, G. (1964): *Development of the Labour Surplus Economy: Theory and Practice* (Homewood, Ill.: Irwin).

George, S. and Paige, N. (1982): *Food for Beginners* (London: Writers and Readers Publishing Cooperative).

Ghose, A. (1979): 'Short term changes in income distribution in poor agrarian economies', ILO Working Paper WEP 10-6/WP 28, Geneva.

Grant, J. (1978): *Disparity Reduction Rates in Social Indicators* (Washington, DC: Overseas Development Council).

Griffin, K. (1978): *International Inequality and National Poverty* (London: Macmillan).

Gwatkin, D. R. (1979): 'Food policy, nutrition planning and survival: the cases of Kerala and Sri Lanka', *Food Policy*, November.

Hirschman, A. O. (1958): *The Strategy of Economic Development* (New Haven, Conn.: Yale University Press).

—— (1970): *Exit, Voice, and Loyalty* (Cambridge, Mass.: Harvard University Press).

—— (1977): *The Passions and the Interests* (Princeton: Princeton Univ. Press).

—— (1981): *Essays in Trespassing: Economics to Politics and Beyond* (Cambridge: Cambridge University Press).

Isenman, P. (1978): 'The relationship of basic needs to growth, income distribution and employment – the case of Sri Lanka', mimeographed, World Bank.

Ishikawa, S. (1981): *Essays on Technology, Employment and Institutions in Economic Development* (Tokyo: Kinokuniya).

Jayawardena, L. (1974): 'Sri Lanka'. In Chenery, H. *et al.* (eds), *Redistribution with Growth* (London: Oxford University Press).

Kynch, J. and Sen, A. K. (1983): 'Indian women: survival and well-being', *Cambridge Journal of Eonomics*, 7, 363-80.

Lappé, F. M. and Collins, J. (1979): *Food First: beyond the Myth of Scarcity* (New York: Ballantine Books).

Lewis, W. A. (1954): 'Economic development with unlimited supplies of labour', *Manchester School*, 22, 139-91.

—— (1955): *The Theory of Economic Growth* (Homewood, Ill.: Irwin).

Little, I. M. D. (1982): *Economic Development: Theory, Policy and International Relations* (New York: Basic Books).

—— Scitovsky, T. and Scott, M. (1971): *Industry and Trade in some Developing Countries* (London: Oxford University Press).

McLellan, D. (1977) (ed.): *Karl Marx: Selected Writings* (Oxford: Oxford University Press).

Mandelbaum (Martin), K. (1945): *The Industrialization of Backward Areas* (Oxford: Blackwell).

Mao Tse-tung (Zedong) (1974): *Mao Tse-tung Unrehearsed, Talks and Letters: 1956-71* (ed. Schram) (London: Penguin Books).

Marga Institute (1974): *Welfare and Growth in Sri Lanka* (Colombo: Marga Institute).

Marglin, S. A. (1976): *Value and Price in the Labour Surplus Economy* (Oxford: Clarendon Press).

Marx, K. and Engels, F. (1846): *The German Ideology*.

Miliband, R. (1977): *Marxism and Politics* (London: Oxford University Press).

Morris, M. D. (1979): *Measuring the Condition of the World's Poor: The Physical Quality of Life Index* (Oxford: Pergamon Press).

Nurkse, R. (1953): *Problems of Capital Formation in Underdeveloped Countries* (Oxford: Blackwell).

Oughton, E. (1982): 'The Maharashtra drought of 1970-73: an analysis of scarcity', *Oxford Bulletin of Economics and Statistics*, 44, 169-97.

Parikh, K. and Rabar, F. (1981) (eds): *Food for All in a Sustainable World* (Laxenburg: IIASA).

People's Republic of China (1981): *Foreign Broadcast Information Service*, no. 58, 26 March.

Rao, V. K. R. V. (1982): *Food, Nutrition and Poverty in India* (Brighton: Wheatsheaf Books).

Ravallion, M. (1983): 'The Performance of Rice Markets in Bangladesh during the 1974 famine', mimeographed, University of Oxford.

Research Group of the Feng Yang County Communist Party Committee (1982): 'An investigation into the household production contract system in Liyuan Commune', *New York Review of Books*, **30** (16 June), 36–8; translated from *Nongye Jingji Congkan* (Collected Material on Agricultural Economics), 25 November 1980.

Rosenstein-Rodan, P. (1943): 'Problems of industrialization in Eastern and South-eastern Europe', *Economic Journal*, **53**, 202–11.

Schultz, T. W. (1964): *Transforming Traditional Agriculture* (New Haven, Conn.: York University Press).

Sen, A. K. (1967): 'Surplus labour in India: a critique of Schultz's statistical tests', *Economic Journal*, **77**, 154–61.

—— (1975): *Employment, Technology and Development* (Oxford: Clarendon Press).

—— (1976): 'Famines as failures of exchange entitlement', *Economic and Political Weekly*, **11**, 1273–80.

—— (1977): 'Starvation and exchange entitlement: a general approach and its application to the Great Bengal Famine', *Cambridge Journal of Economics*, **1**, 33–59.

—— (1981a): *Poverty and Famines: An Essay on Entitlement and Deprivation* (Oxford: Clarendon Press).

—— (1981b): 'Public action and the quality of life in developing countries', *Oxford Bulletin of Economics and Statistics*, **43**, 287–319.

—— (1981c): 'Family and food: sex bias in poverty', mimeographed, 1981. [Essay 15 in this volume.]

—— (1982a): *Choice, Welfare and Measurement* (Oxford: Blackwell, and Cambridge, Mass.: MIT Press).

—— (1982b): 'Food battles: conflict in the access to food', Coromandel Lecture, 13 December 1982. Reprinted in *Mainstream*, 8 January 1983.

—— (1982c): 'How is India doing?' *New York Review of Books*, **29**, Christmas Number, pp. 41–5.

—— (1982d): *Commodities and Capabilities*, Hennipman Lecture, April 1982. To be published by North-Holland, Amsterdam.

—— (1983): 'Poor, relatively speaking', *Oxford Economic Papers*, **35**, 153–69. [Essay 14 in this volume.]

—— and S. Sengupta (1983): 'Malnutrition of rural children and the sex-bias', *Economic and Political Weekly*, **18**.

Singer, H. W. (1952): 'The mechanics of economic development', *Indian Economic Review*; reprinted in *The Economics of Underdevelopment* (ed. A. N. Agarwala and A. P. Singh) (London: Oxford University Press, 1958).

Sinha, R. and Drabek, A. G. (1978) (eds): *The World Food Problem: Consensus and Conflict* (Oxford: Pergamon Press).

Spitz, P. (1978): 'Silent violence: famine and inequality', *International Social Science Journal*, **30**.

Srinivasan, T. N. (1982): 'Hunger: defining it, estimating its global incidence and alleviating it', mimeographed. To be published in *The Role of Markets in the World Food Economy* (ed. D. Gale Johnson and E. Schuh).

Streeten, P. (1981): *Development Perspectives* (London: Macmillan).

—— with Burki, S. J., Mahbub ul Haq, Hicks, N. and Stewart, F. (1981): *First Things First: Meeting Basic Needs in Developing Countries* (New York: Oxford University Press).

Sun Yefang (1981): Article in *Jingji Guanli* (Economic Management), no. 2, 15 February; English translation in People's Republic of China (1981).

Taylor, L. (1975): 'The misconstrued crisis: Lester Brown and world food', *World Development*, **3**, 827–37.

Zhu Zhengzhi (1980): Article in *Jingji Kexue*, no. 3.

20
Goods and People

1 *Introduction*

Hugh MacDiarmid, the Scottish poet, wrote in his *Lament for Great Music*:

> The struggle for material existence is over. It has been won.
> The need for repressions and disciplines have passed.
> The struggle for truth and that indescribable necessity,
> Beauty, begins now, hampered by none of the lower needs.
> No one now needs live less or be less than his utmost.[1]

While the necessity 'to live less or be less than his utmost' may indeed be over in some special sense, the tragic fact remains that the lives of most people of the world fall very far short of that ideal. In contrast with the expectation of life at birth of around the middle seventies in the rich countries, more than two-thirds of the 'low-income' countries have life expectancy below 50 years.[2] The majority of people of the world do not have access to regular medical and hospital services, or to the security of safe water. Literacy rates are still shockingly low in most low-income countries. Even in the rich countries the relatively impoverished have to live a very constrained life in many respects.[3] For a large part of the population of this globe there is no escape from the need to 'live less or be less' – a *great deal* less – than their 'utmost'.

This paper is concerned with some foundational issues in development analysis. It is argued here that the process of economic develop-

1. Hugh MacDiarmid, *Collected Poems* (London: MacGibbon & Kee, 1967).
2. *World Development Report 1982*, Table 21. The 'low-income' countries are defined as those with GNP per head less than US$410. See also Singer and Ansari (1977), Grant (1978) and Morris (1979).
3. See, for example, Jencks (1972), Atkinson (1975), Beckerman (1979), Townsend (1979).

Paper presented at the opening Plenary Session of the Seventh World Congress of the International Economic Association, Madrid, 1983.

ment is best seen as an expansion of people's 'capabilities'. This approach focuses on what people can *do* or can *be*, and development is seen as a process of emancipation from the enforced necessity to 'live less or be less'. The capabilities approach relates to, but fundamentally differs from, characterizing development as either (1) expansion of *goods and services*, or (2) increase in *utilities*, or (3) meeting *basic needs*. These contrasts are taken up first in the next three sections.

Another foundational issue concerns understanding the process of economic expansion and structural change through which capabilities can be expanded. This involves focusing on the 'entitlements' of people, representing the command of households over commodity bundles. These issues are briefly discussed in Sections 5 and 6. That question also requires us to look into the *use* of entitlements and the factors governing it, e.g. division of commodities within the family, use of commodities to generate capabilities. The *conversion* of entitlements into capabilities raises many difficult economic and social problems, a few of which are taken up in Section 7.

In Section 8 the so-called 'world food problem' is discussed in the light of the approach of *capabilities*, and related to it, *entitlements* and *conversion*. The paper ends with some concluding remarks (Section 9).

2   Commodities and Capabilities

It is not uncommon to think of economic development as expansion of the availability of goods and services in the country in question. The focus on the growth of GNP per head is an especially simple version of that general approach. There are some obvious merits in taking that approach. It is, for example, a good antidote to the temptation to build castles in the air — overlooking the commodity basis of prosperity.

But while goods and services are valuable, they are not valuable in themselves. Their value rests on what they can do for people, or rather, what people can do with these goods and services.[4] This question is an important one to emphasize because 'commodity fetishism' — to borrow an expression from Marx (1887) — is such a widespread phenomenon, and the important role that the exchange of commodities plays in modern society tends to sustain that fetishism.

4. Arguments for focusing on 'capabilities' in analysing well-being, equality, living standard and positive freedom have been presented in Sen (1979a, 1980, 1982a, 1983b). The capabilities approach can be traced back at least to Adam Smith and Marx, as is discussed in Sen (1983a, 1983b).

If the capabilities of each person were uniquely (and positively) related to the national availability of goods and services, then there would have been perhaps no great harm in focusing on the total supply of goods and services. But that assumption is a non-starter. There is not only the problem of the division of the national output between families and individuals,[5] but also the fact that the conversion of commodities into capabilities varies enormously with a number of parameters, e.g. age, sex, health, social relations, class background, education, ideology, and a variety of other interrelated factors.

Take the case of food and nutrition. The nutrition of people depends not merely on the availability of food per head in the community, but also on distribution considerations, on the one hand, and on the other on such factors as (i) the person's age and sex (and if a woman, whether pregnant or lactating); (ii) metabolic rates and body size; (iii) activity levels; (iv) medical conditions (including presence or absence of stomach parasites); (v) climatic conditions; (vi) the social needs of entertainment and communal relations (including offering and partaking of food); (vii) education in general, and in particular, knowledge of nutritional and health matters; (viii) access to medical services and the ability to use them, and so on. The capability of a person to be well nourished cannot be identified or linked in a straightforward way with the national supply of food, or even with his or her own individual access to food. The object of the exercise in dealing with the 'food problem' is to expand the ability to be well nourished and also to expand other related capabilities such as eliminating hunger, enjoying food and social intercourse, and so on. To focus on food as such without looking beyond would be a mistake.

The same applies to commodities in general. Development is not a matter, ultimately, of expanding supplies of commodities, but of enhancing the capabilities of people. The former has importance only in an instrumental and strongly contingent way, traceable to the real importance of the latter.

3   Capabilities and Utilities

It might be tempting to think that the above line of reasoning must lead to focusing on utilities as the standard of value, which is what

5. The distributional question raises interesting problems in the characterization of real national income; see Sen (1967a, 1976b).

traditional welfare economics tends to do. But confining attention to utilities amounts to seeing people in a highly limited way. Happiness or desire-fulfilment represents only one aspect of human existence. It can be argued that capabilities are valued ultimately because they reflect freedom, including, *inter alia*, the freedom to achieve happiness. It is a question of the command that people have over their lives.[6] Hunger, starvation and famines are awful social phenomena not just because they cause disutility. An elementary failure of freedom is involved in this, and we do not judge the seriousness of the situation by the precise extent of the unhappiness, or dissatisfaction.

It is inevitable that on a fundamental subject like this there would be differences of approach. It is not my purpose in this essay to present detailed arguments as to why the utilitarian basis of traditional welfare economics is fundamentally flawed. I have discussed this question more extensively elsewhere,[7] and will not further pursue the debate here. But there is a practical issue related to this question that has not been much discussed in the literature and which happens to be very important in evaluating and assessing development and structural change. Judging importance by the mental metric of happiness or desire-fulfilment can take a deeply biased form due to the fact that the mental reactions often reflect defeatist compromises with harsh reality induced by hopelessness. The insecure sharecropper, the exploited landless labourer, the overworked domestic servant, the subordinate housewife, may all come to terms with their respective predicaments in such a way that grievance and discontent are submerged in cheerful endurance by the necessity of uneventful survival.[8] The hopeless underdog loses the courage to desire a better deal and learns to take pleasure in small mercies. The deprivations appear muffled and muted in the metric of utilities.

In such situations discontent and disutility, instead of being tragic outcomes (as in utilitarian assessment), would have constituted a positive assertion of creative potentiality. Since economic development has much to do with making structural changes to conquer the inequities and exploitations that characterize the world, the importance of questioning the utilitarian method of accounting cannot be overemphasized.

6. The roots of this approach go back at least to Smith (1776) and Marx (1887).

7. See Sen (1970, 1979a, 1979b, 1982b). See also Rawls (1971), Williams (1973) and Sen and Williams (1982). For defences of the utility-based approach, see Ng (1981) and the papers by Hare, Harsanyi and Mirrlees in Sen and Williams (1982), in which see also the anti-utilitarian arguments presented by Dasgupta, Elster, Hahn, Hammond, Hampshire, Rawls, Scanlon, Taylor and others.

8. See Sen (1981b, 1982c), and Essay 13 in this volume, and Elster (1982).

The ability to achieve happiness is, of course, of importance on its own, and it can certainly be seen as one of many capabilities of relevance to development. The difference with utilitarianism arises in the insistence of the latter that everything – including all other capabilities – be judged exclusively in the metric of utilities. Judging the importance of anything is thus identified with measuring the utilities associated with it. Removal of starvation, poverty, inequity, exploitation, illiteracy, and other deprivations, is seen as unimportant in itself and rendered important only if – and to the extent that – there is a net utility gain through that removal. It is this utility-based narrow vision of traditional welfare economics that is fundamentally inadequate as a basis for evaluating action and policy, in general, and development and structural change, in particular.

4 Capabilities and Basic Needs

The approach of meeting 'basic needs',[9] which has played an important part in the recent literature on economic development, has some similarities with the capabilities approach. As Paul Streeten (1981) has pointed out, 'the basic needs concept is a reminder that the objective of the development effort is to provide all human beings with the *opportunity* for a full life' (p. 21). It involves the rejection of both utility-based welfare economics and commodity-based growth calculus. These characteristics are shared by the basic needs approach with the capabilities approach, and more specifically the focus on 'nutrition, health, shelter, water and sanitation, education, and other essentials' in the basic needs approach makes it directly concerned with a number of important capabilities.

There are, however, significant differences as well. First, the 'basic needs' are defined in terms of commodities (in Streeten's (1981) words, 'particular goods and services required to achieve certain results'), even though attention is paid to differences in the commodities needed by different persons to satisfy the same human requirements. Thus the focus remains on commodities even though the contingent nature of commodity requirements is fully acknowledged. But often commodity requirements may not be at all derivable from a specified set of capabilities, since the relation between commodity bundles and capability bundles may quite plausibly be a *many–one* correspondence, with the same capabilities being achievable

9. See Pant (1962), Haq (1976), Herrera *et al.* (1976), ILO (1976), Ghai *et al.* (1977), Griffin (1978), Streeten and Burki (1978), Chichilnisky (1980), Streeten (1981), for various ways of characterizing basic needs.

by more than one particular bundle of goods and services. (For example, different combinations of food and health services may produce the same level of nutrition.) Operating on the commodity space rather than directly on the space of capabilities involves additional problems.

Second, the commodity requirements for specific capabilities may not be independently decidable for each person, due to social interdependence. For example, such capabilities as the ability to appear in public without shame (discussed by Adam Smith, 1776), or taking part in the life of the community (discussed by Peter Townsend, 1979), depends on the consumption of others. This has not merely the consequence that *absolute* deprivation in capabilities may take the form of *relative* deprivation in terms of commodities and incomes (see Sen, 1983a), but also that the needs of commodities may not be absolutely specifiable at all.

Third, basic needs are 'interpreted in terms of *minimum* specified quantities' of particular commodities, and the implicit framework is that of reaching a *minimum* level of capabilities (see Streeten, 1981, pp. 25–6). The capability approach, in contrast, is not confined to that use only, and indeed can be used for judging individual 'advantage' at any level.[10] In this sense the basic needs approach involves one particular application of the capabilities framework. The capabilities approach is applicable in judging advantage and deprivation in rich countries as well as poor ones (Sen, 1983a), and it can also be used for such other purposes as judging the real extent of inequality (Sen, 1980).

Fourth, 'needs' is a more passive concept than 'capability', and it is arguable that the perspective of positive freedom links naturally with capabilities (what can the person *do*?) rather than with the fulfilment of their needs (what can be *done for* the person?). The perspective of fulfilling needs has some obvious advantages in dealing with dependents (e.g. children), but for responsible adults the format of capabilities may be much more suitable in seeing what is involved and in linking it with the issue of freedom. This distinction is really a matter of outlook and emphasis, but it can be quite important in analysing general objectives of development.

The controversies on the use of the basic needs approach has tended to be concerned with strategic issues rather than with foundational

---

10. This can be done through vector comparisons (yielding a partial order) or through weighting and indexing (leading to a more complete ordering). The underlying technical issues as well as some empirical problems are discussed in my forthcoming monograph *Commodities and Capabilities*, Hennipman Lecture, Sen (1983b).

ones. It has, for example, been argued that concentrating on basic needs may interfere with building a solid material basis of economic prosperity. However, economic prosperity is not sought for its own sake, and the concern with it can be seen to be based ultimately on worry about capabilities in the future, which might not be achievable in the absence of economic expansion. The debate can thus be cast in terms of the conflicts between immediately enhancing capabilities now (reflected in meeting *basic needs*) and long-term expansion of capabilities in the future (*through* economic prosperity). Thus analysed, the debate can be seen to be of the traditional form – familiar in the literature on planning[11] – of capabilities now *versus* a bigger expansion of capabilities in the future. Though the object of value is changed here from the traditional concentration on utilities (utilities now versus more utilities later), the intertemporal conflict must be seen to be of the familiar type.

Another criticism of the basic needs approach arises from the worry that a concentration on just the minimum requirements may lead to a softening of the opposition to inequality in general. 'Minimum needs and no more' is a familiar – and unfair – caricature. But if the basic needs approach is seen as just one application of the capabilities approach, it would be clear that other issues related to capabilities (including that of the *equality* of capabilities, see Sen, 1980), is not prejudiced by the special concern with basic needs at a certain stage of development.

What is needed is to take the basic needs approach out of the arbitrarily narrow box into which it seems to have got confined. To see it as just one part of the capabilities approach – to which it is motivationally linked – would do just that. All the standard issues of efficiency, equality, etc. can be seen as arising within the capabilities approach.[12] (The contribution of that approach is mainly to make the metric of advantage and achievement avoid both the fetishism of the commodity focus and the subjectivism of the utility focus, rather than to lead to undue concentration on minimality or immediacy.) The basic needs approach would cease to appear one-sided and distracting if it is seen to be a part of a more general approach and if that recognition is allowed to have its due impact in policy formulation.

11. See Chakravarty (1970), Heal (1973), Dasgupta (1982).
12. This includes problems of incentives and the conflicts between efficiency and equality. How important these conflicts are is an empirical question that is both important and complex and this question has to be faced just as much within the capabilities approach as under the more traditional approaches.

5 *Entitlements, Famines and Hunger*

The capabilities of persons depend, among other things, on the bundles of commodities over which they can establish command. In each society there are rules that govern who can have the use of what, and people pursue their respective objectives subject to these rules. For example, in a private ownership economy, use depends on ownership and exchange. The set of all bundles of commodities from which a person can choose one bundle can be called the person's 'entitlement'.[13]

To illustrate, suppose person i owns initially 20 units of commodity 1 and 30 units of commodity 2. This can be called his endowment vector. He can stick to that bundle if he so chooses, but he can also exchange that bundle into another through trade or production. Any other bundle of goods that would cost no more than what 20 units of commodity 1 and 30 units of commodity 2 would fetch in the market is included in his entitlement set. So is every other bundle within that budget constraint. And so are other bundles that he can acquire through production ('exchange with nature'), or a mixture of production and trade. The trade and production possibilities are summarized by an 'exchange entitlement mapping', which specifies, for each endowment bundle, all the different bundles any one of which he can command (e.g. through the use of trade or production).[14] A person's endowment vector and the exchange entitlement mapping together determine his over-all entitlement, representing the actual opportunity of acquiring commodity bundles in his particular situation.

The entitlement of a person also includes what can be obtained through claims against the state, e.g. the entitlement to unemployment benefit (if the person fails to find a job), or to social subsidy (if his income falls below a certain minimum figure). In many economies these entitlements are substantial enough to provide a person with a good deal of security, but in others they are tiny or just absent. In situations of distress, e.g. a slump, the existence of such claims against the state might well be vital for survival.

13. The concept of entitlements has been more fully presented, explored and used for analysis in Sen (1977b, 1981a). See also Arrow (1982).

14. Formally, if x is a person's endowment vector and $f(\cdot)$ a set-valued function specifying for each endowment vector a set of vectors over which he can establish command, then $f(x)$ is the person's endowment set. The characteristic of the exchange entitlement mapping $f(\cdot)$ in different economic systems and circumstances have been explored in Appendices A and B in Sen (1981a).

The entitlement approach concentrates on relating a person's or a household's actual command over goods and services to the rules of entitlement in that system and the person's or household's actual position in the system (e.g. the initial ownership or endowment). This way of approaching the issue contrasts with approaches that avoid the question of command by making some general assumption about the over-all availability of goods for distribution among the population. This includes theories (such as Malthusian population theory) that concentrate on average food output per head as the key indicator determining famines and other disasters,[15] as well as those that explicitly assume a given unequal pattern of distribution without going into the causation of that distribution. Since these distributions have been known to change sharply over a short period (and not only over the longer run), the case for a causal analysis of the type demanded by the entitlement approach seems to be strong.

Whether a person is able to establish command over, say, enough food to avoid starvation depends on the nature of the entitlement system operating in the economy in question and on the person's own position in that society. Even when the over-all ratio of food to population is high, particular occupation groups can perish because of their inability to establish command over enough food. To see the food problem in terms of, say, the Malthusian focus on food output or supply per head can be a deadly mistake − literally so.[16]

To illustrate this point, I shall make brief references to a number of particular experiences of hunger and famine in the modern world, based on some of the detailed case studies that I have presented elsewhere (Sen, 1981a; see also Essay 18 in this volume).

(1) In the Great Bengal Famine of 1943, in which about 3 million people died, food availability per unit of population was not particularly low and was, in fact, about 9 per cent higher than in 1941 when there was no famine. The famine victims (e.g. landless rural labourers, fishermen) suffered a drastic decline in their market entitlements due to their wages and money earnings not keeping up with the rise in food prices, resulting from demand-fed inflationary pressure in a war-boom economy (with urban expansion being supplemented by exclusively urban food rationing at controlled prices, largely insulating

15. Malthus (1978). However, see also Malthus (1800), in which he outlines an entitlement system, albeit in a rudimentary form; on this see Sen (1981a), pp. 174–9.

16. On related issues, see Aziz (1975, 1982), Taylor (1975), Lipton (1977), Griffin (1978), Sinha and Drabek (1978), Ghose (1979), Parikh and Rabar (1982), Oughton (1982), Srinivasan (1982), Ravallion (1983).

urban purchasers from the rise in food prices in the rest of the economy).[17]

(2) During the Ethiopian famine in Wollo of 1972, the food availability per head in Ethiopia as a whole was normal. Though the food output in Wollo itself was much lower due to drought, food did not move much into Wollo from elsewhere in the country, and some food actually moved *out of* Wollo, which experienced a famine with largely stationary prices (since the ability of the Wollo population to buy food had fallen along with the decline of agricultural output).[18]

(3) In the Ethiopian famine in Harerghe in 1974, the most-affected victim-group, viz. the pastoralists, were hit not merely by the loss of animals due to drought, but also – quantitatively more importantly – by the change in the relative prices of animals and animal products vis-à-vis foodgrains, which affected their basis of subsistence in the form of selling animals and animal products to buy normally cheaper calories in foodgrains. The market mechanism played a decimating role in this famine, through the general fall in incomes (agricultural and pastoral) making consumers shift from richer animal products to basic foodgrains, driving up the relative price of the latter.[19]

(4) In the Bangladesh famine in 1974 the food availability per head was higher than in any other year during 1971–75. Rural labourers were affected by the loss of employment due to floods, which later affected output to be harvested, but which had an immediate and devastating impact on the entitlement of the wage labourers. Rise in rice prices due to general inflationary pressure also made the market entitlements go down.[20]

The cases of famines bring out dramatically the importance of variations of entitlements in matters of life and death – a role that cannot be taken over by such variables as the index of food avail-

17. See Sen (1981a, Chapter 6). There were other factors supplementing this picture, e.g. powerful speculative rises in food prices partly engineered by a few traders, and totally inept government policy adding to panic rather than providing relief.

18. See Sen (1981a, Chapter 7). Food 'counter-movement', i.e. food moving *out of* the famine areas, has also been observed in other famines, e.g. the Irish famines of 1840s and the Bangladesh famine of 1974. It is characteristic of certain types of famines in which the effective demand falls more than the supply of food (Sen, 1981a, pp. 160–2).

19. See Sen (1981a, Chapter 7). The market-oriented development of commercial agriculture also contributed to the decline by affecting the availability of good grazing grounds for the Ethiopian pastoralists to use.

20. See Sen (1981a, Chapter 9). See also Alamgir (1980); also Islam (1977). A further adverse development was the decision of the United States government to discontinue food aid to Bangladesh (because of her trade with Cuba) precisely when it was most needed – with a famine threatening and food stocks in the public distribution system being very low (on this see McHenry and Bird, 1977, and Sobhan, 1979). The introduction of public relief, creating entitlements against the state, was delayed crucially as a result.

ability or of food output per head. The relevance of entitlements is, however, much more pervasive than might appear from these examples. For example, in determining the causation of endemic malnutrition in many developing economies, such as India, the entitlement system provides a helpful format for analysing the mechanism of the failure to establish command over an adequate bundle of food on the part of many occupation groups. For example, for landless labourers the only endowment worth the name is labour power, and their fortunes depend crucially on the working of the labour market. For sharecroppers, in contrast, there is also the issue of the right to cultivate the land in question, and the substance of entitlements related to it depends on the legal and practical status of that right and the economic circumstances governing them.

6   Incomes and Entitlements

Since food is bought and sold in the market in a straightforward way, and since much of the income of the very poor is expended on food, it may be helpful to see the entitlement to food in terms of *incomes*. Indeed, it has become quite widely recognized in recent years that hunger is very often caused by shortage of incomes rather than by the over-all shortage of food. This rather simple way of seeing the entitlement problem is a bit incomplete since income has to be earned and the causes of the inability to earn enough income would have to be studied, investigating endowments (including labour power) and exchange possibilities (including employment and wages). Nevertheless the level of income is a crucial variable in understanding the entitlement to food and can be treated as such without losing the essentials of a more complete approach.

The commanding power of incomes depends, naturally, on prices, and as such we have to look at some notion of 'real income' (that is, corrected for prices). The real income is, of course, a weight-based index, and much depends on what weights are chosen. In dealing with food command in distress situations it may be appropriate to put a greater weight on food, and indeed in some contexts it is useful to get a straightforward estimate of the total amount of food command if all income were expended on food.[21] Since the weight of food is in any case very high in the budget of the poor in the developing countries, the issue of weighting is not such a complex

21. See Sen (1981a, pp. 63-70, 104-11, 145-50).

one in dealing specifically with the entitlement to food in that context.

However, for other goods and services (e.g. education, health services, transport), real income may provide quite a distant way of viewing entitlement. The expenditure on these commodities may not be a large part of the total budget so that their weight on the price index may be relatively small. A change in the price or availability of these goods and services may not thus be strongly reflected in the real income index. Further the existence of quantity restrictions make the income-based view very opaque. If there is no hospital in the neighbourhood or no school within easy reach − or if there are hospitals and schools but with highly limited capacity − the income of the would-be purchaser may not give much of an idea as to whether the person can or cannot acquire these commodities.

Entitlements have to be studied in a more elaborate way in these cases and the short-cut of making do with an income-based picture will give little clue as to what people can or cannot acquire. In examining the enormous differences in the access to health services, medicine, education, etc., in different poor countries, the approach of entitlement has to be more fully applied (see Sen, 1983c).

This problem may not be very serious for the *entitlement to food*, but it can be nevertheless extremely serious for the *capability to be well nourished*, which − as was discussed earlier − is the real concern in being interested in the entitlement to food. The capability to be well nourished depends, among other things, on the medical condition of the people (e.g. the presence or absence of parasitic diseases in the stomach),[22] and it depends also on nutritional education and knowledge. The entitlements to these other goods and services (e.g. health and educational services) are not well approximated by over-all indices of real income. Thus when it comes to the capability to be well nourished, income ceases to be an adequate parameter of analysis, and considerations of food entitlement have to be supplemented by those of entitlements to complementary goods and services. This is an important qualification to bear in mind while applauding the fact that in recent years the importance of income shortage in hunger has − rightly − come to be widely recognized.

7 Intra-family Distribution and Capabilities

Capability to be nourished, as was argued in the last section, is not a matter of entitlement to food only, but depends also on entitlements

22. See, for example, Scrimshaw (1977).

to other goods and services such as health services, medicine and education. In fact, even when the entitlements to all these commodities have been fully taken into account, there remain other sources of variation of the capability to be nourished, as was discussed in Section 2.

One issue concerns the distribution of food and other commodities *within* the family. While we have been talking of entitlements of *persons*, the usual procedures of production and exchange apply to *households* only, with the distribution within the household being determined by other procedures.[23] It is the entitlements of households that have to be then translated into actual consumption of members of the household. There is a good deal of evidence that in poor countries in different parts of the world, food is often distributed very unequally within the family (see, for example, the surveys by den Hartog (1973) and Schofield (1975)).

An important difficulty in studying this problem arises from the fact that the relationship between consumption of food and capability to be well nourished varies with age, sex, activity level, pregnancy, lactation and other variables. For example, an observed lower intake of food by women vis-à-vis men has often not been taken as evidence of sex bias, on the ground that the calorie requirements of men are also higher. However, the so-called calorie requirements specified by the FAO/WHO Expert Committee (1973) are extremely arbitrary both in general methodology (relying simply on body size and activity level) and in the particular way activity levels are specified (especially underestimating the energy use in home-based work).[24] The fact that the lower food intake of women may appear to be more than counterbalanced by the lower 'requirements' of women is thus not as definitive evidence of the absence of anti-female bias in household allocation as it has sometimes been taken to be.

In fact, as was argued in the context of discussing the 'basic needs' approach (Section 4), the idea of commodity 'requirements' for particular 'capabilities' is itself unsustainable. There are possibilities of 'multiple equilibria' of energy and work, and also considerable variations in these relations between one person and another.[25] There are 'many–one' correspondences between commodity bundles (food, health, education, etc.) and nutritional levels.

23. The theory that argues that non-market transactions can be fruitfully seen in terms of *as if* market exchanges has a long way to go to be convincing either in theory or in empirical application, even though it has provided some useful insights on some particular issues (see Becker, 1981).

24. See Chen, Huq and D'Souza (1980) and Sen (1981c), among others.

25. See Sukhatme (1977), Davidson, Passmore, Brock and Truswell (1979), and Srinivasan (1982).

The simple formulae of 'requirements' are less scientific than they might look, and they have sometimes simply helped to justify systematic biases in the treatment of different groups, such as men and women.

In judging the well-being of different groups and the deal they get in the society, it would be more sensible to go directly towards observing achievements rather than commodity consumption. For example, it is more sensible to look for medical signs of under-nourishment and nutrition-related morbidity and mortality, than to estimate, first, personal food intake, and then, see how that relates to the assumed 'requirements'.

In terms of the capabilities approach, observing morbidity or undernourishment is clearly the right direction to go, since our ultimate concern is not with who eats how much, but largely with the capabilities of nourishment that the persons in question enjoy. Two objections can, however, be raised. First, the capabilities can be difficult to measure, and it can be argued that they are not as straight-forward as intakes of food. This is, up to a point, a sustainable objection. However, observational problems in ascertaining who eats how much are also very serious. To get accurate data on the intake of calories and other nutrients of each member of the family, it would be necessary not only to *see* who is eating how much in a family meal, but also to *weigh* exactly all the food items consumed by each, and it is a little difficult to assume that the eating activities would be unaffected by such interference. Ascertaining nutritional charac-teristics and getting morbidity and mortality data may be a *relatively* simpler operation.[26]

The second objection takes the form of pointing out that observ-ing nutritional characteristics may not tell us much about inequalities in the distribution of food. That is indeed so, but since ultimately interest in food consumption largely rests in its effects on nutrition and its consequences, the loss may not be very great.[27] The essence of the capabilities approach is to see commodity consumption as no more than a means to generating capabilities, and if the capabilities

26. It should, however, be emphasized that assessing capability, which represents a *set* of possibilities, is not identical with assessing the actual use that is made of the capabilities, reflected in the particular outcome. In the case of avoiding serious undernourishment or high morbidity or mortality, the problem may be less difficult than it is in other cases. On this general question, see Sen (1983b).

27. Note, however, the ability to enjoy consuming food or using it for various social purposes can also be quite an important capability, and this cannot be identified with nutrition. See Douglas and Isherwood (1979). But nor is the quantity of food consumed in itself a good indicator of these functional uses of food. A more sophisticated analysis of capabilities is called for.

and their use can be directly ascertained, the absence of detailed information on commodity consumption may not be much regretted.

It should be conceded that when dealing with less elementary capabilities than the ability to be well nourished, the observational problems may be more serious. Indeed, it will sometimes be the case that commodity inputs may be much easier to observe than capabilities and their use, and there may then be some practical advantage in using adjusted commodity data as 'proxy' for capabilities (see Sen, 1983b). However, that is a tactical issue and does not overturn the basic fact that it is capabilities that we are interested in, and even in these cases, observing commodity consumption would be motivated by treating it as a possibly convenient indicator of capabilities.

The importance of entitlements rests in the role they play in the determination of capabilities. From the point of view of policy this role can be sometimes crucial, and in dealing with such extreme problems as famines, an almost exclusive concentration on entitlements and their variations may sometimes make sense. On the other hand, in dealing with less extreme problems, e.g. endemic malnutrition, high morbidity and mortality, it is very important to remember that entitlements constitute no more than one part of the story. It is, to be sure, a part that undoubtedly deserves serious attention, especially in dealing with policy issues related to land reform, employment policy, social security, food for work programmes, etc., but the incompleteness of the entitlement picture has to be kept in view for a more comprehensive attack on deprivation (and on the enforced necessity of people to 'live less or be less' than what society can organize).

8   Remarks on the Food Problem

Malthusian pessimism has had a great revival in recent decades, and the so-called 'world food problem' has become a subject of great concern. Model-based reasoning has outlined various scenarios of collapse of 'material existence' on this planet,[28] and the prospect of worldwide starvation has been forcefully portrayed. These analyses have had a great impact on the way the food problem and the future of the world are viewed by the general public, fed by hair-raising reports in the media, blowing up and distorting the pronouncements of specialist experts. As I write this paper, *The Times* of Friday

---

28. See, for example, Forrester (1971), Meadows *et al.* (1972), Mesarovic and Pestel (1974), Brown and Eckholm (1974).

17 June 1983, reports under the eye-catching heading, 'Starvation Threat to 65 Nations': 'More than half of the world's developing nations will be unable to feed their people by the end of this century, according to a United Nations survey, published today.' We are told: 'Data about soils and climate in 117 lands was fed into a complex computer programme to produce the "grim conclusion", according to the UN Fund for Population Activities which sponsored the survey in collaboration with the UN Food and Agriculture Organisation' (p. 5).

It is right that worries about the economic future of the world should engage serious attention. However, serious attention has not typically confirmed the pessimism. Models of collapse are not, of course, difficult to construct (with or without 'a complex computer programme'!). But most of the serious studies of long-run prognostication (including the FAO report *allegedly* summarized by *The Times*) have not prophesied such a coming doom, and have indicated much greater scope for decisive policy response.[29] There are obvious scopes for disagreement on various assumptions used in these models, but the case for Malthusian pessimism looks far from plausible.

The neo-Malthusian resurgence does, in fact, seriously misguide economic thinking in two important ways. First, by focusing on such misleading variables as food output per unit of population, the Malthusian approach profoundly misspecifies the problems facing the poor in the world, as was discussed in Section 5 above. The question of entitlements in general and food entitlements in particular get submerged in the crude picture of supply and availability. It is often overlooked that what may be called 'Malthusian optimism' has actually killed millions of people. Focusing attention on the Malthusian variable of food output per head, the food situation has often appeared to be comfortable even when there have been good economic grounds for expecting terrible troubles for particular occupation groups, and in such circumstances public policy based on smugness (related to food output per head) has tended to permit the development of a widespread famine when it could have been easily averted.

Second, by concentrating attention on the alleged long-run decline in the future, neo-Malthusianism distracts attention from the already existing sufferings and miseries in the world. The need for a positive advance gets overshadowed by an imagined need for countering a hypothetical future decline. The real problem is not that the world

29. See Parikh and Rabar (1981), and also Leontief *et al.* (1977), Herrera *et al.* (1977), Interfutures (1979), Linnemann (1981). See also Aziz (1975, 1982), Taylor (1975), Griffin (1978), Sinha and Drabek (1978), Swaminathan (1983).

will *turn* beastly, but that it *is* beastly already; and it has been so throughout history, with human life being nasty, brutish and short.

Food output per head has been steadily rising in the world as a whole. It has, however, been falling in particular countries, most of them in parts of Africa. In itself this is not a pointer to disaster. Not every country has to grow all the food it eats – many of the rich ones (e.g. Britain) do not. The real problem is that the decline in food output per head in many of these countries is going hand in hand with a decline in real income per head, and the entitlement to food is also slipping for many of the occupation groups in these countries. Such an occurrence can and does take place in many countries through the decline of *other* economic variables such as non-food crops, industrial output and employment, and mining activities. What is really worrying about the so-called 'African food problem' is this decline in economic power to *command* goods and services, especially food. The fact that in many of these countries this economic decline is associated with a decline in food output per head is not *in itself* of overwhelming significance.

This way of looking at the problem in terms of entitlements also suggests that in deciding on policy response there is no *a priori* reason to pursue expansion of food output only, and it is rather a matter of deciding what type of economic expansion would lead to a steady rise of real income in general and that for poor and vulnerable groups in particular. The seriousness of the problem of survival and nutrition should not turn us all into Physiocrats.

The question of food output is, however, of importance in itself in two particular respects, within the entitlement approach. First, the relative prices of food will depend on the supply, and if there is a decline in the world food output this would be reflected in prices being higher than what would have otherwise been the case. But this line of reasoning points not to the necessity that every country should grow its own food, but that the world supply should keep in line with world demand, which is a very different type of requirement. Indeed, given the fact that incomes are rising in many poor countries leading to an increase in food consumption per head, the issue of demand and supply calls for a substantially *faster* rate of expansion of food output in the world than the growth of population.

The second direct role of food output as such relates to the fact that given inefficiencies and the uncertainties of the market mechanism, particular occupation groups may be safer by growing their own food than by depending on income from other sources.[30] This

30. See Chapters 7, 8 and 10 in Sen (1981a).

is a matter of economic judgement, and the issue once again is not the size of food output as such but the minimum food command that vulnerable groups might be able to secure.[31]

The question of food entitlements represents one side of the food problem, and in this, food production has an important, though contingent, role. But as was argued earlier, the capability to be well nourished does not depend on food entitlement only. There is also the question of entitlement to complementary goods and services such as health services and education, and furthermore the problem of distribution of food within the family. The success of some countries in eliminating endemic malnutrition and the related morbidities and mortality (e.g. China, Sri Lanka) has been based on a policy package in which a more equal access to food has been supplemented by widespread access to health services and elementary education. Policies of free or subsidized food distribution have been supplemented by an active public policy of health and education. I have discussed these questions elsewhere (Sen, 1981c, 1983c), and here I shall only note that on the basis of these policies China and Sri Lanka have been able to achieve levels of health and longevity that are very much higher than in countries with comparable GNP per head (such as Pakistan or India), and at least as high as many countries that are many times richer in terms of GNP per head (such as Brazil or Mexico).

The part of the food policy that is most difficult to deal with concerns the issue of distribution of food within the family. Evidence of a systematic bias against women, and even against girls vis-à-vis boys, is quite strong in many developing countries, especially in Asia.[32] This applies to observed differences in capability failure with respect to nutrition,[33] and seems also to relate to the fact that despite the biological advantages of the female in survival, in many of these countries women have lower longevity (and higher mortality at most ages).

The problem is particularly acute in Asia. It is interesting to note that while the ratio of female to male population is 1.02 in Africa and 1.05 in Europe and North America, that ratio is 0.99 in Latin America, 0.96 in East Asia (including China), 0.96 in Southwest Asia, and 0.93 in South Asia (including India).[34] There are a number

31. See Sinha and Drabek (1978) and Aziz (1982).
32. See, for example, Bardhan (1974), den Hartog (1973), Schofield (1975), Chen, Huq and D'Souza (1980), Mitra (1980), Sen (1981), Kynch and Sen (1982).
33. See Kynch and Sen (1982) and Sen and Sengupta (1983).
34. See United Nations, *Demographic Year book 1981* (New York: UN, 1982). The latest Chinese census seems to suggest an even lower female–male ratio for China, just over 0.94.

of complex causal factors in this contrast, but the relative neglect of the female in intra-family distribution (involving both food and health services) is possibly an important influence.[35] Just as there might be a special 'African food problem', with persistent production problems, there might even be a peculiarly 'Asian food problem', involving intra-family biases in the distribution of food (and of complementary goods and services).[36]

The policy issues related to this 'Asian food problem' are very complex, since changing the modes of family behaviour is no mean task. The role of education, especially *political* education, is important in the long-run solution of the problem, as is the question of female employment and economic power.[37] In the short run there might be considerable scope for reducing the extent of the discrimination against little girls through supplementary feeding of children in direct nutritional intervention (through school meals and other programmes of public feeding of children). There is, in fact, some evidence that such intervention might reduce the excess female undernourishment and morbidity, aside from reducing undernourishment in general.[38]

There is no one 'world food problem'. There are many distinct — though interrelated — problems of food entitlement and the capability to be nourished. The policy issues include, among others:

(1) generating and guaranteeing entitlement to food of households in different occupation groups (involving not merely issues of food production, but also of income security, employment policy, public distribution, land reform, and related structural changes in the economy);

(2) generating and guaranteeing entitlement to complementary goods and services (especially health services and education, possibly through public policy);

(3) working towards the elimination of biases against women and children where they exist (involving long-run economic, political and social change, and in the short-run possibly various types of feeding programmes, especially of children).

35. See Kynch and Sen (1982).
36. It should be mentioned, however, that nutritional sex bias seems to be less present in Southeast Asia. Also, the female–male ratio in Southeast Asia is, in fact, around 1.01 — much higher than in the rest of Asia.
37. See Sen (1983d, 1984).
38. See Sen and Sengupta (1983), for a case study.

9   *Concluding Remarks*

In this paper there has been an attempt to discuss the case for, and the implications of, seeing development as expansion of capabilities of people. This perspective differs from taking a commodity-centred view, of which concentration on GNP and its growth rate is an especially simple case (Section 2). It also involves the rejection of a utility-based view, common in welfare economics (Section 3). Further, it differs from the 'basic needs' approach, though it facilitates seeing that approach in a wider perspective (Section 4). It is important to go into these foundational issues for understanding and analysing the requirements of development, including the nature of the structural changes that are called for.

The generation of capabilities relates to entitlements, in the form of command over goods and services. Economic analyses based on such gross variables as food availability per head, or GNP per head, can be very misleading in understanding starvation and hunger, and deprivation in general. Entitlement systems and the positions of particular occupation groups in such systems deserve careful analysis (Section 5).

While *income* is a good intermediate variable in studying food entitlement, it often provides an unhelpful perspective in dealing with entitlements to other goods and services, including those complementary to food. It can also be very misleading as a basis for causal analysis of nutritional differences (Section 6).

The problem of distribution of food within the household raises a particularly complex set of questions. Given the firm evidence of sex bias in some parts of the world, especially in much of Asia, the policy issues can be particularly serious. Sex bias is best analysed in terms of differences of capabilities and nutritional achievements rather than in terms of differences in consumption (including food intake). The former relates better to the ultimate objectives and it also avoids the absurdly difficult problem of observing individual consumption in a joint family meal (Section 7).

While the 'world food problem' has attracted, in recent decades, a lot of attention, the nature of the difficulties has often been misspecified. There are several distinct 'food problems' which require separate, but not independent, analysis. Some remarks have been made on these problems (Section 8), including that of food entitlements, entitlements of complementary goods and services (such as health services, medicine and education), and conversion of household entitlements into personal capabilities (including the important problem of distribution within the family).

The process of development is not primarily one of expanding the supply of goods and services but of enhancing the capabilities of people. Focusing on capabilities forces us to see the theoretical questions and policy issues in a particular light. There is a need to pay specific attention to the generation and security of entitlements and their conversion into capabilities. Some of the underlying policy issues are as complex as the basic approach is simple. That, of course, is not unusual in economics.

References

Alamgir, M. (1980): *Famine in South Asia — Political Economy of Mass Starvation in Bangladesh* (Cambridge, Mass.: Oelgeschlager, Gunn and Hain).

Arrow, K. J. (1982): 'Why People Go Hungry', *New York Review of Books*, 29 (15 July).

Atkinson, A. B. (1975): *The Economics of Inequality* (Oxford: Clarendon Press).

Aziz, S. (ed.) (1975): *Hunger, Politics and Markets: The Real Issues in the Food Crisis* (New York: NYU Press).

—— (ed.) (1982): 'The Fight Against World Hunger', Special number of *Development*, 4.

Bardhan, P. (1974): 'On Life and Death Questions', *Economic and Political Weekly* (4 September).

Becker, G. (1981): *A Treatise on the Family* (Cambridge, Mass.: Harvard University Press).

Beckerman, W. (1979): *The Impact of Income Maintenance Programmes on Poverty in Four Developing Countries* (Geneva: ILO).

Brown, L. R. and Eckholm, E. P. (1974): *By Bread Alone* (Oxford: Pergamon Press).

Chakravarty, S. (1969): *Capital and Development Planning* (Cambridge, Mass.: MIT Press).

Chen, L. C., Huq, E. and D'Souza, S. (1980): 'A Study of Sex-Biased Behaviour in the Intra-family Allocation of Food and the Utilization of Health Care Services in Rural Bangladesh' (Harvard School of Public Health).

Chichilnisky, G. (1980): 'Basic Needs and Global Models: Resources, Trade and Distribution', *Alternatives*, **VI**.

Dasgupta, P. (1982): *The Control of Resources* (Oxford: Blackwell).

Davidson, S., Passmore, R., Brock, J. F. and Truswell, A. S. (1979): *Human Nutrition and Dietectics* (Edinburgh: Churchill Livingstone).

den Hartog, A. P. (1973): 'Unequal Distribution of Food within the Household', *FAO Newsletter*, **10** (4) (October–December).

Douglas, M. and Isherwood, B. (1979): *The World of Goods* (New York: Basic Books).

Elster, J. (1982): 'The Sour Grapes', in Sen and Williams (1982).

FAO/WHO Expert Committee (1973): *Energy and Protein Requirements* (Rome: FAO).

Forrester, J. W. (1971): *World Dynamics* (Cambridge, Mass.: Wright-Allen).

Ghai, D., Khan, A. R., Lee, E. and Alfthan, T. A. (1977): *The Basic Needs Approach to Development* (Geneva: ILO).

Ghose, A. (1979): *Short Term Changes in Income Distribution in Poor Agrarian Economies* (Geneva: ILO).

Gorman, W. M. (1956): 'The Demand for Related Goods', *Journal Paper J3129*, Iowa Experimental Station, Ames, Iowa.

Grant, J. P. (1978): *Disparity Reduction Rates in Social Indicators* (Washington, DC: Overseas Development Council).

Griffin, K. (1978): *International Inequality and National Poverty* (London: Macmillan).

—— and Khan, A. R. (1977): *Poverty and Landlessness in Rural Asia* (Geneva: ILO).

Haq, Mahbubul (1976): *The Poverty Curtain* (New York: Columbia University Press).

Heal, G. M. (1973): *The Theory of Economic Planning* (Amsterdam: North Holland).

Herrera, A. O. *et al.* (1976): *Catastrophe or New Society? A Latin American World Model* (Ottawa: IDRC).

ILO (1976): *Employment, Growth and Basic Needs: A One-World Problem* (Geneva: ILO).

Islam, N. (1977): *Development Planning in Bangladesh: A Study in Political Economy* (London: Hurst).

Interfutures (1979): *Facing the Future* (Paris: OECD).

Jencks, C. (1972): *Inequality* (New York: Basic Books).

Kynch, J. and Sen, A. (1982): 'Indian Women: Well-being and Survival', mimeographed. Forthcoming in *Cambridge Journal of Economics*.

Lancaster, K. J. (1966): 'A New Approach to Consumer Theory', *Journal of Political Economy*, **74**.

Leontief, W. *et al.* (1977): *The Future of the World Economy* (New York: Oxford University Press).

Linnemann, H. (1981): *MOIRA: A Model of International Relations in Agriculture* (Amsterdam: North-Holland).

Lipton, M. (1977): *Why Poor People Stay Poor* (London: Temple Smith).

McHenry, D. F. and Bird, K. (1977): 'Food Bungle in Bangladesh', *Foreign Policy*, No. 27 (Summer).

McNicoll, G. and Nag, M. (1982): 'Population Growth: Current Issues and Strategies', *Population and Development Review*, **8**.

Malthus, T. R. (1798): *Essay on the Principle of Population* (London).

—— (1800): *An Investigation of the Cause of the Present High Price of Provisions*.

Marx, K. (1887): *Capital: A Critical Analysis of Capitalist Production*. Translated by S. Moore and E. Aveling; F. Engels (ed.) (London: Sonnenschein).

—— (1977): *Karl Marx: Selected Writings*, D. McLellan (ed.) (Oxford: Oxford University Press).

Meadows, D. N. *et al.* (1972): *The Limits to Growth* (Washington, DC: Potomac).

Mesarovic, M. D. and Pestel, E. (1974): *Mankind at Turning Point* (New York: Dutton).

Mitra, A. (1980): *Implications of Declining Sex-Ratio in India's Population* (Bombay: Allied Publishers).

Morris, M. D. (1979): *Measuring the Conditions of the World's Poor: The Physical Quality of Life Index* (Oxford: Pergamon Press).

Ng, K. (1981): 'Welfarism: A Defence Against Sen's Attack', *Economic Journal*, **91**.

Oughton, E. (1982): 'The Maharashtra Drought of 1970-73: An Analysis of Scarcity', *Oxford Bulletin of Economics and Statistics*, **44**.

Pant, P. *et al.* (1962): 'Perspective of Development: 1961-1976, Implications of Planning for a Minimum Level of Living', Perspective Planning Division, Planning Commission of India, New Delhi.

Parikh, K. and Rabar, F. (eds) (1981): *Food For All in a Sustainable World* (Laxenberg: IIASA).

Rao, V. K. R. V. (1982): *Food, Nutrition and Poverty in India* (Brighton: Harvester Press).

Ravallion, M. (1983): 'The Performance of Rice Markets in Bangladesh during the 1974 Famine', mimeographed, Oxford University.

Rawls, J. (1971): *A Theory of Justice* (Cambridge, Mass.: Harvard University Press).

Schofield, S. (1975): *Village Nutrition Studies: An Annotated Bibliography* (Brighton: IDS, University of Sussex).

Scrimshaw, N. S. (1977): 'Effect of Infection on Nutrient Requirements', *American Journal of Clinical Nutrition*, **30**.

Sen, A. K. (1970). *Collective Choice and Social Welfare* (San Francisco: Holden-Day; Amsterdam: North-Holland).

—— (1976a). 'Real National Income', *Review of Economic Studies*, **43** [reprinted in Sen (1982a)].

—— (1976b): 'Poverty: An Ordinal Approach to Measurements', *Econometrica*, **44** [reprinted in Sen (1982a)].

—— (1977a): 'On Weights and Measures: Informational Constraints in Social Welfare Analysis', *Econometrica*, **45** [reprinted in Sen (1982a)].

—— (1977b): 'Starvation and Exchange Entitlement: A General Approach and Its Application to the Great Bengal Famine', *Cambridge Journal of Economics*, **1**.

—— (1979a): 'Personal Utilities and Public Judgment: Or What's Wrong with Welfare Economics?', *Economic Journal*, **89** [reprinted in Sen (1982a)].

—— (1979b): 'Utilitarianism and Welfarism', *Journal of Philosophy*, **76**.

—— (1980): 'Equality of What?', in S. McMurrin (ed.), *Tanner Lectures on Human Values*, vol. I (Cambridge: Cambridge University Press) [reprinted in Sen (1982a)].

—— (1981a): *Poverty and Famines: An Essay on Entitlement and Deprivation* (Oxford: Clarendon Press).

—— (1981b): 'Family and Food: Sex-Bias in Poverty?', mimeographed, 1981 [Essay 15 in this volume].

—— (1981c): 'Public Action and the Quality of Life in Developing Countries', *Oxford Bulletin of Economics and Statistics*, **43**.

—— (1982a): *Choice, Welfare and Measurement* (Oxford: Blackwell; and Cambridge, Mass.: MIT Press).

—— (1982b): 'Rights and Agency', *Philosophy and Public Affairs*, **11**.

—— (1982c): 'Food Battles: Conflicts in the Access to Food', Coromandel Lecture, 12 December; reprinted in *Mainstream* (8 January 1983).

—— (1983a). 'Poor, Relatively Speaking', *Oxford Economic Papers*, **35** [Essay 14 in this volume].

—— (1983b): *Commodities and Capabilities*, Hennipman Lecture 1982 (to be published by North-Holland, Amsterdam).

—— (1983c): 'Development: Which Way Now?' *Economic Journal*, **93** [Essay 19 in this volume].

—— (1983d): 'Economics and the Family', *Asian Development Review*, **1** [Essay 16 in this volume].

—— (1984): 'Women, Technology and Sexual Divisions', Working Paper, Technology Division, UNCTAD, Geneva.

—— and Sengupta, S. (1983): 'Malnutrition of Rural Children and the Sex Bias', mimeographed. Forthcoming *Economic and Political Weekly*.

—— and Williams, B. (eds) (1982): *Utilitarianism and Beyond* (Cambridge: Cambridge University Press).

Sinha, R. and Drabek, A. G. (1978): *The World Food Problem: Consensus and Conflict* (Oxford: Pergamon Press).

Singer, H. and Ansari, J. (1977): *Rich and Poor Countries* (London: Allen & Unwin).

Smith, Adam (1776): *An Inquiry into the Nature and Causes of the Wealth of Nations*.

Sobhan, R. (1979): 'Politics of Food and Famine in Bangladesh', *Economic and Political Weekly*, **14**.

Srinivasan, T. N. (1982): 'Hunger: Defining It, Estimating Its Global Incidence and Alleviating It', mimeographed. To be published in D. Gale Johnson and E. Schuh (eds), *Role of Markets in the World Food Economy*.

Streeten, P. (1981): With S. J. Burki, Mahbub ul Haq, N. Hicks and F. Stewart, *First Things First: Meeting Basic Needs in Developing Countries* (New York: Oxford University Press).

—— and Burki, S. (1978): 'Basic Needs: Some Issues', *World Development*, **6**.

Sukhatme, P. V. (1977): *Nutrition and Poverty* (New Delhi: Indian Agricultural Research Institute).

Swaminathan, M. S. (1983): 'Agricultural Progress: Key to Third World Prosperity', Third World Lecture, Third World Foundation.

Taylor, L. (1975): 'The Misconstrued Crisis: Lester Brown and World Food', *World Development*, **3**.

Townsend, P. (1979): *Poverty in the United Kingdom* (Harmondsworth: Penguin).

Williams, B. (1973): 'A Critique of Utilitarianism', in J. Smart and B. Williams, *Utilitarianism: For and Against* (Cambridge: Cambridge University Press).

Name Index

Subject Index